PENGUIN ACADEMICS

CANADIAN LITERATURE IN ENGLISH Texts and Contexts

VOLUME II

Laura Moss
University of British Columbia

Cynthia Sugars
University of Ottawa

PEARSON
Longman

Toronto

Library and Archives Canada Cataloguing in Publication

Canadian literature in English : texts and contexts/edited by Cynthia Sugars, Laura Moss.

Includes bibliographical references and index.
ISBN 978-0-321-31362-1 (v. 1). — ISBN 978-0-321-49400-9 (v. 2)

1. Canadian literature (English).   I. Sugars, Cynthia Conchita, 1963–
II. Moss, Laura F. E. (Laura Frances Errington), 1969–

PS8231.C36 2008   C810.8   C2008-900022-6

ISBN-13: 978-0-321-49400-9
ISBN-10: 0-321-49400-8

Vice President, Editorial Director:
    Gary Bennett
Editor-in-Chief: Ky Pruesse
Acquisitions Editor: Christopher Helsby
Marketing Manager: Loula March
Supervising Developmental Editor:
    Suzanne Schaan
Production Editor: Richard di Santo
Copy Editor: Martha Breen
Proofreaders: Nancy Carroll,
    Barbara Czarnecki

Production Coordinator: Janis Raisen
Composition: Integra
Permissions Research: Beth McAuley
Photo Research: Sandy Cooke
Art Director: Miguel Acevedo
Interior and Cover Design:
    Sharon Lucas
Cover Image: Alex Colville, *Horse and Train*, 1954; Glazed tempera on hardboard; Copyright A.C. Fine Art Inc.

About the cover: This painting was inspired by lines from South African poet Roy Campbell's 1949 poem "Dedication to Mary Campbell": "Against a regiment I oppose a brain/And a dark horse against an armoured train."

5 2020

contents

| SECTION VII | Contemporary Canada, 1985–Present   517 |

INTRODUCTION: THE LOCAL, THE NATIONAL, AND THE GLOBAL   517

Figures for Section VII   539

preface

"Hey, what are you doing?"
she said, and he said
"I'm just standing here
being a Canadian"
and she said "Wow
is that really feasible?"
and he said "Yes
but it requires plenty of imagination."
　　—Lionel Kearns, "Public Poem for Manitoulin Island Canada Day"

This anthology has its origins at a conference in Hamilton, Ontario. Both of us happened to be staying at the same B&B, and one morning we started to talk about the kind of anthology that might be more appropriate than the Canadian literature collections already available, given the type of teaching we actually do. As we continued chatting, we realized that we shared a similar vision for this, as yet, "imaginary" text. The anthology, we agreed, would include visual materials and contextual pieces alongside important writings by canonical and non-canonical, literary and "non-literary" Canadian authors. It would include the kinds of contextual information we regularly bring to class or include in course packs. It would take into account the history of the settlement of Canada, while also representing a diversity of voices. It would provide a good sense of the debates surrounding the growth of Canadian literature, including a recognition of the ways this literature was inevitably linked to shifting notions of national identity. Moreover, it would provide substantial cultural-historical commentary on each period and its authors. And it would be fun! We wanted to dispel the myth of the humourless Canadian writer. By the end of the conference, we had decided to co-edit a new anthology of Canadian literature.

Over the past five years we have tried to create something that resembles our vision. Along the way we have struggled with issues of balance, representation, artistic merit, historical significance, and space. Inevitably, there are many fine writers and poets we have not had the space to include. Further, permission was not granted for specific pieces by all of the authors we had originally approached. Above all, during selection we have been mindful that this is primarily a teaching anthology, and so we have tried to balance an inclusion of widely taught texts with materials that are less well known but which offer unique opportunities for classroom pedagogy.

In order to facilitate readability, within each section authors are ordered chronologically by year of birth. When some authors' lives span two or even three sections (P.K. Page and Margaret Avison, for instance), we have placed them in the section where they had their earliest impact. Under each author's name, poems and short stories are arranged chronologically according to first book publication, unless otherwise noted; the date appears in square brackets following each item. When we want to signal the first magazine or journal publication of a poem for chronological purposes, two dates are provided: the first represents the original publication date; the second the first book publication date. However, within the selections from a given volume, the order in the book has not necessarily been duplicated. This offered us a little more flexibility to provide logical groupings of poems. Poems and stories are gathered separately under each author's name; in other words, we do not break up the poems with a short story simply because the publication date of the story falls somewhere amidst the poem dates. In the two volumes, we have gathered works into seven sections: I. Narratives of Encounter; II. Narratives of Emigration, Settlement, and Invasion; III. Post-Confederation Period; IV. Turn of the Century; V. Modernism; VI. Contemporary Canada, 1960–1985; and VII. Contemporary Canada, 1985–Present.

A note on language: We have used the terms "Aboriginal" and "Native" peoples interchangeably in this text to refer to indigenous people in Canada; "First Nations" refers to indigenous peoples who are neither Inuit nor Métis. These descriptors are capitalized in order to acknowledge that they refer to nations. In the excerpts, we have retained historically specific terms used by the authors (whether ironically or not) even though these may be considered derogatory and/or outdated. We have also chosen to capitalize the terms "Black" and "White" when used with reference to "race" categories in order to signal the constructedness of both labels.

This two-volume anthology of Canadian literature has six main aims:

1. To provide a chronological survey of English-Canadian poetry, short fiction, pamphlets, nonfiction, and essays, ranging from the sixteenth century to the present. The range of works included in this anthology attests to the richness of the history of Canadian literature. Because we are attempting to cover a large span of time and space, we have had to construct some parameters to limit the inclusions. We have chosen not to include any excerpts from novels or plays, on the assumption that they will be assigned as additional texts in most Canadian literature courses. We have thus not included work by some prominent writers who are known primarily as novelists or playwrights. Also for practical reasons, this is an anthology of Canadian literature written in English, so we do not include literary works in translation. Thus, regrettably, we do not include stories originally told/written in First Nations languages or Inuktitut, or works originally written in French, or, for example, Icelandic, or Ukrainian. Further, courses in French- and English-Canadian literature tend to be separate in most university literature programs, a division that informs our restriction to the literary history of English-Canadian writing.

2. To include contextual materials to accompany the wide range of literary texts, including materials that might be used in classroom teaching, such as political speeches, government documents, photographs, paintings, cartoons, songs, popular culture texts, and essays. Because of space and permissions

restrictions, we could not include as many of these items as we would have liked. However, we have tried to provide enough of this material to create a sense of the important intellectual debates and socio-cultural concerns of each period, and to provide useful materials for teaching individual items (e.g., the painting to accompany Mavis Gallant's story "The Doctor," the photograph of John Torrington to supplement Margaret Atwood's "The Age of Lead," and Thomas King's self-portrait as the Lone Ranger).

3. To provide extensive introductions to each section that include information about literary, political, cultural, and social history, print culture, and the "history of the book." We trace the intellectual and aesthetic debates over the various periods. The introductions are complemented by biographical and literary headnotes for each author. Our hope is that these materials will be of use as background reading as well as constituting distinct teaching documents in themselves.

4. To chart the central debates surrounding the formation of Canadian national literary and cultural traditions, particularly debates about the links between literary production and national identity. In other words, this is a book in part about the consolidation and often contentious definition of Canadian literature. Three key questions keep arising: What, if anything, is distinctive about Canadian literature (and, by extension, how does one define the qualifier "Canadian")? What is the connection between literature and community? How does Canadian literature fit within an international literary context? These questions continue into the present day, when nation-based designations have become increasingly problematized in the context of diasporic migration, global culture, and transnationalism. Yet, as the historical snapshots of the debates included here reveal, transnationalism is not a new phenomenon, as many of the earlier writers knew only too well. Moreover, the difficulty—or impossibility, or undesirability, according to various points of view—of extracting an overarching Canadian national identity from a mix of highly disparate peoples was present in the formulation of the BNA Act in 1867 and continued into the debates surrounding Canada's official multiculturalism policy in the 1970s and '80s, as well as in the discussions around cultural and institutional citizenship in recent years. Tracing these central debates over the past several hundred years reminds us that the issues we consider vital today are not necessarily new, even if they are differently formulated.

5. To gather works that make intertextual reference to one another. For example, John Franklin's disastrous expeditions are taken up in the twentieth century by Rudy Wiebe's essay "Exercising Reflection," Stan Rogers's 1981 song "Northwest Passage," and Atwood's short story "The Age of Lead." Duncan Campbell Scott's poems about Native peoples are given a new twist when placed beside Armand Garnet Ruffo's poem about Scott; Louis Riel's speech to the jury in 1885 is picked up by bpNichol in his poem "The Long Weekend of Louis Riel." Similarly, Morley Callaghan's "Loppy Phelan's Double Shoot" and Ruffo's "Grey Owl" poems look back to the earlier selections by Grey Owl (Archibald Belaney), and all three can be considered in terms

of the concept of "imposture" beside the work of Frederick Philip Grove and Robert Kroetsch's poem about Grove. Susanna Moodie's account of her settlement in the backwoods finds subsequent treatment in Atwood's poetry sequence *The Journals of Susanna Moodie*; it is also interesting to consider these texts alongside George Copway's writing, Laura Goodman Salverson's *Confessions*, and Alice Munro's story "Meneseteung." In addition, we have tried to make conceptual or thematic links across time and geography. P.K. Page's concerns for the environment in "Planet Earth" sit well beside the recent poetry of Rita Wong, and Anne Carson's "Audubon" speaks to the avian aesthetics of Don McKay's work. Texts in Volume I by Agnes Maule Machar, Sara Jeannette Duncan, Nellie McClung, and L.M. Montgomery showcase gender issues with similar conviction to Atwood's "The Female Body" and Munro's "Meneseteung," as well as the distinct feminisms of Daphne Marlatt, M. NourbeSe Philip, Dionne Brand, and Carol Shields. Intertextuality also highlights authors' notions of community and literary history. It is important to note the vitality and mutual influence of groups of writers—whether the Confederation Group of the 1880s, the McGill Group of the 1920s, TISH of the 1960s, or the Kootenay School of Writing of the 1990s—to show how much writing happens in linked communities.

6. To be representative of different regions, ethnicities, histories, and gender identities. We have tried to present a range of genres as well, expanding the purview of literature to include non-fiction and broadly defining poetry and prose forms. In keeping with the changing demographics of Canada, we have tried to reflect the increasingly multicultural presence in the country's literatures (as well as the vibrant debates around topics such as racism, citizenship, institutions, multiculturalism, and belonging). We have also included a substantial representation of writing by Aboriginal authors across the sections of this anthology.

∗ ∗ ∗

We wish to thank many people for contributing ideas and suggestions to this anthology. Legions of people have commented on the project from conception to actualization. We would like to note in particular several occasions of academic generosity and would like to thank Janice Fiamengo for the idea of including different versions of A.J.M. Smith's "The Lonely Land"; Roy Miki for suggesting specific letters from his edited book of Muriel Kitagawa's letters; Patrick Langston and Ian McLeish for their help with the Bob and Doug McKenzie material; Jeremy Rios for acting as a biblical consultant; Daisy Neijmann for translating the Icelandic prayer in Laura Goodman Salverson's story; and George Elliott Clarke for providing context for his historical poems. We also appreciate the generosity of the following people who deserve our sincere thanks for their input into Volume II: Jennifer Andrews, Robert Brown, Alison Calder, Mary Chapman, Carrie Dawson, Glenn Deer, Jennifer Delisle, Debra Dudek, Nancy Earle, Margery Fee, Janice Fiamengo, Sherrill Grace, Bev Haun, Jennifer Henderson, Erin Hurley, Dean Irvine, Gillian Jerome,

Brian Johnson, Larissa Lai, Virginia Lavin, Gerald Lynch, Travis Mason, Leslie Monkman, John Moss, Bill New, Laurie Ricou, Duffy Roberts, Robert Stacey, Tony Tremblay, Richard Van Camp, Brenda Vellino, and Glenn Willmott.

We are indebted to the numerous peer reviewers who formally commented on the project proposal and/or Volume II at various stages along the way; they included Alison Calder, University of Manitoba; Gregory Chan, Kwantlen University College; Carrie Dawson, Dalhousie University; Candace Fertile, Camosun College; Janice Fiamengo, University of Ottawa; Manina Jones, University of Western Ontario; Mary Beth Knechtel, Langara College; Sophie McCall, Simon Fraser University; Tanis MacDonald, Wilfrid Laurier University; Sam McKegney, Queen's University; Kevin McNeilly, University of British Columbia; Seymour Mayne, University of Ottawa; Wendy Roy, University of Saskatchewan; Sam Solecki, University of Toronto; and others who prefer to remain anonymous.

We are grateful for the detailed work of our research assistants: at UBC, Travis Mason, Maryann Martin, Laura Potter, Genevieve Gagne-Hawes, and Melanie Sanderson; at the University of Ottawa, Jessica Langston, Kathleen Patchell, and Tania Aguila-Way. Laura would like to thank her colleagues in the Department of English and the Faculty of Arts at the University of British Columbia for their support. Cynthia would like to express her gratitude to the Department of English and Faculty of Arts at the University of Ottawa. We would also like to thank our editors at Pearson Education Canada, Suzanne Schaan, Chris Helsby, and Richard di Santo, for their dedication to the book from start to finish.

Above all, we thank our families for their love and support throughout this process. Our six children (all currently under the age of 9) have provided fun, grounding, and balance in our lives as we have worked on this project. Cynthia's Neve, Abbey, and Morgan and Laura's Simon, Owen, and Charlie have enjoyed the piles of recycled paper and revelled in the poems of Dennis Lee. Charlie and Morgan, born within weeks of each other and a year into this project, will forever be our CanLit anthology babies. We'd most like to thank our husbands, Paul Keen and Fred Cutler, for providing boundless critical insights, advice, coffee, dinners, glasses of wine, pep talks, encouragement, love, and an unfailing, and ironic, enthusiasm for things Canadian.

The creation of this anthology has been a truly collaborative project and has been one of the most rewarding, and tiring, academic experiences either of us has had. We have also helped each other over crises at home and at work and have forged a solid friendship out of it all. Over the course of thousands of email messages (with 2007 messages sent to each other in 2007 alone) between Ottawa, Vancouver, and Sydney, we have created this anthology together. We are both responsible for its strengths and weaknesses. That we have listed Volume I as edited by Cynthia Sugars and Laura Moss and Volume II as edited by Laura Moss and Cynthia Sugars is meant to reflect the collaborative nature of this venture. Enjoy!

Dedication

To SIMON, OWEN, and CHARLIE
To NEVE, ABBEY, and MORGAN

Modernism

Introduction: Making It New in Canada

> Modernity and tradition alike demand that the contemporary artist who survives adolescence shall be an intellectual. Sensibility is no longer enough, intelligence is also required. Even in Canada.
>
> —A.J.M. Smith, "Wanted: Canadian Criticism" (1928)

In Search of a New Poetics: Modernism in Canada

"While our young nation is striving to find its soul, there is sure to be much uncouth gesturing," wrote Albert Durrant Watson and Lorne Pierce in their introduction to *Our Canadian Literature* in 1923 (xvii). Indeed, much of the next 40 years can be read as a time of national soul-searching in Canadian writing. The writers and poets in these years often gestured rudely at convention and thumbed their noses at tradition. In the period following the First World War, through the affluence of the 1920s, the economic depression of the 1930s, the Second World War, and the postwar boom, Canadian literature developed alongside the growing confidence in the nation. This was a result of a generation of writers who actively rejected both the driving aesthetics and the prevailing ideologies of the previous generations in favour of something more recognizably modern in subject matter, tone, and form. There was also a push toward artistic independence and an acknowledgement of the need to unhinge Canadian writing from a colonial mentality. The 40 years between 1920 and 1960 saw significant changes in Canadian culture, society, technology, foreign policy, national identity, and, concurrently, literature.

As in other former colonies reaching states of independence, art in Canada was instrumental in effecting cultural and psychic decolonization. Artists in this period in particular were trying to create works that were not derivative, and not naively nationalistic, but which were maturely "Canadian" in some way. In the 1920s two young renegade modernist poets from Montreal named F.R. Scott and A.J.M. Smith argued for the need to advance beyond the mediocrity which they insisted confined Canadian literature to the status of a colonial literature. Novelist Hugh MacLennan, two decades later, argued that "a colonial literature can at best be but a pale reflection of the mother-literature, without authority of any sort, until the colony has matured" ("New Country" 139). Poet Irving Layton's comment at the end of the period summarizes the attitude of the times: "It is not simply enough to survive; one has to be able to grow, to push the soil apart and come up unstunted or at least as unstunted as possible" (Thomas, "Interview" 66).

The young Smith barely remains civil to the well-established poets of the previous generation—such as Bliss Carman, Charles G.D. Roberts, and Duncan Campbell Scott—when he writes that "the most popular experience [in their poetry] is to be pained, hurt, stabbed, or seared by beauty—preferably by the yellow flame of a crocus in the spring or the red flame of a maple leaf in autumn" (see "Rejected Preface"). The vehemence of such a damnation of the reigning kings of Canadian letters cannot be underestimated. It was just such a rejection of the literary status quo that drove Smith, Scott, and Leon Edel to launch *The McGill Fortnightly Review* (1925–27) as a venue for new poetry and then, shortly after, with Leo Kennedy, to publish the *Canadian Mercury* (1928–29) as an avant-garde "little magazine." Indeed, in the opening editorial of the *Canadian Mercury* the editors called for nothing short of the "emancipation of Canadian literature from the state of amiable mediocrity and insipidity" in which they insisted it languished (3). Along with their contemporary A.M. Klein, these poets have come to be known as the McGill Group or the Montreal School. *The McGill Fortnightly Review,* while very much a student paper publishing articles and opinion pieces on McGill University affairs, launched the careers of several key modernist poets, including Smith and Scott themselves but also Klein and Edel.

In his 1936 "Rejected Preface" for the poetry collection he co-edited with Scott, *New Provinces: Poems of Several Authors*—arguably the first collection of avowedly modernist poetry in Canada—Smith outlines the editors' intention to "overthrow" the prevailing mode of sentimental poetry in Canada and to position contemporary poetry in relation to international modernist movements inspired particularly by the distinct styles of poetry of poets as far apart as W.B. Yeats and T.S. Eliot. Smith was actively involved in making a new space in Canadian poetry for himself and his like-minded friends. *New Provinces* included work by Scott and Smith, as well as by the more established poet E.J. Pratt and younger poets Klein, Kennedy, and Robert Finch. Smith's preface (included here) was rejected by the publisher and also by Pratt and Finch as too incendiary. They did not want to cause trouble with established writers and readers. Scott was more understated in his claims for the book. In his letter of

11 January 1934 to Pratt, Scott writes: "We are not aiming at anything extraordinarily experimental, but so far as possible we would like to indicate that we are all post-Eliot" (qtd. in Gnarowski xi). Like those who followed American poet Ezra Pound's dictum to "make it new," they eschewed older forms of authority as decayed and obsolete. This psychic rupture with the old was mirrored in formal experimentation. In short, modernism in art and in literature was characterized by innovation, a rejection of tradition, a belief in progress, and a sense of alienation from the past.

The poetry of this period is marked by an interest in politics and social concerns, with much of the new poetry containing social criticism, commentary on urban or industrial life, and strong criticisms of the economic inequalities of the day (see Scott's poem "A Social Register" as an example). Indeed, like Scott, most of these young writers were members of the political left, and were interested in combining the principles of socialism with the innovations of modernist aesthetics. Kennedy summed up the tenor of the times well when he wrote, "We need poetry that reflects the lives of our people, working, loving, fighting, groping for clarity. We need satire—fierce, scorching, aimed at the abuses which are destroying our culture and which threaten life itself. Our poets have lacked direction for their talents and energies in the past—I suggest that today it lies right before them" (qtd. in Morley 102). With a focus on material conditions rather than sentiment, such a concerted effort at linking art, culture, and social protest is characteristic of much of the literature of the inter-war period.

Some of the most politically charged poetry came from the pens of modernist women poets. However, in spite of the presence of well-respected poets such as Dorothy Livesay, P.K. Page, Margaret Avison, Miriam Waddington, Anne Marriott, and Anne Wilkinson, the modernist movement was dominated by male writers, and writing was defined by the influential critics in clearly gendered terms. Whereas "feminine" writing was dismissed as sentimental, romantic, and flowery (all characteristics of the previous generation of poetry that were being so strongly eschewed by Smith and his cohort), "masculine" writing was championed for its virility, sparseness, and muscularity (Gerson 48). Needless to say, the modernist women did not necessarily write in the so-called "feminine" styles, just as Roberts and Lampman hadn't written in these "masculine" forms. The fact that the charge of being "feminine" in voice was an artificial construction that was then marked as derogatory reveals something about the gender politics of the times.

It is not without a sense of irony that the most celebrated post-Confederation poet, Charles G.D. Roberts, composed "A Note on Modernism" at this time. In it he astutely writes that "Modernism, a strictly relative term, has gone by different names in different periods, but always it has been, and is, a reaction of the younger creators against the too long domination of their older predecessors" (296). This central figure of the old guard then goes on to show how the poets so derided by Smith, such as Carman, D.C. Scott, and Archibald Lampman, "had already initiated a departure, a partial departure, from the

Victorian tradition of poetry, years before the movement began in England" (298). In Roberts's view, it is important to place the trends in poetry and art on a longer historical plane. What Roberts does not acknowledge here, however, is the influence of the American poetic movements of the day on the younger poets in Canada.

Although it is difficult to pinpoint an exact date for the birth of modernism in America, several critics have argued that it began in 1913 with the Armory Show in a New York City building formerly used for military purposes. The show toured the country and had an impact on hundreds of thousands of people. It exhibited works by a number of European artists (including Marcel Duchamp, Pablo Picasso, Paul Cézanne, Paul Gauguin, and Georges Braque) who were experimenting with form, subject matter, and style. The radical spirit of the Armory Show, and of the European art it exhibited, became foundational for the poets, sculptors, writers, and painters who are now seen as constituting a distinct aesthetic movement in the culture of America. This movement includes Ezra Pound, T.S. Eliot, William Faulkner, Ernest Hemingway, William Carlos Williams, H.D., and Gertrude Stein. Many of these writers were noted for their rejection of excess sentimentality and description in their attempt to draw attention to the materiality of the words on the page, thus putting into practice the injunction of Archibald MacLeish in his 1926 poem "Ars Poetica": "A poem should not mean / But be."

The same radical dismissal of the past that appealed to this generation in the United States also appealed to Canadians. The most famous experimentation in art during this period was that of the Group of Seven painters (see the headnote for Lawren Harris for details). One sees in their work a desire for new forms of representation of the local in both art and poetry. This was accomplished technically by breaking with the dominant realist mode of representation by using bold brush strokes of heavy paint in unusual colours. The Group dared to paint purple skies, orange water, and blue trees, evoking the emotional essence of the scene rather than attempting to duplicate it realistically. They painted in the form of "expressionism," making use of vibrant colours, sharp lines, dark shadows, and dramatic images. Expressionism is defined by its encapsulation of an emotional or psychological experience, often as this experience is projected onto depictions of landscapes or inanimate objects. The Group of Seven argued that it was impossible to view Canada through the picturesque European lens that dominated Canadian collections, museums, and public appreciation at the time. At first the group met with public disapproval. Gradually, however, tastes changed and the Group became emblematic of the fight for a national art.

The painters inspired the Canadian modernist poets who were, among other things, interested in reframing the relationship between Canadian cultural identity and the landscape. One sees similar concerns in the painting and poetry of the period: both were responding to the conservative and imitative traditions of Canadian art; both rejected conventions of nineteenth-century realism; both felt that the work of art should not only represent an experience, but *be* an experience. The early modernist poets followed the expressionism of the painters by trying to write linguistic equivalents of this approach. One of the best-known instances of influence between painters and poets in Canada is Smith's 1926 poem "The Lonely Land." The painting thought to have inspired this poem is Tom Thomson's *The West Wind* (1917), included in this section (Figure V-1). Smith's poem, like *The West Wind*, illustrates a shift away from picturesque nature description to an aesthetic that was nevertheless still "Romantic" in its invocation of the sublime, untamed, and awe-inspiring land.

Although Smith and Scott were perhaps the most outspoken early advocates of modernist ideas in Canadian poetry, they were not the first. Literary critic Ken Norris argues that "the tenets of Modernism began to be exercised in Canada before there was a successful Modernist Canadian poem produced" (56). He further refers to the modernist commitment to free verse (as opposed to regular meter and rhyme scheme) articulated in the prefaces to both Arthur Stringer's *Open Water* (1914) and F.O. Call's book of verse, *Acanthus and Wild Grape* (1920), although he notes that this emphasis is not sustained in their poetry itself. By the 1920s a handful of poets scattered around the country, such as Dorothy Livesay, W.W.E. Ross, and Raymond Knister, were influenced by experimental work coming from the United States and Europe. Livesay, for example, recalls that her mother, the writer Florence Randal Livesay, subscribed to the modernist literary magazines *The Dial* and *Poetry*: "[T]hat was how, from the beginning, I was influenced by imagism and by Amy Lowell, 'H.D.', Williams, Pound" (Interview). Livesay also cites the influence of Ross, Knister, Finch, and Louise Morey Bowman on her early writing. So when Smith and Scott started *The McGill Fortnightly Review* on 21 November 1925, they were not quite the renegades they thought they were. What they were doing, however, was consolidating interest in emerging modernist aesthetics and experimental poetic techniques.

Nearly two decades later, in his landmark anthology of Canadian poetry, *The Book of Canadian Poetry* (1943), Smith wrote about two prevailing traditions in contemporary poetry: "native" and "cosmopolitan." The first group of poets he characterized as writing poetry that was responsive to what is "individual and unique in Canadian life" (5). He viewed the nationalist basis of this tradition as parochial and risking sentimentality, whereas he saw the work of the second tradition to have made a "heroic effort to transcend colonialism by entering into the universal, civilizing culture of ideas" (5). For Smith, cosmopolitan poetry was excitingly international in spirit, evoking what Canadian life had "in common with life everywhere" (5).

Angered by Smith's suggestion of the superiority of the poetry of the cosmopolitan group over the native group, in 1947 poet John Sutherland produced his own anthology in direct response to Smith's work (*Other Canadians: An Anthology of the New Poetry in Canada 1940–1946*). In it, Sutherland expands "Smith's canon" by including Irving Layton and Louis Dudek, as well as Miriam

Waddington, Patrick Anderson, and James Reaney. Sutherland intended to complicate Smith's evaluations by demonstrating how the cosmopolitan was itself implicated by colonialism because, he argued, it was reliant on foreign trends rather than presenting home-grown articulations of place and space. Sutherland's short essay "Literary Colonialism," published in the little magazine he co-edited called *First Statement*, attacks Smith's position: "Mr. Smith, who apparently sees special virtue in importing other people's ideas and literary forms, believes that the future belongs to the cosmopolitan group, because they respond to every change in fashion" (3). In contrast, Sutherland predicts that in the future Canadian poetry "will be a poetry that has stopped being a parasite on other literatures and has had the courage to decide its own problems in its own way" (3). E.K. Brown was another influential critic who argued against the colonialism he saw as endemic to Canadian writing. However, instead of focusing on the writers, he looked to the Canadian reading public and publishing industry to help support a local literary scene. In *On Canadian Poetry* (1943), Brown links the colonial mentality to what he calls "our neglect of our literature" (306) and maintains that the arts could thrive if only Canadians took Canadian literature, and themselves, more "seriously" (308).

Little Magazines and Political Rivalries

Between the 1920s and the 1950s, there were only a few avenues for the dissemination of literary works in Canada: artist-run presses and general interest magazines that included short stories and poems amongst news articles and essays about the arts, as well as magazines dedicated principally to literature.[1] Still, the poets of the day believed that it was vital to create not only new poetry but new outlets for the new poetry. This inaugurated the now long-standing tradition in Canada of poet-critics or poet-editors collaborating on magazines and founding small presses.

The heart of modernism in Canadian poetry lay in the limited-circulation literary magazines, known as the "little magazines." Such magazines included *Contemporary Verse* (1941–52) out of Vancouver—later revamped as *CV II* (1975–) out of Winnipeg—and rival poetry journals *First Statement* (1942–45) and *Preview* (1942–45) out of Montreal. Because the Depression had forced cutbacks in the publishing programs of the major publishing houses, writers often opted to create their own venues to ensure publication. The small presses linked to these magazines were vital for young writers. Significant books published by Sutherland's First Statement Press, for instance, included Layton's *Here and*

---

[1] For instance, *The Canadian Bookman* (1919–39), *Canadian Forum* (1920–2000), and *The Goblin* (1921–27) were well-circulated magazines that emphasized literary criticism. Indeed, literary historian Sandra Djwa points out that one of the initial aims of the *Forum* was to attempt "to trace and value those developments of art and letters which are distinctively Canadian" (25). There were also commercial and trade publications like *Saturday Night* (1887–), *Maclean's* magazine (1911–), and *Quill and Quire* (1935–) that sat beside magazines of the political left such as *Masses* (1932–34) and *New Frontier* (1936–37).

Now (1945) and *Now Is the Place* (1948), Anderson's *A Tent for April* (1945), and Miriam Waddington's *Green World* (1945), along with collections by Raymond Souster and Anne Wilkinson. In 1945 *The Fiddlehead* magazine started up in Fredericton and in 1952 the University of New Brunswick inaugurated the Fiddlehead Poetry Books Series. To this day, small presses continue to be vital to the development of Canadian literature. The magazines and presses act as focal points for poets and writers, foster collaboration, and engender interaction between key figures.

Small presses and magazines are not without their own politics. In Montreal, for instance, *Preview* and *First Statement* were clearly rival publications. In an article published in *Preview* in October 1942, P.K. Page speaks in patronizing tones of the rival magazine as one published by "young people" with a "wide-eyed uncertain policy of inclusion" ("Canadian Poetry" 8). Writing to Smith from Toronto about his 1943 book, Pratt exclaimed, "I must say that the *Preview* editor [Ruddick] Shaw acted like a shit on your Anthology," and continued, "I didn't mind the criticisms so much as the prejudice. It was so blatantly obvious that the whole article was a build-up for the *Preview* editorial coterie. After damning all Canadian literature up to the present, there came in the last paragraph a eulogy of the Anderson/Scott/Page/Ruddick gang. The new Light had arisen now and Poetry had just been stalling for those bastards to rise in their effulgence" (28 January 1944, Hypertext Edition of Pratt's Complete Letters). This letter illustrates how personal and vituperative Canadian literary politics could get. Somewhat ironically, financial exigencies caused *Preview* and *First Statement* to merge in 1945 to become the *Northern Review* (1946–56), under the editorship of John Sutherland. The battle between *Preview* and *First Statement* in Montreal is said to have invigorated poetry in Canada in the 1940s and bears echoes with the infamous "War between the Poets" of the post-Confederation period between Wilfred Campbell, Charles G.D. Roberts, and Bliss Carman. Personal politics aside, the 1940s were a time of intense excitement and commitment in the world of Canadian poetry. This kind of energy was again revived in the 1960s when fierce discussions about the links between Canadian identity and culture returned to the fore.

Fiction: Divergent Approaches to the Modern Aesthetic

Between the 1920s and 1950s, Canadian fiction developed along less radical but no less passionate lines than poetry. The 1920s saw the publication of several important novels set on the Canadian prairies: Laura Goodman Salverson's *The Viking Heart* (1923), Martha Ostenso's *Wild Geese* (1925), and Frederick Philip Grove's *Settlers of the Marsh* (1925) turned the relatively new provinces of Manitoba and Saskatchewan into places worthy of fiction. The novelists explore the psychological impact of farming and settlement on developing communities as they narrate stories of immigrants adjusting to both the landscape and the people of the prairie provinces.[2] Tame by today's standards, Grove's first novel in English and his first Canadian novel, *Settlers of the Marsh,* was considered indecent. The psychological emphasis on the development of the character of the Swedish immigrant Niels Lindstadt in the novel is balanced by the precision of the realistic descriptions of the setting. Grove's realism has been read by some critics as tempered by a desire to invoke archetypal subjects. In particular, his treatment of the Canadian pioneer is set within his larger concern with "the spiritual versus the material," namely "the universal dilemma of men tempted to gain the world at the price of their own souls" (Keith 21). Although Grove's novels resist categorization (as he variously combines elements of naturalism, romanticism, classicism, and realism), Grove is sometimes cited as one of the earliest writers of "prairie realism," a form that was used to great effect by Sinclair Ross (*As for Me and My House,* 1941) and W.O. Mitchell (*Who Has Seen the Wind,* 1947), a generation later.

In a different vein, Mazo de la Roche's *Jalna* books (1927–60)—a series of 16 romantic novels depicting the trials of generations of the Whiteoaks family living on an English-style estate in rural Ontario—were immensely popular in both Britain and Canada and were subsequently translated into French, German, Swedish, Danish, Norwegian, Czech, Polish, Finnish, and Portuguese. Highly readable, these books presented rather conservative responses to often simplified versions of social and moral dilemmas of the day. The *Jalna* books are perhaps the best contemporary example of the kind of Romantic prose that the modernist writers reacted against. Indeed, de la Roche's novels were not attempting to be realistic but were wrapped up in the romance of the plot and character development; the Canadian setting was largely incidental, and the public loved them. De la Roche was not alone in writing fiction that proved popular with a wide audience. The first 16 books of the wildly successful American boys' detective series (begun in 1926) *The Hardy Boys,* published under the pseudonym Franklin W. Dixon, were ghostwritten by a prolific pulp fiction writer from Carleton Place, Ontario, named Leslie McFarlane.

During this time Morley Callaghan became the first fiction writer to be overtly celebrated for using the elements of poetic modernism (sparseness of language, intensity of psychological engagement, and drive for newness and change) in his fiction. His first novel, *Strange Fugitive* (1928), won him enough praise (and support of a publisher) to help finance a stint living in Paris as part of a bohemian crowd of writers that included Ernest Hemingway, James Joyce, and F. Scott Fitzgerald. On his return to Canada, Callaghan published a trio of novels that are often viewed as his best works: *Such Is My Beloved* (1934), *They Shall Inherit the Earth* (1935), and *More*

[2] Other immigrant writers tackled similar subject matter, sometimes in English and sometimes in the language of their original country. As Eric Thomson notes, these include John Herries McCulloch (*The Men of Kildonan,* 1926), Maurice Constantin-Weyer (*Un Homme se penche sur son passé/A Man Scans His Past,* 1929), Frederick Niven (*The Flying Years,* 1935), Magdelana Rasheviciite-Eggleston (*Mountain Shadows,* 1955), Vera Lysenko (*Men in Sheepskin Coats,* 1947; and *Yellow Boots,* 1954), Illia Kiriak (*Sons of the Soil,* 1959; translation of original from 1939), and Sigmund Bychinsky (*A Flight of Cranes,* composed 1945, published 2007), among others.

Joy in Heaven (1937). Like those of many other modernist writers, Callaghan's works are set in urban landscapes and tackle large moral and social issues, particularly men's struggles with religious faith and ethical choices. In response to Callaghan's trio of novels, Desmond Pacey published "At Last—A Canadian Literature," in the 2 December 1938 *Cambridge Review,* where he argued that emerging writers led by the likes of Callaghan were paving the way for a mature Canadian literature.

Conversely, when Sinclair Ross published his now-celebrated novel *As for Me and My House* in 1941, it met with little fanfare. However, when it was reissued as the fourth title chosen by Malcolm Ross in the McClelland and Stewart New Canadian Library paperback series (1958), it seemed its time had come. Ross's novel about the stagnant marriage of a woman to a tormented artist/preacher husband evokes a dry and withering prairie landscape. A subjective narrative with limited action, the novel is episodic in structure (following the diary entries of the main character), but unified through the recurring use of images (windows, false fronts, wind, trains). The realism of the novel is evident in Ross's representations of the drought, isolation, and poverty of the prairies in the 1930s, while the ambiguity that inheres within the novel's structure over character point-of-view (are Mrs. Bentley's comments reliable?) is in line with many modernist novels worldwide, notably those that revel in psychological complexity such as the novels of Henry James or Virginia Woolf.

While Ross set his fiction firmly in western Canada, it is not primarily nationalist in intent. However, this was not the case for other novelists writing at this time. Echoing the debates of the 1880s and '90s, there was a revival of concern about the place of literature in the constitution of national independence and identity. This was particularly the case among some writers active in the Canadian Authors Association (CAA): Stephen Leacock, Bliss Carman, Robert Service, E.J. Pratt, Mazo de la Roche, and Charles G.D. Roberts, among them. In 1946 William Arthur Deacon, head of the CAA, boldly stated:

> Either Canadian literature triumphs, overcoming all the unique handicaps and obstacles confronting the Canadian writer—and in the result Canada becomes a great nation, realizing her potential; or we fail to manufacture the cement of a strong native literature, and Canada ceases to enjoy a separate existence, becoming merely a northerly extension of the economy of the United States.
>
> *That* is what is in the balance.
>
> Nothing so puny as individual incomes or the kind of work we like; but the *fate* of our *country.* (qtd. in Thomas and Lennox 205)

Deacon's strong words illustrate the urgent tenor of the debates about literature during this period. Reflected in Deacon's speech is the motto of this volunteer, non-profit organization formed in 1921: "Writers helping writers." Over the years the CAA has lobbied for Public Lending Rights payments to authors and for stronger copyright legislation; instituted Canada Book Week, the *Canadian Poetry Magazine,* and the *Poetry Yearbook;* and supported other pressing concerns for writers in Canada. The CAA is also the group on the receiving end of Scott's wrath in his 1927 poem "The Canadian Authors Meet," in which he depicts the group as outdated, posturing, and ineffectual.[3]

When MacLennan wrote that "there is as yet no tradition of Canadian literature" in the foreword to his novel *Barometer Rising* (1941), he was not being facetious. He articulated his own nationalist strategy by explaining the need for Canadian writers to write for two audiences: a Canadian audience and an audience beyond the nation. MacLennan describes his own artistic process when writing *Barometer Rising*:

> It seemed to me that for some years to come the Canadian novelist would have to pay a great deal of attention to the background in which he set his stories. He must describe, and if necessary define, the social values which dominate the Canadian scene, and do so in such a way as to make them interesting to foreigners. Whether he likes it or not, he must for a time be something of a geographer, an historian and a sociologist. (*Thirty & Three* 52)

Like the members of the CAA, MacLennan clearly saw the need for artists to articulate a strong sense of place and belonging. Essays like "Boy Meets Girl in Winnipeg and Who Cares?" eloquently express MacLennan's sense of commitment to a national Canadian literature. Unlike the "cosmopolitan" group of modernist poets, MacLennan argued that "literature is not an international activity in any sense, and though new visions and new techniques can flow across international borders, the substance of any living literature must come out of the society to which the writer belongs" ("New Country" 138). Hence MacLennan's insistence in "Boy Meets Girl" on retaining the Canadian settings for his novels even though American publishers advised against it.

Although the existence of a recognizable Canadian literary tradition was still being debated, the 1940s ushered in some of the most memorable works of fiction in Canada, including Gwethalyn Graham's Governor General's Award-winning novel of the divided worlds of English, French, and Jewish Montrealers, *Earth and High Heaven* (1944), Ethel Wilson's *Hetty Dorval* (1947), Malcolm Lowry's *Under the Volcano* (1947), Robertson Davies's *The Diary of Samuel Marchbanks* (1947), and Elizabeth Smart's remarkable novel *By Grand Central Station I Sat Down and Wept* (1945). The 1940s also saw the birth of the Stephen Leacock Memorial Medal for Humour (est. 1947) and the continuation of the long tradition of Canadian satire begun by Thomas Chandler Haliburton and Thomas McCulloch over a century before, with such works as Paul Hiebert's satirical fictional biography of the "Sweet Songstress of Saskatchewan," *Sarah Binks* (1947), Earle Birney's Second World War satire *Turvey* (1949), Eric Nicol's *The Roving I* (1950) (which earned him the first of three Leacock Medals—1951, 1956, and 1958), and Robertson Davies's Salterton trilogy.

---

[3] The CAA response to Scott appears in Lyn Harrington's *Syllables of Recorded Time: The Story of the Canadian Authors Association 1921–1981*.

Fiction in the 1950s continued to grow in popularity and esteem with the publication of such important works as Hugh Garner's *Cabbagetown* (1950), Ernest Buckler's *The Mountain and the Valley* (1952), Ethel Wilson's *Swamp Angel* (1954), and Adele Wiseman's *The Sacrifice* (1956). Like Smart's *By Grand Central Station*, Sheila Watson's radically experimental *The Double Hook* (written between 1951 and 1953, published in 1959) is a memorable work of modernist fiction that is difficult to categorize. However, unlike Smart's novel, it is consciously set in a Canadian locale. The novel takes place in the Cariboo region of British Columbia as the narrative combines references to the Native trickster figure Coyote, Christian liturgy, and Homer's *Odyssey*. In the novel, the landscape is haunted by the ghost of the dead mother but also by the whispers of the ubiquitous Coyote and the stories that seep out of the dry land. Two decades after it was published, Watson recalled how she began writing *The Double Hook* as an "answer to a challenge" that you could not write about particular places in Canada, "that what you'd end up with was a regional novel of some kind" (qtd. in Davidson 60). Instead, following William Blake's notion that you can see "the world in a grain of sand," Watson argued that in faithfully rendering the particular, you touch on the universal.

Institutional Structures of Canadian Culture and Literature

When Scottish novelist and poet John Buchan, Lord Tweedsmuir, became Governor General of Canada in 1935, literature was clearly a key element on the agenda in his office and his home. His wife, writer Susan Buchan (Lady Tweedsmuir), was also active in promoting literacy in Canada. With her "Lady Tweedsmuir Prairie Library Scheme," Rideau Hall was used as a distribution centre for 40,000 books sent out to readers in remote areas of the economically depressed country. In 1936 Buchan, with the instrumental help of the CAA, created the Governor General's Literary Awards. The awards quickly became the highest distinction awarded to a book in Canada. In the first year, only two awards were given out—the fiction award to Bertram Brooker for *Think of the Earth* (1936), and the non-fiction award to T.B. Robertson for collected newspaper articles. Both were in English. In 1957 the awards were put under the administration of the Canada Council for the Arts, and a cash prize began to be awarded to the winner. The awards for French-language literature were not added until 1959, with André Giroux's *Malgré tout, la joie* winning the inaugural award. There are now seven categories of Governor General's Literary Awards, awarded in both French and English. The inception of the awards reveals the increasing role Canadian literature was playing in public affairs at the close of the 1930s.

A decade after Buchan first instituted the Governor General's Awards, the government of Prime Minister Louis St. Laurent (1948–57) ordered an inquiry into the state of the national development of the arts, letters, and sciences. Following in the spirit of a series of government initiatives that had stemmed from the recommendations of the Aird Commission (1928) on public broadcasting—which had resulted in the creation of the Canadian Broadcasting Corporation (CBC) and the National Film Board in the 1930s—the agenda of St. Laurent's government was one of cultural nationalism, specifically, to promote the development of the arts in Canada. The inquiry, known as the Massey Commission, was a direct response to the years of debate about the need for a distinctly Canadian culture, questions that had been central as far back as the mid-nineteenth century. The Report focuses on the need for an increase in funding and government patronage of a wide range of cultural activities: "[I]f we in Canada are to have a more plentiful and better cultural fare, we must pay for it. Goodwill alone can do little for a starving plant; if the cultural life of Canada is anaemic, it must be nourished, and this will cost money." The Report was taken seriously. Based on the recommendations of the Report (see the excerpt in this section), the Canada Council was established in 1957 and strong cultural nationalism became entrenched.

Riding the wave of nationalism in the arts embraced in the Massey Report and the commercial success of writers like MacLennan, Davies, and Callaghan, literary critic Malcolm Ross teamed up with publisher Jack McClelland of McClelland and Stewart to begin the New Canadian Library Series (NCL). This mass-market paperback reprint series was the first dedicated solely to Canada's literatures. Beginning with Grove's *Over Prairie Trails*, Callaghan's *Such Is My Beloved*, Leacock's *Literary Lapses*, and Ross's *As for Me and My House*, the series now spans more than 200 years of Canadian writing. Critic Robert Lecker notes how the affordable NCL editions "allowed teachers to discuss the work of many Canadian authors who had never been the subject of formal academic study" (656). Lecker suggests that the NCL consolidated an emerging national canon of literary writing. However, it can be argued that this emergent tradition is also evident in the many anthologies and collections of Canadian writing that were published in the period prior to 1958. Depending on how one reads it, the NCL was either an exercise in canon formation or a means of making affordable copies of classic texts available to a large audience. Either way, its list has had an enormous impact on the development of Canadian literature.

In another publishing success story, shortly after the war a Canadian company named Harlequin began to publish romance fiction, or "women's fiction" as they termed it, along with popular westerns, mysteries, and cookbooks. Over the next generation as they focused attention on romances, Harlequin revolutionized book marketing and sales by making their inexpensive novels available for their primarily female audiences in the places that women shopped: drugstores, grocery stores, and department stores. The result was astonishing financial success. According to the Harlequin online home page, the company has shipped approximately 5.22 billion books since its inception. Without question, this makes Harlequin among the most financially successful publishing ventures in Canadian history.

Keeping pace with the production of works of fiction and poetry, in the autumn of 1958 writer-critic George Woodcock was invited by the head of the Department of English at the University of British Columbia to edit a quarterly journal devoted to the critical discussion of Canadian writing. In the autumn of 1959 the first issue of *Canadian Literature: A Quarterly of Criticism and Review* was published. It has since been joined by such critical journals as *Essays on Canadian Writing; Studies in Canadian Literature; The Journal of Canadian Fiction; The Journal of Canadian Poetry: Studies, Documents, Reviews; Open Letter; Prairie Fire; West Coast Line; Antigonish Review;* and a number of others dedicated specifically to the study of Canadian writing. The "explosion" of literature and nationalist sentiment that would mark the 1960s and '70s came out of a firm base of institutional support for literature in the 1950s.

Putting Literature in Context: The Turbulent Inter-War Years

During the 1920s and '30s, Canadians were not just looking inward at new forms of self-expression. In politics, Canada was asserting sovereignty at an international level. At the international peace conference that followed the First World War, Prime Minister Robert Borden was insistent that Canada sign the peace treaty as an independent member and attain its own seat within the League of Nations (an international organization established on the principles of collective security and preservation of peace). It did so in 1920. The league created a forum for international discussion of political and social questions, as well as issues of sovereignty and governance. At the Imperial Conference in 1926, the prime ministers of the participating countries adopted the Balfour Report, which defined the Dominions as "autonomous Communities within the British Empire, equal in status, in no way subordinate to another in any aspect of their domestic or external affairs, though united by common allegiance to the Crown and freely associated as members of the British Commonwealth of Nations" (Commonwealth Secretariat). By 1931 the Statute of Westminster was passed in Britain, granting Canada and the other Dominions—the Irish Free State, Newfoundland, South Africa, and, shortly after, Australia and New Zealand, with India following in 1947 after independence—independent control over foreign policy. This initiative guaranteed these nations' independence within the newly constituted "British Commonwealth." In 1949 the word "British" was dropped to allow for the development of relationships among the former colonies and the many new nations that were emerging out of the decolonization process that continued well into the 1950s and 1960s.

While Canada as a nation was working toward autonomy, women within Canada were doing the same. A quick look at some of the topics covered in one significant Canadian women's magazine highlights some of the social, cultural, and literary changes in the period.[4] In July of the inaugural year of *The Chatelaine* magazine (1928), the magazine ran the provocatively titled article "Only a Super-Woman Can Juggle Both a Family and a Career." Although the

---

[4] Over the years, *Chatelaine* magazine has published work by important Canadian writers including Dorothy Livesay (at 18 years of age), L.M. Montgomery, Nellie McClung, Morley Callaghan, Margaret Atwood, and Adrienne Clarkson. Note that the magazine dropped "The" from the title in the 1930s.

magazine published an article in March 1939 about how "Men Don't Want Clever Wives," by the 1940s sentiments had changed with the necessities brought about by war. Patriotic headlines like "Shopping to Win the War: Buy British, Buy Canadian" (1940) accompany those on how to wear trousers properly "if you MUST wear them" (1943). By the 1950s, there were articles addressing the new needs of women in a changing society, "Makeover for a Working Wife" (1956) and "The Pill That Could Shake the World" (1953), although these articles sat beside "Don't Educate Your Daughter" (1954). By the end of the 1950s, the readership of *Chatelaine* was 1.6 million women for each issue, providing a reasonable indication of public opinion on gender concerns (80th Anniversary, 322). Women's issues, domestically and in the workforce, shifted dramatically over the period, but at the core were concerns for equality, public-private balance, and social rights.

Social and economic rights were sorely tested following the dramatic stock market crash of October 1929, when the New York Stock Exchange sales of stocks accelerated, leading to panic selling and tumbling prices in New York, London, Toronto, Montreal, and around the world. The event shocked the Western industrial world. While the Maritimes had been struggling with difficult economic conditions for years before the crash, the rest of the country had been in an economic boom. The economic depression had a disquieting effect on communities across the nation: all aspects of society were hit hard. In a few short years, the gross national product dropped by approximately 42% and one in five Canadians depended on the government for financial relief. Industrial jobs were difficult to come by, with massive layoffs and work slowdowns or stoppages at most major factories. The prairies were hit particularly hard with the double whammy of low grain prices, due to dismally high international tariffs, and poor crops due to years of drought. By 1933, the total personal income in the hardest-hit province, Saskatchewan, was 70% lower than it had been in 1928 (Alberta was down by 55%, Manitoba by 49%, and the national total by 38%). Due to years of crop failure and the black blizzards of the dust bowl, 66% of the rural population in Saskatchewan was forced onto government relief by the midpoint of the decade.

One offshoot of the economic crisis was a greater public understanding of the need for accessible contraception as a means of managing the population growth. While the birth control movement in Canada was originally started in the 1920s by leftist intellectuals, in the 1930s the economic imperative made the possibility more attractive to a wide range of people. The medical director of the first birth control clinic in the country, Dr. Elizabeth Bagshaw (1881–1982), linked the rise in acceptance of birth control and the economic situation in the 1930s: "There was no welfare and no unemployment payments, and these people were just about half-starved because there was no work, and for them to go on having children was a detriment to the country. They couldn't afford children if they couldn't afford to eat. So the families came to the clinic and we gave them information" ("Bagshaw"). Distributing contraception was not legalized in Canada until Pierre Trudeau, acting as Justice Minister (he became Prime Minister in 1968), introduced his controversial omnibus bill in the House of Commons in 1967 calling for massive changes to the Criminal Code of Canada, including decriminalization of contraception, and allowing some abortions under extremely restricted conditions (which came into effect in 1969).

According to cultural critics Geoff Pevere and Greig Dymond, during this decade of economic despair Hollywood film companies and New York radio shows often played on the public's desire for hope. With "family comedies, superheroics, gangster sagas, urban musicals, and urbane mysteries," people could escape from their own troubles through increasingly popular films, pulp fiction, and radio soap operas (so-called because they were sponsored by companies that manufactured cleaning products) (42). A window into this aspect of the period comes in Richard B. Wright's award-winning novel *Clara Callan* (2001), as he follows the glamorous career of a radio soap opera star in New York and that of her more tranquil sister in small-town Ontario. One real-life event captured the nation's attention as much as any soap opera. On 28 May 1934, five premature baby girls were born to poor farmers Elzire and Oliva Dionne in a log house on the outskirts of North Bay, Ontario. The birth of the Dionne Quintuplets was "arguably the North American pop-cultural event of the decade" (*Mondo* 42). Their survival was seen as miraculous. Citing fear of parental exploitation, the girls were made wards of the state and set up in a theme park named "Quintland" that was open to the public. They soon became international celebrities, appearing on the covers of the immensely popular *Time, Life,* and *Look* magazines, and were used in advertisements to sell everything from cars to cereal. By the time the sisters were four years old, the government of Ontario was making $20 million a year in ticket sales and product endorsements.

When the Depression began, William Lyon Mackenzie King was Prime Minister of Canada. Primarily as a result of his view that the crisis would pass and nothing exceptional was to be done, King was defeated in the 1930 election. The Conservative Party, under the leadership of R.B. Bennett, won on a campaign of government intervention. At first Bennett created make-work programs and instituted social assistance programs. However, due to government overspending and the unprecedented scope of poverty in the country, he had to suspend these actions. When Canadians could not afford gasoline for their cars, they had them pulled by horses. These horse-drawn "Bennett Buggies" have become a lasting symbol of the Depression in Canada. Bennett's Conservatives were defeated by the Liberals in 1935, again under the leadership of King, who now campaigned with the catchy slogan "King or Chaos."

Social unrest and political discontent arose among many young men who could not find employment or who were forced to work in federal relief camps for 20 cents a day. Anger at the impoverished working and living conditions of the work camps led thousands of men on the "On-to-Ottawa Trek." After going on strike in April 1935 and protesting for two months, they journeyed to Ottawa to bring their problems to the attention of the federal government. The Trek stopped in Regina, Saskatchewan, when Prime Minister Bennett asked for eight representatives to meet with him in Ottawa. When the Ottawa contingent returned to Regina to reunite with the other protesters and supporters (over 1500 people), the group was surrounded by Royal Canadian Mounted Police (RCMP) and attacked with clubs and tear gas. These types of clashes emerged out of people's growing awareness of social inequities at the time, but the government's response was part of its general suspicion of anything it labelled "communist," a paranoia that mounted in the 1930s and rose to a height in the Cold War era of the 1950s and '60s. Similar social action is depicted in Irene Baird's novel *Waste Heritage* (1939), based upon the aftermath of the 1938 occupation of the Vancouver Post Office by unemployed "sit-downers" who were evicted by police with tear gas. Later, Earle Birney encapsulated the desperation of the times and the need for grassroots action in his novel *Down the Long Table* (1955).

Still, the 1930s saw the rise of several protest political parties and a political reform movement. For instance, in order to deal with the devastating effects of the drought on western Canadian farmers, William "Bible Bill" Aberhart founded the Social Credit Party of Alberta along the principles of social credit—whereby government grants could be used to supplement the difference between production costs and an individual's purchasing power. Social Credit won the Alberta 1935 election by a landslide. Another party, the Co-operative Commonwealth Federation (CCF), was founded in 1932. Historian J.T. Morley notes that the organization was a "political coalition of progressive, socialist and labour forces anxious to establish a political vehicle capable of bringing about economic reforms to improve the circumstances of those suffering the effects of the Great Depression" ("CCF"). The philosophical basis for the CCF, articulated as the "Regina Manifesto," was composed by members of the League for Social Reconstruction (a left-wing intellectual group that included historian Frank Underhill and poet F.R. Scott) (see the Scott headnote for a fuller description of his role in the CCF). By 1944, under the leadership of Thomas (Tommy) Douglas, who would later become famous as the "father of socialized medicine in Canada," the CCF won the Saskatchewan provincial election and governed for the next 17 years. In 1961, the CCF merged with the Canadian Labour Congress to become the New Democratic Party, with Douglas at the helm.

The socialist politics of the CCF meshed well with the left-leaning mixture of pragmatism and idealism of many of the writers of the day. Livesay, Birney, Scott, and Klein, and also writers like Baird and Anne Marriott, were invested in making strong social statements in their work. Many of the most powerful and long-lasting works of art created at this time challenged the relationship between art, social responsibility, and the larger community. MacLennan's novel *The Watch That Ends the Night*, partially based on the work of noted Canadian socialist doctor Norman Bethune, outlines the trials of living in a state of economic uncertainty in the urban centre of Montreal. MacLennan's narrator recalls the "Thirties":

Of course the sun shone and the rain fell. I was young and there were many days when I was happy. There were nights when I was gay. There were times when, being young, I allowed myself the luxury of hope. But there was poison in the air then, and I think it spread from the rotting corpses of the first war. The Thirties lie behind us like the memory of guilt and shame. (123)

MacLennan's novel, published in 1959, highlights the lingering sense of disillusionment carried over from the 1930s. The Canadian economy improved with Canada's entry into the Second World War in 1939; it was not until the massive state expenditures necessitated by the war that unemployment was finally reduced to minimal levels by 1942.

The Second World War (1939–45)

The Second World War brought Canada out of the economic hardships of the thirties, but it also took a large human toll on the young nation. The global military event joined what had initially been two separate conflicts: the "Second Sino-Japanese War" (Japan had invaded China in 1937) and the war in Europe (declared in 1939). During the war, many of the world's nations aligned themselves with one of two opposing military alliances: the Allies (including Britain, France, Canada, America, and China) and the Axis Powers (Germany, Japan, and Italy). When Adolf Hitler and his National Socialist German Workers' Party (commonly known as the Nazi Party) army attacked Poland in September 1939, Britain and France declared war on Germany. On 10 September 1939, Canada officially declared war as an independent nation (unlike in the First World War, when Canada followed Britain into war without consulting Parliament to debate the nation's involvement). Over the next six years, the Canadian military played a vital role in the international conflicts. During the course of the war, over a million Canadian men and women served in the Canadian Army, the Royal Canadian Navy, the Royal Canadian Air Force, and with other Allied Forces. Over forty thousand Canadian men and women died for the cause. Canadian involvement in the war involved the defence of Britain from what appeared to be imminent Nazi invasion; the defence of Hong Kong against Japanese invasion; and many front-line offensives in Europe, including those at Dieppe (1941) and Juno Beach (1944) and in Italy. Canadian soldiers also played a key role in the liberation of Holland.

Canadians supported the war in Europe and the war against Japan as allies of Britain, but also for reasons of Canadian national security. Further, the effects of the Depression still lingered at the beginning of the war and thousands of single unemployed young men welcomed the possibility of employment that the war provided. In the opening months of the war, more than 50,000 Canadians volunteered to fight in Europe. As with the First World War, however, support was lower in Quebec than in the rest of Canada. At the outbreak of war, Prime Minister Mackenzie King promised that there would be no conscription. Along with European leaders, King had supported the policy of "appeasement" of Germany in the late 1930s, accepting Hitler's aggressive moves (the annexation of Austria in 1938 and the victory over Czechoslovakia in 1939), hoping that Germany would be satisfied with the consolidation of the German-speaking areas of Europe. When Canada entered the war, the idea was that Canadian involvement would be limited. However, following the "blitzkrieg" (massive attacks on Belgium, the Netherlands, and France in May 1940), and worried that Britain would be next, the Canadian government decided that the Axis Powers had to be stopped and committed more resources and more troops. With the occupation of France, British Prime Minister Winston Churchill resisted pressure to surrender Britain to Germany and called on "our empire beyond the seas" for assistance. The United States maintained a neutral position in the war until Japan bombed Pearl Harbor in December of 1941. Although Canada made a significant contribution to the war and was one of Britain's largest allies, Churchill and American President Franklin Delano Roosevelt primarily directed the Western allies.

As the war continued, King ordered a national registration for home defence and maintained his position against conscription, but added his famously equivocal statement "Conscription if necessary, but not necessarily conscription." His government ended up passing the National Resources Mobilization Act, requiring all single men to register for home defence, but stopped short of conscription for overseas service. King also commanded factories to begin 24-hour-a-day, seven-day-a-week production of war supplies. Everyone was encouraged to do his or her part at home and overseas. Women and families in Canada were urged to knit sweaters, recycle cans and bottles for metal and glass for the factories, share resources, and tend small "Victory Gardens" to grow food for the war effort. The government created propaganda posters in order to raise funds for the war effort by drawing on a sense of Canadian community and common values worthy of sacrifice (Figures V-8 and V-9). It also helped manufacture consent amongst the populace by whipping up anti-German and anti-Japanese fervour. The majority of Canadians believed the war to be a worthy cause, one where valour was rewarded and the enemy Axis Powers were clearly considered to be in the wrong. It was for this reason, as well, that many Canadians supported the sanctions against Canadians of Japanese heritage, which included the creation of a *cordon sanitaire* of 100 miles from the coast of B.C., the internment of tens of thousands of people, the confiscation of goods and property, and the separation of family members from each other (see Figure V-7). In retrospect, it is now widely acknowledged that the Canadian government's treatment of Canadians of Japanese ancestry during the war went far beyond issues of national security and was in fact a case of prejudice (Canadians of German heritage were not treated in the same systematic manner) and large-scale injustice (see Muriel Kitagawa's letters in this section for more details). The war came to an end in Europe on VE Day (Victory in Europe), 8 May 1945, when, just days after Hitler committed suicide, German forces in Italy surrendered. Three months later, on 15 August 1945, Japan surrendered to the Allied forces following the American atomic bombings of Hiroshima and Nagasaki. The horrors wrought in Japan by these bombs, the death of over 200,000 civilians and the disfigurement of countless others, led in part to the fears of subsequent generations around the possibility of nuclear war in the new "Atomic Age."

One of the most horrific events of the Second World War was the Holocaust, the state-organized murder of approximately six million Jewish men, women, and children by Nazi Germany and its collaborators. The extermination of the Jewish population of German-controlled Europe was planned and executed in stages during Hitler's rule. Legislation for the removal of Jews from civil society began well before the war. Hitler's belief in racial purity, German nationalism, and Aryan superiority led to the creation of concentration camps and, after his introduction of "the Final Solution" in late 1941, extermination camps. Inmates in concentration camps such as Dachau were used as slave labour until they died of exhaustion or disease. Camps such as Auschwitz and Treblinka were places where millions of men, women, and children were taken to die of starvation or to be murdered in gas chambers. Historian Donald Niewyk notes that in addition to the systematic persecution of Jews, the Nazis also targeted millions of people belonging to other groups: Gypsies (Romas), the physically and mentally handicapped, Soviet prisoners of war, religious dissenters, and homosexuals. The legacy of Nazi persecution in Europe during the war is long-standing and deeply felt even today.

In recognition of the atrocities of the war, in December 1948 the General Assembly of the United Nations adopted and proclaimed *The Universal Declaration of Human Rights*. For the first time, an international group set forth the inalienable rights and fundamental freedoms of each and every person on earth. Arguing that "disregard and contempt for human rights have resulted in barbarous acts which have outraged the conscience of mankind," the Declaration is a strong indictment of humanity's capacity for discrimination. Alongside negotiators from France, the United States, Lebanon, and China, a Canadian lawyer named John Humphrey played a key role in the creation and adoption of the landmark UN document. The Declaration became central in the development of the 1982 Canadian Charter of Rights and Freedoms.

Of the many Canadian writers and poets of this period, A.M. Klein was perhaps the most vocal opponent of the Canadian government's position against accepting refugees from Europe in the 1930s. Canada at the time had arguably the worst record of all possible receiving states in the admission of refugees from Nazi Germany, as Irving Abella and Harold Troper record in *None Is Too Many* (vii), accepting only 5,000 Jews who had escaped from Nazi-controlled Europe between 1933 and 1939. Abella and Troper also infer that the rejection of refugees by democratic countries was understood by the Nazis to be approval of their anti-Semitic policies. When the *St Louis* sailed from Germany with 930 Jewish refugees on board in 1939, no country in the Americas would allow them to land. Klein's scathing satire of the government's anti-Semitic position, "A Modest Proposal" (included in this section; see his headnote for a complete discussion of his position in defence of Europe's fleeing Jews), lambastes Canada for ignoring the problems in Europe. In 1944 Klein published *The Hitleriad*, a savagely satiric indictment of Hitler written in mock epic form (in the style of Alexander Pope's *The Dunciad*).[5]

Postwar Immigration: "A Calculated Kindness"

Following Canada's successful war effort, and in keeping with the Canadian government's bid for complete autonomy, Canada introduced legal Canadian citizenship. Until 1947, those living in Canada were designated British subjects resident in Canada. When the Canadian Citizenship Act came into effect on 1 January 1947, those who had previously been "subjects of the Crown" were now "Canadian citizens." Mackenzie King received the first certificate of Canadian citizenship. Henceforth, in a precursor to the Charter of Rights and Freedoms (1982), under the law all Canadians were to be regarded as equal, irrespective of whether they were Canadian-born or naturalized citizens, regardless of heritage, religion, national origin, or any proprietary claim that one group might make to being more Canadian than another.

During the economic turmoil of the 1930s, immigration rates plummeted to a virtual standstill with both the government and the public balking at the prospect of new immigration. However, following the war, with increased economic prosperity and an ever-rising demand for labour, immigration was once again seen as an economic necessity. The postwar immigrants were needed to fill jobs in agriculture, the new urban-based manufacturing sector, the construction of affordable housing, and the skilled labour professions. While industry required workers, the government initially retained its preference for British, Dutch, and Northern European immigrants as the "best" kinds of workers and the most easily assimilable future Canadians. On 1 May 1947, King argued in the House of Commons that Canada is "perfectly within her rights in selecting the persons whom we regard as desirable future citizens. Large-scale immigration from the Orient would change the fundamental composition of the Canadian population." However, that same month the Chinese Immigration Act was finally repealed (see Volume I, Section III). It took until 1 April 1949 for Japanese Canadians to regain their freedom to live anywhere in Canada.

Business interests in Canada warned that economic prosperity was in jeopardy if there were not enough people willing to assume low-wage and low-status positions rejected by "preferred" immigrants and native-born Canadians. They urged the government to "skim off the cream of the almost one-million-strong labour pool languishing in the displaced persons (DP) camps in Germany,

---

[5] The legacy of war permeates generations of Canadian writing. Many novels deal with the war, the Holocaust, human rights abuses, and the atomic bomb: Hugh Garner's *Storm Below* (1949); Earle Birney's *Turvey* (1949); Douglas LePan's *The Deserter* (1964); Roch Carrier's *La Guerre, Yes Sir!* (1968); Joy Kogawa's *Obasan* (1981); Timothy Findley's *Famous Last Words* (1981) and *The Telling of Lies* (1986); Matt Cohen's *Emotional Arithmetic* (1990); Michael Ondaatje's *The English Patient* (1992); Wayson Choy's *The Jade Peony* (1995); Anne Michaels's *Fugitive Pieces* (1996); Dennis Bock's *The Ash Garden* (2001); and Michael Crummey's *The Wreckage* (2005) figure among the works that respond to the war and its aftermath.

Austria, and Italy before other labour-short nations—including the United States and Australia—beat Canada to the punch" (Troper 28). Canada thus admitted over 180,000 Displaced Persons (individuals made homeless by the war or who refused repatriation) between 1947 and 1952. These men and women accepted what Troper calls "Canada's calculated kindness" and agreed to work in prescribed industrial, service sector, or domestic jobs in order to gain entry to Canadian society and the promise the country held for future generations. The labour importation scheme that led to the influx of Displaced Persons to Canada greatly added to the heterogeneity of the nation. Such heterogeneity, however, by and large did not become evident in mainstream Canadian literature until the next generation.

In 1952, the government updated immigration law to focus recruitment not on farmers, but rather on industrial and urban labour. The new Immigration Act that came into effect on 1 June 1953 still provided for the refusal of admission on the grounds of nationality, ethnic group, geographical area of origin, and unsuitability with regard to the climate. With business still concerned over possible labour shortages, immigrant recruitment expanded to include Southern Europe. The label "enemy alien" was discarded for Italians in 1947 and for Germans in 1950 (the marker was a holdover from the Second World War). Further, in the early 1950s, immigration to Canada from Greece and Portugal increased markedly. The influx of people from Southern Europe helped develop religious, cultural, and social pluralism in the urban centres.

Canada also became more attuned to its role in international crises. Following the Soviet Red Army's bloody repression of the Hungarian Revolt, for instance, Canada welcomed 37,000 Hungarian refugees (Whitaker and Hewitt 244). Although the Canadian government promoted the assimilation of immigrants into mainstream Canadian society, many immigrants rejected the notion of total assimilation and opted instead to retain significant cultural, religious, and social practices of their ancestral lands. Moreover, some stories of immigration reveal the racism that new immigrants faced in Canada during these years. In his essay from the late 1920s, "Canadians New and Old" (included here), Frederick Philip Grove was critical of the double standard in the Canadian mainstream's reluctant reception of new immigrants. A.M. Klein, Irving Layton, and later Mordecai Richler also highlight the prevalence of Canadian anti-Semitism even as they note the country's need for Jewish workers. As Canada moved into the 1960s with a loosening of immigration restrictions for people from Asia, South America, and South East Asia, the country also moved toward the official Multiculturalism Policy of 1971. This, too, would lead to a reshaping of Canada in more inclusive terms.

Newfoundland Joins Confederation

Canada also grew in another significant way at the end of the 1940s. When the four provinces of New Brunswick, Nova Scotia, Ontario, and Quebec united to form Canada in 1867, Newfoundland had decided not to join. Instead, it opted to remain a self-governing British colony (see "The Anti-Confederation Song" in Volume I). In spite of revived talks of confederation with Canada in 1895, Newfoundland remained independent. In the early twentieth century the Newfoundland government spent heavily on the construction of railway lines and public services that drew on funds far beyond its means. Newfoundland also suffered devastating, and expensive, losses in the First World War.[6] Such spending continued into the 1920s. When the Depression hit in the 1930s, the colony was in grave debt. In a desperate situation, Newfoundland appealed to Britain for assistance. A Commission of Government responsible for the administration of the colony replaced the system of responsible government (home rule) that had been in place so that now authority rested with the British Parliament.

Following the prosperity that came with the Second World War, many Newfoundlanders decided it was time to move on from the Commission. The question became a heated one over what form the new government should take. The American military presence established in the colony in the 1940s worried some Newfoundlanders (and some Canadians) that America was creating a stronghold in the region. The Newfoundland National Convention was struck to evaluate the possibilities for Newfoundland's future and make recommendations to the British government. On one side were those who argued for a return to independent responsible government (led by delegate Peter Cashin); on another side were those who wished to form a union with Canada (led by delegate Joseph "Joey" Smallwood). Yet another side argued that it was best to hold the course and retain the Commission of Government. It was decided to put the vote to a citizens' referendum, in which voters were asked to choose one of the three options. Smallwood emphasized the increased social services that Newfoundlanders would receive through a union with Canada, whereas Cashin appealed to the patriotism of Newfoundlanders and stressed the loss of independence. See Figures V-10 and V-11 for propagandistic political cartoons supporting both sides of the debate.

When the results of the first referendum were inconclusive, it was deemed necessary to hold a second vote. The second referendum (22 July 1948) resulted in a narrow victory for Confederation, with approximately 78,000 votes (52.3%) claiming victory over a total of slightly greater than 71,000 votes (47.7%) for responsible government. The British North America Act, 1949 was put into effect on 31 March 1949 to confirm the union of Canada and Newfoundland. While public ceremonies celebrated Confederation in both Ottawa and St. John's, there were also black flags of mourning draped on the windows of many buildings in the new province. In the end, Newfoundland's union with Canada caused deep and lasting rifts within the "colony of unrequited dreams," as Wayne Johnston

---

[6] Of particular note is the devastation faced by the 1st Newfoundland Regiment on 1 July 1916 at Beaumont-Hamel, on the first day of the battle of the Somme, when hundreds of Newfoundlanders were injured or killed in the single most deadly day of the war for the colony. In Newfoundland today, the first of July is marked by some as Memorial Day, rather than as Canada Day, to remember the fallen at Beaumont-Hamel.

put it in his 1998 novel of the same title. Smallwood, self-dubbed "the Last Father of Confederation," became the premier of the new province and governed in that role until 1972.

The Cold War and the Suburban Fifties

Between the end of the Second World War in 1945 and the fall of the Berlin Wall in 1989, the "Cold War" was waged on political, economic, and diplomatic terms between two superpowers and their allies. The United States and the Soviet Union (USSR) stood ready to initiate a nuclear apocalypse. In 1948, External Affairs Minister (and future Prime Minister) Louis St. Laurent bluntly stated that foreign policy must "be based on a recognition of the fact that totalitarian communist aggression endangers the freedom and peace of every democratic country, including Canada" (Bliss 322). The world became loosely divided along ideological lines: Democracy and Capitalism vs. Communism. In response to fears of nuclear war, Canada was an original signatory to the North Atlantic Treaty Organization (NATO 1949)—Canada's first peacetime military alliance—and a participant in a military alliance against the Soviet bloc. Still, the presence of the Cold War within the nation took Canada by surprise when the 1945 defection of Igor Gouzenko, a cipher clerk in the Soviet Embassy in Ottawa, brought out evidence of espionage against the Canadian state. It was difficult for Canadians to believe that a "Russian spy" was actually operating in Ottawa. In response to Gouzenko's allegations of a substantial spy ring in the Canadian civil service, Prime Minister King established the Kellock-Taschereau Royal Commission (1946) and half a dozen people were charged. While Senator Joseph McCarthy chaired the U.S. "House Committee on Un-American Activities" (1947), accusing hundreds of left-wing Americans of being disloyal and treasonous, and of being "Communists," in Canada the RCMP were policing Canadian politics (Whitaker and Hewitt 12). As in the United States, the Kellock-Taschereau Commission in Canada linked the threat of Soviet espionage to the internal threat of Communist subversion, contributing to an escalating paranoia as the government attempted to stamp out anything deemed subversive as they searched for the "enemy within."

In *Love, Hate, and Fear in Canada's Cold War* (2004), Richard Cavell argues that it is vital to recognize that while there is overlap with the McCarthy witch hunt and the Red Scare in the United States, the Cold War was articulated differently in Canada. Drawing on the work of Robert Corber, Cavell notes how the labelling of left-wing intellectuals and activists as "homosexual" led to a culture of containment and regulation within the Canadian civil service. Morality was thus linked to state security during this time. As cultural historian Mary Louise Adams documents, in response to fears of the "representations of sexuality in so-called indecent or lewd publications" (139), a special parliamentary committee on "salacious and indecent literature" reported that "the freedom-loving, democratic countries have need of all the strength in their moral fibre to combat the evil threat, and anything that undermines the morals of our citizens and particularly the young is a direct un-Canadian threat" (qtd. in Adams 139). Movements such as these contributed to a general atmosphere of paranoia: no one wanted to be considered "un-Canadian" in this time of heightened national defence.

As the Cold War hostilities between the West and the East intensified over the course of the 1950s, another international conflict arose. The war in Korea, between the Communist People's Republic to the north and the pro-Western Republic of Korea to the south, resulted in millions of civilian deaths as U.S. airpower reduced North Korea to rubble (Whitaker and Hewitt 71). It also claimed the lives of over 300 Canadians serving with United Nations forces (1950–53). In 1956, Canada once again entered an international conflict as Canadian diplomat (and future Prime Minister, 1963–68) Lester B. Pearson stepped onto the world stage when he mediated a settlement between Great Britain (which threatened to invade Egypt to keep the Suez Canal open) and Egypt. Pearson's solution was to have a UN-led peace force, neither British nor Egyptian, guard the canal. Canada's commitment to peacekeeping was born. It has since become a defining element of Canadian foreign policy and a popular element of the contemporary Canadian self-image. Canadians were filled with pride when Pearson's role in averting war in the Suez Crisis was acknowledged with a Nobel Prize for Peace. When he became Prime Minister, Pearson continued to position Canada as a peacekeeping middle power, arguing that the "essential purpose" of Canadian foreign policy was "the promotion, by every means within its power, of accord between London and Washington" (Bliss 326).

The new Conservative Prime Minister, John Diefenbaker (1957–63), who wrested power from the hands of the Liberals after 22 years in control (1935–57), did not share Pearson's views on diplomacy with the United States. He had particularly cold relations with President John F. Kennedy. The populist from Saskatchewan was elected with a vision of Canada as a strong northern nation. He also worked diligently to make the west an equal participant in the Confederation (in practice as well as on paper). A dazzling orator, the "Chief" electrified crowds with his passion for a unified nation. With "Dief" and Pearson (now leader of the Liberal Party) at loggerheads at the end of the decade, Canada moved into the political refashioning that was to follow in the 1960s with the birth of medicare and the new Canadian flag.

To understand the subsequent liberation movements of the 1960s and '70s, and the inter-generational gap that arose as a result, it is helpful to consider how many of the ideals and attitudes of the 1960s were sowed in the postwar period immediately following the Second World War. The war had shown people the horrors to which racism and intolerance could lead, and this awareness arguably informed many of the civil rights and peace movements of the decades to follow. In the 1950s, people embraced the incredible affluence and prosperity that abounded following the war—the high degree of employment, the relative wealth among the middle classes, the increase in the number of universities, the sense of having left the Depression era far behind. People were abandoning rural livelihoods for urban living, and in North America, families were moving in huge numbers to the newly developed suburbs on the outskirts of cities (Don Mills, outside Toronto, was the first in Canada), buying large houses in clean, orderly neighbourhoods. Such instant communities, where homogeneity of architectural form mirrored the expectations of social conformity, exemplified the postwar ethos (see Margaret Atwood's poem "The City Planners").

This period was also marked by the integration of technology into everyday life in the home and neighbourhood with fast cars, accessible air travel, long distance telephones, the advent of take-out food, drive-in movies, indispensable time-saving household appliances, portable radios, and finally televisions that could bring politics, music, and fashion right into people's living rooms. Indeed, it is hard to overestimate the cultural and social impact of television. As Marshall McLuhan was quick to point out in his pronouncement in *Understanding Media* in 1964, "The medium is the message." Television changed the way people experienced the world: it was powerful, immediate, inside one's home. Although television was invented in the 1920s, it was initially a very expensive luxury. In the late 1950s fewer than 50% of Canadian homes had a television set; by 1965, over 90% owned one.[7] Many Canadians who could afford it revelled in the "conspicuous consumption" that came with 1950s life in Canada. Yet there was still an alarming rate of poverty among First Nations people and in immigrant communities.

This indulgence in "conspicuous consumption" was accompanied by a need for security—indeed, the underside of the conventionalism and homogeneity of the 1950s was an anxiety that these new acquisitions could be easily undermined. As historian Todd Gitlin puts it, this generation was "formed in the jaws of an extreme and wrenching tension between the assumption of affluence and its opposite, a terror of loss, destruction, and failure" (12). Individual families, fearing an imminent Communist attack and a replay of the atom bomb (still with the lingering image of the final days of the Second World War in their minds), built bomb shelters in their basements or on their properties. It was a time when a sense of public morality and decency was paramount, and when the older generation began to worry about the gyrating hips of a singer like Elvis Presley and the flow of "sexy" magazines across the border. Mary Louise Adams, writing about newly imposed obscenity laws, shows how the success of "trashy novels and dirty magazines contradicted the many efforts to build 'fine moral citizens' that were popular in postwar Canada, such as sports clubs, teen canteens, and lectures on family life education" (154). The family became the retreat of security and comfort.

During the war, thousands of women had worked in offices and in factories, and had served in the armed forces, often as nurses or interpreters. After the war, gender expectations reverted to prewar ideals. The myth that advertisers and

[7] Canada first began broadcasting colour television programs in 1966.

television producers perpetuated of the patient, well-dressed domestic woman, martini in hand, waiting at the door for her tired husband to return from a tough day at the office—as in the American television program *Leave It to Beaver* (1957–63)—was raged against by feminists in the decades to come, most memorably by Betty Friedan in her compelling exposé of the postwar decades, *The Feminine Mystique* (1963). At the heart of the family-centred world stood the mother in the role of "homemaker." This assertion of women's role in the home in turn meant larger families. Postwar birth rates soared in Canada, the United States, Australia, and New Zealand until well into the 1960s. This phenomenon, known as the "baby boom," was perhaps the biggest influence on the period that was to follow, for it was this generation of children who would become the activists and writers of the next decades. The "boomers," born in the period roughly between 1948 and 1960, constituted an enormous group and would initiate the "revolution" of the next two decades.

The seeds of a counterculture movement were already evident in the 1950s. This was the beginning of rock 'n' roll—when Elvis Presley, Buddy Holly, Chuck Berry, Little Richard, and Fats Domino took America by storm. It was also the period of the disaffected young, male anti-hero—the "angry young man"—epitomized in the characters played by Hollywood actors such as James Dean (*Rebel Without a Cause*, 1955) and Marlon Brando (*A Streetcar Named Desire*, 1951); the period that saw the rise of the "Beat generation" and the road novel; J.D. Salinger's cult novel, *The Catcher in the Rye* (1951), with its existentially tormented anti-hero Holden Caulfield; and the tragedy of the American "everyman" Willy Loman in Arthur Miller's *Death of a Salesman* (1949). It is easy to see in these writers the seeds of such iconic 1960s/'70s authors as Leonard Cohen, bpNichol, and Margaret Atwood. Gitlin refers to many of these 1950s texts as "parables of estrangement" (29), which they were, but in the 1960s this estrangement became funnelled into specifically political ends, as the counterculture and civil rights movements sought to "speak truth to power" in their championing of marginal voices. By the late 1950s, the radicalism of modernist poets like Smith and Klein no longer seemed cutting-edge. As Fidel Castro's revolutionaries came to power in Cuba in 1959, a new generation of artists in Canada entered a decade that would bring changes no one had anticipated.

FIGURE V-1 *The West Wind* **(1917), Tom Thomson (1877–1917)**

Tom Thomson was a friend and mentor of the artists who later formed the Group of Seven. In 1917, three years before the Group of Seven had their first group exhibition, Thomson died tragically in a canoeing accident in Algonquin Park. Thomson's *The West Wind* is one of the most enduring images in the history of Canadian landscape painting. With its fierce treatment of the environment, the painting is said to have inspired a generation of modernist painters and poets to rethink their relationship to the Canadian landscape. In an essay in the *McMaster Monthly* (1934), Group of Seven member Arthur Lismer explains that "Tom Thomson's *The West Wind* is the spirit of Canada made manifest in a picture. It is a symbol of our Canadian character." A.J.M. Smith's poem "The Lonely Land" was likely inspired by *The West Wind*. In both works, the pine tree is used as an emblem of a hardy, and humble, northern spirit. Although today the painting is regularly reproduced and sold as a quintessential image of the nation, at the time it was painted it represented a bold and innovative depiction of the Canadian landscape.

Source: Tom Thomson, Canadian, 1877–1917; *The West Wind*, 1917; oil on canvas; 120.7 x 137.9 cm; Art Gallery of Ontario, Toronto; Gift of the Canadian Club of Toronto, 1926; © 2008 Art Gallery of Ontario.

FIGURE V-2 *Indian Church* (1929), Emily Carr (1871–1945)

Emily Carr painted *Indian Church* on a trip to Nootka Island. This painting, which can be viewed alongside her story of a visit to a missionary church in "Ucluelet," illustrates Carr's attempt to locate art squarely in British Columbia with a style suited to the West Coast landscape. The painting evokes the power of the forest as the trees engulf the small church below. The contrast of the green and grey pines and the still whiteness of the church unsettles the naturalness of the building, and the religion it stands for. The painting joins a sublime view of nature (or the sense of nature as inspiring awe or reverence, by reason of its immensity or grandeur) with the picturesque (framing nature in a domesticated context). Carr's artistic credo from 1912 still rings true in this work: "Art is art, nature is nature, you cannot improve upon it."

FIGURE V-3 *Mt. Lefroy, 1930,* **Lawren Harris (1885–1970)**

According to Group of Seven founding member Lawren Harris, "If we view a great mountain soaring into the sky, it may excite us, evoke an uplifted feeling within us. . . . The artist takes that response and its feelings and shapes it on canvas with paint so that when finished it contains the experience." This portrait showing Mt. Lefroy in Banff National Park, on the Alberta/British Columbia border, evokes a sense of wonder and fear. It echoes the description of the mountain in Earle Birney's poem "Bushed": "Then he knew though the mountain slept the winds / were shaping its peak to an arrowhead / poised." See Lawren Harris's essay "Revelation of Art in Canada" for more details on his views on art and the nation.

Source: Lawren S. Harris, 1885–1970; *Mt. Lefroy*, 1930; oil on canvas; 133.5 x 153.5 cm; Purchase 1975; McMichael Canadian Art Collection; 1975.7.

FIGURE V-4 Archie Belaney, c. 1901

These two photographs convey the transformation of Archibald Belaney from a proper English schoolboy in Hastings, England, to a Canadian wilderness man and "Indian" named Grey Owl. The 12-year-old Archie Belaney, "posing stiffly in his dark woollen Sunday suit / beside his Aunt's collie," as Armand Garnet Ruffo writes in his poem "Imagined Country," "has the ability to see himself / (as you see him) clear across the ocean, all the way / into the heart of the imagined country called Canada."

Source: Library and Archives Canada, PA 147585.

FIGURE V-5 Archibald Belaney/Grey Owl

As an adult, Belaney fashioned himself as an "Indian" conservationist, lover of animals, and naturalist named Grey Owl (Wa-Sha-Quon-Asin). Many non-Native observers were convinced that he was Aboriginal because he conformed to romanticized Western notions of what an "Indian" should look like. This photograph originally accompanied Grey Owl's story of the rescue of the beaver kittens (included here) in *Pilgrims of the Wild* (1934) with the following caption: "Jelly Roll asleep on Grey Owl's knee. 'She would rest her head on my knee . . . Talking meanwhile in her uncanny language.'"

Source: Glenbow Archives, NA4868-214.

FIGURE V-6 "The Last Spike" (1885)
This famous photograph was staged as the official publicity shot to mark the completion of the Canadian Pacific Railway on 7 November 1885. The photo shows company director Donald Smith hammering in the ceremonial "last spike," in Craigellachie, B.C. To his right stands CPR general manager William Cornelius Van Horne; between them is chief engineer Sandford Fleming. This is the photo that is commemorated in the conclusion to E.J. Pratt's 1952 epic poem "Towards the Last Spike," where the reverberations from the hammer's blow initiate "a massed continental chorus."

Source: Glenbow Archives, NA1494-5.

FIGURE V-7 Confiscated Boats, British Columbia 1942
As part of the invocation of the War Measures Act immediately after the bombing of Pearl Harbor in 1941, fishing boats owned by Japanese Canadians were impounded at the Annieville Dyke on the Fraser River, near Vancouver. Approximately 1200 boats were seized and sold by order-in-council of the B.C. Securities Commission during January and February 1942. See also Muriel Kitagawa's letters in this section.

Source: Studio: Leonard Frank photo, Vancouver Public Library, Special Collections, VPL31890.

**Figures V-8 and V-9 World War II Victory Bonds Posters: "Keep These Hands Off"
and "I'm Making Bombs and Buying Bonds"**

These Second World War posters were created to help raise funds for the war effort. War
bonds are debt security bonds issued by the government in times of war for the purpose of
raising money to finance military operations. The campaign for Victory Bonds had been so
successful in the First World War that the government returned to them in the Second World
War. Such posters were to help mobilize public opinion on the home front in support of the
war. The promotional material contains an emotional appeal to patriotism, urging citizens to
support the war effort by investing their savings in the bonds. The posters are meant to be a
reminder of what is at stake in the war effort. The hands in "Keep These Hands Off" have
symbols of the enemies embedded in them. The Nazi swastika and the Japanese setting sun
loom over the vulnerable young woman and child. "I'm Making Bombs and Buying Bonds"
shows two ways in which women could participate in the war effort—working in munitions
factories and lending savings to the government.

Source: Library and Archives Canada, C-90883 (top); Library and Archives Canada, C-91436
bottom).

"Shall We Say Grace?"

FIGURE V-10 "Shall We Say Grace" (1947), by Herbert Block ("Herblock")

This cartoon, in support of Newfoundland joining Canada in Confederation, was originally published in the 10 October 1947 *Washington Post* to promote the Marshall Plan (for the United States to provide financial aid to the governments and citizens of America's European allies and to help the millions left homeless and impoverished in Europe after the Second World War). The depiction of starving faces looking longingly at the wealthy as they feast would have appealed to the passionate feelings of those in Newfoundland, led by Joey Smallwood, who argued that it was time for the struggling colony to benefit from the prosperity of Canada. The Confederate Association, supporting union with Canada, was formed on 21 February 1948 and immediately began publishing *The Confederate*. The cartoon was placed in *The Confederate* three months later, on 20 May 1948.

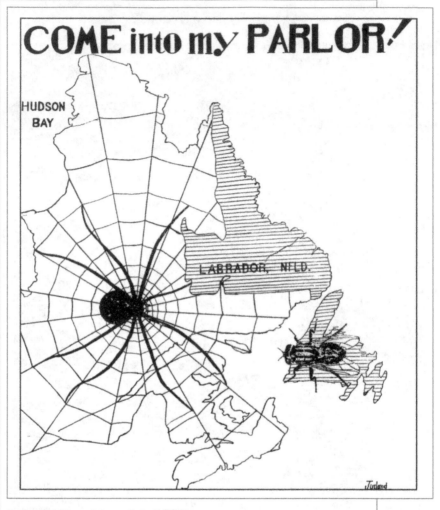

Figure V-11 "Come into my Parlor!" (1948)

Shortly after *The Confederate* published Herblock's "Shall We Say Grace," the Responsible Government League (led by Peter Cashin), supporting an independent Newfoundland, responded with "Come into my Parlor!" (published in *The Independent*, 31 May 1948). Drawing on the lyrics of the popular song "The Spider and the Fly" by English author Mary Howitt (1799–1888), the cartoon depicts Newfoundland as a vulnerable fly waiting to be eaten in the web of Canada. Both cartoons touch on the fiery emotions that were involved in the debate over whether Newfoundland should join Canada (which it did in 1949). See the introduction to Section V for more details.

Source: Jutland, published in *The Independent*, May 31, 1948.

Emily Carr is perhaps the most famous painter in British Columbia today. Indeed, she has become an icon of Canadian art and culture. The leading school of fine art and design in the province is named after her, and the Vancouver Art Gallery has a permanent gallery dedicated to her work. Yet it was only later in her lifetime that her art gained national recognition.

Her artistic acclaim has tended to overshadow her achievement, also arrived at late in life, as a writer. Although she did not publish her first book until just before her 70th birthday, within a few years she published *Klee Wyck* (1941) (which won the Governor General's Award for non-fiction), *The Book of Small* (1942), and *The House of All Sorts* (1944), followed by four other major works published posthumously. Born in Victoria, B.C., Carr was the daughter of English merchants who came to Canada via the California goldfields. After her mother died when she was 12 and her father when she was 14, she was raised by her strict older sisters. Victoria was a small town for someone like Carr, who was known for keeping a pet monkey (named Woo) and for pushing her art supplies around the city in a baby carriage.

Although she spent most of her life on Vancouver Island, Carr also studied in the United States, England, and France. However, when she returned to B.C. following her studies, she could not earn a living from selling her paintings, so she turned her home into a boarding house, bred sheepdogs, taught art classes to children, and made ceramics to sell to tourists. Writer Ethel Wilson recalls taking private art lessons from Carr in Vancouver in 1906–07: "But as the lessons consisted entirely of conversation, and I did not recognize genius, and I earned only $47.50 a month and had no talent, I could not afford to buy conversation." Wilson adds that "there were things about her parrots that I did not like."

In 1927 Carr was invited to the National Gallery in Ottawa for her first major show outside of British Columbia. At the show, she had the opportunity to meet several members of the Group of Seven, and was particularly taken with Lawren Harris's paintings. She wrote in her diary: "Oh, God, what have I seen? Where have I been? Something has spoken to the very soul of me, wonderful, mighty, not of this world." Harris and the Group of Seven had a profound influence on Carr's work, in large part because they made her feel less isolated in her own artistic endeavours. Harris, in turn, recognized Carr's importance and lamented her lack of public recognition. Like the Group of Seven, Carr was invested in finding a mode of expression that suited Canadian landscapes and contexts. In the *McGill News* in June 1929, Carr called for the formation of a uniquely Canadian art: "What are we Canadian artists of the west going to do with our art? We are young yet, and are only slowly finding a way, but are we obliged to bedeck ourselves in borrowed plumes and copy art born of other countries and not ours?" The answer for her was clearly no.

Carr turned to two things for inspiration in her painting: what her biographer Doris Shadbolt calls the "material presence of the aboriginal culture of the past" (totem poles, masks, and ruins of houses) and the distinctive local West Coast landscape (trees, brush, water, and skies). Carr's paintings are examples of colourful and dramatic expressionism.

Her striking use of heavy greens, blues, and greys with bold brush strokes creates landscapes that surge with motion and intensity. Her art captures the sublime power of the rain forests and islands of the North American West Coast (see Figure V-2).

In the late 1930s she turned from painting to writing and published her first autobiographical work, *Klee Wyck,* in 1941. It tells the story of her life and travels in short literary vignettes. Her work is part of the Canadian tradition of short story cycles following D.C. Scott's *In the Village of Viger* (1896), Stephen Leacock's *Sunshine Sketches of a Little Town* (1912), and F.P. Grove's *Over Prairie Trails* (1922). In "Ucluelet," the first story in *Klee Wyck,* Carr recalls her early visit to Ucluelet on the west coast of Vancouver Island to visit her older sister Lizzie, who was living among the people of the Ucluelet First Nation (the Maa-nulth people) as a missionary. The visit ignited Carr's enduring fascination with the Indigenous peoples of British Columbia.

Over the course of her life she visited many communities up and down the coast of B.C., Alaska, and the Queen Charlotte Islands. Following the prevailing belief at the time that the Northwest Coast Nations and cultures were inevitably disappearing due to European encroachment on their lands, Carr chose to document aspects of coastal First Nations cultures (particularly of the Haida, Gitksan, and Tlingit Nations), especially the totem poles and longhouses, before they were gone.

Following in Carr's footsteps, in the 1920s and '30s a number of eastern Canadian and American artists explored the totem villages: Langdon Kihn, A.Y. Jackson, Edwin Holgate, and Ann Savage took sketching trips to Gitksan villages on the Skeena River to paint portraits of the totem poles. These artistic treatments of First Nations cultures and symbols have been subject to much debate over the past years. Some feel that such art is an instance of cultural appropriation of Native subjects by non-Native artists, while others find the depictions to be respectful portraits of local communities. Art historian Gerta Moray has called Carr's treatment of First Nations imagery "aestheticized nostalgia," referring to Carr's perpetuation of the notion that the First Nations cultures were in decline by painting them in decline. It has been argued, in response, that she did so in an effort to preserve the cultural artifacts aesthetically. The debate can be fruitfully extended to a reading of "Ucluelet" and the picture Carr paints of this community and the missionary church in the late nineteenth century.

Ucluelet

The lady missionaries expected me. They sent an enormous Irishman in a tiny canoe to meet the steamer. We got to the Ucluelet wharf soon after dawn. Everything was big and cold and strange to me, a fifteen-year old school-girl. I was the only soul on the wharf. The Irishman did not have any trouble deciding which was I.

It was low tide, so there was a long, sickening ladder with slimy rungs to climb down to get to the canoe. The man's big laugh and the tippiness of the canoe were even more frightening than the ladder. The paddle in his great arms rushed the canoe through the waves.

We came to Toxis, which was the Indian name for the Mission House. It stood just above high-tide water. The sea was in front of it and the forest behind.

The house was of wood, unpainted. There were no blinds or curtains. It looked, as we paddled up to it, as if it were stuffed with black. When the canoe stuck in the mud, the big Irishman picked me up in his arms and set me down on the doorstep.

The missionaries were at the door. Smells of cooking fish jumped out past them. People lived on fish at Ucluelet.

Both the missionaries were dignified, but the Greater Missionary had the most dignity: the Lesser Missionary was fussy. They had long pale faces. Their hair was licked from their foreheads back to buns on the scruffs of their necks. They had long noses straddled by spectacles, thin lips, mild eyes, and wore straight, dark dresses buttoned to the chin.

There was only two of everything in the kitchen, so I had to sit on a box, drink from a bowl and eat my food out of a tin pie-dish.

After breakfast came a long Presbyterian prayer. Outside the kitchen window, just a few feet away at the edge of the forest, stood a grand balsam pine tree. It was very tall and straight.

The sizzling of the Missionaries' "trespasses" jumped me back from the pine tree to the Lord's Prayer just in time to "Amen". We got up from our knees to find the house full of Indians. They had come to look at me.

I felt so young and empty standing there before the Indians and the two grave Missionaries! The Chief, old Hipi, was held to be a reader of faces. He perched himself on the top of the Missionaries' drug cupboard; his brown fists clutched the edge of it, his elbows taut and shoulders hunched. His crumpled shoes hung loose as if they dangled from strings and had no feet in them. The stare of his eyes searched me right through. Suddenly they were done; he lifted them above me to the window, uttered several terse sentences in Chinook, jumped off the cupboard and strode back to the village.

I was half afraid to ask the Missionary, "What did he say?"

"Not much. Only that you had no fear, that you were not stuck up, and that you knew how to laugh."

Toxis sat upon a long, slow lick of sand, but the beach of the Indian village was short and bit deep into the shoreline. Rocky points jutted out into the sea at either end of it.

Toxis and the village were a mile apart. The school house was half-way between the two and, like them, was pinched between sea and forest.

The school house called itself "church house" on Sundays, and looked as Presbyterian as it could under the circumstances.

It had a sharp roof, two windows on each side, a door in front, and a wood-shed behind.

The school equipment consisted of a map of the world, a blackboard, a stove, crude desks and benches and, on a box behind the door, the pail of drinking-water and a tin dipper.

The Lesser Missionary went to school first and lit the fire. If the tide were high she had to go over the trail at the forest's edge. It was full of holes where high seas had undermined the big tree roots. Huge upturned stumps necessitated detours through hard-leafed sallal bushes and skunk cabbage bogs. The Lesser Missionary fussed her way jumpily. She hated putting her feet on ground which she could not see, because it was so covered with growing green. She was glad when she came out of the dark forest and saw the unpainted school house. The Greater Missionary had no nerves and a long, slow stride. As she came over the trail she blew blasts on a cow's horn. She had an amazing wind, the blasts were stunning, but they failed to call the children to school, because no voice had ever suggested time or obligation to these Indian children. Then the Greater Missionary went to the village and hand-picked her scholars from the huts.

On my first morning in Ucluelet there was a full attendance at school because visitors were rare. After the Lord's Prayer the Missionaries duetted a hymn while the children stared at me.

When the Missionary put A, B, C on the board the children began squirming out of their desks and pattering down to the drinking bucket. The dipper registered each drink with a clank when they threw it back.

The door squeaked open and shut all the time, with a second's pause between opening and closing. Spitting on the floor was forbidden, so the children went out and spat off the porch. They had not yet mastered the use of the pocket-handkerchief, so not a second elapsed between sniffs. The Lesser Missionary twitched as each sniff hit her ear.

Education being well under way, I slipped out to see the village.

When I did not return after the second's time permitted for spitting, the children began to wriggle from the desks to the drinking bucket, then to the spitting step, looking for me. Once outside, their little bare feet never stopped till they had caught me up. In the empty schoolroom the eyes of the Lesser Missionary waited upon those of the Greater as the shepherd's dog watches for the signal to dash.

"That is all for today," the older woman said quietly and they went home.

After that I was shut up tight at Toxis until school was well started; then I went to the village, careful to creep low when passing under the school windows.

On the point at either end of the bay crouched a huddle of houses—large, squat houses made of thick, hand-hewn cedar planks, pegged and slotted together. They had flat, square fronts. The side walls were made of driftwood. Bark and shakes, weighted with stones against the wind, were used for roofs. Every house stood separate from the next. Wind roared through narrow spaces between.

Houses and people were alike. Wind, rain, forest and sea had done the same things to both—both were soaked through and through with sunshine, too.

I was shy of the Indians at first. When I knocked at their doors and received no answer I entered their houses timidly, but I found that a grunt of welcome was always waiting inside and that Indians did not knock before entering. Usually some old crone was squatted on the earth floor, weaving cedar fibre or tatters of old cloth into a mat, her claw-like fingers twining in and out, in and out, among the strands that were fastened to a crude frame of sticks. Papooses[1] tumbled round her on the floor for she was papoose-minder as well as mat-maker.

Each of the large houses was the home of several families. The door and the smoke-hole were common to all, but each family had its own fire with its own things round it. That was their own home.

The interiors of the great houses were dim. Smoke teased your eyes and throat. The earth floors were not clean.

It amused the Indians to see me unfold my camp stool, and my sketch sack made them curious. When boats, trees, houses appeared on the paper, jabbering interest closed me about. I could not understand their talk. One day, by grin and gesture, I got permission to sketch an old mat-maker. She nodded and I set to work. Suddenly a cat jumped in through the smoke-hole and leaped down from a rafter on to a pile of loose boxes. As the clatter of the topple ceased there was a bestial roar, a pile of mats and blankets burst upwards, and a man's head came out of them. He shouted and his black eyes snapped at me and the old woman's smile dried out.

"Klatawa" (Chinook for "Go")[2] she shouted, and I went. Later, the old wife called to me across the bay, but I would not heed her call.

"Why did you not reply when old Mrs. Wynook called you?" the Missionary asked.

"She was angry and drove me away."

"She was calling, 'Klee Wyck, come back, come back,' when I heard her."

"What does 'Klee Wyck' mean?"

"I do not know."

The mission house door creaked open and something looking like a bundle of tired rags tumbled onto the floor and groaned.

"Why, Mrs. Wynook," exclaimed the Missionary, "I thought you could not walk!"

The tired old woman leaned forward and began to stroke my skirt.

"What does Klee Wyck mean, Mrs. Wynook?" asked the Missionary.

Mrs. Wynook put her thumbs into the corners of her mouth and stretched them upwards. She pointed at me; there was a long, guttural jabber in Chinook between her and the Missionary. Finally the Missionary said, "Klee Wyck is the Indians' name for you. It means 'Laughing One'."

The old woman tried to make the Missionary believe that her husband thought it was I, not the cat, who had toppled the boxes and woke him, but the Missionary, scenting a lie, asked for "straight talk". Then Mrs. Wynook

[1] Young children.

[2] Carr's parenthetical translation.

told how the old Indians thought the spirit of a person got caught in a picture of him, trapped there so that, after the person died, it had to stay in the picture.

"They have such silly notions," said the Missionary.

"Tell her that I will not make any more pictures of the old people," I said. It must have hurt the Indians dreadfully to have the things they had always believed trampled on and torn from their hugging. Down deep we all hug something. The great forest hugs its silence. The sea and the air hug the spilled cries of sea-birds. The forest hugs only silence; its birds and even its beasts are mute.

When night came down upon Ucluelet the Indian people folded themselves into their houses and slept.

At the mission house candles were lit. After eating fish, and praying aloud, the Missionaries creaked up the bare stair, each carrying her own tin candlestick. I had a cot at the foot of their wide wooden bed and scrambled quickly into it. Blindless and carpetless, it was a bleak bedroom even in summer.

The Missionaries folded their clothes, paired their shoes, and put on stout nightgowns. Then, one on each side of the bed, they sank to their knees on the splintery floor and prayed some more, this time silent, private prayers. The buns now dangled in long plaits down their backs and each bowed head was silhouetted against a sputtering candle that sat on an upturned apple-box, one on either side of the bed, apple-boxes heaped with devotional books.

The room was deathly still. Outside, the black forest was still, too, but with a vibrant stillness tense with life. From my bed I could look one storey higher into the balsam pine. Because of his closeness to me, the pine towered above his fellows, his top tapering to heaven like the hands of the praying Missionaries. [. . .]

[1941]

FREDERICK PHILIP GROVE ▪ (1879?–1948)

Twenty-three years after the death of Frederick Philip Grove, Queen's University professor and Grove biographer Douglas Spettigue discovered his "real" identity in documents found in the British Museum. Like Archie Belaney/Grey Owl, Grove transformed himself when he immigrated to Canada and began a life under an assumed identity. Grove's invented Canadian identity—the one under which he wrote and became a significant member of the Canadian literary community— was of an immigrant descended from a wealthy Swedish father and a cosmopolitan Scottish mother, who moved to Manitoba to teach in small prairie communities and write about immigrant life. His Governor General's Award-winning "autobiography," *In Search of Myself* (1946), was found, decades after publication, to be largely fictional. In it, he cryptically writes, "I believe I have hidden myself fairly well."

Contrary to what Grove wrote in his autobiography, Spettigue found that Grove was born Felix Paul Greve in Prussia. Prior to his arrival in Canada, Grove was a minor editor, writer, translator, and literary personality in Europe. In 1903 he was jailed for fraud in Germany for a year. In 1909, it was reported that Greve was dead. In fact, he faked his own "suicide" in order to escape his crushing debt load. He disappeared into the Kentucky farmland with his wife Else, and German commentators accepted the fact of his death.

Around 1911, Greve left both Kentucky and Else for the Canadian prairies. Else went on to become a Dada artist and poet (Baroness Elsa von Freytag-Loringhoven), famous in New York art circles from 1918 to 1923 as the "Dada Baroness." In 1912, a man named "Fred Grove" surfaced in Manitoba and became a teacher, married a Canadian woman named Catherine Wiens, attended the University of Manitoba, and began to write about life on the prairies. For several years he and his wife worked as teachers in several rural communities (Haskett, Virden, Winkler, and Gladstone). When their daughter May died suddenly at the age of 12, the Groves left Manitoba for Ontario. Grove continued to write there until his death.

With Sinclair Ross, Grove is acknowledged for his portraits of pioneer life in the Canadian west. He is especially celebrated for the precision and acuity of his depiction of the Canadian prairies. In addition to his novels about the Canadian prairie and its inhabitants—*Settlers of the Marsh* (1925), *Our Daily Bread* (1928), and *Fruits of the Earth* (1933)—he also published autobiographical writings, including *Over Prairie Trails* (1922), *A Search for America* (1927), and *In Search of Myself* (1946).

Following the publication of his autobiographical collection, *Over Prairie Trails,* Grove undertook a series of speaking tours across Canada. These included a number of talks under the auspices of the Association of Canadian Clubs in 1927, in which Grove spoke from his perspective as an immigrant to Canada, contrasting the "melting pot" ideology of the United States with what he hoped would be a form of mutually beneficial coexistence in a multicultural Canada. "Canadians Old and New," in which Grove addresses two audiences, "Mr. Canadian Citizen" and "Mr. Newcomer" to Canada, was one of these public lectures, and was subsequently published in *Maclean's* (1928). Grove's lecture is hard-hitting, for in it he accuses mainstream Canadians of being intolerant toward "foreigners." His position was rooted in a vision of an ideal multicultural nation, in which all European peoples had an integral role to play in the consolidation of a national Canadian identity. Grove was adamantly opposed to one-sided assimilation, though his vision of a multicultural Canada is unquestionably a European one. It was in Canada, he believed, that the warring factions of Europe should be able to coexist in peace and hence provide an example for the rest of the world.

In *Over Prairie Trails,* from which "Dawn and Diamonds" is drawn, Grove sketches seven autobiographical journeys taken between Gladstone, where he taught, and Falmouth 34 miles away, where his wife taught and lived with their daughter. *Over Prairie Trails* has conventionally been seen as a "documentary" of the author's journeys. Early reviews focused on the author's fidelity to an "authentic description of inland Canadian weather" (*Canadian Forum,* May 1923). Indeed, a 1925 review in *Saturday Night* noted that the book's main concern is meteorological. Later readers emphasize the artifice with which Grove writes. According to literary critic K.P. Stich, Grove's "sly under- and over-statements, his ambiguities, his precision and imprecision, in short, his linguistic mendacities . . . begin in his preface to *Over Prairie Trails.*"

Literary historian W.H. New echoes Stich's emphasis on Grove's "linguistic mendacity" when he writes about the artifice that underscores the documentary nature of the sketches, but he adds that "language is the landscape being traversed, and it is the telling, not just the teller, that cannot quite be believed." New argues that Grove is telling a tall tale, an exaggeration. In "Dawn and Diamonds," the family man is driven by his desire to see his wife and child to celebrate Christmas and is incidentally transformed by the beauty of the moment. Grove's minute and evocative description of winter snow bears comparison with P. K. Page's "Stories of Snow" and Patrick Lane's "Winter" series, both included in this anthology. Robert Kroetsch's 1975 poem "F.P. Grove: The Finding" explores the role of self-invention in Grove's life and writing.

Dawn and Diamonds

Two days before Christmas the ground was still bare. I had a splendid new cutter with a top and side curtains; a heavy outfit, but one that would stand up, I believed, under any road conditions. I was anxious to use it, too, for I intended to spend a two weeks' holiday up north with my family. [. . .] School had closed at noon. I intended to set out next morning at as early an hour as I could. I do not know what gave me my confidence, but I firmly expected to find snow on the ground by that time. I am rather a student of the weather. I worked till late at night getting my cutter ready. I had to adjust my buggy pole and to stow away a great number of parcels. The latter contained the first real doll for my little girl, two or three picture books, a hand sleigh, Pip— a little stuffed dog of the silkiest fluffiness—and as many more trifles for wife and child as my Christmas allowance permitted me to buy. It was the first time in the five years of my married life that, thanks to my wife's co-operation in earning money, there was any Christmas allowance to spend; and since I am writing this chiefly for her and the little girl's future reading, I want to set it down here, too, that it was thanks to this very same co-operation that I had been able to buy the horses and the driving outfit which I needed badly [. . .].

I was going to have the first real Christmas again in twenty-five years, with a real Christmas tree, and with wife and child, and even though it was a poor man's Christmas, I refused to let anything darken my Christmas spirit or dull the keen edge of my enjoyment. [. . .] I went home and to bed and slept about as soundly as I could wish. When the alarm of my clock went off at five in the morning, I jumped out of bed and hurried down to shake the fire into activity.

As soon as I had started something of a blaze, I went to the window and looked out. It was pitch dark, of course, the moon being down by this time, but it seemed to me that there was snow on the ground. I lighted a lamp and held it to the window; and sure enough, its rays fell on white upon white on shrubs and fence posts and window ledge. I laughed and instantly was in a glow of impatience to be off. [. . .]

We drove along—and slowly, slowly came the dawn. You could not define how it came. The whole world seemed to pale and to whiten, and that was all. There was no sunrise. It merely seemed as if all of Nature—very gradually—was soaking itself full of some light; it was dim at first, but never grey; and then it became the whitest, and clearest, the most undefinable light. There were no shadows. Under the brush of the wild land which I was skirting by now there seemed to be quite as much of luminosity as overhead. The mist was the thinnest haze, and it seemed to derive its whiteness as much from the virgin snow on the ground as from above. I could not cease to marvel at this light which seemed to be without a source—like the halo around the Saviour's face. The eye as yet did not reach very far, and wherever I looked, I found but one word to describe it: impalpable—and that is saying what it was not rather than what it was. As I said, there was no sunshine, but the light was there, omnipresent, diffused, coming mildly, softly, but from all sides, and out of all things as well as into them. [. . .]

I have lived in southern countries, and I have travelled rather far for a single lifetime. Like an epic stretch my memories into dim and ever receding pasts. I have drunk full and deep from the cup of creation. The Southern Cross is no strange sight to my eyes. I have slept in the desert close to my horse, and I have walked on Lebanon. I have cruised in the seven seas and seen the white marvels of ancient cities reflected in the wave of incredible blueness. But then I was young. When the years began to pile up, I longed to stake off my horizons, to flatten out my views. I wanted the simpler, the more elemental things, things cosmic in their associations, nearer to the beginning or end of creation. The parrot that flashed through "nutmeg groves" did not hold out so much allurement as the simple grey-and-slaty junco.[1] The things that are unobtrusive and differentiated by shadings only—grey in grey above all—like our northern woods, like our sparrows, our wolves—they held a more compelling attraction than orgies of colour and screams of sound. So I came home to the north. On days like this, however, I should like once more to fly out and see the tireless wave and the unconquerable rock. But I should like to see them from afar and dimly only—as Moses saw the promised land.[2] Or I should like to point them out to a younger soul and remark upon the futility and innate vanity of things.

[1] Slate coloured junco, a bird common in central and eastern North America.

[2] In Deuteronomy and Numbers, as a punishment God prevents Moses from entering the Promised Land; as a concession, he allows Moses to look on the Promised Land.

And because these things take me out of myself, because they change my whole being into a very indefinite longing and dreaming, I wilfully blot from my vision whatever enters. If I meet a tree, I see it not. If I meet a man, I pass him by without speaking. I do not care to be disturbed. I do not care to follow even a definite thought.

There is sadness in the mood, such sadness as enters—strange to say—into a great and very definitely expected disappointment. It is an exceedingly delicate sadness—haughty, aloof like the sun, and like him cool to the outer world. It does not even want sympathy; it merely wants to be left alone.

It strangely chimed in with my mood on this particular and very perfect morning that no jolt shook me up, that we glided along over virgin snow which had come soft-footedly over night, in a motion, so smooth and silent as to suggest that wingless flight. . . .

We spurned the miles, and I saw them not. [. . .] My horses fell into their accustomed walk, and at last I saw.

Now, what I saw, may not be worth the describing, I do not know. It surely is hardly capable of being described. But if I had been led through fairylands or enchanted gardens, I could not have been awakened to a truer day of joy, to a greater realization of the good will towards all things than I was here.

Oh, the surpassing beauty of it! There stood the trees, motionless under that veil of mist, and not their slenderest finger but was clothed in white. And the white it was! A translucent white, receding into itself, with strange backgrounds of white behind it—a modest white, and yet full of pride. An elusive white, and yet firm and substantial. The white of a diamond lying on snow-white velvet, the white of a diamond in diffused light. None of the sparkle and colour play, that the most precious of stones assumes under a definite, limited light which proceeds from a definite, limited source. Its colour play was suggested, it is true, but so subdued that you hardly thought of naming or even recognizing its component parts. There was no red or yellow or blue or violet, but merely that which might flash into red and yellow and blue and violet, should perchance the sun break forth and monopolize the luminosity of the atmosphere. There was, as it were, a latent opalescence.

And every twig and every bough, every branch and every limb, every trunk and every crack even in the bark was furred with it. It seemed as if the hoarfrost still continued to form. It looked heavy, and yet it was nearly without weight. Not a twig was bent down under its load, yet with its halo of frost it measured fully two inches across. The crystals were large, formed like spearheads, flat, slab-like, yet of infinite thinness and delicacy, so thin and light that, when by misadventure my whip touched the boughs, the flakes seemed to float down rather than to fall. And every one of these flat and angular slabs was fringed with hair-like needles, or with feather-like needles, and longer needles stood in between. There was such an air of fragility about it all that you hated to touch it—and I, for one, took my whip down lest it shook bare too many boughs.

Whoever has seen the trees like that—and who has not?—will see with his mind's eye what I am trying to suggest rather than to describe. It was never the single sight nor the isolated thing that made my drives the things of beauty which they were. There was nothing remarkable in them either. They were commonplace enough. I really do not know why I should feel urged to describe our western winters. Whatever I may be able to tell you about them, is yours to see and yours to interpret. The gifts of Nature are free to all for the asking. And yet, so it seems to me, there is in the agglomerations of scenes and impressions, as they followed each other in my experience, something of the quality of a great symphony; and I consider this quality as a free and undeserved present which Chance or Nature shook out of her cornucopia so it happened to fall at my feet. I am trying to render this quality here for you.

On that short mile along the first of the east-west grades, before I again turned into the bush, I was for the thousandth time in my life struck with the fact how winter blots out the sins of utility. What is useful, is often ugly because in our fight for existence we do not always have time or effort to spare to consider the looks of things. But the slightest cover of snow will bury the eyesores. Snow is the greatest equalizer in Nature. No longer are there fields and wild lands, beautiful trails and ugly grades—all are hidden away under that which comes from Nature's purest hands and fertile thoughts alone. Now there was no longer the raw, offending scar on Nature's body; just a smooth expanse of snow-white ribbon that led afar. [. . .]

This morning, however, in this strange light, which was at this very hour undergoing a subtle change that I could not define as yet, mile after mile of road seemed to lift itself up in the far away distance, as if you might drive on for ever through fairyland. The very fact of its straightness, flanked as it was by the rows of frosted trees, seemed like a call. And a feeling that is very familiar to me—that of an eternity in the perpetuation of whatever may be the state I happen to be in, came over me, and a desire to go on and on, for ever, and to see what might be beyond. . . .

But then the turn into the bushy trail was reached. I did not see the slightest sign of it on the road. But Dan[3] seemed infallible—he made the turn. And again I was in Winter's enchanted palace, again the slight whirl in the air that our motion set up made the fairy tracery of the boughs shower down upon me like snow-white petals of flowers, so delicate that to disturb the virginity of it all seemed like profaning the temple of the All-Highest.

But then I noticed that I had not been the first one to visit the woods. All over their soft-napped carpet floor there were the restless, fleeting tracks of the snowflake, lacing and interlacing in lines and loops, as if they had been assembled in countless numbers, as no doubt they had. And every track looked like nothing so much as like that kind of embroidery, done white upon white, which ladies, I think, call the feather stitch. In places I could clearly see how they had chased and pursued each other, running, and there was a merriness

___

[3] Dan is his horse.

about their spoors, a suggestion of swiftness which made me look up and about to see whether they were not wheeling their restless curves and circles overhead. But in this I was disappointed for the moment, though only a little later I was to see them in numbers galore. It was on that last stretch of my road, when I drove along the dam of the angling ditch. There they came like a whirlwind and wheeled and curved and circled about as if they know no enemy, feeding meanwhile with infallible skill from the seed-bearing weeds while skimming along. But I am anticipating just now. In the bush I saw only their trails. Yet they suggested their twittering and whistling even there; and since on the gloomiest day their sound and their sight will cheer you, you surely cannot help feeling glad and overflowing with joy when you see any sign of them on a day like this!

Meanwhile we were winging along ourselves, so it seemed. For there was the second east-west grade ahead. And that made me think of wife and child to whom I was coming like Santa Claus, and so I stopped under a bush that overhung the trail; and though I hated to destroy even a trifling part of the beauty around, I reached high up with my whip and let go at the branches, so that the moment before the horses bolted, the flakes showered down upon me and my robes and the cutter and changed me into a veritable snow man in snow-white garb. [. . .]

And never before had I seen the school and the cottage from quite so far! The haze was still there, but somehow it seemed to be further overhead now, with a stratum of winter-clear air underneath. Once before, when driving along the first east-west grade, where I discovered the vista, I had wondered at the distance to which the eye could pierce. Here, on the dam, of course, my vision was further aided by the fact that whatever of trees and shrubs there was in the way—and a bridge of poplars ran at right angles to the ditch, throwing up a leafy curtain in summer—stood bare of its foliage. I was still nearly four miles from my "home" when I first beheld it. And how pitiably lonesome it looked! Not another house was to be seen in its neighbourhood. I touched the horses up with my whip. I felt as if I should fly across the distance and bring my presents to those in the cottage as their dearest gift. They knew I was coming. They were at this very moment flying to meet me with their thoughts. Was I well? Was I finding everything as I had wished to find it? And though I often told them how I loved and enjoyed my drives, they could not view them but with much anxiety, for they were waiting, waiting, waiting . . . Waiting on Thursday for Friday to come, waiting on Wednesday and Tuesday and Monday—waiting on Sunday even, as soon as I had left; counting the days and the hours, and the minutes, till I was out, fighting storm and night to my heart's content! And then—worry, worry, worry—what might not happen! Whatever my drives were to me, to them they were horrors. There never were watchers of weather and sky so anxiously eager as they! And when, as it often, too often happened, the winter storms came, when care rose, hope fell, then eye was clouded, thought dulled, heart aflutter . . . Sometimes the soul sought comfort from nearest neighbours, and not always was it vouchsafed. "Well," they would say, "if he starts out to-day, he will kill his horses!"—or, "In weather like this I should not care to drive five miles!"—Surely, surely, I owe it to them, staunch, faithful hearts that they were, to set down this record so it may gladden the lonesome twilight hours that are sure to come. . . .

And at last I swung west again, up the ridge and on to the yard. And there on the porch stood the tall, young, smiling woman, and at her knee the fairest-haired girl in all the world. And quite unconscious of Nature's wonder-garb, though doubtlessly gladdened by it, the little girl shrilled out, "Oh, Daddy, Daddy, did du see Santa Claus?" And I replied lustily, "Of course, my girl, I am coming straight from his palace."

[1922]

Canadians Old and New

Like the statues of the ancient Roman deity Janus,[4] this article is going to have two faces, one turned to those who, being born in this country or having lived here long enough to be fully acclimatized, invite through their recognized governmental agencies members of all white nations to come and to make their homes among them; the other, to those who have just arrived in pursuance of that invitation, or who, having arrived some time ago, did not find all they may have expected to find in the way of a welcome. [. . .]

Firstly, then, Mr. Canadian Citizen, let me tell you a few truths about yourself as well as about your guests; for, since you have invited the newcomers, they are plainly your guests, entitled to all the privileges which we commonly accord those whom we thus honor.

What, at the present moment, do you, the average citizen of this country, do in order to make the newcomer feel at home? Anything or nothing? First of all, you call him a 'foreigner'—a title of honor, indeed, since it implies that likely he has seen more of the world than you have seen—unless you have traveled. But it is well-known that this title, within the British Isles, has from time immemorial had a sinister sound. [. . .] [T]he Britisher coming to these shores—in spite of the fact that we cherish our connection with Britain as the motherland and greet our British cousins as next-of-kin—is as much a 'foreigner' when he lands as any man arriving from Central Europe: both are citizens of this country only *in posse*. The Britisher has an enormous advantage over the continental European inasmuch as he speaks one of the two languages which have the right-of-way in Canada; but he is vastly less apt to have a desire to adapt himself and to acknowledge that the way 'we' do these things 'at 'ome' cannot be binding on the country to which he came in order to make his living. The present writer knows a good many districts in the west of this vast Dominion where there are 'little islands' of English or Scotch immigrants

---

[4] In Roman mythology, Janus is the god of transitions, new beginnings, and doorways, often represented by two heads, one looking toward the past, the other toward the future.

who offer as their contribution towards the evolution of a new Canadian mentality chiefly acrid criticism of the destructive kind. So-called 'foreigners' rarely make themselves obnoxious in that way.

Again, what, Mr. Citizen, do you do in order to welcome the 'foreigner' whom you invite? Oh, well you assign him 160 acres of land in the bush or a job in a factory or work on the road-bed of a transportation line, and thereafter you leave him icily alone.

He meets with other 'foreigners'; and if they are farmers, there is soon a 'foreign settlement'; if they are factory hands, there is a 'foreign quarter' in some city; if men of the pick and shovel, there is a 'foreign gang'. The adults in settlement, quarter, or gang are very apt to hang on to their vernacular; they have very little opportunity to acquire any other, especially the women. They have no desire for isolation; but it is forced on to them. [...]

Often these 'foreigners' come from communities with not only a vastly older but a spiritually richer environment than they find among ourselves. It could not be otherwise: our country is young, unfinished, crude. Many of them are readers in their own tongue—readers, that is, not of silly modern sex novels, but of the great literatures that have been indigenous to their own countries for thousands of years. I know a certain Scotch scholar—a member of one of our universities—who, in the declining third of his life, thought it worth his while to acquire a knowledge of Icelandic in order to study Icelandic sagas; he professes himself overwhelmed with their depth and significance. There are many Icelanders living in our midst, especially, of course, in the west, who have been familiar with that literature from their earliest youth. Yet these very men I have seen treated, by a Canadian-born station master who was a dunce, as if they were the scum of the earth because their English accent betrayed their foreign birth. [...]

And now the crucial question, Do you, Mr. Canadian, want to assimilate these people? Do you want them to give up what is theirs and to adapt your vaunted 'high standard of living' which is only a high standard of waste? Do you want them to eclipse themselves and to drop their good as well as their evil? But the question itself is sheer nonsense. It posits as possible what is an impossibility. There is no such thing as a one-sided assimilation. Every action has its reaction. Don't forget that these people who come among us have pluck and enterprise; or they would not be here. Do not forget that they have brains; for most of them were the underdogs in Europe; and it is precisely the underdog who develops his brains. Look at your rural schools in mixed districts: which children lead their classes, yours or those of these 'foreigners'. No, assimilation can only be mutual. Only if you take from them, will they take from you. The friars of the thirteenth century became a power in England, not because they made themselves the hosts, but because they consented to be the guests of the poor. Have you sat down at a Ruthenian table? If so, you have done more to change the hostess' ways than by inviting her to a banquet in a palace. The thing, however, which I wish to underline in this connection is that these 'foreigners', little as most of us realize it, have something to give as well as to receive; and what they have to give is vastly more than the motive power of arm and back: they bring a spiritual heritage as well as their brawn which is at best an economic asset.

But I must cease and let the other face of the Janus-head speak.

Mr. Newcomer, we invited you to come among us, and you followed the call. We bid you welcome. We are bound by a promise. We wanted you to help us till our soil; to swing the pick in order to release the ore that lies buried in the depth of our rocks; to turn the wheels of our industries. In return we promised you freedom.

You have lived in Europe; so you know that there is no freedom without law. Your freedom depends on your attitude toward that law. You must, for the moment, accept and obey it; or the very machinery that is set in motion for your protection will continue moving to your enslavement. That is fundamental, here as in Europe; we have no longer, perhaps we never had, any wild west. But freedom involves opportunity. We are wasteful, you are thrifty; if you were not, you would not have survived; in that lies your opportunity. Do not become Canadian in this one point. The wages we pay in this country offer an ample margin over and above the necessities. What you do with that margin is nobody's business but your own. If you spend it on moving-picture shows, candy, or 'smart' clothes, it will not be available to give you a start as an owner of land, a merchant, or a producer of industrial goods. If you don't it will do so. Could you have become the owner of a quarter-section of land in Europe? If so, you would not be here today. This is one thing we offer. Retain your thrift, and you will prosper.

We offer more. We offer you a partnership in the business of 'running this country'. Live among us for five years without wilfully destroying your opportunities by coming into flagrant conflict with the law, and we will give you a share in forming that law. If there are details of that law as you find it which seem strange, which perhaps seem oppressive to you, you will be able to do your share to change them; and if, in a given point, you do not succeed, you will learn to bear with it because it is part of that law which you helped to shape. In school-district, municipality, province, dominion, we want you to contribute your share and your vote; for, after five years, we will consider you as one of ourselves; till then, you are our guest.

Perhaps you will meet with a man or a woman here and there who will turn away from you because you have betrayed by your accent that you were not born among us. I will give you a piece of confidential advice. Put that man or woman down, in the depth of your heart, as belonging to the riff-raff of this country; you will find such a riff-raff wherever you go. Should you happen to meet them in the mass, as will happen, hold on to this great truth: these people, as a nation, invited you to come; as a nation, therefore, they bid you welcome. They wanted you; they still want you; they are merely momentarily hidden behind that screen of riff-raff. If you doubt, make this test: go to the most prominent, the best educated man—or woman—in your district and ask for sympathy or help; I feel sure both sympathy and help will be given.

Still more. We offer you brotherhood. We do not only want your strong arm or your special skill. We want *you*. If you have knowledge which we lack, we want you to give us that knowledge. If you feel emotions which are strange to us, we want to share those emotions—do not forget those trees whose name lies hidden in the first two syllables of the name of your native Bukowina, nor the ash that is called Ygdrasin[5] in Icelandic saga: if you long for them, we honor that longing; tell us about it so that we can share it. If you have curious dreams, let us see them with you; to those who know, your dreams seem greater and more precious than the brawn of your muscle. I know there lives a song in you: do not forget your language. We may not know that language, as likely you knew no English when you came. It was your own experience that your powers grew as you learned a new tongue. Be proud, then, of the fact that in the knowledge of your native tongue you have a power withheld from many of us. In our high schools and universities we teach our own youths one or two foreign languages—Latin, Greek, German, not to mention French which is not foreign to Canada; we do so for the sake of the mental power such knowledge imparts. It is true that most of our provinces bid you send your children to a school where they learn English. That is as it should be: there must be a common medium of communication.

But the best thing we offer you lies perhaps in this that we offer you a soil in which you yourself can grow. If you think we want you to become in all things like the rest of us Canadians, you are mistaken. By becoming absolutely like ourselves—if such a thing were possible—you would lose the greater part of your value to us. Seventy-five per cent of the population of our west—more in the east—is Anglo-Saxon in origin; that is, they are a blend of Celt, Briton, German, Scandinavian, and Norman-French, not to mention Spanish and colonial infusions. The blend is old; it has stood many tests; it has been successful in history; it has built a not inconsiderable empire. It is a lusty blend, still full of the exuberance of youth. It will stand further blending. The Anglo-Saxon is constitutionally opposed to the narrow theory which places a value on pure racial strains. We consider the admixture which you bring as a useful leaven. Learn our language, obey our laws, and help us to make them when you have qualified for that function: that, Mr. Newcomer, is all we ask of you. Apart from that, remain what you are, except in as much as the newly changed environment, the freer, less crowded air of this continent exerts its unavoidable influence. That unavoidable influence you must not resist, or your own growth will be stunted. But if you withhold from us what you bring—the example of thrift, the ancient viewpoint which sees in life more than the opportunity to accumulate dollars—you stunt *our* growth.

Above all, hold your head high. This country does not claim to be a 'melting pot'. What it does claim is that in it there 'are many mansions'[6]—and one of them, undoubtedly, is the mansion that has been waiting precisely for you.

[1928]

---

[5] Presumably a reference to Buko, the Tree of Life. In Norse mythology, Yggdrasil is the World Tree, the giant ash tree located at the centre of the universe that links and shelters all the worlds in Norse cosmology.

[6] John 14:2: "In my Father's house are many mansions: if it were not so, I would have told you. I go to prepare a place for you."

Often considered a transitional figure between the Confederation Poets and the modernists, E.J. (Edwin John) Pratt was both committed to developing a new sense of Canadian poetry and anchored in a nationalistic documentation of Canadian history, technology, politics, and culture. His work is also infused with stories of the sea and the storytelling traditions of his Newfoundland childhood. In his poetry, Pratt draws on events of history, turning them into the stuff of epic poetry. With the modernists, though, Pratt articulated his belief in innovation: "[R]hyme and meter do not make a poem. . . . The real flesh and blood of poetry lies in turns of phrases, vivid images, new and unusual thoughts and manners of expressing them."

Although he lived most of his adult life in Toronto, Pratt retained an affiliation with his birthplace, the colony of Newfoundland. Born in Western Bay in 1882, he was the son of a Methodist minister from Yorkshire and a Newfoundlander from a sea captain's family. Pratt spent his early years at a variety of parishes around the colony where his father worked (Bonavista, Cupids, Blackhead, Brigus, Fortune, Bay Roberts, Grand Bank, and St. John's). Before leaving Newfoundland at the age of 25, he worked as a draper's apprentice at a dry goods store, as a teacher at Moreton's Harbour for two years, and as a Methodist preacher-probationer serving in parishes around the colony. He claims to have paid for his first year at university by selling "Universal Lung Healer" in Newfoundland—a brew he and a friend concocted out of spruce, cherry bark, sarsaparilla, and rum, selling for the handsome price of $1 a bottle.

Pratt tells of how his Newfoundland experiences stayed with him throughout his life. For instance, he composed "Erosion" from the memory of accompanying his father to the home of a woman whose husband had been lost at sea. Pratt writes of breaking the news to her: "I still remember the change on the woman's face—the pallor and the furrow as the news sank in. 'Erosion' was written more than thirty years after but the memory of the face is as vivid today as it was at the time."

In 1907 Pratt emigrated from Newfoundland to Canada, moving to Toronto where he began his life-long relationship with Victoria College, University of Toronto, as a student of philosophy and "new theology." Over the next 10 years he worked to obtain a B.A., M.A., B.Div., ordination into the Methodist ministry, and finally a Ph.D. in theology. In 1920 he was invited to join the Department of English at Victoria College as a faculty member. He worked there until his retirement 33 years later. Victoria College has honoured Pratt's long association by naming its campus library after him.

While Pratt was lauded nationally (he won the Governor General's Award for poetry for *The Fable of the Goats and Other Poems* in 1937, in 1940 for *Brébeuf and His Brethren,* and again in 1952 for *Towards the Last Spike*), he also invested heavily in the poetry of others. He argued that while there were not yet any "great" Canadian poets, there was hope that there soon would be. Pratt was an exemplary literary citizen, serving as the editor of *Canadian Poetry Magazine* and the president of the Canadian Authors Association. A friend or acquaintance of most of the major critics and writers of the day, Pratt was particularly close with Northrop

Frye, F.R. Scott, and Earle Birney; in turn, many regarded Pratt as the first truly Canadian poet. Literary critic Desmond Pacey claimed that Pratt "laid the foundation of a Canadian poetry."

Committed to the idea of a national Canadian literature, Pratt is best known for his long narrative poems on historical Canadian subjects. Many of these works evince a growing Canadian nationalism, most notably the epic poem "Towards the Last Spike" (1952). On the title page of the book-length poem (53 pages) lies a description of the work: "A verse-panorama of the struggle to build the first Canadian transcontinental from the time of the proposed Terms of Union with British Columbia (1870) to the hammering of the last spike in Eagle Pass (1885)." In this, the last of his major long poems (published when he was 70), Pratt turns Canadian history into national mythology. The poem memorializes the building of the Canadian Pacific Railway (CPR) as a classical epic using elevated and often heroic language. In "Towards the Last Spike," Pratt contributes to the growing mythologization of the transcontinental railway in Canadian culture; that is, he turns what was essentially an economic enterprise into a grand act of nation-building. Although he celebrates those who masterminded the railroad as men of vision, there is a hint of ambiguity at the end of the poem when the Laurentian Shield, in the shape of an immense prehistoric lizard, is momentarily awakened from its slumber and tries to drown out the sound of the railway's triumph. There is also a delightful sense of humour in the poem that acts to deflate the grandeur of the topic. Prime Minister John A. Macdonald ("Sir John" in the poem), waking up from his nightmare with a "hangover at dawn," is clearly a dubi-

ous epic hero; in fact, the poem invites the reader to ask who the hero of the poem really is.

In the excerpts chosen here, Pratt tells the story of Macdonald's dream of uniting the country through a transcontinental link that runs from "sea to sea." The poem details the political conflicts and financial struggles of the intervening years, including the wooing of British Columbia to join Canada. Central to these excerpts is the figure of William Cornelius Van Horne, who was charged with the construction of three major portions of the line: the section from the end of track at Flat Creek (Oak Lake) in western Manitoba to Calgary ("Number One"); the line north of Lakes Huron and Superior from Callander, Ontario, to Thunder Bay ("Number Two"); and gaps in the line between Port Arthur (Thunder Bay) and Winnipeg. Subsequently, Van Horne became the construction manager of the section through the Rockies ("Number Three"). See the introduction to the Post-Confederation section in Volume I for more details on the history of the CPR. The photograph of the CPR's "last spike" driven in at Craigellachie, British Columbia (Figure V-6), is documented by Pratt in the final section of the poem ("The Spike"). Note that the actual labourers on the CPR, the workers who did the back-breaking work, are minor in Pratt's poem (and the thousands of Chinese workers do not figure at all). This absence is criticized in F.R. Scott's short rebuttal poem "All the Spikes but the Last" (see also Figure III-8 in Volume I for the workers' version of the last spike photograph).

Fellow modernist A.J.M. Smith commented that "Pratt is fascinated with magnitude, with immense strength and almost incredible power, natural, monstrous or human, and with geographical if not astronomical distance." It is this fascination with the immense that makes Pratt so central to the modernist period. In a 10 July 1946 letter to William Arthur Deacon, Pratt writes that "the history of literature in its permanent form is a combination of tradition and experiment and that between the two there should be mutual respect." Respected by the modernists and the traditionalists alike, Pratt was central to the development of Canadian literature for over 50 years. Indeed, in 1964, Leonard Cohen wrote "For E.J.P.," a poem dedicated to the memory of this powerful poet (see Section VI).

Newfoundland

Here the tides flow,
And here they ebb;
Not with that dull, unsinewed tread of waters
Held under bonds to move
Around unpeopled shores—
Moon-driven through a timeless circuit
Of invasion and retreat;
But with a lusty stroke of life
Pounding at stubborn gates,
That they might run   10
Within the sluices of men's hearts,
Leap under throb of pulse and nerve,
And teach the sea's strong voice
To learn the harmonies of new floods,
The peal of cataract,
And the soft wash of currents
Against resilient banks,
Or the broken rhythms from old chords
Along dark passages
That once were pathways of authentic fires.   20

Red is the sea-kelp on the beach,
Red as the heart's blood,
Nor is there power in tide or sun
To bleach its stain.
It lies there piled thick
Above the gulch-line.
It is rooted in the joints of rocks,
It is tangled around a spar,
It covers a broken rudder,
It is red as the heart's blood,   30
And salt as tears.

Here the winds blow,
And here they die,
Not with that wild, exotic rage
That vainly sweeps untrodden shores,
But with familiar breath
Holding a partnership with life,
Resonant with the hopes of spring,
Pungent with the airs of harvest.
They call with the silver fifes of the sea,   40
They breathe with the lungs of men,
They are one with the tides of the sea,
They are one with the tides of the heart,
They blow with the rising octaves of dawn,
They die with the largo of dusk,
Their hands are full to the overflow,
In their right is the bread of life,
In their left are the waters of death.   50

Scattered on boom
And rudder and weed
Are tangles of shells;
Some with backs of crusted bronze,
And faces of porcelain blue,
Some crushed by the beach stones
To chips of jade;
And some are spiral-cleft
Spreading their tracery on the sand
In the rich veining of an agate's heart;   60
And others remain unscarred,
To babble of the passing of the winds.

Here the crags
Meet with winds and tides—
Not with that blind interchange
Of blow for blow
That spills the thunder of insentient seas;
But with the mind that reads assault
In crouch and leap and the quick stealth,
Stiffening the muscles of the waves.   70
Here they flank the harbours,
Keeping watch
On thresholds, altars and the fires of home,
Or, like mastiffs,
Over-zealous,
Guard too well.

Tide and wind and crag,
Sea-weed and sea-shell
And broken rudder—
And the story is told   80
Of human veins and pulses,
Of eternal pathways of fire,
Of dreams that survive the night,
Of doors held ajar in storms.

[1923]

Erosion

It took the sea a thousand years,
A thousand years to trace
The granite features of this cliff,
In crag and scarp and base.

It took the sea an hour one night,
An hour of storm to place
The sculpture of these granite seams
Upon a woman's face.

[1932]

From Towards the Last Spike

It was the same world then as now—the same,[1]
Except for little differences of speed
And power, and means to treat myopia
To show an axe-blade infinitely sharp
Splitting things infinitely small, or else
Provide the telescopic sight to roam
Through curved dominions never found in fables.
The same, but for new particles of speech—
Those algebraic substitutes for nouns
That sky cartographers would hang like signboards   10
Along the trespass of our thoughts to stop
The stutters of our tongues with their equations.

As now, so then, blood kept its ancient colour,
And smoothly, roughly, paced its banks; in calm
Preserving them, in riot rupturing them.

---

[1] Pratt calls this section a prologue contrasting conditions of life in the past and the mid-twentieth century present.

Wounds needed bandages and stomachs food:
The hands outstretched had joined the lips in prayer—
"Give us our daily bread, give us our pay."[2]
The past flushed in the present and tomorrow
Would dawn upon today: only the rate   20
To sensitize or numb a nerve would change;
Only the quickening of a measuring skill
To gauge the onset of a birth or death
With the precision of micrometers.
Men spoke of acres then and miles and masses,
Velocity and steam, cables that moored
Not ships but continents, world granaries,
The east-west cousinship, a nation's rise,
Hail of identity, a world expanding,
If not the universe: the feel of it   30
Was in the air—"Union required the Line."[3]
The theme was current at the banquet tables,
And arguments profane and sacred rent
God-fearing families into partisans.
Pulpit, platform and floor were sounding-boards;
Cushions beneath the pounding fists assumed
The hues of western sunsets; nostrils sniffed
The prairie tang; the tongue rolled over texts:
Even St. Paul was being invoked to wring
The neck of Thomas[4] in this war of faith   40
With unbelief. Was ever an adventure
Without its cost? Analogies were found
On every page of history or science.
A nation, like the world, could not stand still.
What was the use of records but to break them?
The tougher armour followed the new shell;
The newer shell the armour; lighthouse rockets
Sprinkled their stars over the wake of wrecks.
Were not the engineers at work to close
The lag between the pressures and the valves?   50
The same world then as now thirsting for power
To crack those records open, extra pounds

[2] This line echoes the words of the Lord's Prayer: "Give us this day our daily bread."

[3] In 1871, the Terms of Union stipulated that British Columbia would join Canadian Confederation if Canada promised that there would be a transcontinental transport link between B.C. and the provinces east of the Rockies within 10 years. Although B.C initially requested a wagon road, Macdonald's government promised a railway.

[4] See John 20:24–29 for the story of Doubting Thomas who would not believe that Jesus had risen from the dead until he had seen him in the flesh. Jesus afterwards chastised him for not having sufficient faith: "Blessed are they that have not seen, and yet have believed."

Upon the inches, extra miles per hour.
The mildewed static schedules which before
Had like asbestos been immune to wood
Now curled and blackened in the furnace coal.
This power lay in the custody of men
From down-and-outers needing roofs, whose hands
Were moulded by their fists, whose skins could feel
At home incorporate with dolomite,   60
To men who with the marshal instincts in them,
Deriving their authority from wallets,
Directed their battalions from the trestles.
[. . .]

The Hangover at Dawn

He[5] knew the points that had their own appeal.
These did not bother him: the patriot touch,
The Flag, the magnetism of explorers,
The national unity. These could burn up
The phlegm in most of the provincial throats.
But there was one tale central to his plan
(The focus of his headache at this moment),
Which would demand the limit of his art—
The ballad of his courtship in the West:
Better reveal it soon without reserve.   70

The Lady of British Columbia[6]

Port Moody and Pacific! He had pledged
His word the Line should run from sea to sea.
"From sea to sea",[7] a hallowed phrase. Music
Was in that text if the right key were struck,
And he must strike it first, for, as he fingered
The clauses of the pledge, rough notes were rasping—
"No Road, No Union", and the converse true.
East-west against the north-south run of trade,
For California like a sailor-lover

---

[5] "He" is the Prime Minister, Sir John A. Macdonald (1815–1891), suffering from middle-of-the-night insomnia.

[6] This section is, to use Pratt's term, a "nightmare" experienced by Macdonald. British Columbia is represented as a beautiful lady courted by California, a suave sailor, and Sir John, his rival. Sir John has to make his long-distance marriage proposal by proxy and is successful only after the lady has negotiated a deal to bring the two parties together. See Figure III-5 in Volume I for an 1879 political cartoon depicting Sir John on his knees wooing British Columbia.

[7] See Psalm 72:8: "He shall have dominion also from sea to sea, and from the river to the ends of the earth." This phrase is also the official motto of Canada.

Was wooing over-time. He knew the ports.   80
His speech was as persuasive as his arms,
As sinuous as Spanish arias—
Tamales, Cazadero, Mendecino,[8]
Curling their baritones around the Lady.
Then Santa Rosa, Santa Monica,
Held absolution in their syllables.
But when he saw her stock of British temper
Starch at ironic sainthood in the whispers—
"Rio de nuestra señora de buena guia,"[9]
He had the tact to gutturalize the liquids,   90
Steeping the tunes to drinking songs, then take
Her on a holiday where she could watch
A roving sea-born Californian pound
A downy chest and swear by San Diego.[10]

Sir John, wise to the tricks, was studying hard
A fresh proposal for a marriage contract.
He knew a game was in the ceremony.
That southern fellow had a healthy bronze
Complexion, had a vast estate, was slick
Of manner. In his ardour he could tether   100
Sea-roses to the blossoms of his orchards,
And for his confidence he had the prime
Advantage of his rival—*he was there.*

The Long-distance Proposal

A game it was, and the Pacific lass
Had poker wisdom on her face. Her name
Was rich in values—*British;* this alone
Could raise Macdonald's temperature: so could
Columbia with a different kind of fever,
And in between the two, *Victoria.*
So the *Pacific* with its wash of letters
Could push the Fahrenheit another notch.
She watched for bluff on those Disraeli features[11]

[8] Towns in California, as are Santa Rosa and Santa Monica later in the stanza. The rival California can offer a link with the California coastal rail line that ran through Cazadero, among other locations.

[9] Pratt's note: "River of Our Lady of Safe Conduct."

[10] Spanish saint, San Diego de Alcala, after whom the city in California is named. The Catholicism of "California" is here portrayed as unappealing to the Lady of B.C.

[11] Macdonald was said to physically resemble Benjamin Disraeli (1804–1881), Prime Minister of England in 1868 and 1874–80.

Impassive but for arrowy chipmunk eyes,   110
Engaged in fathoming a contract time.
With such a dowry she could well afford
To take the risk of tightening the terms—
"Begin the Road in two years, end in ten"—
Sir John, a moment letting down his guard,
Frowned at the Rocky skyline, but agreed.[12]
[. . .]

Number One

Oak Lake to Calgary. Van Horne[13] took off
His coat. The North must wait, for that would mean
His shirt as well. First and immediate
This prairie pledge—five hundred miles, and it
Was winter. Failure of this trial promise
Would mean—no, it must not be there for meaning.
An order from him carried no repeal:
It was as final as an execution.
A cable started rolling mills in Europe:
A tap of Morse sent hundreds to the bush,   120
Where axes swung on spruce and the saws sang,
Changing the timber into pyramids
Of poles and sleepers. Clicks, despatches, words,
Like lanterns in a night conductor's hands,
Signalled the wheels: a nod put Shaughnessy[14]
In Montreal: supplies moved on the minute.
Thousands of men and mules and horses slipped
Into their togs and harness night and day.
The grass that fed the buffalo was turned over,
The black alluvial mould laid bare, the bed   130
Levelled and scraped. As individuals
The men lost their identity; as groups,
As gangs, they massed, divided, subdivided,
Like numerals only—sub-contractors, gangs
Of engineers, and shovel gangs for bridges,

[12] After the Terms of Union were ratified by Parliament, B.C. entered Confederation in July 1871.

[13] American William Cornelius Van Horne (1843–1915) became general manager of the construction of the CPR on 2 January 1882 with the promise that 500 miles of track could be laid in 1882, a distance further than any company had ever built in a single year. Van Horne rose to the position of vice-president of the CPR in 1884, president in 1888 (until 1899), and chairman from 1890 to 1910. For Van Horne, speedy construction of the railway on the prairies was essential as government money and land subsidies were earned only as portions of the line were completed and opened.

[14] Thomas George, first Baron Shaughnessy (1853–1923), was charged with maintaining the flow of supplies during construction.

Culverts, gangs of mechanics stringing wires,
Loading, unloading and reloading gangs,
Gangs for the fish-plates[15] and the spiking gangs,
Putting a silver polish on the nails.
But neither men nor horses ganged like mules: 140
Wiser than both they learned to unionize.
Some instinct in their racial nether regions
Had taught them how to sniff the five-hour stretch
Down to the fine arithmetic of seconds.
They tired out their rivals and they knew it.
They'd stand for overwork, not overtime.
Faster than workmen could fling down their shovels,
They could unhinge their joints, unhitch their tendons;
Jumping the foreman's call, they brayed "Unhook"
With a defiant, corporate instancy.   150
The promise which looked first without redemption
Was being redeemed. From three to seven miles
A day the parallels were being laid,
Though Eastern throats were hoarse with the old question—
Where are the settlements?[16] And whence the gift
Of tongues which could pronounce place-names that purred
Like cats in relaxation after kittens?
Was it a part of the same pledge to turn
A shack into a bank for notes renewed;
To call a site a city when men saw   160
Only a water-tank? This was an act
Of faith indeed—substance of things unseen—
Which would convert preachers to miracles,
Lure teachers into lean-to's for their classes.
And yet it happened that while labourers
Were swearing at their blisters in the evening
And straightening out their spinal kinks at dawn,
The tracks joined up Oak Lake to Calgary.

Number Two

On the North Shore a reptile lay asleep—[17]
A hybrid that the myths might have conceived,

---

[15] A steel plate joining two railway ties.

[16] One of the main charges against building the railway was that there were not enough settlements in the west to support it.

[17] This section contains an extended metaphor in which the Laurentian Shield is described as a monstrous giant reptile asleep within the coils of a giant snake. The "black sand" refers to dynamite.

But not delivered, as progenitor
Of crawling, gliding things upon the earth.
She lay snug in the folds of a huge boa
Whose tail had covered Labrador and swished
Atlantic tides, whose body coiled itself
Around the Hudson Bay, then curled up north
Through Manitoba and Saskatchewan
To Great Slave Lake. In continental reach   170
The neck went past the Great Bear Lake until
Its head was hidden in the Arctic Seas.
This folded reptile was asleep or dead:
So motionless, she seemed stone dead—just seemed:
She was too old for death, too old for life,
For as if jealous of all living forms
She had lain there before bivalves began
To catacomb their shells on western mountains.
Somewhere within this life-death zone she sprawled,
Torpid upon a rock-and-mineral mattress.   180
[. . .]
And the Laurentian monster at the first
Was undisturbed, presenting but her bulk
To the invasion. All she had to do
Was lie there neither yielding nor resisting.
Top-heavy with accumulated power
And overgrown survival without function,
She changed her spots as though brute rudiments
Of feeling foreign to her native hour
Surprised her with a sense of violation
From an existence other than her own—   190
Or why take notice of this unknown breed,
This horde of bipeds that could toil like ants,
Could wake her up and keep her irritated?
They tickled her with shovels, dug pickaxes
Into her scales and got under her skin,
And potted holes in her with drills and filled
Them up with what looked like fine grains of sand,
Black sand. It wasn't noise that bothered her,
For thunder she was used to from her cradle—
The head-push and nose-blowing of the ice,   200
The height and pressure of its body: these
Like winds native to clime and habitat
Had served only to lull her drowsing coils.
It was not size or numbers that concerned her.
It was their foreign build, their gait of movement.

They did not crawl—nor were they born with wings.
They stood upright and walked, shouted and sang;
They needed air—that much was true—their mouths
Were open but the tongue was alien.
The sounds were not the voice of winds and waters,   210
Nor that of any beasts upon the earth.
She took them first with lethargy, suffered
The rubbing of her back—those little jabs
Of steel were like the burrowing of ticks
In an elk's hide needing an antler point,
Or else left in a numb monotony.
These she could stand but when the breed
Advanced west on her higher vertebrae,
Kicking most insolently at her ribs,
Pouring black powder in her cavities,   220
And making not the clouds but her insides
The home of fire and thunder, then she gave
Them trial of her strength: the trestles tottered;
Abutments, bridges broke; her rivers flooded:
She summoned snow and ice, and then fell back
On the last weapon in her armoury—
The first and last—her passive corporal bulk,
To stay or wreck the schedule of Van Horne.
[. . .]

Dynamite on the North Shore

The lizard was in sanguinary mood.
She had been waked again: she felt her sleep
Had lasted a few seconds of her time.
The insects had come back—the ants, if ants
They were—dragging *those* trees, *those* logs athwart
Her levels, driving in *those* spikes; and how
The long grey snakes unknown within her region
Wormed from the east, unstriped, sunning themselves
Uncoiled upon the logs and then moved on,
Growing each day, ever keeping abreast!   230
She watched them, waiting for a bloody moment,
Until the borers halted at a spot,
The most invulnerable of her whole column,
Drove in that iron, wrenched it in the holes,
Hitting, digging, twisting. Why that spot?
Not this the former itch. That sharp proboscis
Was out for more than self-sufficing blood

About the cuticle: 'twas out for business
In the deep layers and the arteries.

And this consistent punching at her belly   240
With fire and thunder slapped her like an insult,
As with the blast the caches of her broods
Broke—nickel, copper, silver and fool's gold,
Burst from their immemorial dormitories
To sprawl indecent in the light of day.
Another warning—this time different.

Westward above her webs she had a trap—
A thing called muskeg, easy on the eyes
Stung with the dust of gravel.
[. . .]
Now was her time. She took three engines, sank them 250
With seven tracks down through the hidden lake
To the rock bed, then over them she spread
A counterpane of leather-leaf and slime.
A warning, that was all for now. 'Twas sleep
She wanted, sleep, for drowsing was her pastime
And waiting through eternities of seasons.
As for intruders bred for skeletons—
Some day perhaps when ice began to move,
Or some convulsion ran fires through her tombs,
She might stir in her sleep and far below   260
The reach of steel and blast of dynamite,
She'd claim their bones as her possessive right
And wrap them cold in her pre-Cambrian folds.
[. . .]

The Spike[18]

Silver or gold? Van Horne had rumbled "Iron."
No flags or bands announced this ceremony,
No Morse in circulation through the world,
And though the vital words like Eagle Pass,
Craigellachie, were trembling in their belfries,
No hands were at the ropes. The air was taut

---

[18] The Last Spike was driven in at Craigellachie, British Columbia, on 7 November 1885 by CPR director Donald Smith. When asked out of what material the last spike in the railway should be made, Van Horne decreed that it should be no different than any other spikes. Many of the details here, including the rigid spruce trees in the background, refer to the famous photograph of the "Last Spike" (see Figure V-6). When Smith struck the "first" last spike, it bent over; it was replaced and he hammered the final one in more gingerly.

With silences as rigid as the spruces
Forming the background in November mist.
More casual than camera-wise, the men
Could have been properties upon a stage,   270
Except for road maps furrowing their faces.

Rogers, his both feet planted on a tie,
Stood motionless as ballast. In the rear,
Covering the scene with spirit-level eyes,
Predestination on his chin, was Fleming.
The only one groomed for the ritual
From smooth silk hat and well-cut square-rig beard
Down through his Caledonian longitude,[19]
He was outstaturing others by a foot,
And upright as the mainmast of a brig.   280
Beside him, barely reaching to his waist,
A water-boy had wormed his way in front
To touch this last rail with his foot, his face
Upturned to see the cheek-bone crags of Rogers.[20]
The other side of Fleming, hands in pockets,
Eyes leaden-lidded under square-crowned hat,
And puncheon-bellied under overcoat,
Unsmiling at the focused lens—Van Horne,
Whatever ecstasy played round that rail
Did not leap to his face. Five years had passed,   290
Less than five years—so well within the pledge.
The job was done. Was this the slouch of rest?
Not to the men he drove through walls of granite.
The embers from the past were in his soul,
Banked for the moment at the rail and smoking,
Just waiting for the future to be blown.

At last the spike and Donald with the hammer!
His hair like frozen moss from Labrador
Poked out under his hat, ran down his face
To merge with streaks of rust in a white cloud.   300
What made him fumble the first stroke? Not age:
The snow belied his middle sixties. Was
It lapse of caution or his sense of thrift,
That elemental stuff which through his life
Never pockmarked his daring but had made

---

[19] A reference to Sandford Fleming's Scottish heritage.
[20] A.B. Rogers (who found a passage through the Rockies) and Edward Mallandaine (the "water boy").

The man the canniest trader of his time,
Who never missed a rat-count, never failed
To gauge the size and texture of a pelt?
Now here he was caught by the camera,
Back bent, head bowed, and staring at a sledge,   310
Outwitted by an idiotic nail.
Though from the crowd no laughter, yet the spike
With its slewed neck was grinning up at Smith.
Wrenched out, it was replaced. This time the hammer
Gave a first tap as with apology,
Another one, another, till the spike
Was safely stationed in the tie and then
The Scot, invoking his ancestral clan,
Using the hammer like a battle-axe,
His eyes bloodshot with memories of Flodden,[21]   320
Descended on it, rammed it to its home.

* * *

The stroke released a trigger for a burst
Of sound that stretched the gamut of the air.
The shouts of engineers and dynamiters,
Of locomotive-workers and explorers,
Flanking the rails, were but a tuning-up
For a massed continental chorus. Led[22]
By Moberly (of the Eagles and *this* Pass)
And Rogers (of *his own*), followed by Wilson,
And Ross (charged with the Rocky Mountain Section), 330
By Egan (general of the Western Lines),
Cambie and Marcus Smith, Harris of Boston,
The roar was deepened by the bass of Fleming,
And heightened by the laryngeal fifes
Of Dug McKenzie and John H. McTavish.
It ended when Van Horne spat out some phlegm
To ratify the tumult with "Well Done"[23]
Tied in a knot of monosyllables.

[21] The battle of Flodden in Northumberland (1513) was fought between the Scots army under King James IV and the English army. It was one of the largest and most bloody battles between the two nations.

[22] The men named here were the engineers, surveyors, politicians, and financiers responsible for the final stages of construction of the CPR who were present at the ceremony: including Walter Moberly (engineer and surveyor who "discovered Eagle Pass"); John Egan (General Superintendent of the CPR's western division in 1885); Henry Cambie (government engineer); Marcus Smith (engineer-in-chief during the absence of Fleming, in charge of B.C. surveys after 1873); George Harris (a director of the CPR); Dug McKenzie (locomotive engineer); and John H. McTavish (land commissioner).

[23] Van Horne's entire celebratory speech consisted of "All I can say is that the work has been well done in every way."

Merely the tuning up! For on the morrow
The last blow on the spike would stir the mould   340
Under the drumming of the prairie wheels,
And make the whistles from the steam out-crow
The Fraser. Like a gavel it would close
Debate, making Macdonald's "sea to sea"
Pour through two oceanic megaphones—
Three thousand miles of *Hail* from port to port;
And somewhere in the middle of the line
Of steel, even the lizard heard the stroke.
The breed had triumphed after all. To drown
The traffic chorus, she must blend the sound   350
With those inaugural, narcotic notes
Of storm and thunder which would send her back
Deeper than ever in Laurentian sleep.

[1952]

LAWREN HARRIS ■ (1885–1970)

Painter and writer Lawren Harris recalls the enthusiasm and passion of his coterie of artists: "We loved this country and loved exploring and painting it." Harris is perhaps best remembered as a founding member of the modern painters known as the Group of Seven. In the early part of the twentieth century eight friends came together in Toronto to explore, through art, the character of Canada. Working as commercial artists and designers, the friends began to take sketching trips to Algonquin Park, Lake Superior, Georgian Bay, and other "remote" parts of the Ontario "North." They also gathered at the Toronto Arts and Letters Club to socialize and discuss new directions in Canadian art. In 1920, following the end of the First World War and the tragic death of one of the key members of the group, Tom Thomson (1877–1917), the remaining friends went on to form the Group of Seven.

The Group consisted of Harris, Franklin Carmichael, A.Y. Jackson, Frank Johnston, Arthur Lismer, J.E.H. MacDonald, and F.H. Varley, all of whom were "stirred by big emotions, born of our own landscape." Influenced by the work of "rebel" Quebec artists J.W. Morrice and Maurice Cullen, these painters were highly experimental, breaking away from the realist represen- tations of the landscape that dominated the art of the day. The group affiliation helped them join forces in the face of criticism. Since the beginning of the century, they had been painting in a style that eschewed European traditions of landscape painting in favour of a more home-grown kind of expressive art that captured the mood of the Canadian landscape. This rejection of European traditions, however, was not initially well appreciated by the critics or the collectors. For instance, in the 1910s, Harris had been a popular painter of Toronto streets and old houses. However, as A.Y. Jackson puts it in his retrospective on the Group, "realizing that popularity usually denotes mediocrity, he switched to painting the stark bare hills of Lake Superior, until critics regarded him as a public menace and declared his pictures of Canada were discouraging immigration."

It did not take long, however, for the boldness of the Group to become fashionable with the young poets and artists of the day, who could sense that something important was happening. The Group of Seven were involved in an artistic movement that had important consequences for Canadian writers who were themselves trying to break from a reliance on the older forms of Europe and America. Thus one sees similar concerns in the painting and the poetry of the period: both were responding to the conservative and imitative traditions of Canadian art; both rejected nineteenth-century realist conventions; both felt that art should not only represent an experience, but be an experience. The Group of Seven painted in the form of "expressionism," defined by its encapsulation of an emotional or psychological experience, often as this experience is projected onto depictions of landscapes or inanimate objects. The early modernist poets followed suit by trying to write linguistic equivalents of this approach. A.J.M. Smith, for instance, composed "The Lonely Land" as a kind of poetic version of Tom Thomson's The West Wind, and projects the quality of "loneliness" onto the scene he describes. Turning away from idyllic representations of pastoral landscapes to the ruggedness of Canadian nature, especially the Canadian Shield, the Group of Seven self-consciously presented themselves as Canada's national school of painters and produced a Canadian art that reflected their experience of the land. The final Group of Seven exhibition was held in 1931.

Harris, a founding member of the Group, was born in Brantford, Ontario, into a wealthy family (of Massey-Harris farm machinery/industrial fortune). After studying painting in Germany for three years, he returned to Canada and began to paint local scenes. "Revelation of Art in Canada," first published in The Canadian Theosophist, 15 July 1926, outlines Harris's desire to "question established ways, all institutions and attitudes of the past and other peoples," in the hopes of finding the "soul" of the nation. In paintings such as Mt. Lefroy (Figure V-3), Harris extends his interest in the landscape to include almost Art Deco-like lines and distinctly northern colours, dark yet luminous.

Harris lived the last 30 years of his life in Vancouver, where he tried to give expression to the West Coast landscape. Long after the Group disbanded, Harris continued to evolve as a painter and remained a patron of the arts in Canada until the end of his life.

Revelation of Art in Canada

Any change of outlook, increase of vision and deepening of conviction in a people shows itself first through some form of art, art being both a clarifying and objectifying process. With us in Canada painting is the only art that so far has achieved a clear, native expression and so the forming distinctive attitude, the creative direction of the genius of our people and their higher aspirations are to be detected in it.

Indeed a new vision is coming into art in Canada. It is a direct effect of the interplay of capacity and environment and moves into manipulation straight through the muddle of perishable imported notions. Furthermore, this creative activity is forming a home-made vortex that steadily grows and intensifies, broadens and ascends, and is destined to draw into itself the creative and responsive growing power of many of our people. It touches into life all that is inherent, and leaves the acquired in the back-waters, away from its flowing. Its results in art are far removed from mere prettiness, from anything ordinarily pleasing, from any solace to the complacencies, and thus are somewhat perturbing to those of our people brought up on imported painting. But our younger folk who seem to live in a swifter rhythm than older generations, a rhythm too swift for sentimentality, and some of our older folk who are still supple of soul, take to it naturally. They accept it as naturally as they do the charged air, the clarity and spaciousness of our north country. For it has in it a call from the clear, replenishing, virgin north that must resound in the greater freer depths of the soul or there can be no response. Indeed, at its best it participates in a rhythm of light, a swift ecstasy, a blessed severity, that leaves behind the heavy drag of alien possessions and thus attains moments of release from transitory earthly bonds.

We in Canada are in different circumstances than the people in the United States. Our population is sparse, the psychic atmosphere comparatively clean, whereas the States fill up and the masses crowd a heavy psychic blanket over nearly all the land. We are in the fringe of the great North and its living whiteness, its loneliness and replenishment, its resignations and release, its call and answer—its cleansing rhythms. It seems that the top of the continent is a source of spiritual flow that will ever shed clarity into the growing race of America, and we Canadians being closest to this source seem destined to produce an art somewhat different from our Southern fellows—an art more spacious, of a greater living quiet, perhaps of a more certain conviction of eternal values. We were not placed between the Southern teeming of men and the ample replenishing North for nothing.

Indeed no man can roam or inhabit the Canadian North without it affecting him, and the artist, because of his constant habit of awareness and his discipline in expression, is perhaps more understanding of its moods and spirit than others are. He is thus better equipped to interpret it to others, and then, when he has become one with the spirit, to create living works in their own right, by using forms, colour, rhythms and moods, to make a harmonious home for the imaginative and spiritual meanings it has evoked in him. Thus the North will give him a different outlook from men in other lands. It gives him a difference in emphasis from the bodily effect of the very coolness and clarity of its air, the feel of soil and rocks, the rhythms of its hills and the roll of its valleys, from its clear skies, great waters, endless little lakes, streams and forests, from snows and horizons of swift silver. These move into a man's whole nature and evolve a growing, living response that melts his personal barriers, intensifies his awareness, and projects his vision through appearances to the underlying hidden reality. This in time, in and through many men creates a persisting, cumulating mood that pervades a land, colouring the life of its people and increasing with every response of those people. It is called the spirit of a people. Spirit, I suppose, because it is felt but not seen. In reality it is the forming, self-created, emotional body of those people.

Now the determining factor in unfolding, for a man at least, is not in adaptation to his environment, or his personality, but in the understanding of it and the control and use of it within himself. This is slowly accomplished by creative activity evolved from his environment. Thus, for us to create, to objectify our feelings and intuitions, our aspirations and devotion in art is a necessary, persisting and unescapable part of the unfolding of our life. Firstly, it is essential to the understanding of our environment and its eliciting power in our souls; and secondly, it is essential to the understanding of our life and the life of all peoples and times; and thirdly, it is essential if we are to comprehend, however little, the swift unfolding power of the creative spirit that gives faith and works within faith. [...]

It is just so that our people may find understanding of eternal values here and now. The long slow transfiguration coiled in the drowse of the ages is thus disclosed and awakened, and our faculties, which are the servants of this transfiguration, are brought to worthy functioning, and we commence to seek beauty and truth, the meaning of life.

The idiom changes, the emphasis shifts. This is the moving surface of life, flowing with the march of time, with ages, races and peoples, guided by the genii of man's evolution. The principles, the laws, the informing spirit, is eternally the same, varying only in the degree of vision, conception and expression of a people. Through the arts, the creative spirit uses and develops the idiom of a day and people, the particular personality, to give them intimations of the play of spontaneous selflessness and a glimpse of the shining power of great faith.

But the personality of a people when it commences to form and grow, as with us now in Canada, seems to run counter to the accepted idioms of the ages. The guided centring of force to a living growth here and now has to meet the insistent, distracting superficial emanations from older growths, from Europe particularly. This should induce us to delve deeper into our souls through the interminable hells of pleasure and pain, and find conviction, find our own song of life. Until we do so more fully the dross of the ages will affect us much more than their gold.

Superficial living on the emanations of other peoples is still much too prevalent with us. Not that we shouldn't view and study the winnowed results of the experience of all peoples, but we must turn to account here and now what we find will help us, convert it into our own living idiom, and not succumb to its far away seeming from fears of inferiority. Indeed fear of inferiority still holds us to old worn grooves. The continual contemplation of the achievements of older peoples, other days, by most of our learned, authoritative individuals, holds us to old notions, waning rhythms, dying institutional modes, dogmas, national creeds, which for us now can have only second hand meaning. Then, too, all the channels of cultural barter flow to us from other countries, other times, and even the glory of the art of the ages gets between us and creative life here and now.

At times, indeed, we seem like a low receptive reservoir into which pours the chaos of ages, the mixed concord and discord of many varied peoples; and until we clean this reservoir by inducing the upwelling of the hidden waters of life through our own positive endeavours, we will remain a confused people.

Of course, most of this flooding from older sources is the continuance of a flow that was inevitable and necessary to us until comparatively recently. In the early days in Canada all ideas, modes, social and state institutions, religious observances came with the settlers. These formed the mechanism of their life and tided them over the period of home-making in the new environment. But since taking root in the new land and with the stimulus of freed and revivified faculties a new outlook was bound to grow until today it is forming a distinct individuality. And this individuality now seeks to grow by its own creative efforts, and the clinging to old modes and the partial lust for imported notions can no longer be of benefit to it. Now indeed we must find our own gift for men, and to do this we must cease to make ideas, beauty and truth, or fabrics of finished civilizations seem remote, far off, glamorous by time and distance, but being all worthy things to life here and now.

There have been signs since our very beginnings in Canada of a new upwelling from deep within, and these increase, both despite and because of the muddled flow from abroad. Our life of manners, thought and feeling is a native creation to the extent that pioneering struggles in a virgin country under great skies altered the European outlook. Our atmosphere is more stimulating to the boldness necessary to question established ways, all institutions and attitudes of the past and other peoples. We are somewhat free from the weariness and consequent doubts and melancholy of Europe, and if we seek first the growing immense zest of this country and continent we will find our own soul and our own unique gift for men.

To some among us the newer zest of this continent is not entirely friendly. Its results appear crude, raucous, ill-formed because forming, and yet to engage however little in aiding the unfolding of its life and directing its energy to lofty ideals within ourselves, is our task and should be our joy. For zest is ever new and charges all things with new meaning. It clears the eyes of the smudge of old darkness, cleanses the soul and makes of faith a mighty generator.

If such is our faith we will find contact with the creative spirit that is ageless, we will come to understand the golden ages of the world rightly, as a forever present reality, because we will have touched the source of their glory. Then we will seek to communicate "at the summit of the soul," where we have seen, however faintly, an inexpressible, familiar majesty, and here and now, through the arts, create a culture worthy the spirit in man.

[1926]

On 14 April 1938, one day after the death of Grey Owl—the "Indian" conservationist, environmentalist, and naturalist—newspaper headlines read: "FAMED INDIAN REALLY A WHITE MAN! FRIEND OF THE BEAVER EXPOSED! GREY OWL A FRAUD! and GREY OWL REALLY AN ENGLISHMAN, OLD FRIENDS INSIST."

The case of Archibald Belaney, or Grey Owl, brings up many questions around issues of authenticity, appropriation of voice, and authority. On the day of his death, 13 April 1938, the *North Bay Nugget* published a story in which Angele Egwuna, Belaney's first and only legal wife, revealed his true identity. What is surprising is that the newspaper had held back on the story for four years out of respect for the importance of Grey Owl's conservationist work.

For a year and a half before his death, Grey Owl had lectured in Britain, Canada, and the United States to more than a quarter of a million people, including the King and Queen at Buckingham Palace. His lectures, books, and films made him one of the best-known Canadians of the 1930s. With the newspaper reports of his imposture, his advocates (most notably his publisher) rushed to his defence, only to discover in a short time that Grey Owl was in fact born as Archibald (Archie) Stansfeld Belaney to English parents in Hastings, England.

Because his father abandoned his teenaged mother, Belaney was raised by his aunts in England. At the age of 17, he journeyed to Canada in search of his father and adventure. In Canada, he remade himself as an "Indian," or as the *Toronto Daily Star* put it, he undertook the "creation in the flesh of an imaginary man." Grey Owl's self-fashioning arose out of his childhood fascination with playing "Indian" in the woods around his home and out of his early love of books that glorified the "Indian" in North America. Based on the stereotypes he read in the works of James Fenimore Cooper and Henry Wadsworth Longfellow, among others, Belaney constructed an idealized version of a strong, brave, fearless "Indian." When he took on the name of Grey Owl, Belaney retained many of these composite "pan-Indian" characteristics of romanticized indigeneity.

In Canada he learned the skills needed to become a trapper and a guide. Over the course of his life, he worked as a government conservationist, an activist for Native rights, and later an author and public speaker promoting the protection of "the beaver people." It is for his writings on his own transformation from trapper to conservationist that he became internationally known. *The Men of the Last Frontier* (1931) and *The Adventures of Sajo and Her Beaver People* (1935) both met with international success. His best-known work, *Pilgrims of the Wild* (1934), from which the excerpts in this anthology are taken, details the shift from animal hunter to animal lover. However, it is mainly for his self-transformation from upper-middle-class Englishman to "Indian" wilderness man that he is remembered (see Figures V-4 and V-5). In its coverage of the story on 14 April 1938, the *Toronto Daily Star* leads: "[I]f it does not turn out to be the greatest literary hoax of the century, it will at least prove to be one of the most extraordinary examples of self-dramatization on record."

The invented version of himself that Grey Owl disseminated included a mother who was an Apache Indian and a Scottish father who travelled around the United States as an itinerant worker. Grey Owl maintained that he'd been born in Texas near the Mexican border (or in Mexico near the border with Texas, depending on which version you read) and as a boy had been a knife thrower with Buffalo Bill's circus, touring the United States and England. He was, he claimed, briefly educated in England (to justify his lifelong "Cockney accent"). At this point the story drifts toward more verifiable facts. It was in Temagami, Ontario, that he learned to speak Ojibway, was given his Ojibway name (Wa-Sha-Quon-Asin or Grey Owl) because of his propensity to travel at night, and was adopted into an Ojibway band. Following three years serving in the First World War (and a marriage in England), he returned to the Canadian wilderness to work as a trapper, a ranger, and a guide. In 1928 he adopted two orphaned beaver kittens, and he devoted the rest of his life to the preservation and conservation of wildlife. Grey Owl's letter to William Arthur Deacon, excerpted here, outlines a version of this story and illustrates the conviction with which he perpetuated it.

In her memoir, *Devil in Deerskins* (1972), Anahareo, Grey Owl's third wife and partner in the conservation of the beaver, responded to the headlines after his death: "The more Archie did, the more Indian he became in the eyes of the public, and he went along with it and became more Indian than Tecumseh himself. One may as well go the limit should it happen to facilitate the job at hand." In *Wilderness Writers* (1972), James Polk defends Belaney by pointing to the racial politics of the most vehement responses to Belaney's assumed identity: "Perhaps deep down, people were disturbed by the thought that a white man would actually prefer a more primitive culture to his own 'advanced' society." Controversially, Polk continues, "[I]f ever a white man had earned the right to speak for the Indian, the wilderness, and the beaver, that man was Grey Owl." Whether Belaney was justified in speaking "for the Indian" is still up for debate. What is certain is that he successfully passed as an "Indian" for many years, was listened to as an authority on the dangers of a vanishing wilderness and the extinction of the beaver at least partially because of his invented heritage, and was discredited when he was found to be other than he said he was.

The enigma of Grey Owl/Belaney has sparked several literary responses: Morley Callaghan's "Loppy Phelan's Double Shoot" (included in this section), Robert Kroetsch's *Gone Indian* (1973), Gwendolyn MacEwen's "Grey Owl's Poem" (1987), and Armand Garnet Ruffo's collection *Grey Owl: The Mystery of Archie Belaney* (1996), in Section VII, number prominently among them.

From Pilgrims of the Wild

I had long ago invested the creatures of the forest with a personality. This was the inevitable result of a life spent wandering over the vast reaches of a still, silent land in which they were the only form of animate life, and sprang from early training and folklore. Yet this concession gained them no respite, and although I never killed needlessly and was as merciful as was possible under the circumstances, the urge of debts to be paid, money to spend, and prestige to be maintained, lent power to the axe handle and cunning to the hands that otherwise might have faltered on occasion. Always I had pitied, but had closed my mind to all thoughts of compassion save in retrospect.

But my point of view was slowly changing. Forced at last to stop and look around and take stock, obliged now to think of someone else besides myself, I stepped out of my case hardened shell and rubbed my eyes to get a clearer vision, and saw many things that had hitherto escaped me in my remorseless striving for achievement. My surroundings began to have a different aspect. Up till now the fate of those creatures amongst whom my life had been spent had mattered only in so far as they contributed to my prowess as a hunter. Now my newly awakened consideration for something else besides myself was branching out most disastrously it seemed. I began to have a faint distaste for my bloody occupation. This was resolutely quenched, though the eventual outcome was inescapable.

Even in those less enlightened days, at a time when I actually believed that radio was spoiling the hunt by affecting the climate, I was perhaps not without a certain sense of justice which, though not recognized as such at the time, evinced itself in strange ways. A primitive and imaginative ancestry had not been without its influence. There were certain precepts, amounting to superstitions, that were strictly adhered to at no matter what cost in time and trouble. You may not take them very seriously, but to me they amounted to a good deal, and were often performed with quite a solemn ritual. No bear was killed without some portion of the carcass, generally the skull or shoulder bones, being hung up in a prominent place somewhere in his former range. The bodies of beaver were laid in supposedly comfortable positions and the hands, feet and tail, severed for convenience in skinning, were laid beside or on the body. Whenever possible the body, with these appendages securely tied to it, was committed to the water through a hole laboriously cut in the ice. Those eaten had the knee-caps, unusual adjuncts for an animal, removed and most religiously burnt. All these ceremonies are practised by semi-civilized, and even more advanced Indians over a wide area; and should anyone be tactless enough to enquire the reason why they do these things, the answer if any, will be:

"Ozaam tapskoche anicianabé, mahween—because they are so much like Indians."

I had however other customs of my own invention, and kept rigidly two self-imposed rules. I would allow no sportsman I guided to photograph a wounded animal until it was dead, and any animal that should chance to be brought to camp alive, must be resuscitated and let go. So when I one Spring captured a month old wolf cub I took him home to the cabin and kept him alive, intending to free him when he was old enough to fend for himself. He was a forlorn little creature, and although I was kind to him he was never happy. He had two sole amusements: one was chewing an old moccasin under the bed, the nearest approach to playing that he ever got; the other was staring by the hour at the cabin walls, staring with his slanting, inscrutable eyes unfocused as though gazing, not at the dark walls of his prison but on beyond them, on into the far distance, to some far distant prospect of his earlier memory. He paid me scant attention save to accept food, but kept on gazing with his veiled eyes until his view was shut off by the sides of the box in which he lay and died.

And so perhaps he came at last to his Promised Land, upon which he had looked so wistfully and so long.[1]

At the termination of the Winter trapping season we went out to sell our fur. Prices had fallen, and were going down every week or so. Although we did not realize it, the day of the trapper was almost done. The handwriting was on the wall, but although it had been painstakingly inscribed there by ourselves, none of us were able to read it.

The hunting ground we were working had been previously trapped over by a noted hunter the Winter before, and between that and the low prices we only took fur to the value of about six hundred dollars; not a great sum in comparison to what I had been in the habit of making during these boom years. There would be little left over after the debt was settled and a summer's provisions purchased, not enough to start out in pursuit of that willow-the-wisp [sic], the virgin, untapped hunting ground that every trapper sees visions of, gets reports about, sees on maps, but never quite catches up to. So I decided on a Spring hunt to replenish the exchequer, something that went a little against even my principles, as a hunt at that time of the year was looked on as both destructive and cruel by the better class of trapper. But there was a family of beaver remaining over from the organized slaughter of the year before, and like too many of my kind, I salved my conscience by saying that I may as well to clean them out before someone else stepped in and took them.

Delayed over a week at the post by the late arrival of a buyer, and more time being consumed by the journey in, we did not arrive back at our ground until the last of May. The hunt should have been over by now, and I was a little disturbed over the hardship I could not now avoid inflicting, as the young beaver were most certainly born by now, and would perish after the old ones were removed. This proved to be the case. Whilst making a set at an old, renovated beaver house where I knew the female to be, I heard faintly the thin piping voices of kitten beavers. In apparent clumsiness, I allowed my paddle to drop with a rattle on the canoe gunnell with the intention of hiding the sound, but Anahareo had heard it and begged me to lift the trap, and allow the baby beaver to have their mother and live. I felt a momentary pang myself, as I had never before killed a beaver at this time on that account, but continued with my work. We needed the money.

The next morning I lifted the bodies of three drowned beaver. The mother was missing however, one trap being unaccounted for. I found where the chain had been broken, and dragged for the body unsuccessfully, later breaking the dam and partly draining the pond, but without avail. She would be the largest and most valuable, so I bemoaned my loss and forgot the life that had been

---

[1] See Deuteronomy 3:21–29, where Moses looks on the Promised Land without being allowed to enter.

destroyed for nothing, and the helpless kittens left to starve. After a whole day spent in a fruitless search, I removed all traps and equipment and proceeded to camp, having no intention whatever of returning; but the next day, after skinning and stretching the catch, for no reason at all I changed my mind. So inauspiciously do important events intrude themselves into our lives. I portaged back to the ruined pond that would never again be good for anything, and we paddled over to the old beaver house in an effort to discover if the female had succeeded in getting back there, but could find no indication either by sight or sound of her presence.

So we turned to go, finally and for good. As we were leaving I heard behind me a light splash, and looking back saw what appeared to be a muskrat lying on top of the water along side of the house. Determined to make this wasted day pay, I threw up my gun, and standing up in the canoe to get a better aim, prepared to shoot. At that distance a man could never miss, and my finger was about to press the trigger when the creature gave a low cry, and at the same instant I saw, right in my line of fire another, who gave out the same peculiar call. They could both be gotten with the one charge of shot. They gave voice again, and this time the sound was unmistakeable—they were young beaver! I lowered my gun and said:

"There are your kittens."

The instinct of a woman spoke out at once.

"Let us save them," cried Anahareo excitedly, and then in a lower voice, "It is up to us, after what we've done."

And truly what had been done here looked now to be an act of brutal savagery. And with some confused thought of giving back what I had taken, some dim idea of atonement, I answered,

"Yes; we have to. Let's take them home." It seemed the only fitting thing to do.

This was not such an easy matter as the kittens were well able to take care of themselves in the water, being older than I had thought. By the exercise of considerable patience and ingenuity we eventually caught them, and dropped them aboard, two funny-looking furry creatures with little scaly tails and exaggerated hind feet, that weighed less than half a pound apiece, and that tramped sedately up and down the bottom of the canoe with that steady, persistent, purposeful walk that we were later to know so well. We looked at them in a kind of dumbfounded bewilderment, feeling much as if we had caught a pair of white elephants, hardly knowing what to do with them. And certainly we had not the faintest inkling of the far-reaching effects their unceremonious entry into our affairs was to have.

Had my finger pressed but lightly on the trigger that fateful morning, these two tiny creatures, whose coming saved from slaughter so many of their kin who followed them and materially changed the lives of several people, would have passed like two wisps from some wandering breeze, back into the Great Unknown from which they had so short a time before set out.

[1934]

Letter to William Arthur Deacon[2]

Beaver Lodge
Prince Albert National Park,
Saskatchewan
May 10, 1935

Dear Mr. Deacon:

Received your kind letter & the Australian review. [. . .] Now about my friend who suggests I have no Indian blood, but am all Scotch. Firstly, the only people who have known me real well since I came to Canada 30 years ago, are bush people & Indians of the type who do not go to Toronto, nor speak of "artistic effect." No one living in this country knows anything of my antecedents except what I have chosen to tell them.

If I have not analysed my blood-mixture quite as minutely as some would wish, let me say here & now that here are the component parts.

Mother—	1/2 Scotch (American)
	1/2 Indian
Father—	Full White, American,
	reputed Scotch descent.

Therefore I am a quarter Indian, a quarter Scotch & the rest reputed Scotch, tho unproven.

Now there it is. You may know that all persons of 1/2 breed "nationality," also all persons having less divisions of Indian blood, are known as half-breeds. I never even stopped to figure the thing out. My friend whom you met, has only my word for it that I have a drop of Scotch blood. Some people, you must know, object to having a "native" accomplish anything. As my whole life-training, my mentality, methods, & whole attitude is undeniably Indian, I have given credit for anything I may have accomplished to the people whom I look on as my own. Unfortunately most men of my type, in whom the Indian, at first glance, is not so strikingly apparent, spend much time denying their Indian blood, & claiming to be French or smoked Irish or something. This I refuse to do. Give all credit for my small success to the white people, (no offence intended) & leave the Indians, who taught me what I know, holding the bag? No sir. It is the admixture of Indian blood that I carry, with some pride, that has enabled me to penetrate so deeply into the heart of Nature; yet undoubtedly the White part has enabled me to express it adequately.

[2] William Arthur Deacon (1890–1977), Canadian editor and literary critic, books editor of *Saturday Night* from 1922 to 1928, the Toronto *Mail and Empire* from 1928 to 1936, and the *Globe and Mail* from 1936 to 1960. Deacon wrote to Grey Owl stating that he had met an acquaintance of his who insisted that "you are all Scotch without a drop of Indian blood in you. . . . Do you want to deny this charge?" This was Grey Owl's response.

There are thousands of mixed bloods like myself kicking around the North; some favour the Indian, some the white; those that favour the white deny their Indian blood which makes me mad as a wet hen. It is a strange anomaly that my wife who is nearly fullblood Indian, could not, when she married me, speak 10 words in any Indian language, even her own, & knew no more about bush life than a young miss from the sidewalk on Yonge Street. I, who was 3 parts white, was the better Indian. Civilization plays strange tricks on us. Right now, so quickly she picked things up, Anahareo can shade many a practiced woodsman, both in skill & courage. This last attribute is her most outstanding characteristic.

When I first commenced to write a few articles, the Editor asked who & what I was & I said I was a bushwhacker, a man of Indian blood. What I meant was, I was tarred with the brush, & felt I was admitting something. I expected he would at once turn me down. This has happened, socially, before, & often since. The artistic effect I never even thought of. I figured I would write a few articles till I got enough money to move the beaver to Ontario, & then quit, & follow my natural way. That the writing business would assume the proportions it since has, never even occurred to me. When the Government took me up, they used the word Indian in describing me, as they said "breed" was derogatory, God knows why. I did not figure I should call myself a white man, because when it was found out, as it eventually might be, that I had Indian blood, down I go with a wollop [sic]. I feel as an Indian, think as an Indian, all my ways are Indian, my heart is Indian. They, more than the whites, are to me, my people.

[. . .] Though nothing has been decided, there is talk of me touring Great Britain on a lecture tour. If it materializes I intend to stop off in Toronto, & may call on you for a little advice.

Pardon this very long & very dull letter. Blame it on nostalgia; it is a hobby of mine. I suppose a man of any strength of character would push it out of his life, but I can't; too firmly rooted in the pine lands, & white water, & the smoky, balsam scented scents of the Ojibway Indians . . .

With best wishes I am,

Yours sincerely,

Grey Owl

[1935]

LAURA GOODMAN SALVERSON ■ (1890–1970)

Laura Goodman was the daughter of Icelandic immigrants who came to Canada in 1887. Born three years after their arrival in Winnipeg, she was raised in a peripatetic household in various Icelandic communities in Canada and the United States. Her father was an idealist who was ill-fitted to work the drudge jobs reserved for immigrants at this time. Although she did not learn to speak

English until she was 10 years old, Salverson grew up with the goal of becoming a writer. According to literary scholar Daisy Neijmann, it was not unusual for a child of an itinerant working-class family to want to become a chronicler of life stories: "The Icelandic immigrant community was teeming with writers, most of them self-educated, and Icelandic immigrant writing was flourishing. Icelandic immigrant papers circulated widely and formed an outlet for these literary outpourings, among them regular columns by Laura's father." Many of these authors sought to give "literary expression to the immigrant experience," though in most cases they wrote in Icelandic. After she married George Salverson, who worked for the railway, Laura continued her transient life and published several important books in English about Icelandic Canadian communities.

Along with Frederick Philip Grove, Salverson is among the first writers to explore the experiences of immigrants in western Canada. With the publication of *The Viking Heart* (1923), a saga of nation-building following Norse storytelling traditions to document the experiences of Icelandic immigrants to Manitoba, Salverson helped to establish the stories of new Canadians as viable stuff of fiction.

When asked to write a new preface for her Governor General's Award-winning autobiography, *Confessions of an Immigrant's Daughter* (1939), set on the Canadian prairies in the first decades of the twentieth century, she noted that her purpose in writing the autobiography was "to make of a personal chronicle a more subjective and therefore more sensitive record of an age now happily past. For the past was difficult indeed for the immigrant who had the temerity to value his own traditions and dared to dream of justifying those traditions to the enrichment of his adopted country." Writing the new preface in 1948, a scant nine years after the original publication of the book, she argued that "today our attitude is less insular, and I cannot help but feel that any newcomer to our Dominion has only himself to blame if he fails to find some measure of human satisfaction. How many opportunities he will find which did not exist in the days of which I write in this book!" Her perspective thus bears comparison to that of Grove in "Canadians Old and New."

"Those Child Transgressions," an early chapter from *Confessions of an Immigrant's Daughter,* intertwines the complexities of family, humour, and memory as the narrator tells the story of her young self learning to read in order to "join in the journey" to see the world.

From Confessions of an Immigrant's Daughter

Those Child Transgressions

My mother could never quite believe that I was not meant for the realms above. So sure was she of my early demise that I began to be a little impatient for the heavenly event. I used to imagine myself setting forth in great state in the Little White Hearse—for of course I was much too big to be taken away in a hack. After that I would flit about in a variety of wings, doing nothing in particular, for my imagination failed me completely when it came to a working programme in Paradise. It was really quite a jolly game, that helped me immensely when I was bored with living cooped up in the house while other children whooped and hollered around the village pump. My greatest disappointment centred in that pastime. If only I might have trampled that delicious mud, I felt that even death would not be too big a price. My second disappointment was God.

God kept a very jealous eye on wilful children. That I was a victim of this pestiferous sin I discovered one lovely morning when the sun was a bristling disk in the sky, and the local children especially merry, splashing through the puddles. Of course, I could not go out. There was a cold wind, my mother said, and if I caught a chill, what might not happen! It was all very sad. But, I thought to myself, just to open the window and hang out for a moment would hardly amount to a very heinous sin. It was a thrilling experience—I even yelled a little, just to show that after all I was not lacking in social graces. Perhaps I wriggled. At any rate, down came the window with a terrifying clop right on my wicked neck!

My screams brought mother on the run. No doubt she was frightened and envisioned who knows what injuries. When she saw that nothing much was amiss, however, her temper, always quick, rose to the occasion.

'Now you see how God punishes naughty girls!' she cried. 'Perhaps, after this, you'll do as you're told!'

Well, for the most part, I always did. My mother had a sharp tongue as well as a sharp eye. That I did not so much resent—mamma had so many soft moments. But that God should plunk the window down on my neck struck me as both ungentlemanly and unjust. From that day I had no use for the Deity. The angels were exempt from this condemnation—they seemed to be a cheerful lot with cheerful duties. And Jesus, the perennial Christmas Babe who later had to die for the sins of the world wrung many tears from my heart. I could never understand why God treated him so badly—except that God was just that kind of deity.

But though my mother was apprehensive that every season was my last (and who can blame her, when I was the only one of her babies born in those arduous years to survive infancy, and then only to fall prey to awful sickness) it was no excuse for ignorance. I had to learn a multitude of poems and prayers and scriptural verses. That was not very difficult if the words had a musical sound and a fitting rhythm. 'Lift up your heads, O ye hills' and 'Yea, though ye slay me, yet will I believe in Him'—such phrases had a fascination for me, entirely apart from any meaning. And of all the many sacred verses, I loved best the lyric passage:

> Dröttin blessi mig or mína
> Morgun kveld og nött or, dag,
> Dröttin vevji vaengi sína
> Mig um lífs of salar hag.[1]

A beautiful conception of a divinity (which I never connected with an anthropomorphic God) that enfolded every living being in protective wings of love.

---

[1] Untranslated in the original publication. This traditional Icelandic prayer may be translated from the Icelandic as "God bless me and mine / Morning, evening, night, and day / God wrap his wings / Around my life and the good of my soul."

It was fun to learn these things, even if it seemed a little silly to roll them off so regularly every night. Where I rebelled, with sad consequences, was at the business of learning to read. Not that I was not thrilled with the general idea, but when my mother brought out the old yellow-paged family Bible for a text-book I struck for liberty and licence. I would *not* learn to read that musty volume. Besides, my mother's choice was sadly inept.

'And it came to pass after these things, that God did tempt Abraham, and said unto him, Abraham: and he said, Behold, here I am. And he said, Take now thy son, thine only son Isaac, whom thou lovest, and get thee into the land of Moriah; and offer him there for a burnt offering upon one of the mountains which I will tell thee of.'[2]

Slowly and seriously my mother read, her slender finger tracing the words for me. Simple little words that brought a curious chill and as swift rebellion to my mind.

'Now, child,' said she, 'see how far you can go. Spell out the letters, and it won't be hard.'

Bleakly I looked at her. Well, let the heavens fall and all dark doom swallow me up—my mind was set. 'I won't read,' I said. 'I won't read a single word, mamma.'

I think she would have been less surprised if I had bitten her.

'You won't read?' she repeated helplessly, and, snatching at saving reason, quickly asked, 'Are you sick? Does your head ache?'

'No, mamma, I am not sick.'

'What's the matter with you then? Stop being silly and do as you are told.'

She might as well have spoken to a stone: neither argument nor reprimand moved me. I was wicked, I knew, and resigned to an evil fate, but not to reading such mischievous stuff. That fate, in the guise of a dark cupboard under the stairs quickly befell me. It was frightfully black, and I was sure that a thousand mice were nibbling in the corners. I sat there with my sins and waited for eternity to pass. I did not cry. I just sat there listening to the imaginary mice, and wondering how long it would be until they had eaten everything else, and would begin on me.

At least a hundred years had dragged by when I heard my father come home, and the next moment found myself hauled up before him in all my dusty iniquity. Said my indignant mother, when the chronicle of my unconscionable revolt ended, 'Now, young lady, perhaps you'll think differently, and obey like a sensible child.'

To which I instantly replied—quite as though she had pressed a button and released a prepared answer: 'Now I'll never learn to read, mother.'

It may have been her unfailing sense of humour which saved me from further pressure, which undoubtedly would have had a serious psychological effect. Or there may have been something in my strained white face that actually

---

[2] Genesis 22:1–2.

frightened her. She was never one to understand mental complexes or straitened emotional states. So now, rather than cope with something at once ridiculous and incredible, for I was usually obedient and completely ruled by her influence, she left me where I was, disgraced and contemptible, and hurried to the kitchen. Father said nothing, and quietly slipped out of the house. When he returned there was a whimsical smile on his face, and in his hand a small pink book. Quite as though nothing unusual were afoot, he exhibited his purchase so that I should see in all its shining wonder the fine frontispiece. There, bold as you please, stood a chubby little chap with a bundle on a stick jauntily perched over one shoulder. His cap sat crookedly, and his round face beamed. He was utterly adorable, and I promptly fell in love with him.

'This is Master Neils,' father told me. 'A gay young fellow, with adventure in his soul. He is setting forth to see the world. Now, how would you like to join in the journey, little miss?'

I was already upon his knees, my eyes glued to the charming creature. I was speechless for the thumping in my breast.

'Ah, I see that you do,' said papa. 'Well, then, you must learn to read. That, my dear, is the very best way to journey about the world.'

Thus was I saved, and, needless to say, I loved that little pink book above any other. It was not only my key to dreams, but a passport into a kingdom of understanding that has to do with charities to which the Marthas of this world remain for ever blind.[3] I was to remember that trifling incident many times, and out of it grew the perception that, like liberty, true benevolence is a quality of mind.

That my mother had assumed the role of a commanding executive in our household was not exactly her fault. By nature she was gay and instinctively averse from conventional strictures that loom so all-important to the average woman. There was no sacred order in her house. If the weekly paper arrived in the midst of washday she would let the water cool and read the serial with no qualms whatsoever. Water could always be reheated, but enthusiasm, once cooled, was stale as a dry herring. We had our meals at the prescribed hours, although, for herself, she cherished no such boresome ritual. No one ever had less interest in food. How she managed to keep so healthy on such sketchy fare is still a mystery. 'If I'm not hungry, why should I eat?' she would say, and sit down with a cup of poisonously strong coffee and her endless knitting. It was the same with clothes. Now, why should she bundle up against the weather, when she never took a chill? In zero weather she hung out the steaming wash, dressed in nothing warmer than a cotton gown and undergarments made from carefully bleached flour sacking. 'Well, what of it?' she would parry. She never caught cold, and, besides, was immune to all diseases.

For her children, it was another story. I, at least, was swaddled in clothes, made to eat when I had no appetite, and, it now seems to me, actually was

[3] See Luke 10:38–42.

coddled into the invalidism she meant to avoid. Indeed, it became a kind of sin for me to even think of behaving like other children—a frightful challenge to evil fate even to dream of being well. I suspect there was a wide streak of jealous possessiveness in her character which fixed upon the one thing the world could not snatch from her—the affection of her children. Yet even in this she was not altogether successful. In my case, at least, it was papa who figured actively in my infant brooding. For no matter how gentle and kind mamma might be, and everlastingly concerned for my health, I knew quite well that it was papa who came nearer to understanding me. That this incipient understanding was not permitted to grow and outlast childhood was, I think, my mother's fault. In the end, she weaned me completely away, made an alien of the parent whose vagaries I share, and, as I now know, diverted my normal instincts into channels of activity for which I had no natural talents.

None of this my loving mother meant to do. She was always pathetically eager to plan some happiness for us, to join in the gaiety, however tired she might be. Those early years of unrelieved privation had concentrated into one unbearable memory. Her small son weeping out his heart because on Christmas Eve, when he had set out so stoutly through the storm to attend the church concert, there was not even so much as a red apple on the tree for him. She had not wanted him to go, but he had argued so defensively out of his child's high faith. He had been so good—and did not God love good children? He had watched little sister while mamma worked and tried his best to wait on papa, who was sick in bed. Oh, there would be something on the Christ Child's lovely tree for him—he would not be forgotten because he was little and shy and so very poor.

So now, when things were a little easier —when there was sometimes as much as seven dollars in the weekly pay envelope—why, she naturally was determined to make the most of every festival. My birthday was always a great occasion. I think it marked a sort of conquest over the fear that dogged her mind. I might be doomed, as one doctor had hinted to perish before I ever reached the teens, but each birthday was a milestone conquered. [. . .]

[1939]

F.R. SCOTT ■ (1899–1985)

Born in Quebec City in the last year of the nineteenth century, Francis Reginald Scott (known as Frank) was anything but a Victorian. Never afraid to state his mind, Scott positioned himself at the vanguard of art, letters, and politics in modern Canada. Scott's early work is that of a radical poet breaking through the sentimentality of the past in order to articulate a place for art in the nation of the future. Throughout his career as a poet, lawyer, and social activist, Scott worked to unsettle Canadian culture from the colonial mentality that he thought stifled it. Influenced by the artistic philosophy of the Group of Seven and echoing American poet Ezra Pound's dictum to "make it new," Scott insisted on the absolute need to bring new forms of expression to the Canadian context.

One of the "McGill Group" (or the "Montreal Group") of poets to emerge out of McGill University in the mid-1920s (Scott, A.J.M. Smith, Leo Kennedy, Leon Edel, and A.M. Klein), Scott was committed to bringing modernism to Canada. While at McGill, Scott, Smith, and Edel established a short-lived but influential journal called *The McGill Fortnightly Review* (1925–27) to promote modernist poetry in Canada. Scott was subsequently part of the group of poets who established the "little magazine" *Preview* (1942–45) (see his minutes of the meeting transcribed here) and fostered its amalgamation with the rival publication *First Statement* (1942–45) to form the joint publication *Northern Review* (1945–56).

With Smith, Scott co-edited the first modernist collection of poetry in Canada: *New Provinces: Poems of Several Authors* (1936). Although it was not a commercial success (selling only 82 copies—of which Scott purchased 10), it is now thought to represent a defining moment in Canadian poetry. In addition to Scott and Smith, it included work by Kennedy and Klein in Montreal, and E.J. Pratt and Robert Finch in Toronto. Scott states his position in his manifesto "New Poems for Old" (1931): "[T]he modernist poet, like the socialist, has thought through present forms to a new and more suitable order. He is not concerned with destroying, but with creating, and being a creator he strikes terror into the hearts of the old and decrepit who cannot adjust themselves to that which is to be. The modernist poet

frequently uses accepted forms, and only discards them when he discovers that they are unsuited to what he has to say. Then he creates a new form, groomed to his thought." According to critic Sandra Djwa, Scott's career as a poet exemplifies the transition from Victorian Romanticism to the modern. But, as with most modernists, she continues, there is a strong infusion of Romanticism in his poetry, primarily in his use of nature as symbol, but also in his belief that poetry can change society. As he writes in the short "Note on Colonialism" (*Preview* 1943), the "duty of the poet is to help in the enfranchisement" of the people.

Scott's famous poem from 1927, "The Canadian Authors Meet," is widely known for its disparaging dismissal of the previous generation of Canadian poets and their acolytes. With the arrogance and presumption typical of a newly formed, and self-appointed, avant-garde toward its predecessors, Scott's poem is striking for its audacity, particularly given that his own father was a part of the group he mocks (F.G. Scott was a contemporary of Bliss Carman, Archibald Lampman, Charles G.D. Roberts, and Wilfred Campbell, all named in the poem). What Scott didn't acknowledge were the many similarities between his generation and that of the Confederation period. Both groups were influenced by a wave of nationalist sentiment and a desire to create a distinctive, internationally viable Canadian literature; both were concerned with form and workmanship in the craft of writing; both sought to supersede the body of supposedly mediocre Canadian work that had preceded them; both saw themselves as members of an avant-garde who would contribute to Canada's international standing; both were predominantly masculine in membership and attitudes. The poem criticizes sentimentalism and high seriousness ("the air is heavy"); artificial boosterism ("self-unction"); a lack of talent ("Miss Crotchet's muse"); allegiance to Britain ("portrait of the Prince of Wales"); pretentiousness and snobbery (the feeling of "mixing with the *literati*"); mindless routine ("puppets"); naive patriotism ("paint the native maple"); and most significantly, derivative poetry ("selfsame welkin ringing"). The final stanza, included in the poem when first published in the April 1927 *McGill Fortnightly Review* but deleted from subsequent publication of the poem, highlights Scott's own ironic, and indeed brazen, self-positioning.

Unlike the Confederation Poets, Scott added social activism to his position as a rebellious poet. As a professor of constitutional law (a Rhodes Scholar, he was educated at Bishop's, Oxford, and McGill), Scott was keenly interested in many aspects of social justice. His most famous case, in a literary framework, was his defence of D.H. Lawrence's *Lady Chatterley's Lover* (1928) against charges of obscenity in the Supreme Court of Canada. In a 1963 interview in the *McGill News,* Scott notes that the two key periods in his intellectual development were working on *The McGill Fortnightly Review* and, following the stock market crash of 1929, the creation of the League for Social Reconstruction (LSR) in 1931–32.

A committed socialist, Scott joined historian Frank Underhill, Eugene Forsey, and E.A. Havelock, among others, to form the LSR. They described themselves as an organization "working for the establishment in Canada of a social order in which the basic principle regulating production, distribution and service will be the common good rather than private profit." In 1935 Scott also participated in the composition of *Social Planning for Canada,* a book which maps the socialist

itinerary that was to become the platform of the Co-operative Commonwealth Federation (CCF). Scott was also heavily involved in the creation of the "Regina Manifesto" (the program the CCF adopted at its first national convention held in Regina, Saskatchewan, in 1933). It called for "a planned and socialized economy in which our natural resources and principal means of production and distribution are owned, controlled and operated by the people." Scott was the national chairman of the CCF from 1942 to 1950 and was involved in the transition of the CCF to the NDP (New Democratic Party). His commitment to socialist politics is echoed by other writers in this period, including Klein, Dorothy Livesay, and Earle Birney.

A long-standing member of the McGill Faculty of Law (1928–68), he served as Dean of Law from 1961 to 1964, as well as technical-aid representative for the United Nations in Burma, and from 1963 to 1971 as a member of the Royal Commission on Bilingualism and Biculturalism. As an Anglo-Quebecker, Scott was vitally interested in supporting Canada as a truly bilingual and bicultural nation. He sought this in his own work through translations of writing by Anne Hébert and Hector de Saint-Denys Garneau.

Acknowledged as a leader in both law and literature, Scott received two Governor General's Awards: the first in 1977 for his work as a social philosopher in *Essays on the Constitution: Aspects of Canadian Law and Politics,* and the second for his poetry collection, *The Collected Poems of F.R. Scott* (1981). Scott often linked his social vision with his poetic one in the form of satire. Satire, he notes, is "inverted positive statement": criticize something and thus recommend its opposite as a solution. In the introduction to *The Blasted Pine: An Anthology of Satire, Invective, and Disrespectful Verse*

(1957), which Scott co-edited with Smith, the editors write that the poems in the collection are sharply critical "of bourgeois respectability, Tory imperialism, mercantile or sectarian hypocrisy, and complacent materialism." These are also the topics that fall under the satiric edge of Scott's own sword ("The Canadian Authors Meet" and "The Canadian Social Register"). As "a man for all seasons" (as critic George Woodcock labelled him)—a poet, editor, lawyer, activist, and critic—Scott was never afraid to make his voice count. He was, according to poet Louis Dudek, "the clearest poetic voice of this century in Canada."

The Canadian Authors Meet

Expansive puppets percolate self-unction
Beneath a portrait of the Prince of Wales.
Miss Crotchet's muse has somehow failed to function,
Yet she's a poetess. Beaming, she sails

From group to chattering group, with such a dear
Victorian saintliness, as is her fashion,
Greeting the other unknowns with a cheer—
Virgins of sixty who still write of passion.

The air is heavy with Canadian topics,
And Carman, Lampman, Roberts, Campbell, Scott,   10
Are measured for their faith and philanthropics,
Their zeal for God and King, their earnest thought.

The cakes are sweet, but sweeter is the feeling
That one is mixing with the *literati*;
It warms the old, and melts the most congealing.
Really, it is a most delightful party.

Shall we go round the mulberry bush, or shall
We gather at the river, or shall we
Appoint a Poet Laureate this Fall,
Or shall we have another cup of tea?   20

O Canada, O Canada, Oh can
A day go by without new authors springing
To paint the native maple,[1] and to plan
More ways to set the selfsame welkin ringing?

[1927, rev. 1936]

[1] The 1927 and 1936 (*New Provinces*) versions have "lily." In subsequent versions, Scott changed this to "maple." "Welkin," in the last line, is an archaic word for "sky."

Far in a corner sits (though none would know it)
The very picture of disconsolation,
A rather lewd and most ungodly poet
Writing these verses, for his soul's salvation.

[1927]

Trans Canada

Pulled from our ruts by the made-to-order gale
We sprang upward into a wider prairie
And dropped Regina below like a pile of bones.[2]

Sky tumbled upon us in waterfalls,
But we were smarter than a Skeena salmon
And shot our silver body over the lip of air
To rest in a pool of space
On the top storey of our adventure.

A solar peace
And a six-way choice.   10

Clouds, now, are the solid substance,
A floor of wool roughed by the wind
Standing in waves that halt in their fall.
A still of troughs.

The plane, our planet,
Travels on roads that are not seen or laid
But sound in instruments on pilots' ears,
While underneath
The sure wings
Are the everlasting arms of science.   20

Man, the lofty worm, tunnels his latest clay,
And bores his new career.

This frontier, too, is ours.
This everywhere whose life can only be led
At the pace of a rocket

F.R. SCOTT

86

[2] "Pile of Bones" was an early name for Regina, describing the huge piles of buffalo bones that were gathered after the hunts.

Is common to man and man,
And every country below is an I land.

The sun sets on its top shelf,
And stars seem farther from our nearer grasp.

I have sat by night beside a cold lake   30
And touched things smoother than moonlight on still water,
But the moon on this cloud sea is not human,
And here is no shore, no intimacy,
Only the start of space, the road to suns.

[1945]

Laurentian Shield

Hidden in wonder and snow, or sudden with summer,
This land stares at the sun in a huge silence
Endlessly repeating something we cannot hear.
Inarticulate, arctic,
Not written on by history, empty as paper,
It leans away from the world with songs in its lakes
Older than love, and lost in the miles.

This waiting is wanting.
It will choose its language
When it has chosen its technic,   10
A tongue to shape the vowels of its productivity.

A language of flesh and of roses.[3]

Now there are pre-words,
Cabin syllables,
Nouns of settlement
Slowly forming, with steel syntax,
The long sentence of its exploitation.

The first cry was the hunter, hungry for fur,
And the digger for gold, nomad, no-man, a particle;

---

[3] In British poet Stephen Spender's 1946 essay "The Making of a Poem," he explores the ways the human mind imposes itself on landscapes and language. For Spender, the kind of language that humans seek is one of "flesh and of roses," which echoes the ways Scott's poem imagines landscape and language to be mutually determining. In his essay, Spender cites his own line "the language of flesh and roses" as an example of poetic "inspiration," recalling how it came to him while he was standing in the corridor of a train looking at a pit-filled landscape.

Then the bold commands of monopoly, big with machines,   20
Carving its kingdoms out of the public wealth;
And now the drone of the plane, scouting the ice,
Fills all the emptiness with neighbourhood
And links our future over the vanished pole.

But a deeper note is sounding, heard in the mines,
The scattered camps and the mills, a language of life,
And what will be written in the full culture of occupation
Will come, presently, tomorrow,
From millions whose hands can turn this rock into children.

[1954]

Bonne Entente

F.R. SCOTT

The advantages of living with two cultures
Strike one at every turn,
Especially when one finds a notice in an office building:
'This elevator will not run on Ascension Day';
Or reads in the *Montreal Star*:
'Tomorrow being the Feast of the Immaculate Conception,
There will be no collection of garbage in the city';
Or sees on the restaurant menu the bilingual dish:

DEEP APPLE PIE

TARTE AUX POMMES PROFONDES

[1954]

The Canadian Social Register[4]

(*A Social Register for Canada was promoted in Montreal in 1947. On the Advisory Committee were names like the Rt Hon. Louis St Laurent, Sir Ellsworth Flavelle, Air Marshal Bishop, Rear Admiral Brodeur, the Hon. J. Earl Lawson, Hartland Molson, and others. A Secret Committee was to screen all applicants. All quotations in this poem are taken verbatim from the invitation sent out to prospective members.*)

Reader, we have the honour to invite you to become a
    "Member of the Social Register",

---

[4] A social register is a directory of names and addresses of prominent families who form the social elite of a community. The New York Social Register was the first, published in 1886. In 1958, the first edition of *The Social Register of Canada* was published. The preface explains that it lists "Canadians who, either as individuals or as members of worthy families, have contributed markedly to the social development of their nation."

For the paltry fee of $125 per annum.
This "work of art, done in good taste", and listing
    annually the "Notables of the Dominion",
Will contain nothing but "Ladies and Gentlemen pre-
    eminent in the Higher Spheres",
A list, indeed, of "First Families",
Who are "the very fabric of our country".
Thus shall we "build up in the Nation's First Families   10
A consciousness of their rôle in the life of a civilized
    democracy".
Thus shall we bring "added dignity and profound
    significance
To our cultural way of life".
Through deplorable lack of vision, in times past,
Men who were "great Canadians, have everlastingly
    passed into oblivion",
Leaving no "footprints on the sands of time".[5]
Somehow, despite their pre-eminence, they have   20
    disappeared.
Shall we, through "tragic shortsightedness", let the
    leaders of this era
"Disappear into the realm of eternal silence?"
"Shall there be no names, no achievements, to hearten
    and strengthen on-coming generations in time of
    stress?"
If they have failed to make history, shall they fail to make
    The Canadian Social Register?
No—not if they can pay $125 annually,   30
And pass our Secret Committee.
For there is a "Secret Committee of seven members",
Who will "determine the eligibility of those applying for
    membership".
Thus will the Social Register be "accepted in the most
    fastidious circles".
And to aid the Secret Committee you will send
The name of your father and the maiden name of your
    mother,
And the address of your "summer residence"   40
(For of course you have a summer residence).

---

[5] Quotation from American poet Henry Wadsworth Longfellow's (1807-1882) "A Psalm of Life": "Lives of great men all remind us / We can make our lives sublime, / And, departing, leave behind us / Footprints on the sands of time."

You may also submit, with a glossy print of yourself,
"Short quotations from laudatory comments received on
    diverse public occasions".
When printed, the Register will be sent,
Free, gratis, and not even asked for,
To (among many others) the "King of Sweden", the
    "President of Guatemala", and the "Turkish Public
    Library".

Reader, this will be a "perennial reminder"   50
Of the people (or such of them as pass the Secret
    Committee)
Who "fashioned this Canada of ours",
For "One does not live only for toil and gain",
Not, anyway, in First Families. It is comforting to believe
That while we "walk the earth", and pay $125,
And "after we have passed on", there will remain
"In the literature of the Universe", and particularly in the
    "Turkish Public Library",
This "de luxe edition", "these unique and dignified annals",   60
"These priceless and undying memories", with laudatory
    comments chosen by ourselves,
To which "succeeding First Families and historians alike
    will look"
For "knowledge, guidance and inspiration".
Lives rich in eligibility will be "written large"
(But within "a maximum of one thousand words")
"For all men to see and judge".
The "glorious dead", too,
These "selfless and noble defenders of Canada's honour",   70
Will be incorporated in the Social Register
"Without any financial remuneration",
Assuming, of course, that they are all
"Sons and daughters of its Members".

Reader, as you may guess, the Register
Was not "a spur of the moment idea".
It was "long and carefully nurtured".
And "counsel was sought in high and authoritative
    places",
So that it may "lay a basis upon which prominent   80
    Canadians will henceforth be appraised
As they go striding down the years",
Paying their $125,

And receiving a "world-wide, gratuitous distribution",
Even unto "the Turkish Public Library".

"Si monumentum requiris, circumspice!"[6]
On this note, we both end.

[1954]

All the Spikes But the Last

Where are the coolies in your poem, Ned?[7]
Where are the thousands from China who swung
   their picks with bare hands at forty below?

Between the first and the million other spikes
   they drove, and the dressed-up act of
   Donald Smith,[8] who has sung their story?

Did they fare so well in the land they helped to
   unite? Did they get one of the 25,000,000 CPR acres?

Is all Canada has to say to them written in the Chinese
   Immigration Act?

[1957]

Minutes from *Preview* Editorial Meeting[9]

PAT: "We want to take [the] rigid statement in *Preview*, March 1942, and see what
   changes we feel ought to be made in it. (Reads) That statement is rather glib
   and experience has not borne out the views.[10] [. . .]
KLEIN: Were you not too nationalist?[11]

---

[6] Latin: "If you seek a monument, look around."

[7] The poem is written in response to E.J. ("Ned") Pratt's epic poem "Towards the Last Spike" (1952). Scott focuses on the unacknowledged work of the 10,000 Chinese workers (the "coolies") who arrived in Canada between 1880 and 1885 to provide labour for the construction of the railway. Hundreds of these workers lost their lives doing such dangerous work. As soon as construction was complete, upon pressure from British Columbians afraid of losing their jobs to people who would work for low wages in dangerous conditions, the Canadian government issued the Chinese head tax ($50) as part of the Act to Restrict and Regulate Chinese Immigration to Canada, 1885 (see Volume I, Section III for the history of the head tax and excerpts from the Chinese Immigration Act).

[8] Donald Smith (1820–1913) was the CPR Director who hammered the "last spike" in the railway and is pictured in the famous "Last Spike" photograph (see Figure V-6).

[9] These minutes from the *Preview* magazine editorial meeting, held in Montreal on 13 March 1944, were handwritten in a small notebook by F.R. Scott. Present at the meeting were Scott, Patrick Anderson (Pat. And.), P.K. Page, Bruce Ruddick, Neufville Shaw, and A.M. Klein.

[10] The initial editorial outlines three goals shared by the group: to overcome Montreal's cultural and artistic isolation, to effect a "fusion between the lyric and the didactic elements in modern verse, a combination of vivid, arresting imagery and the capacity to 'sing' with social content and criticism," and to make contact with other writers.

[11] Klein was not a member of the editorial board in 1942 so he can say "you" here.

SCOTT: Not at all—where did we write about moose and canoes? All we were concerned with was the development of art in Canada. Art in Canada is different from 'Canadian art.'

SHAW: We want literature written in Canada that is "literature." Naturally much of it will deal with Canadian things.

ANDERSON: It is possible to have cultural nationalism + an internationalism at the same time. Internationalism is part of our culture, but so too is Canadian life and landscape.

SHAW: We must have a poetry that is vivid and concrete. Immediate. A good poem has a physical quality, like a peach or an orange. In that sense it is Canadian.

SCOTT: Poetry draws on all experiences—some [are] more universal than others. Landscape is local: philosophy is not.

KLEIN: What is the difference between poetry in Windsor and Detroit?

SCOTT: If poems are about better boxes, one will be red and one green.

PAGE: Subject matter is not much different in two closely related places.

ANDERSON: Montreal is crying out to be written about. If we were socially aware we would write about them.

PAGE: Yes—he could not help drawing upon his environment, + that would be Canadian.

RUDDICK: Canadians used to take moose and use it as a symbol. It had an associational use. This was false, as it was not a direct writing.

SCOTT: We have never had a great poem about a moose yet. We just use the moose as a piece of shorthand. The real moosiness has never come out. I think we shd [sic] discuss why there has not been more poetry and more interest in poetry in Canada.

SHAW: There has been a revival lately. Preview, First Statement, + Con. Verse all appeared within a year. Why did that happen?

AND.: Canada took some time to be influenced by the new poetic influences. English group did not start till 1930's [...]

RUDDICK: Society regards poetry as shameful—they won't go after it. It is not regarded as a worthwhile activity in Canada.

SHAW: Still, we do little to make our stuff known.

SCOTT: After all, that is the purpose of this meeting—to get at the source of the problem of creative literature in Canada, + to publish the results in the hope that it will evoke a response.

AND.: People look on poetry as a jig saw puzzle with a meaning.

PAGE: That is because we make it that way.

RUDDICK: I don't think so. In U.S. no poetry sells very much (even verse that is plain reading).

PAGE: I still think that to [an] average reader our poetry is a puzzle. The poetry they read in school is not a puzzle. So they don't start looking for a puzzle.

RUDDICK: All poetry today is suggestive and a poetry of implication.

SCOTT: Today poetry has moved on from its former base and people are not trained to keep up with it. Poets write in the newer manner + hence are further and further away from the common reader.

AND.: If we were really "singing with social content", people would like the singing + would read it anyway.

SCOTT: There is too much virtuosity in modern poetry. Poets too easily get effects they like.

AND.: Yes—and the poets are escapist in enjoying their own poetry because they cannot enjoy much else. Formerly they used 1. to enjoy writing + 2. enjoy the fact that others would enjoy it.

SCOTT: Poets today know the old order is passing. They have not found their new universals. They are struggling for a new order, knowing only they cannot accept the old. The ordinary people have not yet gone so far forward, + the gap between the poet + public is wide. Not till a new age dawns with a new equilibrium will poet + public walk in tune.

SHAW: Poets of 20's had destruction to occupy them. That was easy. We have to construct—that is difficult.

RUDDICK: Poets today have no faith, no attitude.

KLEIN: That is irrelevant. Good poetry can be made out of unbelief as well as belief. E.G. Baudelaire[12]

RUDDICK: We are marginal men—caught between the old + the new.

SCOTT: I think we are obscure because the present and the future are obscure.

KLEIN: Past present and futures have been obscure, + yet their poetry was transparent.

AND.: Yes, but we have more obscure things to deal with. Psychology has upset us. [. . .]—for the first time with new scientific analysis. This confuses us.

KLEIN: In the writing which shows the most promise there is a contradiction. Poets are socially conscious and seek to give us universals, yet they use a restricted technique. They cannot speak to the masses they love. Richness of imagery is o.k. but it is not communicated. These people are also aware of their schizophrenia.

SCOTT: Why should poets write in language of the old order of society? People have not seen as much of the new world as the poet does. The poet is out ahead. In time, the people will catch up. [. . .]

[1944]

---

[12] Charles Baudelaire (1821–1867) was a nineteenth-century poet whose book *Les Fleurs du mal* (1857) met with scandal because of its treatment of sexuality and death.

"Modernity and tradition alike demand that the contemporary artist who survives adolescence shall be an intellectual. Sensibility is no longer enough, intelligence is also required. Even in Canada." Thus wrote A.J.M. Smith in "Wanted: Canadian Criticism" in April 1928.

Such bold sentiments helped lead Smith to become one of the most significant figures in twentieth-century Canadian literature. As a critic, anthologist, and poet, he helped introduce, track, and install modernism in Canada. For the critic Desmond Pacey, Smith effected nothing short of a revolution in Canadian poetic theory and practice as he "stemmed the tide of lush romantic verse and replaced it with a clear, cold, intense and complex classicism." Responding to the poetry of the generation before him, in the late 1920s and early 1930s, Smith actively sought a new space in Canadian poetry for himself and his friends. In 1936, *New Provinces: Poems of Several Authors,* co-edited by Smith and F.R. Scott, was released. While it contained poems by Smith, Scott, E.J. Pratt, A.M. Klein, Robert Finch, and Leo Kennedy, upon publication it did not include the incendiary preface that Smith had written for the book in which he outlined how outdated and outmoded previous generations of poetry had been.

Smith's "Rejected Preface" for *New Provinces,* included here, takes a radical stand against the Confederation Poets Charles G.D. Roberts, Bliss Carman, and Archibald Lampman. Smith barely remains civil when he writes that "the most popular experience [in their poetry] is to be pained, hurt, stabbed, or seared by beauty—preferably by the yellow flame of the crocus in the spring or the red flame of the maple leaf in autumn." The vehemence of such a damnation of the reigning kings of Canadian letters cannot be underestimated. Smith's mandate was to repudiate the poetry of the past and to set a course for poetry in the future. Regardless of whether he succeeded or not, his criticism and poetry were highly influential for much of the twentieth century.

Born in Westmount, Quebec, in 1902, Arthur James Marshall Smith was a core member of what is often referred to as the Montreal school of poetry (the "Montreal Group" or the "McGill Group"). In his final year as an undergraduate student at McGill University, he was the editor of the *McGill Daily Literary Supplement* (1924–25). When the student council decided not to support the literary supplement the following year, Smith (now a graduate student) and his friend F.R. Scott (and later Leon Edel) founded *The McGill Fortnightly Review* (1925–27). In its two years, it published poetry by Klein and Kennedy, as well as Scott and Smith. The editors wanted to locate contemporary poetry in Canada within the international modernist movement. They were highly critical of the Romanticism of Canadian verse, which they viewed as derivative of late Victorian and Edwardian sources. At this time Smith was also publishing in magazines and journals around the English-speaking world, including *The Dial* (where editor and poet Marianne Moore said she "greatly admired" his poem "The Lonely Land"), *New Republic, New Verse, The Nation,* and even the highly acclaimed *Poetry, a Magazine of Verse* out of Chicago.

Smith's best-known poem, "The Lonely Land," first published in *The McGill Fortnightly Review,* was later republished in the *Canadian Forum* (1927) and *The Dial* (1928), and has since been anthologized widely. The image of the tree in Smith's poem, which is embodied in the elongated shape of the poem, has been held up as a potent symbol of the prototypical Canadian character moulded by the harsh climate. In Smith's words, the hardy Canadian spirit is marked by "a beauty of dissonance." In an interview in the *McGill News*, Autumn 1963, Smith tells the background story of the poem: "I saw the paintings of the Group of Seven and it was from Tom Thomson's painting [see Figure V-1] that I wrote the 'Lonely Land.' I've been in the North Country and, as I say, I do know a cedar from a pine tree but that's about all." He also explains some of the practical reasons behind the evolving versions of the poem. When he found out that you got paid per line for *The Dial,* he cut the lines of the poem in half and was paid twice as much money ($40 total). Smith explains, "It made the poem twice as good as well as twice as valuable." He continues, "It's a curious example of good avarice, I suppose: the poem needed to be run that way and it's got the rhythm now which it didn't have at first." Two versions of the poem are included here to illustrate the stages of revision the poem underwent.

After McGill, Smith went to the University of Edinburgh to do his Ph.D. (on the metaphysical poets) and then to teach at universities in the United States (Ball State and University of Nebraska), before settling for the next 36 years teaching literature at Michigan State University.

Over his career, Smith published many collections of his own poetry, including *News of the Phoenix and Other Poems* (1943), for which he won the Governor General's Award, and *A Sort of Ecstasy* (1954), as well as many anthologies that played a large role in the development of a recognizable Canadian canon. The most influential of his anthologies were *The Book of Canadian Poetry: A Critical and Historical Anthology* (1943), *The Blasted Pine* (1957, co-edited with F.R. Scott), and *The Oxford Book of Canadian Verse in English and French* (1960).

Smith's introduction to *The Book of Canadian Poetry* (1943) marked an important moment in the history of poetry in Canada. In it he outlines his controversial theory of the "native" and the "cosmopolitan" schools of poetry (see the introduction to this section). Smith's assessment had many supporters, including Northrop Frye, who reviewed the book in the *Canadian Forum* in 1943, but it also sparked fierce opposition, namely from John Sutherland, who published an alternative anthology in 1947, *Other Canadians: An Anthology of the New Poetry in Canada, 1940–1946,* to counter Smith. Although Smith's anthology was criticized by some reviewers for its modernist and elitist bias, it was recognized by others as a landmark of Canadian literature, making possible the teaching of Canadian poetry. Still, Smith's influence as an anthologist of Canadian literature was not appreciated by all. The poet Phyllis Webb has said, "When I look back on the way that the history of Canadian literature has been written, it's been documented mainly by Frank Scott and A.J.M. Smith themselves and they have created their own little history."

Of course, Smith's own lively criticism also provoked criticism. Poet and critic Anne Compton notes how the responses to Smith's role as poet and anthologist run the extremes: "Based on at least part of the oeuvre, the critics have claimed that Smith is (and is not) religious, is (and is not) derivative, articulates (fails to articulate) something Canadian, is an optimist (a pessimist), and can (and cannot) express emotion. The diversity of critical responses to Smith's work is positively dizzying." The dizzying diversity of responses is a testament to the centrality of Smith in the larger framework of Canadian literature.

To Hold in a Poem

I would take words
As crisp and as white
As our snow; as our birds
Swift and sure in their flight;

As clear and as cold
As our ice; as strong as a jack pine;
As young as a trillium, and old
As Laurentia's long undulant line;

Sweet-smelling and bright
As new rain; as hard   10
And as smooth and as white
As a brook pebble cold and unmarred;

To hold in a poem of words
Like water in colourless glass
The spirit of mountains like birds,
Of forests as pointed as grass;

To hold in a verse as austere
As the spirit of prairie and river,
Lonely, unbuyable, dear,
The North, as a deed, and forever.   20

[1925, 1954]

The Lonely Land [First Version][1]

Group of Seven

Cedar and jagged fir uplift
Accusing barbs against the grey
And cloud-piled sky;
And in the bay
Blown spume and windrift
And thin, bitter spray
Snap at the whirling sky;
And the pine trees lean one way.

Hark to the wild duck's cry
And the lapping of water on stones   10

[1] This version was published in *The McGill Fortnightly Review* in 1926.

Pushing some monstrous plaint against the sky
While a tree creaks and groans
When the wind sweeps high.

It is good to come to this land
Of desolate splendour and grey grief,
And on a loud, stony strand
Find for a tired heart relief
In a wild duck's bitter cry,
In grey rock, black pine, shrill wind
And cloud-piled sky.   20

[1926]

The Lonely Land[2]

Cedar and jagged fir
uplift sharp barbs
against the gray
and cloud-piled sky;
and in the bay
blown spume and windrift
and thin, bitter spray
snap
at the whirling sky;
and the pine trees   10
lean one way.

A wild duck calls
to her mate,
and the ragged
and passionate tones
stagger and fall,
and recover,
and stagger and fall,
on these stones—
are lost   20
in the lapping of water
on smooth, flat stones.

This is a beauty
of dissonance,

[2] The poem was modified and published in 1927 in *Canadian Forum* and in 1929 in *The Dial*. It was also published in *New Provinces* in 1936. This has become the standard version of the poem.

this resonance
of stony strand,
this smoky cry
curled over a black pine
like a broken
and wind-battered branch   30
when the wind
bends the tops of the pines
and curdles the sky
from the north.

This is the beauty
of strength
broken by strength
and still strong.

                                                    [1926, rev. 1929, 1936]

The Wisdom of Old Jelly Roll[3]

How all men wrongly death to dignify
Conspire, I tell. Parson, poetaster,[4] pimp,
Each acts or acquiesces. They prettify,
Dress up, deodorize, embellish, primp,
And make a show of Nothing. Ah, but met-
aphysics laughs: she touches, tastes, and smells
—Hence knows—the diamond holes that make a net.
Silence resettled testifies to bells.
'Nothing' depends on 'Thing', which is or was:
So death makes life or makes life's worth, a worth   10
Beyond all highfalutin' woes or shows
To publish and confess. 'Cry at the birth,
Rejoice at the death,'[5] old Jelly Roll said,
Being on whisky, ragtime, chicken, and the scriptures fed.

                                                                [1962]

---

[3] Jelly Roll Morton, born Ferdinand Joseph Lamothe (1890?–1941), was an American jazz pianist, bandleader, composer, and, as his business card said, "Originator of Jazz."

[4] A writer of poor or petty verse.

[5] In a 1938 interview with music historian Alan Lomax (published as *Mister Jelly Roll: The Fortunes of Jelly Roll Morton, New Orleans Creole and Inventor of Jazz*, 1950), Morton describes how his jazz quartet would seek out funerals to play at in turn-of-the-century Louisiana because they ensured a good meal for the musicians: "In New Orleans they believed truly to stick right close to the Scripture. That means rejoice at the death and cry at the birth" (18).

A Rejected Preface[6]

The bulk of Canadian verse is romantic in conception and conventional in form. Its two great themes are nature and love—nature humanized, endowed with feeling, and made sentimental; love idealized, sanctified, and inflated. Its characteristic type is the lyric. Its rhythms are definite, mechanically correct, and obvious; its rhymes are commonplace.

The exigencies of rhyme and rhythm are allowed to determine the choice of a word so often that a sensible reader is compelled to conclude that the plain sense of the matter is of only minor importance. It is the arbitrarily chosen verse pattern that counts. One has the uncomfortable feeling in reading such an anthology as W.W. Campbell's *The Oxford Book of Canadian Verse* [1913] or J.W. Garvin's *Canadian Poets* [1916] that the writers included are not interested in saying anything in particular; they merely wish to show that they are capable of turning out a number of regular stanzas in which statements are made about the writer's emotions, say 'In Winter,' or 'At Montmorenci Falls,' or 'In A Birch Bark Canoe.' Other exercises are concerned with pine trees, the open road, God, snowshoes or Pan.[7] The most popular experience is to be pained, hurt, stabbed or seared by beauty—preferably by the yellow flame of a crocus in the spring or the red flame of a maple leaf in autumn.

There would be less objection to these poems if the observation were accurate and its expression vivid, or if we could feel that the emotion was a genuine and intense one. We could then go on to ask if it were a valuable one. But, with a negligible number of exceptions, the observation is general in these poems and the descriptions are vague. The poet's emotions are unbounded, and are consequently lacking in the intensity which results from discipline and compression; his thinking is of a transcendental or theosophical sort that has to be taken on faith. The fundamental criticism that must be brought against Canadian poetry as a whole is that it ignores the intelligence. And as a result it is dead.

Our grievance, however, against the great dead body of poetry laid out in the mortuary of the *Oxford Book* or interred under Garvin's florid epitaphs is not so much that it is dead but that its sponsors in Canada pretend that it is alive. Yet it should be obvious to any person of taste that this poetry cannot now, and in most cases never could, give the impression of being vitally concerned with real experience. The Canadian poet, if this kind of thing truly represents his feelings and his thoughts, is a half-baked, hyper-sensitive, poorly adjusted, and frequently

---

[6] The preface that Smith originally wrote for the collection he co-edited with F.R. Scott: *New Provinces: Poems of Several Authors* (1936). In a letter to Scott on 7 Nov. 1934, E.J. Pratt writes: "I have just received a letter from Hugh Eayrs of Macmillan. [. . .] Eayrs objects to the Preface. He says it is unwise. It would stir up unnecessary antagonisms. Let the Scott Roberts group alone and let the volume stand on its own feet without the initial 'nose-tweaking' as he describes it." "A Rejected Preface" was finally published by Smith in 1973.

[7] Pan, Greek god of shepherds and woodlands who is depicted as having the hindquarters of a goat (like a faun). He is often associated with fertility and nature and figures in many Romantic pastoral poems.

neurotic individual that no one in his senses would trust to drive a car or light a furnace. He is the victim of his feelings and fancies, or of what he fancies his feelings ought to be, and his emotional aberrations are out of all proportion to the experience that brings them into being. He has a soft heart and a soft soul; and a soft head. No wonder nobody respects him, and few show even the most casual interest in his poetry. A few patriotic professors, one or two hack journalist critics, and a handful of earnest anthologists—these have tried to put the idea across that there exists a healthy national Canadian poetry which expresses the vigorous hope of this young Dominion in a characteristically Canadian style, but the idea is so demonstrably false that no one but the interested parties has been taken in.

We do not pretend that this volume contains any verse that might not have been written in the United States or in Great Britain. There is certainly nothing specially Canadian about more than one or two poems. Why should there be? Poetry today is written for the most part by people whose emotional and intellectual heritage is not a national one; it is either cosmopolitan or provincial, and for good or evil, the forces of civilization are rapidly making the latter scarce.

A large number of the verses in this book were written at a time when the contributors were inclined to dwell too exclusively on the fact that the chief thing wrong with Canadian poetry was its conventional and insensitive technique. Consequently, we sometimes thought we had produced a good poem when all we had done in reality was not produce a conventional one. In Canada this is a deed of some merit.

In attempting to get rid of the facile word, the stereotyped phrase and the mechanical rhythm, and in seeking, as the poet today must, to combine colloquialism and rhetoric, we were of course only following in the path of the more significant poets in England and the United States. And it led, for a time, to the creation of what, for the sake of brevity, I will call 'pure poetry.'

A theory of pure poetry might be constructed on the assumption that a poem exists as a thing in itself. It is not a copy of anything or an expression of anything, but is an individuality as unique as a flower, an elephant or a man on a flying trapeze. Archibald MacLeish[8] expressed the idea in *Ars Poetica* when he wrote

A poem should not mean, but be.

Such poetry is objective, impersonal, and in a sense timeless and absolute. It stands by itself, unconcerned with anything save its own existence.

Not unconnected with the disinterested motives that produce pure poetry are those which give rise to imagist poetry. The imagist seeks with perfect objectivity and impersonality to recreate a thing or arrest an experience as precisely and vividly and simply as possible. Kennedy's 'Shore,' Scott's

[8] Archibald MacLeish (1892–1982), American modernist poet and literary critic. The line Smith cites is from one of MacLeish's best-known poems, "Ars Poetica" (1926).

'Trees in Ice,' my own 'Creek' are examples of the simpler kind of imagist verse; Finch's 'Teacher,' tiny as it is, of the more complex. In 'Shore' and 'Creek' the reader may notice that the development of the poem depends upon metrical devices as much as on images; the music is harsh and the rhythm difficult.

Most of the verses in this book are not, however, so unconcerned with thought as those mentioned. In poems like 'Epithalamium,' 'The Five Kine,' 'Words for a Resurrection,' and 'Like An Old Proud King' an attempt has been made to fuse thought and feeling. Such a fusion is characteristic of the kind of poetry usually called metaphysical. Good metaphysical verse is not, it must be understood, concerned with the communication of ideas. It is far removed from didactic poetry. What it is concerned with is the emotional effect of ideas that have entered so deeply into the blood as never to be questioned. Such poetry is primarily lyrical; it should seem spontaneous. Something of the quality I am suggesting is to be found in such lines as

The wall was there, oh perilous blade of glass[9]

or

This Man of April walks again.[10]

In the poems just mentioned thought is the root, but it flowers in the feeling. They are essentially poems of the sensibility, a little bit melancholy, perhaps a little too musical. A healthier robustness is found in satirical verse, such as Scott's much needed counterblast against the Canadian Authors' Association,[11] or in the anti-romanticism of Klein's

And my true love,
She combs and combs,
The lice from off
My children's domes.[12]

The appearance of satire, and also of didactic poetry that does not depend upon wit, would be a healthy sign in Canadian poetry. For it would indicate that our poets are realizing, even if in an elementary way, that poetry is more concerned with expressing exact ideas than wishy-washy 'dreams.' It would indicate, too, that the poet's lofty isolation from events that are of vital significance to everybody was coming to an end.

Detachment, indeed, or self-absorption is (for a time only, I hope) becoming impossible. The era of individual liberty is in eclipse. Capitalism can hardly be expected to survive the cataclysm its most interested adherents are blindly

[9] A line from Robert Finch's "The Five Kine," the lead poem in *New Provinces*.

[10] A line from Leo Kennedy's "Words for a Resurrection." "Epithalamium," mentioned earlier, is also by Kennedy; "Like an Old Proud King" is by Smith.

[11] See Scott's "The Canadian Authors Meet," included in this section.

[12] A stanza from A.M. Klein's poem "Soirée of Vevel Kleinburger," included in *New Provinces*.

steering towards, and the artist who is concerned with the most intense of experiences must be concerned with the world situation in which, whether he likes it or not, he finds himself. For the moment at least he has something more important to do than to record his private emotions. He must try to perfect a technique that will combine power with simplicity and sympathy with intelligence so that he may play his part in developing mental and emotional attitudes that will facilitate the creation of a more practical social system.

Of poetry such as this, there is here only the faintest foreshadowing—a fact that is not unconnected with the backwardness politically and economically of Canada—but that Canadian poetry in the future must become increasingly aware of its duty to take cognizance of what is going on in the world of affairs we are sure.

That the poet is not a dreamer, but a man of sense; that poetry is a discipline because it is an art; and that it is further a useful art: these are propositions which it is intended this volume shall suggest. We are not deceiving ourselves that it has proved them.

[1973]

MORLEY CALLAGHAN ▪ (1903–1990)

In his memoir *That Summer in Paris* (1963), Morley Callaghan recalls the summer of 1929 when he and his wife Loretto lived in the middle of the burgeoning literary scene of Montparnasse, Paris, that included such writers as Ernest Hemingway, F. Scott Fitzgerald, Zelda Fitzgerald, Ford Madox Ford, and James Joyce—the "Lost Generation," as Gertrude Stein called them. Hemingway and Callaghan had been friends since they worked together at the Toronto *Star* newspaper in the 1920s. When Hemingway moved to Paris he encouraged Callaghan to join him. In his memoir, Callaghan describes how their "tangled friendship" came to an end with a bloody boxing match. Callaghan was considerably shorter and lighter, but, according to his own account, he was also a better boxer. The author of *The Great Gatsby* (1925), F. Scott Fitzgerald, was the timekeeper, and apparently became so enthralled with the boxing that he forgot the clock—until the exhausted Hemingway made a desperate lunge at Callaghan, and got knocked on his back by a hard cross to the jaw. In his memoirs, Hemingway remembers the fight differently. From this point on, the friendship between Hemingway and Callaghan cooled.

Callaghan was born and raised in a Catholic family in Toronto. He attended the University of Toronto (St. Michael's College) and Osgoode Hall Law School, but he never practised law, choosing instead to be a full-time writer. Callaghan's first novel, *Strange Fugitive,* appeared in 1928 to such good reviews that by the following year he had signed a contract with the New York publishing house Scribner's for his first collection of short stories, *A Native Argosy* (1929). It was at that point that he and his new bride Loretto went to Europe. Over the course of his career Callaghan published many novels, short stories, plays, and non-fiction articles for various newspapers and periodicals (including regular contributions to *The

New Yorker, Scribner's Magazine, Esquire, Redbook Magazine, Atlantic Monthly, and Maclean's). For much of his career he worked as a journalist and broadcaster. Callaghan's most celebrated work is the triptych of novels published in the mid-1930s, *Such Is My Beloved* (1934), *They Shall Inherit the Earth* (1935), and *More Joy in Heaven* (1937), which question conventional morality and profess a kind of Christian humanism. He won the Governor General's Award for fiction in 1951 for his novel about an interracial love affair in Montreal, *The Loved and the Lost*. While it was applauded nationally, this novel was also viewed by some critics as "snobbishly liberal." Primarily a realist who concentrates on ordinary characters in ordinary settings, Callaghan was one of Canada's best-known writers in the '40s and '50s, grouped with such writers as Hugh MacLennan and Sinclair Ross.

In a review of Callaghan's four-volume *Complete Stories* (2003), W.J. Keith provides a useful overview of the extremes of criticism of Callaghan's work. He notes that prominent American critic Edmund Wilson posited that Callaghan's writing could "be mentioned without absurdity in association with Chekhov's and Turgenev's," and even concluded that Callaghan was "the most unjustly neglected novelist in the English-speaking world." Keith juxtaposes this view with that of Canadian writer and critic John Metcalf who considered Callaghan's stories overly sentimental.

Callaghan's best stories, such as "A Sick Call," "The Blue Kimono," "All the Years of Her Life," and "Last Spring They Came Over," illustrate his direct style. His stories range in setting from small-town Ontario to Paris, and in topic from ethical responsibility to pride and regret. "Loppy Phelan's Double Shoot," from *The Lost and Found Stories of Morley Callaghan* (1985), is one of his less anthologized stories. It is characteristic of Callaghan's style in its understated use of language and straightforward narrative flow, as well as the thematic focus on a single incident in the mundane life of a small-town man. While the story is clearly inspired by the tale of the famous "Indian" conservationist and naturalist Archie Belaney/Grey Owl, Callaghan shifts the emphasis from the impostor to a childhood friend. It is interesting to read this story beside the selections from Grey Owl in this anthology for another perspective on what is at stake when personal history is erased. When doubts about Grey Owl's "Indian" identity began to appear even before his death from pneumonia in 1938, his friend and publisher Lovat Dickson tried to prove his identity and ended up exposing the truth instead. Sam Crowther in the story is similarly determined to find the truth, though ultimately he appears to want Snow Bird's acknowledgement more than anything else. The story becomes an entangled psychological study, not only of friendship and guilt, but of the ways all identity is self-fashioned.

Loppy Phelan's Double Shoot

In those days when grain boats from Chicago, Cleveland, and cities at the head of the Lakes came regularly to the Georgian Bay port of Collingwood, and the shipyard there worked overtime, two boys sat on the rotting stumps at the end of the dock dreaming of lives for themselves far beyond the town.

One of the boys, Sam Crowther, whose father owned the flour and feed store on the main street, was fair-haired, had eager blue eyes, a mild manner, and he dreamed of going to the university and then getting a job in the diplomatic service which would give him a chance to live in Brazil or Chile or Mexico.

The other boy, Hal McGibbney, who had straight black hair, wild and restless narrow brown eyes, and a skin that was always tanned a dark brown, had been living in town about two years. He had come from north of the lakes. His mother and father were dead and he lived with his uncle, Henry Bryant, who worked in the shipyard. He dreamed of living with trappers and fishermen, of remaining alone and untouched by the tame life of the shipyard workers and the town storekeepers.

When they sat together on the dock that summer, looking out beyond the rim of the bay, the two boys talked about baseball. The town had a good team that played against teams made up from the crews of ships loading grain in the harbor. These ships had names like The City of Cleveland, Garden City, Missouri, and these names taken by the crew teams made the games with the town seem important.

On an evening when there was to be a big game at the fairground, Sam Crowther would go down by the railroad station and across the tracks to Henry Bryant's frame cottage, then give a long whistle for Hal McGibbney, who came out wearing his first-baseman's glove. He would pound the pocket of the glove three or four times, spit in it, then pound it again, frown, then smile a little. He never laughed out loud. "Come on, let's go, Sam," he would say and then walk rapidly, as if he were in a hurry to get far away from the cottage. He didn't get along with his uncle, who wanted to beat him but was afraid of him now that he was fourteen and big-boned.

Getting close to the fairground, they started to talk about baseball, and soon they were talking about the stories of Burt L. Standish, which all the boys read, and about his fabulous pitcher, Frank Merriwell, and his bewildering curve ball.[1]

The two boys had a regular place just back of the third base bag, but they stayed there only about twenty-five minutes. "Let's watch Loppy for a while now," Hal said. "Yeah, let's see what he's got tonight," Sam agreed, and they withdrew to where Loppy Phelan, the town's relief pitcher, was warming up. They had never seen Loppy pitch in a real game, and they used to wonder why the manager of the town team kept him warming up game after game without ever using him.

Loppy worked in the shipyard. He was tall, gangling, and his mouth seemed to hang open with a surprised innocence whenever anybody spoke to him. He had large, sad brown eyes and wore a strange, faded pinkish ball shirt. Word had gone around among the boys that the shirt was part of the uniform of the Cincinnati Reds in the National League.

The two boys stood behind Loppy and watched every pitch he made with a rapt interest, and one night Hal said, "I wonder if Loppy can throw a double shoot."

[1] Burt Standish was the pseudonym of Gilbert Patten (1866–1945), a popular fiction writer who wrote more than 200 baseball stories starring the fictional brothers Frank and Dick Merriwell.

"I think he's got all kinds of stuff," Sam said. "Maybe he *could* throw a double shoot."

It was the curve ball of their hero, Frank Merriwell, of Yale. Only Merriwell could throw a double shoot, which was a ball that curved out sharply, and then, as it got close to the batter, suddenly curved in at him. It was the greatest curve of all time.

"Hey, Loppy," Hal called eagerly.

"Eh?" Loppy grunted and he hardly paused in his lackadaisical wind-up.

"Can you throw a double shoot, Loppy?"

Looking a little puzzled, Loppy stopped, put his hands on his hips, grinned, then started his wind-up again. As the ball sped to his catcher, the boys, standing behind him, leaned forward expectantly.

"You see it, Hal?" Sam asked. "What was on it?"

"Boy, oh, boy," Hal said softly.

"Did you see it?'

"Sure," Hal said excitedly.

"Maybe it went too fast for me."

"Throw it again, Loppy."

Hardly heeding them, Loppy let go another fast ball.

"There!" Hal said excitedly.

"Sure," Sam said.

"Holy cow," Hal said. "Loppy Phelan's got a double shoot. Imagine a guy in this town having a double shoot."

After that night, Loppy had his own audience whenever the town team played. They brought all the boys to where Loppy warmed up, telling them about the double shoot and making them watch each pitch Loppy made. One by one the kids who lined up behind Loppy agreed they saw the ball take a twist. Loppy became their hero. When the kids trooped over to line up behind him, he scratched his head and grinned happily.

One night, in a game with the City of Cleveland, the town's regular pitcher weakened. Everything he threw was knocked out of the lot, but he stayed on the mound; the manager acted as if he didn't have another pitcher. But Hal McGibbney, rushing to the third base line and followed by all the kids, began to shout, "Put in Loppy. Use Loppy. Let him throw his double shoot."

Loppy stopped warming up and waited, but the players on the town team only looked mystified. They put their hands on their hips, then shrugged and grinned, and the manager, too, smiled a little. Loppy wasn't called to the pitcher's mound. On other occasions the same thing happened. Then, toward the end of the summer, Loppy Phelan got a job on one of the lake boats and sailed away and never returned. It seemed right to Hal McGibbney that Loppy sailed away.

With other kids, Hal lay in the thick grass under the corner light by Johnson's grocery store and talked about the great pitcher who had been among them and who had never been able to show his class. One by one the boys began to doubt that Loppy Phelan could throw the double shoot, but they were too afraid to argue with Hal. He was too bright, too quick, too intelligent for them.

Then, one night when Hal and Sam had gone down to the dock for a swim and afterward were sitting on the stumps at the end of the pier, Hal said dreamily, "I wonder where Loppy is now?"

"Maybe he's in Cleveland," Sam said. "Maybe he's in Chicago."

"Maybe he's in the big leagues, Sammy, really pitching that double shoot."

"Say," Sam began hesitantly, "I don't think any of the ballplayers around here believed Loppy could throw that old double shoot."

"We know he could."

"Oh, sure."

"He could have been the greatest pitcher this town ever saw. But a guy can't be anything around here," Hal said contemptuously.

With his arms locked around his knees and the last of the twilight touching the side of his lean, brown face, he stared grimly at the glowing surface of the water. He looked lonely, yet proud of his own loneliness. Sam thought he was dreaming of cities where Phelan would be given a chance to pitch, but suddenly Hal laughed. "Well, I know what I should be," he said sharply. "If you do, too, you'll get moving. I hate my uncle's guts. I'm clearing out of here at the end of the week, heading north. I don't know what's going to happen to me, but I like the woods and the rivers. I'll make something out of myself, all by myself. I never belonged around here, Sammy." At the end of the week he went off without saying good-bye to anyone and the town soon forgot Hal McGibbney.

Sam Crowther stayed at home, forced to forget about his ambitious dreams of life in strange countries. He finished high school, but he did not go to the university, for his father died, and Sam's mother wanted him to take over the flour and feed store, which he did. Shortly afterward, he married Louella Chipman, whose father had come to town to manage the new grain elevator. She was an eager little blonde girl, with a timid streak. She liked church work and euchre[2] parties, and she grew plump and pale.

Sam lost most of his hair, wore glasses, wished he had children, and became, by the time he was forty-four, a dignified figure who had run for mayor, been defeated in a close election, and whose store was a center for political gossip.

One summer afternoon, Sam was sitting on the stool behind his counter glancing at the city newspaper while he talked idly with young Tom Stevens, the redheaded, ambitious reporter for the town paper.

"Look at this," Sam said suddenly, as he looked at a story in which a woman who had been married to the celebrated naturalist, Snow Bird, now claimed that he was not an Ojibwa Indian, but a white man, an impostor. The woman said

[2] A type of card game.

Snow Bird had divorced her ten years ago and had custody of their son, John Snow Bird.[3] Now she claimed to be destitute. Snow Bird had a great audience and had just returned to New York from a triumphal tour of England. His beautifully written books on the wolves and the deer of the north shore of Lake Superior had been highly praised and had had a big sale.

"A phony. Another phony," Tom Stevens said, with the cynical satisfaction of a young newspaperman.

"Just a minute," Sam said slowly, staring at the picture of Snow Bird and his son.

Snow Bird looked like a dignified, superior Mohawk or Ojibwa, with a thin, high-bridged nose and shrewd, narrow eyes. He wore his hair in two braids with a single feather. The son, who looked like his father and was about fourteen, was obviously a proud, confident boy, and he had been sent to a good private school.

"Hey, you read this?" Tom suddenly asked, quickly looking up from his own copy of the paper. "The woman says Snow Bird came from some town around here—maybe Parry Sound or Midland—and that his real name is McKechnie."

"Well, I'll be damned!" Sam said softly, his eyes bright with excitement. He covered the feather in the Snow Bird picture and studied the picture of the boy alone, and he whistled softly. "The woman's got it a little wrong, Tom," he said. "It wasn't Parry Sound or Midland. It was right here. And the name wasn't McKechnie. It was McGibbney."

"You sure?" Tom asked. "It says here Snow Bird's New York publisher says the woman's story's malicious blackmail. You sure, Sam?"

"I'm not so sure of that picture of Snow Bird," Sam admitted, trembling, "not with the feather and long hair. And thirty years is a long time. But it's the boy. He looks too much like Hal McGibbney."

"But there are no McGibbneys around here, Sam."

"That's right. Hal lived here with his uncle, Henry Bryant, for about three years. Hell, we were both boys together. Bryant's dead now, and his wife is, too, but lots of people around here remember the Bryants."

"If you're right, Sam —"

"Sure, I'm right."

"Look, let's go up to the library," Tom said, "and see what we can find out about Snow Bird."

Telling his wife to look after the store, Sam left with Tom Stevens. They walked along the sunlit main street and around the corner to the red brick library, where the librarian gave them three of Snow Bird's books and a short account of his life written for a popular magazine. They sat down at the big oaken table and began to read together. The account was straightforward enough; he claimed he was born in a village near James Bay and came down to the north shore of Lake Superior when he was a boy. There was no doubt he had lived in a village called

[3] The events here are loosely based on the life of Grey Owl/Archie Belaney, who married an Anishinaabe woman named Angele Egwuna in 1910 whom he subsequently abandoned with a young daughter. In later years, Angele came forward with the information that Grey Owl was actually an Englishman.

The Mission, at the mouth of the Michipicotten River, for half-breed families there remembered him. He still went back to that Algoman hill country. Most of the Indians on the north shore were Ojibwas, and he spoke their language.

"That all ties in," Sam said eagerly. "He showed up in that north country when he was a boy; after he was a kid around here."

Then he picked up a Snow Bird book about the pursuit of deer by a wolf. "Come on, Sam. Let's go," Tom said.

"Imagine a kid from around here writing stuff like this, and having such a life, a philosopher, too," Sam said in a melancholy tone. "I remember when Hal and I used to sit at the end of the dock talking about the kind of lives we were going to lead when we grew up. Yeah, and we always went up to the park together to watch the ball games." He smiled a little. "There was a pitcher around here named Loppy Phelan. We made him our hero. We used to talk about him all the time. I wonder if Hal ever thinks about Loppy now?"

"Who knows?"

"Hal always knew what he wanted," Sam said, tapping the book, "and it looks as if he headed right for it." A faraway look came into his eyes. "I had crazy dreams, too. I used to talk to him about going to Brazil or Mexico. Well, here I am, stuck here."

Tom walked as far as the store with Sam, and then he left and began to make inquiries about the Bryant family and a boy named Hal McGibbney. Then he wrote the story, and it appeared next day in the local paper. It was a clever story with pictures of Sam and Snow Bird and an account of the days when the two boys used to follow the fortunes of the ballteam and celebrate Loppy Phelan's greatness as a pitcher. "I wonder if Snow Bird ever thinks of Loppy Phelan now," was the heading for the story, which delighted the town when it appeared. It was picked up by the news services and reprinted all over the continent.

"I don't like all this, Tom. In fact, I wish I hadn't shot my mouth off to you," Sam said when Tom Stevens came into his store three days later. "I've got nothing but admiration for what Hal McGibbney has done with his life."

"Take it easy," Tom said. "I thought you'd like to have a look at these clippings." In New York, Snow Bird's publisher had issued a statement, dismissing Sam Crowther as an obvious exhibitionist seeking local notoriety. Snow Bird's statement was briefer. "I was never in Collingwood," he said. "I never played baseball. I never heard of this man, Sam Crowther."

"What else can the man say?" Sam asked. "He can't say now that I told the truth." But his pride was hurt. "I mean, he might have said I was only mistaken."

His neighbors agreed. "Sam's no liar," they insisted when they read what Snow Bird had said. "If he made a mistake he'll admit it later on. Nobody should laugh at him." But when they came to the store they smiled indulgently. This sympathetic respect exasperated him. His wife's fear of what would happen disgusted him. "You'll get us into terrible trouble," she cried, wringing her hands, her moist and startled blue eyes shining with anger. All her life she had been uneasy about anything that might cause gossip about her. "You'll have us dragged into court, and we'll lose everything."

A week later, an attractive young woman in a brown gabardine suit came into Sam's store at three in the afternoon and said she was Miss James from the *Montreal Star*.

"I'm sorry, Miss James," Sam said gruffly. "I'm through making a fool of myself in the newspaper."

"But you told the truth, didn't you, Mr. Crowther?"

"Of course I did."

"After checking around here, that's the way I figure it," Miss James said. She had a casual manner. "You've got a fine reputation, Mr. Crowther. So we're convinced Snow Bird is a phony."

"Just a minute," Sam said sharply. "The man who wrote the beautiful stuff he wrote is no phony."

"So he's a real Indian?"

"No. Like I said, he's Hal McGibbney."

"Snow Bird," she said, smiling, "is in Montreal next Saturday night."

"Yeah," Sam said.

"Why not come to Montreal, Mr. Crowther? My paper will pay your expenses. It's in the public interest."

"Yeah," Sam said, confused. He felt he had cheapened himself, yet he had a wondering admiration for the man he believed he had known as a boy.

"Look here," he began carefully, "you have to agree to get him off to one side and not say anything more than, 'Mr. Crowther believes he knew you a few years ago.'"

"Okay, swell," Miss James said. "I'll get the tickets."

She fled because Sam's wife, who had been listening, suddenly rushed in, crying, "What kind of a fool are you?"

Sam knew she would never understand or care that he had dreamed of a different kind of life. "I am going to Montreal, Lou. That's settled," he said quietly.

Sam wore his good blue serge suit. It was a pleasant trip. Miss James was an amusing girl. After cocktails and dinner at the hotel, they took a taxi to the building where Snow Bird was lecturing, and when Snow Bird came on to the stage, Sam put on his glasses and leaned forward, trembling. Snow Bird, thin and frail and suffering from tuberculosis, was wearing a white dinner jacket and braided hair with a single feather. He had a grave, unaffected dignity.

He talked of a journey he had made in the winter to the country around James Bay and a battle he had witnessed between a lynx and a bear in the twilight.

"I'm not fooled by the look of him," Sam thought stubbornly as he leaned forward, trying to see something that would remind him surely of the boy he had known. But gradually he forgot where he was and his resentment disappeared and his feeling of admiration seemed to come out of a pride in his own youth. When Snow Bird finished and the applause died down and some went to the platform to have Snow Bird autograph books, Miss James said, "Come on, Mr. Crowther, we'll speak to him."

"Please remember, Miss James," Sam said while they were waiting, "we'll just mention my name. We'll leave it up to him. If he says I'm mistaken, all right. I think he'll want to have a talk with me."

Then Snow Bird came toward them. "Snow Bird," Miss James said, trying not to sound too eager. "I'm from the *Montreal Star*. This is Sam Crowther, a friend of yours, I believe."

"Really," Snow Bird said gravely. He looked at Sam, and the muscles around his narrow eyes twitched. He looked steadily at Sam for a long time and then he smiled with an unassailable dignity. "I don't know Mr. Crowther," he said.

"He's from Collingwood," Miss James said quickly. Snow Bird's unruffled dignity had upset her; she felt like a flustered young girl being brushed aside. She forgot her promise to Sam: "Mr. Crowther was sure you had been boys together, played baseball, and that you both used to talk a lot about a great pitcher named Loppy Phelan."

"Does he think so?" Snow Bird asked.

"Maybe I was mistaken," Sam said quickly, searching for some little flicker of recognition. "It's easy to make a mistake," Sam said, nodding. "I thought if we could have a little talk. . . ."

People were edging closer, trying to hear every word, including the black-haired boy in the expensive suit who was Snow Bird's son. "Yes, we know about you, Mr. Crowther," he whispered bitterly. "I know you're out to destroy my father. You are just a cheap liar."

"Wait a minute, son," Sam began, but the hatred in the boy's eyes made him feel soiled and ashamed. He turned to Miss James, who was watching, bright-eyed, and then he abruptly fled from the hall and along the street and down the hill to his hotel, where he packed his bag and caught the night train for home.

But the story of his furtive flight was written faithfully by Miss James. In time, it appeared in the town paper, and Sam's wife cried when she read it. "Oh, you fool, Sam," she moaned. "They'll never ask you to run for mayor again around here. Now we're the laughingstock of the town."

Grabbing his hat, he hurried along the main street to the town paper, and he tried to explain it all to Tom Stevens. "It was the boy that upset me," he began. "He had such faith in his father."

When he saw that Tom hardly believed him, his heart filled with bitterness. "Look, Tom. Print this, have it printed all over the world. The man is a phony. A first-rate phony."

He said this again and again to customers who came to his store. At first they listened, but then he became a bore. When he saw that he had lost all dignity, he suddenly stopped talking about Snow Bird. He hid his bitterness but nursed it in his heart. He began to read the New York papers, particularly the book sections. All that autumn and on through the winter, as if he were pursuing the man, when he came across an item about Snow Bird he cut it out and pasted it in a scrapbook he kept in a locked trunk in his cellar.

In the spring, Snow Bird's New York publishers wrote Sam a dignified letter in which they pointed out that his story, told and retold by malicious gossips, had gravely damaged not only a man's reputation but a very valuable publishing property. They had made inquiries about him and were convinced he was a reputable and esteemed citizen in his community, unlike Snow Bird's former wife, who was simply a grasping, disgruntled, vindictive woman. As an honorable citizen would he not, therefore, be generous enough to state formally that he had made a mistake, and in that way undo some of the damage done to a man who had never harmed him?

Smiling to himself, Sam wrote to the publisher, saying that his own reputation had been gravely damaged in his own home town.

Then, in the early summer, Snow Bird collapsed on Madison Avenue in New York, and his picture was in the paper. They said he did not have the temperament of a man who could stand the long confinement of sanatorium treatment for tuberculosis. Sam Crowther read about it in his store in Collingwood with a strange mixture of sadness, excitement, and a feeling that he was being cheated.

A week later, Sam got another letter from the New York publisher. Snow Bird was dying of tubercular pneumonia, the publisher wrote. His nurse had reported that several times during the night fever, he had mumbled the name, "Sam Crowther." The publisher pointed out that the unhappy question of Snow Bird's identity had been revived, and that they believed he wanted to clear his name for the sake of his son, John Snow Bird. Would Mr. Crowther be good enough to come to New York at their expense? . . .

Sam arrived in New York on a Friday morning when it was raining and was met by Mr. Gilbey, a gray, polite man. "We might as well go right to the hospital," he said. "The poor fellow. It's only a matter of days. Maybe hours."

In the taxi, the publisher was fascinated by the grim, stubborn expression on Sam's face, and he began to feel unhappy as they entered the hospital and went along the corridor to Snow Bird's room. A nurse at the door whispered, "We've given him a sedative that eases the cough, Mr. Gilbey. He may fall into a sleep."

Before he had a chance to look at Snow Bird on the bed, Sam saw the black-haired boy get up from a chair by the window.

"Mr. Crowther, I believe you've met Snow Bird's son," the publisher said gently.

"Yes," Sam said, turning away.

"Snow Bird," the publisher called as they moved closer to the bed. "Snow Bird, this is Sam Crowther. We thought you wanted to see him."

"Sam Crowther," Snow Bird repeated in a hoarse whisper. There was the flicker of a smile at the corner of his mouth. "Sam Crowther," he whispered again. Then, with that name on his lips he seemed to drift away to the edge of sleep or dreaming recollection. Sam, shaken, wanted to cry out and compel his recognition. The boy, standing tensely at the foot of the bed, suddenly cried, "Why did you come down on us? Why did you want to persecute us, Mr. Crowther?"

"What?" Sam asked. He saw Snow Bird open his eyes, watching the boy anxiously. "No matter what you say," the boy whispered, "there are things you can't take away from us. My father has the Indian blood. I know he has it. Isn't that right, Dad?"

Snow Bird, his eyes on Sam, whispered so faintly that his words were a blur of sound, "Yes—and Loppy Phelan had the double shoot."

"I couldn't quite make that out," the publisher said. "I heard, 'yes,' but what was the rest?"

"He said 'yes' Mr. Crowther, and you heard him," the boy insisted.

"Yes," Sam agreed. But he was shocked. He saw young Hal McGibbney sitting on the stumps of the dock that evening many years ago, talking about their pitcher, Loppy Phelan, and he heard himself say: "Hal, maybe he didn't really have that double shoot!" Sam turned to the boy as if he were going to explain, but he could not. He rubbed the back of his neck slowly with his right hand. Then he went closer to the bed, to the man who called himself Snow Bird, whose eyes were now closed.

"Mr. Crowther," the publisher said hesitantly, "so little was said—I mean, can you be satisfied in your own mind?"

"Yes. I'm satisfied," Sam said simply. But then the sudden pain of regret about the way his own life had gone bewildered him. Sam shook his head and hurried out of the room, nursing his terrible loneliness.

[1985]

EARLE BIRNEY ■ (1904–1995)

"I should say at the start that I don't any longer like the words 'poet,' 'poems,' etc. They've developed pretentious connotations. I prefer 'maker' and 'makings.' They mean the same but the texture's plainer, oatmeal, not manna." So writes Earle Birney in his "Preface" to *Ghost in the Wheels* (1977).

Born in 1904 in a log cabin on the banks of the Bow River in Calgary (when it was still part of the Northwest Territories), Alfred Earle Birney was raised in Banff, Alberta, and Creston, B.C. He was an only child who spent what he called a "solitary and Wordsworthian childhood" on a subsistence farm learning to read from the Bible, John Bunyan's *Pilgrim's Progress,* and the poems of Robert Burns. An avid outdoorsman

in his youth, Birney climbed mountains, hunted fossils, cut trails, and played hockey. Although he was a renegade who liked a fight, writing politically hard-hitting and formally experimental poetry, Birney was awarded many honours and was twice a recipient of the Governor General's Award (in 1942 for *David and Other Poems,* and again in 1945 for *Now Is Time*). Altogether he published over a dozen collections of poetry, short stories, and academic criticism.

After high school in Creston, Birney worked in a bank for two years. Not finding fulfillment in that, he decided to go to the University of British Columbia to study engineering. In his second year, however, disenchanted with engineering, he switched to English where he achieved first-class honours in his B.A. After completing a Master's degree at the University of Toronto in 1927, he began a doctorate at the University of California, Berkeley, in Chaucer studies. He left Berkeley to complete his doctoral studies at the University of Toronto (earning a Ph.D. in 1936). While in Toronto he became deeply involved with Marxist politics, and joined a group of Trotskyites (arguing the need for "permanent revolution" among the proletariat). In 1934 Birney was awarded a fellowship to London by the Royal Society. According to his long-time partner Wailan Low, he worked his passage across the Atlantic on a tramp freighter and once in London spent his days in the British Library and his nights working for the Independent Labour Party. He spent five days with the leading socialist Leon Trotsky in 1935, interviewing him in Norway (the interview was transcribed and printed for circulation within the International Labour Party, joining a number of articles in which Birney contributed to the Trotskyite cause). Later that year Birney went to Berlin where he was arrested by the Gestapo for failing to salute a Nazi parade.

While a student at the University of London, Birney met his future wife and fellow Trotskyite Esther Bull. In 1936, Esther emigrated to Canada where she and Birney were married. Together, the Birneys formed a social hub of Canadian poetry for decades to come. For the final years of the Depression, Birney taught in the Department of English at the University of Toronto (University College). From 1936 to 1940 he was literary editor of the *Canadian Forum,* hired, it is said, to liven up the pages of the magazine. Poet E.J. Pratt writes of his plans to visit the Birneys in a 10 August 1936 letter to his wife Viola:

> I [will] spend an hour or two at the Birnies' *[sic]*, the Muscovites, or Marxists, extreme left wing but so

idealistic. You must hear them talk next fall to get the low-down on what the world will be like in the future. University Professors are going to be the world's best paid men with honour & fame. They are to be the crowned heads of the world with enough crowns to go round and poets are sovereigns over the crowned heads. One hundred dollars for a sonnet. So we are all right in the new regime — hot stuff.

Such idealism did not last for Birney. Disillusioned with Marxism and with the advent of the Second World War, he joined the Canadian Army and worked in the personnel selection division (like the hero in his novel *Turvey: A Military Picaresque* [1949], which won the Stephen Leacock Medal for Humour). Even so, Birney never entirely gave up his left-wing beliefs. His second novel, *Down the Long Table* (1955), reflects his continuing indignation at social injustice.

The year he was posted overseas, Birney published *David and Other Poems* (1942) to immediate acclaim. The long poem "David" tells the story of the death of a mountain climber and is a classic treatment of the theme of hubris as the hero of the title pits himself against a formidable natural world (comparable to the man in his poem "Bushed").

When he returned from the war, after spending some time with the CBC's International Service and a year as editor of *Canadian Poetry Magazine,* Birney took a position at UBC where he remained until 1965. During his time at UBC he broke with the English Department and established Canada's first creative writing program. He also revived and edited *Prism International,* a journal to showcase work by young writers.

Although he is said to have been a committed teacher, Birney was disappointed that he could not afford to live by his pen alone. After retirement in 1965, he held several writer-in-residence positions and he lived for periods in France, England, and Mexico. Birney was keenly aware of the international developments in poetry and literature, and he sought to keep up in form and content.

Birney's poetry underwent significant shifts throughout his long career: moving from the narrative poetry of "David" to the playful concrete poetry of his later years ("UP HER CAN NADA," for instance). According to literary critic W.J. Keith, Birney plays a role similar in Canadian literature to E.J. Pratt: "Just as Pratt provided an important link between the Confederation Poets and the early modernists, so Birney spans the period between Pratt and the younger experimentalists of the 1960s." This is particularly true of Birney's satirical verse about Canadian culture. His oft-cited poem "Can. Lit."—in which he makes his famous pronouncement about Canada's "lack of ghosts"—is one example of his critique of the colonial mentality he saw himself struggling to overcome. His two "Canada: Case History" poems have a similar aim, as does his puncturing of central-Canadian presumption in "UP HER CAN NADA." Birney's satires of central Canada emerge from his background as a westerner. Yet notwithstanding his satirical, and indeed cosmopolitan, edge, Birney believed in the importance of local histories and experience. "The true cosmopolite in poetry," Birney proclaimed in "Has Poetry a Future in Canada?" (1946), engaging A.J.M. Smith's idea of the native versus cosmopolitan poetic schools, "always had his roots deep in the peculiar soil of his own country. . . . The most cosmopolitan service a Canadian poet can do is to make himself . . . a clear and memorable and passionate interpreter of Canadians themselves."

His powerful poem "i accuse us," written during the Vietnam War, harnesses his anger at Canadians' "dynamic apathy." In a 1975 interview with poet Al Purdy, Birney argued that the "U.S. is an imperial power, which is difficult to like. They are sloughing off whatever democracy they have left with succeeding waves of reaction, neo-fascism and imperialism. Nothing short of a major catastrophe will stop that drift. . . . We in Canada must have courage and willingness to sacrifice and wait for the time when the U.S. will no longer be able to bully." Never one to fear confrontation, Birney was an adventurous and iconoclastic thinker who criticized Canadian society and politics because he dreamed of a better world, "the *real* civilization" that could perhaps be glimpsed before mankind "crawl[ed] off to join the dinosaurs," as he puts it in his anti-Vietnam War speech "i accuse us" (1973).

Anglosaxon Street[1]

Dawndrizzle ended   dampness steams from
blotching brick and   blank plasterwaste
Faded housepatterns   hoary and finicky
unfold stuttering   stick like a phonograph

---

[1] As with "Can. Lit." and "The Bear on the Delhi Road," Birney revised the original "Anglosaxon Street" for inclusion in *Selected Poems* (1966). The poem, an ironic description of Toronto, shows the influence of Birney's study of Old and Middle English, with its use of a mid-line caesura, alliteration, kennings/metaphorical word compounds, and litotes/ironic understatement.

Here is a ghetto gotten for goyim
O with care denuded of nigger and kike[2]   10
No coonsmell rankles reeks only cellarrot
attar[3] of carexhaust catcorpse and cookinggrease
Imperial hearts heave in this haven
Cracks across windows are welded with slogans
There'll Always Be An England enhances geraniums
and V's for Victory vanquish the housefly

Ho! with climbing sun march the bleached beldames
festooned with shopping bags farded[4] flatarched
bigthewed Saxonwives stepping over buttrivers 20
waddling back wienerladen to suckle smallfry

Hoy! with sunslope shrieking over hydrants
flood from learninghall the lean fingerlings
Nordic nobblecheeked not all clean of nose
leaping Commandowise into leprous lanes

What! after whistleblow! spewed from wheelboat
after daylight doughtiness dire handplay
in sewertrench or sandpit come Saxonthegns[5]
Junebrown Jutekings[6] jawslack for meat

Sit after supper on smeared **doorsteps** 30
not humbly swearing hatedeeds on Huns[7]
profiteers politicians pacifists Jews

Then by twobit magic to muse in movie
unlock picturehoard or lope to alehall
soaking bleakly in beer skittleless

---

[2] Birney ironically employs pejorative and disparaging ethnic slurs for non-Jews ("goyim"), African Canadians ("nigger"), and Jews ("kike").

[3] "Attar" refers to a fragrant essence (usually of roses).

[4] To hide or mask defects of the complexion.

[5] *Thegn* or *thane*, a military attendant, servant, or retainer to Anglo-Saxon lords, but also sometimes used to refer to a nobleman more generally. The archaic and elevated term is here used to refer to husbands coming home from work.

[6] One of the Low German tribes that invaded Britain in the fifth and sixth centuries.

[7] The Asiatic race of nomads who invaded Europe around A.D. 375, and in the middle of the fifth century, under their famous leader Attila, overran a great part of the continent. In the present tense of the poem, the term also refers to the pejorative word for "Germans" used during the two world wars.

Home again to hotbox   and humid husbandhood
in slumbertrough adding   sleepily to Anglekin[8]
Alongside in lanenooks   carling and leman[9]
caterwaul and clip   careless of Saxonry
with moonglow and haste   and a higher heartbeat   40

Slumbers now slumtrack   unstinks cooling
waiting brief for milkmaid   mornstar and worldrise

Toronto 1942[10]
[1942, rev. 1966]

Canada: Case History: 1945[11]

This is the case of a high-school land,
dead-set in adolescence,
loud treble laughs and sudden fists,
bright cheeks, the gangling presence.
This boy is wonderful at sports
and physically quite healthy;
he's taken to church on Sunday still
and keeps his prurience stealthy.
He doesn't like books, except about bears,
collects new coins and model planes,   10
and never refuses a dare.
His Uncle spoils him with candy, of course,
yet shouts him down when he talks at table.
You will note he's got some of his French mother's looks,
though he's not so witty and no more stable.
He's really much more like his father and yet
if you say so he'll pull a great face.
He wants to be different from everyone else
and daydreams of winning the global race.
Parents unmarried and living abroad,   20

---

[8] An Old English word for speakers of "Englisc" or for their home ("Anglecynn" or "Englaland"). Birney is also playing on the sound of the word to evoke "Anglican" and possibly "Angel-kin" (children).

[9] A carling is a churlish or loutish young man. A leman is a lover.

[10] Birney inserted the date and place of composition with almost every poem.

[11] In his own *Twentieth Century Canadian Poetry* (1953), Birney glosses the poem: "Canada is here analyzed as if by a social-worker presenting the history of a 'case'. Canada is a problem adolescent with a rich Uncle (Sam), a French mother and an English father."

relatives keen to bag the estate,
schizophrenia not excluded,
will he learn to grow up before it's too late?

Ottawa, 1945
[1948]

Can. Lit.

(or *them able leave her ever*)[12]

since we'd always sky about
when we had eagles they flew out
leaving no shadow bigger than wren's
to trouble even our broodiest hens

too busy bridging loneliness
to be alone
we hacked in railway ties
what Emily[13] etched in bone

we French&English never lost   10
our civil war
endure it still
a bloody civil bore

the wounded sirened off
no Whitman wanted
it's only by our lack of ghosts
we're haunted

Spanish Banks, Vancouver 1947/1966
[1962, rev. 1966]

Bushed

He invented a rainbow but lightning struck it
shattered it into the lake-lap of a mountain
so big his mind slowed when he looked at it

---

[12] First published in *Ice Cod Bell or Stone* (1962) but substantially revised for the 1966 version published in *Selected Poems*. The original poem is one 10-line stanza. The opening line is a play on the popular nineteenth-century anthem "The Maple Leaf Forever." See Volume I, Section III for the text of "The Maple Leaf Forever" by Alexander Muir.

[13] In the poem Birney contrasts the manual labour of railway building in Canada to the creative work of nineteenth-century American writers Emily Dickinson (1830–1886) and Walt Whitman (1819–1892). See the introduction to Section VI for a further discussion of this poem.

Yet he built a shack on the shore
learned to roast porcupine belly and
wore the quills on his hatband

At first he was out with the dawn
whether it yellowed bright as wood-columbine
or was only a fuzzed moth in a flannel of storm
But he found the mountain was clearly alive   10
sent messages whizzing down every hot morning
boomed proclamations at noon and spread out
a white guard of goat
before falling asleep on its feet at sundown

When he tried his eyes on the lake   ospreys
would fall like valkyries[14]
choosing the cut-throat
He took then to waiting
till the night smoke rose from the boil of the sunset

But the moon carved unknown totems   20
out of the lakeshore
owls in the beardusky woods derided him
moosehorned cedars circled his swamps and tossed
their antlers up to the stars
Then he knew   though the mountain slept   the winds
were shaping its peak to an arrowhead
poised

And now he could only
bar himself in and wait
for the great flint to come singing into his heart   30

Wreck Beach 1951

[1952]

---

[14] In Scandinavian mythology, one or other of the 12 war-maidens, sometimes in the form
of giant birds, supposed to hover over battlefields and conduct the fallen warriors to Valhalla,
the hall assigned to those who have died in battle to feast with Odin. "Cut-throat" is a type of
fish; in terms of the Valkyrie reference, it also alludes to the dead bodies on the battlefield.

The Bear on the Delhi Road

Unreal   tall as a myth
by the road the Himalayan bear
is beating the brilliant air
with his crooked arms
About him two men   bare
spindly as locusts   leap

One pulls on a ring
in the great soft nose   His mate
flicks   flicks with a stick
up at the rolling eyes   10

They have not led him here
down from the fabulous hills
to this bald alien plain
and the clamorous world   to kill
but simply to teach him to dance

They are peaceful both   these spare
men of Kashmir   and the bear
alive is their living   too
If   far on the Delhi way
around him galvanic they dance   20
it is merely to wear   wear
from his shaggy body the tranced
wish forever to stay
only an ambling bear
four-footed in berries

It is no more joyous for them
in this hot dust to prance
out of reach of the praying claws
sharpened to paw for ants
in the shadows of deodars   30
It is not easy to free
myth from reality
or rear this fellow up
to lurch   lurch with them
in the tranced dancing of men

Srinagar 1958—Île des Porquerolles 1959
[1962]

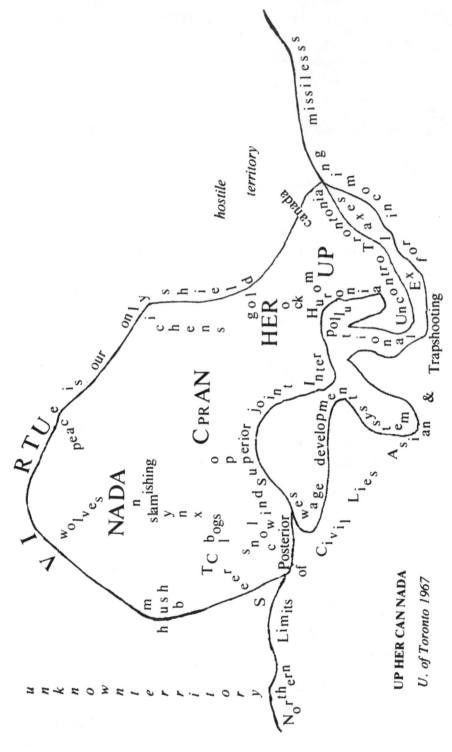

UP HER CAN NADA
U. of Toronto 1967

[*U. of Toronto, 1967*]

i accuse us[15]

(speech, anti-vietnam rally, toronto, 1967)

O.K. so the U.S. is the only country
to move "from barbarism to decadence
without achieving civilization"[16]
& where does that leave us?
what's with us supernorthamericans
who never had the guts
to be either barbaric or decadent?
are we what the Yanks have fostered
instead of a civilization?   10

Hail!   five hundred years
of near-beer British
& sour-wine French
united in building Unamerica
without speaking to each other
(also farewell!   twenty thousand years
of Indian & Inuit
& the creatures they lived with)

Sure we're into our second century
of well-not-quite parasitism   20
& not-quite-independence
Hail!   fellow-hitchhikers
in the limousines of empires
It's been fast smooth riding
but where are we heading?
If we have to be fleas
leaving a dead lion
why choose a sick eagle?
Why not a healthy sheep?
or really live it big: 30
think rape & hunt for elephants?

---

[15] Allusion to Emile Zola's famous open letter of 13 January 1898 to the newspaper *L'Aurore*
entitled "J'accuse." In the letter, Zola accused the French government of anti-Semitism for its
unlawful imprisonment of Alfred Dreyfus, a Jewish officer in the French army, for espionage.
The letter incited a public outcry, shifting public opinion in Dreyfus's favour and calling attention to the scandal worldwide. Zola was charged with libel and had to flee the country for a year.
As a result of this letter, Zola's phrase "J'accuse" is used when people want to lay charges against a
powerful person or institution.

[16] Quotation from Oscar Wilde (1854–1900), author of the play *The Importance of Being Earnest*
(1895), about America.

Sorry   I forgot   we are Canadians
we are the quiet reasoning folk
the blessed peacemakers in fact
who shall inherit
the radioactive earth
Balls!   as neutrals
we're about as phony as they come
We are the experts in waging
neither-war-nor-peace   40
while making up our Canamind

We are the boys who put delegates
on the United Nations' commission
to keep real peace in Vietnam
& secretly told them
not to report the shiploads of arms
the U.S. unloaded weekly in Saigon

We are the owners of the biggest swatch
of "undeveloped resources" in the world
(i.e. uncut trees ungouged earth   50
unkilled fish unscalped animals
unoiled beaches & unblasted rock)
all of which we are hot to unpossess
if only our capital werent tied up
making more explosives to export
for wars abroad than we use at home
for our kind of peace

Yes sir we're the biggest seller
of napalm & phosphorus
the U.S. ever had   60
though of course we howl
every week on television
when the bastards drop it all
on somebody's kids

Don't think we haven't got a conscience—
who sent a whole children's hospital
to South Vietnam?   O sorry no
that was the British   Our doctors
werent allowed to sew new eyelids & skin
on little gooks that got in the road   70
of free enterprise by C.I.L. (Canada)[17]

For Christ's or Buddha's sake or for our Own
let's face us as others do
Even the Americans who've escaped to us
from the earth's most prosperous
& brutal superstate
the unartful dodgers[18] mistaking
our inaction for bravery
& our ambiguities for freedom
find our uniqueness lies   80
in "dynamic apathy"[19]

Hell Vietnam was just a symptom
we've got the disease!
When the Greek army's fascists
murdered Greek democracy[20]
who at once assured the generals
they'd get a loan?
Yep that was Canada my fellow Ca-nadas
that was the frecklecheeked kid sister
beating Big Brother to it   90

Tomorrow it'll be our turn
to help somebody else
help kill more Jews Arabs
Polynesians whathaveyou
or sit firm in words for both sides
while the real Africans stand up
to be shredded down

It's us I accuse   you   me
of failure to become something else
than a dozen separatisms   100
united only by a common war

[17] Birney is ironically using an ethnic slur. According to the Princeton University Dictionary, a "gook" is "a disparaging term for an Asian person (especially for North Vietnamese soldiers in the Vietnam War)." Birney is likely referring to Canadian Industries Limited, also known as C-I-L, a Canadian chemicals manufacturer whose products include paints, fertilizers, pesticides, and explosives.

[18] The Artful Dodger is a young pickpocket in Charles Dickens's (1812–1870) novel *Oliver Twist* (1838). The term "draft dodger" applied to those American men facing conscription for the Vietnam War who decided to flee to Canada rather than serve in the American armed forces. Approximately 20,000 to 30,000 draft-eligible American men came to Canada as immigrants during the era of the Vietnam War.

[19] Diplomatically Canada was "non-belligerent" and did not fight in the Vietnam War.

[20] Reference to the coup d'état of 1967 led by a group of colonels that put in office a military government in Greece from 1967 to 1974.

on our own central government
& by common exploitation
of our poor by our rich

I accuse us
of failure to become a nation—
a nation neither White Red Black Brown or Pink
but its own Rainbow
a nation seeking internationhood
not another empire   a Soul   110
a Human Presence   capable of pity with strength
of less holiness   & more wholeness

I accuse Us
of celebrations without cause
of standing not moving
in passionate urgency
towards the *real* civilization
there may just be time
to glimpse before our species
crawls off to join the dinosaurs.   120

[*1973*]

Canada: Case History: 1973

No more the highschool land
deadset in loutishness
This cat's turned cool
the gangling's gone
guffaws are for the peasants

Inside his plastic igloo now
he watches gooks and yankees bleed[21]
in colour on the telly
But under a faded Carnaby[22] shirt
ulcers knife the rounding belly   10

Hung up on rye and nicotine and sex-
y flicks, kept off the snow and grass
he teeters tiptoe on his arctic roof
(ten brittle legs, no two together)

[21] A reference to the Vietnam War.

[22] In the 1960s, Carnaby Street in London, England, was a hip area for Mod fashion and underground music. The street embodies the swinging sixties.

baring his royal canadian ass
white and helpless in the global winds

Schizoid from birth, and still a sado-masochist
this turkey thinks that for his sins
he should be carved while still alive:
legs to Québec, the future Vietnam;   20
the rest, self-served and pre-digested,
to make a Harvest Home for Uncle Sam. . . .

Teeth shot and memory going
(except for childhood grudges),
one moment murderous, the next depressed,
this youth, we fear, has moved from adolescence
into what looks like permanent senescence.

Toronto 1973

[1975]

HUGH MACLENNAN ▪ (1907–1990)

In 1945 Hugh MacLennan argued that "Canadians are hungry for a spokesman" and obliged in his own novel *Two Solitudes* (1945), which he termed a "novel of Canada." The title of this novel has become a catch phrase in Canadian culture. It is synonymous with the long-standing tensions between French and English Canada. The novel is the story of an emerging artist caught between two worlds: English and French; wealth and poverty; Protestantism and Catholicism; urban and rural life. As a nationalist, MacLennan favoured civic nationalism (with an emphasis on place and citizenship) over ethnic nationalism (with an emphasis on purity of race or homogeneity of a people). Winning five Governor General's Awards for fiction and for non-fiction, he is one of the most decorated authors to have lived in Canada. Poet and critic Eli Mandel named him "the father of the Canadian novel" in 1986. However, his work has also been accused of engaging too heavily in nationalist concerns.

John Hugh MacLennan was born in Glace Bay, Nova Scotia, in 1907. When he was seven years old his father moved his medical practice and his family to Halifax. A central event in MacLennan's childhood was the explosion of a munitions ship in the Halifax Harbour. On 6 December 1917, the *Imo* and the French arms ship the *Mont Blanc* collided, causing a devastating explosion. In his essay "On Being a Maritime Writer," MacLennan remembers that he decided to become a writer when he saw "men dying in the streets" and he wanted to record the memory. Indeed, this event became the subject of MacLennan's first published novel, *Barometer Rising,* in 1941.

After graduating from Dalhousie University in 1928, MacLennan won a Rhodes Scholarship to study at Oxford (where he also became the Oxford University singles tennis champion of 1930, following his victory as the Maritimes singles champion in 1929). Falling in love with his future wife Dorothy Duncan on the boat home from England in 1932, MacLennan headed next to Princeton where he received his Ph.D. in classics in 1935. For the following decade, MacLennan taught at Lower Canada College in Montreal. Intellectually left-leaning all his life, he joined the Co-operative Commonwealth Federation (CCF) in 1937, after meeting F.R. Scott, among others, in Montreal. After the immediate success of *Two Solitudes,* MacLennan resigned from teaching in order to write full time. His novels include *The Precipice* (1948), *Each Man's Son* (1951), *The Watch That Ends the Night* (1959), *Return of the Sphinx* (1967), and *Voices in Time* (1980). As a professional writer, however, he was always in financial straits, so a few years later he joined the English Department at McGill University and remained teaching there until his retirement in 1981. Like Scott, he was a proud Anglo-Quebecker. MacLennan died in North Hatley, Quebec, in 1990.

The economic Depression of the 1930s had a lasting effect on MacLennan. In his novel *The Watch That Ends the Night,* MacLennan shifts his narrative between the 1930s and the 1950s in order to criticize the idealism of the first era and the shallowness of the second. For MacLennan, *The Watch That Ends the Night* was a "requiem for the idealists of the Thirties who had meant so well, tried so hard and went so wrong." The Canadian band The Tragically Hip adapted a passage from *The Watch That Ends the Night* in their song "Courage (for Hugh MacLennan)" on their album *Fully Completely* (1992). Well respected as an author of fiction, MacLennan also received acclaim (including two Governor General's Awards) for his collections of essays. "Boy Meets Girl in Winnipeg and Who Cares?" was published in *Scotchman's Return and Other Essays* (1960) and draws on MacLennan's continuing concerns about the viability of Canadian art, in this case when he was advised by a New York publisher to set his novels in Europe or the United States rather than in Canada. The essay showcases MacLennan's spirited cultural nationalism.

Boy Meets Girl in Winnipeg and Who Cares?

The writing profession has many advantages: no boss breathes down your neck, nobody cares if you are late to work so long as you are not late *with* work, you don't have to co-operate with anyone except yourself and maybe the occasional editor. Along with the uncaught criminal, the artist is, as Somerset Maugham[1] long ago pointed out, one of the few remaining species of *homo sapiens* who can roughly be described as free. Not even the Russians have been able to organize him without making him useless.

For this freedom the writer pays, and with each passing year he pays more, because in any technological society freedom almost prices itself out of the market. The price you pay for freedom today is a total lack of security.

While a book is in train, life can be so exciting for the writer that he never thinks about money unless the bank tells him he is overdrawn, and he thinks about his security only in those ghastly moments when the book bogs down. But

[1] W. Somerset Maugham (1874–1965), English novelist and fiction writer, author of *Of Human Bondage* (1915) and *The Razor's Edge* (1945).

all this changes after the book is completed and sent off to the publishers. Publishers are more human than writers in their cycles: a writer's period of gestation may range from ten days (Erle Stanley Gardner[2]) to five years (myself with the last novel) to the lifetime necessary for the man who intends to produce a masterpiece the moment he can get around to it. But publishers, from the time they receive a script to the time they deliver the first edition to the bookstores, usually consume from seven to nine months.

Nine months can seem pretty long to a waiting man, and during this period I always swear I will reform. I remember my father telling me not to gamble, and I realize that if I have not gambled with money (never having had enough to gamble with) I have certainly gambled with my life, and have done so deliberately with the odds against me. The writer's usual gamble is to bet on hitting the jackpot somewhere along the line, his idea being that if he keeps on writing long enough the probabilities are reasonable that he will do so at least once, and then he can invest the money and attain his security. In the old days this worked pretty well, and in one or two countries it still works up to a point for the very lucky few, in spite of the tax gatherers necessary for the support of the welfare state.

But in Canada the gamble doesn't work at all; in Canada the odds against the jackpot are what they would be in roulette if every tenth slot was a double-zero. I have known this for years, and yet I have contumaciously[3] gone back to the tables again and again. While it is true that our population is rising fast, at least a third of it is not presumed to read English literature in its spare time. A best seller in our market is exceptional if it tops 10,000, and the royalty on 10,000 copies is about $4,500. On the other hand in the United States, where the population now exceeds 170 million, all of them over five taught to read and write and all of them over two to look at television, a best seller cannot only hit the half-million mark but later, and for this very reason, be sold to the movies and television people for sums of money which fatten the tax gatherers as a dead elephant fattens the vultures that roost on Kilimanjaro. But even after the publicans have picked you, if you hit a jackpot like that you have a sizable paycheck to bank.

This simple arithmetic I have always disregarded whenever I have been in train with a novel. To hell with figures, I say, while genius pretends to burn. I write English, I say, and the Americans read English, and as long as I build a better mousetrap the world is sure to beat that famous path to my famous door. Again and again American reviewers, who are more generous to outsiders than any other reviewers in the world, urge their readers to read Canadian books. But in spite of all this goodwill, grass still grows green and thick around the doorsteps of our better Canadian mousetrap builders.

Why shouldn't it? If we insisted on electing Mackenzie King[4] for twenty-two years, why should Americans think us an interesting people? In any case, literature

---

[2] Erle Stanley Gardner (1889–1970) was a pulp fiction writer, the creator of the fictional lawyer Perry Mason, and one of the best-selling authors of all time.

[3] Stubbornly perverse, insubordinate, rebellious.

[4] William Lyon Mackenzie King (1874–1950) was the tenth Prime Minister of Canada.

has always been mixed up with nationalisms and popular assumptions. Citizens of new countries are supposed to break sods instead of typewriters, and Europeans coming to live among them are supposed to furnish them with such culture as they can imbibe. A century ago Melville and Hawthorne[5] had as hard a time crashing the international market as we Canadians have now, and it did their pockets little good, nor did they know about it during their lives, that in our day Harvard students turn out about a dozen theses a year on their work. In the last three generations the United States not only broke through into the international market; for a time it came close to capturing it. But the American writers who developed a mature native literature had an advantage the critics have seldom noted: a huge and growing native population. It was this native population which supported them in the years when they were growing up, for it is natural for people to find their own societies more interesting than the societies of strangers.

Facts such as these I have stubbornly disregarded for more than twenty years. I have known them perfectly; I have known them ever since I received a telegram informing me that two Hollywood studios were interested in my first novel.[6] I saw dollar signs all over the Windsor Station the night I boarded that train for New York, and there were still more of them hanging from the skyscrapers when I drove in a taxi to the old Ritz-Carlton to meet the representative of the studio which was the more interested of the two. He was a man exceedingly affable, though somewhat boiled-looking about the eyelids, and before ordering a thirty-dollar lunch he gave me two cocktails. He also told me the deal was off.

"It's like this," the man explained. "This book of yours, it's about this town Halifax and who's ever heard of Halifax down here except as a word nicely brought-up kids say when what really they mean is hell? 'Go to Halifax', is what nicely brought-up kids down here say. Well, of course, this wouldn't make any difference if this was an ordinary book. We could work a switcheroo. But the trouble is in this book of yours Halifax gets itself blown up in the climax of the story. We fooled around with a switcheroo even on that. We thought of the Johnstown Flood, but that happened so long ago that who cares, so we canned the whole idea." He looked at me in sincere friendship and said: "It's tough, but that's how it is. All you've got to do next time is set the scene in the United States and *then* we'll be really interested."

Being naïve in those days, I asked what difference the locale of a story makes so long as the story is good.

"Well, take Paris," he said, "that's okay for one kind of story. Take London—that's okay for another kind. But take Canada—that's not okay because what do Americans think when they hear that word 'Canada' except cold weather and Mounties or maybe when they hear it they don't know what to think. Now this is not the way it ought to be and it's tough, but look at it like this. A boy meets a girl

---

[5] American writers: Herman Melville (1819–1891), the author of *Moby-Dick* (1851) and Nathaniel Hawthorne (1804–1864), the author of *The Scarlet Letter* (1850).

[6] *Barometer Rising* (1941), about the Halifax explosion.

in Paris, one thing leads to another and they—well, it's interesting. But a boy meets a girl in Winnipeg and they swing into the same routine and who cares? I'm not saying it's not just as good in Winnipeg as it is in Paris. Maybe it's even better because in Winnipeg what else is there to do? But for the American public you've got to see it's a fact that Winnipeg kind of kills interest in the whole thing."

I protested (I was *very* naïve in those days) that my books tended to be serious, what you might call social novels.

"That's exactly what I've been trying to say," he explained. "The way you write, if you want a big market down here, you just haven't got much of a choice. The way you write you've got to make it American. Now let me tell you a little tale to illustrate that point."

One Monday morning on the Coast, he related, in the days of the silents when Hollywood magnates were real magnates and not Organization Men, one of the very biggest of these magnates padded into his office, seated himself behind his twelve-foot desk and pressed down all the buttons it contained. Within five minutes most of his executives, script men, continuity men, cameramen, directors, idea men, editors and press agents were arrayed before him. He advanced his dimpled chin, stared at each of them in turn, and barked:

"Why do I pay you guys one—two—three thousand dollars a week and from you what do I get but strictly nothing?"

After the necessary quarter-minute's silence had been observed, the magnate continued:

"Over the week-end I was with high-class people and they told me of a very wonderful book, the most wonderful story of this century, and from you what do I hear of this story but strictly nothing?"

After the necessary ten seconds of silence, the chief story editor asked if the title of the book might be revealed. It could be, and it was *The Well of Loneliness*.[7] The editor shrugged and said he had read it long ago.

"Then why," stared the boss, "don't I see this *Well of Loneliness* in lights?"

The editor sighed and said it was impossible. The magnate scowled and said the word "impossible" was a word that nobody in his studio was permitted to understand. The editor agreed that this was true, but argued that the censors would not permit *The Well of Loneliness* to be shown in American family theatres, not even with the "Adults Only" sign on the door. The heroine of the book, he explained to the chief, was a Lesbian.

The dimpled chin advanced further across the desk, the wonderful little eyes gleamed.

"Why do I pay for brains when evidently brains is what you do not like to use? So the girl in this story is a Lesbian? So what if she's from Peru? So what if her home is in Costa Rica maybe? In this studio we make her an American!"

The man from Hollywood looked at me mournfully and said: "So now you see the way it is."

---

[7] *The Well of Loneliness* is a 1928 novel by the English author Radclyffe Hall (1880–1943).

Oddly enough I saw exactly how it was, just as I see how it is now, for right here in Canada the situation is little different. Suppose you try to sell a serious social novel about Peru or Costa Rica in Canada, how many Canadians are going to storm the shops to buy that book?

Yet I, fully understanding this situation years ago, have continued to squander my dwindling hopes of security by continually writing books about Canadians living in their own country. Can anybody be stupider about his interests than that? Now, with still another long novel due this month (due as a matter of fact on Friday the Thirteenth of this month and no kidding) I feel like the gambler in the garden at Monte Carlo solemnly telling himself "Never, never again." For five years I have been assuring myself that this novel is by far the best thing I've ever done or dreamed of doing, that its Canadian setting is worked into it like shot silk, that here is a story that should sound just as good in London or New York as in Montreal. Maybe it will; maybe it will! But my Scotch instinct also says, "Maybe it won't!" And as I await the results with Scotch fatalism, I again remember the words of that man from Hollywood, and this time I swear I'm going to act on them the next time I write a novel.

"The thing for you to do," he said, "being a Canadian, is make the best of *both* your worlds. Mix up the English and Americans in the same package, and fix it so somehow this Englishman in this book comes over to the States with certain ideas and he changes them, understand, when he finds out about American women and democracy." He shook my hand warmly as we left the Ritz. "Now just one more little thing and it shouldn't be too hard to do. Try to work Lincoln[8] into the story somehow. Work Lincoln in, you as a Canadian work Lincoln into it with this Englishman, and something very nice ought to come out."

He paused as we passed through the revolving door, wrinkled up his face into a confidential question-mark and spoke again:

"How inhibited are you on sex?" he asked me. "This last book of yours, it had some hints of sex but not half enough in my opinion."

"How much sex do you think I need?"

"Pretty well all you can put in. Of course, it's got to be moral. I mean, if people get it extra-curricularly they've got to pay for it, but you can describe them getting it, and while you're at it, let yourself go. A book with no sex, the reader feels cheated. But you know all that anyway."

Dumas *fils*[9] once told a neophyte the three basic rules of the novelist's trade: "First tell them what to do. Then do it. Then tell them you've done it."

---

[8] Abraham Lincoln (1809–1865), the 16th President of the United States, led the government's Union forces through the American Civil War (1861–65). On 14 April 1865, he was assassinated at Ford's Theatre in Washington. He is remembered as a fighter for freedom and unity.

[9] Alexandre Dumas *fils* (1824–1895), the son of Alexandre Dumas *père* (1802–1970), who was a French author and playwright.

Now, being determined to atone for a mis-spent life before it's too late, I'm going to tell you what I'm going to do, then I'm going to do it, then I'm going to tell you I've done it.

My next novel is going to open in London just as the Hollywood man said, with Lord Peter Sandwich (can't you see him: tall, saturnine[10] and a soldier?) conversing with Lord Palmerston beside a window looking down into the Horse Guards where some very pretty guardsmen are trooping the colour. As everyone knows who knows his Civil War[11] literature, Lord Palmerston[12] is a villain, and if it had not been for the Good Queen and Prince Albert, together with the spirit of English democracy (this book has to be sold in England as well as in the States), Palmerston would long ago have turned the might of the British Empire against Lincoln's embattled Union. So this novel of mine will begin with Lord Palmerston giving Lord Peter Sandwich his instructions, and these instructions, when followed out, are going to be the storyline of the book.

In case you have not guessed it, Sandwich has just been given a secret mission: he is to sail to Havana where he is to proceed immediately to a certain address. There he will be told how to find the transportation which will convey him through the northern blockade into Charleston, whence he is to proceed inland through the Confederacy to President Jefferson Davis whom he will promise (verbally, of course) that if the Confederacy can make one more major successful effort, if it can strike out of its lines into the heart of the Union, the right-thinking people in Her Majesty's Government will be able to sweep aside the protests of the liberals, the milksops[13] and the Good Queen herself. The Royal Navy, the Royal Navy, sir, will be ordered out to sea, and Boston and New York will be blockaded. Then, while Lee strikes north through the Shenandoah, that army of redcoats will strike south from Canada to plunge the dagger into the back of the Great Experiment. "History," says Palmerston in effect, "from now on depends more or less on you."

Lord Peter has still a few days left in London, and these he occupies as a young man does when he is about to set forth on a secret mission. The lady's cries (she is of course nobly born) will be duly recorded in my novel, and Lord Peter's prowess in the culbatizing exercise will be described with what the critics now call clinical accuracy, and rightly too, for "clinic" is derived from a Greek

---

[10] Sluggish, cold, and gloomy in temperament.

[11] American Civil War (1861–65), when 11 Southern states declared their secession from the United States after President Lincoln expressed a desire to arrest the expansion of slavery into the free states and work toward its "ultimate extinction." The pro-slavery Southern states were led by President Jefferson Davis (1808–1889), President of the Confederate States of America (1861–65). The Union forces were led by Lincoln who fought to keep the nation as one. Lincoln issued the Emancipation Proclamation on 1 January 1863. It held that "all persons held as slaves" within the rebellious states "are, and henceforth shall be free." The war ended two years later following the death of Lincoln.

[12] Henry John Temple, 3rd Viscount Palmerston (1784–1865), Prime Minister of the United Kingdom (1859–65). Although he was not pro-slavery, his sympathies in the American Civil War were with the Southern Confederacy because he thought the dissolution of the Union would weaken the power of the United States.

[13] Feeble, timid, or ineffectual person.

word meaning "bed". This will be the first sexual commercial on my programme, and as it will occur around page 20, the reader will be assured at the very beginning that this is a novel in which he will not be cheated, for if the spacing continues at that rate, at least twenty more similar scenes will follow, and he can feel by the weight of it that this is not a short book.

Once this scene is over, Lord Peter takes the train to Southampton (some pretty descriptions of Hampshire scenery, some moral reflections about the immorality of his current life) and thence to the frigate, aboard which Lord Peter is impressively piped.

As nothing can be more monotonous than the description of a sea voyage on a neutral man o' war, this frigate on which Lord Peter sails must encounter a few incidents which will liven up the log. I am not sure of all of them yet, but there are a variety of possibilities. *H.M.S. Atrocious* (the name must exist somewhere on the navy list) may quite possibly run down a Yankee merchantman and create an international incident. Or perhaps a woman has stowed away on board and Lord Peter can discover her? Or perhaps the captain can go mad, and Lord Peter can save the ship from him? As I said, and as you well know, there is a variety of possibilities here. But there is one thing of which I am certainly not going to cheat the reader and that is the flogging scene. A sailor is going to be seized up in the gangway and the bosun is going to give him two dozen with the cat,[14] and the screams of the sailor are going to be recorded and the sound of the cat whistling through the air and snapping against his bare back—first with a dry sound and later on with a kind of splash—are going to be described with all the vividness at my command, and this should put the reader into exactly the right mood for Lord Peter's next amatory adventure, which he consummates with the Cuban lady who arranges his transportation to Charleston.

In Charleston, of course, Lord Peter sees a proud aristocracy on its last legs, its flowers at their prime, and several of these he adds to his collection before finally he goes inland (descriptions of the Confederacy feeling the pinch of the Northern blockade) where he not only meets President Davis, but also shakes hands with General Lee, and although General Lee's nobility makes him uneasy about his own character, the result of Lord Peter's meeting with him is what it has to be: the march to Gettysburg.[15]

By now, as the reader will understand, the mysterious something in the New World has begun to work on the mind of this hard young aristocrat and it occurs to him that he may be a bit of a heel. The first messenger of grace is an American woman. He seduces her, but this time the scene is a little different, for

[14] The cat-o-nine-tails was a whip with nine knotted lashes. Until 1881 it was an authorized instrument of punishment in the British navy.

[15] General Robert E. Lee (1807–1870), senior military adviser to President Davis. Lee was defeated at the Battle of Gettysburg in Pennsylvania (1863). Gettysburg was the site of the largest number of casualties in the war and is often cited as the turning-point of the war.

in the deep of the southern night she breaks into tears and reminds him that her husband is in Lee's cavalry and here she is being disloyal to him in her own bed. Nor is this lady at ease as regards the righteousness of the Southern cause, or in the inevitability of war. In fact she is confused all around. What will she do with herself if her husband finds out about her? What will she do if her husband is killed? What will the South do even if the South wins? And what will happen to the South if any more men are slaughtered in this insensate war? War, she informs Lord Peter, is not quite the manly sport he seems to think it is, and it is with these words ringing in his ears that Lord Peter reaches the field of Gettysburg.

The Battle of Gettysburg has been described so often that it is necessary to re-describe it every February when Lincoln's birthday rolls around. You may be sure it will be described in this novel I am going to write, for it is the turning-point in the life of the novel's hero. We see Lord Peter standing on the knoll with Lee's staff and the other foreign observers; we hear the horses scream and neigh; we see the men fall; we see the mask of tragedy settle on to the face of General Lee as wave after wave of his men die before the Northern sharpshooters; we see the moment approach for Pickett's charge.[16] The bugles blow, and then we see Lord Peter suddenly run away from the knoll and mount a riderless horse, and because he is a superb rider, soon we see him heading the charge against the Union lines.

He gets it, and wakes up with the kindly twang of a Yankee voice saying: "Waal son, I guess you've lost a little bit of weight."

The weight Lord Peter has lost is his left leg, and as he cannot be moved for a while, it is quite consistent with the probabilities that he should still be hanging around Gettysburg when the Presidential party arrives from Washington, and when Lincoln makes that speech, who is present to understand it except this tired, wounded and humbled English aristocrat?[17] The Gettysburg Oration settles almost every problem in Lord Sandwich's guilty, troubled mind, and the little confusion that still lingers is taken care of when the Great Emancipator,[18] visiting the wounded of both sides, puts his hand on Sandwich's shoulder, looks into his eyes and utters a few words. What those words are I do not intend to tell you. You must buy the book if you want to find out.

So there, friends, is the plot of my next novel, and there is only one thing which can prevent it from being written. That is for the Canada Council, which has been established, as everyone knows, to promote the arts in this country, to persuade the Government to agree to pension off every novelist who can prove

---

[16] Pickett's Charge was an infantry assault ordered by Lee.

[17] That speech is the Gettysburg Address made by Lincoln at the dedication ceremony for the Gettysburg National Cemetery (1863). It begins with the famous lines, "Four score and seven years ago our fathers brought forth on this continent a new nation, conceived in Liberty, and dedicated to the proposition that all men are created equal," and ends with the resolution that "this nation, under God, shall have a new birth of freedom—and that government of the people, by the people, for the people, shall not perish from the earth."

[18] Another name for Abraham Lincoln.

he has written at least five novels in his lifetime. If the Government of England in the eighteenth century gave John Cleland a lifetime pension after he wrote *Fanny Hill*,[19] its provision being that *Fanny Hill* should be withdrawn from the bookstalls and that Cleland should never write anything else so long as he lived, why should not the much richer government of twentieth-century Canada do something of the same sort? I have warned them fairly what the alternative is, so the next move is surely up to them. If the Government, however reluctantly, kept a Peter Breughel out of the country in the interests of economy and social security, why should it not, in the same interests (or more or less in the same interests) keep this proposed book of mine out of existence?

[1960]

[19] English novelist John Cleland (1709–1789), author of *Fanny Hill; or Memoirs of a Woman of Pleasure* (1784). The novel, considered to be the first modern erotic novel in English, was deemed obscene and Cleland was arrested for "corrupting the King's subjects." The author was released after he renounced the novel.

SINCLAIR ROSS ■ (1908–1996)

134

Until recently, few novels written in Canada were taught as often as Sinclair Ross's *As for Me and My House* (1941). Read as the "quintessential" Canadian novel of mid-century, Ross's tale exemplifies the prevalent themes of isolation and survival in a harsh unyielding landscape. However, it also probes into issues of sexuality, artistic frustration, and hypocrisy in a haunting exploration of anxiety and marginality.

Born James Sinclair Ross in Prince Albert, Saskatchewan, Ross was a self-proclaimed outsider: he left school with a Grade 11 education; he lived into adulthood with his oppressive mother; he was a private man who was overwhelmed by even the limited attention garnered by his writing; and he was homosexual at a time when it was socially marginalizing and legally forbidden in Canada (decriminalized in 1969). Ross worked professionally as a banker (in a job he is said to have loathed) for 43 years, stopping only to serve in the Second World War. He published four

novels and two short story collections in his lifetime: *As for Me and My House*, *The Well* (1958), *The Lamp at Noon and Other Stories* (1968), *Whir of Gold* (1970), *Sawbones Memorial* (1974), and *The Race and Other Stories* (1982). After he retired in 1968, Ross left Canada to live in Greece and Spain. For the next dozen years he tried his hand at writing full time. He returned to Canada to spend his last years in Vancouver, dying of Parkinson's disease at the age of 88.

Although his first novel met with lukewarm reviews when published, *As for Me and My House* has gone on to become a classic (in part due to Malcolm Ross's decision to republish it as the fourth book in the New Canadian Library Series). Literary critic Alison Calder nicely summarizes the central concerns of the book when she writes that "the novel, narrated as the diary of Mrs. Bentley, a minister's wife in a small prairie town, reveals a claustrophobic world circumscribed by small-town hypocrisy and marked by an unforgiving landscape."

The novel presents an ambivalent view of gender politics, urban/rural divides, and town and church philosophical clashes. Recent approaches to Ross's work have viewed it in the context of queer theory, as critic Peter Dickinson does when he shows how the novel engages with issues of "counter-normative sexuality."

Ross's articulation of prairie space in his work made it seem to be a subject worthy of literary representation for future generations of western Canadian writers. For instance, novelist Margaret Laurence commented that "it was *As for Me and My House* that taught me that one could write out of the known background of a small prairie town and that everything that happens anywhere also in some ways happens there." In "The Moment of the Discovery of America Continues," prairie novelist and poet Robert Kroetsch writes, "I remember responding with shock to Ross's portrait of a marriage, a prairie town, a prairie house." He continues, "Ross and his characters in his town of Horizon became a generating principle, the enabling moment that released me into a memory of the politics and the poverty, of the card parties and the funerals and the wedding dances and the sports days and the auction sales, the silences and the stories of the thirties. Ross, by some alchemy, allowed me to recognize the binary patterns that the human mind uses to construct its day and its labyrinth." Ross's work still resonates with contemporary readers and writers: *As for Me and My House* has inspired three collections of poems by prairie poet Dennis Cooley (*The Bentley Poems* [2000], *Country Music* [2004], and *The Bentleys* [2006]), as well as Lorna Crozier's *A Saving Grace: The Collected Poems of Mrs. Bentley* (1996). Further, his stories "The Painted Door" and "One's a Heifer" were turned into successful films by the National Film Board in 1984 as part of their Canadian Short Story Collection.

"The Painted Door" was published originally in *Queen's Quarterly* in 1939 and subsequently in *The Lamp at Noon* almost 30 years later, alongside his widely anthologized "One's a Heifer," "A Field of Wheat," and the haunting title story of the collection. Ross's narratives are driven by oppressive prairie weather, fractured marriages, frustrated sexuality, crushing loneliness, and the unrelenting restlessness of his characters. As a slow and controlled exploration of a suffocating and claustrophobic home in winter, "The Painted Door" uses pathetic fallacy to illustrate the perils of a stagnant marriage and forms an interesting comparison with F.P. Grove's "Dawn and Diamonds" (included in this section). Critic Andrew Lesk notes that "the crisp sterility of the winter prairie drains the colours of the marriage into a bloodless black and white." Ross is able to turn a blizzard into a scene of temptation, betrayal, and remorse.

The Painted Door

Straight across the hills it was five miles from John's farm to his father's. But in winter, with the roads impassible, a team had to make a wide detour and skirt the hills, so that from five the distance was more than trebled to seventeen.

"I think I'll walk," John said at breakfast to his wife. "The drifts in the hills wouldn't hold a horse, but they'll carry me all right. If I leave early I can spend a few hours helping him with his chores, and still be back by suppertime."

Moodily she went to the window, and thawing a clear place in the frost with her breath, stood looking across the snowswept farmyard to the huddle of stables and sheds. "There was a double wheel around the moon last night," she countered presently. "You said yourself we could expect a storm. It isn't right to leave me here alone. Surely I'm as important as your father."

He glanced up uneasily, then drinking off his coffee tried to reassure her. "But there's nothing to be afraid of—even if it does start to storm. You won't need to go near the stable. Everything's fed and watered now to last till night. I'll be back at the latest by seven or eight."

She went on blowing against the frosted pane, carefully elongating the clear place until it was oval-shaped and symmetrical. He watched her a moment or two longer, then more insistently repeated, "I say you won't need to go near the stable. Everything's fed and watered, and I'll see that there's plenty of wood in. That will be all right, won't it?"

"Yes—of course—I heard you—." It was a curiously cold voice now, as if the words were chilled by their contact with the frosted pane. "Plenty to eat—plenty of wood to keep me warm—what more could a woman ask for?"

"But he's an old man—living there all alone. What is it, Ann? You're not like yourself this morning."

She shook her head without turning. "Pay no attention to me. Seven years a farmer's wife—it's time I was used to staying alone."

Slowly the clear place on the glass enlarged: oval, then round, then oval again. The sun was risen above the frost mists now, so keen and hard a glitter on the snow that instead of warmth its rays seemed shedding cold. One of the two-year-old colts that had cantered away when John turned the horses out for water stood covered with rime at the stable door again, head down and body hunched, each breath a little plume of steam against the frosty air. She shivered, but did not turn. In the clear, bitter light the long white miles of prairie landscape seemed a region strangely alien to life. Even the distant farmsteads she could see served only to intensify a sense of isolation. Scattered across the face of so vast and bleak a wilderness it was difficult to conceive them as a testimony of human hardihood and endurance. Rather they seemed futile, lost. Rather they seemed to cower before the implacability of snow-swept earth and clear pale sun-chilled sky.

And when at last she turned from the window there was a brooding stillness in her face as if she had recognized this mastery of snow and cold. It troubled John. "If you're really afraid," he yielded, "I won't go to-day. Lately it's been so cold, that's all. I just wanted to make sure he's all right in case we do have a storm."

"I know—I'm not really afraid." She was putting in a fire now, and he could no longer see her face. "Pay no attention to me. It's ten miles there and back, so you'd better get started."

"You ought to know by now I wouldn't stay away," he tried to brighten her. "No matter how it stormed. Twice a week before we were married I never missed—and there were bad blizzards that winter too."

He was a slow, unambitious man, content with his farm and cattle, naively proud of Ann. He had been bewildered by it once, her caring for a dull-witted fellow like him; then assured at last of her affection he had relaxed against it gratefully, unsuspecting it might ever be less constant than his own. Even now, listening to the restless brooding in her voice, he felt only a quick, unformulated kind of pride that after seven years his absence for a day should still concern her. While she, his trust and earnestness controlling her again:

"I know. It's just that sometimes when you're away I get lonely . . . There's a long cold tramp in front of you. You'll let me fix a scarf around your face."

He nodded. "And on my way I'll drop in at Steven's place. Maybe he'll come over to-night for a game of cards. You haven't seen anybody but me for the last two weeks."

She glanced up sharply, then busied herself clearing the table. "It will mean another two miles if you do. You're going to be cold and tired enough as it is. When you're gone I think I'll paint the kitchen woodwork. White this time—you remember we got the paint last fall. It's going to make the room a lot lighter. I'll be too busy to find the day long."

"I will though," he insisted, "and if a storm gets up you'll feel safer, knowing that he's coming. That's what you need, Ann—someone to talk to besides me."

She stood at the stove motionless a moment, then turned to him uneasily. "Will you shave then, John—now—before you go?"

He glanced at her questioningly, and avoiding his eyes she tried to explain, "I mean—he may be here before you're back—and you won't have a chance then."

"But it's only Steven—he's seen me like this—"

"He'll be shaved, though—that's what I mean—and I'd like you too to spend a little time on yourself."

He stood up, stroking the heavy stubble on his chin. "Maybe I should all right, but it makes the skin too tender. Especially when I've got to face the wind."

She nodded and began to help him dress, bringing heavy socks and a big woollen sweater from the bedroom, wrapping a scarf around his face and forehead. "I'll tell Steven to come early," he said, as he went out. "In time for supper. Likely there'll be chores for me to do, so if I'm not back by six don't wait."

From the bedroom window she watched him nearly a mile along the road. The fire had gone down when at last she turned away, and already through the house there was an encroaching chill. A blaze sprang up again when the drafts were opened, but as she went on clearing the table her movements were strangely furtive and constrained. It was the silence weighing upon her—the frozen silence of the bitter fields and sun-chilled sky—lurking outside as if alive, relentlessly in wait, mile-deep between her now and John. She listened to it, suddenly tense, motionless. The fire crackled and the clock ticked. Always it was there. "I'm a fool," she whispered hoarsely, rattling the dishes in defiance, going back to the stove to put in another fire. "Warm and safe—I'm a fool. It's a good chance when he's away to paint. The day will go quickly. I won't have time to brood."

Since November now the paint had been waiting warmer weather. The frost in the walls on a day like this would crack and peel it as it dried, but she needed something to keep her hands occupied, something to stave off the encroachments of cold and loneliness. "First of all," she said aloud, opening the paint and mixing it with a little turpentine, "I must get the house warmer. Fill up the stove and open the oven door so that all the heat comes out. Wad something along the window sills to keep out the drafts. Then I'll feel brighter. It's the cold that depresses."

She moved briskly, performing each little task with careful and exaggerated absorption, binding her thoughts to it, making it a screen between herself and the surrounding snow and silence. But when the stove was filled and the windows sealed it was more difficult again. Above the quiet, steady swishing of her brush against the bedroom door the clock began to tick. Suddenly her movements became precise, deliberate, her posture self-conscious, as if someone had entered the room and were watching her. It was the silence again, aggressive, hovering. The fire spit and crackled at it. Still it was there. "I'm a fool," she repeated. "All farmers' wives have to stay alone. I mustn't give in this way. I mustn't brood. A few hours now and they'll be here."

The sound of her voice reassured her. She went on: "I'll get them a good supper—and for coffee to-night after cards bake some of the little cakes with raisins that he likes ... Just three of us, so I'll watch, and let John play. It's better with four, but at least we can talk. That's all I need—someone to talk to. John never talks. He's stronger—he doesn't understand. But he likes Steven—no matter what the neighbours say. Maybe he'll have him come again, and some other young people too. It's what we need, both of us, to help keep young ourselves ... And then before we know it we'll be into March. It's cold still in March sometimes, but you never mind the same. At least you're beginning to think about spring."

She began to think about it now. Thoughts that outstripped her words, that left her alone again with herself and the ever-lurking silence. Eager and hopeful first; then clenched, rebellious, lonely. Windows open, sun and thawing earth again, the urge of growing, living things. Then the days that began in the morning at half-past four and lasted till ten at night; the meals at which John gulped his food and scarcely spoke a word; the brute-tired stupid eyes he turned on her if ever she mentioned town or visiting.

For spring was drudgery again. John never hired a man to help him. He wanted a mortgage-free farm; then a new house and pretty clothes for her. Sometimes, because with the best of crops it was going to take so long to pay off anyway, she wondered whether they mightn't better let the mortgage wait a little. Before they were worn out, before their best years were gone. It was something of life she wanted, not just a house and furniture; something of John, not pretty clothes when she would be too old to wear them. But John of course couldn't understand. To him it seemed only right that she should have the clothes—only right that he, fit for nothing else, should slave away fifteen hours a day to give them to her. There was in his devotion a baffling, insurmountable humility that made him feel the need of sacrifice. And when his muscles ached, when his feet dragged stolidly with weariness, then it seemed that in some measure at least he was making amends for his big hulking body and simple mind. That by his sacrifice he succeeded only in the extinction of his personality never occurred to him. Year after year their lives went on in the same little groove. He drove his horses in the field; she milked the cows and hoed potatoes. By dint of his drudgery he saved a few months' wages, added a few dollars more each fall to his payments on the mortgage; but the only real difference that it all made was to deprive her of his companionship, to make him a little duller, older, uglier than he might otherwise have been. He never saw their lives objectively. To him it was not what he actually accomplished by means of the sacrifice that mattered, but the sacrifice itself, the gesture—something done for her sake.

And she, understanding, kept her silence. In such a gesture, however futile, there was a graciousness not to be shattered lightly. "John," she would begin sometimes, "you're doing too much. Get a man to help you—just for a month—" but smiling down at her he would answer simply, "I don't mind. Look at the hands on me. They're made for work." While in his voice there would be a stalwart ring to tell her that by her thoughtfulness she had made him only the more resolved to serve her, to prove his devotion and fidelity.

They were useless, such thoughts. She knew. It was his very devotion that made them useless, that forbade her to rebel. Yet over and over, sometimes hunched still before their bleakness, sometimes her brush making swift sharp strokes to pace the chafe and rancor that they brought, she persisted in them.

This now, the winter, was their slack season. She could sleep sometimes till eight, and John till seven. They could linger over their meals a little, read, play cards, go visiting the neighbours. It was the time to relax, to indulge and enjoy themselves; but instead, fretful and impatient, they kept on waiting for the spring. They were compelled now, not by labour, but by the spirit of labour. A spirit that pervaded their lives and brought with idleness a sense of guilt. Sometimes they did sleep late, sometimes they did play cards, but always uneasily, always reproached by the thought of more important things that might be done. When John got up at five to attend to the fire he wanted to stay up and go out to the stable. When he sat down to a meal he hurried his food and pushed his chair away again, from habit, from sheer work-instinct, even though it was only to put more wood in the stove, or go down cellar to cut up beets and turnips for the cows.

And anyway, sometimes she asked herself, why sit trying to talk with a man who never talked? Why talk when there was nothing to talk about but crops and cattle, the weather and the neighbours? The neighbours, too—why go visiting them when still it was the same—crops and cattle, the weather and the other neighbours? Why go to the dances in the schoolhouse to sit among the older women, one of them now, married seven years, or to waltz with the work-bent, tired old farmers to a squeaky fiddle tune? Once she had danced with Steven, six or seven times in the evening, and they had talked about it for as many months. It was easier to stay at home. John never danced or enjoyed himself. He was always uncomfortable in his good suit and shoes. He didn't like shaving in the cold weather oftener than once or twice a week. It was easier to stay at home, to stand at the window staring out across the bitter fields, to count the days and look forward to another spring.

But now, alone with herself in the winter silence, she saw the spring for what it really was. This spring—next spring—all the springs and summers still to come. While they grew old, while their bodies warped, while their minds kept shrivelling dry and empty like their lives. "I mustn't," she said aloud again. "I married him—and he's a good man. I mustn't keep on this way. It will be noon before long, and then time to think about supper. . . . Maybe he'll come early— and as soon as John is finished at the stable we can all play cards."

It was getting cold again, and she left her painting to put in more wood. But this time the warmth spread slowly. She pushed a mat up to the outside door, and went back to the window to pat down the woollen shirt that was wadded along the sill. Then she paced a few times round the room, then poked the fire and rattled the stove lids, then paced again. The fire crackled, the clock ticked. The silence now seemed more intense than ever, seemed to have reached a pitch where it faintly moaned. She began to pace on tiptoe, listening, her shoulders drawn together, not realizing for a while that it was the wind she heard, thin-strained and whimpering through the eaves.

Then she wheeled to the window, and with quick short breaths thawed the frost to see again. The glitter was gone. Across the drifts sped swift and snakelike little tongues of snow. She could not follow them, where they sprang from, or where they disappeared. It was as if all across the yard the snow were shivering awake—roused by the warnings of the wind to hold itself in readiness for the impending storm. The sky had become a sombre, whitish grey. It too, as if in readiness, had shifted and lay close to earth. Before her as she watched a mane of powdery snow reared up breast-high against the darker background of the stable, tossed for a moment angrily, and then subsided again as if whipped down to obedience and restraint. But another followed, more reckless and impatient than the first. Another reeled and dashed itself against the window where she watched. Then ominously for a while there were only the angry little snakes of snow. The wind rose, creaking the troughs that were wired beneath the eaves. In the distance sky and prairie now were merged into one another linelessly. All round her it was gathering; already in its press and whimpering there strummed a boding of eventual fury. Again she saw a mane of snow spring up, so dense and high this time that all the sheds and stables were obscured. Then others followed, whirling fiercely out of hand; and, when at last they cleared, the stables seemed in dimmer outline than before. It was the snow beginning, long lancet shafts of it, straight from the north, borne almost level by the straining wind. "He'll be there soon," she whispered, "and coming home it will be in his back. He'll leave again right away. He saw the double wheel—he knows the kind of storm there'll be."

She went back to her painting. For a while it was easier, all her thoughts half-anxious ones of John in the blizzard, struggling his way across the hills; but petulantly again she soon began, "I knew we were going to have a storm—I told him so—but it doesn't matter what I say. Big stubborn fool—he goes his own way anyway. It doesn't matter what becomes of me. In a storm like this he'll never get home. He won't even try. And while he sits keeping his father company I can look after his stable for him, go plowing through snowdrifts up to my knees—nearly frozen—."

Not that she meant or believed her words. It was just an effort to convince herself that she did have a grievance, to justify her rebellious thoughts, to prove John responsible for her unhappiness. She was young still, eager for excitement and distractions; and John's steadfastness rebuked her vanity, made her complaints seem weak and trivial. Fretfully she went on, "If he'd listen to me sometimes and not be so stubborn we wouldn't be living still in a house like this. Seven years in two rooms—seven years and never a new stick of furniture . . . There—as if another coat of paint could make it different anyway."

She cleaned her brush, filled up the stove again, and went back to the window. There was a void white moment that she thought must be frost formed on the window pane; then, like a fitful shadow through the whirling snow, she recognized the stable roof. It was incredible. The sudden, maniac raging of the storm struck from her face all its pettishness. Her eyes glazed with fear a little; her lips blanched. "If he starts for home now," she whispered silently—"But he won't—he knows I'm safe—he knows Steven's coming. Across the hills he would never dare."

She turned to the stove, holding out her hands to the warmth. Around her now there seemed a constant sway and tremor, as if the air were vibrating with the violent shudderings of the walls. She stood quite still, listening. Sometimes the wind struck with sharp, savage blows. Sometimes it bore down in a sustained, minute-long blast, silent with effort and intensity; then with a foiled shriek of threat wheeled away to gather and assault again. Always the eavetroughs creaked and sawed. She started towards the window again, then detecting the morbid trend of her thoughts, prepared fresh coffee and forced herself to drink a few mouthfuls. "He would never dare," she whispered again. "He wouldn't leave the old man anyway in such a storm. Safe in here—there's nothing for me to keep worrying about. It's after one already. I'll do my baking now, and then it will be time to get supper ready for Steven."

Soon, however, she began to doubt whether Steven would come. In such a storm even a mile was enough to make a man hesitate. Especially Steven, who, for all his attractive qualities, was hardly the one to face a blizzard for the sake of someone else's chores. He had a stable of his own to look after anyway. It would be only natural for him to think that when the storm rose John had turned again for home. Another man would have—would have put his wife first.

But she felt little dread or uneasiness at the prospect of spending the night alone. It was the first time she had been left like this on her own resources, and her reaction, now that she could face and appraise her situation calmly, was gradually to feel it a kind of adventure and responsibility. It stimulated her. Before nightfall she must go to the stable and feed everything. Wrap up in some of John's clothes—take a ball of string in her hand, one end tied to the door, so that no matter how blinding the storm she could at least find her way back to the house. She had heard of people having to do that. It appealed to her now because suddenly it made life dramatic. She had not felt the storm yet, only watched it for a minute through the window.

It took nearly an hour to find enough string, to choose the right socks and sweaters. Long before it was time to start out she tried on John's clothes, changing and rechanging, striding around the room to make sure there would be play enough for pitching hay and struggling over snowdrifts; then she took them off again, and for a while busied herself baking the little cakes with raisins that he liked.

Night came early. Just for a moment on the doorstep she shrank back, uncertain. The slow dimming of the light clutched her with an illogical sense of abandonment. It was like the covert withdrawal of an ally, leaving the alien miles unleashed and unrestrained. Watching the hurricane of writhing snow rage past the little house she forced herself, "They'll never stand the night unless I get them fed. It's nearly dark already, and I've work to last an hour."

Timidly, unwinding a little of the string, she crept out from the shelter of the doorway. A gust of wind spun her forward a few yards, then plunged her headlong against a drift that in the dense white whirl lay invisible across her path. For nearly a minute she huddled still, breathless and dazed. The snow was in her mouth and nostrils, inside her scarf and up her sleeves. As she tried to straighten a smothering scud flung itself against her face, cutting off her breath a second time. The wind struck from all sides, blustering and furious. It was as if the storm had discovered her, as if all its forces were concentrated upon her extinction. Seized with panic suddenly she threshed out a moment with her arms, then stumbled back and sprawled her length across the drift.

But this time she regained her feet quickly, roused by the whip and batter of the storm to a quick, retaliative anger. For a moment her impulse was to face the wind and strike back blow for blow; then, as suddenly as it had come, her frantic strength gave way to a limp and overpowering exhaustion. Suddenly, a comprehension so clear and terrifying that it struck all thoughts of the stable from her mind, she realized in such a storm her puny insignificance. And the realization gave her new strength, stilled this time to a desperate persistence. Just for a moment the wind held her, numb and swaying in its vise; then slowly, buckled far forward, she groped her way again towards the house.

Inside, leaning against the door, she stood tense and still a while. It was almost dark now. The top of the stove glowed a deep, dull red. Heedless of the storm, self-absorbed and self-satisfied, the clock ticked on like a glib little idiot. "He shouldn't have gone," she whispered silently. "He saw the double wheel— he knew. He shouldn't have left me here alone."

For so fierce now, so insane and dominant did the blizzard seem, that she could not credit the safety of the house. The warmth and lull around her was not real yet, not to be relied upon. She was still at the mercy of the storm. Only her body pressing hard like this against the door was staving it off. She didn't dare move. She didn't dare ease the ache and strain. "He shouldn't have gone," she repeated, thinking of the stable again, reproached by her helplessness. "They'll freeze in their stalls—and I can't reach them. He'll say it's all my fault. He won't believe I tried."

Then Steven came. Quickly, startled to quietness and control, she let him in and lit the lamp. He stared at her a moment, then flinging off his cap crossed to where she stood by the table and seized her arms. "You're so white—what's wrong? Look at me—." It was like him in such little situations to be masterful. "You should have known better than to go out on a day like this. For a while I thought I wasn't going to make it here myself—."

"I was afraid you wouldn't come—John left early, and there was the stable—."

But the storm had unnerved her, and suddenly at the assurance of his touch and voice the fear that had been gripping her gave way to an hysteria of relief. Scarcely aware of herself she seized his arm and sobbed against it. He remained still a moment, unyielding, then slipped his other arm around her shoulder. It was comforting and she relaxed against it, hushed by a sudden sense of lull and safety. Her shoulders trembled with the easing of the strain, then fell limp and still. "You're shivering,"—he drew her gently towards the stove. "There's nothing to be afraid of now, though. I'm going to do the chores for you."

It was a quiet, sympathetic voice, yet with an undertone of insolence, a kind of mockery even, that made her draw away quickly and busy herself putting in a fire. With his lips drawn in a little smile he watched her till she looked at him again. The smile too was insolent, but at the same time companionable; Steven's smile, and therefore difficult to reprove. It lit up his lean, still-boyish face with a peculiar kind of arrogance: features and smile that were different from John's, from other men's—wilful and derisive, yet naively so—as if it were less the difference itself he was conscious of, than the long-accustomed privilege that thereby fell his due. He was erect, tall, square-shouldered. His hair was dark and trim, his young lips curved soft and full. While John, she made the comparison swiftly, was thick-set, heavy-jowled, and stooped. He always stood before her helpless, a kind of humility and wonderment in his attitude. And Steven now smiled on her appraisingly with the worldly-wise assurance of one for whom a woman holds neither mystery nor illusion.

"It was good of you to come, Steven," she responded, suddenly. "Such a storm to face—I suppose I can feel flattered."

For his presumption, his misunderstanding of what had been only a momentary weakness, instead of angering quickened her, roused from latency and long disuse all the instincts and resources of her femininity. She felt eager, challenged. Something was at hand that hitherto had always eluded her, even in the early days with John, something vital, beckoning, meaningful. She didn't understand, but she knew. The texture of the moment was satisfyingly dreamlike: an incredibility perceived as such, yet acquiesced in. She was John's wife—she knew—but also she knew that Steven standing here was different from John. There was no thought or motive, no understanding of herself as the knowledge persisted. Wary and poised round a sudden little core of blind excitement she evaded him, "But it's nearly dark—hadn't you better hurry if you're going to do the chores? Don't trouble—I can get them off myself—."

An hour later when he returned from the stable she was in another dress, hair rearranged, a little flush of colour in her face. Pouring warm water for him from the kettle into the basin she said evenly, "By the time you're washed supper will be ready. John said we weren't to wait for him."

He looked at her a moment, "But in a storm like this you're not expecting John?"

"Of course." As she spoke she could feel the colour deepening in her face. "We're going to play cards. He was the one that suggested it."

He went on washing, and then as they took their places at the table, resumed, "So John's coming. When are you expecting him?"

"He said it might be seven o'clock—or a little later." Conversation with Steven at other times had always been brisk and natural, but now suddenly she found it strained. "He may have work to do for his father. That's what he said when he left. Why do you ask, Steven?"

"I was just wondering—it's a rough night."

"He always comes. There couldn't be a storm bad enough. It's easier to do the chores in daylight, and I knew he'd be tired—that's why I started out for the stable."

She glanced up again and he was smiling at her. The same insolence, the same little twist of mockery and appraisal. It made her flinch suddenly, and ask herself why she was pretending to expect John—why there should be this instinct of defence to force her. This time, instead of poise and excitement, it brought a reminder that she had changed her dress and rearranged her hair. It crushed in a sudden silence, through which she heard the whistling wind again, and the creaking saw of the eaves. Neither spoke now. There was something strange, almost terrifying, about this Steven and his quiet, unrelenting smile; but strangest of all was the familiarity: the Steven she had never seen or encountered, and yet had always known, always expected, always waited for. It was less Steven himself that she felt than his inevitability. Just as she had felt the snow, the silence and the storm. She kept her eyes lowered, on the window past his shoulder, on the stove, but his smile now seemed to exist apart from him, to merge and hover with the silence. She clinked a cup—listened to the whistle of the storm—always it was there. He began to speak, but her mind missed the meaning of his words. Swiftly she was making comparisons again: his face so different to John's, so handsome and young and clean-shaven. Swiftly, helplessly, feeling the imperceptible and relentless ascendancy that thereby he was gaining over her, sensing sudden menace in this new, more vital life, even as she felt drawn towards it irresistibly.

The lamp between them flickered as an onslaught of the storm sent shudderings through the room. She rose to build up the fire again and he followed her. For a long time they stood close to the stove, their arms almost touching. Once as the blizzard creaked the house she spun around sharply, fancying it was John at the door; but quietly he intercepted her. "Not to-night—you might as well make up your mind to it. Across the hills in a storm like this—it would be suicide to try."

Her lips trembled suddenly in an effort to answer, to parry the certainty in his voice, then set thin and bloodless. She was afraid now. Afraid of his face so different from John's—of his smile, of her own helplessness to rebuke it. Afraid of the storm, isolating her here alone with him in its impenetrable fastness. They tried to play cards, but she kept starting up at every creak and shiver of the walls. "It's too rough a night," he repeated. "Even for John. Just relax a few minutes—stop worrying and pay a little attention to me."

But in his tone there was a contradiction to his words. For it implied that she was not worrying—that her only concern was lest it really might be John at the door.

And the implication persisted. He filled up the stove for her, shuffled the cards—won—shuffled—still it was there. She tried to respond to his conversation, to think of the game, but helplessly into her cards instead she began to ask, Was he right? Was that why he smiled? why he seemed to wait, expectant and assured?

The clock ticked, the fire crackled. Always it was there. Furtively for a moment she watched him as he deliberated over his hand. John, even in the days before they were married, had never looked like that. Only this morning she had asked him to shave. Because Steven was coming—because she had been afraid to see them side by side—because deep within herself she had known even then. The same knowledge, furtive and forbidden, that was flaunted now in Steven's smile. "You look cold," he said at last, dropping his cards and rising from the table. "We're not playing, anyway. Come over to the stove for a few minutes and get warm."

"But first I think we'll hang blankets over the door. When there's a blizzard like this we always do." It seemed that in sane, commonplace activity there might be release, a moment or two in which to recover herself. "John has nails in to put them on. They keep out a little of the draft."

He climbed upon a chair for her, and hung the blankets that she carried from the bedroom. Then for a moment they stood silent, watching the blankets sway and tremble before the blade of wind that spurted around the jamb. "I forgot," she said at last, "that I painted the bedroom door. At the top there, see—I've smeared the blankets coming through."

He glanced at her curiously, and went back to the stove. She followed him, trying to imagine the hills in such a storm, wondering whether John would come. "A man couldn't live in it," suddenly he answered her thoughts, lowering the oven door and drawing up their chairs one on each side of it. "He knows you're safe. It isn't likely that he'd leave his father, anyway."

"The wind will be in his back," she persisted. "The winter before we were married—all the blizzards that we had that year—and he never missed—."

"Blizzards like this one? Up in the hills he wouldn't be able to keep his direction for a hundred yards. Listen to it a minute and ask yourself."

His voice seemed softer, kindlier now. She met his smile a moment, its assured little twist of appraisal, then for a long time sat silent, tense, careful again to avoid his eyes.

Everything now seemed to depend on this. It was the same as a few hours ago when she braced the door against the storm. He was watching her, smiling. She dared not move, unclench her hands, or raise her eyes. The flames crackled, the clock ticked. The storm wrenched the walls as if to make them buckle in. So rigid and desperate were all her muscles set, withstanding, that the room around her seemed to swim and reel. So rigid and strained that for relief at last, despite herself, she raised her head and met his eyes again.

Intending that it should be for only an instant, just to breathe again, to ease the tension that had grown unbearable—but in his smile now, instead of the insolent appraisal that she feared, there seemed a kind of warmth and sympathy. An understanding that quickened and encouraged her—that made her wonder why but a moment ago she had been afraid. It was as if the storm had lulled, as if suddenly she were transported to shelter and incredible calm.

Or perhaps, the thought seized her, perhaps instead of his smile it was she that had changed. She who, in the long, wind-creaked silence, had emerged from the increment of codes and loyalties to her real, unfettered self. She who now felt suddenly his air of appraisal as but an understanding of the unfulfilled woman that until this moment had lain within her brooding and unadmitted, reproved out of consciousness by the insistence of an outgrown and routine fidelity.

For there had always been Steven. She understood now. Seven years— almost as long as John—ever since the night they first danced together.

The lamp was burning dry, and through the dimming light, isolated in the fastness of silence and storm, they watched each other. Her face was white and struggling still. His was handsome, clean-shaven, young. Her eyes were fanatic, believing desperately, fixed upon him as if to exclude all else, as if to find justifi-cation. His were cool, bland, drooped a little with expectancy. The light kept dimming, gathering the shadows round them, hushed, conspiratorial. He was smiling still. Her hands again were clenched up white and hard.

"But he always came," she persisted. "The wildest, coldest nights—even such a night as this. There was never a storm—"

"Never a storm like this one." There was a quietness in his smile now, a kind of simplicity almost, as if to reassure her.

"You were out in it yourself for a few minutes. He would have five miles, across the hills . . . I'd think twice myself, on such a night, before risking even one."

Long after he was asleep she lay listening to the storm. As a check on the draft up the chimney they had left one of the stovelids partly off, and through the open bed-room door she could see the flickerings of flame and shadow on the kitchen wall. They leaped and sank fantastically. The longer she watched the more alive they seemed to be. There was one great shadow that struggled towards her threaten-ingly, massive and black and engulfing all the room. Again and again it advanced, about to spring, but each time a little whip of light subdued it to its place among the others on the wall. Yet though it never reached her still she cowered, feeling that gathered there was all the frozen wilderness, its heart of terror and invincibility.

Then she dozed a while, and the shadow was John. Interminably he advanced. The whips of light still flicked and coiled, but now suddenly they were the swift little snakes that this afternoon she had watched twist and shiver across the snow. And they too were advancing. They writhed and vanished and came again. She lay still, paralyzed. He was over her now, so close that she could have touched him. Already it seemed that a deadly, tightening hand was on her throat. She tried to scream but her lips were locked. Steven beside her slept on heedlessly.

Until suddenly as she lay staring up at him a gleam of light revealed his face. And in it was not a trace of threat or anger—only calm, and stonelike hopelessness.

That was like John. He began to withdraw, and frantically she tried to call him back. "It isn't true—not really true—listen, John—" but the words clung frozen to her lips. Already there was only the shriek of wind again, the sawing eaves, the leap and twist of shadow on the wall.

She sat up, startled now and awake. And so real had he seemed there, standing close to her, so vivid the sudden age and sorrow in his face, that at first she could not make herself understand she had been only dreaming. Against the conviction of his presence in the room it was necessary to insist over and over that he must still be with his father on the other side of the hills. Watching the shadows she had fallen asleep. It was only her mind, her imagination, distorted to a nightmare by the illogical and unadmitted dread of his return. But he wouldn't come. Steven was right. In such a storm he would never try. They were safe, alone. No one would ever know. It was only fear, morbid and irrational; only the sense of guilt that even her new-found and challenged womanhood could not entirely quell.

She knew now. She had not let herself understand or acknowledge it as guilt before, but gradually through the wind-torn silence of the night his face compelled her. The face that had watched her from the darkness with its stonelike sorrow—the face that was really John—John more than his features of mere flesh and bone could ever be.

She wept silently. The fitful gleam of light began to sink. On the ceiling and wall at last there was only a faint dull flickering glow. The little house shuddered and quailed, and a chill crept in again. Without wakening Steven she slipped out to build up the fire. It was burned to a few spent embers now, and the wood she put on seemed a long time catching light. The wind swirled through the blankets they had hung around the door, and struck her flesh like laps of molten ice. Then hollow and moaning it roared up the chimney again, as if against its will drawn back to serve still longer with the onrush of the storm.

For a long time she crouched over the stove, listening. Earlier in the evening, with the lamp lit and the fire crackling, the house had seemed a stand against the encroaching wilderness, against its frozen, blizzard-breathed implacability, a refuge of feeble walls wherein persisted the elements of human meaning and survival. Now, in the cold, creaking darkness, it was strangely extinct, looted by the storm and abandoned again. She lifted the stove lid and fanned the embers till at last a swift little tongue of flame began to lick around the wood. Then she replaced the lid, extended her hands, and as if frozen in that attitude stood waiting.

It was not long now. After a few minutes she closed the drafts, and as the flames whirled back upon each other, beating against the top of the stove and sending out flickers of light again, a warmth surged up to relax her stiffened limbs. But shivering and numb it had been easier. The bodily well-being that the warmth induced gave play again to an ever more insistent mental suffering. She remembered the shadow that was John. She saw him bent towards her, then retreating, his features pale and overcast with unaccusing grief. She re-lived their seven years together and, in retrospect, found them to be years of worth and dignity. Until crushed by it all at last, seized by a sudden need to suffer and atone, she crossed to where the draft was bitter, and for a long time stood unflinching on the icy floor.

The storm was close here. Even through the blankets she could feel a sift of snow against her face. The eaves sawed, the walls creaked. Above it all, like a wolf in howling flight, the wind shrilled lone and desolate.

And yet, suddenly she asked herself, hadn't there been other storms, other blizzards? And through the worst of them hadn't he always reached her?

Clutched by the thought she stood rooted a minute. It was hard now to understand how she could have so deceived herself—how a moment of passion could have quieted within her not only conscience, but reason and discretion too. John always came. There could never be a storm to stop him. He was strong, inured to the cold. He had crossed the hills since his boyhood, knew every creek-bed and gully. It was madness to go on like this—to wait. While there was still time she must waken Steven, and hurry him away.

But in the bedroom again, standing at Steven's side, she hesitated. In his detachment from it all, in his quiet, even breathing, there was such sanity, such realism. For him nothing had happened; nothing would. If she wakened him he would only laugh and tell her to listen to the storm. Already it was long past mid-night; either John had lost his way or not set out at all. And she knew that in his devotion there was nothing foolhardy. He would never risk a storm beyond his endurance, never permit himself a sacrifice likely to endanger her lot or future. They were both safe. No one would ever know. She must control herself—be sane like Steven.

For comfort she let her hand rest a while on Steven's shoulder. It would be easier were he awake now, with her, sharing her guilt; but gradually as she watched his handsome face in the glimmering light she came to understand that for him no guilt existed. Just as there had been no passion, no conflict. Nothing but the sane appraisal of their situation, nothing but the expectant little smile, and the arrogance of features that were different from John's. She winced deeply, remembering how she had fixed her eyes on those features, how she had tried to believe that so handsome and young, so different from John's, they must in themselves be her justification.

In the flickering light they were still young, still handsome. No longer her justification—she knew now—John was the man—but wistfully still, wondering sharply at their power and tyranny, she touched them a moment with her fingertips again.

She could not blame him. There had been no passion, no guilt; therefore there could be no responsibility. Suddenly looking down at him as he slept, half-smiling still, his lips relaxed in the conscienceless complacency of his achievement, she understood that thus he was revealed in his entirety—all there ever was or ever could be. John was the man. With him lay all the future. For to-night, slowly and contritely through the days and years to come, she would try to make amends.

Then she stole back to the kitchen, and without thought, impelled by overwhelming need again, returned to the door where the draft was bitter still. Gradually towards morning the storm began to spend itself. Its terror blast became a feeble, worn-out moan. The leap of light and shadow sank, and a chill crept in again. Always the eaves creaked, tortured with wordless prophecy. Heedless of it all the clock ticked on in idiot content.

They found him the next day, less than a mile from home. Drifting with the storm he had run against his own pasture fence, and overcome had frozen there, erect still, both hands clasping fast the wire.

"He was south of here," they said wonderingly when she told them how he had come across the hills. "Straight south—you'd wonder how he could have missed the buildings. It was the wind last night, coming every way at once. He shouldn't have tried. There was a double wheel around the moon."

She looked past them a moment, then as if to herself said simply, "If you knew him, though—John would try."

It was later, when they had left her a while to be alone with him, that she knelt and touched his hand. Her eyes dimmed, still it was such a strong and patient hand; then, transfixed, they suddenly grew wide and clear. On the palm, white even against its frozen whiteness, was a little smear of paint.

[1939, 1968]

A.M. KLEIN ■ (1909–1972)

A.M. Klein was the first internationally recognized Jewish poet in Canada. In 1909 Abraham Moses Klein was born to Kalman and Yetta Klein, orthodox Jews from Ratno, Ukraine. He was raised in Montreal where he acquired, in addition to knowledge from a secular education, an understanding of Hebrew, Yiddish, the Torah, and the Talmud. When he attended McGill University, he majored in classics, political science, and economics (studying with Stephen Leacock). At McGill, Klein became associated with the "Montreal Group" of poets (A.J.M. Smith,

F.R. Scott, Leo Kennedy, and Leon Edel) although he was younger than they. Before he turned 20 he published his first poems in the New York *Menorah Journal,* the *Canadian Forum,* Chicago's *Poetry* magazine, the *Canadian Mercury,* and elsewhere. He edited *The Judean,* the monthly magazine of Canadian Young Judaea, from 1928 to 1932. Further, he and his friend David Lewis (future leader of the New Democratic Party) founded a campus magazine called *McGilliad* in 1930. During this time he also tutored the young Irving Layton in high school Latin.

After graduating from McGill and then studying law at the Université de Montréal (1933), Klein opened a law practice that he maintained until the late 1950s. As the editor of the *Canadian Zionist* in 1936, Klein's commitment to Zionism is clear. He also had a long-standing relationship with the *Canadian Jewish Chronicle,* first as a contributor in the 1920s and then, from 1938 to 1955, as its editor and principal columnist, writing weekly columns on Jewish life, culture, and politics. At this time he was also a speech writer and public relations consultant for Samuel Bronfman, the noted distiller, philanthropist, and president of the Canadian Jewish Congress. Throughout his career, Klein's Jewish heritage remained paramount in his work. As Klein himself stated, "[W]ithout a knowledge of our traditions, without a grasp of the chain of intellectual being which extends back though generations, our Judaism is but an accident of birth, a genealogical distinction, and not a positive heritage."

Included in Smith and Scott's *New Provinces: Poems of Several Authors* (1936) as one of the new modernist poets of Canada, Klein was well respected by other young poets. In 1940 he published his first collection of

poetry, *Hath Not a Jew . . .* (1940) (the title refers to Shylock's soliloquy in *The Merchant of Venice),* to quiet critical acclaim. During the 1940s he associated with the *Preview* group of poets—Scott, Patrick Anderson, P.K. Page, and others—and with the *First Statement* group, in particular Irving Layton. (See Klein's comments in the minutes of the *Preview* meeting included in the F.R. Scott section.) In 1948 he published his Governor General's Award-winning collection *The Rocking Chair and Other Poems.* It was at this time that he showed his disdain for the parochialism of the kind of nationalism that was being promoted by other writers. In reply to a questionnaire about writing in Canada by poet Raymond Souster, Klein notes influences on his writing coming from the "single entity" of "all English writing—Australian, South African, Canadian, and American." He also argues that the "writer who is concerned with his writing, and not his passport, neither stresses nor ignores" Canadian backgrounds in his work because "paysage is important only insofar as it affects the man upon it."

Unable to enlist in the Second World War because of poor eyesight, Klein contributed to the war effort through his articles for the *Canadian Jewish Chronicle* and through his poetry. "A Modest Proposal" is modelled directly on Jonathan Swift's satire of the same title, which proposes solving the problems of poverty in Ireland by using the babies of the poor for food and leather. In the midst of the war, Klein also published a savage satire of Hitler and his followers, *The Hitleriad* (1944). Klein also fought anti-Semitism closer to home in Quebec. When a newly built synagogue was set on fire and no one was arrested, Klein scathingly wrote, "The dubious honor—burning synagogues—which hitherto characterized only Nazi cities, is now shared by the capital of our province."

Although he was nominated as a candidate for the CCF (Co-operative Commonwealth Federation, a precursor of today's New Democratic Party) for the 1944 election, he withdrew before the election. However, in the 1949 federal election Klein ran, and lost, as a CCF candidate in the largely Jewish Montreal-Cartier riding.

In recognition of his growing significance as a poet, Klein was hired to teach English at McGill from 1945 to 1948. He was widely recognized as a dynamic young poet but he also wrote fiction. His only published novel, *The Second Scroll,* modelled on the structure of the Torah, was released in 1951. In it he engages with the aftermath of the Holocaust in Europe. Some consider this book his greatest literary achievement, although others reserve this honour for his poetry. The most public honour of his literary career came in 1957, with the award of the Lorne Pierce Gold Medal by the Royal Society of Canada. It serves as testimony to his sustained and distinguished contribution to Canadian writing over a period of years.

During the 1950s, following a lecture tour of Canada and the United States on the subject of Israel, Klein turned away from writing, from practising law, and from public life. It is said that for the final 18 years of his life A.M. Klein was silent. His silence was, according to biographer Naïm Kattan, "total and permanent." What is generally agreed to have been a state of depression is read by Kattan metaphorically when he proposes that "for the poet who had taken part in human struggles, human joys, and human suffering, silence is probably the ultimate act of self-expression." In "Portrait of the Poet as Landscape," Klein writes of the neglected artist in an indifferent society who must come to terms with his own art and voice. Such a figure haunts much of Klein's work, as it must have haunted the poet himself.

In his use of language Klein is a poet's poet. Poet and anthologist Gary Geddes considers how Klein's "tools included French, English, Yiddish, Latin, and Hebrew and a love of language that expressed itself in infectious wit, outrageous word-play, and a propensity for exotic vocabularies and frequent allusions to religious and literary classics." A lover of James Joyce's *Ulysses* and the poetry of Gerard Manley Hopkins, Klein clearly enjoyed the challenge of language. And yet he was also political—actively invested in documenting life for Jewish Canadians and, as in the poetry of Scott, engaging in the large social and political issues of the day in Quebec. "Indian Reservation: Caughnawaga," for instance, shows Klein to be an astute commentator on the injustices of the province and its political actors: here he considers the death of dignity in a Mohawk community near Montreal.

In her study of Klein, poet Miriam Waddington follows his work through three literary and cultural traditions: Jewish, English, and Canadian. She also notes that after studying Klein and "examining the important critical writing on English Canadian literature, I came to the conclusion that no single homogeneous Canadian literary tradition exists." In this way Waddington helps delineate the complexity of Klein's poetry as central to the growing diversity of the field of Canadian literature in the postwar period.

Heirloom

My father bequeathed me no wide estates;
No keys and ledgers were my heritage;
Only some holy books with *yahrzeit*[1] dates
Writ mournfully upon a blank front page—

Books of the Baal Shem Tov,[2] and of his wonders;
Pamphlets anent the devil and his crew;
Prayers against road demons, witches, thunders;
And sundry other tomes for a good Jew.

Beautiful: though no pictures on them,[3] save
The Scorpion crawling on a printed track;   10
The Virgin floating on a scriptural wave,
Square letters twinkling in the Zodiac.

The snuff left on this page, now brown and old,
The tallow stains of midnight liturgy—
These are my coat of arms, and these unfold
My noble lineage, my proud ancestry!

And my tears, too, have stained this heirloomed ground,
When reading in these treatises some weird
Miracle, I turned a leaf and found
A white hair fallen from my father's beard.   20

[1940]

The Still Small Voice[4]

The candles splutter; and the kettle hums;
The heirloomed clock enumerates the tribes;
Upon the wine-stained table-cloth lie crumbs

---

[1] In a 21 January 1943 letter to A.J.M. Smith, reprinted as Smith's contribution to *The A.M. Klein Symposium* (1975), Klein composed notes on this and other poems. Klein's note for *yahrzeit*: "Literally anniversary. It is customary to inscribe the date of passing of an ancestor on the flyleaf of some sacred book. Special prayers are said on that anniversary date."

[2] Yisroel Ben Eliezer (1698–1760), known as the Baal Shem Tov. Klein's note: "Literally, the Master of the Good Name—a saintly rabbi of the eighteenth century, founder of the movement known as Chassidism; he placed good works above scholarship. He was a simple good man, a St. Francis of Assisi, without birds or flowers."

[3] Klein's note: "Hebrew prayer books are never illustrated. The only drawings that appear in the liturgy are the signs of the Zodiac illustrating the prayers for rain and fertility."

[4] One in the section of poems entitled "Haggadah" in *Hath Not a Jew* ... (1940).

Of matzoh[5] whose wide scattering describes
Jews driven in far lands upon this earth.
The kettle hums; the candles splutter; and
Winds whispering from shutters tell re-birth
Of beauty rising in an eastern land,
Of paschal sheep driven in cloudy droves;
Of almond-blossoms colouring the breeze;   10
Of vineyards upon verdant terraces;
Of golden globes in orient orange-groves.
And those assembled at the table dream
Of small schemes that an April wind doth scheme,
And cry from out the sleep assailing them:
Jerusalem, next year! Next year, Jerusalem!

[1940]

Portrait of the Poet as Landscape

I

Not an editorial writer, bereaved with bartlett,[6]
mourns him, the shelved Lycidas.[7]
No actress squeezes a glycerine tear for him.
The radio broadcast lets his passing pass.
And with the police, no record. Nobody, it appears,
either under his real name or his alias,
missed him enough to report.

It is possible that he is dead, and not discovered.
It is possible that he can be found some place
in a narrow closet, like the corpse in a detective story,   10
standing, his eyes staring, and ready to fall on his face.
It is also possible that he is alive
and amnesiac, or mad, or in retired disgrace,
or beyond recognition lost in love.

We are sure only that from our real society
he has disappeared; he simply does not count,

---

[5] An unleavened flatbread, used especially during Passover, which commemorates the Exodus of the Jews from enslavement in Egypt. The poem makes reference to the scattering of the Tribes of Israel, which, it was predicted, would be reunited in the New Jerusalem.

[6] John Bartlett's *Familiar Quotations: A Collection of Passages, Phrases, and Proverbs Traced to Their Sources in Ancient and Modern Literature* (1855).

[7] Klein draws on the tradition of the pastoral elegy as a lament for a dead young poet, signalled here with reference to John Milton's (1608–1674) poem "Lycidas" (1638). Klein's poem concerns what Margaret Atwood calls the "modern poet's ignominious obscurity" in *Negotiating with the Dead*.

except in the pullulation[8] of vital statistics—
somebody's vote, perhaps, an anonymous taunt
of the Gallup poll, a dot in a government table—
but not felt, and certainly far from eminent—   20
in a shouting mob, somebody's sigh.

O, he who unrolled our culture from his scroll—
the prince's quote, the rostrum-rounding roar—
who under one name made articulate
heaven, and under another the seven-circled air,[9]
is, if he is at all, a number, an x,
a Mr. Smith in a hotel register,—
incognito, lost, lacunal.[10]

II

The truth is he's not dead, but only ignored—
like the mirroring lenses forgotten on a brow   30
that shine with the guilt of their unnoticed world.
The truth is he lives among neighbours, who, though
        they will allow
him a passable fellow, think him eccentric, not solid,
a type that one can forgive, and for that matter, forego.

Himself he has his moods, just like a poet.
Sometimes, depressed to nadir,[11] he will think all lost,
will see himself as throwback, relict, freak,
his mother's miscarriage, his great-grandfather's ghost,
and he will curse his quintuplet senses, and their tutors   40
in whom he put, as he should not have put, his trust.

Then he will remember his travels over that body—
the torso verb, the beautiful face of the noun,
and all those shaped and warm auxiliaries!
A first love it was, the recognition of his own.
Dear limbs adverbial, complexion of adjective,
dimple and dip of conjugation!

And then remember how this made a change in him
affecting for always the glow and growth of his being;

---

[8] Sprouting, budding, germinating, or producing.
[9] In the pre-Copernican universe, there were seven spheres surrounding the earth.
[10] Of a blank or missing portion, of a gap or empty space.
[11] The lowest or worst point (of something).

how suddenly was aware of the air, like shaken tinfoil,   50
of the patents of nature, the shock of belated seeing,
the lonelinesses peering from the eyes of crowds;
the integers of thought; the cube-roots of feeling.

Thus, zoomed to zenith, sometimes he hopes again,
and sees himself as a character, with a rehearsed role:
the Count of Monte Cristo,[12] come for his revenges;
the unsuspected heir, with papers; the risen soul;
or the chloroformed prince awaking from his flowers;
or—deflated again—the convict on parole.

III

He is alone; yet not completely alone.   60
Pins on a map of a colour similar to his,
each city has one, sometimes more than one;
here, caretakers of art, in colleges;
in offices, there, with arm-bands, and green-shaded;
and there, pounding their catalogued beats in libraries,—

everywhere menial, a shadow's shadow.
And always for their egos—their outmoded art.
Thus, having lost the bevel in the ear,
they know neither up nor down, mistake the part
for the whole, curl themselves in a comma,   70
talk technics, make a colon their eyes. They distort—

such is the pain of their frustration—truth
to something convolute and cerebral.
How they do fear the slap of the flat of the platitude!
Now Pavlov's[13] victims, their mouths water at bell,
the platter empty.
                    See they set twenty-one jewels
into their watches; the time they do not tell!

Some, patagonian[14] in their own esteem,
and longing for the multiplying word,   80

---

[12] *The Count of Monte Cristo* (1845–46), an adventure novel by Alexandre Dumas *père* (1802–1870), telling the story of a young sailor accused of treason and imprisoned on his wedding day who escapes and plots his revenge.

[13] A reference to the famous psychology experiment by Ivan Pavlov (1849–1936) where dogs were conditioned to salivate at the sound of a bell, in anticipation of being fed, as an example of "classical conditioning."

[14] Gigantic, huge, immense.

join party and wear pins, now have a message,
an ear, and the convention-hall's regard.
Upon the knees of ventriloquists, they own,
of their dandled brightness, only the paint and board.

And some go mystical, and some go mad.
One stares at a mirror all day long, as if
to recognize himself; another courts
angels,—for here he does not fear rebuff;
and a third, alone, and sick with sex, and rapt,
doodles him symbols convex and concave.   90

O schizoid solitudes! O purities
curdling upon themselves! Who live for themselves,
or for each other, but for nobody else;
desire affection, private and public loves;
are friendly, and then quarrel and surmise
the secret perversions of each other's lives.

IV

He suspects that something has happened, a law
been passed, a nightmare ordered. Set apart,
he finds himself, with special haircut and dress,
as on a reservation. Introvert.   100
He does not understand this; sad conjecture
muscles and palls thrombotic[15] on his heart.

He thinks an impostor, having studied his personal
    biography,
his gestures, his moods, now has come forward to pose
in the shivering vacuums his absence leaves.
Wigged with his laurel, that other, and faked with his face,
he pats the heads of his children, pecks his wife,
and is at home, and slippered, in his house.

So he guesses at the impertinent silhouette   110
that talks to his phone-piece and slits open his mail.
Is it the local tycoon who for a hobby
plays poet, he so epical in steel?
The orator, making a pause? Or is that man
he who blows his flash of brass in the jittering hall?

[15] Coagulating or curdling of the blood.

Or is he cuckolded by the troubadour
rich and successful out of celluloid?
Or by the don who unrhymes atoms? Or
the chemist death built up? Pride, lost impostor'd pride,
it is another, another, whoever he is,   120
who rides where he should ride.

V

Fame, the adrenalin: to be talked about;
to be a verb; to be introduced as *The:*
to smile with endorsement from slick paper; make
caprices anecdotal; to nod to the world; to see
one's name like a song upon the marquees played;
to be forgotten with embarrassment: to be—
to be.

It has its attractions, but is not the thing;
nor is it the ape mimesis who speaks from the tree   130
ancestral; nor the merkin joy . . .[16]
Rather it is stark infelicity
which stirs him from his sleep, undressed, asleep
to walk upon roofs and window-sills and defy
the gape of gravity.

VI

Therefore he seeds illusions. Look, he is
the nth Adam taking a green inventory
in world but scarcely uttered, naming, praising,
the flowering fiats in the meadow, the
syllabled fur, stars aspirate, the pollen   140
whose sweet collision sounds eternally.
For to praise

the world—he, solitary man—is breath
to him. Until it has been praised, that part
has not been. Item by exciting item—
air to his lungs, and pressured blood to his heart.—
they are pulsated, and breathed, until they map,
not the world's, but his own body's chart!

---

[16] A merkin is a type of wig used to cover the pubic area, in some cases to disguise the private parts (as when, in performances during Shakespeare's time, men played the roles of women). Here the meaning would be a "false joy." *Mimesis* is a Greek word meaning *imitation*, often used in literary critical discourse to refer to realism.

And now in imagination he has climbed
another planet, the better to look   150
with single camera view upon this earth—
its total scope, and each afflated[17] tick,
its talk, its trick, its tracklessness—and this,
this he would like to write down in a book!

To find a new function for the declassé craft
archaic like the fletcher's;[18] to make a new thing;
to say the word that will become sixth sense;
perhaps by necessity and indirection bring
new forms to life, anonymously, new creeds—
O, somehow pay back the daily larcenies of the lung!   160

These are not mean ambitions. It is already something
merely to entertain them. Meanwhile, he
makes of his status as zero a rich garland,
a halo of his anonymity,
and lives alone, and in his secret shines
like phosphorus. At the bottom of the sea.

                                                              [1948]

Indian Reservation: Caughnawaga[19]

Where are the braves, the faces like autumn fruit,
who stared at the child from the coloured frontispiece?
And the monosyllabic chief who spoke with his throat?
Where are the tribes, the feathered bestiaries?—
Rank Aesop's[20] animals erect and red,
with fur on their names to make all live things kin'—
Chief Running Deer, Black Bear, Old Buffalo Head?

Childhood, that wished me Indian, hoped that
one afterschool I'd leave the classroom chalk,

---

[17] Breathed upon; inspired.

[18] Maker of bows and arrows.

[19] Caughnawaga, or the Kahnawake (Kahnawákeró:non) Mohawk Territory, is on the south shore of the St. Lawrence River across from Montreal. In this poem, Klein questions the construction of what critic Daniel Francis has called the "Imaginary Indian" (1992), or the romanticized portrait of the brave, noble "Indian" derived from literature. Remembering the romantic stereotypes of his youth, the speaker laments the commodification of "Indian" culture in the present. See also the Grey Owl and Armand Garnet Ruffo selections in this book.

[20] Aesop's Fables is a collection of stories using anthropomorphized animals. The fables include "The Fox and the Grapes," "The Hare and the Tortoise," and "The Town Mouse and the Country Mouse."

the varnish smell, the watered dust of the street,   10
to join the clean outdoors and the Iroquois track.
Childhood; but always,—as on a calendar,—
there stood that chief, with arms akimbo, waiting
the runaway mascot paddling to his shore.

With what strange moccasin stealth that scene is
          changed!
With French names, without paint, in overalls,
their bronze, like their nobility expunged,—
the men. Beneath their alimentary shawls
sit like black tents their squaws; while for the tourist's   20
brown pennies scattered at the old church door,
the ragged papooses jump, and bite the dust.

Their past is sold in a shop: the beaded shoes,
the sweetgrass basket, the curio Indian,
burnt wood and gaudy cloth and inch-canoes—
trophies and scalpings for a traveller's den.
Sometimes, it's true, they dance, but for a bribe;
after a deal don the bedraggled feather
and welcome a white mayor to the tribe.

This is a grassy ghetto, and no home.   30
And these are fauna in a museum kept.
The better hunters have prevailed. The game,
losing its blood, now makes these grounds its crypt.
The animals pale, the shine of the fur is lost,
bleached are their living bones. About them watch
as through a mist, the pious prosperous ghosts.

[1948]

A Modest Proposal   14 July 1939

Many readers no doubt will recall that the great satirist Dean Swift,[21] in seeking
to heap ridicule upon his contemporaries, suggested by way of 'modest proposal'
a *reductio ad absurdum*[22] of the customs of his fellow-men then current. Having

---

[21] Dean of St. Patrick's, Dublin. Jonathan Swift (1667–1745) was an Irish satirist, author of *Gulliver's Travels* (1726) and the shocking pamphlet "A Modest Proposal: For Preventing the Children of Poor People in Ireland from Being a Burden to Their Parents or Country, and for Making Them Beneficial to the Public" (1729).

[22] Latin: reduction to the absurd.

neither the wit nor the Irish of the Dean, it does seem to us, nonetheless, that there is a crying need for such a 'modest proposal' anent the destiny of the Jewish homeland and the fate of Jewish refugees.

It appears that great numbers of the wanderers have willy-nilly taken to the high seas. The *St. Louis*[23] floats upon the Atlantic for two months, freighted with unhappy human cargo. Another ship leaves some Greek port, and arrives in Palestine only to see its passengers interned in a concentration camp. But a little while ago there came to the shores of Erez Israel a ship which Jews in Danzig had bought and manned, and directed to the Holy Land; when they arrived at the Port of Haifa they were towed out of the harbour and left floating along the sea-coast.

Here then is the opportunity for some grim humorist to win himself a place in immortality beside Dean Swift. Let him suggest a homeland for Jews upon the face of the waters!

If there was room for a 'Jewish Territorial Movement,' perhaps a Hebrew Oceanic Society can be organized!

Perhaps, too, the British Government, realizing the error of its ways, will revise the Balfour Declaration,[24] and issue a new one, a liquid one: 'His Majesty's Government views with favour the "floating" of a "National Jewish Homewater,"[25] anywhere upon the surface of those waves which Britannia rules, and will use its best endeavours to facilitate the achievement of this proposal, it being clearly understood that nothing will be done to injure the rights of non-Jews in the said waters.'

Upon the issuance of such a proclamation, shiploads of Jews would issue. They would always stay at anchor, a floating state joined, ship to ship, cruiser to cruiser, liner to liner, a floating state.

A couple of years thereafter, as this naval country would begin to prosper, the British Government would send forth a Royal Commission to investigate. The Commission would bring in a report that the Jewish Homewater was not properly docked, and that the Jewish ships were destroying the national independence of the neighboring fish. Tons of pamphlets would then be circulated about the

[23] The S.S. *St. Louis* was a German transatlantic ocean liner that left Hamburg, Germany, for Havana, Cuba, in May 1939 with almost 1000 passengers, mostly German-Jewish families seeking refuge from Nazi Germany. The passengers were denied entry into Cuba and the United States and the ship was forced to return to Europe.

[24] The Balfour Declaration (2 November 1917), a statement of policy by Arthur James Balfour, a representative of the British government, states that "His Majesty's Government view with favour the establishment in Palestine of a national home for the Jewish people, and will use their best endeavours to facilitate the achievement of this object, it being clearly understood that nothing shall be done which may prejudice the civil and religious rights of existing non-Jewish communities in Palestine or the rights and political status enjoyed by Jews in any other country."

[25] Klein's proposal, to create a "National Jewish Homewater," ridicules the shifting British position on the creation of a Jewish state. The Jewish Territorial Organization Klein refers to is a 1903 breakaway group from the Zionist Movement aimed at establishing autonomous Jewish settlements not limited to Israel. According to Usher Caplan and M.W. Steinberg (the editors of a collection of Klein's essays from the *Canadian Jewish Chronicle* entitled *Beyond Sambation* [1982]), Klein bases his satire on the phrase "Om Isroel" (the nation of Israel) as he turns it into "Yom Yisroel!" (the ocean of Israel). He adds "Chai" (lives) to "Yom Isroel" to play with the phrase "Om Isroel Chai," meaning "the nation of Israel lives."

problem of 'the landless fish.' The chairman of the aforementioned Commission would insist, with all the logic he could muster, that the phrase 'nothing will be done to injure the rights of non-Jews,' obviously referred to the local marine life, which apparently did not subscribe to the Mosaic creed.

Ship-building would continue, and the Homewater would expand. Another Commission would be then sent to examine the area of 'Yom Yisroel' and would look with disapproval upon the 'immigration waves.' Recommendations would be made that there should be a Partition of the waves, the learned Commissioner, indeed, would support his viewpoint by citing from the biography of Moses who performed a similar procedure on the Red Sea.

But the Homewater would still flourish. 'Yom Yisroel Chai!' would be the slogan of a national Jewry. Whereupon the Colonial Office, completely fed up with the manner in which these *chalutzim*[26] would be making a success even out of water, would begin to study the above-mentioned Declaration again. Finally, it would issue a White Paper, made out of rubber—the better to float with, my child. The gist of this White Paper would be that when the Government promised a Homewater on the surface of those waves which Britannia rules, it really meant a different thing entirely. Instead of 'on the surface,' read, 'at the bottom'; otherwise they stick by all their commitments.

[1939]

[26] Pioneers, early Zionists.

DOROTHY LIVESAY ■ (1909–1996)

Dorothy Livesay's career spans the development of modern poetry in Canada. Born into a literary household in Winnipeg in 1909, Livesay was, as critic Desmond Pacey argued in 1957, one of the most important poets of the generation that came to maturity between the wars. Her father, John Frederick Bligh Livesay, was the first general manager of the Canadian Press after the First World War, while her mother, Florence Randal Livesay, was a significant figure in the early twentieth-century Canadian literary scene who published prose, poetry, fiction, translations of Ukrainian literature, and journalism. In a 1978 interview, Livesay recalled how as a child she was surrounded by writing: her father bought her the works of Virginia Woolf,

Katherine Mansfield, and Dorothy Richardson (giving her Woolf's *A Room of One's Own* [1929] and saying "Go thou and do likewise"); and her mother subscribed to American modernist literary magazines of the time. These early influences had a clear effect on her own poetry.

Livesay received a B.A. from the University of Toronto (1927–31) and a Diplôme d'études supérieures from the Sorbonne in Paris (1931–32). She returned to Canada to study at the School of Social Work at the University of Toronto (1932–34), and over three decades later, she achieved her M.Ed. at the University of British Columbia (1966). Throughout her eclectic life—writing poetry and working as an editor and journalist, raising two children, doing social work, and teaching—Livesay was governed by a commitment to social justice and women's rights.

Livesay's dictum that "every decade we become a different person" is certainly evident in her poetry, although there is consistency across the decades as well. In the 1920s her clear, direct, and unsentimental poetry shows the influence of the imagist poets as well as an engagement with the other young Canadian modernists. In retrospect, Livesay remarks on her first two collections (*Green Pitcher* [1928] and *Signposts* [1932]) as "brief, imagistic and lyrical" but laments their lack of social engagement.

Throughout the 1930s Livesay was heavily influenced by Marxism and what she called "internationalism." In a 1978 interview she recalled that "the whole nationalist thing suddenly fell away completely in the Depression years because we believed that there had to be international revolution which would change every country and make it socialist." During this decade she turned to Communism as an answer to the social and economic injustice she saw around her. Both her experience of working with the poor as a social worker and her reading of such left-wing writers as C. Day Lewis, Stephen Spender, and W.H. Auden led her to turn from the imagism of her early work to write more committed social and political poetry. After practising social work in Montreal and New Jersey, she moved to Vancouver to become the western editor of the left-wing journal *New Frontier*. Livesay retrospectively documents her activism and journalistic work in the 1930s In *Right Hand Left Hand* (1977). Her essay "Proletarianitis in Canada," published in *New Frontier* in 1936, develops Livesay's criticism of the

absence of a social realist tradition in Canadian literature that gives voice to working-class experience. In the "Foreword" to *Documentaries* (1968), Livesay recalls that with the Depression and threats of war and dictatorship, she was "fired with the desire to set down in documentary form what was happening in my Canadian generation, histori-cally and socially." She continues, "I am 'ornery' and like authenticity in reportage. The plain language used, the traditional iambic metres and the ideol-ogy expressed were characteristics of that period in Canada."

With the 1940s came the Second World War and a focus on labour issues, anti-authoritarianism, and the concerns of contemporary women. In 1941, Livesay was a founding editor of *Contemporary Verse* in Vancouver (1941–52). Under the general editorship of Alan Crawley, the magazine was one of the first "little" magazines dedicated to the publication of poetry in Canada. The 1940s also brought national recognition for Livesay. She won the Governor General's Award for her documentary poem condemning the exploitation of workers in a factory, *Day and Night* (1944), and again for *Poems for People* (1947). This early recognition of her work culminated in her receiving the Royal Society of Canada's Lorne Pierce Medal in 1947 for distinguished contribution to Canadian literature.

A particularly poignant example of Livesay's documentary form came in *Call My People Home* (1950). Livesay wrote this poem in 1948 as, she says, "a tribute to the endurance and tolerance of the Japanese-Canadians who so roughly and so violently, in the year 1941, were uprooted from their fishing villages and fishing boats." Her hus-band, Duncan McNair, was an active member of a committee of Canadian citizens formed to protest the evacuation and fight the government's position on internment. Livesay combines findings from the committee with newspaper accounts of the day, archival documents, and the personal recollections of a formerly interned Japanese Canadian student who lived in Livesay's home as a foster child after the war. Like many of her other documentaries, *Call My People Home* was broadcast on CBC Radio before it was printed in textual form. Her long narrative poems are, according to Livesay, "a conscious attempt to create a dialectic between the objective facts and the subjective feelings of the poet."

In the 1950s and '60s, Livesay's poetry turned again to questions of personal identity, sexuality, and religion. After her husband died in 1959, Livesay travelled extensively and incorporated her travels into her poetry. In poetic response to her years (1959–63) teaching at a teachers' training college in Northern Rhodesia (which became the independent nation of Zambia in 1964), for instance, Livesay composed *The Colour of God's Face* (1964). The collection that many consider to be Livesay's finest came out near the end of the decade. In *The Unquiet Bed* (1967), she engages with sexuality and love as few before her had in Canadian literature. As poet and critic Frank Davey notes, "[A]mong her works are the most sensitive and powerful poems of feminine sexuality in our literature." The music behind the rhythm of Livesay's words is enhanced by the repetition of her central recurring symbols, which she lists in the introduction to her *Collected Poems* (1972) as "the seasons, day and night; sun, wind, and snow; the garden with its flowers and birds; the house, the door, the bed."

In the 1970s and '80s Livesay continued writing about relationships between the sexes, motherhood, children, female sexuality, and independence. During these decades, Livesay held a number of writer-in-residence positions across Canada. While at the University of Manitoba in 1975, she was central in the founding of *Contemporary Verse II* as a kind of reincarnation of Crawley's *Contemporary Verse*. She was also the magazine's first editor. In her first editorial for *CV II* (1975), Livesay composed what can be read as her poetic vision:

> The poetry we want to praise and to print must have the authority of experience and action from all levels of society: the deprived, the enslaved, the sheltered, the brainwashed; as well as the fat, sleek, jaded. It must spring from all ethnic (and immigrant) sources, whose roots will nourish us.

In spite of the shifts in emphasis, Livesay's poetry is consistent in advocating the responsibility of the writer to the community "to seek better things for humanity."

Throughout her career, Livesay was committed to exploring and promoting the social impact of poetry. Writing, she believed, was both a political act and an artistic one. A highly symbolic writer, she draws on both conventionally recognized symbols and contextual ones in order to engage with both public and private issues. Livesay was named an officer of the Order of Canada in 1987 and of the Order of British Columbia in 1992. She spent her final years on Galiano Island and in Victoria, B.C. A remarkable element of her legacy lies in the fact that the B.C. book prize for poetry is named the Dorothy Livesay Prize.

Fire and Reason

I cannot shut out the night—
Nor its sharp clarity.

The many blinds we draw,
You and I,
The many fires we light
Can never quite obliterate
The irony of stars,
The deliberate moon,
The last, unsolved finality
Of night.   10

                                                      [1928]

Day and Night

                        I

Dawn, red and angry, whistles loud and sends
A geysered shaft of steam searching the air.
Scream after scream announces that the churn
Of life must move, the giant arm command.
Men in a stream, a human moving belt
Move into sockets, every one a bolt.
The fun begins, a humming whirring drum—
Men do a dance in time to the machines.[1]

One step forward
Two steps back   10
Shove the lever,
Push it back

While Arnot whirls
A roundabout
And Geoghan shuffles
Bolts about

One step forward
Hear it crack

[1] In her "Commentary" on the poem, Livesay writes: "This documentary is dominated by themes of struggle: class against class, race against race. The sound of Negro spirituals mingled in my mind with Cole Porter's 'Night and Day.'"

Smashing rhythm—
Two steps back.

Your heart-beat pounds
Against your throat
The roaring voices
Drown your shout

Across the way
A writhing whack
Sets you spinning
Two steps back—

One step forward
Two steps back.

II

Day and night rising and falling
Night and day shift gears and slip rattling
Down the runway, shot into storerooms
Where only eyes and a notebook remember
The record of evil, the sum of commitments.
We move as through sleep's revolving memories
Piling up hatred, stealing the remnants
Doors forever folding before us—
And where is the recompense, on what agenda
Will you set love down? Who knows of peace?

Day and night
Night and day
Light rips into ribbons
What we say

I called to love
Deep in dream:
Be with me in the daylight
As in gloom.

Be with me in the pounding
In the knives against my back
Set your voice resounding
Above the steel's whip crack.

High and sweet
Sweet and high
Hold, hold up the sunlight
In the sky!

Day and night
Night and day
Tear up all the silence
Find the words I could not say. . .   60

III

We were stoking coal in the furnaces; red hot
They gleamed, burning our skins away, his and mine.
We were working together, night and day, and knew
Each other's stroke; and without words exchanged
An understanding about kids at home,
The landlord's jaw, wage-cuts and overtime.

We were like buddies, see? Until they said
That nigger is too smart the way he smiles
And sauces back the foreman; he might say
Too much one day, to others changing shifts.   70
Therefore they cut him down, who flowered at night
And raised me up, day hanging over night—
So furnaces could still consume our withered skin.

Shadrack, Mechak and Abednego[2]
Turn in the furnace, whirling slow.

> Lord, I'm burnin' in the fire
> Lord, I'm steppin' on the coal
> Lord, I'm blacker than my brother
> Blow your breath down here.

> Boss, I'm smothered in the darkness   80
> Boss, I'm shrivellin' in the flames
> Boss, I'm blacker than my brother
> Blow your breath down here.

Shadrack, Mechak and Abednego
Burn in the furnace, whirling slow.

[2] See Daniel 3, where Shadrach, Meshach, and Abednego refuse to worship a golden idol, are thrown into a furnace, but do not burn because of the strength of their faith. They emerge from the furnace unharmed.

IV

Up in the roller room, men swing steel
Swing it, zoom; and cut it, crash.
Up in the dark the welder's torch
Makes sparks fly like lightning's reel.

Now I remember storm on a field: 90
The trees bow tense before the blow
Even the jittering sparrow's talk
Ripples into the still tree shield.

We are in storm that has no cease
No lull before, no after time
When green with rain the grasses grow
And air is sweet with fresh increase.

We bear the burden home to bed
The furnace glows within our hearts:
Our bodies hammered through the night   100
Are welded into bitter bread.

Bitter, yes:
But listen, friend,
We are mightier
In the end

We have ears
Alert to seize
A weakness in
The foreman's ease.

We have eyes   110
To look across
The bosses' profit
At our loss.

Are you waiting?
Wait with us
Every evening
There's a hush

Use it not
For love's slow count:
Add up hate   120
And let it mount—

One step forward
Two steps back
Will soon be over:
Hear it crack!

The wheels may whirr
A roundabout
And neighbour's shuffle
Drown your shout

The wheel must limp   130
Till it hangs still
And crumpled men
Pour down the hill:

Day and night
Night and day—
Till life is turned
The other way!

[1944]

Bartok and the Geranium[3]

She lifts her green umbrellas
Towards the pane
Seeking her fill of sunlight
Or of rain;
Whatever falls
She has no commentary
Accepts, extends,
Blows out her furbelows,[4]
Her bustling boughs;

And all the while he whirls   10
Explodes in space,
Never content with this small room;
Not even can he be
Confined to sky
But must speed high
From galaxy to galaxy,

[3] In this poem, the voices are those of the stationary female geranium and the kinetic music of Béla Bartók (1881–1945), Hungarian composer and pianist. First published in *Contemporary Verse* 39.3 (1947), republished in a chapbook of 10 poems edited by Jay Macpherson, *New Poems* (1955), and revised before publication in Livesay's *Selected Poems* (1957). This version is from *Selected Poems*.

[4] Anything resembling a flounce.

Wrench from the stars their momentary calm,
Stir music on the moon.

She's daylight;
He is dark.   20
She's heaven's held breath;
He storms and crackles
Spits with hell's own spark.

Yet in this room, this moment now
These together breathe and be:
She, essence of serenity,
He in a mad intensity
Soars beyond sight
Then hurls, lost Lucifer,[5]
From heaven's height.   30
And when he's done, he's out:

She lays a lip against the glass
And preens herself in light.

[1955, rev. 1957]

The Three Emily's[6]

These women crying in my head
Walk alone, uncomforted:
The Emily's, these three
Cry to be set free—
And others whom I will not name
Each different, each the same.

Yet they had liberty!
Their kingdom was the sky:
They batted clouds with easy hand,
Found a mountain for their stand;   10
From wandering lonely they could catch
The inner magic of a heath—
A lake their palette, any tree
Their brush could be.

[5] Lucifer, meaning "light-bearer"; another name for Satan, who in John Milton's *Paradise Lost* (1667) rebels against God and is hurled from the height of heaven to take up residence in hell.

[6] Canadian painter Emily Carr (1871–1945), American poet Emily Dickinson (1830–1886), and English novelist Emily Brontë (1818–1848), author of *Wuthering Heights* (1847). First published in *Canadian Forum* (1953), this poem was not published in book form until *Collected Poems* (1972).

And still they cry to me
As in reproach—
I, born to hear their inner storm
Of separate man in woman's form,
I yet possess another kingdom, barred
To them, these three, this Emily.   20
I move as mother in a frame,
My arteries
Flow the immemorial way
Towards the child, the man;
And only for brief span
Am I an Emily on mountain snows
And one of these.

And so the whole that I possess
Is still much less —
They move triumphant through my head:
I am the one
Uncomforted.

[1953, 1972]

Lament

For J.F.B.L.[7]

What moved me, was the way your hand
Lay in my hand, not withering,
But warm, like a hand cooled in a stream
And purling still; or a bird caught in a snare
Wings folded stiff, eyes in a stare,
But still alive with the fear,
Heart hoarse with hope—
So your hand, your dead hand, my dear.

And the veins, still mounting as blue rivers,
Mounting towards the tentative finger-tips,   10
The delta where four seas come in—
Your fingers promontories into colourless air
Were rosy still—not chalk (like cliffs
You knew in boyhood, Isle of Wight):
But blushed with colour from the sun you sought

---

[7] J.F.B. Livesay, the poet's father, who died in 1944.

And muscular from garden toil;
Stained with the purple of an iris bloom,
Violas grown for a certain room;
Hands seeking faïence, filagree,[8]
Chinese lacquer and ivory—   20
Brussels lace; and a walnut piece
Carved by a hand now phosphorus.

What moved me, was the way your hand
Held life, although the pulse was gone.
The hand that carpentered a children's chair,
Carved out a stair
Held leash upon a dog in strain
Gripped wheel, swung sail,
Flicked horse's rein
And then again   30
Moved kings and queens meticulous on a board,
Slashed out the cards, cut bread, and poured
A purring cup of tea;

The hand so neat and nimble
Could make a tennis partner tremble,
Write a resounding round
Of sonorous verbs and nouns—
Hand that would not strike a child, and yet
Could ring a bell and send a man to doom.

And now unmoving in this Spartan room   40
The hand still speaks:
After the brain was fogged
And the tight lips tighter shut,
After the shy appraising eyes
Relinquished fire for the sea's green gaze—
The hand still breathes, fastens its hold on life;
Demands the whole, establishes the strife.

What moved me, was the way your hand
Lay cool in mine, not withering;
As bird still breathes, and stream runs clear—   50
So your hand; your dead hand, my dear.

[1957]

[8] Glazed earthenware and porcelain; delicate jewel work, usually of gold and silver.

The Unquiet Bed

The woman I am
is not what you see
I'm not just bones
and crockery

the woman I am
knew love and hate
hating the chains
that parents make

longing that love
might set men free   10
yet hold them fast
in loyalty

the woman I am
is not what you see
move over love
make room for me

[1967]

IRVING LAYTON ■ (1912–2006)

Irving Layton lived by his famous dictum: "They dance best who dance with desire." Layton is one of the most controversial and outspoken Canadian poets of the twentieth century. Loved, admired, and loathed, Layton is an important figure for the modernist period and for subsequent generations. He wrote with passion, contempt, humour, and severity. In the foreword to his Governor General's Award-winning collection of poems, *A Red Carpet for the Sun* (1959), Layton states: "[I]n a world where corruption is the norm and enslavement universal, all art celebrates [the free individual], prepares the way for his coming. Poetry, by giving dignity and utterance to our distress, enables us to hope, makes compassion reasonable." This philosophy of art is evident throughout Layton's poetry as he strives to be more than those he labels as "insufferable blabbermouth" poets who are "too patient, courteous, and civilized." Indeed, many of his 40 published volumes of poetry are prefaced by words to his critics and words to those he criticizes. However, even as he critiqued the pretensions of the Canadian literati, Layton was steeped in a classicist and humanist tradition. As W.J. Keith puts it, "Some of his most brilliant effects arose out of a supreme expression of crude subject matter that is no longer crude when he has transformed it by means of his art."

IRVING LAYTON

172

Layton was born Israel Lazarovitch in 1912 in Tirgu Neamt, Romania. He immigrated to Montreal with his family in his first year of life. The son of an "ineffectual dreamer and visionary," as Layton called his father Moishe, and a mother (Keine/Klara) of "indomitable strength and vigour," he grew up the youngest child in a large Jewish family in the St. Urbain Street neighbourhood of Montreal (later made famous by Mordecai Richler in his novel *St. Urbain's Horseman* [1971]). While still in high school, after meeting political activist David Lewis and poet A.M. Klein, Layton joined the Young People's Socialist League. Klein tutored Layton in Latin, teaching him to appreciate the music in the hexameters of Virgil. He was then educated at Macdonald College in Montreal, earning a B.Sc. in agriculture, and later, after serving briefly in the Canadian Army in the Second World War (1942–43), at McGill, where he earned an M.A. (1946) in economics and political science.

Throughout his life Layton was a poet, but he also taught English to immigrants and taught at a Jewish high school in Montreal; one of his students was poet and songwriter Leonard Cohen. He later lectured at Sir George Williams (now Concordia) University. From 1969 to 1978 he was a professor at York University in Toronto. Returning to Montreal, he lived his last decades there.

His second wife, Betty Sutherland, was introduced to him by her brother, John Sutherland, with whom she had co-founded the little magazine *First Statement* (1942–45). Layton became involved with the periodical and with other Montreal poets of the 1940s, particularly Louis Dudek and Raymond Souster. With these two poets he founded the co-operative publishing outlet Contact Press in 1952. More than other poets of his generation, however, Layton positioned himself in the media spotlight. He appeared on a CBC television debating show and spoke often on radio and at public events, never shying away from controversy. Layton was a public poet who (however narcissistically) saw himself as a servant of poetry. He spoke of the need for a new kind of poetry and for a more vigorous place for the poet in society. Some critics saw this as shameless self-promotion, while others saw it as beneficial to raising the profile of Canadian literature.

In a 2006 Harbourfront Reading Series tribute to Layton's life, the poet Pier Giorgio Di Cicco claimed that the subjects of Layton's poetry are "love, sex, death, and more love, defiance of time, lust for life, contempt for tyranny, and more love." Layton sought, as he himself said, "peace, social justice, and the end of human alienation" through poetry. His poetry is sometimes direct and sometimes difficult. In a CBC television broadcast in 1956, Layton declared that "the essence of poetry lies in the condensation, the concentration, to say so much more in so little time" than a novelist. "The Fertile Muck," for instance, challenges existing poetic representations of life, death, and the poetic process. It also urges the reader to engage with Layton's theories of the creative process. Similarly concerned with poetic process, "The Birth of Tragedy" draws on Friedrich Nietzsche's *The Birth of Tragedy out of the Spirit of Music* (1872) in order to comment on the poet's role in redeeming the tragedy of human suffering by giving it form within a work of art.

In many ways, Layton's philosophical stance can be described as existentialist, for he preached living life to its fullest, in the present moment, even in the face of absurdity and suffering. In his view, it was the poet who was able to uncover the "primal energies" of existence. His poem "The Fertile Muck" describes the poet's mission to translate "muck" or chaos into something wondrous.

One of the most fiercely debated elements of Layton's work is his representation of women, sexuality, and love. While some call the poems attacks on puritan prudishness and social inhibitions and applaud his forthright use of language (Louis Dudek made this argument in the 1940s), others call the poems sexist, and some have gone so far as to call Layton a misogynist. In the "Foreword" to *A Red Carpet for the Sun,* Layton writes, "Modern women I see cast in the role of furies striving to castrate the male; their efforts aided by all the malignant forces of a technological civilization that has rendered the male's creative role of revelation superfluous. . . . We're being feminized and proletarianized at one and the same time." He continues, "This is the inglorious age of the mass-woman. Her tastes are dominant everywhere—in theatres, stores, art, fiction, houses, furniture—and these tastes are dainty and trivial." In a 1988 article, critic Joanne Lewis argues that to call him a "male chauvinist does little but to state the obvious." Because Layton often links sexuality with violence and pain, she argues that "the language of Layton's poetry does more than break the puritan embargo on writing about sexuality in sexually explicit terms; it degrades both women and human sexuality." His words speak for themselves on this topic in the foreword and in his poetry (see "The Tamed Puma," "He Saw Them, At First,"

"Lust," or "Sourwine Sparkle," or see the sad and tender poem "Berry Picking," which is included here).

The life and poetry of Irving Layton are of much critical interest today. A passionate man, he responded bitterly to Elspeth Cameron's controversial biography of him entitled *Irving Layton: A Portrait* (1985). His son David Layton's *Motion Sickness: A Memoir* (1999) presents a conflicted portrait of the man as a father and as a public figure. McClelland and Stewart recently issued *A Wild Peculiar Joy: The Selected Poems* (2004), edited by Sam Solecki, as well as his ironically titled memoir *Waiting for the Messiah* (2006).

Following Layton's death in January 2006, former Canadian poet laureate George Bowering eulogized that Layton "had an energy that blew apart the lah-dee-dah approach to poetry that was offered to us then. I think that maybe he was one of those guys who opened the way for poets who were better than him. You certainly wouldn't have seen an Al Purdy without Layton." Layton was made an officer of the Order of Canada in 1976 and was nominated for the Nobel Prize in Literature in 1981. Critic and poet Stephen Scobie writes, "[A]s capable of genius as he is of utter triviality, Layton remains one of the most rewarding and infuriating of Canadian poets."

The Birth of Tragedy[1]

And me happiest when I compose poems.
    Love, power, the huzza of battle
    are something, are much;

---

[1] Reference to German philosopher Friedrich Nietzsche's (1844–1900) work *The Birth of Tragedy out of the Spirit of Music* (1872), in which he discusses two aspects of human creativity: the Apollonian (associated with rationality and order) and the Dionysian (associated with instinct, irrationality, and energy). The power of great art comes from its ability to unite both forces. Nietzsche's view, like Layton's, was that Western culture had repressed Dionysian energies in favour of Apollonian control.

yet a poem includes them like a pool
        water and reflection.
In me, nature's divided things—
        tree, mould on tree—
        have their fruition;
I am their core. Let them swap,
bandy, like a flame swerve   10
I am their mouth; as a mouth I serve.

And I observe how the sensual moths
        big with odour and sunshine
        dart into the perilous shrubbery;
or drop their visiting shadows
        upon the garden I one year made
of flowering stone to be a footstool
        for the perfect gods:
        who, friends to the ascending orders,
sustain all passionate meditations   20
and call down pardons
for the insurgent blood.

A quiet madman, never far from tears,
        I lie like a slain thing
        under the green air the trees
inhabit, or rest upon a chair
        towards which the inflammable air
tumbles on many robins' wings;
        noting how seasonably
        leaf and blossom uncurl   30
and living things arrange their death,
while someone from afar off
blows birthday candles for the world.

[1954]

From Colony to Nation

A dull people,
but the rivers of this country
are wide and beautiful

A dull people
enamoured of childish games,
but food is easily come by
and plentiful

Some with a priest's voice
in their cage of ribs: but
on high mountain-tops and in thunderstorms   10
the chirping is not heard

Deferring to beadle and censor;
not ashamed for this,
but given over to horseplay,
the making of money

A dull people, without charm
or ideas,
settling into the clean empty look
of a Mountie or dairy farmer
as into a legacy   20

One can ignore them
(the silences, the vast distances help)
and suppose them at the bottom
of one of the meaner lakes,
their bones not even picked for souvenirs.

[1956]

The Fertile Muck

There are brightest apples on those trees
        but until I, fabulist, have spoken
they do not know their significance
or what other legends are hung like garlands
        on their black boughs twisting
like a rumour. The wind's noise is empty.

Nor are the winged insects better off
        though they wear my crafty eyes
wherever they alight. Stay here, my love;
you will see how delicately they deposit   10
        me on the leaves of elms
or fold me in the orient dust of summer.

And if in August joiners and bricklayers
        are thick as flies around us
building expensive bungalows for those

who do not need them, unless they release
          me roaring from their moth-proofed cupboards
their buyers will have no joy, no ease.

I could extend their rooms for them without cost
          and give them crazy sundials
to tell the time with, but I have noticed   20
how my irregular footprint horrifies them
          evenings and Sunday afternoons:
they spray for hours to erase its shadow.

How to dominate reality? Love is one way;
          imagination another. Sit here
beside me, sweet; take my hard hand in yours.
We'll mark the butterflies disappearing over the hedge
          with tiny wristwatches on their wings:
our fingers touching the earth, like two Buddhas.

[1956]

Berry Picking

Silently my wife walks on the still wet furze
Now darkgreen the leaves are full of metaphors
Now lit up is each tiny lamp of blueberry.
The white nails of rain have dropped and the sun is free.

And whether she bends or straightens to each bush
To find the children's laughter among the leaves
Her quiet hands seem to make the quiet summer hush—
Berries or children, patient she is with these.

I only vex and perplex her; madness, rage
Are endearing perhaps put down upon the page;   10
Even silence daylong and sullen can then
Enamour as restraint or classic discipline.

So I envy the berries she puts in her mouth,
The red and succulent juice that stains her lips;
I shall never taste that good to her, nor will they
Displease her with a thousand barbarous jests.

How they lie easily for her hand to take,
Part of the unoffending world that is hers;
Here beyond complexity she stands and stares
And leans her marvellous head as if for answers.   20

No more the easy soul my childish craft deceives
Nor the simpler one for whom yes is always yes;
No, now her voice comes to me from a far way off
Though her lips are redder than the raspberries.

[1958]

Keine Lazarovitch[2]

1870–1959

When I saw my mother's head on the cold pillow,
Her white waterfalling hair in the cheeks' hollows,
I thought, quietly circling my grief, of how
She had loved God but cursed extravagantly his creatures.

For her final mouth was not water but a curse,
A small black hole, a black rent in the universe,
Which damned the green earth, stars and trees in its stillness
And the inescapable lousiness of growing old.

And I record she was comfortless, vituperative,
Ignorant, glad, and much else besides; I believe   10
She endlessly praised her black eyebrows, their thick weave,
Till plagiarizing Death leaned down and took them for his mould.

And spoiled a dignity I shall not again find,
And the fury of her stubborn limited mind;
Now none will shake her amber beads and call God blind,
Or wear them upon a breast so radiantly.

O fierce she was, mean and unaccommodating;
But I think now of the toss of her gold earrings,
Their proud carnal assertion, and her youngest sings
While all the rivers of her red veins move into the sea.   20

[1961]

Whom I Write For

When reading me, I want you to feel
    as if I had ripped your skin off;
Or gouged out your eyes with my fingers;
Or scalped you, and afterwards burnt your hair

---

[2] An elegy for the poet's mother.

IRVING LAYTON

in the staring sockets; having first filled them
with fluid from your son's lighter.
I want you to feel as if I had slammed
    your child's head against a spike;
And cut off your member and stuck it in your
    wife's mouth to smoke like a cigar.   10

For I do not write to improve your soul;
    or to make you feel better, or more humane;
Nor do I write to give you any new emotions;
Or to make you proud to be able to experience them
    or to recognize them in others.
I leave that to the fraternity of lying poets
    —no prophets, but toadies and trained seals!

How much evil there is in the best of them
    as their envy and impotence flower into poems
And their anality into love of man, into virtue: 20
Especially when they tell you, sensitively,
    what it feels like to be a potato.

I write for the young man, demented,
    who dropped the bomb on Hiroshima;[3]
I write for Nasser and Ben Gurion;[4]
For Krushchev and President Kennedy;[5]
    for the Defence Secretary[6]
voted forty-six billions for the extirpation
    of humans everywhere.
I write for the Polish officers machine-gunned   30
    in the Katyn forest;[7]

[3] In this stanza, Layton refers to major world political events, conflicts, and leaders of the past 20 years. The atomic bombing of Hiroshima, Japan, on 6 August 1945, killed an estimated 140,000 people and brought an end to the Second World War.

[4] Gamal Abdel Nasser (1918–1970), Arab nationalist and socialist President of Egypt (1954–70). David Ben-Gurion (1886–1973), the first Prime Minister of Israel. He led Israel to victory in the 1948 Arab-Israeli War. Layton lists the leaders on both sides of the conflict.

[5] Premier of the Soviet Union, Nikita Khrushchev (Layton misspells his name) (1894–1971), and American President John F. Kennedy (1917–1963). A reference to the Cuban Missile Crisis (October 1962), a confrontation between the United States, the Soviet Union, and Cuba during the Cold War after Soviet missiles were discovered by the Americans in Cuba.

[6] Presumably a reference to American government support for nuclear weapons under Robert McNamara (1916–), U.S. Secretary of Defense from 1961 to 1968.

[7] Reference to the Katyn Forest massacre, a mass execution of an estimated 4,000 Polish Army officers (prisoners-of-war) ordered by Soviet authorities in early 1940.

I write for the gassed, burnt, tortured,
 and humiliated everywhere;
I write for Castro and tse-Tung,[8] the only poets
 I ever learned anything from;
I write for Adolph Eichmann,[9] compliant clerk
 to that madman, the human race;
For his devoted wife and loyal son.

Give me words fierce and jagged enough
 to tear your skin like shrapnel;   40
Hot and searing enough to fuse
 the flesh off your blackened skeleton;
Words with the sound of crunching bones or bursting
    eyeballs;
 or a nose being smashed with a gun butt;
Words with the soft plash of intestines
 falling out of your belly;
Or cruel and sad as the thought which tells you
    "This is the end"
And you feel Time oozing out of your veins   50
 and yourself becoming one with the weightless dark.

                        [1963]

[8] Communist leaders. Fidel Castro (1926–), the revolutionary leader of the Cuban People's Party, overthrew the government of Cuba in 1959 and ruled the country until his retirement in 2008. Mao Tse-tung (1893–1976), the Chinese military and political leader who led the Communist Party of China to victory in the Chinese civil war, was the leader of the People's Republic of China from its establishment in 1949 until his death in 1976.

[9] Adolf Eichmann (1906–1962), Nazi war criminal, architect of the "Final Solution." He headed the Gestapo Department for Jewish Affairs, responsible for sending approximately five million Jews to ghettos and extermination camps in Nazi-occupied Eastern Europe during the Second World War. After the war, Eichmann escaped to Argentina using a false passport, where he was joined by his wife and sons. In 1960, he was captured in Argentina and tried in an Israeli court on 15 charges of crimes against the Jewish people, crimes against humanity, and war crimes. His defence was that he was just following orders. In 1962, he was convicted and hanged.

MURIEL KITAGAWA ■ (1912–1974)

In the spring of 1941, every Japanese Canadian over the age of 16 was finger-printed and photographed by the RCMP and made to carry a registration card at all times. These cards noted whether the person was "Canadian born" or not. Shortly after Japan's entry into the Second World War on 7 December 1941 (with the bomb-ing of Pearl Harbor), the War Measures Act was invoked, meaning that civil rights could be suspended in the interest of wider national security. Japanese Canadians were deemed a threat to security in the country, and were branded "enemy aliens," even though approximately 75 per cent of the "enemy aliens" were either Canadians by birth or naturalized subjects. A sunset-to-sunrise curfew was imposed on "every person of the Japanese race," as the Minister of Justice (and future Prime Minister) Louis St. Laurent put it in the public notice of the curfew dated at Ottawa, 26 February 1942. The Notice clarifies that the term "persons of the Japanese race" also includes any "person not wholly of the Japanese race if his father or mother is of the Japanese race." Personal property—listed in the St. Laurent Notice as "motor vehicles, cameras, transmitter radios, radio receivers, firearms, ammunition, and explosives"—was confiscated. At short notice the further "systematic expulsion of the Japanese [sic] from the area within 100 miles of the B.C. coast" began. Many of the 21,000 men, women, and children who were in the "restricted area" at the time and who were forced to leave their homes were housed in degrading and unsanitary conditions in the former livestock barns at Hastings Park (the Pacific National Exhibition fairgrounds). The people were then moved to internment camps in the B.C. interior (Kaslo, Greenwood, Sandon, New Denver, and Slocan, among them) or were forced to join work camps in Ontario and western Canada. Later, some families had to work as "farm labour reinforcements" on sugar beet farms in Alberta and Manitoba in order to keep the families together. The confiscated property (including the fishing boats in Figure V-7) was sold at auction without the owners' knowledge or consent in order to pay for the administrative costs of the sale and living expenses of the internees (who were forced to pay for their own internment, unlike prisoners of war, who were protected under the Geneva Convention). Although the war ended in 1945, the internees were asked to "test their loyalty to Canada" and move further east of the

Rockies or be voluntarily "repatriated" to Japan. Of the 4,000 people who were "repatriated" by 1947, half were born in Canada. In 1948, Japanese Canadians were able to apply for citizenship and gain the right to vote. On 1 April 1949, four years after the war ended, the last of the wartime restrictions were lifted, allowing Japanese Canadians to travel freely and return to the West Coast.

Tsukiye Muriel Kitagawa (née Fujiwara) was born in Vancouver in 1912 and raised in New Westminster, B.C. In 1932 she helped to found *The New Age,* a newspaper dedicated to the news and ideas of the Nisei (second-generation Japanese Canadians). In her articles for the newspaper she addresses inequalities among Canadians—including the right to vote (the demand for Nisei franchise as Canadian-born people was denied in 1936 because of opposition from politicians in British Columbia). By 1938 she was contributing prolifically to the English-language newspaper *The New Canadian: An Independent Weekly for Canadians of Japanese Origin* (which ran from 1938 to 2001 and, during the war, was the only Japanese-Canadian paper allowed to publish, thereby becoming the main source of community news and government policy directives). In 1938, she married Ed (Eddie) Kitagawa. Over the next few years they had four children, including twins born during the upheaval. In 1942, she and her family were forced to leave all their possessions and flee to Toronto to join her brother. She continued to write for years after the war.

The federal Order-in-Council posted a Notice to "Male Enemy Aliens" stating "[t]hat no Enemy Alien shall after [the last day of April, 1942], enter, leave or return to such protected area except with the permission of the Commissioner of the Royal Canadian Mounted Police Force" (issued on 7 February 1942). Kitagawa's letters, published here, date from the month following this Notice. In these letters to her brother, Wesley Fujiwara, who was attending university in Toronto, she describes the changing scenes of her life in Vancouver with increasing horror. As a keen documenter of social injustice before the war, Kitagawa's early writings retain a sense of hope in the Canadian system of peace and fairness. A disbelief that Canadian citizens could be treated as enemies is sustained throughout her writings and yet that is what she so powerfully documents. The 2 March letter contains a sense of outrage that her personal space is being violated. In the letter of 20 April 1942, which describes the conditions of the livestock pen at Hastings Park where thousands of women and children were incarcerated, there is a sense of despair and sadness accompanied by anger at the debased living conditions. The letters were collected and edited by poet Roy Miki as *This Is My Own: Letters to Wes and Other Writings on Japanese Canadians, 1941–1948* (1985). Author Joy Kogawa also drew on Kitagawa's letters in the research for her groundbreaking novel about the Japanese-Canadian internment, *Obasan* (1981).

On 22 September 1988, Prime Minister Brian Mulroney acknowledged in the House of Commons that "in the crisis of wartime, the government of Canada wrongfully incarcerated, seized the property, and disenfranchised thousands of Canadians of Japanese ancestry" and announced a comprehensive redress settlement reached with the National Association of Japanese Canadians on behalf of their community (after years of work by the association fighting to reach such a settlement).

From This Is My Own

March 2, 1942.

Dear Wes:

What a heavenly relief to get your letter. I was just about getting frantic with worry over you. That's why I hope you'll forgive me for writing to Jim Carson. Eddie and I thought that was the only way to find out what really was happening to you. Oh Wes, the things that have been happening out here are beyond words, and though at times I thank goodness you're out of it, at other times I think we really need people like you around to keep us from getting too wrought up for our own good.

Eiko and Fumi[1] were here yesterday, crying, nearly hysterical with hurt and outrage and impotence. All student nurses have been fired from the [Vancouver] General.

They took our beautiful radio ... what does it matter that someone bought it off us for a song? ... it's the same thing because we had to do that or suffer the ignominy of having it taken forcibly from us by the RCMP. Not a single being of

---

[1] Kitagawa's friends.

Japanese race in the protected area will escape. Our cameras, even Nobi's toy one, all are confiscated. They can search our homes without warrant.

As if all this trouble wasn't enough, prepare yourself for a shock. We are forced to move out from our homes, Wes, to where we don't know. Eddie was going to join the Civilian Corps but now will not go near it, as it smells of a daemonic, roundabout way of getting rid of us. There is the very suspicious clause 'within and *without*' Canada that has all the fellows leery.[2]

The Bank is awfully worried about me and the twins, and the manager has said he will do what he can for us, but as he has to refer to the main office which in turn has to refer to the Head Office, he can't promise a thing, except a hope that surely the Bank won't let us down after all these years of faithful service.[3] Who knows where we will be now tomorrow next week. It isn't as if we Nisei were aliens,[4] technical or not. It breaks my heart to think of leaving this house and the little things around it that we have gathered through the years, all those numerous gadgets that have no material value but are irreplaceable. My papers, letters, books and things . . . the azalea plants, my white iris, the lilac that is just beginning to flower . . . so many things.

Oh Wes, the Nisei are bitter, too bitter for their own good or for Canada. How can cool heads like Tom's prevail when the general feeling is to stand up and fight.

Do you know what curfew means in actual practice? B.C. is falling all over itself in the scramble to be the first to kick us out from jobs and homes. So many night-workers have been fired out of hand. Now they sit at home, which is usually just a bed, or some cramped quarters, since they can't go out at night for even a consoling cup of coffee. Mr. Shimizu is working like mad with the Welfare society to look after the women and children that were left when their men were forced to volunteer to go to the work camps. Now those men are only in unheated bunk-cars, no latrines, no water, snow 15' deep, no work to keep warm with, little food if any. They had been shunted off with such inhuman speed that they got there before any facilities were prepared for them. Now men are afraid to go because they think they will be going to certain disaster . . . anyway, too much uncertainty. After all, they have to think of their families. If snow is 15' deep there is no work, and if there is no work there is no pay, and if there is no pay no one eats. The *Province* reports that work on frames with tent-coverings is progressing to house the 2,000

---

[2] Miki's note: The strongest rumour running through the community at this time was that the eastern road and lumber camps did not exist, and that Nisei men would end up in the North Atlantic working on tankers which were targets for German submarines (Interview, Thomas Shoyama).

[3] Miki's note: Ed Kitagawa started working at the bank in 1922.

[4] In 1940, an Order-in-Council was passed that defined "enemy aliens" as "all persons of German or Italian racial origin who have become naturalized British subjects since September 1, 1922." The term "enemy alien" was updated to include persons of Japanese heritage in 1942. They were considered British subjects because until the Citizenship Act of 1947 was passed, people in Canada were British subjects. She is pointing out that Nisei were born in Canada so were not naturalized subjects.

expected. Tent coverings where the snow is so deep! And this is Democracy! You should see the faces here, all pinched, grey, uncertain. If the Bank fails Eddie, do you know what the kids and I have to live on? $39. For everything . . . food, clothing, rent, taxes, upkeep, insurance premiums, emergencies. They will allow for only two kids for the Nisei. $6 per., monthly. It has just boiled down to race persecution, and signs have been posted on all highways . . . JAPS . . . KEEP OUT. Mind you, you can't compare this sort of thing to anything that happens in Germany. That country is an avowed Jew-baiter, totalitarian. Canada is supposed to be a Democracy out to fight against just the sort of thing she's boosting at home.

And also, I'll get that $39 only if Eddie joins the Chain Gang, you know, *forced to volunteer* to let the authorities wash their hands of any responsibilities. All Nisei are liable to imprisonment I suppose if they refuse to volunteer . . . that is the likeliest interpretation of Ian MacKenzie's[5] "volunteer or else." Prisoners in wartime get short shrift . . . and to hell with the wife and kids. Can you wonder that there is a deep bitterness among the Nisei who believe so gullibly in the democratic blah-blah that's been dished out. I am glad Kazuma [Uyeno] is not here.

There are a lot of decent people who feel for us, but they can't do a thing.

And the horrors that some young girls have already faced . . . outraged by men in uniform . . . in the hospital . . . hysterical. Oh we are fair prey for the wolves in democratic clothing. Can you wonder the men are afraid to leave us behind and won't go unless their women go with them? I won't blame you if you can't believe this. It *is* incredible. Wes, you have to be here right in the middle of it to really know.

How can the hakujin[6] face us without a sense of shame for their treachery to the principles they fight for? One man was so damned sorry, he came up to me, hat off, squirming like mad, stuttering how sorry he was. My butcher said he knew he could trust me with a side of meat even if I had no money. These kind people too are betrayed by the Wilsonites[7] . . . God damn his soul! Yet there are other people who, while they wouldn't go so far as to persecute us, are so ignorant, so indifferent they believe we are being very well treated for what we are. The irony of it all is enough to choke me. And we are tightening our belts for the starvation to come. The diseases . . . the crippling . . . the twisting of our souls . . . death would be the easiest to bear.

The Chinese are forced to wear huge buttons and plates and even placards to tell the hakujin the difference between one yellow peril and another. Or else they would be beaten up. It's really ridiculous.

And Wes, we are among the fortunate ones, for above that $39 we may be able to fill it out by renting this house. Now I wish I hadn't given my clothes to

---

[5] Ian Alistair Mackenzie (1890–1949), Minister of Pensions and National Health in Prime Minister William Lyon Mackenzie King's government. His campaign slogan for the 1944 election was "No Japs from the Rockies to the seas."

[6] Japanese term designating a person of European descent, literally meaning White person or people.

[7] Vancouver Alderman Halford Wilson, who served from 1935 to 1972, was a civic leader in the campaign against Japanese Canadians remaining in coastal B.C.

Kath. We will need them badly. Uncle has been notified to get ready to move. Dad will be soon too.

There's too much to say and not enough time or words.

Can't send you pictures now unless some hakujin takes the snaps . . . STRENG VERBOTEN[8] to use even little cameras to snap the twins . . . STRENG VERBOTEN is the order of the day.

My apologies to Jim Carson.

Love,

Mur.

April 20, 1942.

Dear Wes:

I went to the Pool yesterday to see Eiko who is working there as steno.[9] I saw Sab too who is working in the baggage . . . old Horseshow Building. Sab showed me his first paycheque as something he couldn't quite believe . . . $11.75.[10] He's been there for an awful long time. Eiko sleeps in a partitioned stall, she being on the staff, so to speak. This stall was the former home of a pair of stallions and boy oh boy, did they leave their odour behind. The whole place is impregnated with the smell of ancient manure and maggots. Every other day it is swept with dichloride of lime or something, but you can't disguise horse smell, cow smell, sheeps and pigs and rabbits and goats. And is it dusty! The toilets are just a sheet metal trough, and up till now they did not have partitions or seats. The women kicked so they put up partitions and a terribly makeshift seat. Twelve-year old boys stay with the women too. The auto show building, where there was also the Indian exhibit, houses the new dining room and kitchens. Seats 3000. Looks awfully permanent. Brick stoves, 8 of them, shining new mugs . . . very very barrack-y. As for the bunks, they were the most tragic things I saw there. Steel and wooden frames with a thin lumpy straw tick, a bolster, and three army blankets of army quality . . . no sheets unless you bring your own. These are the 'homes' of the women I saw. They wouldn't let me into the men's building. There are constables at the doors . . . no propagation of the species . . . you know . . . it was in the papers. These bunks were hung with sheets and blankets and clothes of every hue and variety, a regular gipsy tent of colours, age, and cleanliness, all hung with the pathetic attempt at privacy. Here and there I saw a child's doll and teddy bear . . . I saw babies lying there beside a mother who was too weary to get up . . . she had just thrown herself across the bed . . . I felt my throat thicken . . . an old old lady was crying,

---

[8] German: Strictly forbidden.

[9] The Pool is a part of Hastings Park Exhibition Grounds in Vancouver, where thousands of people were held. Stenographer: a shorthand writer or typist.

[10] In an earlier letter she notes that her friend "Sab earns about $2 a day at the Pool helping out, minus board, of course."

saying she would rather have died than have come to such a place . . . she clung to Eiko and cried and cried. Eiko has taken the woes of the confinees on her thin shoulders and she took so much punishment she went to her former rooms and couldn't stop crying. Fumi was so worried about her. Eiko is really sick. The place has got her down. There are ten showers for 1500 women. Hot and cold water. The men looked so terribly at loose ends, wandering around the grounds, sticking their noses through the fence watching the golfers, lying on the grass. Going through the place I felt so depressed that I wanted to cry. I'm damned well not going there. They are going to move the Vancouver women first now and shove them into the Pool before sending them to the ghost towns.[11]

I'm getting kind of frantic because we haven't heard yet from the Bank. The manager wrote again on the 17th. If they would only hurry up and say something one way or the other. If they say no, I shall send you a wire and then you know what to do. If only Eddie can get a job that pays enough to make it worthwhile staying out of the work camps, something we can eat on and save a little. He's quick with his hands, but he knows figures best. He's worked 21 years with the Bank of Montreal. If I can, I am going to take Eiko with me as nursemaid. I don't think it would be wise to take Obasan[12] with us because she is a national's wife, and she is going back to Japan anyway as soon as she can, while Eiko and we have no such intentions.

The other day at the Pool, someone dropped his key before a stall in the Livestock Building, and he fished for it with a long wire and brought to light rotted manure and maggots!!! He called the nurse and then they moved all the bunks from the stalls and pried up the wooden floors. It was the most stomach-turning nauseating thing. They got fumigators and tried to wash it all away and got most of it into the drains, but maggots still breed and turn up here and there. One woman with more guts than the others told the nurse (white) about it and protested. She replied: "Well, there's worms in the garden aren't there?" This particular nurse was a Jap-hater of the most virulent sort. She called them "filthy Japs" to their faces and Eiko gave her 'what-for' and Fumi had a terrible scrap with her, both girls saying: "What do you think we are? Are we cattle? Are we pigs you dirty-so-and-so!" You know how Fumi gets. The night the first bunch of Nisei were supposed to go to Schreiber[13] and they wouldn't, the women and children at the Pool milled around in front of their cage, and one very handsome mountie came with his truncheon and started to hit them, yelling at them, "Get the hell back in there." Eiko's blood boiled over. She strode over to him and shouted at him: "You put that stick down! What do you think you're doing! Do you think these women and children are so many cows that you can beat them back into their place?" Eiko was shaking mad and raked him with fighting words. She has taken it on her to

[11] Internment camps in Kaslo, New Denver, Roseberry, Slocan City, Lemon Creek, Sandon, and Greenwood, B.C.

[12] Miki's note: Japanese for "Aunt," here a reference to Aunt Sei Toyofuku.

[13] Schreiber, B.C., a road construction camp.

fight for the poor people there, and now she is on the black list and reputed to be a trouble-maker. Just like Tommy and Kunio.[14] I wish I too could go in there and fight and slash around. It's people like us who are the most hurt . . . people like us, who have had faith in Canada, and who have been more politically minded than the others, who have a hearty contempt for the whites.

[. . .]

I'll write again soon.

With love,

Mur.

[14] Kitagawa's friends.

DOUGLAS LEPAN ■ (1914–1998)

Born in Toronto, Douglas LePan is one of only a few writers to win the Governor General's Award for both poetry (in 1953, for *The Net and the Sword*) and fiction (in 1964, for *The Deserter*). Both works concern the experiences of the Second World War, in which LePan served as an artilleryman. Critic William Toye posits that LePan's writing about the war presents in a "paradox the utter meaninglessness of war and the indestructible meaning of the intrinsically human." In his early, high modernist writing, LePan repeatedly engages such a paradox.

A writer and a diplomat, LePan mingled with the important artistic and political figures of his day. From 1945 to 1959, he served in the Department of External Affairs in London (as special assistant to Lester Pearson in the late 1940s), as well as in Washington and Ottawa. Educated at the University of Toronto, Harvard, and Oxford, in 1959 he returned to academia and taught literature at Queen's University (1959–64); he served as the principal of University College in the University of Toronto (1964–70) (when Robertson Davies was at Massey College and Northrop Frye

was at Victoria College) and as professor there from 1970 to 1979.

The most anthologized of LePan's poems is his "A Country Without a Mythology," first published in *The Wounded Prince and Other Poems* (1948) alongside "*Coureurs de Bois*." In this provocative poem LePan uses an extended metaphor of an explorer entering the threatening land of Canada to describe a prototypical Canadian experience. Canada is figured as a dangerous and savage land empty of history and mythology. Coming out of the war at a time when many writers were obsessed with the idea of finding a national identity, LePan typifies in his comments the view of Canada as a blank slate in need of articulation. More recently, however, LePan's figuration of Canada as a country without a mythology has been criticized because its Eurocentric view neglects to account for the long history of First Nations peoples on/in the land.

LePan's term for Canada has been adopted and refuted by critics and writers alike. In 1965 Northrop Frye argued in the conclusion to the *Literary History of Canada* that it is necessary for the writer to withdraw from the "country without a mythology into a country of mythology." Davies takes up the title of LePan's poem in his well-known essay "Literature in a Country Without a Mythology" (1988), where he concludes that "Canada has a mythology, but it is only now, after four hundred years of history, forced to decide what it is going to do about it." Davies's 1977 essay "The Canada of Myth and Reality" (included in Section VI), concludes with a discussion of LePan's poem "*Coureurs de Bois,*" which Davies believes contains an emblematic description of the Canadian prototype, "Wild Hamlet with the features of Horatio," whose modest features mask a hidden power.

In 1990, at age 76, LePan published his final collection of poems (*Far Voyages*), in which he "came out" as a gay poet with a passionate extended elegy for a former lover. "Passacaglia" is from this collection. This slim volume has been seen by poet John Barton as a landmark book in Canadian queer studies. Barton and Billeh Nickerson include LePan's poetry in *Seminal: The Anthology of Canada's Gay Male Poets* (2007) along with work by Patrick Anderson, bill bissett, Robin Blaser, John Glassco, Daniel David Moses, Stan Persky, Shane Rhodes, Bill Richardson, Gregory Scofield, and Michael V. Smith.

A Country Without a Mythology

No monuments or landmarks guide the stranger
Going among this savage people, masks
Taciturn or babbling out an alien jargon
And moody as barbaric skies are moody.

Berries must be his food. Hurriedly
He shakes the bushes, plucks pickerel from the river,
Forgetting every grace and ceremony,
Feeds like an Indian, and is on his way.

And yet, for all his haste, time is worth nothing.
The abbey clock, the dial in the garden.   10
Fade like saint's days and festivals.
Months, years, are here unbroken virgin forests.

There is no law — even no atmosphere
To smooth the anger of the flagrant sun.
November skies sting sting like icicles.
The land is open to all violent weathers.

Passion is not more quick. Lightnings in August
Stagger, rocks split, tongues in the forest hiss,
As fire drinks up the lovely sea-dream coolness.
This is the land the passionate man must travel.   20

Sometimes—perhaps at the tentative fall of twilight—
A belief will settle that waiting around the bend
Are sanctities of childhood, that melting birds
Will sing him into a limpid gracious Presence.

The hills will fall in folds, the wilderness
Will be a garment innocent and lustrous
To wear upon a birthday, under a light
That curls and smiles, a golden-haired Archangel.

And now the channel opens. But nothing alters.
Mile after mile of tangled struggling roots,   30
Wild-rice, stumps, weeds, that clutch at the canoe,
Wild birds hysterical in tangled trees.

And not a sign, no emblem in the sky
Or boughs to friend him as he goes; for who
Will stop where, clumsily constructed, daubed
With war-paint, teeters some lust-red manitou?[1]

[1948]

Coureurs de Bois

Thinking of you, I think of the *coureurs de bois*,[2]
Swarthy men grown almost to savage size
Who put their brown wrists through the arras[3] of the woods
And were lost—sometimes for months. Word would come back:
One had been seen at Crêve-coeur, deserted and starving,
One at Sault Sainte Marie shouldering the rapids.
Giant-like, their labours stalked in the streets of Quebec
Though they themselves had dwindled in distance: names only;
Rumours; quicksilvery spies into nature's secrets;
Rivers that seldom ran in the sun. Their resource   10
Would sparkle and then flow back under clouds of hemlock.

---

[1] Term used to designate a spirit among Algonquin cultures.

[2] *Coureurs de bois*, literally "wood-runners," were itinerant, unlicensed fur traders, usually of French origin. When the fur trade began, furs were brought to trading posts by Aboriginal men. The *coureurs de bois* worked at the trading posts, learned the ways of the woods from the First Nations' trappers, and became trappers themselves. LePan describes them in heroic indigenized terms as men of adventure and exploration touched by the wildness of the woods. The exoticized language of the poem begs the question of the identity of "you."

[3] A heavy wall hanging or tapestry.

So you should have travelled with them. Or with La Salle.[4]
He could feed his heart with the heart of a continent,
Insatiate, how noble a wounded animal,
Who sought for his wounds the balsam of adventure,
The sap from some deep, secret tree. But now
That the forests are cut down, the rivers charted,
Where can you turn, where can you travel? Unless
Through the desperate wilderness behind your eyes,
So full of falls and glooms and desolations,   20
Disasters I have glimpsed but few would dream of,
You seek new Easts. The coats of difficult honour,
Bright with brocaded birds and curious flowers,
Stowed so long with vile packs of pemmican,[5]
Futile, weighing you down on slippery portages,
Would flutter at last in the courts of a clement country,
Where the air is silken, the manners easy,
Under a guiltless and reconciling sun.

You hesitate. The trees are entangled with menace.
The voyage is perilous into the dark interior.   30
But then your hands go to the thwarts. You smile. And so
I watch you vanish in a wood of heroes,
Wild Hamlet with the features of Horatio.[6]

[1948]

Passacaglia[7]

I love it when you tell me you love me. But there's no need.
I can tell that from the way you move when we're alone.
But what's harder is trying to figure out *why* you love me,
someone so weatherbeaten, so morose, so footsore and heartsore

[4] René-Robert Cavelier, Sieur de La Salle (1643–1687), was a French explorer who travelled the Great Lakes region of the United States and Canada, the Mississippi River, and the Gulf of Mexico. Critic Eli Mandel reads this as a reference to "that demon of North America, who tore the heart out of the continent."

[5] Dried and powdered meat, usually buffalo, mixed with fat. Fur traders carried pemmican on long voyages in leather bags because it did not spoil.

[6] Reference to William Shakespeare's play *Hamlet* (1601). Horatio is Hamlet's close friend and confidant who works as a sensible, cautious foil to Hamlet's madness. When the trustworthy Horatio sees the ghost of Hamlet's father, we understand that we are to believe in its theatrical existence. See the conclusion to Robertson Davies's essay "The Canada of Myth and Reality" in Section VI for his discussion of this phrase as it applies to the Canadian character generally.

[7] A passacaglia is a musical form of continuous variation in 3/4 time, usually grave in tone, originating in early seventeenth-century Spain. The poet plays with musical opposites throughout the poem.

from the journey, living only from day to day, accustomed
to loss and disappointment, hardly expecting anything else,
with hardly anything more than a soldier's low horizons.
But even now that you've utterly changed the prospect,
and (with a little help from me) broken down my dour carapace
and mollified the proud flesh round my wounds, there's still   10
plenty of scar-tissue left. So . . . why? But the very question
may well be rather ridiculous, a hangover from a different
life and a different habit of discourse, before the old terms
and categories were radically altered. As well ask perhaps,
Why are the upper staves of the passacaglia in love
with the seemingly sullen bass? Or, why is the aria
in love with the accompaniment? The free-floating tenor
or coloratura aria, that has a wealth of playful
or spirited *fioriture* and brilliant cadenzas;[8] the accompaniment
that simply seems to rock back and forth, back and forth,   20
and has little more to say for itself than that. Yet together
they make something out of this world, with its own pulse
and breathing, different from ours, yet leading us on,
showing us the way into a delectable transient clearing,
the skies a halcyon[9] azure, but with traces of passionate scarlet.
Now I'm learning to stop asking questions and simply
to listen to the music. And it's full of surprises. Sometimes
it's rowdy with kettledrums, sometimes placid as a sunlit lake,
sometimes as deftly inconsequent as a long poem by Frank
O'Hara.[10] But whatever it is, you make it all *cantabile*.[11]   30
I waken to ethereal music, to bird-song as though
flutes were conversing with oboes, or to murmurings,
raptures, that seem even more heavenly, more profound.
I look up surprised, to see that there's a helicopter overhead,
trailing a long sign that reads lazily, "No more questions, please."

[1990]

---

[8] *Fioriture*, a florid ornament or embellishment in music; cadenza, a flourish of indefinite form given to a solo voice or instrument at the close of a movement.

[9] Calm, quiet, peaceful, undisturbed.

[10] Frank O'Hara (1926–1966), American poet of the New York school of poetry.

[11] In a smooth, flowing singing style.

P.K. PAGE

P.K. Page's exceptional poetic career spans almost 70 years. Originally a modernist, associated with the Montreal Poets of the 1940s, Page has kept apace with poetic development in Canada. Her most recent work, concerning environmental responsibility, sits well beside contemporary eco-poets such as Don McKay, Robert Bringhurst, Tim Lilburn, and Rita Wong. Her 1994 poem "Planet Earth" illustrates how timely and topical, yet distinctively her own, her poetry remains. Lately, Page has also turned to what critic Kevin McNeilly calls "autobiographical poetics" in her *Brazilian Journal* (1987) and *Hand Luggage: A Memoir in Verse* (2006).

Born in England in 1916, Patricia Kathleen Page came to Canada when she was two years old and settled with her family in Red Deer, Alberta. While working as a filing clerk and historical researcher in Montreal, she joined the modernist literary magazine *Preview* (1942–45) in its second number, along with poets Patrick Anderson, A.M. Klein, F.R. Scott, Neufville Shaw, and John Sutherland (see Page's comments in the "Minutes of the *Preview* Meeting" in the F.R. Scott section). Between April 1942 and August 1945, she published dozens of stories and poems in *Preview* (including "The Stenographers" in July 1942). Having also published poems in periodicals such as *The Observer, The Canadian Author and Bookman,* and *Poetry* (Chicago), she turned to the Vancouver magazine *Contemporary Verse* as a venue for publication as the decade wore on. As literary critic Medrie Purdham points out, Page's first book of poetry, *As Ten As Twenty* (1946), expresses socialist concerns in a compact,

imagist style as she "vividly protest[s] against a world of nosy landladies, cramped apartments, stultifying work, social alienation, and the repressive morality codes of a conservative culture." Page's poetry is also remarkable for its intense visual imagery, as her evocative poem "Stories of Snow," threaded through with references to colour, demonstrates with its account of the power of memory to probe where "unrefractive whiteness lies."

Page began her eclectic career in 1946 as a scriptwriter at the National Film Board of Canada in Ottawa. Following her marriage in 1950 to Arthur Irwin (who died in 1999), she accompanied him on his diplomatic postings: as Canadian High Commissioner to Australia (1953–56), as ambassador to Brazil (1957–59), and ambassador to Mexico and Guatemala (1960–64). As a diplomat's wife she met many of the major political and cultural figures of the twentieth century. During this time she continued to write poetry and prose, albeit sporadically—receiving the Governor General's Award for poetry for *The Metal and the Flower* (1954) and critical acclaim for *Cry Ararat!—Poems New and Selected* (1967). Since 1964, she has lived in Victoria, B.C., and has published stories, poems, children's books, essays, art criticism, and drawings in various magazines and anthologies around the world. As P.K. Irwin, her married name, Page has exhibited her paintings and mounted solo exhibitions in Canada and Mexico and has pieces in the National Gallery and the Art Gallery of Ontario.

The Stenographers[1]

After the brief bivouac of Sunday,
their eyes, in the forced march of Monday to Saturday,
hoist the white flag, flutter in the snow-storm of paper,
haul it down and crack in the mid-sun of temper.

In the pause between the first draft and the carbon[2]
they glimpse the smooth hours when they were children—
the ride in the ice-cart, the ice-man's name,
the end of the route and the long walk home;

remember the sea where floats at high tide
were sea marrows growing on the scatter-green vine   10
or spools of grey toffee, or wasps' nests on water;
remember the sand and the leaves of the country.

Bell rings and they go and the voice draws their pencil
like a sled across snow; when its runners are frozen
rope snaps and the voice then is pulling no burden
but runs like a dog on the winter of paper.

Their climates are winter and summer—no wind
for the kites of their hearts—no wind for a flight;
a breeze at the most, to tumble them over
and leave them like rubbish—the boy-friends of blood.

In the inch of the noon as they move they are stagnant.   20
The terrible calm of the noon is their anguish;
the lip of the counter, the shapes of the straws
like icicles breaking their tongues, are invaders.

Their beds are their oceans—salt water of weeping
the waves that they know—the tide before sleep;
and fighting to drown they assemble their sheep
in columns and watch them leap desks for their fences
and stare at them with their own mirror-worn faces.

In the felt of the morning the calico-minded,
sufficiently starched, insert papers, hit keys,   30

[1] A shorthand writer or typist. Page turns the quotidian world of office workers into the subject of poetry.

[2] Carbon paper was placed between sheets of paper so copies of documents could be made.

efficient and sure as their adding machines;
yet they weep in the vault, they are taut as net curtains
stretched upon frames. In their eyes I have seen
the pin men of madness in marathon trim
race round the track of the stadium pupil.

[1946]

The Landlady

Through sepia air the boarders come and go,
impersonal as trains.   Pass silently
the craving silence swallowing her speech;
click doors like shutters on her camera eye.

Because of her their lives become exact:
their entrances and exits are designed;
phone calls are cryptic.   Oh, her ticklish ears
advance and fall back stunned.

Nothing is unprepared. They hold the walls
about them as they weep or laugh. Each face   10
is dialled to zero publicly. She peers
stippled with curious flesh;

pads on the patient landing like a pulse,
unlocks their keyholes with the wire of sight,
searches their rooms for clues when they are out,
pricks when they come home late.

Wonders when they are quiet, jumps when they move,
dreams that they dope or drink, trembles to know
the traffic of their brains, jaywalks their street
in clumsy shoes.   20

Yet knows them better than their closest friends:
their cupboards and the secrets of their drawers,
their books, their private mail, their photographs
are theirs and hers.

Knows when they wash, how frequently their clothes
go to the cleaners, what they like to eat,
their curvature of health, but even so
is not content.

And like a lover must know all, all, all.
Prays she may catch them unprepared at last
and palm the dreadful riddle of their skulls—
hoping the worst.

[1946, rev. 1974]

Stories of Snow

Those in the vegetable rain retain
an area behind their sprouting eyes
held soft and rounded with the dream of snow
precious and reminiscent as those globes—
souvenir of some never-nether land—
which hold their snow-storms circular, complete
high in a tall and teakwood cabinet.

In countries where the leaves are large as hands
where flowers protrude their fleshy chins
and call their colours,
an imaginary snow-storm sometimes falls
among the lilies.
And in the early morning one will waken
to think the glowing linen of his pillow
a northern drift, will find himself mistaken
and lie back weeping.
And there the story shifts from head to head,
of how in Holland, from their feather beds
hunters arise and part the flakes and go
forth to the frozen lakes in search of swans—
the snow-light falling white along their guns,
their breath in plumes.
While tethered in the wind like sleeping gulls
ice-boats wait the raising of their wings
to skim the electric ice at such a speed
they leap jet strips of naked water,
and how these flying, sailing hunters feel
air in their mouths as terrible as ether.
And on the story runs that even drinks
in that white landscape dare to be no colour;
how flasked and water clear, the liquor slips
silver against the hunters' moving hips.
And of the swan in death these dreamers tell
of its last flight and how it falls, a plummet,
pierced by the freezing bullet

and how three feathers, loosened by the shot,
descend like snow upon it.
While hunters plunge their fingers in its down
deep as a drift, and dive their hands
up to the neck of the wrist   40
in that warm metamorphosis of snow
as gentle as the sort that woodsmen know
who, lost in the white circle, fall at last
and dream their way to death.

And stories of this kind are often told
in countries where great flowers bar the roads
with reds and blues which seal the route to snow—
as if, in telling, raconteurs unlock
the colour with its complement and go
through to the area behind the eyes   50
where silent, unrefractive whiteness lies.

[1946]

Photos of a Salt Mine

How innocent their lives look,
how like a child's
dream of caves and winter, both combined;
the steep descent to whiteness
and the stope[3]
with its striated walls
their folds all leaning as if pointing to
the greater whiteness still,
that great white bank
with its decisive front,   10
that seam upon a slope,
salt's lovely ice.

And wonderful underfoot the snow of salt
the fine
particles a broom could sweep,
one thinks
muckers might make angels in its drifts
as children do in snow,

---

[3] A step-like excavation in the side of a pit.

lovers in sheets,
lie down and leave imprinted where they lay   20
a feathered creature holier than they.

And in the outworked stopes
with lamps and ropes
up miniature matterhorns[4]
the miners climb
probe with their lights
the ancient folds of rock—
syncline and anticline[5]—
and scoop from darkness an Aladdin's cave:[6]
rubies and opals glitter from its walls.   30

But hoses douse the brilliance of these jewels,
melt fire to brine.
Salt's bitter water trickles thin and forms,
slow fathoms down,
a lake within a cave,
lacquered with jet—
white's opposite.
There grey on black the boating miners float
to mend the stays and struts of that old stope
and deeply underground   40
their words resound,
are multiplied by echo, swell and grow
and make a climate of a miner's voice.

So all the photographs like children's wishes
are filled with caves or winter,
innocence
has acted as a filter,
selected only beauty from the mine.
Except in the last picture,
it is shot   50
from an acute high angle. In a pit
figures the size of pins are strangely lit
and might be dancing but you know they're not.

[4] Reference to the Matterhorn mountain in the Swiss Alps.

[5] Folds in rock layers that are used to determine the age of the rock.

[6] A reference to the story of Aladdin and the magic lamp from *The Book of One Thousand and One Nights.*

Like Dante's vision of the nether hell[7]
men struggle with the bright cold fires of salt,
locked in the black inferno of the rock:
the filter here, not innocence but guilt.

[1954]

Stefan

Stefan
aged eleven
looked at the baby and said
When he thinks it must be pure thought
because he hasn't any words yet
and we
proud parents
admiring friends
who had looked at the baby

looked at the baby again   10

[1981]

Planet Earth

It has to be spread out, the skin of this planet,
has to be ironed, the sea in its whiteness;
and the hands keep on moving,
smoothing the holy surfaces.

In Praise of Ironing   Pablo Neruda[8]

It has to be loved the way a laundress loves her linens,
the way she moves her hands caressing the fine muslins
knowing their warp and woof,[9]
like a lover coaxing, or a mother praising.
It has to be loved as if it were embroidered   10

---

[7] Dante Alighieri (1265–1321), Italian poet whose central work is *The Divine Comedy*. In the first part of the poem, the *Inferno*, Dante describes the nine circles of Hell in the form of an inverted cone where the lowest circle contains a frozen lake.

[8] Pablo Neruda (1904–1973), Chilean poet and politician who won the Nobel Prize for Literature in 1971.

[9] "Warp and woof" literally refers to the two sets of interwoven threads in weaving; it is often used metaphorically to refer to the "fabric" or essence of something. Here Page is able to invoke both usages.

with flowers and birds and two joined hearts upon it.
It has to be stretched and stroked.
It has to be celebrated.
O this great beloved world and all the creatures in it.
It has to be spread out, the skin of this planet.

The trees must be washed, and the grasses and mosses.
They have to be polished as if made of green brass.
The rivers and little streams with their hidden cresses
and pale-coloured pebbles
and their fool's gold   20
must be washed and starched or shined into brightness,
the sheets of lake water
smoothed with the hand
and the foam of the oceans pressed into neatness.
It has to be ironed, the sea in its whiteness

and pleated and goffered,[10] the flower-blue sea
the protean,[11] wine-dark, grey, green, sea
with its metres of satin and bolts of brocade.
And sky—such an O! overhead—night and day
must be burnished and rubbed   30
by hands that are loving
so the blue blazons forth
and the stars keep on shining
within and above
and the hands keep on moving.

It has to be made bright, the skin of this planet
till it shines in the sun like gold leaf.
Archangels then will attend to its metals
and polish the rods of its rain.
Seraphim will stop singing hosannas[12]   40
to shower it with blessings and blisses and praises
and, newly in love,
we must draw it and paint it
our pencils and brushes and loving caresses
smoothing the holy surfaces.

[1994]

---

[10] Fluted, crimped.

[11] Changing, unpredictable. The "wine-dark sea" is a recurring phrase in Homer's *Odyssey*.

[12] Seraphim are angels, distinguished especially by the fervour of love; hosanna, a shout of praise or adoration.

Like that of P.K. Page and Dorothy Livesay, Margaret Avison's poetry spans many decades. And as with the poetry of Page and Livesay, the reader of Avison's poetry is rewarded in persevering through its dense complexity. When Volume III of *Always Now: The Collected Poems* appeared in 2005, reviewers rushed to call for renewed attention to Avison's work. Reviewer Anne Burke suggests that Avison's poetry, with its hard, abstract, and learned verse, under-cuts the conventional view that mod-ernism in Canada was a masculinist stronghold.

Born in Galt, Ontario, in 1918, Avison was the daughter of a Methodist minister who led parishes in Regina and Calgary. Avison recalls how the open landscape of southern Alberta perma-nently defined her sense of space where "The snow outside / glittered like mica-shavings / in the Alberta sunshine," as she puts it in "The Seed of History." A student at Victoria College—a hub of poetry in the 1930s as the academic home of poet E.J. Pratt and a young Northrop Frye—Avison published her first poem in *Canadian Poetry Magazine* in 1939, the year before she received her B.A. After attending schools of creative writing at the Universities of Indiana (1955) and Chicago (1956–57) where she was a Guggenheim fellow, she received an M.A. from the University of Toronto in 1965.

Critical accolades span Avison's publishing career, with almost three decades between her two Governor General's Award-winning collections *Winter Sun* (1960) and *No Time* (1989). She continued writing until her death in 2007, publishing *Not Yet but Still* (1997) and *Concrete and Wild Carrot* (2002),

which won the lucrative 2003 Griffin Prize—Avison was lauded by the judges for the "many decades she has forged a way to write, against the grain, some of the most human, sweet and profound poetry of our time"—and *Momentary Dark* (2006), issued the year before she died. An officer of the Order of Canada since 1985, she is remembered by poet Dennis Lee as a "titan" of modernism in Canada.

Although Avison's first collection did not appear until 1960, her poems were regularly included in the "little magazines" of the 1940s, including *Contemporary Verse* and *First Statement*. A.J.M. Smith adopted her work as a model of cosmo-politan poetry and included four of her poems in *The Book of Canadian Poetry* (1943), while John Sutherland highlighted her work in his *Other Canadians* (1947). Cosmopolitan mod-ernism is evident in the early sonnet "Snow," which encapsulates her poetic credo about the ways in which the imagi-nation overcomes the limitations of sen-sory perception. As critic David Stouck puts it, the imagination, or what Avison termed "the optic heart," stands on the borderline between what is felt and what is perceived.

The focus of Avison's writing changed when she embraced Christianity and Christian salvation in the early 1960s. Her collections following *Winter Sun—The Dumbfounding* (1966) and *sunblue* (1978), in particular—reflect the reverence and wonder of Christian beliefs. While there is a sense of awe in her later poetry, it is not sentimental or romantic. In the spiritual resonance of her poems one can find the influence of the nineteenth-century English poet Gerard Manley Hopkins (as well as in her convoluted word play and sense of revelation in the natural world glorifying God) and the metaphysical poets of the seventeenth century such as John Donne, Andrew Marvell, and George Herbert. Like the metaphysical poets, Avison has an astute command of irony and of the metaphorical "conceit." Her poetry is concerned with issues of spirituality and moral sensibility, but it does not proselytize. Poet Mary di Michele writes that "the surprised and surprising in vision and in language is the reward awaiting the attentive reader of Avison's poetry."

The Apex Animal

A Horse, thin-coloured as oranges ripened in freight-
    cars
which have shaken casements through the miles of
    night
across three nights of field and waterfront ware-
    houses—
rather, the narrow Head of the Horse
with the teeth shining and white ear-tufts:
It, I fancy, and from experience
commend the fancy to your inner eye,   10
It is the One, in a patch of altitude
troubled only by clarity of weather,
Who sees, the ultimate Recipient
of what happens, the One Who is aware
when, in the administrative wing
a clerk returns from noon-day, though
the ointment of mortality
for one strange hour, in all his lustreless life,
has touched his face.

(For that Head of a Horse there is no question   20
whether he spent the noon-hour with a friend,
below street-level, or on the parapet—
a matter which may safely rest
in mortal memory.)

                                                    [1960]

The Swimmer's Moment

For everyone
The swimmer's moment at the whirlpool comes,
But many at that moment will not say

"This is the whirlpool, then."
By their refusal they are saved
From the black pit, and also from contesting
The deadly rapids, and emerging in
The mysterious, and more ample, further waters.
And so their bland-blank faces turn and turn
Pale and forever on the rim of suction   10
They will not recognize.
Of those who dare the knowledge
Many are whirled into the ominous centre
That, gaping vertical, seals up
For them an eternal boon of privacy,
So that we turn away from their defeat
With a despair, not for their deaths, but for
Ourselves, who cannot penetrate their secret
Nor even guess at the anonymous breadth
Where one or two have won: 20
(The silver reaches of the estuary).

[1960]

Snow

Nobody stuffs the world in at your eyes.
The optic heart must venture: a jail-break
And re-creation. Sedges and wild rice
Chase rivery pewter. The astonished cinders quake
With rhizomes. All ways through the electric air
Trundle candy-bright disks; they are desolate
Toys if the soul's gates seal, and cannot bear,
Must shudder under, creation's unseen freight.
But soft, there is snow's legend: colour of mourning
Along the yellow Yangtze[1] where the wheel   10
Spins an indifferent stasis that's death's warning.
Asters of tumbled quietness reveal
Their petals. Suffering this starry blur
The rest may ring your change, sad listener.

[1960]

From Now—On?

The family car has come
for the son who believed

---

[1] River in China. In many Asian countries, including China, white is the colour of mourning.

he had left home.
His college luggage heaved
into the back too leaves,
with two of them, still room
in the front seat for him.

Is it his last year?
Where are his companions
to gather and conspire   10
falsely about reunions?
It's good there's no-one there
to witness these old tensions,
old bonds, new fear.

The future closes down
with the slammed trunk.
Dazed by distractions
and like a drunk
awash suddenly with affection
and close to tears, he thinks   20
of the long-lost home town.

For him, is this disruption?
"An end and no beginning"
now his life's caption?
Ice on bright puddles, birds all singing
to mock the nothingness suction,
the spiritless direction,
his flattened pinions?

In the vague inattention of a too
long life, out walking by   30
that college: how
many spring term-ends have I
seen the cars load, the shy
parents reclaiming their boy.
And this "how many" is also,
for me, disruption.

[1997]

On 8 April 1949, the government of Louis St. Laurent ordered an inquiry into the state of national development of the arts, letters, and sciences. The expressed agenda of the official Order-in-Council was one of cultural nationalism, specifically, to promote the development of the arts in Canada: "[I]t is desirable that the Canadian people should know as much as possible about their country, its history and traditions; and about their national life and common achievements; . . . it is in the national interest to give encouragement to institutions which express national feeling, promote common understanding and add to the variety and richness of Canadian life, rural as well as urban." Vincent Massey (1887–1967) was appointed chair of the Commission.

The Commission's mandate came about because of a great transition in Canadian cultural affairs. According to Richard Stursberg, the current head of CBC television, "Although the country's prewar cultural life was primarily focused on amateur, community-oriented, voluntary activities, the commission foresaw that these activities were giving way to a more urban, impersonal and national orientation; the overall character of the final report is a strange mixture of mourning for an age that was rapidly passing and of excitement at the new era of professional 'mass culture' that lay ahead."

The Commissioners toured the major cities of Canada between August 1949 and July 1950, travelling nearly 16,000 kilometres, holding public hearings in 16 cities in the 10 provinces (224 meetings, 114 of these in public session), and reviewing 462 briefs, in the presentation of which over 1,200 witnesses appeared before the Commission. The briefs included submissions from 13 federal government institutions, seven provincial governments, 87 national organizations, 262 local bodies, and 35 private commercial radio stations. The Commissioners invited experts in various fields to prepare special studies as well. In the realm of literature this consisted of an English literature specialist (E.A. McCourt) and a French literature specialist (René Garneau), as well as reports by the Canadian Authors Association, Société des Écrivains Canadiens, Canadian Writers' Committee, and the members of the First Statement Press collective.

The Report issued in 1951 by the Commission became known publicly as the "Massey Report." It is an important document in the cultural history of Canada because it is where the need for public support of the arts and culture was clearly spelled out, with specific recommendations on how to achieve greater cultural independence and prosperity. The Massey Commission was thus a direct response to the years of debate about the need for a distinctly Canadian culture, questions that had been central as far back as the mid-nineteenth century. The Report describes the problems facing the arts in Canada in the postwar period, arguing that culture plays a critically important role in nation building and that the federal government has an obligation to better support cultural development. It focuses on the need for an increase in funding and government patronage of a wide range of cultural activities: "[I]f we in Canada are to have a more plentiful and better cultural fare, we must pay for it. Goodwill alone can do little for a starving plant; if the cultural life of Canada is anaemic, it must be nourished, and this will cost money."

Perhaps most importantly for literature in Canada, the Commission also recommended "that a body be created to be known as the Canada Council for the Encouragement of the Arts, Letters, Humanities and Social Sciences to stimulate and to help voluntary organizations within these fields, to foster Canada's cultural relations abroad, to perform the functions of a national commission for UNESCO, and to devise and administer a system of scholarships." Based on the recommendations of the Report, the Canada Council was established in 1957.

The Report met with general approval and all of its major recommendations (concerning broadcasting, the creation of the Canada Council, the support of a national library, and financial aid to universities) were implemented by 1957. However, according to the "Notes on the Massey Report" by historian Frank Underhill (1885–1971), co-founder of the CCF and co-writer of the "Regina Manifesto" with F.R. Scott (see the Scott section), the report focuses too much on the threat of American cultural annexation. That, of course, is open to debate. Included here are excerpts from the section of the Report that deals most closely with the threat of American culture to Canadian culture and the section that outlines the state of literature in Canada.

From The Massey Report: A Royal Commission on National Development in the Arts, Letters and Sciences, 1949–1951

The Forces of Geography

CANADIANS, with their customary optimism, may think that the fate of their civilization is in their own hands. So it is. But this young nation, struggling to be itself, must shape its course with an eye to three conditions so familiar that their significance can too easily be ignored. Canada has a small and scattered population in a vast area; this population is clustered along the rim of another country many times more populous and of far greater economic strength; a majority of Canadians share their mother tongue with that neighbour, which leads to peculiarly close and intimate relations. One or two of these conditions will be found in many modern countries. But Canada alone possesses all three. What is their effect, good or bad, on what we call Canadianism? [. . .]

23. Every intelligent Canadian acknowledges his debt to the United States for excellent films, radio programmes and periodicals. But the price may be excessive. Of films and radio we shall speak in more detail later, but it may be noted in passing that our national radio which carries the Sunday symphony from New York also carries the soap-opera. In the periodical press we receive indeed many admirable American journals but also a flood of others much less admirable which, as we have been clearly told, is threatening to submerge completely our national product. [. . .]

24. The Canadian Periodical Press Association tells the same tale. Although during the last generation our periodicals have maintained and greatly strengthened their position, the competition they face has been almost overwhelming. Canadian magazines with much difficulty have achieved a circulation of nearly forty-two millions a year as against an American circulation in Canada of over eighty-six millions. "Canada . . . is the only country of any size in the world," one of their members has observed, "whose people read more foreign periodicals then they do periodicals published in their own land, local newspapers excluded." The Canadian periodical cannot in its turn invade the American market; for Americans, it seems, simply do not know enough about Canada to appreciate Canadian material.[1] Our periodicals cannot hold their own except in their limited and unprotected market, nine million English-speaking readers. These must be set against the one hundred and sixty millions served by their competitors in the whole North American continent.

25. The American invasion by film, radio and periodical is formidable. Much of what comes to us is good and of this we shall be speaking presently. It has, however, been represented to us that many of the radio programmes have in fact no particular application to Canada or to Canadian conditions and that some of them, including certain children's programmes of the "crime" and "horror" type, are positively harmful. News commentaries too, and even live broadcasts from American sources, are designed for American ears and are almost certain to have an American slant and emphasis by reason of what they include or omit, as well as because of the opinions expressed. We think it permissible to record these comments on American radio since we observe that in the United States many radio programmes and American broadcasting in general have recently been severely criticized. It will, we think, be readily agreed that we in Canada should take measures to avoid in our radio, and in our television, at least those aspects of American broadcasting which have provoked in the United States the most out-spoken and the sharpest opposition.[2]

26. American influences on Canadian life to say the least are impressive. There should be no thought of interfering with the liberty of all Canadians to enjoy them. Cultural exchanges are excellent in themselves. They widen the choice of the consumer and provide stimulating competition for the producer. It cannot be denied, however, that a vast and disproportionate amount of material coming from a single alien source may stifle rather than stimulate our own creative effort; and, passively accepted without any standard of comparison, this may weaken critical faculties. We are now spending millions to maintain a

[1] See Hugh MacLennan's "Boy Meets Girl in Winnipeg and Who Cares?" and Sara Jeannette Duncan's "American Influence on Canadian Thought" (Volume I, Section III).

[2] See the discussion of CanCon regulations in the introduction to Section VI.

national independence which would be nothing but an empty shell without a vigorous and distinctive cultural life. We have seen that we have its elements in our traditions and in our history; we have made important progress, often aided by American generosity. We must not be blind, however, to the very present danger of permanent dependence. [...]

Literature

1. The ancient capital of Canada was founded in 1608. Half a century earlier Jacques Cartier published in France an account of his voyage up the St. Lawrence in 1534. This was the first work, or to be more precise, the first important literary document inspired by Canada. It would, perhaps, be going too far to claim the great explorer from St. Malo as the first Canadian man of letters, but at least we can maintain that Canada has enjoyed an association with literature from its earliest beginnings.[3]

2. But this early association did not produce any precocious results. In fact, from the evidence we have received from writers' societies, from editors, from literary organizations and from the authors of the two Special Studies prepared for us on Canadian literature, we must conclude that, among the various means of artistic expression in Canada, literature has taken a second place, and indeed has fallen far behind painting. We have found general agreement that Canadian letters have no such great names as Morrice, Jackson, Harris, Thomson, Gagnon and Pellan[4] in painting, names as famous abroad as in their own country.

IS THERE A NATIONAL LITERATURE?

3. Is it true, then, that we are a people without a literature? To this question we have had similar replies from different sources. Defining the term "Canadian literature" as the reflection in works of imagination of the interests, the ideals and the character of our people, the author of one of our studies states that Canada cannot yet show an adequate number of works that correspond to this description. [...]

9. Not only the critics but the briefs agree that Canadian literature has not yet achieved the status of a "national literature". "The inarticulate nature of the average Canadian's patriotism results from the lack of a native literature commensurate with Canada's physical, industrial, scientific and academic stature, and with the proved character of its people"; this we read in the brief of the Canadian Authors Association. [...]

---

[3] See Volume I for an excerpt from Cartier's *Voyages*.

[4] Canadian painters: James Wilson Morrice (1865–1924), Tom Thomson (1877–1917), A.Y. Jackson (1882–1974), Lawren Harris (1885–1970), Clarence Gagnon (1881–1942), and Alfred Pellan (1906–1988).

10. If, on the other hand,[5] one accepts the views of the young writers of the First Statement Press,[6] Canadian letters for some years have been proceeding steadily towards the beginning of a truly national literature. Since the 1930's when the publication of a book was not too frequent an event, the situation has much improved. Then too, periodical reviews and magazines were practically closed to Canadian writers who, in consequence, had no means of conveying their ideas to the reading public. Criticism at that time, so far as it existed at all, was confined to writers of a previous age. There has been a great change. In the opinion of the young writers of the First Statement Press, Canadian poetry, turning away from the theme of nature to the theme of human experience, has had a constantly increasing influence. In prose, too, we are told, English-speaking writers have finally succeeded in bridging partly the gulf between Canadian literature and Canadian society.

11. In short, although all our informants agree that Canada has not yet established a national literature, there is also general agreement that, in spite of the obstacles in the way, much progress has recently been made. We were particularly impressed by the optimism of our younger writers.

THE FUTURE OF CANADIAN LETTERS

12. One association expressed regret at the delay in the appearance of a national literature since this is the greatest of all forces making for national unity. But our literature must first find its centre of gravity. At the moment, so the critics have told us, our writers are subject to the pull of a variety of forces. Traditions still strong and vigorous exert an influence upon our letters from England and France; Canadian writers still feel the pull of these historic ties. On the other hand, the literature of the United States, which in the last thirty years has acquired an increasing international reputation, exercises an impact which is beneficial in many respects no doubt, but which, at the same time, may be almost overpowering. The author of our special study on letters in French Canada referred to "a crisis of orientation", a crisis which he would like to see resolved by more energetic efforts to maintain those fundamental characteristics common to the literatures of Great Britain and France. On the other hand, there are those who deplore the respect paid to those principles and forms which come to us from Europe as literary survivals of the spirit of colonialism.

13. Without taking sides on this matter we do think it important to comment on the efforts of those literary groups belonging to various schools of thought which strive to defend Canadian literature against the deluge of the less worthy

---

[5] The first hand is not actually mentioned. Paragraph 10 follows on statements by the Canadian Writers' Committee and the Canadian Authors Association that are pessimistic about the state of "national" literature. The CWC, for instance, argues, "As an agricultural and industrial nation Canada ranks high in the world. But as a cultured nation exploring the human mind and soul she ranks low."

[6] Such as John Sutherland, Betty Sutherland, Irving Layton, Raymond Souster, and Louis Dudek.

American publications. These, we are told, threaten our national values, corrupt our literary taste and endanger the livelihood of our writers. According to the Canadian Writers' Committee:

> "A mass of outside values is dumped into our cities and towns and homes. . . . We would like to see the development of a little Canadian independence, some say in who we are, and what we think, and how we feel and what we do. . . . The fault is not America's but ours."

14. Immunity from alien influences would not, of course, be sufficient in itself to create a national literature; but it would at least make possible a climate in which the Canadian writer would find himself more at home, where he would be better understood, and where he would find the opportunity for more frequent spiritual contacts with a society which would be more fully Canadian. For if our writers are uncertain of the road ahead, their uncertainty, it seems, is derived from the general confusion in a society with no fixed values and no generally accepted standards.

CANADIAN LITERARY TALENT

15. It may be that the Canadian writer, whether in English or French, has not yet reached that level of universalism which would permit his work to awaken echoes outside our country as well as within it; he may still have some way to go before finding "a Canadian cadence" to borrow the expression of an English-speaking critic; it may be that he is producing novels too naive in their structure, lacking dramatic and poetic force, novels which are too descriptive and not sufficiently analytic, that the tempo of our books is not sufficiently rapid and warm, that true poetry is rare with us and the theatre almost non-existent. In spite of these weaknesses it remains true that we have an important number of writers finely gifted who, if their work were sustained by greater interest and sympathy in their own country, might succeed in giving to our literature the stimulus which has hitherto been lacking. [. . .]

18. If we have properly understood what we have been told, the Canadian writer suffers from the fact that he is not sufficiently recognized in our national life, that his work is not considered necessary to the life of his country; and it is this isolation which prevents his making his full contribution. It seems therefore to be necessary to find some way of helping our Canadian writers to become an integral part of their environment and, at the same time, to give them a sense of their importance in this environment.

19. Interested societies and groups of writers have made a variety of proposals to us. The Canadian Authors Association would like to extend the present system of awards now offered to writers, such as the annual awards of the Governor General, but also to have them accompanied by a prize in

money to be granted by the Canadian Government. It has also been proposed that fellowships, such as those of the Guggenheim Foundation, should be established to enable writers of proven competence to devote an entire year or more to the preparation of a serious literary work. Finally, while it was recognized that the C.B.C. had already given help to our writers by commissioning scripts from them, by presenting book reviews, and in general by recognizing them and their place in our national life, it has been proposed to us that the national radio call even more frequently upon the services of Canadian writers.

[1951]

Notes on the Massey Report[7]

Frank Underhill

[. . .] There is one theme in the Report about which some searching questions should be asked. The Commissioners seek a national Canadian culture which shall be independent of American influences. Several times they speak of these influences as "alien". This use of the word "alien" seems to me to reveal a fallacy that runs through much of Canadian nationalistic discussion. For we cannot escape the fact that we live on the same continent as the Americans, and that the longer we live here the more are we going to be affected by the same continental influences which affect them. It is too late now for a Canadian cultural nationalism to develop in the kind of medieval isolation in which English or French nationalism was nurtured. These so-called "alien" American influences are not alien at all; they are just the natural forces that operate in the conditions of twentieth-century civilization.

The fact is that if we produced Canadian movies for our own mass consumption, they would be as sentimental and vulgar and escapist as are the Hollywood variety; and they would be sentimental, vulgar, and escapist in the American way, not in the English or French or Italian way. Our newspapers which are an independent local product do not differ essentially from the American ones; the kind of news which the Canadian Press circulates on its own origination is exactly like that originated by A.P. or U.P.[8] Like the American ones, they become progressively worse as the size of the city increases, up to a certain point. Somewhere between the size of Chicago and the size of New York another force comes into operation, producing a different kind of newspaper. We haven't any daily as bad as the *Chicago Tribune*, because we haven't any city as big as Chicago; but also we haven't anything as good as the *New York Times* or *Herald Tribune*. If *Macleans Magazine* achieved its ambition, and American competition were shut out from its constituency, it would continue to be what it is now, only more so,

---

[7] "Notes on the Massey Report" was originally published in *Canadian Forum* (Aug. 1951).

[8] A.P. is short for American Press; U.P. stands for United Press.

i.e., a second-rate *Saturday Evening Post* or *Colliers*. It is mass-consumption and the North American continental environment which produce these phenomena, not some sinister influences in the United States.

If we could get off by ourselves on a continental island, far away from the wicked Americans, all we should achieve would be to become a people like the Australians. (And even then the American goblin would get us in the end, as he is getting the Australians.) Let us be thankful, then, that we live next door to the Americans. But if we allow ourselves to be obsessed by the danger of American cultural annexation, so that the thought preys on us day and night, we shall only become a slightly bigger Ulster.[9] The idea that by taking thought, and with help of some government subventions, we can become another England—which, one suspects, is Mr. Massey's ultimate idea—is purely fantastic. No sane Canadian wants us to become a nation of Australians or Ulsterites. So, if we will only be natural, and stop going about in this eternal defensive feat of being ourselves, we shall discover that we are very like the Americans both in our good qualities and in our bad qualities. Young Canadians who are really alive make this discovery now without going through any great spiritual crisis.

The root cultural problem in our modern mass-democracies is this relationship between the mass culture, which is in danger of being further debased with every new invention in mass communications, and the culture of the few. The United States is facing this problem at a rather more advanced stage than we have yet reached, and the more intimately we can study American experience the more we shall profit. What we need, we, the minority of Canadians who care for the culture of the few, is closer contact with the *finest* expressions of the American mind. The fear that what will result from such contact will be our own absorption is pure defeatism. We need closer touch with the best American universities (*not* Teachers College) and research institutions, closer touch with American experimental music and poetry and theatre and painting, closer personal touch with the men who are leaders in these activities. The Americans are now mature enough to have come through this adolescent phase of believing that the way to become mature is to cut yourself off from the older people who are more mature than you are. It is about time that we grew out of it also. I think that the Massey commissioners should use their leisure now to study the Americans much more closely than they seem to have done hitherto.

[1951]

9 Northern Ireland.

Contemporary Period, 1960–1985

Introduction: Nationalists, Intellectuals, and Iconoclasts

[W]e need to know about here, because here is where we live.
—Margaret Atwood, *Survival* (1972)

THE 1960s AND 1970s in Canada are widely heralded as a time of resurgent cultural nationalism. Of course, Canadians had experienced similar nationalist fervour and self-definition in the late nineteenth century, during the years following Confederation when people were striving to decide Canada's political future in relation to Britain and the United States. The late nineteenth century was also a period marked by intense, and often contentious, debates about Canadian cultural identity, a question that would be revived with equal passion by Canadian modernists ranging from the Group of Seven to A.J.M. Smith and John Sutherland between the 1920s and '50s. However, there was something unique about the form these questions would take in the late 1960s.

As never before, the quest for Canadian identity had a truly pan-national dimension. The fervour was felt in Toronto as well as in Winnipeg, in Halifax and in Vancouver (though markedly less so in Quebec, which was experiencing a nationalist movement of its own). Moreover, the language of the day was infused with the liberatory and revolutionary rhetoric that characterized the

1960s and '70s more generally. This was going to be a freedom movement: anti-imperialist in tenor, invigorating in spirit, and idealistic in tone. But none of this would be possible, poet and critic Dennis Lee observed, until Canadian culture had managed to shed its inferiority complex and come out from under the shadow of the United States.

The nationalist fervour of the late '60s and early '70s, which peaked in the cross-national centennial celebrations of 1967 (commemorating the 100th anniversary of Confederation) and the international success of Expo 67 in Montreal, was bolstered by an avid, at times somewhat blinkered, anti-Americanism, a desire to establish Canada as everything that the United States was not. Of course, anti-Americanism had long historical roots in Canada, reaching back to the period when the United States rebelled against England (and, hence, against British North America) at the time of the American Revolution. Early literary works such as Thomas Chandler Haliburton's *The Clockmaker* (1836), Susanna Moodie's *Roughing It in the Bush* (1852), and Sara Jeannette Duncan's "American Influence on Canadian Thought" (1887) had condemned the "Yankees" for their blatant opportunism and amorality (see Volume I). However, the threat of American cultural imperialism became palpably evident in the post-Second World War era. The influential Massey Report of 1951, with its recommendations for cultural protection in Canada, assumed that American culture imperilled Canadian sovereignty (see Section V). In 1973, Lee warned of "the American tidal-wave that inundates us, in the cultural sphere as much as in the economic and political" (47). If in previous periods Canadian authors had been concerned to distinguish their writings from the influence of British traditions and British colonial history, in the post-Second World War period, it was the United States that had emerged as the new world superpower, a development that seemed all the more ominous because of its proximity to Canada. Works such as George Grant's *Lament for a Nation* (1965) and Lee's "Cadence, Country, Silence" (1973) and such poems as Margaret Atwood's "Backdrop Addresses Cowboy" (1968), John Newlove's "America" (1970), and Earle Birney's "i accuse us" (1973) express anxiety about the destructive influence of the United States. People began to speak of the American Empire, much as they had invoked the British Empire some decades before, but this new concern about an imperial threat emerged in the context of the "Cold War" between the United States and Communist governments worldwide. The American reach extended into South Asia, the Caribbean (notably Cuba), and Latin America. Canadians' sense of distinctiveness from the United States was clarified and given additional force during the Vietnam War (1965–73).[1] Canada took an independent position on the war, and actively welcomed American draft dodgers who fled over the border to be given sanctuary here.

---

[1] The dates for the Vietnam War vary depending on how one marks the beginning and end of the conflict. These dates represent American involvement in the war, from the first American full-scale attack on the North Vietnamese in March 1965 to the American withdrawal of troops in January 1973.

Nevertheless, critics have written about the failure of the emancipatory project of the 1960s, noting how the period of optimism and idealism soon metamorphosed into disillusionment as the 1960s, and the Vietnam War, progressed. While there is some truth to this notion, it ignores the long-lasting impact the period had on the ways subsequent generations viewed—and continue to view—their world. The post-Second World War era was marked by massive decolonization and civil liberties movements worldwide. Indeed, the period of the 1960s and '70s was foundational to the ways people today view the world from a postcolonial, transnational, global, and sometimes postmodern perspective.

The North American Context: Appraising the 1960s and '70s

It is impossible to speak about the 1960s and '70s in Canada without considering the period in a North American context. The leftist political ideals and civil liberties movements taking place in the United States extended across the border. However, these ideals and movements took very different forms in Canada (for example, the *séparatiste* movement in Quebec, Canadian nationalism and cultural protectionism, the fight for Canadian faculty within Canadian universities, and the support of Vietnam War draft dodgers). The 1960s were sparked by a sense of a gap between the institutional rhetoric of freedom and equality and the reality of lived experience—the experience of the urban poor, racial minorities (Aboriginal people did not have the unconditional right to vote in federal elections until 1960),[2] and the position of women. Poets such as Irving Layton, Earle Birney, bill bissett, bpNichol, and Leonard Cohen, among others, took a hard look at the moral hypocrisy of Canadian society during these years and questioned mainstream assumptions and preferences in their writing. Cohen's 1964 poem "What I'm Doing Here" provides a vivid sense of this hypocrisy in the liberal rhetoric of the day as he denounces the "universal alibi" that governs easy protestations of innocence in the post-Second World War era. Atwood's "It is dangerous to read newspapers" (1968) and Birney's powerful poem "i accuse us" (1973) are hard-hitting accounts of Canada's complicity in the horrors of Vietnam. The disaffection with institutional structures came to a head in the United States during the Watergate scandal of 1972–74, when it was discovered that President Richard Nixon had sanctioned a series of illegal activities—which included fraud, wire-tappings, burglary, intimidation, and bribery.

In effect, the left-wing political movements of this period sought to revive a more convincing meaning of "democracy," as opposed to the hollowed-out use of the word that so many political figures of the period were invoking. The rhetoric in the air was one of revolution and anti-imperialism. In the context of this renewed democratic spirit came changes not only to social structures—namely in the

[2] Aboriginal groups were able to vote in federal elections prior to 1960 under the condition that they relinquish their status under the Indian Act. According to Elections Canada, 1960 is the date when the practice of using Aboriginal political enfranchisement as a tool of assimilation finally came to an end.

treatment of minorities as a result of the extensive civil rights movements of the period and of women, following the advent of the Women's Liberation Movement and the period that we today refer to as Second Wave Feminism—but in the area of cultural expression as well. Radical changes were to emerge in literature and other art forms. This was the period of concrete poetry, sound poetry, folk music, and pop art. It was also the period that launched what we think of as the beginnings of postmodernism in the arts and critical theory. Such postmodernism was based on the counterculture notions of questioning authority, repudiating the universals sought in modernism, and performing, as French theorist Jean-François Lyotard put it, an "incredulity toward metanarratives" (xxiv), that is, a critique of overarching truth-claims such as national histories and religious systems.

One can discern the growing roots of an "anti-colonial" awareness during this period as well. The aftermath of the Second World War had exposed the horrifying results of anti-Semitism, and the Berlin Wall, built in 1961, became a symbol of the dangers of totalitarianism and intolerance. At the same time, many former British and French colonies around the world were gaining their independence, including Nigeria in 1960; Algeria, Jamaica, and Uganda in 1962; Kenya in 1963; and Singapore in 1965. Margaret Laurence's writings during this period engage explicitly with the colonial legacy in Africa. *This Side Jordan* (1960), for example, exposes the transfer of power in Ghana in the days leading up to its independence from British rule (reached in 1957). People were beginning to think of themselves as sharing a global planet, hence the catchphrase for Montreal's Expo 67, "Man and His World," and the popular logo that pictured people of various nations and ethnicities holding hands around the globe.

Connected to this emergent sense of global responsibility was the growing environmental movement of the period. Acid rain and toxic pesticides (especially DDT) were the subject of Rachel Carson's unprecedented exposé, *The Silent Spring*, published in 1962. In the 1970s a scandal arose around the situation in Love Canal, a neighbourhood in Niagara Falls, New York, in which residents, whose children were being born with severe birth defects, learned that their community was sitting on top of a toxic chemical dump. Canadian writer, naturalist, and environmental activist Farley Mowat published many of his major environmental texts during these years, including *Never Cry Wolf* in 1963. The international environmentalist organization Greenpeace was founded in Vancouver in 1971, and David Suzuki, the well-known Canadian geneticist-environmentalist, began his broadcasting career devoted to building public awareness of scientific and ecological issues in the 1970s. Later in the period, the Academy Award-winning National Film Board documentary *If You Love this Planet* (1982) caused a stir when physician Helen Caldicott warned about the environmental dangers posed by nuclear weapons.

The prime legacy of the 1960s is the crusade for social equality. The platitudes of democracy rang hollow for many who continued to find themselves disenfranchised: African Americans, especially in the ghettoes of the United States; Aboriginal peoples, who in the 1950s in Canada still did not have the right to vote without losing "Indian" status; women, who continued to find themselves victims of sexual inequality and subjugation; and gays and lesbians, who were subjected to criminal sanction for being homosexual. The huge mass of "baby boomers," now beginning to enter university and colleges, staged sit-ins and marches to protest infringements on democratic rights. These protests extended to an international scale as people protested the rise of American imperialism, especially in Vietnam and countries in Latin America. Accompanying this was the popular protest movement in the form of folk music, which included such figures as Bob Dylan, Joan Baez, and Pete Seeger in the United States, and Neil Young, Bruce Cockburn, Buffy Sainte-Marie, Gordon Lightfoot, and Joni Mitchell in Canada. Dylan's 1964 song "The Times They Are A-Changin'" expressed the sense of having entered a new revolutionary era. A protest against the American invasion of Cambodia in 1970 led to the massacre at Kent State University when the National Guard opened fire on student protesters, killing four, a shocking event that inspired Neil Young's famous song "Ohio" (1970) as well as the moving poem by Canadian poet Gary Geddes "Sandra Lee Scheuer." In response there was a nationwide student strike as millions of students closed down colleges and schools to protest the event.

Foremost of these international protests, and the longest-running, was the massive protest movement (combined with a more general peace movement) against the Vietnam War, which raged from 1965 to 1973. The North Vietnamese, backed by the Soviets, fought against the U.S.-backed South Vietnamese. The war, which effectively pitted Americans against the Soviets as part of the general Cold War ethos of the period, revealed the status of the United States as an oppressive, and often ruthless, world superpower. After 10 years, and millions of deaths (counting soldiers and civilians on both sides), the Americans finally withdrew and the North Vietnamese won, leading to the establishment of a Communist government in the country.

For Canada, the Vietnam War had two major impacts. First, it established Canadian pride in being distinct from the United States, since Canada did not officially support the conflict; as Frank Davey wrote in 1973, it provided proof that Canada was "in some important ways an 'un-American' place" (*From* 16). Second, Canada provided refuge to over 20,000 American draft dodgers, many of whom remained in the country after the end of the war. Indeed, this was the first time American immigration to Canada outnumbered the reverse. According to John Hagan, it was "the largest politically motivated migration from the United States since the United Empire Loyalists moved north to oppose the American Revolution" (qtd. in Turner 69). The opposition of most Canadians to the war sparked numerous anti-war protests across the country, which were supported by many artists and musicians. The Vietnam War was a catalytic moment for Canadian nationalism as it highlighted the views of Canadians as distinct from those of Americans.

Concurrent with these international events was the struggle for racial and social equality on the North American home front. Before the 1960s, African Americans experienced many infringements of their civil rights, including being barred from attending the same colleges and universities as White Americans and segregation on buses and in restaurants. In the early 1960s, Reverend Martin Luther King Jr. led a peaceful march against segregation in Birmingham, Alabama, and was attacked by riot police. In 1962, a series of race riots occurred in Oxford, Mississippi, when an African-American man, James Meredith, tried to enrol in a Whites-only college. A civil rights march in Washington in 1963 culminated in King's eloquent speech in which he proclaimed: "I have a dream that my four little children will one day live in a nation where they will not be judged by the color of their skin but by the content of their character. . . ." After King was assassinated in Memphis on 4 April 1968, 150,000 people attended his funeral. King's central role in the fight for racial equality and harmony had enormous impact in the United States and Canada, countries where the White majority was not used to listening to the powerful words of a Black man.

The 1960s also saw the formation of an important Native American activist movement, which continues into the present. As Bruce Trigger notes, "For almost three centuries White North Americans had assumed that native peoples were doomed to be culturally assimilated or to perish as a superior European civilization spread inexorably across the continent" (3). Writings about Aboriginal peoples at the turn of the twentieth century had proclaimed them to be a "weird and waning race" (see Duncan Campbell Scott's poem "The Onondaga Madonna" in Volume I), condemned to "vanish" naturally into the mists of time. However, by the 1960s, not only had Aboriginal people survived in huge numbers, but Native activists took it upon themselves to protest their inequitable treatment under government policy. Native activism in Canada cannot be seen outside its larger North American context. (Indeed, many Aboriginal people today regard the Canada-U.S. border as an artificial marker across traditional territory. See Thomas King's story "Borders" in Section VII.) The American Indian Movement (AIM) was formed in 1968 and rallied around the cause of treaty rights, land claims, and police brutality. In 1972, the movement gained international attention when it seized control of the Bureau of Indian Affairs in Washington, D.C. The movement's activities reached their culmination in 1973 when a standoff between Native Americans and police took place at Wounded Knee, South Dakota (the location of a previous massacre of Native people in 1890).

In 1960, Aboriginal people had finally won the right to vote in federal elections without losing their status rights. Following on the heels of the unsuccessful national lobby group the North American Indian Brotherhood (NAIB), established in the late 1940s, the National Indian Council was formed in 1961 to represent treaty and status Indians, non-status Indians, and Métis people (the Inuit were not included). Subsequently, after trouble finding common ground of concerns with such a large constituency, the National Indian Brotherhood was founded in the late 1960s as an alliance of status and treaty Aboriginal groups to lobby for collective demands to provincial and federal governments. The non-status and Métis groups united and formed the Native Council of Canada. Today, the Assembly of First Nations is the highest level of political representation for First Nations people in Canada.

In 1969 the federal government introduced its controversial "White Paper," which was meant to replace the Indian Act and to relieve the government of responsibility for Aboriginal people. The White Paper called for the end of treaties, claiming that this would mean equality for Aboriginal peoples, but it was interpreted by many, most notably by the well-known Cree activist Harold Cardinal, as a move toward assimilation. Not only did it renege on treaty promises, but it did not address social and economic problems in Aboriginal communities. The "Red Paper" of 1970 was launched by Cardinal as a response to the White Paper, which was put aside by the government in 1971. This triumph was a key moment in Aboriginal activism, anticipating many future Aboriginal gains in Canadian politics, most notably the refusal to ratify Brian Mulroney's Meech Lake Accord in 1990 by Manitoba MLA Elijah Harper. Another equally important political intervention occurred in the early 1970s when Jeanette Corbière Lavell challenged the section of the Indian Act that mandated women's loss of status upon marrying non-Native men (see the excerpt from the Indian Act in Volume I). The ramifications of this law meant that Native mothers could not leave land to their children, nor could their children go to school on reserves with their relatives. It also meant that the Human Rights Act (section 66) did not apply to the Indian Act, since Native women were not allowed to appeal for matrimonial property rights. The case was taken to the Supreme Court in 1973 and lost by one vote. After a decade-long struggle, Lavell finally succeeded: in 1985, with Bill c-31, her Indian status was reinstated.

The 1960s and '70s also saw the birth of the "Women's Liberation Movement" (often referred to as Second Wave Feminism), one of the most important legacies to emerge out of the period. In the United States, the National Organization for Women (NOW) became established in 1966, with popular feminist spokesperson Gloria Steinem campaigning for women's rights across North America. In 1971, Steinem founded *Ms.* magazine, which was a significant venue for women's issues at the time. In Canada, the women's magazine *Chatelaine* came under the editorship of Doris Anderson, who extended the feminist scope of the magazine by inviting articles on topics such as divorce laws and abortion. Such texts as Betty Friedan's *The Feminine Mystique* (1963) and Kate Millett's *Sexual Politics* (1968) made a splash as feminist thinkers articulated the sense of disjunction that women were experiencing between the so-called "freedom" of twentieth-century America and their sense of being continually secondary to their male counterparts—not only in terms of wages and career opportunities, but also in terms of the ways they were regarded, what was expected of them, and how they were treated. This disjunction became readily apparent to a young Atwood in the early 1960s when she began to make a name for herself as a published poet. According to literary biographer Rosemary Sullivan, Atwood and other women poets of the day experienced a closing of the ranks because many male writers, such as Irving Layton, believed female writers to be encroaching on traditional male territory: "Modern women I see cast in the role of furies striving to castrate the male," wrote Layton in his Foreword to *A Red Carpet for the Sun* (1959).

Even though this period is often referred to as the "sexual revolution"—largely because of the loosening of sexual mores as a result of the birth control pill, first made available in North America in 1960—the "revolution" did not really change the status of women in male-female relationships. While women were at last able to control their reproduction, they were often still treated as sexual objects by many of the men they encountered. This was the era of mini-skirts and go-go girls dancing in cages, a period marked by the onset of female anorexia and bulimia as fashion models, such as the famous English model Twiggy, became thinner and thinner. Women were still often expected to serve men, earned substantially less than men for work of equal value, had fewer opportunities, and were rarely considered men's intellectual equals. Women's fiction of the period is replete with exposures of this kind of condescending double standard, evident in such works as Atwood's *The Edible Woman* (1969), *Surfacing* (1972), and *Lady Oracle* (1977), Laurence's *The Diviners* (1974), and Marian Engel's *Bear* (1978). Traditionally women had very fixed roles in relation to men. They were still conditioned to view marriage as the culmination of life experience, a fantasy that flew in the face of realistic expectations; writers such as Laurence, Atwood, and Alice Munro, as well as poets of the previous generation such as Dorothy Livesay and P.K. Page, composed piercing critiques of the ways romantic illusions can destroy the women, and men, who are caught up in them. As Sullivan notes, "no one seemed to notice at the time that the one area that had hardly changed at all was sexual politics. Where were women in the sixties revolution? They were the same adjuncts they had always been in the past. . . . [T]he sixties hadn't solved the power dynamic in sexual relationships" (193, 197). The tensions that informed male-female relationships became the focus of Atwood's 1971 poetry collection *Power Politics*. Nevertheless, Atwood's and Laurence's ambivalent relation to the women's movement, expressed in the 1971 letter from Laurence to Atwood included here, was based on their reluctance to engage in group politics that might ossify into prescriptive intolerance. Like most writers, they were committed to freedom of expression, yet they had also lived with sexism firsthand.

National Politics: Canada in the 1960s and '70s

The rise in Canadian nationalist sentiment during the 1960s and '70s can be attributed to a number of factors: global decolonization movements, post-Second World War affluence, a public that was eager to read and hear more about themselves, the centennial celebrations of 1967, the Vietnam War, a loosening of immigration restrictions, increased subsidization of the arts in Canada, and the election, in 1968, of a prime minister, Pierre Trudeau, who was flamboyant, sophisticated, cosmopolitan, yet also an avid Canadian nationalist. This increase in national self-consciousness was part of the context of independence movements worldwide. Suddenly it was no longer pejorative to call oneself "local" or "provincial" or "native." What set one apart (as an individual, as a nation) was also what made one fit in (into a global context of united nations and multicultural identities). For Northrop Frye, writing in *The Bush Garden* in 1971, national unity (as opposed to "uniformity") was something that was "regional" in definition, and Canada was seen to be defined by its constituent parts and perspectives. A.J.M. Smith's condescension toward the "native school" of poets and critics in the 1940s was now superseded by a group of writers and critics who embraced the label for its "postcolonial" impetus toward independent self-expression (i.e., moving beyond a dependence on British and American influence). As Atwood states in her 1971 article "Nationalism, Limbo and the Canadian Club," "Canada ceased to be a kind of limbo you were stuck in if unlucky or not smart enough and became a real place" (84) with valued local traditions and histories. These appeals to national identity or national independence were wrapped up in a rhetoric of radical politics: anti-imperialist, anti-establishment, anti-status quo, avant-garde.

The global context of decolonization movements following the Second World War was a crucial part of this newly inflected sense of national liberation. Postcolonial expression in countries such as India, Nigeria, and Algeria contributed to a wider discourse internationally that promoted and infused national independence movements. This rhetoric entered Canada through the ideas of many notable postcolonial and postmodern thinkers, such as Frantz Fanon, Michel Foucault, and, in the late 1970s, Edward Said. The "de-colonization" movement in Canada was launched partly in response to the holdover of British traditions, but primarily in opposition to the cultural imperialism of the United States, whose culture and politics were dominating the Canadian scene, and whose imperialist policies internationally (in Latin America, Cuba, and Vietnam) revealed a disturbing trend of coercion and violence that Canadians were loath to condone after the atrocities of the Second World War. In 1970, the Committee for an Independent Canada (1970–81) was founded by prominent Canadian public figures Peter Newman, Walter Gordon, and Mel Hurtig as a citizens' committee to promote cultural and economic independence from the United States.

Another factor contributing to the rise of Canadian nationalism during this period was the general increase in the standard of living for most middle-class Canadians during the postwar era, many of whom had moved to the suburbs to take advantage of affordable housing and large, family-sized lots. Ordinary families could afford most modern conveniences such as cars, televisions, and vacations. An important unifying link during this period was the opening of the Trans-Canada Highway in 1962. Its impact paralleled that of the building of the CPR in the late nineteenth century. It was now possible to travel by car from St. John's, Newfoundland, to Victoria, British Columbia (almost 8000 km), with a ferry ride at either end. The longest national highway in the world, the Trans-Canada made it possible for Canadians to move easily across provinces, but more importantly, it conjured in people's minds a sense of a national whole, an array of distinct geographical regions unified within a national context that stretched across the country.

The drive for progress, technological advancement, and "globalization" that characterized this period is epitomized in the work of Marshall McLuhan, whose critical assessment of the speed with which communications technologies were changing had significant ramifications for the way people talked about their world. McLuhan's monumental work *The Gutenberg Galaxy: The Making of Typographic Man*, published in 1962, analyzed the impact that technological changes in the realm of print and electronic media would have on human cognition and social organization. His prescient coining of the phrase "the global village" in this work warned people to beware of the potential totalitarian effects of such global media technologies. McLuhan's equally groundbreaking *Understanding Media: The Extensions of Man* came out in 1964 and set the intellectual world abuzz. His chapter entitled "The Medium Is the Message" insisted that it was not the content so much as the medium itself that had concrete social effects, particularly in the ways it affected how humans perceived the world around them. In his account, people had to be armed with an understanding of the effects of the new communications media if they were not to come under its thrall. The infamous television debate between John F. Kennedy and Richard Nixon in 1960, which sealed Kennedy's election as president, was won because Kennedy had used the medium of television to his own advantage; those who heard the debate on radio overwhelmingly felt that Nixon had won.

However, many people continued to be left behind in this newly acquired affluence. Many Aboriginal communities, for example, still lived in conditions of poverty on nationally instituted reserves. Many immigrants worked in factories and industries for very low wages. Urban ghettoes proliferated. The early 1960s saw the founding of the federal New Democratic Party (1961) under the leadership of Tommy Douglas (from 1961 to 1971). A blend of the old CCF (Co-operative Commonwealth Federation) and the unions in the Canadian Labour Congress, the NDP supported many socialized programs such as medicare, pensions, and unemployment insurance. Canadians still reap the benefits of the initiatives led by Douglas in the 1960s; during the federal leadership of Lester Pearson, a national pension plan (1965) and a universal health care system (1966) were introduced (a medicare system had first been implemented in the province of Saskatchewan in 1962). John Porter's controversial investigation of pervasive racial and class inequality in Canada in his book *The Vertical Mosaic*, published in 1965, was crucial in underscoring the continuing inequities in the popular sense of Canada as a "just" society and cultural mosaic. As Porter's investigation revealed, citizenship in Canada meant different things for different people. In Porter's view, Canada was a self-perpetuating hierarchy, where those of British origin occupied the top positions while other groups, such as French Canadians, Indigenous peoples, immigrants, and visible minorities, were relegated to the bottom rungs of the class system. In a similar vein, Harold Cardinal's important 1969 exposé, *The Unjust Society*, explored the hypocrisy of government treatment of Canada's Aboriginal people.

Although it seems contradictory, the critique of overarching institutional structures went hand in hand with a Canadian nationalist ethos, one that opposed the powerful American "colonizer" beyond Canada's borders. The most vocal Canadian nationalists of the period were also self-proclaimed leftists, and cultural nationalism, in practice, often found itself in support of local independence movements, promoting Aboriginal land claims or regional expression. Nevertheless, the cultural nationalist movement (like the hippie movement more generally) was largely a middle-class and mainstream one. The belief that life was good and prosperous fostered a growing sense of national pride, which in turn provided the security from which to critique different forms of state oppression.

The readiness of the Canadian populace to embrace their distinct culture and identity fed into the cultural awakening that was taking place on a national scale. Publishers were releasing more Canadian books, government grants were available to Canadian artists and musicians, Canadian plays were being produced (*Anne of Green Gables*, the longest continually running play in Canadian history, had its premiere in 1965), Canadian literary magazines were proliferating, new universities were springing up. In short, Canadians were becoming interested in their world, their words, their history, and were eager to read about and celebrate their own. As part of this general wave of celebratory nationalism and increased desire for self-definition, and in preparation for the upcoming centennial celebrations, Lester Pearson opened negotiations to institute "O Canada!" as Canada's official national anthem and to introduce a new Canadian flag that would not be based on a British prototype. Before this the "Red Ensign," a modified version of the British flag (and still the basis for the provincial flag of Ontario), had been Canada's national flag. What followed was a heated and testy debate, in which many English Canadians lamented the loss of the British connection should the flag be changed, while French Canadians insisted that the new flag *not* contain symbols of English power. After much rancour from both sides of the controversy, Pearson unfurled the new flag in Parliament on 15 February 1965, based on a design by George Stanley. Because of copyright entanglements, however, "O Canada!" was not proclaimed the official national anthem until 1980.

Perhaps the most notable nationalist event of this period was the 100th anniversary of Confederation in 1967. The nationwide festivals, theatricals, songs, events, and publications caught Canadians up in a kind of national mania. Gordon Lightfoot was commissioned to write a song to commemorate the centenary, which resulted in his famous anthem "The Canadian Railroad Trilogy," included here. It was also in this year that Dolores Claman composed the theme song for CBC's *Hockey Night in Canada*. Chief Dan George was asked to write a poem and speak at the centennial celebration in Vancouver; this was the impetus behind his powerful "Lament for Confederation" (included in this section) in which he took Canada to task for its treatment of First Peoples.

The celebrations were heightened by the crowning achievement of the centenary year, the international World's Fair, Expo 67, held in Montreal. Between April and October 1967, Canadians from across the country thronged to Montreal to take part in the festivities. International celebrities, including Queen Elizabeth II, Jackie Kennedy, Bing Crosby, and French President Charles de Gaulle, visited the exposition, which included performances by such Canadian celebrities as Marshall McLuhan and Leonard Cohen. According to the *Montreal Star* at the time, Expo was "the most staggering Canadian achievement since this vast land was finally linked by a transcontinental railway." The exposition, which boasted 90 pavilions from 62 countries, put Canada on the global map as a "modern" and multicultural nation. In total, over 50 million people visited the site. There was a sense, as historian Charlotte Gray expresses it, that "anything was possible, that Canada really was the promised land" (*Canada* 414). Implicit in Expo 67 was the theme of "progress" (its overarching theme was "Man and His World," but there were numerous sub-themes related to technology and exploration: "Man the Explorer," "Man the Producer," and "Man the Creator"); the spectacle revelled in modernity and saw itself as embracing the "future." In many ways, the Expo site resembled a futuristic cityscape or space station. The architecture and decor of the pavilions made use of avant-garde geometric patterns, such as the famous geodesic dome built by Buckminster Fuller (Figure VI-1), not to mention Moshe Safdie's offbeat Habitat 67 building, a design for living quarters for the future. Even the telephone booths resembled space capsules.

The design of the Expo site was part of the general craze for space exploration and technology at the time. Prior to Expo, the first man had been launched into space in April 1961 (a Russian named Yuri Gagarin). Over the next few years, Russia and the United States were engaged in a "space race" to put the first man on the moon. The United States won, with Neil Armstrong making his famous moon landing on 20 July 1969, an event that was broadcast simultaneously around the world. Television programs of the period capture the mania for space travel: shows such as *The Jetsons* (1962–63), *Lost in Space* (1965–68), and *Star Trek* (1966–69) were produced in the 1960s; even *The Flintstones* (1960–66) sported a character who was an alien from outer space.

One of the most important Canadian political events of the early 1960s, and one that was to have a major effect on government policy and Canadian cultural dynamics for generations after, was Prime Minister Lester B. Pearson's decision to establish a Royal Commission on Bilingualism and Biculturalism in 1963. The commission recommended that francophones should have access to federal services in French and that francophone minorities outside of Quebec should have educational opportunities in French. This inquiry ultimately led to the passing of the Official Languages Act in 1969, which made French and English joint official languages. As a result, federal offices and courts had to offer services in both languages, food labels had to be bilingual, and French had to be taught in English schools. The original Royal Commission of 1963 had been struck because of a growing sense of dissatisfaction among French Canadians with their position within the Canadian nation-state. This period in French Canadian nationalism, referred to as the "Quiet Revolution," emerged under the political reign of Quebec Liberal Premier Jean Lesage, whose motto upon his election in 1960 was "Il faut que ça change!" ("Things must change!"). These years were marked by the secularization of French-Canadian society and an increased sense of cultural and political self-awareness. On the one hand, Quebeckers had to overturn the restrictive control of the Catholic Church, which was holding French Canadians back from taking part in the modern, secular world. On the other hand, they had to overthrow the dominance of English rule, since the English-speaking élites in Quebec held most of the economic and political power in the province. Many French Canadians began to support the idea of separation from Canada in order to realize their potential as a distinct, historical people. The nationalist sentiment that was washing over Canada at this time was echoed in Quebeckers' growing sense of themselves as a unique culture and people, at the same time as English-speaking Canadians held up Quebec as a crucial component of Canadian national and cultural identity. Ironically, the Quebec nationalist movement received an unexpected boost during the centennial celebrations when in July 1967, while in Montreal for Expo 67, French President Charles de Gaulle uttered his infamous slogan from the balcony of Montreal's city hall: "Vive le Québec libre!" His words became the rallying cry for the separatist movement thereafter.

However, the liberationist movement took a dark turn a few years later with the October Crisis of 1970, when members of the separatist FLQ (Front de Libération du Québec) kidnapped two political figures, James Cross (a British diplomat) and Pierre Laporte (Quebec's minister of labour). In response, Pierre Trudeau, who had been elected as prime minister in 1968, invoked the controversial War Measures Act, which restricted people's civil liberties and led to the arrest of hundreds of people. On October 17, the body of Laporte, who was murdered by the FLQ, was found in the trunk of a parked car. The event shocked the nation. Up to then, French-English relations had sometimes been strained in Canada, but there had never been this kind of violence. French and English citizens alike were appalled, both by the reality of terrorist activity right at their own doorstep, and by the forceful use of the War Measures Act against innocent people. A few years later, the provincial separatist party, the Parti Québécois, was established, and the party leader, René Lévesque, was elected as the provincial premier in 1976 (see Figure VI-3). The controversial Bill 101 (an extension of Bill 22 from 1974) came into effect the next year, which made French the single official language of Quebec. Lévesque had been elected on the promise that he would hold a sovereignty referendum in Quebec, and so, in 1980, Quebeckers voted on whether or not to withdraw from Confederation; the result was a "No." For the time being, the majority of Quebeckers wanted to keep Quebec in Canada.

An unexpected secondary effect of the 1963 B&B Commission was the bringing of multicultural issues to the forefront of discussions of Canadian society. As the Commissioners travelled across Canada, they were struck by the number of people who wanted cultural recognition to extend beyond the two "charter groups" (French and English) in Canada. Many of these groups, such as the Ukrainian community in Manitoba, Jewish communities in Montreal and Toronto, and Italian, Greek, Japanese, and Chinese Canadians across the country, argued that their ancestors had also contributed to the establishment of Canada in the early days of nation-building. Section IV of the Royal Commission report, "The Cultural Contribution of the Other Ethnic Groups," outlines the necessity of recognizing Canada's multicultural diversity. In response, Trudeau introduced a proposal for an official multicultural policy to Parliament in 1971 that was unanimously supported, leading to the establishment of a Ministry for Multiculturalism (1971) and the eventual formulation of the Multiculturalism Act, which came into effect in 1988 (see the excerpt in Section VII). Trudeau's vision was of a bicultural nation defined by "multiculturalism within a bilingual framework." To many, this was a problem. French Canadians felt that the multiculturalism policy represented a way for the federal government to ignore their political claims and initiate what they viewed as the inevitable assimilation of French Canadians into English Canada. Others argued that it disempowered Quebec by rendering French culture just one among many. Aboriginal Canadians were still not recognized as one of the charter peoples, even though their participation in the "founding" of Canada is indisputable. Many ethnic groups felt that official multiculturalism led to a form of exoticization of "others" within the Canadian state, superficially celebrating cultural differences (with an official emphasis on "ethnocultural" elements such as food, dance, and music) but not attending to economic and political inequities (see the discussion of these issues in the introduction to Section VII). However, notwithstanding some of the problems inherent in the policy, it brought increased awareness of issues of cultural and social inequality within Canada.

In part, the growing awareness of Canada's multicultural society emerged during these decades as a result of the loosening of immigration restrictions and the concomitant rise in immigration from non-European countries, especially from Asia and the Caribbean. In 1962 there was a major shift in immigration policy, one that emphasized skills and education rather than race or national origin by instituting a point system for applicants. Country of origin had been the focus of immigration policies in the late nineteenth and early twentieth centuries, as, for example, Clifford Sifton outlined in his article "The Immigrants Canada Wants" in 1922 (see Volume I). In the 1960s, 46,000 West Indian immigrants settled in Canada. When the Soviets invaded Czechoslovakia in August 1968, over 11,000 Czech refugees arrived in Canada, many of whom were well educated and highly skilled. The shift in immigration policy, Elspeth Cameron notes, "ushered in an era in which 'visible minorities' increasingly constituted a large proportion of new Canadians" (xx), which in turn led to renewed attention to issues of discrimination and racism. Austin Clarke's hard-hitting story "Canadian Experience" confronts head-on the difficulty of newly arrived immigrants attempting to enter the Canadian workforce. Clarke's work presents a quite different view of the multicultural "mosaic" from that promoted in the official rhetoric. Indeed, since the 1980s, issues of discrimination have been explored by Canadian authors and have led to important and enabling public discussions about racism, multiculturalism, and national citizenship.

One of the major Canadian "postcolonial" initiatives during this period was Trudeau's success in having the Canadian Constitution "patriated" back to Canada in 1982. Up to that point, any amendments to the Canadian Constitution had to be made by the parliament of the United Kingdom (see the excerpt from the BNA Act in Volume I). In effect, the Constitution itself was changed little from the BNA Act of 1867, but the Constitution Act of 1982 initiated Canada's legal right to make amendments to its Constitution without the approval of the British sovereign. However, the only province not to sign the new Constitution was Quebec, which contributed to Quebec's marginalization from Canadian state deliberations. Nor were Aboriginal communities consulted. One of the major additions to the Constitution was the Canadian Charter of Rights and Freedoms, a list of fundamental human rights that are considered integral to Canada's status as a democratic society. The Charter protects such things as freedom of expression, freedom to move and live anywhere within Canada, and the right to use either official language. The context leading up to the formation of the Charter was the international human rights movement that gained impetus following the Second World War; the United Nations was founded in 1945 under a widely held sense that it was necessary to prevent such horrific acts against humanity as took place during the war. The Canadian Charter of Rights and Freedoms has been used as a model for national human rights legislation worldwide.

Cultural Nationalism: Writing in (Post)Colonial Space

One of the most distinctive aspects of the 1960s and '70s era in Canada was the rise of political and cultural nationalism, a phenomenon that was echoed in many other postcolonial nations worldwide. Margaret Laurence's incisive writings about Africa in the 1960s testify to a growing awareness in Canada of international anti-colonial issues. Laurence herself noted in her 1970 autobiographical essay "A Place to Stand On" that she had transposed her experiences in Africa onto the Canadian context. Laurence and many other writers of this period lamented the fact that Canadians in the 1950s and '60s had grown up without a clear sense of their own history or identity. In keeping with the discourse of the period, what people had in view was the "liberation" of the Canadian mindset from the cultural and psychological inferiority complex that had come to dominate Canadians in the 1950s and early '60s, especially in relation to the United States. Not only were Canadians largely influenced by American culture and attitudes, but many had come to believe that they were inferior. Dennis Lee's account of the prevailing attitude in the 1950s and '60s is disturbing: "Canadians were by definition people who looked over the fence and through the windows at America, and un-self-consciously learned from its movies, comics, magazines and TV shows how to go about being alive" ("Cadence" 48). S.M. Crean, writing in her 1976 book *Who's Afraid of Canadian Culture?*, launched an attack on those Canadians who insisted on the dichotomy between two poles, "excellent" and "Canadian." Earle Birney's poem "Can. Lit." (1962/66), included in Section V, expresses this mindset succinctly in its satirical account of these colonial attitudes, especially Canadians' debilitating insecurity in the face of American culture: "it's only by our lack of ghosts / we're haunted." Birney's poem may seem to endorse such attitudes, but in fact it is a challenge to Canadians (comparable to Haliburton's double-edged challenge to self-satisfied Nova Scotians in the 1830s) to wake up and take their place in the world.

At the base of many of these cultural pronouncements was a widely shared belief, previously articulated in the Massey Report in 1951, that a national literature should reflect a national identity, indeed that a national consciousness was impossible without a cultural context to back it up. Atwood and Lee are famous for their political manifestos during this period—*Survival* (1972) and "Cadence, Country, Silence" (1973)—which proclaimed an end to this colonial state of mind. As Lee put it in 1973, the worst realization was "the recognition that the sphere of imperial influence was not confined to the pages of newspapers. It also included my head" (49–50). Even more upsetting was the sense that this "brainwashing" and self-loathing had in many ways been allowed to happen by Canadians themselves. Atwood wrote in her 1971 essay "Nationalism, Limbo and the Canadian Club" that "[i]t was our own choices, our own judgements, that were defeating us" (89). For Lee it was George Grant who had most clearly elucidated the historical roots of the current colonial condition in Canada. Grant believed that Canadians' rejection of the "American dream" in the eighteenth century had influenced the building of a distinct Canadian set of values, including a reverence for a sense of the "good" rather than a pursuit of happiness—in short, a distinct sense of "what it meant to be a human being" (Lee 51). Grant's idealized sense of Canadians' inherent humanity is echoed by Lee and Atwood.

Nevertheless, anxiety about the power and proximity of the United States led to Grant's famous pronouncement in his 1965 *Lament for a Nation*, in which he foretold the potential demise of Canada and Canadian culture. Bemoaning the decline of traditional values generally, Grant predicted that the technological modernity epitomized by the United States, informed by rampant individualism and materialism, would signal the end of Canadian sovereignty (see excerpts from *Lament for a Nation* in this section). In effect, the cultural nationalist movements of the late '60s and early '70s in Canada were an attempt to ensure that Grant's prophecy did not come true. And the movement took place on a massive scale—not only through the political initiatives of the period, but in the massive output of energy and money that went into the formation, promotion, and production of a Canadian literature during these decades. This movement was made possible because of the general affluence of the period and because of the sheer numbers and energy of the "baby boomers." Not only was there a marked increase in the number of Canadian writers, but more importantly, there was a sizable increase in the number of Canadian *readers* who were eager to learn about and take part in the literary renaissance that was occurring around them. In particular, readers wanted works that would offer a reflection of their own world, their own communities, their own experiences.

A commitment to the promotion and protection of Canadian culture had already taken place at the end of the previous decade, particularly with the foundation of the Canada Council in 1957 (see the excerpts from the Massey Report in Section V). The 1960s and '70s witnessed tremendous development in Canadian writing and publishing. There was a concerted effort on the part of the Canadian government, artists' organizations, and individual artists to promote the cause of Canadian culture. Thousands of government dollars were poured into the promotion of the arts in Canada. Regional theatre companies were established across the country, including the Vancouver Playhouse and Halifax's Neptune Theatre (1963), the Citadel in Edmonton (1965), the Saidye Bronfman Centre in Montreal (1967), Theatre New Brunswick (1968), and Ottawa's National Arts Centre (1969). The 1960s marked the inauguration of the Shaw Festival in Niagara-on-the-Lake (1962) and the Charlottetown Festival in P.E.I. (1965). Musicians, painters, and dancers were funded by the Canada Council, as were numerous publishing projects and individual authors. Many of the writers who received support from the Canada Council in the 1960s are well-known figures in Canadian literature today: Leonard Cohen, Mordecai Richler, Irving Layton, and Anne Hébert among them.

A particularly important source of support for Canadian writers during this time was CBC Radio, which was developing arts programs that would promote Canadian artists. Central among these was Robert Weaver's program "Anthology," which ran from 1953 to 1985 and broadcast many known and unknown Canadian writers of the time. Weaver was fiercely committed to promoting Canadian literature in the public sphere. His interest in Canadian writing led him to found the *Tamarack Review* in 1956 and to publish numerous anthologies of Canadian fiction in the 1960s and '70s. After his death in 2008, many prominent writers argued that they might not have been able to support themselves from their writing if it hadn't been for Weaver's encouragement.

At the same time, there was an enormous struggle to introduce Canadian literature as a permanent subject within university English departments across the country. This is difficult to understand in today's context, when courses in Canadian literature are part of all Canadian university English departments. However, there was a time when the introduction of such courses, and the dearth of faculty qualified to teach them (since there were few places where one could receive training in the subject), was met with fierce antipathy by faculty members who saw Canadian literature as a sign of the demise of the great tradition of English literature. At Queen's University in the 1950s, for example, and at the University of Toronto as late as the 1970s, Canadian literature was taught as an adjunct at the end of the course in American literature. An established curriculum in Canadian literature did not become solidly established in English departments across the country until the late 1960s.

Such programs were dependent on the availability of professionals trained in the field of Canadian literature as well as on the availability of anthologies, journals, and critical studies devoted to Canadian authors, a phenomenon that was in turn dependent on what many saw to be the necessary "decolonization" of the academic study of English in Canada more generally. Concurrent with these pedagogical initiatives was the fervent and controversial fight over the hiring of teaching faculty in Canadian universities. The battle waged by Robin Mathews and James Steele at Carleton University against the over-hiring of American professors to the exclusion of Canadian candidates caused a furor, resulting in their controversial publication, *The Struggle for Canadian Universities*, in 1969. To confront the lingering inferiority complex that remained in Canadian cultural institutions, a legal requirement was instituted making it mandatory to first consider Canadian applicants for all academic jobs in Canada.

In 1968, A.B. Hodgetts's study *What Culture? What Heritage?* sparked a nation-wide controversy when he critiqued the inadequacy of Canadian content in Canada's public schools. In response, in 1972 the Association of Universities and Colleges of Canada established a Commission on Canadian Studies headed by T.H.B. Symons to investigate the state of teaching about Canada in the Canadian school system. The publication to emerge from this venture, *To Know Ourselves* (1975), was an extensive account of Canadian content in university curricula and a series of recommendations to correct the imbalance the Commission discovered. Symons' conclusion was far from sanguine: "[T]here is no developed country in the world with comparable resources that devotes as little attention [as does Canada] to the support of its own culture and of education relating to itself" (15). Atwood's guide for secondary-school teachers of Canadian literature, *Survival* (1972), was part of this movement to ensure that Canadians became educated about themselves. The battle for Canadian literature in schools and universities was thus a battle for self-expression (see the excerpt from *Survival* included here). As Stan Fogel has argued, the teaching of Canadian literature began as an "oppositional practice" (155).

In *Survival*, Atwood maintained that Canadians needed to see a reflection of themselves in their literature in order to have any meaningful sense of who they were. This sounds very similar to the romantic nationalism propounded by many nineteenth-century Canadian authors, including Thomas D'Arcy McGee, who proclaimed in 1857: "No literature, no national life,—this is an irreversible law." Authors in the 1970s were putting this belief into practice with an energy that seems remarkable today. Some of the works that are today considered "classics" of Canadian fiction were first published during these nationalistic decades.[3]

Alongside the growing attention to Canadian writing during this period was an explosion of critical materials related to the study of Canadian literature. In 1965, Carl F. Klinck edited the important critical historical study *Literary History of Canada*, a volume that has become a central text in Canadian literary scholarship. By the 1970s, the New Canadian Library series at McClelland and Stewart, established in 1958 under the editorship of Malcolm Ross to put Canadian literary works

---

[3] Examples include Laurence's *The Stone Angel* (1964) and *The Diviners* (1974), Cohen's *Beautiful Losers* (1966), Michel Tremblay's *Les Belles Soeurs* (1968), Roch Carrier's *La Guerre, Yes Sir!* (1968), Robert Kroetsch's *The Studhorse Man* (1969), Atwood's *The Journals of Susanna Moodie* (1970) and *Surfacing* (1972), Ondaatje's *The Collected Works of Billy the Kid* (1970) and *Coming Through Slaughter* (1976), Davies's *Fifth Business* (1970), Munro's *Lives of Girls and Women* (1971), Richler's *St Urbain's Horseman* (1971), Antonine Maillet's major novels of Acadian culture and history *La Sagouine* (1971) and *Pélagie-la-Charrette* (1979), Rudy Wiebe's *The Temptations of Big Bear* (1973), and Timothy Findley's *The Wars* (1977).

into wide circulation (see the introduction to Section V), was undergoing renewal. At the Calgary Conference on the Canadian Novel in 1978, Ross distributed a survey to the participants asking them to rank the most important works of Canadian literature. Margaret Laurence's novel *The Stone Angel* won. The results helped determine a list of Canadian novels that would become part of the curriculum in Canadian university courses (and in turn would be published in the NCL series to provide texts for these courses). This interest in Canadian scholarship was accompanied by the founding of many scholarly Canadian literature journals, beginning with *Canadian Literature* in 1959 (the first journal committed to critical writing on Canadian literature), but including such later journals as *Journal of Canadian Studies* (1966), *The Journal of Canadian Fiction* (1972), *Essays on Canadian Writing* (1974), *Canadian Theatre Review* (1974), *Studies in Canadian Literature* (1976), *Canadian Poetry* (1977), and *Journal of Canadian Poetry* (1978). Accompanying this wealth of activity on the part of Canadian writers and publishers was the foundation of the Writers' Union of Canada in 1973. In 1971, a small group of writers including Mowat, Atwood, Graeme Gibson, and June Callwood met to discuss the need for an organization to represent the rights and professional concerns of Canadian authors. The Union, officially founded in Ottawa in 1973, promotes intellectual and artistic freedom and protects the collective interests of writers. The Union attracted an enormous membership from across the country, and was chaired by such prominent Canadian authors as Laurence, Engel, Timothy Findley, Pierre Berton, Matt Cohen, Callwood, Gibson, and Atwood. Christopher Moore's history of the Writers' Union on the official website describes the enormous initiative that the Union's members undertook in order to support Canadian writing:

> In the early years, promoting Canadian writing was a controversial act. "Canadian Literature" remained almost unknown as a subject of academic and critical study. Union members picketed bookstores [and] . . . agitated for more Canadian books in Canadian schools and university courses. When teachers complained that there were no texts from which to teach Canadian Literature, the early Union's can-do spirit kicked in: Union members organized teams of teachers as consultants [and] . . . promoted public readings by Canadian writers for Canadian audiences, eventually supporting hundreds of readings a year.

In response to some of the same issues in other arts arenas, in 1968 the Canadian Radio-television and Telecommunications Commission (CRTC) was established to regulate various aspects of Canadian broadcasting in order to offer protection to Canadian cultural expression. The most famous, and most influential, of its policies was the "Canadian Content" or "CanCon" policy, which stipulated that Canadian broadcasters had to air a certain percentage of work by Canadian artists during peak hours. The policy emerged out of a sense that American popular culture was dominating the airwaves, since it was almost impossible for Canadian artists to have their music or films broadcast in Canada unless they had previously achieved recognition in the United States. The policy was meant to provide institutional support for musicians and film-makers, to energize the Canadian music and film industries on the whole, and to provide more choice for consumers by exposing listeners/viewers to more than just mainstream (i.e., non-Canadian) artists. Nevertheless, many broadcasters sought to dodge the CanCon requirements through ingenious methods. The iconic portion of the television program *SCTV* (1976–1984) that featured "Bob and Doug McKenzie" in their "Great White North" segment was introduced to meet CanCon regulations. Canadian television had fewer commercials than American television, and *SCTV* was told that it had to provide two extra minutes for its Canadian edition that contained content that was "distinctly Canadian" (Pevere 105). Peeved at the absurdity of having to add extra Canadian content to a show that was written by Canadians, Rick Moranis (who played Bob McKenzie) snidely proposed a segment that exhibited such classic props of "Canadiana" as cases of beer and some sides of back bacon roasting on a barbecue (Figure VI-9). In an ironic twist, *SCTV* decided to fill the extra time with the "CanCon" that they felt was being forced on them, creating what became the single most popular segment of the program: two beer-swilling, toque-bearing, dim-witted "hosers." Within weeks of the first broadcast, Bob and Doug McKenzie were on their way to becoming pop culture icons. The unanticipated success of Bob and Doug McKenzie points to the widespread enthusiasm for confirmations of Canadian identity (the more ironic and self-reflexive, even self-deprecating, the better) that the public at large seemed to hunger for. This phenomenon was later echoed in the popular success of the Molson Canadian beer advertisement "I AM Canadian" (2000) included in Section VII.

In keeping with the drive to secure an identifiable Canadian identity was a form of literary "essentialism" that dictated that literature was a direct reflection of a national consciousness or national way of being. The literary critical trend in Canada during this period was therefore less focused on aspects of form and style (though these did remain a concern) than on the content of literary works, particularly their symbolic cultural resonance. This critical movement, referred to as "thematic criticism," sought to identify distinctive themes or motifs in Canadian literature that were indicative of a national mode of thought (and hence provided a window onto Canadian identity). Initially influenced by the critical writings of Northrop Frye, the thematic approach explored prevailing patterns and archetypes that were evident in Canadian writing and, by extension, indicative of predominant Canadian modes of perception. The most well-known critical texts in this category are D.G. Jones's *Butterfly on Rock* (1970), Atwood's *Survival* (1972), and John Moss's *Patterns of Isolation* (1974). Atwood's identification of the common theme of survival in Canadian writing has its origins in Frye's conceptualization of the Canadian "garrison mentality," a notion that described the inherent paranoia and protectiveness of the Canadian psyche (exemplified in the ways Canadian settlers had sought to protect themselves in the threatening wilderness by cordoning themselves off from the outside world). Frye's theory, which he outlined in his influential Conclusion to the *Literary History of Canada*

(1965), like Frye's writings on Canada generally, revealed a distinct discomfort with Canadian writing (what postcolonial theorists refer to more generally as "colonial cringe"), thus substantiating Lee's recognition of this mentality in many Canadians of the period. A number of writers and critics fell back on this self-castigating mode, Robertson Davies and Mordecai Richler in their caustic remarks about Canadian parochialism being foremost among them.

While Frye's terms were pejorative, the writings of other thematic critics, such as Jones, Moss, and Atwood, were not. Moss, for instance, writes about the "processes of our emergence into national being" and, like Atwood, outlines some distinguishing themes of Canadian fiction: "Whether they define concepts of exile, express what I would call the geophysical imagination, or arise from the ironic conflicts of individual consciousness, they equally reflect the progress of the Canadian imagination towards a positive identity" (*Patterns* 7). Here, the link between literature and the imperative of a unified sense of national identity is clear. However, as the decade wore on it was evident that not all critics endorsed this approach, and "thematics" became the favoured target of the next generation of Canadian literary theorists. In 1976, Frank Davey published his influential attack on thematic criticism, "Surviving the Paraphrase," in *Canadian Literature*. With its parodic allusion to Atwood's survival thesis, Davey's essay charged the thematic approach with being more social commentary than literary analysis. Davey favoured a formalist approach to literature that did not succumb to sociological analysis, one more in keeping with the New Critical movement that had come to predominate the field in the United States. The year after the appearance of Davey's essay, Barry Cameron and Michael Dixon published their "Mandatory Subversive Manifesto" to introduce a special issue of *Studies in Canadian Literature* (1977). The subtitle of their essay, "Canadian Criticism vs. Literary Criticism," highlighted their attitude toward the dominance of thematic criticism in Canadian literary studies. Like Davey, they favoured an approach that would concentrate on form, structure, and genre, a preference that is echoed in some of the experimental poetry of the period (including Davey's own), such as the work of bpNichol, bill bissett, George Bowering, and Fred Wah. In spite of these critiques, the thematic approach holds a significant place in Canadian literary history. As Stephanie Bolster puts it in her article for *Northern Poetry Review*, "Surviving Survival," "[I]ts practice was inseparable from the task of convincing the world—and Canadians—that there was indeed such a thing as Canadian literature" (2006).

Indeed, the approach of the thematic critics in the 1960s and '70s was integrally connected to the nationalist agenda of the period, for Canadian literature was taken as evidence of Canada's cultural identity and maturity. Like the literary approach, the cultural nationalist movement in general was critiqued for its rhetoric of homogenization, namely because it attempted to articulate characteristics that were shared by all members of the community. Atwood's claim in her Afterword to *The Journals of Susanna Moodie* (1970) that the Canadian mode of thought was one of "paranoid-schizophrenia" in relation to its divided colonial predicament (articulated as an ambivalent response to one's habitation of Canada) and her identification of the "survival" motif in Canadian literature are examples of this kind of unifying mode of perception that thematic critics were interested in. Such approaches, like the cultural nationalist movement more generally, have been charged with a misrepresentation and silencing of the many constituencies that made up late-twentieth-century Canada. Indeed, the rhetoric of national unity was belied by the wider context of the '60s and '70s in which marginal voices were striving to be heard against such cultural homogenization: the voice of Aboriginal peoples who rightly did not see themselves as equal partners in the "just society" nor in the renaissance of mainstream Canadian writing; Québécois nationalists, like Pierre Vallières in 1968, who identified themselves as "white niggers of America" ("nègres blancs d'Amérique") and hence did not include themselves in this largely English-Canadian nationalist project of cross-national self-expression. Québécois writer Michèle Lalonde's famous polemical poem of 1968, "Speak White," decried the imposition of English-Canadian language and culture on Quebeckers of the period. Despite the attempt of many English-Canadian writers to foster a "bicultural" vision of Canada in their literary works and writing—such as F.R. Scott's 1954 poem "Bonne Entente," David Fennario's 1979 play *Balconville,* or D.G. Jones's commitment to bilingual publications in his anthologies of Canadian writing and in his founding of the bilingual literary journal *Ellipse* in 1969—the quest for an identifiable pan-national Canadian identity was a project that was fraught from the start. The introduction of the multicultural policy by the Trudeau government in 1971 was coterminous with a wealth of writing by Canadian authors of non-mainstream ethnicities, including such well-known figures as Austin Clarke, Michael Ondaatje, and Joy Kogawa, a shift that would become even more significant in the final decades of the twentieth century.

This period also saw the foundation of numerous independent Canadian publishing houses and literary magazines which became central in providing publication venues for the writers of the period. Before this time, publishing opportunities within Canada were very limited, and Canadians often had to seek publication in American or British journals for their work. Karl H. Siegler, recent president of Talonbooks, describes the dire circumstances for the Canadian book trade at the beginning of the 1960s: "Back then, their dismissal was based on a colonial perception of our shared reality—most Canadian books in all genres were to be found on a single shelf near the back of the bookstore under the rubric 'Canadiana,' much as Canadian movies are now most commonly found in the 'foreign films' sections of our video-rental stores—strangers in our own land, our books were back then, as our films still are today" (promotional letter). As had been the case for over a century, many writers (e.g., Charles G.D. Roberts, Bliss Carman, Sara Jeannette Duncan) felt that they had to leave Canada in order to achieve international success. Such a motivation led to the exodus of such notable Canadians as Mordecai Richler (who moved to London in 1954 and lived there for 20 years), Margaret Laurence (who lived in England for more than 10 years), and Mavis Gallant (who moved to Paris in 1950 and continues to live there). Many of the more ardent Canadian nationalists, such as Atwood and Findley, made a point of remaining in Canada to assert their ties with Canadian culture.

Two of the most important publishing houses to be established during this time were Coach House Press and House of Anansi Press, both of which became gathering places for Canadian writers. The significance of these publishing houses to the development of Canadian literature cannot be overestimated, for they provided much needed support to up-and-coming (and often experimental) Canadian writers who otherwise would likely have had to look outside of Canada for a means to publish their work. Coach House was founded by Stan Bevington (literally in an old coach house in a Toronto back lane) in 1965, and soon acquired a reputation for artistic experimentation and finely crafted design. Its focus was Canadian poetry, especially the graphic and concrete poetry of such seminal Canadian literary figures as bpNichol, Roy Kiyooka, Michael Ondaatje, Henry Beissel, Daphne Marlatt, and George Bowering. House of Anansi Press was founded by Dennis Lee and Dave Godfrey in 1967 in order to provide a much-needed publishing venue for Canadian writers, especially novelists and nonfiction writers. Up to that time, "foreign-owned or branch-plant houses had a very bad track record in publishing original Canadian books" (Sullivan 199), and Godfrey was exasperated at "being made to feel like a colonial in his own country" (MacSkimming 175). Under Lee's leadership, Anansi's reputation grew so that it soon became one of the most sought-after publishers by Canadian authors (it is still publishing Canadian books today). Initially produced out of the basement of Godfrey's house on Spadina Avenue in Toronto, it helped launch the careers of such prominent Canadians as Matt Cohen (*Korsoniloff*, 1969), Graeme Gibson (*Five Legs*, 1969), and Ondaatje (*The Collected Works of Billy the Kid*, 1970), as well as publishing important critical works including Grant's *Technology and Empire* (1969) and Frye's *The Bush Garden* (1971). Anansi was also dedicated to current political causes, and achieved notoriety in 1968 when it published a guide for Vietnam War draft dodgers, *Manual for Draft-Age Immigrants to Canada*, which became the press's best-selling title of the 1960s and resulted in the press undergoing police investigation. For Canadian literary scholars, Anansi's most famous publication was Atwood's infamous guidebook to Canadian literature, *Survival* (1972). Atwood had undertaken the project under Lee's instigation, in part because her experience teaching Canadian literature at York University in 1971 had brought home to her how little her colleagues knew about the subject. The book, while controversial, became a bestseller, both within Canada and abroad, and sold more than 50,000 copies within three years of publication. Other significant literary presses to emerge during this period were Oberon (1966), Talonbooks (1967), Exile Editions (1976), Black Moss Press (1969), and blewointment (1967), the latter established by bill bissett in Vancouver. Soon after, Brick Books was established by Stan Dragland and Don McKay (1975). The dynamic blend of aesthetic experimentation and cultural consolidation helped to ensure the unparalleled growth of a national literary scene. The passion and commitment of the innumerable people who worked in these operations, many of whom were unpaid, testify to the intensity of the belief in Canadian culture that governed the period.

Connected to the growth in literary publishing in Canada was the explosion of little magazines across the country—magazines such as *Prism* (1959), *Alphabet* (1960), *TISH* (1961), *blewointment* (1963), *Open Letter* (1965), *West Coast Review* (1966), *Wascana Review* (1966), *Malahat Review* (1967), *Ellipse* (1969), *Antigonish Review* (1970), *Descant* (1970), *Books in Canada* (1971), *Canadian Fiction Magazine* (1971), *event* (1971), *Exile* (1972), *Capilano Review* (1972), and *CV II* (1975). *TISH: A Magazine of Vancouver Poetry* was started by UBC students George Bowering, Frank Davey, Fred Wah, Jamie Reid, and Dave Dawson in 1961. The group was influenced by prominent American poets Robert Duncan, Robert Creeley, and Charles Olson, particularly after the 1961 series of lectures given at UBC by Duncan, and the 1963 Vancouver Poetry Festival attended by Creeley, Olson, Duncan, Denise Levertov, and Allen Ginsberg. The experimental poetry of the Black Mountain poets in particular inspired Bowering, Wah, Davey, and Lionel Kearns to put into effect the theories of the group, namely the evocation of direct experience (without the reinforcement of myth or symbol) via very specific "images" and the rhythms of the spoken word. They were also indebted to the earlier imagist style of American modernist poets Ezra Pound and William Carlos Williams. In the 13 January 1962 issue of *TISH*, Davey put it evocatively when he stated that the group sought to explore "the correspondence between breath and line" (97). This emphasis on the materiality of the words and sounds on the page set the *TISH* approach in opposition to what is sometimes called the "mythopoeic" school of Canadian poetry, which emphasized universal symbolic and mythic elements: a group that included such writers as Gwendolyn MacEwen, Jay Macpherson, James Reaney, and Atwood. Moreover, along with bissett, *TISH* is important for bringing attention to west coast writers of the period at a time when much of the national literary activity in Canada was centralized in Toronto and Montreal. Concerned with articulating a western sensibility rather than a national voice, Davey writes that "*TISH* marks the turning point of British Columbia poetry away from the shadows of derived, humanistic, Toronto-focused writing and toward the light of its own energies" (159).

A move toward experimentation was generally evident in the writing of this period, especially in poetry, an approach that was in keeping with the counter-culture and "postmodern" spirit of the 1960s and '70s generally. The radical poetry movement of this period challenged not only centralized authority structures and nationalist paradigms, but the very conventions of literary poetics themselves, through its use of disrupted syntax, atypical spelling and punctuation, fragmentation, multiple perspectives, and a sometimes jarring combination of rhythm and dissonance. "Concrete" poetry focused on the physical form and materials of the poem, highlighting the visual effect of letters upon the page or the sound of words as a crucial component of "meaning making." The lines or the letters of the poem draw a picture that evokes the subject matter in some way. With its emphasis on a synthesis of image and language, form and content, it echoed the abstract and pop art movements in painting (showing the influence of American pop artists Andy Warhol and David Hockney, and Canadian artists such as Greg Curnoe and

Jack Chambers). Nichol is perhaps Canada's most well-known concrete poet; his poem "Blues" (included here) is one of the most famous visual poems in Canadian literature. Nichol's production of radically experimental ways of disseminating his poetry—through film, tape recordings, comic strips, and oral sound performances—have earned him a reputation as one of the most innovative poets of the generation. Together with Steve McCaffery, Paul Dutton, and Rafael Barreto-Rivera, Nichol established the sound performance group known as the "Four Horsemen," whose presentations incorporated grunts, moans, and shrieks in order to foreground the potential of language as pure sound. These poets stretched what seemed to be an infinity of sounds out of individual words and performed their range of possible signification.

Other writers during this period were influenced by the language-centred poets. Earle Birney's concrete poetry, as seen in his 1967 poem "UP HER CAN NADA" (Section V), is indicative of the extensive influence of the new poetics. One of the most well-known experimental poetic works of this period was Michael Ondaatje's *The Collected Works of Billy the Kid* (1970), which won the Governor General's Award that year (shared with Nichol for his book *The True Eventual Story of Billy the Kid*, 1970), much to the chagrin of former prime minister John Diefenbaker, whose nationalist sentiments led him to object that the book should not have won because its central character was not Canadian. Generically the work is difficult to categorize as it offers a collage of poetry, prose pieces, photographs, and newspaper segments, the cumulative effect of which is to undermine any attempt to settle on the "facts" of Billy the Kid's life and actions. The "collected works" ultimately do not contain their subject but leave him open to any number of proliferating interpretations. Ondaatje's book had an immense influence on subsequent poetic sequences of the period, including Daphne Marlatt's *Steveston* (1974) and Robert Kroetsch's *Seed Catalogue* (1977), and its influence is evident into the present day, as, for example, in the intriguing poetic sequence by Armand Garnet Ruffo, *Grey Owl: The Mystery of Archie Belaney* (1996) and Lorna Crozier's *A Saving Grace* (1996).

The beginnings of the experimental, postmodern novel are evident during this period as well. Critics often identify the first postmodern Canadian novels as Elizabeth Smart's *By Grand Central Station I Sat Down and Wept* (1945) and Sheila Watson's *The Double Hook* (1959), both of which were published before the heyday of North American postmodernism (although both novels have also been seen as central modernist works). In the 1960s, three prominent postmodern novels were Leonard Cohen's *Beautiful Losers* (1966), Graeme Gibson's *Five Legs* (1969), and Dave Godfrey's *The New Ancestors* (1970), to be followed by the many historical metafictions (fiction about the writing of fiction) of the 1970s and early '80s, including Wiebe's *The Temptations of Big Bear* (1973), Ondaatje's *Coming Through Slaughter* (1976), Findley's *The Wars* (1977) and *Famous Last Words* (1981), and Bowering's *Burning Water* (1980). See the introduction to Section VII for a discussion of Linda Hutcheon's theory of "historiographic metafiction."

The same period saw the foundation of the influential alternative theatre company Theatre Passe Muraille, which was founded in Toronto in 1968 by Jim Garrard.

The group used innovative methods to break down the divide between actors and audience. Under the direction of Paul Thompson, it became known for its nationalist concerns and its process of collective creation, in which a group of actors would "workshop" ideas for pieces and then collaboratively "write" the final play. Thompson's role in Theatre Passe Muraille was groundbreaking, particularly his concept of creating a distinctive voice for Canadian drama by taking theatre out into small communities and creating plays in consultation with community members. Like much of the creative work of this period, his approach was both regionalist and nationalist at the same time, the idea being that national identity was constituted by its regional and cultural diversity. The most famous example of these theatrical events was the 1972 performance of *The Farm Show*, where the group worked and lived in a rural Ontario farming community, interviewing people, working on their farms, listening to their stories, and finally turning it all into a play which premiered for the local community first. This emphasis on local or regional experience was part of the incipient "postmodern" ethos of the period, which saw itself writing back to centralized national narratives and manifesting an insistence on the local, evident in such works from the period as George Bowering's *Rocky Mountain Foot* (1968), Daphne Marlatt's *Steveston* (1974), and Robert Kroetsch's *Seed Catalogue* (1977).

The early 1970s also saw the beginning of a surge of writing by Aboriginal authors, many of whom gained mainstream attention. Tradition has it that Louis Riel predicted that 100 years following his death Indigenous people in North America would rise up and "the artists, musicians, poets, and visionaries" would lead the way (Acoose, "Post *Halfbreed*" 40). This prediction has turned out to be true in the explosion of Indigenous writing and other art forms in the late twentieth century. In 1973, Maria Campbell's autobiographical text *Halfbreed* was a radical intervention for its explicit treatment of the ways Aboriginal people (specifically Métis communities in Manitoba) had been oppressed for generations in Canada, thereby testing Trudeau's myth of Canada as the "just society" and the reputation of Canada as an inclusive multicultural nation. According to Janice Acoose, Campbell's book "encouraged many Indigenous people to begin writing, and her text initiated the process of representing Indigenous women both positively and knowledgeably" ("Post *Halfbreed*" 29). *Halfbreed* was also an important text for its subversion of the stereotypes about Aboriginal people that had been for so long propagated by White authors and anthropologists. Her work is thus part of the period's concern with civil rights, social change, and identity politics, and is complemented by many feminist writers in the period who sought to reclaim their voice in White patriarchal society. Other important Native-authored works of this period include Lee Maracle's *Bobbi Lee: Indian Rebel* (1975), Basil Johnston's *Moose Meat & Wild Rice* (1978), and Rita Joe's *Poems of Rita Joe* (1978), all of which helped to raise consciousness about the subjection of Indigenous people in Canada. These texts have become some of the foundational works for what is now an exciting body of work by Aboriginal poets and fiction writers—as well as painters and film-makers—in Canada. Prominent among Aboriginal painters of this period are

Norval Morrisseau, who is widely celebrated for his spiritual and shamanistic paintings based on Ojibwa-Midewewin tradition, and Daphne Odjig, whose work is based on images of women and family in Ojibwa culture (see Figure VI-6). In 1973, Odjig founded the Professional Native Indian Artists Association (sometimes referred to as the "Indian Group of Seven"), which included Jackson Beardy, Carl Ray, Joseph Sanchez, Eddy Cobiness, Norval Morrisseau, and Alex Janvier. The paintings of these artists often contain overt political critiques of the colonization of Indigenous people.

This engagement with Indigenous cultures and political concerns is evident in many writings by non-Native writers during these years as well. Rudy Wiebe's Governor General's Award-winning novel from 1973, *The Temptations of Big Bear*, expressly sought to write Indigenous people back into Canadian history. It was followed by his 1977 novel about Louis Riel, *The Scorched Wood People* (which echoed Maria Campbell's "revisioning" of the Riel story at the beginning of *Halfbreed*). Margaret Laurence's *The Fire-Dwellers* (1969) and *The Diviners* (1974) also sought to highlight the importance of Métis communities on the prairies and to expose the racism against Aboriginal people that continued to pervade Canadian society. In *The Diviners* the Scottish-Canadian heroine Morag Gunn falls in love with a Métis man, Jules Tonnerre, and together they have a child who must find her place, as a mixed-race woman, in Canadian society. Robert Kroetsch's *Gone Indian* (1973) and Marian Engel's *Bear* (1976) are examples of other novels that engage with Indigenous cultures. The story of Louis Riel, in particular, caught the interest of many non-Native authors during this period as they sought to "write back" to national histories that had depicted Riel as an enraged outlaw who posed a threat to national unity.[4] In Canadian theatre, George Ryga's momentous play *The Ecstasy of Rita Joe* (1970), which was commissioned by the Vancouver Playhouse for the centennial year in 1967, became an important consciousness raiser with its graphic depiction of institutional and physical violence against a Native woman. The fact that the play was commissioned for Canada's centennial indicates the degree to which the nationalist agenda of this period coexisted with an anti-establishment critique of oppressive national institutions. Sharon Pollock's 1973 play *Walsh*, based on negotiations in the late 1800s between Sioux Chief Sitting Bull and North West Mounted Police superintendent James Walsh, shared a similar concern with Canada's unjust treatment of Aboriginal peoples.

While many of the experimental writers of this generation sought to interrogate or de-centre the cultural nationalist agenda that had come to dominate the Canadian literary scene, an interest in inheritance and history, particularly as

[4] These works include John Robert Colombo's "The Last Words of Louis Riel" (1967), John Newlove's "Crazy Riel" (1968), Dorothy Livesay's "Prophet of the New World" (1972), Don Gutteridge's *Riel: A Poem for Voices* (1972), Raymond Souster's "Louis Riel Addresses the Jury" (1977), and Nichol's "The Long Weekend of Louis Riel" (1978). Later texts include Frank Davey's "Riel" (1985), Beth Cuthand's "Seven Songs for Uncle Louis" (1989), Kim Morrissey's *Batoche* (1989), Margaret Sweatman's novel *When Alice Lay Down with Peter* (2001), and Chester Brown's graphic novel *Louis Riel: A Comic-Strip Biography* (2003).

these related to place, was also a concern of the writing of this period. Jeff Derksen outlines some of the central themes in Canadian literature at this time, including metaphors of survival, relationship to the landscape and to national space, national identity, and mytho-spatial poetics of a land with contested histories and lingering colonial relations. Canadian literature, writes Derksen, sought to "bring the nation into historical presence and spatial legibility" (240–41). Birney had proclaimed, in 1962, that it was "only by our lack of ghosts / we're haunted," a suggestion either that Canada did not have an enticing enough past, or that Canadians had not been taught to see it. Certainly, many Canadians had a sense that they had been deprived of a sense of their own past. "We were people who had been deracinated," wrote George Bowering in 1976 (qtd. in Blaser 17). One of the earliest and most memorable expressions of this kind was Wallace Stegner's 1962 fictional memoir *Wolf Willow*, a work that reclaims the rich history of the southern Saskatchewan frontier. Stegner laments the generalized sense of complacency and indifference that had disinherited him a knowledge of the region's past: "The very richness of that past as I discover it now makes me irritable to have been cheated of it then. . . . I was an unpeopled and unhistoried wilderness, I possessed hardly any of the associations with which human tradition defines and enriches itself" (112, 122). Similarly, in his 1974 essay "On the Trail of Big Bear," Wiebe expresses anger at the way Canadians had been deprived of their history: "The stories we tell of our past are by no means merely words: they are meaning and life to us as *people*, as a *particular* people; the stories are there, and if we do not know of them we are simply, like animals, memory ignorant, and the less are we people" (134). This concern links his work with that of fellow prairie writer Robert Kroetsch, whose poetry reveals a similar focus on unearthing a buried past, or "unhiding the hidden" as he terms it, especially as its trace remains in the landscape and relics that surround us.

As part of the general interest in nationalist topics during this period, and in response to a perceivable "malaise" or void in Canadians' sense of themselves, writers became interested in resuscitating what they perceived to be a lost or suppressed Canadian history as a way of filling the perceived gap in identity and consciousness. The attempt to consolidate a cohesive national consciousness was achieved through these gestures toward a shared history. Some of the most prominent writers of the 1960s and '70s undertook a kind of recuperation of Canadian history—or thematized its absence—as part of this quest for "authentic" Canadian cultural expression. Many of these works sought to resurrect symbolic ancestors or articulate an ambivalence at the heart of Canadians' sense of themselves—a sense that they were on the fringes of cosmopolitan civilization, yet nevertheless aware of there being something distinctive about Canadian experience (see Purdy's poem "Home Thoughts"). Most famously, Atwood's 1970 poetry sequence *The Journals of Susanna Moodie* sought to emblematize the historical figure of Canadian settler and author Susanna Moodie as a kind of symbolic ancestor for contemporary Canadians. It held up the nineteenth-century pioneer as an archetype for Canadians' divided sense of their emplacement in

Canada, embodying the integral "schizophrenia" of the Canadian national mindset, caught between England and North America, and in the 1970s, between the United States and "home." The ghosts of ancestors that hover over the city of Toronto in Dennis Lee's 1968 poetry sequence *Civil Elegies* (Elegy 1), a long poem that laments the decline of Canadian independence and self-knowledge, echoes that of Atwood's Moodie who lurks on modern buses or speaks from "underground" (see Figure VI-7). Atwood's description of Lee's *Civil Elegies* evokes the sense of urgency that accompanied this quest: "What must happen is a claiming, a 'will to be' in this country. . . . [W]hich comes first, rebellion against the dominating Empire or the individual and group self-confidence . . . required to sustain such a rebellion. [Both], it appears, are necessary if we are not to live forever on 'occupied soil'" (*Survival* 244).

This concern to reclaim Canada's past is evident in much of the writing from this period, and continues into the twenty-first century as a preoccupation of Canadian authors. Laurence's protagonist Morag Gunn in *The Diviners* (1974) must learn about her past through oblique means, as a way of learning about the early settlers on the Canadian prairies. Morag's symbolic journey to the Old World "homeland," Scotland, reveals to her, in retrospect, that her home—and history—is really in Canada. Likewise, Al Purdy's famous poem, "The Country North of Belleville," as well as his series of "Roblin's Mills" poems, highlights the disappearance of Canada's past before it has been adequately recorded and assimilated. In his correspondence with Laurence, Purdy lamented the loss of these historical traces and Canadians' blithe disinterest in preserving them. Gordon Lightfoot's "The Canadian Railroad Trilogy" (1967), John Newlove's "Samuel Hearne in Wintertime" (1968), George Bowering's "George, Vancouver" (1970), Daphne Marlatt's *Steveston* (1974), Kroetsch's "Stone Hammer Poem" (1975), Michael Ondaatje's "Pig Glass" (1979), and Jon Whyte's "Henry Kelsey" (1981) are also evidence of a growing interest in Canadian history as an inspiration for both regional and national expression.

One of the most important historical novels of this period was Joy Kogawa's *Obasan* (1981), which took as its subject the forced internment of Japanese Canadians during the Second World War in Canada. Kogawa's novel was a major inspiration for the Redress Movement in Canada, which led to an apology and financial settlement for Japanese Canadians from the Canadian government in 1988. This interest in "re-searching" Canadian history is evident in the work of two prominent popular historians from this period as well, Peter Newman and Pierre Berton, especially Newman's histories of the fur trade (such as *The Company of Adventurers* [1985]) and Berton's popular histories and television programs on the building of the CPR (*The National Dream* [1970] and *The Last Spike* [1971]).

The hippies, intellectuals, and iconoclasts of the 1960s and '70s whose efforts helped to fuel this period of cultural innovation may have ascended to the ranks of revered literary icons, but as a direct result of their groundbreaking efforts, Canadians could no longer complain that they were haunted by a lack of ghosts.

FIGURE VI-I Expo 67: United States Pavilion, Geodesic Dome designed by Buckminster Fuller

Source: Damie Stillman

FIGURE VI-2 Expo 67: Ontario Pavilion with Canadian Pavilion in the background

Source: Library and Archives Canada/Canadian Corporation for the 1967 World Exhibition fonds/e000996019. © Government of Canada. Reproduced with the permission of the Minister of Public Works and Government Services (2008).

FIGURE VI-3 "René Lévesque vs. The British North America Act"

This cartoon by Jan Kamienski that appeared in the *Winnipeg Tribune* tapped into the sense in English Canada that Lévesque's *séparatiste* policies were destroying the foundations of the country. In most political cartoons, Lévesque was depicted as a chain-smoker; here he is shown rolling a cigarette in a torn-off piece of the British North America Act, the document that forged Canada as a union of French and English settlers in 1867.

Source: Jan Kamienski, Winnipeg Tribune

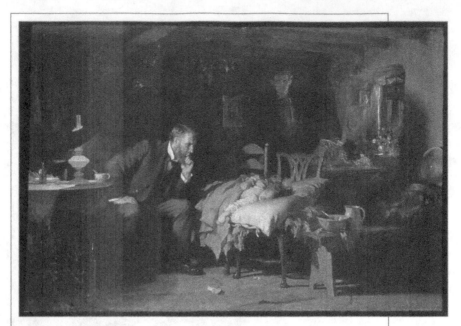

FIGURE VI-4 *The Doctor* **(1891), Sir Luke Fildes (1843–1927)**

This is the painting that features in Mavis Gallant's story "The Doctor." Fildes was an English social realist painter who depicted scenes of poverty and deprivation; his work was a central influence on the writings of Charles Dickens, among others. This painting was inspired by the death of Fildes's own son in 1877. Here it is not clear whether the child will survive or not, although the symbolic detail of the dawn light shining on the child gives the image an element of hope. The painting was popular with Victorian audiences, who admired the lowly doctor's humble heroism and diligence as he watches over his patient.

Source: Sir Luke Fildes, *The Doctor*, 1981; oil on canvas; The Granger Collection, New York.

FIGURE VI-5 *Reason over Passion* (1968), Joyce Wieland (1931–1998)

This icon of Canadian second-wave feminism by Joyce Wieland satirizes Pierre Trudeau's famous slogan from the 1968 Liberal convention: "Reason over Passion." Wieland turns this into a feminist commentary by claiming the slogan for women, while also making it ironic, by creating it in a conventionally female medium: quilting. The fact that women were stereotypically associated with "passion" or "emotion," as opposed to the male attributes of rationality or "reason," is further parodied here—though paradoxically the slogan is "written" onto a bed cover, the place of "passionate" activity. The fact that reason is placed "over" passion might suggest the continuation of male domination during the so-called sexual revolution.

Source: Joyce Wieland, *Reason over Passion*, 1968; photo © National Gallery of Canada, Ottawa.

FIGURE VI-6 *The Indian in Transition* (1978), Daphne Odjig (1919–)

Daphne Odjig (Potawatomi, Odawa, and English) is one of the most important Aboriginal painters in Canada to emerge during the 1970s. *The Indian in Transition*, commissioned by the Canadian Museum of Civilization, charts the history of Native peoples in North America, beginning before the arrival of Europeans, continuing through the attempted destruction of Aboriginal cultures, and ending on an expression of rejuvenation and hope. Odjig's story unfolds with the figure on the left playing the drum, which symbolizes strong Aboriginal cultural traditions, while overhead is a protective Thunderbird. In the centre, a boat, whose bow is a serpent, has arrived filled with pale-skinned people. Aboriginal people are then shown to be caught in a chaotic world of disease and despair. Four ethereal figures rise above the fallen cross and broken drums, one of which, to the right, protectively shelters the sacred drum and struggles free, under the protection of the Thunderbird and the eye of Mother Earth depicted in the top left. Odjig ends the story as it began, with a message of hope and mutual understanding for the future. The story in the painting echoes the "seventh-generation prophecy," which predicts that Native peoples and cultures will regain their voice seven generations after the arrival of Christopher Columbus in the New World.

Source: *The Indian in Transition*, by Daphne Odjig; photo © Canadian Museum of Civilization, Artifact III-M-15, Image S79-3830.

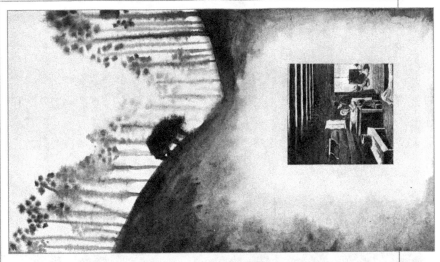

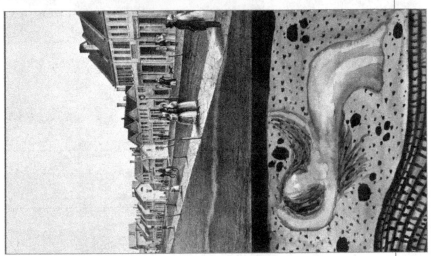

FIGURE VI-7 Margaret Atwood's illustrations to *The Journals of Susanna Moodie* (1970)

These illustrations were created by Margaret Atwood to accompany her poems in *The Journals of Susanna Moodie* (1970). The first one gives a sense of the "garrisoned" and fearful state of the settler in the midst of a vaguely threatening landscape. The second shows Susanna Moodie buried underneath the burgeoning city, now a part of the landscape she so resisted.

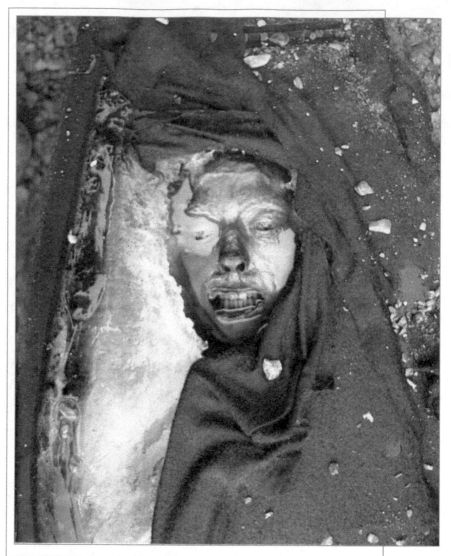

FIGURE VI-8 Photograph of the exhumed body of John Torrington, one of the sailors on the Franklin Expedition of 1845

This photograph of John Torrington, who died 1 January 1846, was taken in the 1980s by the forensic team led by Owen Beattie to chart the exhumation of the buried sailors from John Franklin's fatal expedition of 1845. Because the bodies had been buried in the permafrost, they had been almost perfectly preserved. The image shows Torrington's body moments after it was uncovered. This photograph is described in Margaret Atwood's short story, "The Age of Lead."

Source: Photo by Owen Beattie. From Owen Beattie and John Geiger, *Frozen In Time: The Fate of the Franklin Expedition*, Greystone Books, 2004.

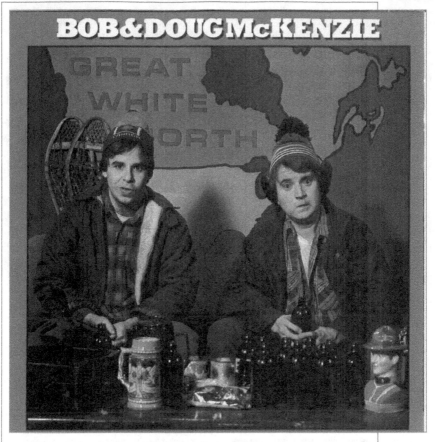

Figure VI-9 Bob and Doug McKenzie, *The Great White North* album cover (1981)
In 1980, the Canadian television comedy program *SCTV* introduced its "Great White North" segment as a way of meeting "CanCon" requirements. The segment featured the two dim-witted "hoser" brothers Bob and Doug McKenzie, played by Rick Moranis and Dave Thomas, who discussed such authentic "Canadian" topics as beer and back bacon, and repeatedly tagged the Canadianism "eh" onto the end of their sentences. In 1981, the pair released their *Great White North* record album, which vaulted to number one within a month of its release and sported the following tongue-in-cheek attestation on its back cover:

> 100% CCIC
> CANADIAN CONTENT CERTIFICATION
> This recording is certified 100% Canadian Content by the Canadian Cultural Identity Commission. Any broadcasts of any portion of this recording qualifies as 100% Canadian between the hours 6 A.M. and 12 Midnite.

Source: SRO Management and Anthem Entertainment Inc.

The MacPatriation Brothers

Figure VI-10 "The MacPatriation Brothers" (1981), Roy Peterson
Originally published in the *Vancouver Sun* on 28 October 1981, this political cartoon of Prime Minister Pierre Trudeau and Minister of Justice (later Prime Minister) Jean Chrétien makes fun of the seemingly endless constitutional negotiations by representing the two politicians as the famous "hosers" Bob and Doug McKenzie.

Source: Roy Peterson

CHIEF DAN GEORGE (GESWANOUTH SLAHOOT) ■ (1899–1981)

Born in North Vancouver into the Tsleil Waututh nation (Coast Salish band), Dan George, or Geswanouth Slahoot, became an iconic actor and writer in the 1960s and '70s. His given name at birth, Teswahno, translates as "thunder coming up over the land from the water." When he attended boarding school as a child, his name was changed to its English form, Dan George. He became Chief of the Tsleil Waututh on the Burrard Reserve in 1951, taking over the position from his father, and was made an honorary chief of two other bands, the Squamish and the Shuswap.

His first acting roles came in the 1960s, in both television and film. In recognition of his work with Dustin Hoffman in *Little Big Man* (1970), he became the first Native actor to be nominated for an Academy Award. He also had an illustrious stage career, acting in the original 1967 production of

George Ryga's groundbreaking play about Native people, *The Ecstasy of Rita Joe*.

Alongside his acting career, Dan George took seriously his role as a spokesperson and inspiration for Aboriginal people. He published two books of poetry, *My Heart Soars* (1974) and *My Spirit Soars* (1982), which call on Indigenous people to use "the instruments of the white man's success" while maintaining Aboriginal cultural traditions. As part of the 1 July 1967 Centennial festivities, Dan George performed his powerful poem, "A Lament for Confederation," in Vancouver's Empire Stadium to a crowd of 35,000 people. The poem is an indictment of Canada's oppression of Aboriginal people, and the losses they had experienced in the 100 years since Confederation. Yet, like his poem "If the Legends Fall Silent," it also ends with a vision of Native people's resurgence in the years to come.

A LAMENT FOR CONFEDERATION

251

A Lament for Confederation

How long have I known you, Oh Canada? A hundred years? Yes, and many many *seelanum* more. And today, when you celebrate your hundred years, Oh Canada, I am sad for all the Indian people throughout the land.

For I have known you when your forests were mine; when they gave me my meat and my clothing. I have known you in your streams and rivers where your fish flashed and danced in the sun, where the waters said come, come and eat of my abundance. I have known you in the freedom of your winds. And my spirit, like the winds, once roamed your good lands.

But in the long hundred years since the white man came, I have seen my freedom disappear like the salmon going mysteriously out to sea. The white man's strange customs which I could not understand, pressed down upon me until I could no longer breathe.

When I fought to protect my land and my home, I was called a savage. When I neither understood nor welcomed this way of life, I was called lazy. When I tried to rule my people, I was stripped of my authority.

My nation was ignored in your history textbooks—they were little more important in the history of Canada than the buffalo that ranged the plains. I was ridiculed in your plays and motion pictures, and when I drank your firewater I got drunk—very, very drunk. And I forgot.

Oh Canada, how can I celebrate with you this centenary, this hundred years? Shall I thank you for the reserves that are left me of my beautiful forests? For the canned fish of my rivers? For the loss of my pride and authority, even among my own people? For the lack of my will to fight back? No! I must forget what's past and gone.

Oh God in Heaven! Give me back the courage of the olden Chiefs. Let me wrestle with my surroundings. Let me again, as in the days of old, dominate my environment. Let me humbly accept this new culture and through it rise up and go on.

Oh God! Like the Thunderbird of old I shall rise again out of the sea; I shall grab the instruments of the white man's success—his education, his skills, and with these new tools I shall build my race into the proudest segment of your society. Before I follow the great chiefs who have gone before us, Oh Canada, I shall see these things come to pass.

I shall see our young braves and our chiefs sitting in the houses of law and government, ruling and being ruled by the knowledge and freedoms of *our* great land. So shall we shatter the barriers of our isolation. So shall the *next* hundred years be the greatest in the proud history of our tribes and nations.

[1967]

NORTHROP FRYE ■ (1912–1991)

According to literary theorist Murray Krieger, Northrop Frye had a hold "on a generation of developing literary critics greater and more exclusive than that of any one theorist in recent critical history." From the 1940s to the 1990s, Frye established himself as one of the most important critics of the twentieth century, gaining an international reputation for his organization of literary phenomena into cohesive patterns. Within Canada, he influenced generations of literary critics and authors, including Margaret Atwood (whose own critical work *Survival* [1972] is indebted to Frye) and Robertson Davies.

However, it is not for his writings on Canadian literature that Frye is best known. Frye has been widely described as an "archetypal" or "myth critic," and was directly influenced by anthropologist

James Frazer's synthesis of world mythology in *The Golden Bough* (1922), the visionary writings of the English Romantic poet William Blake, and the psychological theories of Carl Jung. Renowned for his 1957 work *The Anatomy of Criticism,* a study that systematizes literary approaches into definitive, universal categories, Frye is also known for his critical studies of Blake (*Fearful Symmetry* [1947]) and the Bible (*The Great Code* [1982]).

Throughout his work, Frye stated that his approach had a scientific basis rather than a subjective, evaluative one. He also insisted that literature was an autonomous realm outside the influence of ideology and historical context. However, it is debatable whether he applied these principles to his criticism of Canadian literature. Robin Mathews, in "Literature, the

Universities and Liberal Ideology" (1978), charges Frye with "anaemic resignation" and "quiet colonialism" when commenting on Canadian culture. Nevertheless, Frye felt that he was firmly rooted in a Canadian environment and that Canada had significantly influenced his thought.

Born in Sherbrooke, Quebec, Frye had an introverted and bookish temperament from early on. The family's Methodist background undoubtedly influenced his subsequent interest in Biblical scripture, though not from a doctrinal perspective but from a literary one. In 1919, the family moved to Moncton, N.B., where Frye's father worked as a hardware salesman. Frye attended Victoria College in the University of Toronto, where he was taught by poet E.J. Pratt, graduating in 1933 with a degree in philosophy and English. He then obtained a theology degree from Emmanuel College, University of Toronto. Although he was ordained as a United Church minister in 1936, Frye was more suited to an academic profession and subsequently received a Master's degree in English from Oxford University in England. He returned to Toronto to take up a teaching position at Victoria College in 1939, where he taught for more than 40 years.

Throughout his career, Frye was an active contributor to discussions of Canadian literature and culture. From 1948 to 1952, he was the editor of the important magazine *Canadian Forum,* and contributed a yearly essay on Canadian poetry to the *University of Toronto Quarterly,*

"Letters in Canada," throughout the 1950s. In 1971, he collected his critical writings on Canadian literature in *The Bush Garden: Essays on the Canadian Literary Imagination.* In the book, Frye confronted the lingering "colonialism" in Canadian culture and attempted to define what he saw as an emergent Canadian literary tradition. In his Preface to *The Bush Garden,* Frye offers a distinction between "unity" and "uniformity," which he thinks is crucial to understanding Canadian cultural expression. One of the Canadian works for which Frye is best known is his Conclusion to the *Literary History of Canada,* in which he identifies the central preoccupation of the "Canadian sensibility" in terms of the "garrison mentality," a defensive response to a hostile environment, or, as Frye puts it, a "deep terror in regard to nature." This idea was subsequently developed by Atwood, in 1972, in her notion of the central theme of "survival" in Canadian literature.

Frye's second collection of essays on Canadian culture, *Divisions on a Ground,* appeared in 1982. His commentaries on Canadian literature were often harsh, comparable to those of Davies and Mordecai Richler, which has led critics to note Frye's ambivalence about the social and cultural environment in which he had grown up. Interestingly, a good deal of Canadian literary criticism of the 1970s and '80s, what became known as the "thematic" school of Canadian criticism, was indebted to the archetypal approach of Frye, even as it sought to place Canadian literature in its specific historical and social context.

Conclusion to *Literary History of Canada*

[. . .] It seems to me that Canadian sensibility has been profoundly disturbed, not so much by our famous problem of identity, important as that is, as by a series of paradoxes in what confronts that identity. It is less perplexed by the question "Who am I?" than by some such riddle as "Where is here?"

We are obviously not to read the mystique of Canadianism back into the pre-Confederation period. Haliburton,[1] for instance, was a Nova Scotian, a Bluenose: the word "Canadian" to him would have summoned up the figure of someone who spoke mainly French and whose enthusiasm for Haliburton's own political ideals would have been extremely tepid. The mystique of Canadianism was specifically the cultural accompaniment of Confederation and the imperialistic mood that followed it. But it came so suddenly after the pioneer period that it was still full of wilderness. To feel "Canadian" was to feel part of a no-man's-land with huge rivers, lakes, and islands that very few Canadians had ever seen. "From sea to sea, and from the river unto the ends of the earth"—if Canada is not an island, the phrasing is still in the etymological sense isolating. One wonders if any other national consciousness has had so large an amount of the unknown, the unrealized, the humanly undigested, so built into it. Rupert Brooke speaks of the "unseizable virginity" of the Canadian landscape.[2] What is important here, for our purposes, is the position of the frontier in the Canadian imagination. In the United States one could choose to move out to the frontier or to retreat from it back to the seaboard. The tensions built up by such migrations have fascinated many American novelists and historians. In the Canadas, even in the Maritimes, the frontier was all around one, a part and a condition of one's whole imaginative being. The frontier was primarily what separated the Canadian, physically or mentally, from Great Britain, from the United States, and even more important, from other Canadian communities. Such a frontier was the immediate datum of his imagination, the thing that had to be dealt with first. [. . .]

It has often been remarked that Canadian expansion westward had a tight grip of authority over it that American expansion, with its outlaws and sheriffs and vigilantes and the like, did not have in the same measure. America moved from the back country to the wild west; Canada moved from a New France held down by British military occupation to a northwest patrolled by mounted police. [. . .] Otherwise, the conquest, for the last two centuries, has been mainly of the unconscious forces of nature, personified by the dragon of the Lake Superior rocks in Pratt's *Towards the Last Spike:*

On the North Shore a reptile lay asleep—
A hybrid that the myths might have conceived,
But not delivered.[3]

Yet the conquest of nature has its own perils for the imagination, in a country where the winters are so cold and where conditions of life have so often been bleak and comfortless, where even the mosquitoes have been described as "mementoes of the fall." I have long been impressed in Canadian poetry by a tone of deep terror in regard to nature, a theme to which we shall return. It is

[1] Thomas Chandler Haliburton (1796–1865), nineteenth-century Nova Scotian author. See Volume I.

[2] Rupert Brooke (1887–1915), English poet who died in the First World War. The quotation is from Brooke's 1916 text *Letters from America,* in which he describes his experience in the Canadian west.

[3] See E.J. Pratt's "Towards the Last Spike" (1952) in Section V.

not a terror of the dangers or discomforts or even the mysteries of nature, but a terror of the soul at something that these things manifest. The human mind has nothing but human and moral values to cling to if it is to preserve its integrity or even its sanity, yet the vast unconsciousness of nature in front of it seems an unanswerable denial of those values. [. . .]

If we put together a few of these impressions, we may get some approach to characterizing the way in which the Canadian imagination has developed in its literature. Small and isolated communities surrounded with a physical or psychological "frontier," separated from one another and from their American and British cultural sources: communities that provide all that their members have in the way of distinctively human values, and that are compelled to feel a great respect for the law and order that holds them together, yet confronted with a huge, unthinking, menacing, and formidable physical setting—such communities are bound to develop what we may provisionally call a garrison mentality. In the earliest maps of the country the only inhabited centres are forts, and that remains true of the cultural maps for a much later time. Frances Brooke, in her eighteenth-century *Emily Montague*, wrote of what was literally a garrison;[4] novelists of our day studying the impact of Montreal on Westmount write of a psychological one.

A garrison is a closely knit and beleaguered society, and its moral and social values are unquestionable. In a perilous enterprise one does not discuss causes or motives: one is either a fighter or a deserter. Here again we may turn to Pratt, with his infallible instinct for what is central in the Canadian imagination. The societies in Pratt's poems are always tense and tight groups engaged in war, rescue, martyrdom, or crisis, and the moral values expressed are simply those of that group. In such a society the terror is not for the common enemy, even when the enemy is or seems victorious. [. . .] The real terror comes when the individual feels himself becoming an individual, pulling away from the group, losing the sense of driving power that the group gives him, aware of a conflict within himself far subtler than the struggle of morality against evil. [. . .]

Literature is conscious mythology: as society develops, its mythical stories become structural principles of storytelling, its mythical concepts, sun-gods and the like, become habits of metaphorical thought. [. . .]

I keep coming back to the feeling that there does seem to be such a thing as an imaginative continuum, and that writers are conditioned in their attitudes by their predecessors, or by the cultural climate of their predecessors, whether there is conscious influence or not. [. . .] The more such monuments or such contemporaries there are in a writer's particular cultural traditions, the more fortunate he is; but he needs those traditions in any case. He needs them most of all when what faces him seems so new as to threaten his identity.

[1965, rev. 1971]

---

[4] Frances Brooke (1724–1789) is the author of *The History of Emily Montague* (1769), often identified as the first English-Canadian novel and set during the early "garrison" years following the conquest of Quebec.

Robertson Davies stands apart from many other Canadian writers for treating the parochialism of small-town central Canada alongside the realms of myth and magic. As Davies himself stated in an interview with Donald Cameron, he was "trying to record the bizarre and passionate life of the Canadian people." As a result, his works are difficult to categorize, for they are neither realist nor fabulist. While they contain withering critiques of social and cultural posturing, they indulge in esoteric subject matter and elevated themes, which, compounded by Davies's eccentric and witty public persona, earned him a reputation as a formidable Old World polymath. His fascination with the invisible emerges in his interview with Cameron, where he states that he was "immensely conscious of powers of which I can have only the dimmest apprehension." It is this focus that characterizes the genre that became known as "Southern Ontario Gothic," a term that has been applied to the writings of Davies, Alice Munro, and playwright James Reaney. Each of these writers is fascinated by what is popularly considered the apparent incommensurability of appearance and reality, or history and myth.

Of central concern in Davies's writing is the existence of evil—a theme he considers in his best-selling novel *Fifth Business* (1970)—and the grandeur of human moral dilemmas. His interest in Jungian psychology and archetypal patterns overlaps with the critical views of Northrop Frye, who was for many years his contemporary at the University of Toronto. Davies is also widely described as a satirist, who mocked conventional Canadian proprieties, in the tradition of Stephen Leacock, whose work he admired; he wrote a critical study of Leacock's work, *Stephen Leacock* (1970),

and edited anthologies of Leacock's writings. His insistence on the need to reject conventional attitudes toward such things as religion, social manners, and sex is part of his larger endeavour to revel in the mysteries of the human spirit. In so doing, Davies saw himself to be criticizing Canadian petty moralities while offering the possibility of a redefinition of Canadian identity and culture.

Davies was born in Thamesville, Ontario. His father was the owner of the *Thamesville Herald* and later editor, from 1919 to 1925, of the *Renfrew Mercury.* The family moved to Renfrew when Davies was five years old, and later to Kingston, Ontario, where Davies attended high school. He received a B.A. in literature from Oxford University in 1938, after which he joined the Old Vic Theatre company in London. There he met his future wife, Brenda Mathews, who was the stage manager for the company. Davies returned to Canada in 1940 and became literary editor of *Saturday Night* from 1940 to 1942, and again from 1953 to 1959. During this time, he earned a reputation as a playwright and journalist. He began writing for the *Peterborough Examiner,* becoming editor of the paper in 1942, and eventually acquired partial ownership of the paper, with his two brothers, in 1946. He wrote a regular column for the *Examiner* entitled "The Diary of Samuel Marchbanks" (1943–53), very much in the tradition of Thomas McCulloch's *Letters of Mephibosheth Stepsure,* in which he commented on Canadian politics and social life. These pieces were later published as a series of books, including *The Diary of Samuel Marchbanks* (1947) and *The Table Talk of Samuel Marchbanks* (1949). The Massey Commission extensively quotes S. Marchbanks from the *Peterborough Examiner* (4 March 1950) in its Report.

Davies also submitted a special study of theatre in Canada to the Commission. An important moment in Davies's academic career came in 1960, when he was invited by Vincent Massey, chancellor of the University of Toronto, to become the first Master of Massey College at the university. He held the position alongside his appointment as Professor of English and drama until his retirement in 1981. It is in the Massey College library that "The Great Queen Is Amused" is set.

Davies's international reputation rests on his fiction. He wrote an early trio of satirical novels known as the "Salterton Trilogy" that are united by their setting in the university town of Salterton (loosely based on Kingston). These novels, which satirize Canadian provincialism, include *Tempest-Tost* (1951), *Leaven of Malice* (1954), and *A Mixture of Frailties* (1958). Davies became heavily influenced by the psychological writings of Carl Jung in the 1960s and '70s, and brought this interest to his subsequent novels, most notably "The Deptford Trilogy," which uses the notion of unconscious archetypes as an important unifying theme. The first novel of the trilogy, *Fifth Business* (1970), solidified Davies's international reputation with its tale of Dunstan Ramsay, a retired schoolmaster, who becomes obsessed with the history of saints. The next novel in the series, *The Manticore* (1972), which includes an extended Jungian analysis of one of its characters, won Davies the Governor General's Award. The final novel is *World of Wonders* (1975), in which Ramsay is writing the biography of famous magician Magnus Eisengrim, a man whose destiny has been intimately interconnected with his own. The Cornish Trilogy, which includes *The Rebel Angels* (1981), *What's Bred in the Bone* (1985), and *The Lyre of Orpheus* (1988), is set in the fictional town of Blairlogie (based on Davies's childhood experiences in Renfrew) and represents Davies's attempt to revisit, and come to

terms with, the Canada of his childhood. He died before finishing the third novel of his last trilogy, which includes *Murther and Walking Spirits* (1991) and *The Cunning Man* (1994).

Davies's 1982 collection, *High Spirits,* gathers the ghost stories that he wrote for Massey College's annual Christmas "Gaudy Night" celebrations from 1963 to 1980. The humorous story included here, "The Great Queen Is Amused," is taken from this collection, and shows Davies toying with the colonial connection between Canadian authors and their British predecessors. Davies's perspective on the colonial cultural scene in Canada is difficult to sum up, since he was often contradictory in his views. Although he was clearly an anglophile who loved British literary tradition and elite ritual, he was also vocal in his insistence that Canadian writers (and readers) had to break free from the psychological hold of Britain and create a worthy Canadian literature. In his 1977 talk to the Association for Canadian Studies in the United States, included here, Davies engaged with the self-righteous provincialism of the Canadian mindset (and its colonial mentality) by countering two of the central myths about Canada: the myth of moral superiority and the myth of Canadian difference from the United States. The essay works well when read alongside such similarly critical pieces as Irving Layton's "From Colony to Nation," Earle Birney's "Canada: Case History," and Frank Underhill's critique of the Massey Report, all of which are also included in Section V. Citing Douglas LePan's poem "*Coureurs de Bois*," included in Section V, Davies sums up his sense of the Canadian character this way: "Wild Hamlet with the features of Horatio." Appropriately, this also sums up many of Davies's most memorable fictional characters, characters who play the role of "fifth business," operating from the margins yet having crucial, if unacknowledged, influence on the plotline.

The Great Queen Is Amused

ROBERTSON DAVIES

The first Christmas we celebrated in College I told a Ghost Story on this occasion because I had had an odd experience just before the Gaudy,[1] and thought it might amuse you. The second Christmas I told another, only because it was true and a footnote to the first. It was never my intention that these stories should multiply. The last thing I desire for Massey College is the shabby notoriety of being haunted. I am not a man who particularly likes, or seeks, ghosts: I never saw a ghost till I came here—came to a brand-new building, every brick of which I had seen set in place, and all the furnishings of which have been known to me since they came from the makers. I had always thought that ghosts were superstitions. I wish I thought so still.

It happened a week ago last Sunday. I perceive that you have gone at once to the heart of the matter; it is a pleasure to address a truly perceptive audience. You have recognized immediately that the date was December the fifth—the Vigil of Saint Nicholas, patron of scholars, and therefore an unseen but real presence in this College. It was near to midnight, and I lay in my bed, reading myself to sleep, when I felt stealing over me that special uneasiness which I have learned—but only since I came here—to associate with a particular kind of trouble. In university life one quickly becomes expert in identifying several sorts of disquiet; I have one which I believe is all my own, and I call it the Ghost Chill. My temperature drops suddenly; my breathing is laboured; my vision is disturbed so that stable objects seem to advance and retreat before my eyes, and I feel a stirring in my scalp, as though my hair were rising. I see some medical men in the audience smirking; simple fright, they think. Oh no, nothing so easy as that; I am not frightened, but disagreeably *aware*. I know that something quite out of the ordinary—something untoward—something both inescapable and exhausting—is about to happen to me. I know that I have slipped out of the groove of one sort of life and am trapped for a time in an alien realm.

The Ghost Chill also makes one sensitive to sounds which other people do not hear. As I lay in my bed I became conscious of sobbing and sighing and wailing—as of a great number of people shaken with grief and despair and (this was the worst of it) expecting something of me. How did I know this? I cannot tell you. But I knew it, quite clearly. I was not frightened, but I was deeply disturbed and depressed. I knew that things would be worse before they were better, and I knew also that I could not escape whatever lay before me. So I rolled up my book, put it back in its locked case, put on my dressing-gown and slippers, and set out for the scene of the disturbance.

How did I know where to look? That is another of the characteristics of the Ghost Chill. One knows where to go. I do not make any pretentious claim that one is guided to a particular spot; one just knows where to go. So I trudged downstairs, and through the passage on the lowest floor that leads to the Lower Library.

[1] The annual Christmas feast and party held by the college.

The lights are always burning there, with a hard, charmless blaze that should be enough to discourage the most insensitive ghost. I could see at once that there was nobody in the Reference Room, but from the room which is marked 'Press Room and Stacks' the sound that was drawing me was audible—to my sensitive ear, you understand—in dreadful volume. As I unlocked the door I felt fear for the first time.

How does fear manifest itself in you? With me it is like being stabbed with a cruelly cold knife; for an instant it is a paralysis, then a pain, then a shock. Why was I afraid now? Because I had remembered something that was in the stacks.

Our library has, from time to time, been given generous gifts of books. Even before the College opened one gift came to us of a hundred or more volumes, of which all but five were works of Canadian literature. We are already modestly famous for our collection of Canadian literature, you know. But those five were books to which the Librarian paid scant attention, because they did not fit into any of the categories of our collection. They were the works of a man of whom some of you will have heard, and whose name may raise a smile. It was Aleister Crowley;[2] he died not long ago, putting an end to a life that had been spent in trying to impose himself on the world as a magician. Most people laughed at him, but there is no doubt that his career was an unsavoury one, and he was involved in scandals that were disastrous, and sometimes fatal, to people who had come under his influence. There were five of Aleister Crowley's books in the stacks, piled together on a shelf of unclassified volumes, and once or twice I had suggested to the Librarian that we should get rid of them, or put them in the vault. But I had forgotten them, and so had he. I remembered them now with the terrible onset of fear that I have already described.

But as I have told you, when the Ghost Chill is upon me, I have to do what lies before me, afraid or not. So I turned the key in the lock, pushed back the heavy door, and walked inside.

There I saw a scene of such complex disorder that I do not know where to begin to describe it. The light was extraordinary, to begin with; it was not the electric glare of the Reference Room, but a wavering blue light, as though I stood in the middle of a gas flame. There was one other living creature in the stacks, and I recognized her with dismay. I cannot reveal her name, for she is well-known to many of you, and I do not wish to involve her in unseemly gossip. I must say, however, that she knows our library well, for she has spent many hours in the stacks, doing some research in Canadian literature for her husband. She stood, tall, straight and unafraid, looking about her in wonder, and as the door slammed into place she turned to look at me.

'You had better step inside this circle if you don't want to get into trouble,' she said, in the soft, yet deliberate and pleasing accents which tell of a childhood spent in the Hebrides. I saw that she stood in a chalk circle that had been carefully drawn

[2] Aleister Crowley (1875–1947), a notorious British occult writer and philosopher known for his shocking opinions and behaviour.

on the floor, and I hastened to her side. She was calm in the midst of the frantic disturbance that surrounded us. I suppose President's wives are always calm before scenes of despair and tumult; they learn that art at faculty receptions.

'What on earth are you doing?' I demanded.

'I'm afraid I've been careless with the books,' she replied, and in her hand I recognized one of Crowley's volumes, opened at a drawing that looked like a mathematical diagram. 'I just wanted to see if this recipe worked as well as the author said it did, and it seems to have caused a little trouble.'

A little trouble! I detest understatement; it always seems to me to be dangerous frivolity. A little trouble! My eyes were now accustomed to the strange light, and I could see that the whole area of the stacks was filled with agitated, insubstantial figures; each one was clear to the eye, but it was also transparent. The floor stood thick with them, leaping, writhing, shoving and jostling as they attempted to stand on their hands and fell to the floor every time with shrieks of despair. Some others danced about on their hands, laughing in derisive triumph, and still others crowded all the space immediately below the ceiling. These were even stranger than the dervishes on the floor, for they were curled into balls, their heads tucked into their stomachs, their legs drawn up toward their bodies, and their hands clasped loosely before them, as they bobbed, somersaulted and turned gently in the air, like hideous balloons. And, most extraordinary circumstance of all, every one of these figures was stark naked.

What does one say under such circumstances? Almost any remark one can think of is unequal to the occasion. Undoubtedly mine was so. 'What in the world have you done?' I said.

'Well, I've been reading a lot of these Canadian books, getting together material for Claude's anthology,[3] she replied. 'I got a bit curious about some of the authors— thought what fun it would be to talk to them, and all that—foolishness, I suppose. Then to-day I came across this book by this man Crowley, and he says it isn't hard to bring back the dead if you go about it in a respectful and proper manner. For the past two weeks I've been wishing I could have a word or two with Sara Jeannette Duncan;[4] there's a bit in The Imperialist that always sounds to me as if something had been cut out of it and the gap never properly patched, and I thought—'

'You thought you'd get hold of Miss Duncan and ask her,' I interrupted. The leisureliness of the beautiful anthologist's explanation nettled me.

'Well, Crowley didn't seem to think there was much to it,' she said.

'I think that before monkeying with Crowley you might have had the courtesy to speak to me,' said I.

'Oh don't be so pompous,' said she.

---

[3] Claude Bissell (1916–2000), president of the University of Toronto from 1958 to 1971 and afterwards a professor in the English Department. His anthology of Canadian writing, entitled Great Canadian Writing: A Century of Imagination, was published in 1966.

[4] Sara Jeannette Duncan (1861–1922), Canadian fiction writer and journalist, whose novel The Imperialist (1904) is an important early text of Canadian literature. See Volume I, Section III, for some of Duncan's writings.

Women always think that if they tell a man not to be pompous they will shut him up, but I am an old hand at that game. I know that if a man bides his time his moment will come. 'Well,' I said, 'if you and Crowley are such a great pair, suppose you explain what has happened.'

'That's just the difficulty,' she said, with terrible Scottish patience; 'I don't understand what has happened. I did all the right things, and called the name of Sara Jeanette Duncan, and these articles began to appear. Look at them, would you! Did you ever see such a sight in your life? What do you suppose they are?'

This was my moment of triumph. You see, I knew what they were.

It has been a lifelong habit of mine to read myself to sleep. Some people read light books—mystery stories and the like—in bed, but my custom has always been to read works of greater substance before sleeping. And not just to read them once, carelessly, but to read and re-read a group of selected classics over and over again, year in and year out, for in this way they become a part of oneself. For many years a bedtime favourite of mine has been that very famous commentary on the Pentateuch, the *Midrash of Rabbi Tanhuma bar Abba*, most learned of the fourth century Talmudic mystics and sages.[5] My copy of the Midrash is rather a nice one—a fine tenth century scroll, beautifully illuminated though not particularly suited to reading in bed, because it is fourteen feet long, and as it must be read from right to left this means a lot of winding and rewinding. It is encased at both ends in copper and gold; the rubies on the casing scratch my hands now and then, but I don't greatly mind. It is a small price to pay for keeping my Hebrew alive. As luck would have it, I had been reading the scroll of Rabbi Tanhuma when the Ghost Chill came upon me.

Of course you have guessed what the explanation was. Not all of you will have read the great Midrash, but certainly you have read Louis Ginzberg's seven volume compilation of Jewish legends, and will have formed your own conclusions.[6] But Hebrew studies are neglected in the Hebrides and so, for the sake of completeness, I must continue exactly as if you were as much in the dark as was my companion.

She had asked me what I supposed these apparitions were. 'Why,' I said, 'this is hell, and these are spirits of the dead.'

'Don't be silly,' she replied, 'it isn't a bit like hell, except perhaps for the noise.'

'What do you suppose hell to be?' said I. 'The word merely means a dark and enclosed place, inhabited by spirits. A perfect description of the stacks in Massey College Library. Rabbi Tanhuma says it is indistinguishable from Paradise; both damned and saved pass a few millennia there. I suppose you called up a single spirit, and have received a wholesale delivery; Crowley is a most untrustworthy guide.'

'But who are they?' said she.

'It is only too clear that they are the ghosts of the Canadian authors whose books are here," said I.

[5] An ancient exegetical text on the Pentateuch (the first five books of the Old Testament) that contains a mixture of sermons, stories, and legal discussions.

[6] Louis Ginzberg (1873–1923) was a major Talmudic scholar of the twentieth century, author of *The Legends of the Jews* (1909).

'Then why are they so noisy?' she asked. Every time I think of it, I realize what a wealth of national feeling was compressed into that one enquiry.

'They are clamouring to be reborn,' I explained, for my long acquaintance with Rabbi Tanhuma was at last showing its practical applicability. 'Look, you see those who are floating in that strange, curled-up posture; they have placed themselves in the foetal position, so that, when a child is conceived, they are ready at once to take possession of it in the womb, and come to earth again.'

'Whatever for?' said she.

'Perhaps they hope that this time they might be born American authors,' said I.

Our conversation had not been unnoticed by the spirits, who now began to float uncomfortably near us. Ernest Thompson Seton,[7] though foetal in posture, was still clearly recognizable by the obstreperous outdoorsiness of his appearance; one spirit, naked like the rest, was walking on her hands, and it was only by the invincible dignity of her person, back and front, that I recognized Mrs. Susanna Moodie. Robert Barr looked particularly smug, and I knew why; a Junior Fellow of Massey College is making a fullscale study of him, and he was flattered. A floating foetus bumped me—though spectrally—and I turned just in time to see that it was Nellie McClung, avid for rebirth. It was an eerie experience, I can tell you. I had just time to reflect that Canadian authors appeared, on the whole, to have been neglectful of their physiques.

'You don't suppose they mean us any harm, do you?' said my companion, with the first show of nervousness that I had observed in her.

I do not think that I am a cruel man, but I confess that there is a streak of austerity in my character, and it showed itself now. 'They certainly do not mean *me* any harm,' I replied; 'I have not disturbed their rest; I have not frivolously routed them out of Paradise. What their intentions may be toward *you* I have no way of telling.'

'What are you going to do to get us out of here?' she asked, as if I had not spoken. It is thus that women rule the world.

'There is a practical difficulty,' I said. 'These ghosts can be put to rest only by the command of a king—a Hebrew king. They are uncommon nowadays, even in Massey College. We have one or two men of aristocratic birth, but they are unfortunately Aryan. We have a man whom I strongly suspect of being a chieftain in his homeland, but I am quite sure that an African chief would not fill the bill. Even a royal ghost might help us, but you know Canadian literature—no use looking there.'

'I'm not so sure,' said she. From the triumph in her voice I knew that she had an idea. The circle in which we stood was not too far from the stacks for her to

---

[7] The names listed here are all prominent Canadian authors: Ernest Thompson Seton (1860–1946) was a popular naturalist writer around the turn of the century, author of *Wild Animals I Have Known* (1898) and *Two Little Savages* (1906); Susanna Moodie (1803–1885), an early Canadian pioneer and author of the settler classic *Roughing It in the Bush* (1852); Robert Barr (1850–1912), Canadian journalist and fiction writer, author of *The Triumphs of Eugene Valmont* (1906), which featured a detective of the same name; Nellie McClung (1873–1951), Canadian feminist author who wrote the bestselling novel *Sowing Seeds in Danny* (1908) and was one of the "Famous Five" who petitioned the Canadian Parliament to have women legally recognized as persons (see Volume I for writings by Moodie and McClung).

reach over into what the Librarian calls the Matthews Collection, and this is what she did now, handing me two weighty volumes bound in half-calf. I looked at the title. It was *Leaves from the Journal of Our Life in The Highlands*; the date, 1868.

'But this is by Queen Victoria,' said I.

'Of course,' said she; 'and a queen worth a dozen ordinary kings, and I'm pretty certain that she even qualifies as a Hebrew ruler. Disraeli[8] used to tell her that she was descended from King David, and I doubt if a rabble of middle-class Canadian ghosts can say she wasn't. What's more, she also qualifies as a Canadian author. Wasn't she Queen of Canada?'

Women are very, very remarkable people.

'Come on,' she said; 'get to work. See what you can do.'

I was glad of my long acquaintance with the works of the great Rabbi Tanhuma; it meant that I knew how to raise a spirit without resorting to the slip-shod conjurations of Aleister Crowley. I did what was necessary with, I think I may say, a certain style, and gently and slowly there appeared, between me and the beautiful anthologist that small, immensely dignified figure, familiar from a hundred portraits and statues. She wore the well-known tiny crown, from the back of which depended a beautiful veil; across her bosom was a sash of a splendid blue, and on her left shoulder was pinned the Order of the Garter.

I am a democrat. All of my family have been persons of peasant origin, who have wrung a meagre sufficiency from a harsh world by the labour of their hands. I acknowledge no one my superior merely on grounds of a more fortunate destiny, a favoured birth. I did what any such man would do when confronted with Queen Victoria; I fell immediately to my knees.

'Rise at once,' said the silvery voice with the beautiful, actress-like clarity of articulation, which has been so often described that it sounded almost familiar in my ears. 'We have work to do that cannot wait. We presume that you wish to set at rest this disorderly group of my colonial subjects.'

'If you would be so good, Your Majesty,' said I. 'These are Canadian writers, and here in Massey College our library is, it appears, a Paradise for the repose of all such as are represented on our shelves. The blessed in Paradise invariably appear to mortals either walking on their hands, or in a posture convenient for re-birth—'

'Master,' said Queen Victoria; 'do not presume to teach the great-great-grandmother of your Sovereign how to suck eggs—or to lay ghosts either. We shall have these spirits right-side up and safely at rest in the squeezing of a lemon—to use an expression dear to our faithful ghillie, John Brown.[9] But look what has happened. We wish an explanation.'

---

[8] Benjamin Disraeli (1804–1881), British Prime Minister from 1874 to 1880 and noted novelist, who was on good terms with Queen Victoria (1819–1901) as both were committed to promoting the glory of the British Empire. Though baptized as an Anglican, Disraeli was of Jewish descent, which explains his interest in identifying the Queen as having Hebrew lineage.

[9] John Brown (1826–1883) was the personal servant of Queen Victoria who became very close to her after her husband's death; the term *ghillie* is Scottish Gaelic for *servant*.

I had been so occupied with Queen Victoria (who, even though I could see right through her, was, I assure you, much the most imposing and awesome person I have ever seen through in this world or any other) that I had not noticed what was going on among the ghosts. I saw that there had been a great reversal; those who had formerly been standing on their hands were now on their feet; those who had formerly been foetal in posture were now normally postnatal: but the others—those who had been trying to stand on their hands before—were now standing on their heads, and bitter tears were pouring from their eyes.

'Who can they be?' I murmured to myself.

'Those, Master,' said Queen Victoria, 'are impostors in Paradise—persons loosely attached to literature who are not themselves authors but who fatten upon authors. What place have they in Paradise? Surely you recognize them? Those, when they lived, were literary critics!'

I looked more closely, and indeed it was so. I saw—never mind who, and with him was—but the less said, the better. They were critics, all right.

'Away with them,' cried the Queen, and the effect of her words was horrible. There was a roaring, as of a mighty rushing wind, and a tumult filled the room. I was thrown to the ground, but even as I fell I saw a figure, black and glistening, as of a naked man of extraordinary but frightening beauty, carrying a cruel scourge, who swooped upon the unfortunate critics. I thought I heard Queen Victoria say 'Good evening, Rhadamanthus,'[10] in a tone of genial politeness, as one monarch to another, but I cannot be sure, for the howls of the critics mounted to a scream. 'No!' they shrieked, 'it's unfair. We really *were* authors. We too were creative! Living critics say so!' But it was unavailing. In an instant the critics were gone, and stillness filled the room. But, in our shelves, there were smoking, blackened gaps where their books had stood.

Then the great Queen made a splendid gesture of dismissal, and all the Canadian authors made their farewell. It took a long time, for they did so one by one, basking in the royal presence. The ladies curtsied—some like Sara Jeannette Duncan and Frances Brooke[11] with quite a fashionable air, and others—as though they were improvising. Nakedness is unfriendly to a clumsy curtsy. The men bowed—all sorts of bows, from Kerby's splendid gesture with hand on heart and his right foot advanced, to Ralph Connor's strange giving at the knees. But at last all of them had gone back into the shelves, and there we stood—Queen Victoria, the beautiful anthologist and myself, in a room cleansed and calmed.

'You may leave us,' said the Queen.

---

[10] In Greek legend, Rhadamanthus was the son of Zeus and Europa. He was also the wise King of Crete (before Minos) who went on to become one of the judges of the dead. The term *rhadamanthine* has come to refer to a just but severe judgment, which applies to Victoria's actions here.

[11] Frances Brooke (1724–1789), British author who published what is often considered to be the first Canadian novel, *The History of Emily Montague* (1769), following a stay in Quebec. "Kerby" is a reference to William Kirby (1817–1906), Canadian novelist who wrote the historical novel *The Golden Dog* (1877). Ralph Connor (1860–1937), the pseudonym of Rev. Charles William Gordon, was a popular Canadian short story writer and novelist, author of *The Man from Glengarry* (1901) and *Glengarry School Days* (1902).

I bowed. 'I cannot sufficiently express my gratitude—' I began, but as I spoke a smile of extraordinary sweetness broke over the royal features, which had already begun to fade, and before she vanished altogether there came to my ears, unmistakably—'The Queen was very much amused.'

[1982]

The Canada of Myth and Reality

[. . .] What do I mean when I speak of myth? In national terms I mean the sort of attitude which most people take for granted, the belief that nobody questions because nobody troubles to put it in concrete terms. The myth of national character is familiar to us all: in your country[12] it is summed up in the figure of Uncle Sam, a Down-East Yankee in the dress of 1830 or thereabouts, totally unlike most of your citizens in every way, though now and then, on the streets or in a photograph, one spies the reality on which the stereotype was founded. We all know John Bull, who is not at all like any Englishman we have ever met, and Marianne, that generous-hearted, big-breasted female who is such an incongruous symbol for modern France. But where is the Canadian stereotype? We had one once, a grinning fellow called Jack Canuck, who looked as if he were engaged in wheat-farming on a large scale, but we got rid of him because he simply didn't do.[13] [. . .]

Does this mean, then, that Canada has no national character, no myth by which it lives and from which it approaches the rest of mankind? No, it does not. It means only that Canada achieved adulthood comparatively recently, in an era of the world's history that has been immensely complicated by universal education, international social and political concern, and the sort of sophistication that relates to a highly developed technology. [. . .]

But where, you may ask, are the myths? Demonstrable differences are easily understood: what have you to say about those things which are more truly divisive, because they exist not in politics or law or banking or even in the arts, but in the less accessible realm of the spirit?

Our myths, or 'life-supporting illusions', as your great scholar of the mythic world Joseph Campbell calls them,[14] are many, and I cannot explore them all. There is, for instance, our Myth of Innocence or Moral Superiority:

---

[12] This was originally a talk given to the Association for Canadian Studies in the United States, so Davies is speaking to an American audience.

[13] Johnny or Jack Canuck was an early personification of Canada. From 1869 onwards he was depicted as a wholesome farmer or lumberjack who resisted the bullying of England (allegorized by John Bull) and the United States (Uncle Sam), but by the early twentieth century he had largely disappeared from view, briefly reappearing as the cartoon war hero Johnny Canuck in the 1940s and as the superhero Captain Canuck in the 1970s. Marianne is the personification of the French Republic who stands for Liberty and Reason.

[14] Joseph Campbell (1904–1987), influential American scholar of comparative mythology whose works, informed by the writings of Carl Jung, include The Hero with a Thousand Faces (1949) and his four-volume The Masks of God (1959–1968).

deep in our hearts we Canadians cherish a notion—you see that I do not call it an idea, because an idea may be carefully formulated, whereas a notion is an elusive thing that takes form from every mind that embraces it—we cherish a notion that we are a simple folk, nourished on the simpler truths of Christianity, in whom certain rough and untutored instincts of nobility assert themselves. Now, of course you are rather in that line yourselves, so you will readily understand what I am talking about. But you will not understand it quite as a Canadian understands it, because of course such a Myth of Innocence is really a manifestation of pride, and it means Innocence in comparison with the flawed virtue of somebody else. And for us the somebody else is you. [. . .]

Perhaps you are ready to say that my Myth of Innocence is nothing but a disagreeable self-righteousness, and certainly that plays its part in the myth, though I do not think it is the whole thing. But self-righteousness is part of the blood and bone of this continent, and I think it is somewhat stronger in Canada than it is among you. Self-righteousness is bound to be a characteristic of colonizing peoples; a grabber always wants moral backing when he grabs. [. . .]

Humble people: how we exalt them in our history books and in our popular literature! And rightly so, for to their bravery and endurance we owe much of what we now are. They are, unquestionably, the salt of the earth. But as my own ancestry was indisputably humble, I may be permitted to say that a small quantity of salt is enough; it is the manifest duty of humble people to stop being humble just as fast as they can, because the shadow of their humility is a know-nothing, cantankerous self-righteousness. The very moment that humble people realize that they are humble and that humility is a very fine thing, their goose is cooked. In Canada we have had more than enough of such vaunting humility, and the neglect of intellectual and spiritual aspiration that it fosters. I do not suggest that the alternative is the grasping, self-serving spirit that is the shadow of aristocracy, but surely we can find a model for Modern Man that avoids both these extremes. We must rid ourselves of the Myth of Innocence on both sides of our border, for it is a potent source of mischief and a breeding-ground for many dangerous sorts of stupidity. Innocence preserved too long sours into ignorance.

What other myths have we? [. . .]

[T]here is one, very apparent in our national life now, and a mighty mischief-maker, on which I wish to spend some time. It is our Myth of Difference.

We are more like you than we are like any other nation on earth. Yet how quick we are to contradict an Englishman, let us say, who calls one of us an American. And when he says, as he often does, What's the difference? we are puzzled to give a short answer. If you ask a Swiss how he differs from a Frenchman, or an Italian, or a German, he can tell you at once, and probably he will say that, long years ago, he fought for his difference. I have spoken of the War of 1812, in which we fought for our difference; Canadians have fought in many wars [. . .] but we have only fought on that one occasion to preserve our own land and our own difference.[15] In the light of what was going on in the world at the time, it was not a fight that bulks very large in the chronicles. But there is more than one kind of fighting, and anybody who reads the newspapers with his eyes open knows that the great battles of our time are the psychological battles, though these are often disguised as ideological battles. You made a great advance in your nationhood when you fought an ideological battle—for that was what it was, though it was fought with shot and shell—at the time of your Civil War.[16] We are fighting our Civil War right now, and we are fighting it on what appear to be ideological grounds. Below that level, however, it is a psychological war, and the contestants are not only the Province of Quebec against the remainder of Canada, but the provinces against the Dominion government, the rich areas against the poor areas, and an unformed New Canada against an Old Canada that has served its turn. [. . .]

One of the tasks of the Canadian writer is to show Canada to itself. He is not obliged to do this, but it is one of his options. Canadians—perhaps I should say the critical and academic world of Canada—are anxious for this kind of revelation, and so there is a strong temptation to fake it. Very few people seem to be aware how strong the pull of public opinion and public expectation is on an artist of any sort, and when he tries to give his public what it wants he is not perhaps a conscious faker, but what he produces is certainly a fake. The artist who binds himself to what might be called the national service can only do worthy and effective work if he is wholly true to himself: if his allegiance is to some form of public expectation, he is not serving his country as an artist should. [. . .]

To show Canada to itself—a serious and heavy task, and it cannot be undertaken by anyone whose determination is to wipe out the past. The odd thing is that so many Canadians who are eager to bring forth a new spirit seem to think either that we have no past, or that it is unworthy of consideration. I do not speak of an historical past in terms of lands seized and conquered, battles fought, and political crises endured, because nobody can deny the existence of such things: I mean a cultural past. [. . .]

But at present the uproar is for a Canadian identity. What is it, and where is it to be sought? [. . .]

For me, for many years, the answer has best been formulated in a Canadian poem by one of our finest poets, who has already spoken to you in one of these

[15] The War of 1812, which lasted from 1812 to 1815, was fought between the United States and Britain; as part of the war, the United States made a number of attempts to invade British North America in both Upper and Lower Canada. For Canadians, two of the most famous battles of the war were the capture of Detroit in 1812 (aided by the Shawnee leader Tecumseh) and the repulsion of the American forces at the Battle of Queenston Heights (1812), both British successes under the leadership of Major-General Isaac Brock (who was killed during the latter battle). The War of 1812 is often celebrated as a unifying victory for Canadians (a united front of British, Irish, French, and Aboriginal forces). It led to a number of defensive initiatives, including the building of the Rideau Canal and the construction of Fort Henry (in Kingston) and the citadels in Quebec City and Halifax to protect against future incursions from the Americans.

[16] The American Civil War (1861–65) was fought between the southern slave-owning states (the Confederates) and the "Union" states in the north led by Abraham Lincoln. One of the deadliest conflicts in American history, resulting in over 600,000 soldier deaths, the war led to the abolition of slavery in the United States.

meetings, Douglas LePan. It is in a poem, published in 1948, called 'Coureurs de bois'. It speaks of only one Canadian, but as a true poem should, it speaks also for many thousands. [. . .][17]

The Canadian is the *coureur de bois* who must understand—understand, not tame—the savage land. And is it the savage land of rocks and forests only penetrable by the patient explorer? Only in the sense that this is a metaphor for that equally savage land of the spirit— 'the desperate wilderness behind your eyes,/So full of falls and glooms and desolations,/Disasters I have glimpsed but few would dream of . . . ' The Canadian voyage, I truly believe, is this perilous voyage into the dark interior of which the poet speaks. [. . .]

But why Canada? Why should this nation so wanting in the rich sense of the past—of an individual self-made past—that is the prized possession of other nations be specially suited to undertake explorations that belong to all men? Because, I think, the Canadian travels very light; he can strip off the cast-offs and the lendings of the other nations more readily than they can rid themselves of garments that have taken on the quality of skins.

Who is this voyager? Again the poem tells us. 'Wild Hamlet with the features of Horatio'. There is the Canadian. The appearance is that of the secondary character, the hero's friend, the confidant; but the opportunity and heart—if he has the courage to trust it—is that of one who may be a hero, and a new kind of hero, a hero of conscience and spirit, in the great drama of modern man.

[1977]

[17] Davies includes the complete text of the poem in this essay. See Section V of this anthology for LePan's poem, which Davies cites in the subsequent paragraphs.

GEORGE GRANT ■ (1918–1988)

George Parkin Grant was an inspirational force for many Canadian writers and thinkers during the 1960s, particularly following the publication of *Lament for a Nation: The Defeat of Canadian Nationalism* in 1965. Announcing the imminent "death" of Canada as a viable nation, *Lament* is one of the most important anti-colonial Canadian statements of this period.

The essay was sparked by the defeat of Prime Minister John Diefenbaker in 1963, and with it what Grant saw to be the end of the long-standing tradition of "conservatism" that had grounded Canada's establishment as a distinct North American nation. In the book, Grant goes even further to bemoan Canada's subordination to the materialist ethic of "modernity" and technological progress, which he associates with the material individualism of the United States. Grant's political stance is known as "Red Toryism," for it is a form of conservatism grounded in ideals of tradition and left-leaning conceptions of social responsibility. Grant distinguishes between Canada and the United States by arguing that "Canada was predicated on the rights of nations as well as on the rights of individuals."

Grant was born in Toronto and attended Upper Canada College, where his father was principal, then Queen's University, where his grandfather, George

Munro Grant, had been a principal. In 1939 he received a Rhodes Scholarship and enrolled in the University of Oxford. After the war, having experienced a conversion to Christianity (an intensity of belief that would stay with him throughout his life), he completed a D.Phil. in religious philosophy at Oxford. After obtaining his degree, Grant took up a professorship in philosophy at Dalhousie University from 1947 to 1960, and again from 1980 to 1984. Also during this time he began to earn a reputation as a public intellectual and commentator on education, particularly with his radio broadcasts for the CBC. His popular book *Philosophy in the Mass Age* (1959) originated as a series of radio talks.

Grant's concern about the colonialism of Canadian society, the threat of an increasingly technological society, and the inevitable end of Canada as an individual nation has echoes in other writers of the period, most notably in the critical writings of Northrop Frye, Robertson Davies, and Dennis Lee. According to Lee's essay "Cadence, Country, Silence" (1973), included here, Grant's analysis of the Canadian predicament "seemed to be speaking the words of our civil condition." After encountering Grant's work in 1967, Lee was himself inspired to articulate the Canadian position in his long poem, *Civil Elegies,* published in 1968.

Under Lee's editorial guidance at House of Anansi Press, Grant put together an important collection of essays entitled *Technology and Empire* (1969). The book is in large part a condemnation of the "religion of progress" that governs the West: "This is the belief that the conquest of human and non-human nature will give existence meaning." Ironically, it was also this belief system that guided the imperialist mission of the early explorers, traders, and settlers in Canada—embodied in E.J. Pratt's epic celebration of technological advance in "Towards the Last Spike" (1952). This approach was criticized by the romantically influenced Confederation Poets of the late nineteenth century, linking them to the romanticism of 1960s radicalism in the next century.

Grant concluded his 1967 essay "Canadian Fate and Imperialism," the article that had so influenced Lee, with praise for Canada's non-participation in the Vietnam War. As he sees it, the defence of Canadian independence from the United States is urgent, even though Canada is intimately associated with American policy: "[O]ur non-involvement in the imperial adventures elsewhere will continue to depend on the possible maintenance of [our] waning sovereignty."

From Lament for a Nation: The Defeat of Canadian Nationalism

[. . .] I have implied that the existence of a sovereign Canada served the good. But can the disappearance of an unimportant nation be worthy of serious grief? For some older Canadians it can. Our country is the only political entity to which we have been trained to pay allegiance. Growing up in Ontario, the generation of the 1920's took it for granted that they belonged to a nation. The character of the country was self-evident. To say it was British was not to deny it was North American. To be Canadian was to be a unique species of North American. [. . .] We were grounded in the wisdom of Sir John A. Macdonald, who saw plainly more than a hundred years ago that the only threat to nationalism was from the South, not from across the sea. To be a Canadian was to build, along with the French, a more ordered and stable society than the liberal experiment in the United States. [. . .]

A society only articulates itself as a nation through some common intention among its people. The constitutional arrangements of 1791, and the wider arrangements of the next century, were only possible because of a widespread determination not to become part of the great Republic.[1] Among both the French and the British, this negative intention sprang from widely divergent traditions. What both peoples had in common was the fact they both recognized, that they could only be preserved outside the United States of America. The French were willing to co-operate with the English because they had no alternative but to go along with the endurable arrangements proposed by the ruling power. Both the French and the British had limited common ground in their sense of social order—belief that society required a high degree of law, and respect for a public conception of virtue. Both would grant the state much wider rights to control the individual than was recognized in the libertarian ideas of the American constitution. [. . .]

British conservatism [. . .] led the settlers to try to build on the northern half of this continent an independent society. British conservatism is difficult to describe because it is less a clear view of existence than an appeal to an ill-defined past. The writings of Edmund Burke are evidence of this.[2] Yet many of the British officials, many Loyalists, and later many immigrants felt this conservatism very strongly. It was an inchoate desire to build, in these cold and forbidding regions, a society with a greater sense of order and restraint than freedom-loving republicanism would allow. It was no better defined than a kind of suspicion that we in Canada could be less lawless and have a greater sense of propriety than the United States. The inherited determinism not to be Americans allowed these British people to come to a *modus vivendi* with the more defined desires of the French. English-speaking Canadians have been called a dull, stodgy, and indeed costive lot. [. . .] Yet our stodginess has made us a society of greater simplicity, formality, and perhaps even innocence than the people to the south. Whatever differences there were between the Anglicans and the Presbyterians, and however differently their theologians might interpret the doctrine of original sin, both communities believed that the good life made strict demands on self-restraint. Nothing was more alien to them than the "emancipation of the passions" desired in American liberalism. An ethic of self-restraint naturally looks with suspicion on utopian movements, which proceed from an ethic of freedom. The early leaders of British North America identified lack of public and personal restraint with the democratic Republic. Their conservatism was essentially the social doctrine that public order and tradition, in contrast to freedom and experiment, were central to the good life. [. . .] In our early

[1] The Constitutional Act of 1791 amended the Quebec Act to divide Quebec into Upper and Lower Canada.

[2] Edmund Burke (1729–1797), a British literary and political figure whose influential tract denouncing the French Revolution, entitled *Reflections on the Revolution in France* (1790), was a nostalgic lament for a lost golden age.

expansions, this conservative nationalism expressed itself in the use of public control in the political and economic spheres. Our opening of the West differed from that of the United States, in that the law of the central government was used more extensively, and less reliance was placed on the free settler. Until recently, Canadians have been much more willing than Americans to use governmental control over economic life to protect the public good against private freedom. To repeat, Ontario Hydro, the CNR, and the CBC were all established by Conservative governments. [. . .]

Many levels of argument have been used to say that it is good that Canada should disappear. In its simplest form, continentalism is the view of those who do not see what all the fuss is about. The purpose of life is consumption, and therefore the border is an anachronism. The forty-ninth parallel results in a lower standard of living for the majority to the north of it. Such continentalism has been an important force throughout Canadian history. Until recently it was limited by two factors. Emigration to the United States was not too difficult for Canadians, so that millions were able to seek their fuller future to the south. Moreover, those who believed in the primacy of private prosperity have generally been too concerned with individual pursuits to bother with political advocacy. Nevertheless, this spirit is bound to grow. One has only to live in the Niagara peninsula to understand it. In the mass era, most human beings are defined in terms of their capacity to consume. All other differences between them, like political traditions, begin to appear unreal and unprogressive. As consumption becomes primary, the border appears an anachronism, and a frustrating one at that. [. . .]

It can only be with an enormous sense of hesitation that one dares to question modern political philosophy. If its assumptions are false, the age of progress has been a tragic aberration in the history of the species. To assert such a proposition lightly would be the height of irresponsibility. Has it not been in the age of progress that disease and overwork, hunger and poverty, have been drastically reduced? Those who criticize our age must at the same time contemplate pain, infant mortality, crop failures in isolated areas, and the sixteen-hour day. As soon as that is said, facts about our age must also be remembered: the increasing outbreaks of impersonal ferocity, the banality of existence in technological societies, the pursuit of expansion as an end in itself. Will it be good for men to control their genes? The possibility of nuclear destruction and mass starvation may be no more terrible than that of man tampering with the roots of his humanity. Interference with human nature seems to the moderns the hope of a higher species in the ascent of life; to others it may seem that man in his pride could corrupt his very being. The powers of manipulation now available may portend the most complete tyranny imaginable. [. . .]

If the best social order is the universal and homogenous state, then the disappearance of Canada can be understood as a step toward that order. If the universal and homogenous state would be a tyranny, than the disappearance of even this indigenous culture can be seen as the removal of a minor barrier on the road to that tyranny.

[1965]

Al Purdy has achieved an almost iconic stature in Canadian literature. Critic Sam Solecki, in calling him "the last Canadian poet," signalled Purdy's status as one of the last great visionaries of a unifying "Canadian experience." Poet Dennis Lee described him as "the major explorer of the Canadian experience of being-here."

Purdy's reputation rests largely on the distinctive quality of his poetry, which has a remarkable ability to merge the commonplace and the exalted, the colloquial and the lyrical, all in the erudite but ironic voice of the speaking poet. Seeking to accommodate "his own large clumsy aching generous eloquent awe-stricken self in words," Lee writes in his Afterword to *The Collected Poems* (1986), Purdy sought to "throw over the whole of traditional poetry."

Critics have especially highlighted Purdy's use of the "vernacular" or every-day language in his work. As Margaret Atwood put it in her Foreword to *Beyond Remembering: The Collected Poems of Al Purdy* (2000), "In a Purdy poem, high diction can meet the scrawl on the washroom wall." This aspect of Purdy's poetry, in fact, has a long history in Canadian writing, from the early jibes aimed at Old World gentility evident in the writings of Thomas Chandler Haliburton or Sara Jeannette Duncan, to, closer to his time, the poems of Irving Layton, Earle Birney, and Alden Nowlan.

Alfred Wellington Purdy was born in Wooler, Ontario, in 1918. His father died two years later, and Purdy was raised by his mother in Trenton. During the height of the Depression in 1936, as a 17-year-old high school dropout Purdy hopped a freight train and travelled across Canada as far as the West Coast. He lived as a hobo for many months before return-ing to Ontario, and eventually joined the

Air Force when the Second World War broke out in 1939. Purdy was posted to British Columbia in the early 1940s, and was eventually joined there by his wife Eurithe, whom he had married in 1941. Following the war, he worked at various jobs, including as a "wage slave," as he calls it, in a Vancouver mattress factory.

Purdy was a self-taught man, whose expansive reading and prodigious beer consumption earned him a reputation as a kind of visionary philosopher-poet, very much like Irving Layton and Malcolm Lowry, both of whom Purdy met during these years. He read widely in world literature, from T.S. Eliot, W.H. Auden, and D.H. Lawrence, to the Russian novelists, to Marcel Proust, to his many Canadian influences. Central among the Canadian writers who had a direct impact on his work were Bliss Carman, E.J. Pratt, Earle Birney, Irving Layton, and Milton Acorn. As Purdy put it in his Preface to *The Collected Poems* (1986), "I think I've learned from everyone I've read, on some level, though I've digested their writing in ways that make it impossi-ble for me to recognize it in my own work. All of us who write are indebted to everyone else who writes for our enthusi-asms and craft."

Although he published his first book of poems, *The Enchanted Echo,* in 1944, it was some years before Purdy really estab-lished himself as a poet. He rose to promi-nence in 1965, at the age of 47, with the publication of *The Cariboo Horses,* for which he received the Governor General's Award. According to Lee in his Afterword to Purdy's *Collected Poems* (1986), *The Cariboo Horses* contained all of the ele-ments that would become Purdy's signa-ture approach: "the portraits; the vignettes; the early memories; poems of place; jokey breakneck yarns; on-the-spot reportage; har-de-har asides; delicate evocations of love and the natural world; broad satire; distant times and places; sex and death and poetry, the galaxy and Roblin Lake." Subsequent important collections include *Wild Grape Wine* (1968), *North of Summer: Poems from Baffin Island* (1967), *Sex and Death* (1973), *The Stone Bird* (1981), *Piling Blood* (1984), and *Naked with Summer in Your Mouth* (1994). The poems in *North of Summer*, from which "Lament for the Dorsets" is taken, are based on Purdy's stay in Baffin Island in the summer of 1965.

Purdy's work evokes a sense of being surrounded by ghosts in the landscape, ancestral memories that may be conjured by a solitary artifact (as in "Lament for the Dorsets"), or by architectural ruins (as in "Roblin's Mills" and "Cariboo Horses"). Often his poems fuse historical time with the present moment, thereby aligning the poem's speaker with a figure from a distant past and highlighting the links between past and present. This technique is evident in many of his poems, from "Method for Calling Up Ghosts" to "Lament for the Dorsets" to "Cariboo Horses" to "Grosse Isle."

Some of Purdy's most powerful poems are those about Roblin Lake and Ameliasburgh, Ontario, where he and his wife settled in the late 1950s. He was drawn to write about the local history of settlement in Ontario, an interest that is evident in one of his most famous poems, "The Country North of Belleville," and also in "Wilderness Gothic." A collection entitled *In Search of Owen Roblin* (1974) provides a meditation on the human geography of the area, in Purdy's imaginary construction of the Roblin family as symbolic Canadian ancestors (comparable to Margaret Atwood's *The Journals of Susanna Moodie* [1970] from the same period). Purdy's work thus counters Birney's famous assertion that Canada was haunted by "a lack of ghosts."

The focus on identity and collective memory, so central to Purdy's work and often expressed in elegiac terms, is evident in his many overtly nationalist poems, such as "Home Thoughts." Purdy was baffled by the many public protestations about the absence of Canadian identity in the 1960s and '70s. As he put it in the Introduction to his 1968 collection of Canadian commentary on the United States, *The New Romans*, "[T]here are few things I find more irritating about my own country than this so-called 'search for an identity,' an identity which I've never doubted having in the first place." In his view a Canadian culture was self-evident. As he put it in *The New Romans*, "The environment, the land, the people, and the flux of history have made us what we are; these have existed since Canada's beginning, along with a capacity for slow evolvement into something else. . . . Their total is all that any nation may possess. I think it is enough."

While he accomplished his best work as a poet, Purdy also published one novel, *A Splinter in the Heart* (1990), and an autobiography, *Reaching for the Beaufort Sea* (1993), dedicated to Stan Rogers, from whose song "Northwest Passage" Purdy took the title of his book. Purdy had close and long-lasting friendships with numerous Canadian writers, including Earle Birney, Milton Acorn, Margaret Laurence, Dennis Lee, and Steven Heighton. He inspired immense admiration and accolades from his fellow writers for his expansive, generous, and unpretentious spirit. In 2003, his poem "At the Quinte Hotel" was made into a short film starring the Tragically Hip lead singer Gord Downie. Numerous poets have noted the immense impact that Purdy had on their work, and many were themselves inspired to write poems in Purdy's honour, including such noteworthy Canadian poets as George Bowering, Doug Jones, F.R. Scott, and Tom Wayman. The lively and funny correspondence between Purdy and Laurence has been published as *Margaret Laurence–Al Purdy: A Friendship in Letters* (1993), edited by John Lennox.

When Purdy died of cancer in April 2000, he was sorely mourned. As Purdy wrote in his Preface to his 1986 *Collected Poems,* "I have enjoyed being alive and writing a great deal, being ashamed and prideful, making mistakes and stumbling on answers before I knew the questions existed."

The Country North of Belleville

Bush land scrub land—
      Cashel Township and Wollaston
Elvezir McClure and Dungannon
green lands of Weslemkoon Lake
where a man might have some
      opinion of what beauty
is and none deny him
      for miles—

Yet this is the country of defeat
where Sisyphus[1] rolls a big stone   10
year after year up the ancient hills
picnicking glaciers have left strewn
with centuries' rubble
      days in the sun
when realization seeps slow in the mind
without grandeur or self deception in
      noble struggle
of being a fool—

A country of quiescence and still distance
a lean land   20
      not fat
with inches of black soil on
      earth's round belly—
And where the farms are it's
      as if a man stuck
both thumbs in the stony earth and pulled

[1] Sisyphus, King of Corinth, was punished for acts of hubris against the gods by being sentenced in the Underworld to roll an enormous rock up a hill, only to have the rock roll back down as soon as he reached the top. He is sometimes considered an emblem of the modern existentialist predicament because he endures futility, persisting in his task against all odds.

           it apart to make room
enough between the trees
for a wife
         and maybe some cows and   30
         room for some
of the more easily kept illusions—
And where the farms have gone back
to forest
         are only soft outlines and
         shadowy differences—
Old fences drift vaguely among the trees
         a pile of moss-covered stones
gathered for some ghost purpose
has lost meaning under the meaningless sky   40
         —they are like cities under water and
the undulating green waves of time are
         laid on them—

This is the country of our defeat and
         yet
during the fall plowing a man
might stop and stand in a brown valley of the furrows
         and shade his eyes to watch for the same
         red patch mixed with gold
         that appears on the same   50
         spot in the hills
         year after year
         and grow old
plowing and plowing a ten acre field until
the convolutions run parallel with his own brain—

And this is a country where the young
           leave quickly
unwilling to know what their fathers know
or think the words their mothers do not say—

Herschel Monteagle and Faraday   60
lakeland rockland and hill country
a little adjacent to where the world is
a little north of where the cities are and
sometime
we may go back there
           to the country of our defeat

Wollaston Elvezir Dungannon
and Weslemkoon lake land
where the high townships of Cashel
                    McClure and Marmora once were—   70
But it's been a long time since
and we must enquire the way
                    of strangers—

                                                    [1965]

Wilderness Gothic

Across Roblin Lake, two shores away,
they are sheathing the church spire
with new metal. Someone hangs in the sky
over there from a piece of rope,
hammering and fitting God's belly-scratcher,
working his way up along the spire
until there's nothing left to nail on—
Perhaps the workman's faith reaches beyond:
touches intangibles, wrestles with Jacob,[2]
replacing rotten timber with pine thews,   10
pounds hard in the blue cave of the sky,
contends heroically with difficult problems
of gravity, sky navigation and mythopeia,
his volunteer time and labor donated to God,
minus sick benefits of course on a non-union job—

Fields around are yellowing into harvest,
nestling and fingerling are sky and water borne,
death is yodeling quiet in green woodlots,
and bodies of three young birds have disappeared
in the sub-surface of the new county highway—   20

That picture is incomplete, part left out
that might alter the whole Dürer[3] landscape:
gothic ancestors peer from medieval sky,
dour faces trapped in photograph albums escaping
to clop down iron roads with matched greys:
work-sodden wives groping inside their flesh
for what keeps moving and changing and flashing
beyond and past the long frozen Victorian day.

[2] In Genesis 32: 24–29, Jacob wrestles with an angel in the night until the angel blesses him.
[3] Albrecht Dürer (1471–1528), German painter and engraver.

A sign of fire and brimstone? A two-headed calf
born in the barn last night? A sharp female agony?   30
An age and a faith moving into transition,
the dinner cold and new-baked bread a failure,
deep woods shiver and water drops hang pendant,
double yolked eggs and the house creaks a little—
Something is about to happen. Leaves are still.
Two shores away, a man hammering in the sky.
Perhaps he will fall.

[1968]

Lament for the Dorsets

(Eskimos extinct in the 14th century A.D.)[4]

Animal bones and some mossy tent rings
scrapers and spearheads   carved ivory swans
all that remains of the Dorset giants
who drove the Vikings back to their long ships
talked to spirits of earth and water
—a picture of terrifying old men
so large they broke the backs of bears
so small they lurk behind bone rafters
in the brain of modern hunters
among good thoughts and warm things   10
and come out at night
to spit on the stars

The big men with clever fingers
who had no dogs and hauled their sleds
over the frozen northern oceans
awkward giants
                    killers of seal
they couldn't compete with little men
who came from the west with dogs
Or else in a warm climatic cycle   20
the seals went back to cold waters
and the puzzled Dorsets scratched their heads
with hairy thumbs around 1350 A.D.
—couldn't figure it out
went around saying to each other

---

[4] The Dorsets were an ancient northern people who disappeared between 1000 and 1100 A.D. during a period of warming climate change. The Thule people emerged next, the ancestors of modern-day Inuit. The Dorset left many aesthetic artifacts, notably carved figures in ivory and bone.

plaintively
                "What's wrong? What happened?
                Where are the seals gone?"
And died

Twentieth century people   30
apartment dwellers
executives of neon death
warmakers with things that explode
—they have never imagined us in their future
how could we imagine them in the past
squatting among the moving glaciers
six hundred years ago
with glowing lamps?
As remote or nearly
as the trilobites[5] and swamps   40
when coal became
or the last great reptile hissed
at a mammal the size of a mouse
that squeaked and fled

Did they ever realize at all
what was happening to them?
Some old hunter with one lame leg
a bear had chewed
sitting in a caribou skin tent
—the last Dorset?   50
Let's say his name was Kudluk
carving 2-inch ivory swans
for a dead grand-daughter
taking them out of his mind
the places in his mind
where pictures are
He selects a sharp stone tool
to gouge a parallel pattern of lines
on both sides of the swan
holding it with his left hand   60
bearing down and transmitting
his body's weight
from brain to arm and right hand
and one of his thoughts
turns to ivory

[5] A fossil marine arthropod.

The carving is laid aside
in beginning darkness
at the end of hunger
after a while wind
blows down the tent and snow   70
begins to cover him
After 600 years
the ivory thought
is still warm

[1968]

The Dead Poet

I was altered in the placenta
by the dead brother before me
who built a place in the womb
knowing I was coming:
he wrote words on the walls of flesh
painting a woman inside a woman
whispering a faint lullaby
that sings in my blind heart still

The others were lumberjacks
backwoods wrestlers and farmers   10
their women were meek and mild
nothing of them survives
but an image inside an image
of a cookstove and the kettle boiling
—how else explain myself to myself
where does the song come from?

Now on my wanderings:
at the Alhambra's lyric dazzle[6]
where the Moors built stone poems
a wan white face peering out   20
—and the shadow in Plato's cave[7]
remembers the small dead one
—at Samarcand[8] in pale blue light

[6] An elaborately ornamented palace and fortress, built in the fourteenth century by the Muslim monarchs (the "Moors"), in what is today Granada, Spain.

[7] In *The Republic*, Plato provides the parable of the cave, in which Socrates describes human perception of reality as being comparable to the vision of shadows on the wall of a cave. Humans, the parable suggests, are never able to perceive the essence of things, but only their traces.

[8] One of the oldest cities in Asia, Samarcand (sometimes spelled Samarkand), located in modern-day Uzbekistan, was situated on the ancient trade route between China and Europe. In its day it was considered one of the most vibrant and glorious cities in Asia.

the words came slowly from him
—I recall the music of blood
on the Street of the Silversmiths
Sleep softly spirit of earth
as the days and nights join hands
when everything becomes one thing
wait softly brother   30
but do not expect it to happen
that great whoop announcing resurrection
expect only a small whisper
of birds nesting and green things growing
and a brief saying of them
and know where the words came from

[1981]

Home Thoughts

The lakes I suppose
are not unusual
except in numbers alone
but if you were able to stand on
a great height wherever you are
able to see all that water at once
it would still be difficult to find words
describing anything but quantity:
anyway it's hard to work up much enthusiasm
for large bodies of water   10
they tend to just lie there being inert

And our mountains are neither higher
nor more beautiful than the mountains
praised and loved by other nations
Moving from east to west the land
rises in successive giant steps
like prairie billiard tables
where players of sufficient stature
can't be found in the immediate vicinity
These mountains however are comparatively recent   20
in the geological scale altho what distinction
that confers seems quite dubious
But if mountains may be considered
among a nation's most valued possessions
one could say that we are not poverty-stricken

The rivers too are only rivers
taking as much pleasure in their
progress to the salt sea as foreign rivers
but are mostly in no special hurry
giving the freshwater fish plenty   30
of time to turn back to their homeland

One hears often the lyrical praise
lavished on other nations by their
fortunate citizens—with hands
laid over their hearts for example
attending stirring renditions of the national
anthem with adjectives piled high
paean after paean attaining hallelujah
their valour in war and steadfast practice
of all the arts especially glorious   40
Sometimes it seems that people of nations
outside my own country's boundaries are dancing
and shouting in the streets for joy
at their great good fortune in being citizens
of whatever it is they are citizens of—
And at other times it seems we are the only
country in the world whose people
do not dance in the streets very much
but sometimes stand looking at each other
in morning or evening as if to see there   50
something about their neighbours
overlooked by anthropologists
born of the land itself perhaps
what is quietly human and will remain so
when the dancing has ended

[1986]

Grosse Isle

Look, stranger, at this island now
The leaping light for your delight discovers—

—W.H. Auden[9]

Look stranger
a diseased whale in the St. Lawrence
this other island than Auden's

---

[9] This excerpt is from English poet W.H. Auden's (1907–1973) poem "On This Island" (1936), in which he describes the view of England from a boat in the English channel.

dull grey when the weather is dull grey
and an east wind brings rain
this Appalachian outcrop[10]
a stone ship foundered in the river estuary   10
now in the care and keeping of Parks Canada
—a silence here like no mainland silence
at Cholera Bay where the dead bodies
awaited high tide and the rough kindness[11]
of waves sweeping them into the dark—

Look stranger
at this other island
weedgrown graves in the three cemeteries
be careful your clothes don't get hooked
by wild raspberry canes and avoid the poison ivy   20
—here children went mad with cholera fever
and raging with thirst they ran into the river
their parents following a little way
before they died themselves
—and don't stumble over the rusted tricycle
somehow overlooked at the last big cleanup
or perhaps left where it is for the tourists?

Look stranger
where the sea wind sweeps westward
down the estuary   30
this way the other strangers came
potato-famine Irish and Scotch crofters
refugees from the Highland clearances
and sailing ships waited here
to remove their corpses
and four million immigrants passed through
—now there's talk of a Health Spa and Casino
we could situate our billboard
right under the granite cross by the river:
                    UNLIMITED INVESTMENT OPPORTUNITIES   40

AL PURDY

282

[10] The Appalachians are a mountain system that runs along the eastern side of North America, reaching into Canada's Atlantic provinces and the St. Lawrence Valley.

[11] Grosse Isle, an island near the mouth of the St. Lawrence River, was a cholera quarantine station in the early nineteenth century where thousands of immigrants, most of them Irish, died and were buried. See Susanna Moodie's "A Visit to Grosse Isle," an obvious intertext for this poem, in Volume I, Section II.

Look stranger
see your own face reflected in the river
stumble up from the stinking hold
blinded by sunlight and into the leaky dinghy
only half-hearing the sailors taunting you
                          "Shanty Irish! Shanty Irish!"
gulp the freshening wind and pinch yourself
trying to understand if the world is a real place
stumble again and fall when you reach the shore
and bless this poisoned earth   50
but stranger no longer
for this is home

[1994]

MAVIS GALLANT ■ (1922–)

With Alice Munro, Mavis Gallant is one of the pre-eminent short story writers of the twentieth century. Having made her home in Paris for more than 50 years, Gallant often writes stories that are international in scope, and that frequently centre on the world of expatriates in Europe. Her writings focus on themes of displacement, alienation, and exile, and frequently include meditations on the notion of "home." Exile, in Gallant's stories, can refer to a literal sense of displacement, or it can refer to a psychological state as a result of having cut oneself off from other people, as her 1981 story "Varieties of Exile" demonstrates.

Born and raised in Montreal, Gallant also makes bilingualism an important factor in her writing. Her stories of Montreal, such as "The Doctor" included here, are particularly interesting for their perspective on a person with a foot in both anglophone and francophone societies. As Gallant puts it in her Introduction to her story collection *Home Truths,* "What I do not understand is the hatred and fear of another sound, or even the lack of

curiosity: how can one not want to know what other people think and feel, stated on their own terms?"

Gallant's stories are highly polished and condensed pieces. They are usually marked by a detachment from her characters, who are often socially awkward or inhibited in some way. She is expert at conveying the nuances of dialogue that reveal unconscious meaning. Her precision is particularly evident in "The Doctor," which conveys in wonderful detail scenes of 1930s Montreal from the hazy but prescient perspective of a child. There is something unsettling about the protagonist's powers of perception: "Unconsciously, everyone under the age of ten knows everything."

Mavis de Trafford Young was born in Montreal in 1922 into an English family, but was sent to a French boarding school where she became fluently bilingual. As a child she developed serious complications following a bout of scarlet fever, and was treated by a French-Canadian doctor, who became a close friend of the family; it is this event that forms the basis of her fictional story "The Doctor."

After graduating from high school, she worked as a journalist for the Montreal *Standard*. After a brief marriage to John Gallant, she left Canada for Europe in 1950, eventually settling on Paris's Left Bank. In 1951, she published her first short story in *The New Yorker* and, like Munro, has been a regular contributor to the magazine ever since. Gallant has published numerous short story collections, including *The Other Paris* (1956), *The Pegnitz Junction* (1973), *From the Fifteenth District* (1979), *Overhead in a Balloon: Stories of Paris* (1985), and *In Transit* (1988). Her collection of stories set in Canada, *Home Truths: Selected Canadian Stories* (1981), won the Governor General's Award. The sequence from this collection entitled the "Linnet Muir" stories, of which "The Doctor" is one, has been especially popular with Canadian readers. Each of the stories is linked by the character of Linnet, who is returning to her childhood home of Montreal after years abroad and feels a sense of disjunction as she revisits the haunts of her past.

In her Introduction to *Home Truths*, Gallant responds directly to the expectations, so prevalent during the 1960s and '70s (but also a central concern during the post-Confederation and modernist periods), that Canadian artists should "paint Canadian." As an expatriate writer, she has been pegged as being somehow insufficiently Canadian. "I often have the feeling with Canadian readers that I am on trial," she writes. She also responds directly to the demands of cultural nationalism: "No division is allowed between the writer's citizenship, with its stationary and emotional ties, and his wider allegiance as an artist." She resolves the puzzle of Canadian identity thus: "[A] Canadian is someone who has a logical reason to think he is one." In this sense, Gallant's perspective is very much a cosmopolitan one, yet as she herself admits, one that is grounded in her Quebec childhood and sense of Canadian citizenship. Gallant has garnered numerous awards and honorary degrees over the course of her career. She continues to live and write in Paris.

The Doctor

Who can remember now a picture called "The Doctor"? From 1891, when the original was painted, to the middle of the Depression, when it finally went out of style, reproductions of this work flowed into every crevice and corner of North America and the British Empire, swamping continents.[1] Not even "The Angelus" supplied as rich a mixture of art and lesson. The two people in "The Angelus" are there to tell us clearly that the meek inherit nothing but seem not to mind; in "The Doctor" a cast of four enacts a more complex statement of Christian submission or Christian pessimism, depending on the beholder: God's Will is manifested in a dying child, Helpless Materialism in a baffled physician, and Afflicted Humanity in the stricken parents. The parable is set in a spotless cottage; the child's bed, composed of three chairs, is out of a doll's house. In

---

[1] A reference to *The Doctor* (1891) by Sir Luke Fildes (1843–1927), an English social-realist painter whose sentimentalized portraits of poverty and destitution were popular during the Victorian era. The painting is held in the Tate Gallery, London, as the narrator mentions later. See Figure VI-4 for a reproduction of this painting. *The Angelus* (1859), mentioned in the next sentence, is a painting by Jean-François Millet (1814–1875) in which two peasants are saying a prayer over their crops.

much of the world—the world as it was, so much smaller than now—two full generations were raised with the monochrome promise that existence is insoluble, tragedy static, poverty endearing, and heavenly justice a total mystery.

It must have come as a shock to overseas visitors when they discovered "The Doctor" incarnated as an oil painting in the Tate Gallery in London, in the company of other Victorian miseries entitled "Hopeless Dawn" and "The Last Day in the Old Home." "The Doctor" had not been divinely inspired and distributed to chasten us after all, but was the work of someone called Sir Luke Fildes—nineteenth-century rationalist and atheist, for all anyone knew. Perhaps it was simply a scene from a three-decker novel, even a joke. In museum surroundings—classified, ticketed— "The Doctor" conveyed a new instruction: Death is sentimental, art is pretense.

Some people had always hated "The Doctor." My father, for one. He said, "You surely don't want *that* thing in your room."

The argument (it became one) took place in Montreal, in a house that died long ago without leaving even a ghost. He was in his twenties, to match the century. I had been around about the length of your average major war. I had my way but do not remember how; neither tears nor temper ever worked. What probably won out was his wish to be agreeable to Dr. Chauchard, the pediatrician who had given me the engraving. My father seemed to like Chauchard, as he did most people—just well enough—while my mother, who carried an uncritical allegiance from person to person, belief to belief, had recently declared Chauchard to be mentally, morally, and spiritually without fault.

Dr. Chauchard must have been in his thirties then, but he seemed to me timeless, like God the Father. When he took the engraving down from the wall of his office, I understood him to be offering me a portrait of himself. My mother at first refused it, thinking I had asked; he assured her I had not, that he had merely been struck by my expression when I looked at the ailing child. "*C'est une sensible,*" he said—an appraisal my mother dismissed by saying I was as tough as a boot, which I truly believe to have been her opinion.

What I was sensitive to is nearly too plain to be signalled: the dying child, a girl, is the heart of the composition. The parents are in the shadow, where they belong. Their function is to be sorry. The doctor has only one patient; light from a tipped lampshade falls on her and her alone.

The street where Dr. Chauchard lived began to decline around the same time as the popularity of "The Doctor" and is now a slum. No citizens' committee can restore the natural elegance of those gray stone houses, the swept steps, the glittering windows, because, short of a miracle, it cannot resurrect the kind of upper-bourgeois French Canadians who used to live there. They have not migrated or moved westward in the city—they have ceased to exist. The handful of dust they sprang from, with its powerful components of religion and history, is part of another clay. They were families who did not resent what were inaccurately called "the English" in Montreal; they had never acknowledged them. The men read a newspaper sometimes, the women never. The women had a dark version of faith for private drama, a family tree to memorize for intellectual exercise, intense family affection for the needs of the heart. Their houses, like Dr. Chauchard's, smelled of cleanness as if cleanness were a commodity, a brand of floor wax. Convents used to have that smell; the girls raised in them brought to married life an ideal of housekeeping that was a memory of the polished convent corridor, with strict squares of sunlight falling where and as they should. Two sons and five daughters was the average for children; Simone, Pauline, Jeanne, Yvonne, and Louise the feminine names of the decade. The girls when young wore religious medals like golden flower petals on thin chains, had positive torrents of curls down to their shoulder blades, and came to children's parties dressed in rose velvet and white stockings, too shy to speak. Chauchard, a bachelor, came out of this world, which I can describe best only through its girls and women.

His front door, painted the gloomy shade my father called Montreal green, is seen from below, at an angle—a bell too high for me during the first visits, a letter box through which I called, "Open the door; *c'est moi*," believing still that *moi* would take me anywhere. But no one could hear in any language, because two vestibules, one behind the other, stood in the way. In the first one overshoes dripped on a mat, then came a warmer place for coats. Each vestibule had its door, varnished to imitate the rings of a tree trunk, enhanced by a nature scene made of frosted glass; you unbuckled galoshes under herons and palm trees and shed layers of damp wool under swans floating in a landscape closer to home.

Just over the letter box of the green door a large, beautifully polished brass plate carried, in sloped writing:

> Docteur Raoul Chauchard
> Spécialiste en Médecine Infantile
> Ancien Externe et Interne
> des Hôpitaux de Paris
> Sur Rendez-vous

On the bottom half of the plate this information was repeated in English, though the only English I recall in the waiting room was my mother's addressed to me.

He was not Parisian but native to the city, perhaps to the street, even to the house, if I think of how the glass-shaded lamps and branched chandeliers must have followed an evolution from oil to kerosene to gas to electricity without changing shape or place. Rooms and passages were papered deep blue fading to green (the brighter oblong left by the removal of "The Doctor" was about the color of a teal), so that the time of day indoors was winter dusk, with pools of light like uncurtained windows. An assemblage of gilt-framed pictures began between the heron and swan doors with brisk scenes of Biblical injustice—the casting-out of Hagar,[2] the swindling of Esau[3]—and moved along the hall with European history:

[2] Hagar was the slave woman who was given to Abraham by his wife Sarah to bear him a child. When Sarah gave birth to Isaac, Hagar and her son Ishmael were expelled into the desert. The story is told in Genesis 16 and 21, and was a favourite subject of many nineteenth-century painters and engravers.

[3] In the biblical story of the twin brothers Jacob and Esau (Genesis 25 and 27), Jacob is the second-born son who uses a number of ruses to cheat Esau out of his birthright as the firstborn. One of these includes disguising himself as his brother in order to receive their father Isaac's blessing.

Vercingetorix surrendering to the Romans,[4] the earthquake at Lisbon,[5] Queen Victoria looking exactly like a potato pancake receiving some dark and humble envoy; then, with a light over him to mark his importance, Napoleon III reviewing a regiment from a white horse.[6] (The popularity of "Napoléon" as a Christian name did not connect with the first Bonaparte, as English Canadians supposed—when any thought was given to any matter concerning French Canadians at all—but with his nephew, the lesser Bonaparte, who had never divorced or insulted the Pope, and who had established clerical influence in the saddle as firmly as it now sat upon Quebec.) The sitting-room-converted-to-waiting-room had on display landmarks of Paris, identified in two languages:

> Le Petit Palais—The Petit Palais
> Place Vendôme—Place Vendôme
> Rue de la Paix—Rue de la Paix

as if the engraver had known they would find their way to a wall in Montreal.

Although he had trained in Paris, where, as our English doctor told my mother, leeches were still sold in pharmacies and babies died like flies, Chauchard was thought modern and forward-looking. He used the most advanced methods imported from the United States, or, as one would have said then, "from Boston," which meant both stylish and impeccably right. Ultraviolet irradiation was one, recommended for building up delicate children. I recall the black mask tied on, and the danger of blindness should one pull it off before being told. I owe him irradiation to the marrow and other sources of confusion: it was he who gave my mother the name of a convent where Jansenist discipline still had a foot on the neck of the twentieth century and where, as an added enchantment, I was certain not to hear a word of English. He never dreamed, I am sure, that I would be packed off there as a boarder from the age of four. Out of goodness and affection he gave me books to read—children's stories from nineteenth-century France which I hated and still detest. In these oppressive stories children were punished and punished hard for behavior that seemed in another century, above all on another continent, natural and right. I could never see the right-and-wrong over which they kept stumbling and only much later recognized it in European social fiddle-faddle—the trivial yardsticks that measure a man's character by the way he eats a boiled egg. The prose was stiff, a bit shrill, probably pitched too high for a North American ear. Even the bindings,

---

[4] Vercingetorix was the leader of the Gauls who led a revolt against the Romans during the age of Julius Caesar and was captured and executed in 46 B.C. He was held up as a symbol of Gallic (i.e., French) heroism and courage.

[5] One of the most destructive earthquakes in history, killing over 90,000 people, the great Lisbon earthquake took place on 1 November 1755 and almost completely destroyed the city. The event had a marked effect on European philosophers and theologians of the time, influencing German philosopher Immanuel Kant's concept of the sublime.

[6] Louis-Napoléon Bonaparte (1808–1873), who became the first President of the French Republic in 1848 (and later Emperor of France), was the nephew of Napoléon I. His support of the papacy in Rome earned him the loyalty of Roman Catholics in France.

a particularly ugly red, were repellent to me, while their gilt titles lent them the ceremonial quality of school prizes. I had plenty of English Victorian books, but the scolding could be got over, because there was no unfairness. Where there was, it was done away with as part of the plot. The authors were on the side of morality but also of the child. For a long time I imagined that most of my English books had been written by other children, but I never made that mistake with French; I saw these authors as large, scowling creatures with faces as flushed with crossness as the books' covers. Still, the books were presents, therefore important, offered without a word or a look Dr. Chauchard would not have bestowed on an adult. They had been his mother's; she lived in rooms at the top of the house, receiving her own friends, not often mingling with his. She must have let him have these treasures for a favored patient who did not understand the courtesy, even the sacrifice, until it was too late to say "Thank you." Another child's name—his mother's—was on the flyleaf; I seldom looked at it, concentrated as I was on my own. It is not simply rhetoric to say that I see him still—Fildes' profile, white cuff, dark sleeve, writing the new dedication with a pen dipped in a blue inkwell, hand and book within the circle cast by the lamp on his desk. At home I would paste inside the front cover the plate my father had designed for me, which had "Linnet: Her Book" as ex libris, and the drawing of a stream flowing between grassy banks—his memory of the unhurried movement of England, no reflection of anything known to me in Quebec—bearing a single autumn leaf. Under the stream came the lines

> Time, Time which none can bind
> While flowing fast leaves love
>> behind.

The only child will usually give and lend its possessions easily, having missed the sturdy training in rivalry and forced sharing afforded by sisters and brothers, yet nothing would have made me part willingly with any of the grim red books. Grouped on a special shelf, seldom opened after the first reading, they were not reminders but a true fragment of his twilit house, his swan and heron doors, Napoleon III so cunningly lighted, "Le Petit Palais—The Petit Palais," and, finally, Dr. Chauchard himself at the desk of his shadowy room writing *"Pour ma chère petite Linnet"* in a book that had once belonged to another girl.

Now, how to account for the changed, stern, disapproving Chauchard who in that same office gave me not a book but a lecture beginning "Think of your unfortunate parents" and ending "You owe them everything; it is your duty to love them." He had just telephoned for my father to come and fetch me. "How miserable they would be if anything ever happened to you," he said. He spoke of my *petit Papa* and my *petite Maman* with that fake diminution of authority characteristic of the Latin tongues which never works in English. I sat on a chair still wearing outdoor clothes—navy reefer over my convent uniform, HMS *Nelson* sailor hat held on by a black elastic—neither his patient nor his guest at this dreadful crisis, wondering,

What does he mean? For a long time now my surprise visits to friends had been called, incorrectly, "running away." Running away was one of the reasons my parents gave when anyone asked why I had been walled up in such a severe school at an early age. Dr. Chauchard, honored by one of my visits, at once asked his office nurse, "Do her parents know she's here?" Women are supposed to make dangerous patients for bachelor doctors; besotted little girls must seem even worse. But I was not besotted; I believed we were equals. It was he who had set up the equality, and for that reason I still think he should have invited me to remove my coat.

The only thing worth remarking about his dull little sermon is that it was in French. French was his language for medicine; I never heard him give an opinion in English. It was evidently the language to which he retreated if one became a nuisance, his back to a wall of white marble syntax. And when it came to filial devotion he was one with the red-covered books. Calling on my parents, not as my doctor but as their friend, he spoke another language. It was not merely English instead of French but the private dialect of a younger person who was playful, charming, who smoked cigarettes in a black-and-silver holder, looking round to see the effect of his puns and jokes. You could notice then, only then, that his black-currant eyes were never still.

The house he came to remained for a long time enormous in memory, though the few like it still standing—"still living," I nearly say—are narrow, with thin, steep staircases and close, high-ceilinged rooms. They were the work of Edinburgh architects and dated from when Montreal was a Scottish city; it had never been really English. A Saturday-evening gathering of several adults, one child, and a couple of dogs created a sort of tangle in the middle of the room— an entwining that was surely not of people's feet: in those days everyone sat straight. The women had to, because their girdles had hooks and stays.

Men sat up out of habit, probably the habit of prosperity; the Depression created the physical slump, a change in posture to match the times. Perhaps desires and secrets and second thoughts threading from person to person, from bachelor to married woman, from mother of none to somebody's father, formed a cat's cradle—matted, invisible, and quite dangerous. Why else would Ruby, the latest homesick underpaid Newfoundland import, have kept tripping up as she lurched across the room with cups and glasses on a tray?

Transformed into jolly Uncle Raoul (his request), Dr. Chauchard would arrive with a good friend of his, divorced Mrs. Erskine, and a younger friend of both, named Paul-Armand. Paul-Armand was temporary, one of a sequence of young men who attended Mrs. Erskine as her bard, her personal laureate. His role did not outlive a certain stage of artless admiration; at the first sign of falling away, the first mouse squeak of disenchantment from him, a replacement was found. All of these young men were good-looking, well brought up, longing to be unconventional, and entirely innocent. Flanked by her pair of males, Mrs. Erskine would sway into the room, as graceful as a woman can be when she is boned from waist to thigh. She would keep on her long moleskin coat, even though like all Canadian rooms this one was vastly overheated, explaining that she was chilly. This may have been an attempt to reduce the impression she gave of general largeness by suggesting an inner fragility. Presently the coat would come off, revealing a handwoven tea-cozy sort of garment—this at a time when every other woman was showing her knees. My mother sat with her legs crossed and one sandal dangling. Her hair had recently been shingled; she seemed to be groping for its lost comfortable warmth. Other persons, my father apart, are a dim choir muttering, "Isn't it past your bedtime?" My father sat back in a deep, chintz-covered chair and said hardly anything except for an occasional "Down" to his dogs.

In another season, in the country, my parents had other friends, summer friends, who drank Old-Fashioneds and danced to gramophone records out on the lawn. Winter friends were mostly coffee drinkers, who did what people do between wars and revolutions—sat in a circle and talked about revolutions and wars. The language was usually English, though not everyone was native to English. Mrs. Erskine commanded what she called "*good* French" and rather liked displaying it, but after a few sentences, which made those who could not understand French very fidgety and which annoyed the French Canadians present exactly in the way an affected accent will grate on Irish nerves, she would pick her way back to English. In mixed society, such little of it as existed, English seemed to be the social rule. It did not enter the mind of any English speaker that the French were at a constant disadvantage, like a team obliged to play all their matches away from home. Dr. Chauchard never addressed me in French here, not even when he would ask me to recite a French poem learned at my convent school. It began, "If I were a fly, Maman, I would steal a kiss from your lips." The nun in charge of memory work was fiddly about liaison, which produced an accidentally appropriate "*Si j'étaiszzzzzzzune mouche, Maman.*" Dr. Chauchard never seemed to tire of this and may have thought it a reasonable declaration to make to one's mother.

It was a tactless rhyme, if you think of all the buzzing and stealing that went on in at least part of the winter circle, but I could not have known that. At least not consciously. Unconsciously, everyone under the age of ten knows everything. Under-ten can come into a room and sense at once everything felt, kept silent, held back in the way of love, hate, and desire, though he may not have the right words for such sentiments. It is part of the clairvoyant immunity to hypocrisy we are born with and that vanishes just before puberty. I knew, though no one had told me, that my mother was a bit foolish about Dr. Chauchard; that Mrs. Erskine would have turned cartwheels to get my father's attention but that even cartwheels would have failed; that Dr. Chauchard and Mrs. Erskine were somehow together but never went out alone. Paul-Armand was harder to place; too young to be a parent, he was a pest, a tease, to someone smaller. His goading was never noticed, though my reaction to it, creeping behind his chair until I was in a position to punch him, brought an immediate response from the police: "Linnet, if you don't sit down I'm afraid you will have to go to your room." "If" and "I'm afraid" meant there was plenty of margin. Later: "Wouldn't you be happier if you just went to bed? No? Then get a book and sit down and read it."

Presently, "Down, I said, sit down: did you hear what I've just said to you? I said, sit down, *down*." There came a point like convergent lines finally meeting where orders to dogs and instructions to children were given in the same voice. The only difference was that a dog got "Down, damn it," and, of course, no one ever swore at me.

This overlapping in one room of French and English, of Catholic and Protestant—my parents' way of being, and so to me life itself—was as unlikely, as unnatural to the Montreal climate as a school of tropical fish. Only later would I discover that most other people simply floated in mossy little ponds labelled "French and Catholic" or "English and Protestant," never wondering what it might be like to step ashore; or wondering, perhaps, but weighing up the danger. To be out of a pond is to be in unmapped territory. The earth might be flat; you could fall over the edge quite easily. My parents and their friends were, in their way, explorers. They had in common a fear of being bored, which is a fear one can afford to nourish in times of prosperity and peace. It makes for the most ruthless kind of exclusiveness, based as it is on the belief that anyone can be the richest of this or cleverest of that and still be the dullest dog that ever barked. I wince even now remembering those wretched once-only guests who were put on trial for a Saturday night and unanimously condemned. This heartlessness apart, the winter circle shared an outlook, a kind of humor, a certain vocabulary of the mind. No one made any of the standard Montreal statements, such as "What a lot of books you've got! Don't tell me you've read them," or "I hear you're some kind of artist. What do you really *do?*" Explorers like Dr. Chauchard and Mrs. Erskine and my mother and the rest recognized each other on sight; the recognition cut through disguisements of class, profession, religion, language, and even what polltakers call "other interests."

Once you have jumped out of a social enclosure, your eye is bound to be on a real, a geographical elsewhere; theirs seemed to consist of a few cities of Europe with agreeable-sounding names like Vienna and Venice. The United States consisted only of Boston and Florida then. Adults went to Florida for therapeutic reasons—for chronic bronchitis, to recover from operations, for the sake of mysterious maladies that had no names and were called in obituaries "a long illness bravely borne." Boston seemed to be an elegant little republic with its own parliament and flag. To English Montreal, cocooned in that other language nobody bothered to learn, the rest of the continent, Canada included, barely existed; travellers would disembark after long, sooty train trips expressing relief to be in the only city where there were decent restaurants and well-dressed women and where proper English could be heard. Elsewhere, then, became other people, and little groups would form where friends, to the tune of vast mutual admiration, could find a pleasing remoteness in each other. They resembled, in their yearnings, in their clinging together as a substitute for motion, in their craving for "someone to talk to," the kind of marginal social clans you find today in the capitals of Eastern Europe.

I was in the dining room cutting up magazines. My mother brought her coffee cup in, sat down, and said, "Promise me you will never be caught in a situation where you have to compete with a younger woman."

She must have been twenty-six at the very most; Mrs. Erskine was well over thirty. I suppose she was appraising the amount of pickle Mrs. Erskine was in. They had become rivals. With her pale braids, her stately figure, her eyes the color of a stoneware teapot, Mrs. Erskine seemed to me like a white statue with features painted on. I had heard my mother praising her beauty, but for a child she was too large, too still. "Age has its points," my mother went on. "The longer your life goes on, the more chance it has to be interesting. Promise me that when you're thirty you'll have a lot to look back on."

My mother had on her side her comparative youth, her quickness, her somewhat giddy intelligence. She had been married, as she said, "for ever and ever" and was afraid nothing would even happen to her again. Mrs. Erskine's chief advantage over my mother—being unmarried and available—was matched by an enviable biography. "Ah, don't ask me for my life's story now," she would cry, settling back to tell it. When the others broke into that sighing, singing recital of cities they went in for, repeating strings of names that sounded like sleigh bells (Venice, London, Paris, Rome), Mrs. Erskine would narrow her stoneware eyes and annihilate my mother with "But Charlotte, I've *been* to all those places, I've *seen* all those people." What, indeed, hadn't she seen—crown princes dragged out of Rolls-Royces by cursing mobs, duchesses clutching their tiaras while being raped by anarchists, strikers in England kicking innocent little Border terriers.

". . . And as for the Hung*a*rians and that Béla *Kun*, let me tell *you* . . . tore the uniforms right off the Red Cross *nurses* . . . made them dance the Charleston naked on top of *street*cars . . ."

"Linnet, wouldn't you be better off in your room?"

The fear of the horde was in all of them; it haunted even their jokes. "Bolshevik" was now "Bolshie," to make it harmless. Petrograd had been their early youth: the Red years just after the war were still within earshot. They dreaded yet seemed drawn to tales of conspiracy and enormous might. The English among them were the first generation to have been raised on *The Wind in the Willows*.[7] Their own Wild Wood was a dark political mystery; its rude inhabitants were still to be tamed. What was needed was a leader, a Badger. But when a Badger occurred they mistrusted him, too; my mother had impressed on me early that Mussolini was a "bad, wicked man." Fortunate Mrs. Erskine had seen "those people" from legation windows; she had, in another defeat for my mother, been married twice, each time to a diplomat. The word "diplomat" had greater cachet then than it has now. Earlier in the century a diplomat was believed to have attended universities in more than one country, to have two or three languages at his disposal and some slender notion of geography and

---

[7] Kenneth Grahame's popular children's novel, *The Wind in the Willows* (1908), tells the story of four animal characters (Rat, Badger, Mole, and Toad) who have a series of adventures in the English countryside.

history. He could read and write quite easily, had probably been born in wedlock, possessed tact and discretion, and led an exemplary private life. Obviously there were no more of these paragons then than there might be now, but fewer were needed, because there were only half as many capitals. Those who did exist spun round and round the world, used for all they were worth, until they became like those coats that outlast their buttons, linings, and pockets: your diplomat, recalled from Bulgaria, by now a mere warp and woof, would be given a new silk lining, bone buttons, have his collar turned, and, after a quick reading of Norse myths, would be shipped to Scandinavia. Mrs. Erskine, twice wedded to examples of these freshened garments, had been everywhere— everywhere my mother longed to be.

"My *life*," said Mrs. Erskine. "Ah, Charlotte, don't ask me to tell you everything— you'd never believe it!" My mother asked, and believed, and died in her heart along with Mrs. Erskine's first husband, a Mr. Sparrow, shot to death in Berlin by a lunatic Russian refugee. (Out of the decency of his nature Mr. Sparrow had helped the refugee's husband emigrate accompanied by a woman Mr. Sparrow had taken to be the Russian man's wife.) In the hours that preceded his "going," as Mrs. Erskine termed his death, Mr. Sparrow had turned into a totally other person, quite common and gross. She had seen exactly how he would rise from the dead for his next incarnation. She had said, "Now then, Alfred, I think it has been a blissful marriage but perhaps not blissful enough. As I am the best part of your karma, we are going to start all over again in another existence." Mr. Sparrow, in his new coarse, uneducated voice, replied, "Believe you me, Bimbo, if I see you in another world, this time I'm making a detour." His last words—not what every woman hopes to hear, probably, but nothing in my mother's experience could come ankle-high to having a husband assassinated in Berlin by a crazy Russian. Mr. Erskine, the second husband, was not quite so interesting, for he merely "drank and drank and *drank*," and finally, unwittingly, provided grounds for divorce. Since in those days adultery was the only acceptable grounds, the divorce ended his ambitions and transformed Mrs. Erskine into someone déclassée; it was not done for a woman to spoil a man's career, and it was taken for granted that no man ever ruined his own. I am certain my mother did not see Mr. Sparrow as an ass and Mr. Erskine as a soak. They were men out of novels—half diplomat, half secret agent. The natural progress of such men was needed to drag women out of the dullness that seemed to be woman's fate.

There was also the matter of Mrs. Erskine's French: my mother could read and speak it but had nothing of her friend's intolerable fluency. Nor could my mother compete with her special status as the only English and Protestant girl of her generation to have attended French and Catholic schools. She had spent ten years with the Ursulines in Quebec City (languages took longer to learn in those days, when you were obliged to start by memorizing all the verbs) and had emerged with the chic little Ursuline lisp.

"Tell me again," my entranced mother would ask. "How do you say 'squab stuffed with sage dressing'?"

"Charlotte, I've told you and told you. *'Pouthin farthi au thauge.'*"

"Thankth," said my mother. Such was the humor of that period.

For a long time I would turn over like samples of dress material the reasons why I was sent off to a school where by all the rules of the world we lived in I did not belong. A sample that nearly matches is my mother's desire to tease Mrs. Erskine, perhaps to overtake her through me: if she had been unique in her generation, then I would be in mine. Unlikely as it sounds today, I believe that I was. At least I have never met another, just as no French-Canadian woman of my period can recall having sat in a classroom with any other English-speaking Protestant disguised in convent uniform. Mrs. Erskine, rising to the tease, warned that convents had gone downhill since the war and that the appalling French I spoke would be a handicap in Venice, London, Paris, Rome; if the Ursuline French of Quebec City was the best in the world after Tours, Montreal French was just barely a language.

How could my mother, so quick and sharp usually, have been drawn in by this? For a day or two my parents actually weighed the advantages of sending their very young daughter miles away, for no good reason. Why not even to France? "You know perfectly well why not. Because we can't afford it. Not that or anything like it."

Leaning forward in her chair as if words alone could not convince her listener, more like my mother than herself at this moment, Mrs. Erskine with her fingertips to her cheek, the other hand held palm outward, cried, "Ah, Angus, don't ask me for my life's story now!" This to my father, who barely knew other people had lives.

My father made this mysterious answer: "Yes, Frances, I do see what you mean, but I have a family, and once you've got children you're never quite so free."

There was only one child, of course, and not often there, but in my parents' minds and by some miracle of fertility they had produced a whole tribe. At any second this tribe might rampage through the house, scribbling on the wallpaper, tearing up books, scratching gramophone records with a stolen diamond brooch. They dreaded mischief so much that I can only suppose them to have been quite disgraceful children.

"What's Linnet up to? She's awfully quiet."

"Sounds suspicious. Better go and look."

I would be found reading or painting or "building," which meant the elaboration of a foreign city called Marigold that spread and spread until it took up a third of my room and had to be cleared away when my back was turned upon which, as relentless as a colony of beavers, I would start building again. To a visitor Marigold was a slum of empty boxes, serving trays, bottles, silver paper, overturned chairs, but these were streets and houses, churches and convents, restaurants and railway stations. The citizens of Marigold were cut out of magazines: Gloria Swanson was the Mother Superior, Herbert Hoover a convent gardener.[8] Entirely villainous, they did their plotting and planning in an empty cigar box.

---

[8] Gloria Swanson (1899–1983), Hollywood film actress during the 1920s and '30s; Herbert Clark Hoover (1874–1964), president of the United States from 1929 to 1933.

Whatever I was doing, I would be told to do something else immediately: I think they had both been brought up that way. "Go out and play in the snow" was a frequent interruption. Parents in bitter climates have a fixed idea about driving children out to be frozen. There was one sunken hour on January afternoons, just before the street lamps were lighted, that was the gray of true wretchedness, as if one's heart and stomach had turned into the same dull, cottony stuff as the sky; it was attached to a feeling of loss, of helpless sadness, unknown to children in other latitudes.

I was home weekends but by no means every weekend. Friday night was given to spoiling and rejoicing, but on Saturday I would hear "When does she go back?"

"Not till tomorrow night."

Ruby, the homesick offshore import, sometimes sat in my room, just for company. She turned the radiator on so that you saw a wisp of steam from the overflow tap. A wicker basket of mending was on her lap; she wiped her eyes on my father's socks. I was not allowed to say to anyone "Go away," or anything like it. I heard her sniffles, her low, muttered grievances. Then she emerged from her impenetrable cloud of Newfoundland gloom to take an interest in the life of Marigold. She did not get down on the floor or in the way, but from her chair suggested some pretty good plots. Ruby was the inspirer of "The Insane Stepmother," "The Rich, Selfish Cousins," "The Death from Croup of Baby Sister" ("Is her face blue yet?" "No; in a minute"), and "The Broken Engagement," with its cast of three—rejected maiden, fickle lover, and chaperon. Paper dolls did the acting, the voices were ours. Ruby played the cast-off fiancée from the heart: "Don't chew men ever know what chew want?" Chaperon was a fine bossy part: "That's enough, now. Sit down; I said, *down*."

My parents said, "What does she see in Ruby?" They were cross and jealous. The jealousness was real. They did not drop their voices to say "When does she go back?" but were alert to signs of disaffection, and offended because I did not crave their company every minute. Once, when Mrs. Erskine, a bit of a fool probably, asked, "Who do you love best, your father or your mother?" and I apparently (I have no memory of it) answered, "Oh, I'm not really dying about anybody," it was recalled to me for a long time, as if I had set fire to the curtains or spat on the Union Jack.

"Think of your unfortunate parents," Dr. Chauchard had said in the sort of language that had no meaning to me, though I am sure it was authentic to him.

When he died and I read his obituary, I saw there had been still another voice. I was twenty and had not seen him since the age of nine. "The Doctor" and the red-covered books had been lost even before that, when during a major move from Montreal to a house in the country a number of things that belonged to me and that my parents were tired of seeing disappeared.

There were three separate death notices, as if to affirm that Chauchard had been three men. All three were in a French newspaper: he neither lived nor died in English. The first was a jumble of family names and syntax: "After a serene and happy life it has pleased our Lord to send for the soul of his faithful servant Raoul Étienne

Chauchard, piously deceased in his native city in his fifty-first year after a short illness comforted by the sacraments of the Church." There followed a few particulars—the date and place of the funeral, and the names and addresses of the relatives making the announcement. The exact kinship of each was mentioned: sister, brother-in-law, uncle, nephew, cousin, second cousin.

The second obituary, somewhat longer, had been published by the medical association he belonged to; it described all the steps and stages of his career. There were strings of initials denoting awards and honors, ending with: "Dr. Chauchard had also been granted the Medal of Epidemics (Belgium)." Beneath this came the third notice: "The Arts and Letters Society of Quebec announces the irreparable loss of one of its founder members, the poet R. É. Chauchard." R. É. had published six volumes of verse, a book of critical essays, and a work referred to as "the immortal 'Progress,'" which did not seem to fall into a category or, perhaps, was too well known to readers to need identification.

That third notice was an earthquake, the collapse of the cities we build over the past to cover seams and cracks we cannot account for. He must have been writing when my parents knew him. Why they neglected to speak of it is something too shameful to dwell on; he probably never mentioned it, knowing they would believe it impossible. French books were from France; English books from England or the United States. It would not have entered their minds that the languages they heard spoken around them could be written, too.

I met by accident years after Dr. Chauchard's death one of Mrs. Erskine's ex-minnesingers, now an elderly bachelor. His name was Louis. He had never heard of Paul-Armand, not even by rumor. He had not known my parents and was certain he had never accompanied Dr. Chauchard and Mrs. Erskine to our house. He said that when he met these two he had been fresh from a seminary, aged about nineteen, determined to live a life of ease and pleasure but not sure how to begin. Mrs. Erskine had by then bought and converted a farmhouse south of Montreal, where she wove carpets, hooked rugs, scraped and waxed old tables, kept bees, and bottled tons of pickled beets, preparing for some dark proletarian future should the mob—the horde, "those people"—take over after all. Louis knew the doctor only as the poet R. É. of the third notice. He had no knowledge of the Medal of Epidemics (Belgium) and could not explain it to me. I had found "Progress" by then, which turned out to be R. É.'s diary. I could not put faces to the X, Y, and Z that covered real names, nor could I discover any trace of my parents, let alone of *ma chère petite Linnet*. There were long thoughts about Mozart—people like that.

Louis told me of walking with Mrs. Erskine along a snowy road close to her farmhouse, she in a fur cape that came down to her boot tops and a fur bonnet that hid her braided hair. She talked about her unusual life and her two husbands and about what she now called "the predicament." She told him how she had never been asked to meet Madame Chauchard *mère* and how she had slowly come to realize that R. É. would never marry. She spoke of people who had drifted through the predicament, my mother among them, not singling her out as someone important, just as a wisp of cloud on the edge of the sky. "Poor Charlotte" was how Mrs. Erskine described the thin little target on which she had once trained her biggest guns. Yet "poor Charlotte"—not even an X in the diary, finally—had once been the heart of the play. The plot must have taken a full turning after she left the stage. Louis became a new young satellite, content to circle the powerful stars, to keep an eye on the predicament, which seemed to him flaming, sulphurous. Nobody ever told him what had taken place in the first and second acts.

Walking, he and Mrs. Erskine came to a railway track quite far from houses, and she turned to Louis and opened the fur cloak and said, smiling, "*Viens voir Mrs. Erskine.*" (Owing to the Ursuline lisp this must have been "Mitheth Erthkine.") Without coyness or any more conversation she lay down—he said "on the track," but he must have meant near it, if you think of the ties. Folded into the cloak, Louis at last became part of a predicament. He decided that further experience could only fall short of it, and so he never married.

In this story about the cloak Mrs. Erskine is transmuted from the pale, affected statue I remember and takes on a polychrome life. She seems cheerful and careless, and I like her for that. Carelessness might explain her unreliable memory about Charlotte. And yet not all that careless: "She even knew the train times," said Louis. "She must have done it before." Still, on a sharp blue day, when some people were still in a dark classroom writing "*abyssus abyssum invocat*" all over their immortal souls, she, who had been through this and escaped with nothing worse than a lisp, had the sun, the snow, the wrap of fur, the bright sky, the risk. There is a raffish kind of nerve to her, the only nerve that matters.

For that one conversation Louis and I wondered what our appearance on stage several scenes apart might make us to each other: if A was the daughter of B, and B rattled the foundations of C, and C, though cautious and lazy where women were concerned, was committed in a way to D, and D was forever trying to tell her life's story to E, the husband of B, and E had enough on his hands with B without taking on D, too, and if D decided to lie down on or near a railway track with F, then what are A and F? Nothing. Minor satellites floating out of orbit and out of order after the stars burned out. Mrs. Erskine reclaimed Dr. Chauchard but he never married anyone. Angus reclaimed Charlotte but he died soon after. Louis, another old bachelor, had that one good anecdote about the fur cloak. I lost even the engraving of "The Doctor," spirited away quite shabbily, and I never saw Dr. Chauchard again or even tried to. What if I had turned up one day, aged eighteen or so, only to have him say to his nurse, "Does anyone know she's here?"

When I read the three obituaries it was the brass plate on the door I saw and "Sur Rendez-vous." That means "no dropping in." After the warning came the shut heron door and the shut swan door and, at another remove, the desk with the circle of lamplight and R.É. himself, writing about X, Y, Z, and Mozart. A bit humdrum perhaps, a bit prosy, not nearly as good as his old winter Saturday self, but I am sure that it was his real voice, the voice that transcends this or that language. His French-speaking friends did not hear it for a long time (his first book of verse was not sold to anyone outside his immediate family), while his English-speaking friends never heard it at all. But I should have heard it then, at the start, standing on tiptoe to reach the doorbell, calling through the letter box every way I could think of, "I, me." I ought to have heard it when I was still under ten and had all my wits about me.

[1981]

MARGARET LAURENCE ■ (1926–1987)

Margaret Laurence is best known for her creation of the fictional prairie world of Manawaka, a small town in Manitoba based upon her childhood home of Neepawa. Four of her novels—*The Stone Angel* (1964), *A Jest of God* (1966), *The Fire-Dwellers* (1969), and *The Diviners* (1974)—are at least partially set in Manawaka, as is her collection of linked short stories, *A Bird in the House* (1970).

The works are notable for their portrayal of small-town hypocrisies, social intolerance, and, as Laurence put it, "hysterical propriety." They are comparable to the depiction of Canadian small towns in the fiction of Sinclair Ross, W.O. Mitchell, Robertson Davies, Alice Munro, and Miriam Toews. As Laurence states in her 1972 essay "Where the World Began," "[T]he seeds of both man's freedom and his captivity are found everywhere, even in the microcosm of a prairie town." Laurence describes Neepawa as "[a] place of shadow-spookiness, inhabited by the unknowable dead. A place of jubilation and of mourning, horrible and beautiful."

The paradox in all of Laurence's Manawaka fiction is that while the town forms part of the protagonist's identity, it is also the place that the character must abandon in order to come to terms with the past and the present. As Laurence told Robert Kroetsch in an interview in 1970, her Manawaka fiction represented an attempt to explore her own "roots and [her] ancestors." However, it is not as disguised autobiography that these works are important, but as texts that explore the relation between writing and memory, particularly the ways people "narrate" themselves in order to make sense of who they are. Laurence's novels and stories are unified by themes of regret, dignity, and forgiveness, as characters look back on the past and confront their mistakes. Many of Laurence's protagonists are writers (Vanessa in *A Bird in the House,* Morag in *The Diviners*) or storytellers (Hagar in *The Stone Angel*), and all try to make sense of the past through acts of memory and interpretation.

Laurence was born Jean Margaret Wemyss in Neepawa. Her mother died when she was four years old, and her father five years later; she was raised by her mother's sister, Aunt Margaret, and her maternal grandfather, John Simpson. Aspects of this early childhood are evident in much of Laurence's writing, including Morag Gunn's orphaning at a young age in *The Diviners,* and the formidable grandfather figure in Laurence's *A Bird in the House,* Timothy Connor.

At the age of 18, Laurence moved to Winnipeg where she attended United

College, from which she graduated in 1947 with Honours in English. For a short period she worked as a reporter for the *Winnipeg Citizen,* and in 1947 she married Jack Laurence, a civil engineer. Together, they moved to East Africa in 1950, where Laurence became interested in African poetry and folktales. She wrote a translation of Somali poetry entitled *A Tree for Poverty* (1954), as well as a study of Nigerian literature, *Long Drums and Cannons* (1968), and a memoir about Somaliland, *The Prophet's Camel Bell* (1963), which offers a subtle meditation on the precarious meeting of two cultures and reveals Laurence's awareness of her Western presuppositions.

During this time Laurence also began a series of short stories based on her African experiences, eventually published as *The Tomorrow-Tamer* (1963), and began her first novel, published in 1960 as *This Side Jordan.* As Laurence notes in her autobiographical essay "A Place to Stand On," her African experiences had an important impact on her subsequent outlook on Canada. Following the struggles of African writers to emerge from a long history of colonial rule and reconnect with their ancestral and cultural pasts (she notes the influence of Chinua Achebe in particular), Laurence applied a similar perspective to Canada, and devoted herself to recording her own locally grounded, western Canadian history.

In 1957, the Laurences returned to Canada and settled in Vancouver. In 1962, after separating from her husband, Laurence moved with her two children to England, where they lived for more than 10 years. It was during these years that she completed the first of the Manawaka novels, *The Stone Angel* (1964), the book that was to ground her reputation as a major Canadian author. By the time of publication of the fourth and final

Manawaka novel, *The Diviners* (1974), Laurence had returned to Canada and settled in Lakefield, Ontario. The book explores the Scottish and Métis history of the town of Manawaka through the emblematic, yet socially ostracized, characters of Morag Gunn and Jules (Skinner) Tonnerre. Acclaimed for its expression of the "decolonizing" of Canadians' attitudes toward their homeland, the novel won the Governor General's Award in 1975.

The most notorious event surrounding *The Diviners,* however, was the banning controversy that arose in 1976. Prior to this, Laurence had received some complaints about the swearing and sex depicted in the book, though she suspected that the objections to the book's relatively few sex scenes were based on the complainants' racism, since the novel depicted sexual relations between the protagonist Morag and her Métis lover, Jules. Following a series of parental complaints, the book was banned from the Lakefield High School English reading list and provoked an uproar in the local press. Exhausted by the controversy, Laurence retreated to her Lakefield home and became reluctant to undertake another novel.

A Bird in the House is a story sequence linked through the character of Vanessa MacLeod who, as an adult, recalls her childhood during the 1930s. The stories can be read together as a unit or individually, and bear some resemblance to Mavis Gallant's Linnet Muir stories in *Home Truths* (1981) and Alice Munro's *Lives of Girls and Women* (1971), in which the central character absorbs scenes and experiences as a child that will inform her vision later on. The stories also deal with the themes of inheritance and acceptance, and how the weight of the past lingers into the present. In the title story of the collection, "A Bird in the

House," Vanessa gets a glimpse behind the tightly restrained fronts that her relatives present to the world; this knowledge, although belated, opens up the possibility of forgiveness and understanding, even if it comes too late to make a difference in the individual characters' lives. As Laurence said of the book in a 1972 conversation with Clara Thomas and Irving Layton, "[O]nly after I had finished writing these short stories did I begin to realise that, although I had detested [my grandfather] at the time. . . . I had come to some kind of terms with him, whereby I could realise that even though he had been a very hard man, he had had a very hard life and he had characteristics of strength and of pride that were admirable. . . ."

Laurence also published a collection of essays in 1976, *Heart of a Stranger,* from which her 1970 essay "A Place to Stand On" is taken, as well as a number of children's books. Her evocative memoir, *Dance on the Earth,* about the generations of women in her family, was published posthumously in 1989, two years after Laurence died of cancer.

Throughout her life and writing, Laurence was committed to representing the struggles and ideals of Canadian women. In a letter to writer Marian Engel

in 1984, Laurence notes, "What stuns me, looking at my own family, is how pitifully little I know about the women, even my grandmothers . . . and how much about the men. Lost histories . . . perhaps we must invent them in order to rediscover them." Her letter to Margaret Atwood of 10 January 1971 outlines her sense of having worked through, years before, many of the issues raised by the Women's Liberation movement of the 1970s. Most prominent in her work is a concern with legacy. Like other writers of her generation, including Al Purdy, Rudy Wiebe, and Robert Kroetsch, Laurence was interested in the ways people are influenced, often without being aware of it, by the intangible memories of place and ancestral inheritance (both genetic and cultural). Her works thus offer a kind of historical uncovering, not just for the individual characters within her fiction, but for Canadian readers seeking to comprehend an often hidden or forgotten past. In "Where the World Began," she asks: "Why on earth did generations of Canadians pretend to believe this country dull? . . . We have only just begun to value ourselves, our land, our abilities. We have only just begun to recognize our legends and to give shape to our myths."

A Bird in the House

The parade would be almost over by now, and I had not gone. My mother had said in a resigned voice, "All right, Vanessa, if that's the way you feel," making me suffer twice as many jabs of guilt as I would have done if she had lost her temper. She and Grandmother MacLeod had gone off, my mother pulling the low box-sleigh with Roddie all dolled up in his new red snowsuit, just the sort of little kid anyone would want people to see. I sat on the lowest branch of the birch tree in our yard, not minding the snowy wind, even welcoming its punishment. I went over my reasons for not going, trying to believe they were good and sufficient, but in my heart I felt I was betraying my father. This was the first time I had stayed away from the Remembrance Day parade. I wondered if he would notice that I was not there, standing on the sidewalk at the corner of River and Main while the parade passed, and then following to the Court House grounds where the service was held.

I could see the whole thing in my mind. It was the same every year. The Manawaka Civic Band always led the way. They had never been able to afford full uniforms, but they had peaked navy-blue caps and sky-blue chest ribbons. They were joined on Remembrance Day by the Salvation Army band, whose uniforms seemed too ordinary for a parade, for they were the same ones the bandsmen wore every Saturday night when they played "Nearer My God to Thee" at the foot of River Street. The two bands never managed to practise quite enough together, so they did not keep in time too well. The Salvation Army band invariably played faster, and afterwards my father would say irritably, "They play those marches just like they do hymns, blast them, as though they wouldn't get to heaven if they didn't hustle up." And my mother, who had great respect for the Salvation Army because of the good work they did, would respond chidingly, "Now, now, Ewen—" I vowed I would never say "Now, now" to my husband or children, not that I ever intended having the latter, for I had been put off by my brother Roderick, who was now two years old with wavy hair and everyone said what a beautiful child. I was twelve and no one in their right mind would have said what a beautiful child, for I was big-boned like my Grandfather Connor and had straight lanky black hair like a Blackfoot or Cree.

After the bands would come the veterans. Even thinking of them at this distance, in the white and withdrawn quiet of the birch tree, gave me a sense of painful embarrassment. I might not have minded so much if my father had not been among them. How could he go? How could he not see how they all looked? It must have been a long time since they were soldiers, for they had forgotten how to march in step. They were old—that was the thing. My father was bad enough being almost forty, but he wasn't a patch on Howard Tully from the drugstore, who was completely grey-haired and also fat, or Stewart MacMurchie, who was bald at the back of his head. They looked to me like imposters, plump or spindly caricatures of past warriors. I almost hated them for walking in that limping column down Main. At the Court House, everyone would sing *Lord God of Hosts, be with us yet, lest we forget, lest we forget*. Will Masterson would pick up his old Army bugle and blow the last Post. Then it would be over and everyone could start gabbling once more and go home.

I jumped down from the birch bough and ran to the house, yelling, making as much noise as I could.

I'm a poor lonesome cowboy
An' a long way from home—

I stepped inside the front hall and kicked off my snow boots. I slammed the door behind me, making the dark ruby and emerald glass shake in the small leaded panes. I slid purposely on the hall rug, causing it to bunch and crinkle on the slippery polished oak of the floor. I seized the newel post, round as a head, and spun myself to and fro on the bottom stair.

I ain't got no father
To buy the clothes I wear.
I'm a poor lonesome—

At this moment my shoulders were firmly seized and shaken by a pair of hands, white and delicate and old, but strong as talons.

"Just what do you think you're doing, young lady?" Grandmother MacLeod enquired, in a voice like frost on a windowpane, infinitely cold and clearly etched.

I went limp and in a moment she took her hand away. If you struggled, she would always hold on longer.

"Gee, I never knew you were home yet."

"I would have thought that on a day like this you might have shown a little respect and consideration," Grandmother MacLeod said, "even if you couldn't make the effort to get cleaned up enough to go to the parade."

I realised with surprise that she imagined this to be my reason for not going. I did not try to correct her impression. My real reason would have been even less acceptable.

"I'm sorry," I said quickly.

In some families, *please* is described as the magic word. In our house, however, it was *sorry*.

"This isn't an easy day for any of us," she said.

Her younger son, my Uncle Roderick, had been killed in the Great War. When my father marched, and when the hymn was sung, and when that unbearably lonely tune was sounded by the one bugle and everyone forced themselves to keep absolutely still, it would be that boy of whom she was thinking. I felt the enormity of my own offence.

"Grandmother—I'm sorry."

"So you said."

I could not tell her I had not really said it before at all. I went into the den and found my father there. He was sitting in the leather-cushioned armchair beside the fireplace. He was not doing anything, just sitting and smoking. I stood beside him, wanting to touch the light-brown hairs on his forearm, but thinking he might laugh at me or pull his arm away if I did.

"I'm sorry," I said, meaning it.

"What for, honey?"

"For not going."

"Oh—that. What was the matter?"

I did not want him to know, and yet I had to tell him, make him see.

"They look silly," I blurted. "Marching like that."

For a minute I thought he was going to be angry. It would have been a relief to me if he had been. Instead, he drew his eyes away from mine and fixed them above the mantelpiece where the sword hung, the handsome and evil-looking crescent in its carved bronze sheath that some ancestor had once brought from the Northern Frontier of India.

"Is that the way it looks to you?" he said.

I felt in his voice some hurt, something that was my fault. I wanted to make everything all right between us, to convince him that I understood, even if I did not. I prayed that Grandmother MacLeod would stay put in her room, and that my mother would take a long time in the kitchen, giving Roddie his lunch. I wanted my father to myself, so I could prove to him that I cared more about him than any of the others did. I wanted to speak in some way that would be more poignant and comprehending than anything of which my mother could possibly be capable. But I did not know how.

"You were right there when Uncle Roderick got killed, weren't you?" I began uncertainly.

"Yes."

"How old was he, Dad?"

"Eighteen," my father said.

Unexpectedly, that day came into intense being for me. He had had to watch his own brother die, not in the antiseptic calm of some hospital, but out in the open, the stretches of mud I had seen in his snapshots. He would not have known what to do. He would just have had to stand there and look at it, whatever that might mean. I looked at my father with a kind of horrified awe, and then I began to cry. I had forgotten about impressing him with my perception. Now I needed him to console me for this unwanted glimpse of the pain he had once known.

"Hey, cut it out, honey," he said, embarrassed. "It was bad, but it wasn't all as bad as that part. There were a few other things."

"Like what?" I said, not believing him.

"Oh—I don't know," he replied evasively. "Most of us were pretty young, you know, I and the boys I joined up with. None of us had ever been away from Manawaka before. Those of us who came back mostly came back here, or else went no further away from town than Winnipeg. So when we were overseas—that was the only time most of us were ever a long way from home."

"Did you want to be?" I asked, shocked.

"Oh well—" my father said uncomfortably. "It was kind of interesting to see a few other places for a change, that's all."

Grandmother MacLeod was standing in the doorway.

"Beth's called you twice for lunch, Ewen. Are you deaf, you and Vanessa?"

"Sorry," my father and I said simultaneously.

Then we went upstairs to wash our hands.

That winter my mother returned to her old job as nurse in my father's medical practice. She was able to do this only because of Noreen.

"Grandmother MacLeod says we're getting a maid," I said to my father, accusingly, one morning. "We're not, are we?"

"Believe you me, on what I'm going to be paying her," my father growled, "she couldn't be called anything as classy as a maid. Hired girl would be more like it."

"Now, now, Ewen," my mother put in, "it's not as if we were cheating her or anything. You know she wants to live in town, and I can certainly see why, stuck out there on the farm, and her father hardly ever letting her come in. What kind of life is that for a girl?"

"I don't like the idea of your going back to work, Beth," my father said. "I know you're fine now, but you're not exactly the robust type."

"You can't afford to hire a nurse any longer. It's all very well to say the Depression won't last forever—probably it won't, but what else can we do for now?"

"I'm damned if I know," my father admitted. "Beth—"

"Yes?"

They both seemed to have forgotten about me. It was at breakfast, which we always ate in the kitchen, and I sat rigidly on my chair, pretending to ignore and thus snub their withdrawal from me. I glared at the window, but it was so thickly plumed and scrolled with frost that I could not see out. I glanced back to my parents. My father had not replied, and my mother was looking at him in that anxious and half-frowning way she had recently developed.

"What is it, Ewen?" Her voice had the same nervous sharpness it bore sometimes when she would say to me, "For mercy's sake, Vanessa, what is it *now?*" as though whatever was the matter, it was bound to be the last straw.

My father spun his sterling silver serviette ring, engraved with his initials, slowly around on the table.

"I never thought things would turn out like this, did you?"

"Please—" my mother said in a low strained voice, "please, Ewen, let's not start all this again. I can't take it."

"All right," my father said, "Only—"

"The MacLeods used to have money and now they don't," my mother cried. "Well, they're not alone. Do you think all that matters to me, Ewen? What I can't bear is to see you forever reproaching yourself. As if it were your fault."

"I don't think it's the comedown," my father said. "If I were somewhere else, I don't suppose it would matter to me, either, except where you're concerned. But I suppose you'd work too hard wherever you were—it's bred into you. If you haven't got anything to slave away at, you'll sure as hell invent something."

"What do you think I should do, let the house go to wrack and ruin? That would go over well with your mother, wouldn't it?"

"That's just it," my father said. "It's the damned house all the time. I haven't only taken on my father's house, I've taken on everything that goes with it, apparently. Sometimes I really wonder—"

"Well, it's a good thing I've inherited some practicality even if you haven't," my mother said. "I'll say that for the Connors—they aren't given to brooding, thank the Lord. Do you want your egg poached or scrambled?"

"Scrambled," my father said. "All I hope is that this Noreen doesn't get married straightaway, that's all."

"She won't," my mother said. "Who's she going to meet who could afford to marry?"

"I marvel at you, Beth," my father said. "You look as though a puff of wind would blow you away. But underneath, by God, you're all hardwood."

"Don't talk stupidly," my mother said. "All I hope is that she won't object to taking your mother's breakfast up on a tray."

"That's right," my father said angrily. "Rub it in."

"Oh, Ewen, I'm sorry!" my mother cried, her face suddenly stricken. "I don't know why I say these things. I didn't mean to."

"I know," my father said. "Here, cut it out, honey. Just for God's sake please don't cry."

"I'm sorry," my mother repeated, blowing her nose.

"We're both sorry," my father said. "Not that that changes anything."

After my father had gone, I got down from my chair and went to my mother.

"I don't want you to go back to the office. I don't want a hired girl here. I'll hate her."

My mother sighed, making me feel that I was placing an intolerable burden on her, and yet making me resent having to feel this weight. She looked tired, as she often did these days. Her tiredness bored me, made me want to attack her for it.

"Catch me getting along with a dumb old hired girl," I threatened.

"Do what you like," my mother said abruptly. "What can I do about it?"

And then, of course, I felt bereft, not knowing which way to turn.

My father need not have worried about Noreen getting married. She was, it turned out, interested not in boys but in God. My mother was relieved about the boys but alarmed about God.

"It isn't natural," she said, "for a girl of seventeen. Do you think she's all right mentally, Ewen?"

When my parents, along with Grandmother MacLeod, went to the United Church every Sunday, I was made to go to Sunday school in the church basement, where there were small red chairs which humiliatingly resembled kindergarten furniture, and pictures of Jesus wearing a white sheet and surrounded by a whole lot of well-dressed kids whose mothers obviously had not suffered them to come unto Him until every face and ear was properly scrubbed. Our religious observances also included grace at meals, when my father would mumble "For what we are about to receive the Lord make us truly thankful Amen," running the words together as though they were one long word. My mother approved of these rituals, which seemed decent and moderate to her. Noreen's religion, however, was a different matter. Noreen belonged to the Tabernacle of the Risen and Reborn, and she had got up to testify no less than seven times in the past two years, she told us. My mother, who could not imagine anyone's voluntarily making a public spectacle of themselves, was profoundly shocked by this revelation.

"Don't worry," my father soothed her. "She's all right. She's just had kind of a dull life, that's all."

My mother shrugged and went on worrying and trying to help Noreen without hurting her feelings, by tactful remarks about the advisability of modulating one's voice when singing hymns, and the fact that there was plenty of hot water so Noreen really didn't need to hesitate about taking a bath. She even bought a razor and a packet of blades and whispered to Noreen that any girl who wore transparent blouses so much would probably like to shave under her arms. None of these suggestions had the slightest effect on Noreen. She did not cease belting out hymns at the top of her voice, she bathed once a fortnight, and the sorrel-coloured hair continued to bloom like a thicket of Indian paintbrush in her armpits.

Grandmother MacLeod refused to speak to Noreen. This caused Noreen a certain amount of bewilderment until she finally hit on an answer.

"Your poor grandma," she said. "She is deaf as a post. These things are sent to try us here on earth, Vanessa. But if she makes it into Heaven, I'll bet you anything she will hear clear as a bell."

Noreen and I talked about Heaven quite a lot, and also Hell. Noreen had an intimate and detailed knowledge of both places. She not only knew what they looked like—she even knew how big they were. Heaven was seventy-seven thousand miles square and it had four gates, each one made out of a different kind of precious jewel. The Pearl Gate, the Topaz Gate, the Amethyst Gate, the Ruby Gate— Noreen would reel them off, all the gates of Heaven. I told Noreen they sounded like poetry, but she was puzzled by my reaction and said I shouldn't talk that way. If you said poetry, it sounded like it was just made up and not really so, Noreen said.

Hell was larger than Heaven, and when I asked why, thinking of it as something of a comedown for God, Noreen said naturally it had to be bigger because there were a darn sight more people there than in Heaven. Hell was one hundred and ninety million miles deep and was in perpetual darkness, like a cave under the sea. Even the flames (this was the awful thing) *did not give off any light.*

I did not actually believe in Noreen's doctrines, but the images which they conjured up began to inhabit my imagination. Noreen's fund of exotic knowledge was not limited to religion, although in a way it all seemed related. She could do many things which had a spooky tinge to them. Once when she was making a cake, she found we had run out of eggs. She went outside and gathered a bowl of fresh snow and used it instead. The cake rose like a charm, and I stared at Noreen as though she were a sorceress. In fact, I began to think of her as a sorceress, someone not quite of this earth. There was nothing unearthly about her broad shoulders and hips and her forest of dark red hair, but even these features took on a slightly sinister significance to me. I no longer saw her through the eyes or the expressed opinions of my mother and father, as a girl who had quit school at grade eight and whose life on the farm had been endlessly drab. I knew the truth—Noreen's life had not been drab at all, for she dwelt in a world of violent splendours, a world filled with angels whose wings of delicate light bore real feathers, and saints shining like the dawn, and prophets who spoke in ancient tongues, and the ecstatic souls of the saved, as well as denizens of the lower regions—mean-eyed imps and crooked cloven-hoofed monsters and beasts with the bodies of swine and the human heads of murderers, and lovely depraved jezebels torn by dogs through all eternity. The middle layer of Creation, our earth, was equally full of grotesque presences, for Noreen believed strongly in the visitation of ghosts and the communication with spirits. She could prove this with her Ouija board. We would both place our fingers lightly on the indicator, and it would skim across the board and spell out answers to our questions. I did not believe wholeheartedly in the Ouija board, either, but I was cautious about the kind of question I asked, in case the answer would turn out unfavourable and I would be unable to forget it.

One day Noreen told me she could also make a table talk. We used the small table in my bedroom, and sure enough, it lifted very slightly under our fingertips and tapped once for *Yes*, twice for *No*. Noreen asked if her Aunt Ruthie would get better from the kidney operation, and the table replied *No*. I withdrew my hands.

"I don't want to do it any more."

"Gee, what's the matter, Vanessa?" Noreen's plain placid face creased in a frown. "We only just begun."

"I have to do my homework."

My heart lurched as I said this. I was certain Noreen would know I was lying, and that she would know not by any ordinary perception, either. But her attention had been caught by something else, and I was thankful, at least until I saw what it was.

My bedroom window was not opened in the coldest weather. The storm window, which was fitted outside as an extra wall against the winter, had three small circular holes in its frame so that some fresh air could seep into the house. The sparrow must have been floundering in the new snow on the roof, for it had crawled in through one of these holes and was now caught between the two layers of glass. I could not bear the panic of the trapped bird, and before I realised what I was doing, I had thrown open the bedroom window. I was not releasing the sparrow into any better a situation, I soon saw, for instead of remaining quiet and allowing us to catch it in order to free it, it began flying blindly around the room, hitting the lampshade, brushing against the walls, its wings seeming to spin faster and faster.

I was petrified. I thought I would pass out if those palpitating wings touched me. There was something in the bird's senseless movements that revolted me. I also thought it was going to damage itself, break one of those thin wing-bones, perhaps, and then it would be lying on the floor, dying, like the pimpled and horribly featherless baby birds we saw sometimes on the sidewalks in the spring when they had fallen out of their nests. I was not any longer worried about the sparrow. I wanted only to avoid the sight of it lying broken on the floor. Viciously, I thought that if Noreen said, *God sees the little sparrow fall*, I would kick her in the shins. She did not, however, say this.

"A bird in the house means a death in the house," Noreen remarked.

Shaken, I pulled my glance away from the whirling wings and looked at Noreen.

"What?"

"That's what I've heard said, anyhow."

The sparrow had exhausted itself. It lay on the floor, spent and trembling. I could not bring myself to touch it. Noreen bent and picked it up. She cradled it with great gentleness between her cupped hands. Then we took it downstairs, and when I had opened the back door, Noreen set the bird free.

"Poor little scrap," she said, and I felt struck to the heart, knowing she had been concerned all along about the sparrow, while I, perfidiously, in the chaos of the moment, had been concerned only about myself.

"Wanna do some with the Ouija board, Vanessa?" Noreen asked.

I shivered a little, perhaps only because of the blast of cold air which had come into the kitchen when the door was opened.

"No thanks, Noreen. Like I said, I got my homework to do. But thanks all the same."

"That's okay," Noreen said in her guileless voice. "Any time."

But whenever she mentioned the Ouija board or the talking table, after that, I always found some excuse not to consult these oracles.

"Do you want to come to church with me this evening, Vanessa?" my father asked.

"How come you're going to the evening service?" I enquired.

"Well, we didn't go this morning. We went snow-shoeing instead, remember? I think your grandmother was a little bit put out about it. She went alone this morning. I guess it wouldn't hurt you and me, to go now."

We walked through the dark, along the white streets, the snow squeaking dryly under our feet. The streetlights were placed at long intervals along the sidewalks, and around each pole the circle of flimsy light created glistening points of blue and crystal on the crusted snow. I would have liked to take my father's hand, as I used to do, but I was too old for that now. I walked beside him, taking long steps so he would not have to walk more slowly on my account.

The sermon bored me, and I began leafing through the Hymnary for entertainment. I must have drowsed, for the next thing I knew, my father was prodding me and we were on our feet for the closing hymn.

Near the Cross, near the Cross,
Be my glory ever,
Till my ransomed soul shall find
Rest beyond the river.

I knew the tune well, so I sang loudly for the first verse. But the music to that hymn is sombre, and all at once the words themselves seemed too dreadful to be sung. I stopped singing, my throat knotted. I thought I was going to cry, but I did not know why, except that the song recalled to me my Grandmother Connor, who had been dead only a year now. I wondered why her soul needed to be ransomed. If God did not think she was good enough just as she was, then I did not have much use for His opinion. *Rest beyond the river*—was that what had happened to her? She had believed in Heaven, but I did not think that rest beyond the river was quite what she had in mind. To think of her in Noreen's flashy Heaven, though— that was even worse. Someplace where nobody ever got annoyed or had to be smoothed down and placated, someplace where there were never any family scenes—that would have suited my Grandmother Connor. Maybe she wouldn't have minded a certain amount of rest beyond the river, at that.

When we had the silent prayer, I looked at my father. He sat with his head bowed and his eyes closed. He was frowning deeply, and I could see the pulse in his temple. I wondered then what he believed. I did not have any real idea what it might be. When he raised his head, he did not look uplifted or anything like that. He merely looked tired. Then Reverend McKee pronounced the benediction, and we could go home.

"What do you think about all that stuff, Dad?" I asked hesitantly, as we walked.

"What stuff, honey?"

"Oh, Heaven and Hell, and like that."

My father laughed. "Have you been listening to Noreen too much? Well, I don't know. I don't think they're actual places. Maybe they stand for something that happens all the time here, or else doesn't happen. It's kind of hard to explain. I guess I'm not so good at explanations."

Nothing seemed to have been made any clearer to me. I reached out and took his hand, not caring that he might think this a babyish gesture.

"I hate that hymn!"

"Good Lord," my father said in astonishment. "Why, Vanessa?"

But I did not know and so could not tell him.

Many people in Manawaka had flu that winter, so my father and Dr. Cates were kept extremely busy. I had flu myself, and spent a week in bed, vomiting only the first day and after that enjoying poor health, as my mother put it, with Noreen bringing me ginger ale and orange juice, and each evening my father putting a wooden tongue-depressor into my mouth and peering down my throat, then smiling and saying he thought I might live after all.

Then my father got sick himself, and had to stay at home and go to bed. This was such an unusual occurrence that it amused me.

"Doctors shouldn't get sick," I told him.

"You're right," he said. "That was pretty bad management."

"Run along now, dear," my mother said.

That night I woke and heard voices in the upstairs hall. When I went out, I found my mother and Grandmother MacLeod, both in their dressing-gowns. With them was Dr. Cates. I did not go immediately to my mother, as I would have done only a year before. I stood in the doorway of my room, squinting against the sudden light.

"Mother—what is it?"

She turned, and momentarily I saw the look on her face before she erased it and put on a contrived calm.

"It's all right," she said. "Dr. Cates has just come to have a look at Daddy. You go on back to sleep."

The wind was high that night, and I lay and listened to it rattling the storm windows and making the dry and winter-stiffened vines of the Virginia creeper scratch like small persistent claws against the red brick. In the morning, my mother told me that my father had developed pneumonia.

Dr. Cates did not think it would be safe to move my father to the hospital. My mother began sleeping in the spare bedroom, and after she had been there for a few nights, I asked if I could sleep in there too. I thought she would be bound to ask me why, and I did not know what I would say, but she did not ask. She nodded, and in some way her easy agreement upset me.

That night Dr. Cates came again, bringing with him one of the nurses from the hospital. My mother stayed upstairs with them. I sat with Grandmother MacLeod in the living room. That was the last place in the world I wanted to be, but I thought she would be offended if I went off. She sat as straight and rigid as a totem pole, and embroidered away at the needlepoint cushion cover she was doing. I perched on the edge of the chesterfield and kept my eyes fixed on *The White Company* by Conan Doyle,[1] and from time to time I turned a page. I had already read it three times before, but luckily Grandmother MacLeod did not know that. At nine o'clock she looked at her gold brooch watch, which she always wore pinned to her dress, and told me to go to bed, so I did that.

I wakened in darkness. At first, it seemed to me that I was in my own bed, and everything was as usual, with my parents in their room, and Roddie curled up in the crib in his room, and Grandmother MacLeod sleeping with her mouth open in her enormous spool bed, surrounded by half a dozen framed photos of Uncle Roderick and only one of my father, and Noreen snoring fitfully in the room next to mine, with the dark flames of her hair spreading out across the pillow, and the pink and silver motto cards from the Tabernacle stuck with adhesive tape onto the wall beside her bed—*Lean on Him, Emmanuel Is My Refuge, Rock of Ages Cleft for Me.*

Then in the total night around me, I heard a sound. It was my mother, and she was crying, not loudly at all, but from somewhere very deep inside her. I sat up in bed. Everything seemed to have stopped, not only time but my own heart and blood as well. Then my mother noticed that I was awake.

I did not ask her, and she did not tell me anything. There was no need. She held me in her arms, or I held her, I am not certain which. And after awhile the first mourning stopped, too, as everything does sooner or later, for when the limits of endurance have been reached, then people must sleep.

In the days following my father's death, I stayed close beside my mother, and this was only partly for my own consoling. I also had the feeling that she needed my protection. I did not know from what, nor what I could possibly do, but something held me there. Reverend McKee called, and I sat with my grandmother and my mother in the living room. My mother told me I did not need to stay unless I wanted to, but I refused to go. What I thought chiefly was that he would speak of the healing power of prayer, and all that, and it would be bound to make my mother cry again. And in fact, it happened in just that way, but when

---

[1] Historical novel (1891) by Sir Arthur Conan Doyle (1859–1930) set in the fourteenth century during the Hundred Years' War.

it actually came, I could not protect her from this assault. I could only sit there and pray my own prayer, which was that he would go away quickly.

My mother tried not to cry unless she was alone or with me. I also tried, but neither of us was entirely successful. Grandmother MacLeod, on the other hand, was never seen crying, not even the day of my father's funeral. But that day, when we had returned to the house and she had taken off her black velvet over-shoes and her heavy sealskin coat with its black fur that was the softest thing I had ever touched, she stood in the hallway and for the first time she looked unsteady. When I reached out instinctively towards her, she sighed.

"That's right," she said. "You might just take my arm while I go upstairs, Vanessa."

That was the most my Grandmother MacLeod ever gave in, to anyone's sight. I left her in her bedroom, sitting on the straight chair beside her bed and looking at the picture of my father that had been taken when he graduated from medical college. Maybe she was sorry now that she had only the one photograph of him, but whatever she felt, she did not say.

I went down into the kitchen. I had scarcely spoken to Noreen since my father's death. This had not been done on purpose. I simply had not seen her. I had not really seen anyone except my mother. Looking at Noreen now, I suddenly recalled the sparrow. I felt physically sick, remembering the fearful darting and plunging of those wings, and the fact that it was I who had opened the window and let it in. Then an inexplicable fury took hold of me, some terrifying need to hurt, burn, destroy. Absolutely without warning, either to her or to myself, I hit Noreen as hard as I could. When she swung around, appalled, I hit out at her once more, my arms and legs flailing. Her hands snatched at my wrists, and she held me, but still I continued to struggle, fighting blindly, my eyes tightly closed, as though she were a prison all around me and I was battling to get out. Finally, too shocked at myself to go on, I went limp in her grasp and she let me drop to the floor.

"Vanessa! I never done one single solitary thing to you, and here you go hitting and scratching me like that! What in the world has got into you?"

I began to say I was sorry, which was certainly true, but I did not say it. I could not say anything.

"You're not yourself, what with your dad and everything," she excused me. "I been praying every night that your dad is with God, Vanessa. I know he wasn't actually saved in the regular way, but still and all—"

"Shut up," I said.

Something in my voice made her stop talking. I rose from the floor and stood in the kitchen doorway.

"He didn't need to be saved," I went on coldly, distinctly. "And he is not in Heaven, because there is no Heaven. And it doesn't matter, see? *It doesn't matter!*"

Noreen's face looked peculiarly vulnerable now, her high wide cheekbones and puzzled childish eyes, and the thick russet tangle of her hair. I had not hurt her much before, when I hit her. But I had hurt her now, hurt her in some inexcusable way. Yet I sensed, too, that already she was gaining some satisfaction out of feeling sorrowful about my disbelief.

I went upstairs to my room. Momentarily I felt a sense of calm, almost of acceptance. *Rest beyond the river.* I knew now what that meant. It meant Nothing. It meant only silence, forever.

Then I lay down on my bed and spent the last of my tears, or what seemed then to be the last. Because, despite what I had said to Noreen, it did matter. It mattered, but there was no help for it.

Everything changed after my father's death. The MacLeod house could not be kept up any longer. My mother sold it to a local merchant who subsequently covered the deep red of the brick over with yellow stucco. Something about the house had always made me uneasy—that tower room where Grandmother MacLeod's potted plants drooped in a lethargic and lime-green confusion, those long stairways and hidden places, the attic which I had always imagined to be dwelt in by the spirits of the family dead, that gigantic portrait of the Duke of Wellington at the top of the stairs.[2] It was never an endearing house. And yet when it was no longer ours, and when the Virginia creeper had been torn down and the dark walls turned to a light marigold, I went out of my way to avoid walking past, for it seemed to me that the house had lost the stern dignity that was its very heart.

Noreen went back to the farm. My mother and brother and myself moved into Grandfather Connor's house. Grandmother MacLeod went to live with Aunt Morag in Winnipeg. It was harder for her than for anyone, because so much of her life was bound up with the MacLeod house. She was fond of Aunt Morag, but that hardly counted. Her men were gone, her husband and her sons, and a family whose men are gone is no family at all. The day she left, my mother and I did not know what to say. Grandmother MacLeod looked even smaller than usual in her fur coat and her black velvet toque. She became extremely agitated about trivialities, and fussed about the possibility of the taxi not arriving on time. She had forbidden us to accompany her to the station. About my father, or the house, or anything important, she did not say a word. Then, when the taxi had finally arrived, she turned to my mother.

"Roddie will have Ewen's seal ring, of course, with the MacLeod crest on it," she said. "But there is another seal as well, don't forget, the larger one with the crest and motto. It's meant to be worn on a watch chain. I keep it in my jewel-box. It was Roderick's. Roddie's to have that, too, when I die. Don't let Morag talk you out of it."

During the Second World War, when I was seventeen and in love with an airman who did not love me, and desperately anxious to get away from Manawaka and from my grandfather's house, I happened one day to be going through the old mahogany desk that had belonged to my father. It had a number of small drawers inside, and I accidentally pulled one of these all the way out. Behind it there was

---

[2] Arthur Wellesley (1769–1852), first Duke of Wellington, famous for defeating Napoleon at the Battle of Waterloo.

another drawer, one I had not known about. Curiously, I opened it. Inside there was a letter written on almost transparent paper in a cramped angular handwriting. It began—*Cher Monsieur Ewen*—That was all I could make out, for the writing was nearly impossible to read and my French was not good. It was dated 1919. With it, there was a picture of a girl, looking absurdly old-fashioned to my eyes, like the faces on long-discarded calendars or chocolate boxes. But beneath the dated quality of the photograph, she seemed neither expensive nor cheap. She looked like what she probably had been—an ordinary middle-class girl, but in another country. She wore her hair in long ringlets, and her mouth was shaped into a sweetly sad posed smile like Mary Pickford's.[3] That was all. There was nothing else in the drawer.

I looked for a long time at the girl, and hoped she had meant some momentary and unexpected freedom. I remembered what he had said to me, after I hadn't gone to the Remembrance Day parade.

"What are you doing, Vanessa?" my mother called from the kitchen.

"Nothing," I replied.

I took the letter and picture outside and burned them. That was all I could do for him. Now that we might have talked together, it was many years too late. Perhaps it would not have been possible anyway. I did not know.

As I watched the smile of the girl turn into scorched paper, I grieved for my father as though he had just died now.

[1970]

A Place to Stand On[4]

"The creative writer perceives his world once and for all in childhood and adolescence, and his whole career is an effort to illustrate his private world in terms of the great public world we all share."

Graham Greene, *Collected Essays*[5]

I believe that Graham Greene is right in this statement. It does not mean that the individual does not change after adolescence. On the contrary, it underlines the necessity for change. For the writer, one way of discovering oneself, of changing from the patterns of childhood and adolescence to those of adulthood, is through the explorations inherent in the writing itself. In the case of a great many writers, this exploration at some point—and perhaps at all points—involves an attempt to understand one's background and one's past, sometimes even a more distant past which one has not personally experienced.

---

[3] Mary Pickford (1892–1979), Canadian-born Hollywood film star of the early 1900s.

[4] Quotation from Al Purdy's poem "Roblin's Mills (II)" in which Purdy considers the ghosts of forgotten inhabitants of the landscape and concludes with the affirmation, "they had their being once / and left a place to stand on."

[5] Graham Greene (1904–1991), English novelist and essayist. This excerpt is from Greene's 1950 essay "The Young Dickens."

This sort of exploration can be clearly seen in the works of contemporary African writers, many of whom re-create their people's past in novels and plays in order to recover a sense of themselves, an identity and a feeling of value from which they were separated by two or three generations of colonialism and missionizing. They have found it necessary, in other words, to come to terms with their ancestors and their gods in order to be able to accept the past and be at peace with the dead, without being stifled or threatened by that past.

Oddly enough, it was only several years ago, when I began doing some research into contemporary Nigerian writing and its background, that I began to see how much my own writing had followed the same pattern—the attempt to assimilate the past, partly in order to be freed from it, partly in order to try to understand myself and perhaps others of my generation, through seeing where we had come from.

I was fortunate in going to Africa when I did—in my early twenties— because for some years I was so fascinated by the African scene that I was prevented from writing an autobiographical first novel. I don't say there is anything wrong in autobiographical novels, but it would not have been the right thing for me—my view of the prairie town from which I had come was still too prejudiced and distorted by closeness. I had to get farther away from it before I could begin to see it. Also, as it turned out ultimately, the kind of novel which I can best handle is one in which the fictional characters are very definitely *themselves*, not me, the kind of novel in which I can feel a deep sense of connection with the main character without a total identification which for me would prevent a necessary distancing.

I always knew that one day I would have to stop writing about Africa and go back to my own people, my own place of belonging, but when I began to do this, I was extremely nervous about the outcome. I did not consciously choose any particular time in history, or any particular characters. The reverse seemed to be true. The character of Hagar in *The Stone Angel* seemed almost to choose me. Later, though, I recognized that in some way not at all consciously understood by me at the time I had had to begin approaching my background and my past through my grandparents' generation, the generation of pioneers of Scots-Presbyterian origin, who had been among the first to people the town I called Manawaka. This was where my own roots began. Other past generations of my father's family had lived in Scotland, but for me, my people's real past—my own real past—was not connected except distantly with Scotland; indeed, this was true for Hagar as well, for she was born in Manawaka.

The name Manawaka is an invented one, but it had been in my mind since I was about seventeen or eighteen, when I first began to think about writing something set in a prairie town. Manawaka is not my hometown of Neepawa— it has elements of Neepawa, especially in some of the descriptions of places, such as the cemetery on the hill or the Wachakwa valley through which ran the small brown river which was the river of my childhood. In almost every way, however, Manawaka is not so much any one prairie town as an amalgam of many prairie towns. Most of all, I like to think, it is simply itself, a town of the mind, my own private world, as Graham Greene says, which one hopes will ultimately relate to the outer world which we all share.

When one thinks of the influence of a place on one's writing, two aspects come to mind. First, the physical presence of the place itself—its geography, its appearance. Second, the people. For me, the second aspect of environment is the most important, although in everything I have written which is set in Canada, whether or not actually set in Manitoba, somewhere some of my memories of the physical appearance of the prairies come in. I had, as a child and as an adolescent, ambiguous feelings about the prairies. I still have them, although they no longer bother me. I wanted then to get out of the small town and go far away, and yet I felt the protectiveness of that atmosphere, too. I felt the loneliness and the isolation of the land itself; and yet I always considered southern Manitoba to be very beautiful, and I still do. I doubt if I will ever live there again, but those poplar bluffs and the blackness of that soil and the way in which the sky is open from one side of the horizon to the other—these are things I will carry inside my skull for as long as I live, with the vividness of recall that only our first home can have for us.

Nevertheless, the people were more important than the place. Hagar in *The Stone Angel* was not drawn from life, but she incorporates many of the qualities of my grandparents' generation. Her speech is their speech, and her gods their gods. I think I never recognized until I wrote that novel just how mixed my own feelings were towards that whole generation of pioneers—how difficult they were to live with, how authoritarian, how unbending, how afraid to show love, many of them, and how willing to show anger. And yet, they had inhabited a wilderness and made it fruitful. They were, in the end, great survivors, and for that I love and value them.

The final exploration of this aspect of my background came when I wrote—over the past six or seven years—A *Bird in the House,* a number of short stories set in Manawaka and based upon my childhood and my childhood family, the only semi-autobiographical fiction I have ever written. I did not realize until I had finished the final story in the series how much all these stories are dominated by the figure of my maternal grandfather, who came of Irish Protestant stock. Perhaps it was through writing these stories that I finally came to see my grandfather not only as the repressive authoritarian figure from my childhood, but also as a boy who had to leave school in Ontario when he was about twelve, after his father's death, and who as a young man went to Manitoba by sternwheeler and walked the fifty miles from Winnipeg to Portage la Prairie, where he settled for some years before moving to Neepawa. He was a very hard man in many ways, but he had had a very hard life. I don't think I knew any of this, really knew it, until I had finished those stories. I don't think I ever knew, either, until that moment how much I owed to him. One sentence, near the end of the final story, may show what I mean. "I had feared and fought the old man, yet he proclaimed himself in my veins."

My writing, then, has been my own attempt to come to terms with the past. I see this process as the gradual one of freeing oneself from the stultifying aspect of the past, while at the same time beginning to see its true value—which, in the case of my own people (by which I mean the total community, not just my particular family), was a determination to survive against whatever odds. [. . .]

If Graham Greene is right—as I think he is—in his belief that a writer's career is "an effort to illustrate his private world in terms of the great public world we all share," then I think it is understandable that so much of my writing relates to the kind of prairie town in which I was born and in which I first began to be aware of myself. Writing, for me, has to be set firmly in some soil, some place, some outer and inner territory which might be described in anthropological terms as "cultural background." But I do not believe that this kind of writing needs therefore to be parochial. If Hagar in *The Stone Angel* has any meaning, it is the same as that of an old woman anywhere, having to deal with the reality of dying. On the other hand, she is not an old woman anywhere. She is very much a person who belongs in the same kind of prairie Scots-Presbyterian background as I do, and it was, of course, people like Hagar who created that background, with all its flaws and its strengths. [. . .]

[1970, 1976]

Letter to Margaret Atwood

Elm Cottage
10 Jan 71

Dear Peggy—
Very many thanks for sending me the Women's Lib publication and the poems of bill bissett. Haven't read the poems yet, but read some of the Women's Lib this morning. I guess I really do not have an ambiguous attitude to Women's Lib this morning—basically, I am in great agreement. I can't go along with some of the attitudes, but probably quite a few women in the movement can't, either. I'm not a joiner in the sense that I shall never find a cause with which I agree over detailed beliefs 100%, but of course that isn't so important. [. . .] I suppose I do find it emotionally trying to read the Women's Lib stuff, not because I disagree with most of it, but because in many ways I wish so profoundly that such a general movement had existed let's say 15 years ago. I feel as tho I have in fact fought every single one of these issues, but alone and therefore not effectually from the point of view of relationships. The only solution for me, therefore, was to take off and learn to accept the fact that at 44, now, and considering the men of my generation, and also considering that my own work is of enormous overwhelming importance to me, there's no way of having a partnership on the only terms I could now bear. Odd . . . I remember figuring it all out about 1962 when I was 36, and on my own for the first time in my life, but with 2 kids, whose presence saves me from despair, and when I got to England, thinking "the only relationship I could possibly now maintain would be a relationship of equals." It seems almost spooky to see the same things now being written about and yelled

out loud . . . one really wants to say hurrah! Personally, from that point of view, I wish I were 15 yrs younger or else that there were a few more men of my own age or older who cottoned on to these views. They are, however, scarce as hen's teeth. Luckily, the acts of "managing" a household and its economy no longer scare me, as I found I could really do all that without much trouble when I had to, and that I wasn't a financial nitwit after all, as I had always somehow believed.

You know, I think a lot of girls in Women's Lib nowadays tend to resent women like myself who have to some extent or other made their own professional lives, as this is like saying "I'll make it for myself, never mind about the rest," but of course when I set about my own mini-revolution, I didn't know there were so many others who felt the same way. And that was less than ten years ago. Have noticed v[ery] sharply in those years, however, that after I'd had a couple of books published, my relationships with men always fell into 1 of 2 categories . . . those who saw me as a woman and would rather not know about my writing, and those who accepted me as a writer and equal (mostly writers these guys) but kind of a quasi-male figure or sort of neuter, and who would cringe slightly if I mentioned, e.g., my children. [. . .]

The whole colonial situation, of course (i.e. the woman as black) I not unnaturally figured out years ago when living in Africa, helped somewhat by the French psychologist Mannoni, whose book "Prospero & Caliban: The Psychology of Colonization" for a time was my bible. [. . .]

Incidentally . . . one point with which I took issue, re: some of the Women's Lib articles [was] the feeling on the part of some women that it was kind of unnatural for women to want to have kids. I would say that if a woman doesn't want to have kids, that is her business and hers only. But if she deeply does, that does not mean she is not interested in anything else. I don't really feel I have to analyse my own motives in wanting children. . . . It's like (to me) asking why you want to write. Who cares? You have to, and that's that. But the kids, like the writing, belong ultimately to themselves, and not to you. In fact, they're very like the writing. A gift, given to you by life, undeserved like all grace is undeserved by its very nature, and not to be owned. . . .

Love to you [. . .]

[1971]

ROBERT KROETSCH ■ (1927–)

"We want to hear our own story," Robert Kroetsch told fellow writer Margaret Laurence in 1970. "In a sense, we haven't got an identity until somebody tells our story. The fiction makes us real." Like many Canadian writers of the 1960s and '70s, including such diverse authors as Dennis Lee and Rudy Wiebe, Kroetsch strove to find a way of writing Canada into existence, particularly western Canada.

Eschewing conventional realist approaches to Canadian fiction, and influenced by the poststructuralist theories of Jacques Derrida, Jean-François Lyotard, Michel Foucault, and Mikhail Bakhtin, Kroetsch sought more experimental forms of capturing the interconnections between identity and landscape, oral and written communication, fact and fiction, words and the world. His works are particularly noted for playing with traditional genre boundaries, including the boundary between criticism and literature, between history and fiction, and thus parallel many of the generic experiments of Michael Ondaatje of the same period. Heralded by Canadian critic Linda Hutcheon as "Mr. Canadian Postmodern," Kroetsch has attained a permanent place in the Canadian literary tradition for his innovative, intertextual, mythic, and frequently parodic writings about the Canadian west.

Born in 1927 on a farm near Heisler, Alberta, Kroetsch studied English and philosophy at the University of Alberta from 1945 to 1948. After graduating, he spent years working at various jobs, including on the Mackenzie River boats (the basis of his first novel, *But We Are Exiles* [1965]) and for the U.S. Air Force in Goose Bay, Labrador. He began studies with Hugh MacLennan at McGill University in 1954, but moved to Middlebury College, Vermont, to complete an M.A., and eventually pursued a Ph.D. in creative writing at the University of Iowa's Writers' Workshop. In 1961, he began teaching English at the State University of New York, Binghamton. He eventually left New York to return to Canada and take up a position at the University of Manitoba in 1978, where he taught until his retirement in 1995.

Kroetsch's interest in mythic structures, oral traditions, and tall tales as applied to the Canadian prairies became governing tropes in his "Out-West triptych," a trilogy of novels that include *The Words of My Roaring* (1966), *The Studhorse Man* (1969), and *Gone Indian* (1973). All three novels make use of surreal events and references to classical and Aboriginal mythology to forge a way of "writing" the prairies. The best-known of the three is the Governor General's Award-

winning second novel of the triptych, *The Studhorse Man,* which tells the story of Hazard Lepage, a rural horse breeder whose travels along his circuit are mapped alongside Homer's *Odyssey. Gone Indian* concerns a literature graduate student obsessed with the Canadian author and conservationist Grey Owl (Archibald Belaney), the Englishman who adopted an identity as a Native man in the 1920s (see Section V). It is a ribald and carnivalesque novel that reveals Kroetsch's increasing commitment to literary postmodernism and postcolonialism at the end of the 1960s, in the way it parodies its protagonist's obsession with Native and western authenticity.

Kroetsch's theoretical interests are evident in his co-founding (with William Spanos) of the critical theory journal *Boundary 2: A Journal of Postmodern Literature* in 1972 while in New York. His work on this journal, and his many critical essays on Canadian writing (some of which are collected in his 1989 book *The Lovely Treachery of Words: Essays Selected and New*), have made Kroetsch a central critic of Canadian literature. Kroetsch's interest in developing a "voice" for Canadian writing—not altogether different from some of the goals of the modernists of the 1920s and '30s—has established him as an important theorist, committed to finding ways of articulating a distinctive Canadian mode of expression while also seeing Canadian literature as partaking in international developments of literary postmodernism. His essay "Disunity as Unity: A Canadian Strategy" (1989), included here, concentrates on the paradox of Canadian cultural expression: that the governing "meta-narrative" is the absence of any overarching narrative. In a way comparable to Dennis Lee's notion of the "silence" of colonial space in his essay "Cadence, Country, Silence" (included in this section), Kroetsch concludes that in Canada the "unnaming allows the naming."

Kroetsch's poetry has been as influential as his fiction, and continues his interest in the interrelations of local history, inheritance, landscape, and language. In this sense, his poems bear comparison with some of Al Purdy's concerns in his Roblin's Mills poems, though formally Kroetsch's poems are more experimental. His interest in the instability of meaning and official histories is evident in many of his poems about Canadian prairie history, particularly "Stone Hammer Poem," which is unified by the governing conceit of the archaeological unearthing of an archaic artifact. Kroetsch's notion of archaeology as an alternative to linear and limited narratives of the past—archaeological fragments allow us to get at the past through snippets and speculation—comes through in many of these poems. The stone maul that is found in the grandfather's wheat field invites a meditation on questions of inheritance, belonging, and history, and the role of art as a connecting link to human lives in the past; the poem works in a comparable way to Purdy's "Lament for the Dorsets." Paradoxically, the stone hammer offers a means of placing the present-day speaker within a historical and geographical continuum while also initiating a distinct un-settling, since it highlights the tenuousness of the settler's present-day claim to the land, in contrast to Aboriginal peoples' longstanding presence there. A similar concern forms the focus of Kroetsch's 1983 essay, "On Being an Alberta Writer," included here. The meditation on "unnaming" provided in "Stone Hammer Poem" finds a correlative in the life of Canadian prairie writer Frederick Philip Grove (see Section V), whose shifting identity is explored in Kroetsch's poem "F.P. Grove: The Finding." Kroetsch is interested in the element of "self-fashioning" that is central to Grove's life story, an interest that is echoed in Armand Ruffo's poetic treatment of Grey Owl's "fictional" identity in *Grey Owl: The Mystery of Archie Belaney* (see Section VII). A similar interest in the paradox of unnaming occurs in Kroetsch's "Elegy for Wong Toy," which concerns a Chinese man, "marginal" in terms of official prairie history, who has acquired a central presence in the speaker's memories of his youth in the prairie small town.

One of Kroetsch's most famous poetic works is his 1977 *Seed Catalogue,* a long poem that "translates" the pages of an actual seed catalogue into a distinctive rural prairie voice. Kroetsch uses some of the words from the catalogue alongside his own poetic reworking of prairie history. As he explains in "On Being an Alberta Writer," the goal of the work was to create a kind of palimpsest that would set a historical object alongside living voices, thus bringing together "the oral tradition and the myth of origins" in a unique layering of local experiences and stories.

Kroetsch's interest in archaeological and archival artifacts continues in his novel from the same period, *Badlands* (1975), which tells the story of a paleontologist searching for dinosaur bones in the Alberta badlands. Subsequent novels include *What the Crow Said* (1978), *Alibi* (1983), and *The Man from the Creeks* (1998), the latter a novel about the story behind Robert Service's well-known poem "The Shooting of Dan McGrew" (1907). Noting the gap between his experience of his surroundings and the authorized history he was taught as a child, Kroetsch determined to make that "absence" his focus. As he puts it, "The connection between the name and the named—the importance and the failure of that connection—is one of my obsessions." This interest forms a continuous thread through all of his writings, and his treatment of the paradox of the "trace" (a remnant that is both present and absent) has formed one of the most compelling images in his work. As he evocatively phrases it in his essay included here, "Even abandonment gives us memory."

Elegy for Wong Toy

Charlie   you are dead now
but I dare to speak because
in China the living speak
to their kindred   dead.
And you are one of my fathers.

Your iron bachelorhood perplexed
our horny youth: we were born
to the snow of a prairie town
to the empty streets of our
longing.   You built a railway   10
            to get there.

You were your own enduring   winter.
You were your abacus, your Chinaman's
eyes.   You were the long reach up
to the top of that bright showcase
where   for a few pennies
we bought a whole childhood.

Only a Christmas calendar
told us your name:
Wong Toy, prop., Canada Cafe: 20
above the thin pad of months,
under the almost naked girl
in the white leather boots
who was never allowed to undress
in the rows of God-filled houses

which you were never
invited to enter.

Charlie, I knew my first touch
of Ellen Kiefer's young breasts
in the second booth from the back   30
            in your cafe.
It was the night of a hockey game.
You were out in the kitchen
making sandwiches and coffee.

You were your own enduring
winter.   You were our spring

and we   like meadowlarks
hearing the sun   boom
under the flat horizon
cracked the still dawn alive   40
with one ferocious   song.

So Charlie   this is a thank you
poem.   You are twenty years
dead.   I hope they buried you
sitting upright in your grave
the way you sat   pot-bellied
behind your jawbreakers
and your licorice plugs,
behind your tins of Ogden's fine cut,[1]
your treasury of cigars,   50

and the heart-shaped box of chocolates
that no one ever took home.

[1975]

F.P. Grove: The Finding[2]

1

Dreaming the well-born   hobo of yourself
against the bourgeois father   dreaming Europe
if only to find   a place to be from

the hobo tragedian   pitching bundles
riding a freight   to the impossible city
the fallen archangel   of Brandon or Winnipeg

---

[1] Reference to Ogden's Fine Cut Tobacco.

[2] This poem contains allusions to a number of works by Frederick Philip Grove, the German author who faked his own death and adopted a fictional identity after he immigrated to North America, eventually settling on the Canadian prairies (see Section V). In Grove's 1927 *A Search for America*, one of Grove's many fictionalized accounts of his life, he recounts how he spent years as a hobo travelling across North America. *In Search of Myself* (1946) contains an account of Grove's work as a teamster when he managed "four aged stallions." In the same book, he provides an account of meeting a French priest who encouraged him to become a teacher after seeing him reading French poet Charles Baudelaire's (1821–1867) work *Les Fleurs du mal* (1857). The second section of the poem contains references to Grove's "Snow," the chapter from *Over Prairie Trails* (1922) following "Dawn and Diamonds" (included in Section V), where Grove drives through a blizzard toward his wife and daughter.

in all your harvesting   real
or imagined   did you really find
four aged stallions   neigh

in your cold undertaking   on those trails north   10
in all the (dreamed) nights   in stooks
in haystacks   dreaming the purified dreamer

who lured you   to a new man (back
to the fatal earth)   inventing (beyond
America) a new world   did you find

did you dream   the French priest who hauled you
out of your *fleurs du mal*   and headlong
into a hundred drafts   real

or imagined   of the sought form
(there are no models)   and always   20
(there are only models)   alone

2

alone in the cutter   in the blizzard
two horses   hauling you into the snow
that buries the road   burying the forest

the layered mind   exfoliating
back to the barren sea   (Greek to us,
Grove)   back to the blank sun

and musing snow to yourself   new
to the old rite of burial   the snow
lifting the taught man   into the coyote self   30

the silence of sight   "as if I were not myself
who yet am I"   riding the drifted snow
to your own plummeting   alone and alone

the *wirklichkeit*[3]   of the word itself
the name under the name   the sought
and calamitous edge   of the white earth

[3] German: reality, essence.

the horses   pawing the empty fall
the hot breath on the zero day   the man
seeing the new man so vainly   alone

we say with your waiting wife   (but she   40
was the world   before you invented it
old liar)   "You had a hard trip?"

[1975]

Stone Hammer Poem

1

This stone
become a hammer
of stone, this maul

is the colour
of bone (no,
bone is the colour
of this stone maul).

The rawhide loops
are gone, the
hand is gone, the   10
buffalo's skull
is gone;

the stone is
shaped like the skull
of a child.

2

This paperweight on my desk

where I begin
this poem   was

found in a wheatfield
lost (this hammer,   20
this poem).

Cut to a function,
this stone was
(the hand is   gone—

3

Grey, two-headed,
the pemmican maul

fell from the travois⁴ or
a boy playing   lost it in
the prairie wool or
a squaw   left it in   30
the brain of a buffalo or

It is a million
years older than
the hand that
chipped stone or
raised slough⁵
water (or blood) or

4

This stone maul
was found.

In the field   40
my grandfather
thought
was his

my father
thought was his

5

It is a stone
old as the last
Ice Age, the
retreating/ the
recreating ice,   50
the retreating
buffalo, the
retreating Indians

⁴ A frame built of two poles, used by many Plains peoples, to pull small loads overland; originally
pulled by people, later by horses or dogs.

⁵ *Slough* (pronounced "slew"), naturally formed freshwater pond on the prairies.

(the saskatoons bloom
white (infrequently
the chokecherries the
highbush cranberries the
pincherries bloom
white along the barbed
wire fence (the   60
pemmican   winter

6

This stone maul
stopped a plow
long enough for one
Gott im Himmel.[6]

The Blackfoot (the
Cree?) not

finding the maul
cursed.

?did he curse   70
?did he try to
go back
?what happened
I have to/ I want
to know (not know)
?WHAT HAPPENED

7

The poem
is the stone
chipped and hammered
until it is shaped   80
. like the stone
hammer, the maul.

8

Now the field is
mine because
I gave it
(for a price)

[6] German, "God in Heaven."

to a young man
(with a growing son)
who did not

notice that the land   90
did not belong
to the Indian who
gave it to the Queen
(for a price) who
gave it to the CPR
(for a price) which
gave it to my grandfather
(for a price) who
gave it to my father
(50 bucks an acre   100
Gott im Himmel I cut
down all the trees I
picked up all the stones) who

gave it to his son
(who sold it)

9

This won't
surprise you.

My grandfather
lost the stone maul.

10

My father (retired)   110
grew raspberries.
He dug in his potato patch.
He drank one glass of wine
each morning.
He was lonesome
for death.

He was lonesome for the
hot wind on his face, the smell
of horses, the distant
hum of a threshing machine,   120
the oilcan he carried, the weight
of a crescent wrench in his hind pocket.

He was lonesome for his absent
son and his daughters,
for his wife, for his own
brothers and sisters and
his own mother and father.

He found the stone maul
on a rockpile in the
north-west corner of what   130
he thought of
as his wheatfield.

He kept it (the
stone maul) on the railing
of the back porch in
a raspberry basket.

11

I keep it
on my desk
(the stone).

Sometimes I use it   140
in the (hot) wind
(to hold down paper)

smelling a little of cut
grass or maybe even of
ripening wheat or of
buffalo blood hot
in the dying sun.

Sometimes I write
my poems for that

stone hammer.   150

[1975]

On Being an Alberta Writer

How do you make love in a new country? I used that question as a refrain in a
paper I read two years ago, at a conference held in Banff under the general
title, "Crossing Frontiers." . . . These conferences, these visits, these occasions

of talk connect in our lives (connect our lives, even); we begin to weave our own significance. . . . How do you make love in a new country? Obviously, I believed that I had an answer. But, alas, no one asked.

One way to make love is by writing. Indeed, without writing, I sometimes suspect, there would be no such thing as love. Surely without the lyric poems of Sappho, the sonnets of the Renaissance—without the pastoral dialogue (of which I still hear traces in prairie fiction) or the long history of theatre, our concept of love would be much diminished. Perhaps the sub-question is, then: How do you write in a new country?

I'll attempt an answer. Perhaps a tangential answer, an evasive answer. Perhaps even a fictitious answer. But an answer that is as honest as I can make it, since memory is a disguise as well as a recollection.

I remember how I first began to be skeptical of the writing that I read.

I was a child—I don't know how old (I was born in 1927, if that helps you to locate these matters)—my parents took me to Spring Lake, to a picnic. Spring Lake is a small round lake, surrounded by willows and poplars; it was the centre of the community that my mother grew up in—in the parklands south-east of Edmonton, a few miles from the valley of the Battle River. I was playing in a large, shallow depression in the ground, a depression that somehow wasn't natural. My father came by, looking for me. I asked about the place where I was playing. He said, casually, that it was a buffalo wallow.

It's where buffalo rolled and scratched, he said. He could tell me a little more—the lake never went dry he explained, the buffalo came here to drink.

What buffalo? I asked. Or wondered, if I didn't ask. I don't remember now. When? From where? . . . Even at that young age I was secure in the illusion that the land my parents and grandparents homesteaded had had no prior occupants, animal or human. Ours was the ultimate tabula rasa. We were the truly innocent.

There was an older boy a mile from our farm who, as we kids liked to put it, knew everything. He was so smart a lot of people thought he'd become a priest. I remember that he could recite the names and dates of kings and prime ministers from whomever was thought to be first to the latest. I asked him about buffalo wallows. He'd never even heard of buffalo wallows. But more: he made considerable show of not caring that he hadn't heard. He was educated.

My sense of the gap between me and history was growing. History as I knew it did not account for the world I lived in. Present here in this landscape, I was taking my first lesson in the idea of absence.

There was, half a mile south from our farm, a ring of stones in the prairie grass. My dad and the hired men, strangely, plowed around it. One day, again when I was a child, I ran away from home; instead of going to a neighbor's house, where I could play, I went to that ring of stones . . . and again I began to wonder. I went back home and asked my mother about those stones. She had, then, never heard of a tipi ring; she said the stones were magical. I suspect now that her notion of magical went back two or three generations to the forests of southern Germany, surviving that long transcription through Wisconsin and Minnesota to the District and then the

Province of Alberta. The connection between the name and the named—the importance and the failure of that connection—is one of my obsessions.

I was that day on my way to embracing the model of archaeology, against that of history. The authorized history, the given definition of history, was betraying us on those prairies. A few years after I sat in that tipi ring and cried and then began to notice and then began to wonder, a gang of dam-builders from a Battle River site came by and picked up the stones, and my father broke the sod. If history betrayed us, we too betrayed it. I remember my father one night at supper, saying out of nowhere, he'd made a mistake, letting those men pick up those stones. For reasons he couldn't understand, he felt guilty. Where I had learned the idea of absence, I was beginning to learn the idea of trace. There is always something left behind. That is the essential paradox. Even abandonment gives us memory.

I had to tell a story. I responded to those discoveries of absence, to that invisibility, to that silence, by knowing I had to make up a story. *Our* story. [. . .]

How do you write in a new country?

Our inherited literature, the literature of our European past and of eastern North America, is emphatically the literature of a people who have *not* lived on prairies. We had, and still have, difficulty finding names for the elements and characteristics of this landscape. The human response to this landscape is so new and ill-defined and complex that our writers come back, uneasily but compulsively, to landscape writing. Like the homesteaders before us, we are compelled to adjust and invent, to remember and forget. We feel a profound ambiguity about the past—about both its contained stories and its modes of perception.

There are, first and always, the questions of form and language. For reasons which are not very clear, the prairies developed a tradition of fiction before developing a tradition of poetry. This seems to be contradictory to the cultural experience of most societies. I suspect it has to do with the nature of the experience—in one word, often harsh (that's two words). And there was available, to record that harshness, the realistic mode of fiction.

But even as I say this I ask: Might it not be possible that we now look back on the experience as having been a harsh one because the realistic (or even naturalistic) mode of fiction pictured it so? What if the prairies had been settled—as much of the United States was in the 19th century—at a time when the Gothic model was easily available to the novelists?

The effect of perceptual models on what we see is now the concern of social and literary critics (thanks to such books as Dick Harrison's *Unnamed Country*).[7] I was living outside of Alberta (and outside of Canada) while writing most of my fiction and poetry. Perhaps for that reason I was constantly aware that we both, and at once, record and invent these new places called Alberta and Saskatchewan.

[7] Dick Harrison's critical study, *Unnamed Country: The Struggle for a Canadian Prairie Fiction* (1977), explores the ways Canadian prairie writers have struggled with finding a vocabulary fit for the prairie landscape. He argues that modern-day writers have inherited early settlers' sense of the incongruities between the new land and the old culture.

That pattern of contraries, all the possibilities implied in *record* and *invent*, for me finds its focus in the model suggested by the phrase: a local pride.

The phrase is from William Carlos Williams—indeed those three words are the opening of his great poem *Paterson*, about Paterson, New Jersey: *a local pride*.[8]

The feeling must come from an awareness of the authenticity of our own lives. People who feel invisible try to borrow visibility from those who are visible. To understand others is surely difficult. But to understand ourselves becomes impossible if we do not see images of ourselves in the mirror—be that mirror theatre or literature or historical writing. A local pride does not exclude the rest of the world, or other experiences; rather, it makes them possible. It creates an organizing centre. Or as Williams put it, more radically: the acquiring of a local pride enables us to create our own culture—"by lifting an environment to expression."

How do we lift an environment to expression? How do you write in a new country?

The great sub-text of prairie literature is our oral tradition. In the face of books, magazines, films and TV programs that are so often someone else, we talk to each other by, literally, talking.

The visit is the great prairie cultural event. People go visiting, or they go to other events in order to visit. This accounts for the predominance of the beer parlor and the church in prairie fiction. Beyond this, we see fictional characters going to stampedes and country dances and summer resorts—those places where we talk ourselves into existence.

Oral history is not likely to go back more than two generations—to parents and grandparents. Beyond that little remains—with huge consequences for our sense of history. Within that time-framework exists an enormous prospect of fiction-making. Individuals in a lifetime become characters. Events become story, become folklore, edge towards the condition of myth. Many of our best novels—the novels of Margaret Laurence and Rudy Wiebe especially—assert the primacy of the act of speech over the act of writing. The poetry of Andy Suknaski acknowledges a huge and continuing debt to the oral tradition. The sophisticated sound poetry of Stephen Scobie and Doug Barbour, in Edmonton, suggests that print is merely the kind of notation for speech, as a musical score is for music.[9]

A local pride leads us to a concern with myths of origin. Obviously, on the prairies, there has been an enormous interest in ethnic roots—that version of the myth of origin. But now, in our growing urban centres, there is a new kind of myth emerging. Again, for writers like Laurence or Wiebe, there is available to our imaginations a new set of ancestors: the native or Métis people, Big Bear,

---

[8] William Carlos Williams (1883–1963), American poet, published his five-volume poem *Paterson* in 1963, an extended meditation on the poet's responsibility to his local American context.

[9] Andy Suknaski (1942–), is a Saskatchewan poet of Polish and Ukrainian background who celebrates the history and diverse ethnic heritage of the Canadian prairies. Stephen Scobie (1943–) and Douglas Barbour (1940–), co-founders of Longspoon Press, are Canadian poets and critics who have collaborated on numerous sound poetry projects.

Riel, the fictional Tonnerre family of *The Diviners*, Dumont.[10] And I would suggest that along with this comes the urban dream that our roots are just over the horizon, in the small towns and the rural communities of the prairies. This dream of origins is already evident in Laurence's work. It is already evident in a larger Canadian context—surely it is no accident that the classics of modern Canadian writing are set in rural areas: Sheila Watson's *The Double Hook* with its setting in the Cariboo Country, Ross's Saskatchewan, Ernest Buckler's Nova Scotia in his novel, *The Mountain and the Valley*.[11] The oral tradition, become a literary tradition, points us back to our own landscape, our recent ancestors, and the characteristic expressions and modes of our own speech.

It is a kind of archaeology that makes *this place,* with all its implications, available to us for literary purposes. We have not yet grasped the whole story; we have hints and guesses that slowly persuade us towards the recognition of larger patterns. Archaeology allows the fragmentary nature of the story, against the coerced unity of traditional history. Archaeology allows for discontinuity. It allows for layering. It allows for imaginative speculation.

I am aware that it is the great French historian, Michel Foucault,[12] who has formalized our understanding of the appropriateness of the archaeological method. But the prairie writer understands that appropriateness in terms of the particulars of place: newspaper files, place names, shoe boxes full of old photographs, tall tales, diaries, journals, tipi rings, weather reports, business ledgers, voting records—even the wrong-headed histories written by eastern historians become, rather than narratives of the past, archaeological deposits.

For me, one of those deposits turned out to be an old seed catalogue. I found a 1917 catalogue in the Glenbow archives in 1975. I translated that seed catalogue into a poem called "Seed Catalogue." The archaeological discovery, if I might call it that, brought together for me the oral tradition and the myth of origins. [. . .]

[1983]

Disunity as Unity: A Canadian Strategy

[. . .] My concern here is with narrative itself. The shared story—what I prefer to call the assumed story—has traditionally been basic to nationhood. As a writer I'm interested in these assumed stories—what I call meta-narratives. It

---

[10] See Rudy Wiebe's novels about Plains Cree Chief Big Bear (*The Temptations of Big Bear*, 1973) and Louis Riel and Gabriel Dumont (*The Scorched-Wood People*, 1977). The Tonnerres are the Métis family in Margaret Laurence's 1974 novel *The Diviners*. Gabriel Dumont (1837–1906) fought alongside Louis Riel as the leader of the Métis army during the Northwest Rebellion of 1885.

[11] Kroetsch refers to three well-known Canadian regional novels: Sheila Watson's *The Double Hook* (1959), set in the interior of B.C.; Sinclair Ross's *As For Me and My House* (1941), set in the fictional town of Horizon, Saskatchewan; and Ernest Buckler's *The Mountain and the Valley* (1952), set in the Annapolis Valley of Nova Scotia.

[12] Michel Foucault (1926–1984), French philosopher, historian, and poststructuralist theorist who wrote *The Archaeology of Knowledge* (1969), in which he outlines his archaeological method, a historical excavation of the ways material instances of language and meaning-making are influenced by often unconscious rules and assumptions that make particular meanings possible.

may be that the writing of particular narratives, within a culture, is dependent on these meta-narratives.

An obvious example is the persistence of The American Dream, with its assumptions about individual freedom, the importance of the frontier, the immigrant experience, as it functions in the literature of the United States. Even the cowboy story, and the American version of the detective story, are dependent on that meta-narrative.

To make a long story disunited, let me assert here that I'm suggesting that Canadians cannot agree on what their meta-narrative is. I am also suggesting that, in some perverse way, this very falling-apart of our story is what holds our story together.

In the 1970s the Conseil des Universités of the government of Quebec invited the French critic Jean-François Lyotard to write a report on the state of universities in the western world. Lyotard's reflections were published in English in 1984 under the title *The Postmodern Condition: A Report on Knowledge*.[13] In that report Lyotard writes: "Simplifying to the extreme, I define *postmodern* as incredulity toward meta-narratives. . . . To the obsolescence of the meta-narrative apparatus of legitimation corresponds, most notably, the crisis of metaphysical philosophy and of the university institution which in the past relied on it. The narrative function is losing its functors, its great hero, its great dangers, its great voyages, its great goal. [. . .]"

I am suggesting that by Lyotard's definition, Canada is a postmodern country. [. . .]

Timothy Findley in his novel *The Wars* gives an account of the particularly Canadian experience.[14] His protagonist, Robert Ross, in the course of being destroyed by and in a marginal way surviving the First World War, acts out for the colonial society the destruction and the loss of its European centres, cultural, political, economic. For Findley, form and content speak each other's plight in *The Wars* as the traditional authority of the novel itself begins to falter. He resorts to an archival approach, using letters, photographs, interviews, family history, to recover the story, allowing the reader in turn to wonder how the fictional narrative centre relates to the writer writing. A doubt about our ability to know invades the narrative. What we witness is the collapse, for North American eyes, of the meta-narrative that once went by the name Europe. Europa. Findley's more recent novels, *Famous Last Words* and *Not Wanted on the Voyage*, in their titles and in their stories remind us of Lyotard's observation that in postmodern writing there appears a scepticism or hesitation about the meta-narrative's great voyages, its great goal. [. . .]

In this postmodern world, we trust a version of archaeology over the traditional versions of history. History, in its traditional forms, insisted too strongly on a coherent narrative. Timothy Findley speaks for many Canadians when he

[13] Jean-François Lyotard (1924–1998), French theorist and philosopher known for his analysis of postmodernity in *The Postmodern Condition* (orig. published in French in 1979).

[14] Timothy Findley (1930–2002) is the Canadian author of the 1977 postmodern novel *The Wars*, set during the First World War.

uses an archival method in *The Wars*, trusting to fragments of story, letting them speak their incompleteness. [. . .]

One of the functions of art, traditionally, is the location and elaboration of the meta-narratives. Canadian writing is obsessively about the artist who can't make art. That model is securely established by Sinclair Ross and Ernest Buckler.[15]

Ross, in his novel of the Saskatchewan prairies during the Depression, *As For Me and My House*, has a minister's wife tell the story in the form of her diary. Her husband is a minister who doubts his ministry and who wants both to paint and to write and who succeeds at neither. The book is in effect a powerful novel about the inability to make art—it is a novel as a set of diary entries about an unwritten novel. The meta-narratives—religious, artistic, social, economic—do not hold. Even the great European meta-narrative about "nature" does not hold here, as nature turns into wind and moving dust and an unreachable horizon. [. . .]

One of the important elements in meta-narratives is the story of the place and moment of origin. In the American story we hear of the apparently infinite crowd that was aboard the "Mayflower," we hear of the moment in July 1776 when there seems to have been no opposition at all to the impulse toward revolution and, regrettably, little toleration for peoples who want to emulate that moment.[16] In Canada we cannot for the world decide when we became a nation or what to call the day or days or, for that matter, years that might have been the originary moments. If we can't be united we can't be disunited. [. . .]

Margaret Laurence attempts some counting of ancestral sources—and her heroine gets stories from the official histories, from the mouths of the veterans who actually fought in the trenches, from the survivors of the trek from the Scottish villages, from her Métis lover in Manitoba, from the professor of English to whom she is married for a while, from her own daughter who has songs of her own to sing.[17] The abundance, the disunity, is her saving unity. Christie Logan is indeed of and in the "real country" of Canadian art and story. He is a garbage man who "reads" what he finds in the nuisance grounds, and as such he is the ultimate archaeologist of that old new place called Canada.

---

[15] Sinclair Ross (1908–1996), Saskatchewan novelist and short story writer, known for his influential novel *As For Me and My House* (1941); see Section V. Ernest Buckler (1908–1984), Nova Scotia author, best known for his novel *The Mountain and the Valley* (1952), in which a prospective artist dies in his youth.

[16] The *Mayflower* was the ship that brought the original Pilgrim settlers to the settlement in New England (Plymouth) in 1620. It is often regarded as a symbolic moment for the origins of America, especially American values of freedom and independence, since the Pilgrims were fleeing religious persecution in England. July 1776 is the date of the United States Declaration of Independence when, during the American Revolution (1775–1783), the United States (originally the Thirteen Colonies) declared its independence from Britain. This war is held up as an instance of American democratic ideals. Kroetsch is noting the irony in the fact that these revolutionary origins have been followed by a new conservatism in the United States that does not tolerate movements that "emulate" this foundational revolutionary initiative.

[17] Kroetsch is referring to incidents in the life of Morag Gunn in *The Diviners* (1974) by Margaret Laurence (1926–1987). Christie Logan, from *The Diviners*, is Morag's adoptive father, the local garbage collector.

The attempt at allowing versions of narrative might explain the extreme intertexuality of Canadian culture. Where the impulse in the U.S. is usually to define oneself as American, the Canadian, like a work of postmodern architecture, is always quoting his many sources. Our sense of region resists our national sense. I hear myself saying, I'm from *western* Canada. Or, even beyond that—because I was born in Alberta and now live in Manitoba—people ask me, seriously, if I think of myself as an Albertan or a Manitoban. We maintain ethnic customs long after they've disappeared in the country of origin. We define ourselves, often, as the cliché has it, by explaining to Americans that we aren't British, to the British that we aren't Americans. It may be that we survive by being skilful shape-changers. But more to the point, we survive by working with a low level of self-definition and national definition. We insist on staying multiple, and by that strategy we accommodate to our climate, our economic situation, and our neighbours. [. . .]

[1989]

ALICE MUNRO ■ (1931–)

A three-time Governor General's Award winner and two-time winner of the Giller Prize, Alice Munro is among the finest short story writers in the world. She is celebrated for the sheer craft of her stories, notably for her precise evocation of detail and her ability to achieve an astonishing condensation of meaning within the restricted framework of the short-story form. These skills enable Munro to probe hidden depths in the lives and settings of ordinary people, revealing secrets with an apparent casualness that is startling. Like Mavis Gallant, Munro is adept at conjuring tortuous social and psychological dissembling. However, unlike the expatriate Gallant's, Munro's stories are most often situated in a recognizably Canadian setting. Like Margaret Laurence, Munro is known for her portrait of a distinctive regional landscape; her fictional southwestern Ontario towns of Jubilee (*Lives of Girls and Women*) and Hanratty (*Who Do You Think You Are?*) parallel Laurence's creation of the town of Manawaka, Manitoba, in her stories and novels.

Along with such authors as Robertson Davies and Graeme Gibson, Munro has been described as a writer of "Southern Ontario Gothic," a subgenre of Canadian fiction that is defined by its focus on the Gothic underside of everyday Ontario reality. Her stories revel in paradox and illusion. Munro's characters are plagued by social unease and secret desires, living lives of quiet desperation even as on the surface they appear to be conducting themselves with competence. Her stories, then, are powerful because of their acuity, their ability to probe beneath human insecurity and self-deception.

Born Alice Laidlaw in Wingham, Ontario, Munro grew up on a fox and mink farm managed by her father. Many of her stories have protagonists who come from relatively poor social backgrounds and the tales chart their yearning, and often painful struggles, to gain entrance into more elite social circles. As a result, there has been a good deal of recent critical interest in the issue of class in Munro's stories, notably by the critic Roxanne Rimstead, as well as in Munro's concern with women's social struggles specifically. Of particular interest in Munro's works is the often tormented relationships between men and women, and mothers and daughters, and the need for coming to terms with one's past.

After high school, Munro left home to attend the University of Western Ontario, and while a student there published her first short story (1950), but she was unable to complete her English degree due to lack of money. In 1951, she married James Munro and moved to British Columbia, where she lived for the next 20 years (and where she raised three daughters). In 1963, the couple opened up a successful (and still running) bookstore in Victoria, Munro's Books, where Munro worked until she and her husband separated in 1972. Munro's first collection of short stories, *Dance of the Happy Shades* (1968), won a Governor General's Award and established her characteristic style. Since the 1960s, Munro's reputation has grown immeasurably, and in recent years has inspired a biography by Robert Thacker, *Alice Munro: Writing Her Lives* (2005), and a memoir by her eldest daughter, Sheila Munro, entitled *Lives of Mothers and Daughters: Growing Up with Alice Munro* (2002).

Munro started writing during her teenage years, a fact that informs her interest in writing sequential stories in the genre of the *Künstlerroman,* a form that delineates the growth from youth into adulthood of a central artist-protagonist. This is true in her widely read collection of linked short stories, *Lives of Girls and Women* (1971), which traces the experiences of Del Jordan, who grows up in the fictional town of Jubilee; the story is narrated by Del, who has become a writer in later life. *Who Do You Think You Are?* (1978) is similar in form but charts the life of its protagonist, Rose, from her childhood in Hanratty well into her adult years and career as an actress, delineating Rose's desperate quest to escape the poverty of her

childhood and the social embarrassment that accompanied it.

Munro continued to publish story collections into the 1980s and '90s, including *The Moons of Jupiter* (1982), *The Progress of Love* (1986), *Friend of My Youth* (1990), *Open Secrets* (1994), and *The Love of a Good Woman* (1998). Many of these stories deal with circumstances associated with middle age, including divorce, death, and parent-child conflicts. In other recent collections, such as *Hateship, Friendship, Courtship, Loveship, Marriage* (2001) and *Runaway* (2004), Munro shifted her focus to the travails of later life, of memory, of women alone, and of the elderly. Munro's work, in short, covers the range and depth of human experience: from disappointment to deception, bigotry to naiveté, manipulation to betrayal, self-importance to self-sacrifice.

In some of her stories, as well as in her 2006 work *The View from Castle Rock,* Munro has turned to the pioneering history of Ontario as a way of exploring historical links between present and past, a metafictional approach that is evident in such stories as "Meneseteung" and "A Wilderness Station." In the former story from *Friend of My Youth,* Munro's speculative biography of the fictive "poetess" Almeda Joynt Roth allows her to explore nineteenth-century notions of decorum, social propriety, women's writing, sexuality, and gender expectations amidst the "documentary" evidence of the poet's milieu and what are presumably samples of her sentimental poetry that form the epigraphs to the six sections of the story. When Almeda refuses Jarvis's offer of a walk to church, Munro asks us to consider the limited realm of nineteenth-century female agency against the sinister *"plop, plup"* of grape jelly.

While much of her work has some autobiographical elements, including *The View from Castle Rock,* which contains segments that are loosely based on her ancestors' history over several centuries, Munro has taken issue with the "autobiography" question as grossly over-simplifying in relation to her work. In her 1982 essay about her fiction writing, "What Is Real?," Munro responds to questions about the distinction between reality and fiction and explains how she uses kernels of reality to create the "feeling" of her stories' worlds. She describes the structure of her stories as a house within which the reader is subjected to a certain "feeling." In the centre is "the black room . . . with all other rooms leading to and away from it." The essay is fascinating for its account, not of Munro's technical skills, which are considerable, but of something far more powerful: the deeply intuitive nature of her approach to writing.

Meneseteung

I

Columbine, bloodroot,
And wild bergamot,
Gathering armfuls,
Giddily we go.

Offerings the book is called. Gold lettering on a dull-blue cover. The author's full name underneath: Almeda Joynt Roth. The local paper, the *Vidette*,[1] referred to her as "our poetess." There seems to be a mixture of respect and contempt, both for her calling and for her sex—or for their predictable conjuncture. In the front of the book is a photograph, with the photographer's name in one corner, and the date: 1865. The book was published later, in 1873.

The poetess has a long face; a rather long nose; full, sombre dark eyes, which seem ready to roll down her cheeks like giant tears; a lot of dark hair gathered around her face in droopy rolls and curtains. A streak of gray hair plain to see, although she is, in this picture, only twenty-five. Not a pretty girl but the sort of woman who may age well, who probably won't get fat. She wears a tucked and braid-trimmed dark dress or jacket, with a lacy, floppy arrangement of white material—frills or a bow—filling the deep V at the neck. She also wears a hat, which might be made of velvet, in a dark color to match the dress. It's the untrimmed, shapeless hat, something like a soft beret, that makes me see artistic intentions, or at least a shy and stubborn eccentricity, in this young woman, whose long neck and forward-inclining head indicate as well that she is tall and slender and somewhat awkward. From the waist up, she looks like a young nobleman of another century. But perhaps it was the fashion.

"In 1854," she writes in the preface to her book, "my father brought us—my mother, my sister Catherine, my brother William, and me—to the wilds of Canada

[1] Munro may be drawing on the short-lived Wingham *Vidette* (1883–85) as an inspiration for a typical small-town Ontario publication in the late nineteenth century.

West (as it then was).[2] My father was a harness-maker by trade, but a cultivated man who could quote by heart from the Bible, Shakespeare, and the writings of Edmund Burke.[3] He prospered in this newly opened land and was able to set up a harness and leather-goods store, and after a year to build the comfortable house in which I live (alone) today. I was fourteen years old, the eldest of the children, when we came into this country from Kingston, a town whose handsome streets I have not seen again but often remember. My sister was eleven and my brother nine. The third summer that we lived here, my brother and sister were taken ill of a prevalent fever and died within a few days of each other. My dear mother did not regain her spirits after this blow to our family. Her health declined, and after another three years she died. I then became housekeeper to my father and was happy to make his home for twelve years, until he died suddenly one morning at his shop.

"From my earliest years I have delighted in verse and I have occupied myself—and sometimes allayed my griefs, which have been no more, I know, than any sojourner on earth must encounter—with many floundering efforts at its composition. My fingers, indeed, were always too clumsy for crochetwork, and those dazzling productions of embroidery which one sees often today—the overflowing fruit and flower baskets, the little Dutch boys, the bonneted maidens with their watering cans—have likewise proved to be beyond my skill. So I offer instead, as the product of my leisure hours, these rude posies, these ballads, couplets, reflections."

Titles of some of the poems: "Children at Their Games," "The Gypsy Fair," "A Visit to My Family," "Angels in the Snow," "Champlain at the Mouth of the Meneseteung," "The Passing of the Old Forest," and "A Garden Medley." There are other, shorter poems, about birds and wildflowers and snowstorms. There is some comically intentioned doggerel about what people are thinking about as they listen to the sermon in church.

"Children at Their Games": The writer, a child, is playing with her brother and sister—one of those games in which children on different sides try to entice and catch each other. She plays on in the deepening twilight, until she realizes that she is alone, and much older. Still she hears the (ghostly) voices of her brother and sister calling. *Come over, come over, let Meda come over.*[4] (Perhaps Almeda was called Meda in the family, or perhaps she shortened her name to fit the poem.)

"The Gypsy Fair": The Gypsies have an encampment near the town, a "fair," where they sell cloth and trinkets, and the writer as a child is afraid that she may

[2] The region now known as Ontario. From 1791 to 1841 it was called Upper Canada; from 1841 to 1867 (Confederation) it was called Canada West.

[3] Edmund Burke (1729–1797), British author and politician. He was a staunch opponent of the French Revolution but was committed to the emancipation of the American colonies (as well as reform in Ireland and India). Burke is also famous for his philosophical treatise on the sublime and the beautiful.

[4] Allusion to the children's game of Red Rover or British Bulldog, in which one team links hands and summons a person from the other team with the chant, "Red Rover, Red Rover, we call [name] over!" If the runner is unable to break through their line, he/she must join ranks with the opposing team.

be stolen by them, taken away from her family. Instead, her family has been taken away from her, stolen by Gypsies she can't locate or bargain with.

"A Visit to My Family": A visit to the cemetery, a one-sided conversation.

"Angels in the Snow": The writer once taught her brother and sister to make "angels" by lying down in the snow and moving their arms to create wing shapes. Her brother always jumped up carelessly, leaving an angel with a crippled wing. Will this be made perfect in Heaven, or will he be flying with his own makeshift, in circles?

"Champlain at the Mouth of the Meneseteung": This poem celebrates the popular, untrue belief that the explorer sailed down the eastern shore of Lake Huron and landed at the mouth of the major river.

"The Passing of the Old Forest": A list of all the trees—their names, appearance, and uses—that were cut down in the original forest, with a general description of the bears, wolves, eagles, deer, waterfowl.

"A Garden Medley": Perhaps planned as a companion to the forest poem. Catalogue of plants brought from European countries, with bits of history and legend attached, and final Canadianness resulting from this mixture.

The poems are written in quatrains or couplets. There are a couple of attempts at sonnets, but mostly the rhyme scheme is simple—a b a b or a b c b. The rhyme used is what was once called "masculine" ("shore"/ "before"), though once in a while it is "feminine" ("quiver"/ "river"). Are those terms familiar anymore? No poem is unrhymed.

II

> White roses cold as snow
> Bloom where those "angels" lie.
> Do they but rest below
> Or, in God's wonder, fly?

In 1879, Almeda Roth was still living in the house at the corner of Pearl and Dufferin streets, the house her father had built for his family. The house is there today; the manager of the liquor store lives in it. It's covered with aluminum siding; a closed-in porch has replaced the veranda. The woodshed, the fence, the gates, the privy, the barn—all these are gone. A photograph taken in the eighteen-eighties shows them all in place. The house and fence look a little shabby, in need of paint, but perhaps that is just because of the bleached-out look of the brownish photograph. The lace-curtained windows look like white eyes. No big shade tree is in sight, and, in fact, the tall elms that overshadowed the town until the nineteen-fifties, as well as the maples that shade it now, are skinny young trees with rough fences around them to protect them from the cows. Without the shelter of those trees, there is a great exposure—back yards, clotheslines, woodpiles, patchy sheds and barns and privies—all bare, exposed, provisional-looking. Few houses would have anything like a lawn, just a patch of plantains and anthills and raked dirt. Perhaps petunias growing on top of a stump, in a round box. Only the main street is gravelled; the other streets are dirt roads, muddy or dusty according to season. Yards must be fenced to keep animals out. Cows are tethered in vacant lots or pastured in back yards, but sometimes they get loose. Pigs get loose, too, and dogs roam free or nap in a lordly way on the boardwalks. The town has taken root, it's not going to vanish, yet it still has some of the look of an encampment. And, like an encampment, it's busy all the time—full of people, who, within the town, usually walk wherever they're going; full of animals, which leave horse buns, cow pats, dog turds that ladies have to hitch up their skirts for; full of the noise of building and of drivers shouting at their horses and of the trains that come in several times a day.

I read about that life in the *Vidette*.

The population is younger than it is now, than it will ever be again. People past fifty usually don't come to a raw, new place. There are quite a few people in the cemetery already, but most of them died young, in accidents or childbirth or epidemics. It's youth that's in evidence in town. Children—boys—rove through the streets in gangs. School is compulsory for only four months a year, and there are lots of occasional jobs that even a child of eight or nine can do—pulling flax, holding horses, delivering groceries, sweeping the boardwalk in front of stores. A good deal of time they spend looking for adventures. One day they follow an old woman, a drunk nicknamed Queen Aggie. They get her into a wheelbarrow and trundle her all over town, then dump her into a ditch to sober her up. They also spend a lot of time around the railway station. They jump on shunting cars and dart between them and dare each other to take chances, which once in a while result in their getting maimed or killed. And they keep an eye out for any strangers coming into town. They follow them, offer to carry their bags, and direct them (for a five-cent piece) to a hotel. Strangers who don't look so prosperous are taunted and tormented. Speculation surrounds all of them—it's like a cloud of flies. Are they coming to town to start up a new business, to persuade people to invest in some scheme, to sell cures or gimmicks, to preach on the street corners? All these things are possible any day of the week. Be on your guard, the *Vidette* tells people. These are times of opportunity and danger. Tramps, confidence men, hucksters, shysters, plain thieves are travelling the roads, and particularly the railroads. Thefts are announced: money invested and never seen again, a pair of trousers taken from the clothesline, wood from the woodpile, eggs from the henhouse. Such incidents increase in the hot weather.

Hot weather brings accidents, too. More horses run wild then, upsetting buggies. Hands caught in the wringer while doing the washing, a man lopped in two at the sawmill, a leaping boy killed in a fall of lumber at the lumberyard. Nobody sleeps well. Babies wither with summer complaint, and fat people can't catch their breath. Bodies must be buried in a hurry. One day a man goes through the streets ringing a cowbell and calling, "Repent! Repent!" It's not a stranger this time, it's a young man who works at the butcher shop. Take him home, wrap him in cold wet cloths, give him some nerve medicine, keep him in bed, pray for his wits. If he doesn't recover, he must go to the asylum.

Almeda Roth's house faces on Dufferin Street, which is a street of considerable respectability. On this street, merchants, a mill owner, an operator of salt wells have their houses. But Pearl Street, which her back windows overlook and her back gate opens onto, is another story. Workmen's houses are adjacent to hers. Small but decent row houses—that is all right. Things deteriorate toward the end of the block, and the next, last one becomes dismal. Nobody but the poorest people, the unrespectable and undeserving poor, would live there at the edge of a boghole (drained since then), called the Pearl Street Swamp. Bushy and luxuriant weeds grow there, makeshift shacks have been put up, there are piles of refuse and debris and crowds of runty children, slops are flung from doorways. The town tries to compel these people to build privies, but they would just as soon go in the bushes. If a gang of boys goes down there in search of adventure, it's likely they'll get more than they bargained for. It is said that even the town constable won't go down Pearl Street on a Saturday night. Almeda Roth has never walked past the row housing. In one of those houses lives the young girl Annie, who helps her with her housecleaning. That young girl herself, being a decent girl, has never walked down to the last block or the swamp. No decent woman ever would.

But that same swamp, lying to the east of Almeda Roth's house, presents a fine sight at dawn. Almeda sleeps at the back of the house. She keeps to the same bedroom she once shared with her sister Catherine—she would not think of moving to the large front bedroom, where her mother used to lie in bed all day, and which was later the solitary domain of her father. From her window she can see the sun rising, the swamp mist filling with light, the bulky, nearest trees floating against that mist and the trees behind turning transparent. Swamp oaks, soft maples, tamarack, bitternut.

III

Here where the river meets the inland sea,
Spreading her blue skirts from the solemn wood,
I think of birds and beasts and vanished men,
Whose pointed dwellings on these pale sands stood.

One of the strangers who arrived at the railway station a few years ago was Jarvis Poulter, who now occupies the next house to Almeda Roth's—separated from hers by a vacant lot, which he has bought, on Dufferin Street. The house is plainer than the Roth house and has no fruit trees or flowers planted around it. It is understood that this is a natural result of Jarvis Poulter's being a widower and living alone. A man may keep his house decent, but he will never—if he is a proper man—do much to decorate it. Marriage forces him to live with more ornament as well as sentiment, and it protects him, also, from the extremities of his own nature—from a frigid parsimony or a luxuriant sloth, from squalor, and from excessive sleeping or reading, drinking, smoking, or freethinking.

In the interests of economy, it is believed, a certain estimable gentleman of our town persists in fetching water from the public tap and supplementing his fuel supply by picking up the loose coal along the railway track. Does he think to repay the town or the railway company with a supply of free salt?

This is the *Vidette*, full of shy jokes, innuendo, plain accusation that no newspaper would get away with today. It's Jarvis Poulter they're talking about—though in other passages he is spoken of with great respect, as a civil magistrate, an employer, a churchman. He is close, that's all. An eccentric, to a degree. All of which may be a result of his single condition, his widower's life. Even carrying his water from the town tap and filling his coal pail along the railway track. This is a decent citizen, prosperous: a tall—slightly paunchy?—man in a dark suit with polished boots. A beard? Black hair streaked with gray. A severe and self-possessed air, and a large pale wart among the bushy hairs of one eyebrow? People talk about a young, pretty, beloved wife, dead in childbirth or some horrible accident, like a house fire or a railway disaster. There is no ground for this, but it adds interest. All he has told them is that his wife is dead.

He came to this part of the country looking for oil. The first oil well in the world was sunk in Lambton County,[5] south of here, in the eighteen-fifties. Drilling for oil, Jarvis Poulter discovered salt. He set to work to make the most of that. When he walks home from church with Almeda Roth, he tells her about his salt wells. They are twelve hundred feet deep. Heated water is pumped down into them, and that dissolves the salt. Then the brine is pumped to the surface. It is poured into great evaporator pans over slow, steady fires, so that the water is steamed off and the pure, excellent salt remains. A commodity for which the demand will never fail.

"The salt of the earth," Almeda says.

"Yes," he says, frowning. He may think this disrespectful. She did not intend it so. He speaks of competitors in other towns who are following his lead and trying to hog the market. Fortunately, their wells are not drilled so deep, or their evaporating is not done so efficiently. There is salt everywhere under this land, but it is not so easy to come by as some people think.

Does this not mean, Almeda says, that there was once a great sea?

Very likely, Jarvis Poulter says. Very likely. He goes on to tell her about other enterprises of his—a brickyard, a limekiln. And he explains to her how this operates, and where the good clay is found. He also owns two farms, whose woodlots supply the fuel for his operations.

Among the couples strolling home from church on a recent, sunny Sabbath morning we noted a certain salty gentleman and literary lady, not perhaps in their first youth but by no means blighted by the frosts of age. May we surmise?

This kind of thing pops up in the *Vidette* all the time.

May they surmise, and is this courting? Almeda Roth has a bit of money, which her father left her, and she has her house. She is not too old to have a couple of children. She is a good enough housekeeper, with the tendency toward fancy iced cakes and decorated tarts that is seen fairly often in old maids. (Honorable mention at the Fall Fair.) There is nothing wrong with her looks, and naturally she is in better shape than most married women of her age, not having been loaded down with work and

[5] A county in Ontario on the southwestern shore of Lake Huron.

children. But why was she passed over in her earlier, more marriageable years, in a place that needs women to be partnered and fruitful? She was a rather gloomy girl—that may have been the trouble. The deaths of her brother and sister, and then of her mother, who lost her reason, in fact, a year before she died, and lay in her bed talking nonsense—those weighed on her, so she was not lively company. And all that reading and poetry—it seemed more of a drawback, a barrier, an obsession, in the young girl than in the middle-aged woman, who needed something, after all, to fill her time. Anyway, it's five years since her book was published, so perhaps she has got over that. Perhaps it was the proud, bookish father encouraging her?

Everyone takes it for granted that Almeda Roth is thinking of Jarvis Poulter as a husband and would say yes if he asked her. And she is thinking of him. She doesn't want to get her hopes up too much, she doesn't want to make a fool of herself. She would like a signal. If he attended church on Sunday evenings, there would be a chance, during some months of the year, to walk home after dark. He would carry a lantern. (There is as yet no street lighting in town.) He would swing the lantern to light the way in front of the lady's feet and observe their narrow and delicate shape. He might catch her arm as they step off the board-walk. But he does not go to church at night.

Nor does he call for her, and walk with her *to* church on Sunday mornings. That would be a declaration. He walks her home, past his gate as far as hers; he lifts his hat then and leaves her. She does not invite him to come in—a woman living alone could never do such a thing. As soon as a man and woman of almost any age are alone together within four walls, it is assumed that anything may happen. Spontaneous combustion, instant fornication, an attack of passion. Brute instinct, triumph of the senses. What possibilities men and women must see in each other to infer such dangers. Or, believing in the dangers, how often they must think about the possibilities.

When they walk side by side, she can smell his shaving soap, the barber's oil, his pipe tobacco, the wool and linen and leather smell of his manly clothes. The correct, orderly, heavy clothes are like those she used to brush and starch and iron for her father. She misses that job—her father's appreciation, his dark, kind authority. Jarvis Poulter's garments, his smell, his movements all cause the skin on the side of her body next to him to tingle hopefully, and a meek shiver raises the hairs on her arms. Is this to be taken as a sign of love? She thinks of him coming into her—*their*—bedroom in his long underwear and his hat. She knows this outfit is ridiculous, but in her mind he does not look so; he has the solemn effrontery of a figure in a dream. He comes into the room and lies down on the bed beside her, preparing to take her in his arms. Surely he removes his hat? She doesn't know, for at this point a fit of welcome and submission overtakes her, a buried gasp. He would be her husband.

One thing she has noticed about married women, and that is how many of them have to go about creating their husbands. They have to start ascribing preferences, opinions, dictatorial ways. Oh, yes, they say, my husband is very par-ticular. He won't touch turnips. He won't eat fried meat. (Or he will only eat fried meat.) He likes me to wear blue (brown) all the time. He can't stand organ music.

He hates to see a woman go out bareheaded. He would kill me if I took one puff of tobacco. This way, bewildered, sidelong-looking men are made over, made into husbands, heads of households. Almeda Roth cannot imagine herself doing that. She wants a man who doesn't have to be made, who is firm already and determined and mysterious to her. She does not look for companionship. Men—except for her father—seem to her deprived in some way, incurious. No doubt that is necessary, so that they will do what they have to do. Would she herself, knowing that there was salt in the earth, discover how to get it out and sell it? Not likely. She would be thinking about the ancient sea. That kind of speculation is what Jarvis Poulter has, quite properly, no time for.

Instead of calling for her and walking her to church, Jarvis Poulter might make another, more venturesome declaration. He could hire a horse and take her for a drive out to the country. If he did this, she would be both glad and sorry. Glad to be beside him, driven by him, receiving this attention from him in front of the world. And sorry to have the countryside removed for her—filmed over, in a way, by his talk and preoccupations. The countryside that she has written about in her poems actually takes diligence and determination to see. Some things must be disregarded. Manure piles, of course, and boggy fields full of high, charred stumps, and great heaps of brush waiting for a good day for burning. The meandering creeks have been straightened, turned into ditches with high, muddy banks. Some of the crop fields and pasture fields are fenced with big, clumsy uprooted stumps; others are held in a crude stitchery of rail fences. The trees have all been cleared back to the woodlots. And the woodlots are all second growth. No trees along the roads or lanes or around the farmhouses, except a few that are newly planted, young and weedy-looking. Clusters of log barns—the grand barns that are to dominate the countryside for the next hundred years are just beginning to be built—and mean-looking log houses, and every four or five miles a ragged little settlement with a church and school and store and a blacksmith shop. A raw countryside just wrenched from the forest, but swarming with people. Every hundred acres is a farm, every farm has a family, most families have ten or twelve children. (This is the country that will send out wave after wave of settlers—it's already starting to send them—to northern Ontario and the West.) It's true that you can gather wildflowers in spring in the wood-lots, but you'd have to walk through herds of horned cows to get to them.

IV

The Gypsies have departed.
Their camping-ground is bare.
Oh, boldly would I bargain now
At the Gypsy Fair.

Almeda suffers a good deal from sleeplessness, and the doctor has given her bromides and nerve medicine. She takes the bromides, but the drops gave her dreams that were too vivid and disturbing, so she has put the bottle by for an emergency. She told the doctor her eyeballs felt dry, like hot glass, and her joints ached. Don't read so much, he said, don't study; get yourself good and tired out with housework, take exercise. He believes that her troubles would clear up if she got married. He believes this in spite of the fact that most of his nerve medicine is prescribed for married women.

So Almeda cleans house and helps clean the church, she lends a hand to friends who are wallpapering or getting ready for a wedding, she bakes one of her famous cakes for the Sunday-school picnic. On a hot Saturday in August, she decides to make some grape jelly. Little jars of grape jelly will make fine Christmas presents, or offerings to the sick. But she started late in the day and the jelly is not made by nightfall. In fact, the hot pulp has just been dumped into the cheesecloth bag to strain out the juice. Almeda drinks some tea and eats a slice of cake with butter (a childish indulgence of hers), and that's all she wants for supper. She washes her hair at the sink and sponges off her body to be clean for Sunday. She doesn't light a lamp. She lies down on the bed with the window wide open and a sheet just up to her waist, and she does feel wonderfully tired. She can even feel a little breeze.

When she wakes up, the night seems fiery hot and full of threats. She lies sweating on her bed, and she has the impression that the noises she hears are knives and saws and axes—all angry implements chopping and jabbing and boring within her head. But it isn't true. As she comes further awake, she recognizes the sounds that she has heard sometimes before—the fracas of a summer Saturday night on Pearl Street. Usually the noise centers on a fight. People are drunk, there is a lot of protest and encouragement concerning the fight, somebody will scream, "Murder!" Once, there was a murder. But it didn't happen in a fight. An old man was stabbed to death in his shack, perhaps for a few dollars he kept in the mattress.

She gets out of bed and goes to the window. The night sky is clear, with no moon and with bright stars. Pegasus hangs straight ahead, over the swamp. Her father taught her that constellation—automatically, she counts its stars. Now she can make out distinct voices, individual contributions to the row. Some people, like herself, have evidently been wakened from sleep. "Shut up!" they are yelling. "Shut up that caterwauling or I'm going to come down and tan the arse off yez!"

But nobody shuts up. It's as if there were a ball of fire rolling up Pearl Street, shooting off sparks—only the fire is noise; it's yells and laughter and shrieks and curses, and the sparks are voices that shoot off alone. Two voices gradually distinguish themselves—a rising and falling howling cry and a steady throbbing, low-pitched stream of abuse that contains all those words which Almeda associates with danger and depravity and foul smells and disgusting sights. Someone—the person crying out, "Kill me! Kill me now!"—is being beaten. A woman is being beaten. She keeps crying, "Kill me! Kill me!" and sometimes her mouth seems choked with blood. Yet there is something taunting and triumphant about her cry. There is something theatrical about it. And the people around are calling out, "Stop it! Stop that!" or "Kill her! Kill her!" in a frenzy, as if at the theatre or a sporting match or a prizefight. Yes, thinks Almeda, she has noticed that before—it is always partly a charade with these people; there is a clumsy sort of parody, an exaggeration, a missed connection. As if anything they did—even a murder—might be something they didn't quite believe but were powerless to stop.

Now there is the sound of something thrown—a chair, a plank?—and of a woodpile or part of a fence giving way. A lot of newly surprised cries, the sound of running, people getting out of the way, and the commotion has come much closer. Almeda can see a figure in a light dress, bent over and running. That will be the woman. She has got hold of something like a stick of wood or a shingle, and she turns and flings it at the darker figure running after her.

"Ah, go get her!" the voices cry. "Go baste her one!"

Many fall back now; just the two figures come on and grapple, and break loose again, and finally fall down against Almeda's fence. The sound they make becomes very confused—gagging, vomiting, grunting, pounding. Then a long, vibrating, choking sound of pain and self-abasement, self-abandonment, which could come from either or both of them.

Almeda has backed away from the window and sat down on the bed. Is that the sound of murder she has heard? What is to be done, what is she to do? She must light a lantern, she must go downstairs and light a lantern—she must go out into the yard, she must go downstairs. Into the yard. The lantern. She falls over on her bed and pulls the pillow to her face. In a minute. The stairs, the lantern. She sees herself already down there, in the back hall, drawing the bolt of the back door. She falls asleep.

She wakes, startled, in the early light. She thinks there is a big crow sitting on her windowsill, talking in a disapproving but unsurprised way about the events of the night before. "Wake up and move the wheelbarrow!" it says to her, scolding, and she understands that it means something else by "wheelbarrow"—something foul and sorrowful. Then she is awake and sees that there is no such bird. She gets up at once and looks out the window.

Down against her fence there is a pale lump pressed—a body.

Wheelbarrow.

She puts a wrapper over her nightdress and goes downstairs. The front rooms are still shadowy, the blinds down in the kitchen. Something goes *plop, plup,* in a leisurely, censorious way, reminding her of the conversation of the crow. It's just the grape juice, straining overnight. She pulls the bolt and goes out the back door. Spiders have draped their webs over the doorway in the night, and the hollyhocks are drooping, heavy with dew. By the fence, she parts the sticky hollyhocks and looks down and she can see.

A woman's body heaped up there, turned on her side with her face squashed down into the earth. Almeda can't see her face. But there is a bare breast let loose, brown nipple pulled long like a cow's teat, and a bare haunch and leg, the haunch showing a bruise as big as a sunflower. The unbruised skin is grayish, like a plucked, raw drumstick. Some kind of nightgown or all-purpose dress she has on. Smelling of vomit. Urine, drink, vomit.

Barefoot, in her nightgown and flimsy wrapper, Almeda runs away. She runs around the side of her house between the apple trees and the veranda; she opens the front gate and flees down Dufferin Street to Jarvis Poulter's house, which is the nearest to hers. She slaps the flat of her hand many times against the door.

"There is the body of a woman," she says when Jarvis Poulter appears at last. He is in his dark trousers, held up with braces, and his shirt is half unbuttoned, his face unshaven, his hair standing up on his head. "Mr. Poulter, excuse me. A body of a woman. At my back gate."

He looks at her fiercely. "Is she dead?"

His breath is dank, his face creased, his eyes bloodshot.

"Yes. I think murdered," says Almeda. She can see a little of his cheerless front hall. His hat on a chair. "In the night I woke up. I heard a racket down on Pearl Street," she says, struggling to keep her voice low and sensible. "I could hear this—pair. I could hear a man and a woman fighting."

He picks up his hat and puts it on his head. He closes and locks the front door, and puts the key in his pocket. They walk along the boardwalk and she sees that she is in her bare feet. She holds back what she feels a need to say next— that she is responsible, she could have run out with a lantern, she could have screamed (but who needed more screams?), she could have beat the man off. She could have run for help then, not now.

They turn down Pearl Street, instead of entering the Roth yard. Of course the body is still there. Hunched up, half bare, the same as before.

Jarvis Poulter doesn't hurry or halt. He walks straight over to the body and looks down at it, nudges the leg with the toe of his boot, just as you'd nudge a dog or a sow.

"You," he says, not too loudly but firmly, and nudges again.

Almeda tastes bile at the back of her throat.

"Alive," says Jarvis Poulter, and the woman confirms this. She stirs, she grunts weakly.

Almeda says, "I will get the doctor." If she had touched the woman, if she had forced herself to touch her, she would not have made such a mistake.

"Wait," says Jarvis Poulter. "Wait. Let's see if she can get up."

"Get up, now," he says to the woman. "Come on. Up, now. Up."

Now a startling thing happens. The body heaves itself onto all fours, the head is lifted—the hair all matted with blood and vomit—and the woman begins to bang this head, hard and rhythmically, against Almeda Roth's picket fence. As she bangs her head, she finds her voice and lets out an openmouthed yowl, full of strength and what sounds like an anguished pleasure.

"Far from dead," says Jarvis Poulter. "And I wouldn't bother the doctor."

"There's blood," says Almeda as the woman turns her smeared face.

"From her nose," he says. "Not fresh." He bends down and catches the horrid hair close to the scalp to stop the head-banging.

"You stop that, now," he says. "Stop it. Gwan home, now. Gwan home, where you belong." The sound coming out of the woman's mouth has stopped. He shakes her head slightly, warning her, before he lets go of her hair. "Gwan home!"

Released, the woman lunges forward, pulls herself to her feet. She can walk. She weaves and stumbles down the street, making intermittent, cautious noises of protest. Jarvis Poulter watches her for a moment to make sure that she's on her way. Then he finds a large burdock leaf, on which he wipes his hand. He says, "There goes your dead body!"

The back gate being locked, they walk around to the front. The front gate stands open. Almeda still feels sick. Her abdomen is bloated; she is hot and dizzy.

"The front door is locked," she says faintly. "I came out by the kitchen." If only he would leave her, she could go straight to the privy. But he follows. He follows her as far as the back door and into the back hall. He speaks to her in a tone of harsh joviality that she has never before heard from him. "No need for alarm," he says. "It's only the consequences of drink. A lady oughtn't to be living alone so close to a bad neighborhood." He takes hold of her arm just above the elbow. She can't open her mouth to speak to him, to say thank you. If she opened her mouth, she would retch.

What Jarvis Poulter feels for Almeda Roth at this moment is just what he has not felt during all those circumspect walks and all his own solitary calculations of her probable worth, undoubted respectability, adequate comeliness. He has not been able to imagine her as a wife. Now that is possible. He is sufficiently stirred by her loosened hair—prematurely gray but thick and soft—her flushed face, her light clothing, which nobody but a husband should see. And by her indiscretion, her agitation, her foolishness, her need?

"I will call on you later," he says to her. "I will walk with you to church."

At the corner of Pearl and Dufferin streets last Sunday morning there was discovered, by a lady resident there, the body of a certain woman of Pearl Street, thought to be dead but only, as it turned out, dead drunk. She was roused from her heavenly—or otherwise— stupor by the firm persuasion of Mr. Poulter, a neighbour and a Civil Magistrate, who had been summoned by the lady resident. Incidents of this sort, unseemly, troublesome, and disgraceful to our town, have of late become all too common.

V

> *I sit at the bottom of sleep,*
> *As on the floor of the sea.*
> *And fanciful Citizens of the Deep*
> *Are graciously greeting me.*

As soon as Jarvis Poulter has gone and she has heard her front gate close, Almeda rushes to the privy. Her relief is not complete, however, and she realizes that the pain and fullness in her lower body come from an accumulation of menstrual blood that has not yet started to flow. She closes and locks the back door. Then, remembering Jarvis Poulter's words about church, she writes on a piece of paper, "I am not well, and wish to rest today." She sticks this firmly into the outside frame of the little window in the front door. She locks that door, too. She is trembling, as if from a great shock or danger. But she builds a fire, so that she can make tea. She boils water, measures the tea leaves, makes a large pot of tea, whose steam and smell sicken her further. She pours out a cup while the tea is still quite weak and adds to it several dark drops of nerve medicine. She sits to drink it without raising the kitchen blind. There, in the middle of the floor, is the cheesecloth bag hanging on its broom handle between the two chairbacks. The grape pulp and juice has stained the swollen cloth a dark purple. *Plop, plup,* into the basin beneath. She can't sit and look at such a thing. She takes her cup, the teapot, and the bottle of medicine into the dining room.

She is still sitting there when the horses start to go by on the way to church, stirring up clouds of dust. The roads will be getting hot as ashes. She is there when the gate is opened and a man's confident steps sound on her veranda. Her hearing is so sharp she seems to hear the paper taken out of the frame and unfolded—she can almost hear him reading it, hear the words in his mind. Then the footsteps go the other way, down the steps. The gate closes. An image comes to her of tombstones—it makes her laugh. Tombstones are marching down the street on their little booted feet, their long bodies inclined forward, their expressions preoccupied and severe. The church bells are ringing.

Then the clock in the hall strikes twelve and an hour has passed.

The house is getting hot. She drinks more tea and adds more medicine. She knows that the medicine is affecting her. It is responsible for her extraordinary languor, her perfect immobility, her unresisting surrender to her surroundings. That is all right. It seems necessary.

Her surroundings—some of her surroundings—in the dining room are these: walls covered with dark-green garlanded wallpaper, lace curtains and mulberry velvet curtains on the windows, a table with a crocheted cloth and a bowl of wax fruit, a pinkish-gray carpet with nosegays of blue and pink roses, a sideboard spread with embroidered runners and holding various patterned plates and jugs and the silver tea things. A lot of things to watch. For every one of these patterns, decorations seems charged with life, ready to move and flow and alter. Or possibly to explode. Almeda Roth's occupation throughout the day is to keep an eye on them. Not to prevent their alteration so much as to catch them at it—to understand it, to be a part of it. So much is going on in this room that there is no need to leave it. There is not even the thought of leaving it.

Of course, Almeda in her observations cannot escape words. She may think she can, but she can't. Soon this glowing and swelling begins to suggest words— not specific words but a flow of words somewhere, just about ready to make themselves known to her. Poems, even. Yes, again, poems. Or one poem. Isn't that the idea—one very great poem that will contain everything and, oh, that will make all the other poems, the poems she has written, inconsequential, mere trial and error, mere rags? Stars and flowers and birds and trees and angels in the snow and dead children at twilight—that is not the half of it. You have to get in the obscene racket on Pearl Street and the polished toe of Jarvis Poulter's boot and the plucked-chicken haunch with its blue-black flower. Almeda is a long way now from human sympathies or fears or cozy household considerations. She doesn't think about what could be done for that woman or about keeping Jarvis Poulter's dinner warm and hanging his long underwear on the line. The basin of grape juice has overflowed and is running over her kitchen floor, staining the boards of the floor, and the stain will never come out.

She has to think of so many things at once—Champlain and the naked Indians and the salt deep in the earth, but as well as the salt the money, the money-making intent brewing forever in heads like Jarvis Poulter's. Also the brutal storms of winter and the clumsy and benighted deeds on Pearl Street. The changes of climate are often violent, and if you think about it there is no peace even in the stars. All this can be borne only if it is channelled into a poem, and the word "channelled" is appropriate, because the name of the poem will be—it *is*—"The Meneseteung." The name of the poem is the name of the river.[6] No, in fact it is the river, the Meneseteung, that is the poem—with its deep holes and rapids and blissful pools under the summer trees and its grinding blocks of ice thrown up at the end of winter and its desolating spring floods. Almeda looks deep, deep into the river of her mind and into the tablecloth, and she sees the crocheted roses floating. They look bunchy and foolish, her mother's crocheted roses—they don't look much like real flowers. But their effort, their floating independence, their pleasure in their silly selves do seem to her so admirable. A hopeful sign. *Meneseteung.*

She doesn't leave the room until dusk, when she goes out to the privy again and discovers that she is bleeding, her flow has started. She will have to get a towel, strap it on, bandage herself up. Never before, in health, has she passed a whole day in her nightdress. She doesn't feel any particular anxiety about this. On her way through the kitchen, she walks through the pool of grape juice. She knows that she will have to mop it up, but not yet, and she walks upstairs leaving purple footprints and smelling her escaping blood and the sweat of her body that has sat all day in the closed hot room.

No need for alarm.

For she hasn't thought that crocheted roses could float away or that tombstones could hurry down the street. She doesn't mistake that for reality, and neither does she mistake anything else for reality, and that is how she knows that she is sane.

VI

> *I dream of you by night,*
> *I visit you by day.*
> *Father, Mother,*
> *Sister, Brother,*
> *Have you no word to say?*

April 22, 1903. At her residence, on Tuesday last, between three and four o'clock in the afternoon, there passed away a lady of talent and refinement whose pen, in days gone by, enriched our local literature with a volume of sensitive, eloquent verse. It is a sad misfortune that in later years the mind of this fine person had become somewhat clouded

[6] In her essay "Everything Here Is Touchable and Mysterious" (1974), Munro recalls the river flowing by her home in Wingham as "a short river the Indians called the Menesetung [*sic*], and the first settlers, or surveyors of the Huron Tract, called the Maitland."

and her behaviour, in consequence, somewhat rash and unusual. Her attention to decorum and to the care and adornment of her person had suffered, to the degree that she had become, in the eyes of those unmindful of her former pride and daintiness, a familiar eccentric, or even, sadly, a figure of fun. But now all such lapses pass from memory and what is recalled is her excellent published verse, her labours in former days in the Sunday school, her dutiful care of her parents, her noble womanly nature, charitable concerns, and unfailing religious faith. Her last illness was of mercifully short duration. She caught cold, after having become thoroughly wet from a ramble in the Pearl Street bog. (It has been said that some urchins chased her into the water, and such is the boldness and cruelty of some of our youth, and their observed persecution of this lady, that the tale cannot be entirely discounted.) The cold developed into pneumonia, and she died, attended at the last by a former neighbour, Mrs. Bert (Annie) Friels, who witnessed her calm and faithful end.

January, 1904. One of the founders of our community, an early maker and shaker of this town, was abruptly removed from our midst on Monday morning last, whilst attending to his correspondence in the office of his company. Mr. Jarvis Poulter possessed a keen and lively commercial spirit, which was instrumental in the creation of not one but several local enterprises, bringing the benefits of industry, productivity, and employment to our town.

So the Vidette runs on, copious and assured. Hardly a death goes undescribed, or a life unevaluated.

I looked for Almeda Roth in the graveyard. I found the family stone. There was just one name on it—Roth. Then I noticed two flat stones in the ground, a distance of a few feet—six feet?—from the upright stone. One of these said "Papa," the other "Mama." Farther out from these I found two other flat stones, with the names William and Catherine on them. I had to clear away some overgrowing grass and dirt to see the full name of Catherine. No birth or death dates for anybody, nothing about being dearly beloved. It was a private sort of memorializing, not for the world. There were no roses, either—no sign of a rosebush. But perhaps it was taken out. The grounds keeper doesn't like such things; they are a nuisance to the lawnmower, and if there is nobody left to object he will pull them out.

I thought that Almeda must have been buried somewhere else. When this plot was bought—at the time of the two children's deaths—she would still have been expected to marry, and to lie finally beside her husband. They might not have left room for her here. Then I saw that the stones in the ground fanned out from the upright stone. First the two for the parents, then the two for the children, but these were placed in such a way that there was room for a third, to complete the fan. I paced out from "Catherine" the same number of steps that it took to get from "Catherine" to "William," and at this spot I began pulling grass and scrabbling in the dirt with my bare hands. Soon I felt the stone and knew that I was right. I worked away and got the whole stone clear and I read the name "Meda." There it was with the others, staring at the sky.

I made sure I had got to the edge of the stone. That was all the name there was—Meda. So it was true that she was called by that name in the family. Not just in the poem. Or perhaps she chose her name from the poem, to be written on her stone.

I thought that there wasn't anybody alive in the world but me who would know this, who would make the connection. And I would be the last person to do so. But perhaps this isn't so. People are curious. A few people are. They will be driven to find things out, even trivial things. They will put things together. You see them going around with notebooks, scraping the dirt off gravestones, reading microfilm, just in the hope of seeing this trickle in time, making a connection, rescuing one thing from the rubbish.

And they may get it wrong, after all. I may have got it wrong. I don't know if she ever took laudanum. Many ladies did. I don't know if she ever made grape jelly.

[1990]

ALDEN NOWLAN ■ (1933–1983)

Friend and fellow New Brunswick writer David Adams Richards describes Alden Nowlan as "a large, imposing, generous, self-deprecating, hard-drinking, chain-smoking, complex, irascible, irritating wonder of a man." Nowlan is one of the best-loved poets of Atlantic Canada, heralded for his distinctive blend of everyday speech and philosophical profundity. His colloquial and often self-ironizing poetry is marked by a vigorous interplay of earnestness and parody, tenderness and melancholy. Combining a colloquial style, rough persona, and compassionate assessment of human experience, together with his working-class background and erudite knowledge of world literature, Nowlan's approach is reminiscent of Al Purdy's. Born during the Depression in Nova Scotia (in a village so poor he called it Desolation Creek) to a teenaged mother, Nowlan was raised by his father and grandmother. His childhood was harsh, and he left school at grade five to work as a lumberman. As a writer he was largely self-taught, working as a night watchman in a saw mill, which afforded him time to satisfy his passion for literature. He discovered a library in Windsor, 32 kilometres away, and walked or hitchhiked there every Saturday. At the age of 19, he acquired a job as a reporter for the New Brunswick newspaper the *Hartland Observer* (on the basis of a letter of recommendation he had written himself), the first of many journalistic jobs, including a position as reporter and later editor of the Saint John *Telegraph-Journal.* Nowlan published a number of collections of poetry during the late 1950s and early '60s, including his first, *The Rose and the Puritan,* in 1958.

In 1967, he received the Governor General's Award for his poetry collection *Bread, Wine and Salt.* The following year, after the success of this collection, Nowlan was appointed writer-in-residence at the University of New Brunswick, Fredericton, a position he held until 1983. He attained the post because poets Fred Cogswell and A.J.M. Smith, along with UNB critic Desmond Pacey, had persuaded the premier of New Brunswick, Richard Hatfield, to agree to have the province sponsor

Nowlan as permanent writer-in-residence. Nowlan and his wife Claudine hosted boisterous literary gatherings at their home that included fellow New Brunswick writers David Adams Richards and Ray Fraser, English Department poets Robert Gibbs and Fred Cogswell, critics John Moss and David Arnason, and the singer Stompin' Tom Connors. On one of these occasions, Nowlan and Leo Ferrari, poet and philosophy professor at Saint Thomas University, founded the Flat Earth Society, an organization whose mandate was to refuse the acceptance of facts on blind faith and to defend "the veracity of sense experience." This perspective informs Nowlan's poetry of these years and is particularly evident in his poems "Ypres: 1915" and "What Colour Is Manitoba?," which juxtapose factual records beside the "truer charts" of personal experience. Gibbs, the editor of Nowlan's 1983 selected poems, *An Exchange of Gifts,* notes that the "simplicity and cadences of common speech [were] not for him a matter of fashion but of allowing his deepest and truest feelings and imaginings their way out." This is true of many of Nowlan's poetry collections from this period, including *The Mysterious Naked Man* (1969), *I'm a Stranger Here Myself* (1974), and *Smoked Glass* (1977), and a semi-autobiographical novel published in 1973, *Various Persons Named Kevin O'Brien.* Louis Dudek celebrates Nowlan's poems for their "sporadic symbolism drawn from reality." The power of many of his poems is derived from the edge of troubling ambiguity that underlies their seemingly easygoing surface, as in "The Mysterious Naked Man" and "The Broadcaster's Poem."

Nowlan had suffered from ill health earlier in his life when he had surgery for lymphatic and throat cancer; however, his death at the age of 50 was a shock. His celebration of life is delightfully captured in the concluding lines to his poem "In Praise of the Great Bull Walrus": "[H]ow unthinkable it would have been / to have missed all this / by not being born."

Warren Pryor

When every pencil meant a sacrifice
his parents boarded him at school in town,
slaving to free him from the stony fields,
the meagre acreage that bore them down.

They blushed with pride when, at his graduation,
they watched him picking up the slender scroll,
his passport from the years of brutal toil
and lonely patience in a barren hole.

When he went in the Bank their cups ran over.
They marvelled how he wore a milk-white shirt   10
work days and jeans on Sundays. He was saved
from their thistle-strewn farm and its red dirt.

And he said nothing. Hard and serious
like a young bear inside his teller's cage,

his axe-hewn hands upon the paper bills
aching with empty strength and throttled rage.

[1961]

The Genealogy of Morals[1]

Take any child dreaming of pickled bones
shelved in a coal-dark cellar understairs
(we are all children when we dream) the stones
red-black with blood from severed jugulars.

Child Francis, Child Gilles went down those stairs,
returned sides, hands and ankles dripping blood,
Bluebeard and gentlest saint.[2] The same nightmares
instruct the evil, as inform the good.

[1962]

The Mysterious Naked Man

A mysterious naked man has been reported
on Cranston Avenue. The police are performing
the usual ceremonies with coloured lights and sirens.
Almost everyone is outdoors and strangers are conversing excitedly
as they do during disasters when their involvement is peripheral.
"What did he look like?" the lieutenant is asking.
"I don't know," says the witness. "He was naked."
There is talk of dogs—this is no ordinary case
of indecent exposure, the man has been seen
a dozen times since the milkman spotted him and now   10
the sky is turning purple and voices
carry a long way and the children
have gone a little crazy as they often do at dusk
and cars are arriving
from other sections of the city.
And the mysterious naked man
is kneeling behind a garbage can or lying on his belly

---

[1] Allusion to German philosopher Friedrich Nietzsche's *On the Genealogy of Morals* (1887) in which Nietzsche explores the origins of moral assumptions by showing how the valuations of good and evil are mutually interlocked and overlapping.

[2] Fifteenth-century serial killer Gilles de Rais is thought to have been the model for French author Charles Perrault's fairy tale about Bluebeard, the aristocrat who keeps the remains of his murdered wives locked in a room. St. Francis of Assisi is said to have had a vision in which he received the "stigmata" or bleeding wounds of Christ. The poem is thus juxtaposing opposites to show their foundations in similar psychic sources.

in somebody's garden
or maybe even hiding in the branches of a tree,
where the wind from the harbour   20
whips at his naked body,
and by now he's probably done
whatever it was he wanted to do
and wishes he could go to sleep
or die
or take to the air like Superman.

[1969]

The Broadcaster's Poem

I used to broadcast at night
alone in a radio station
but I was never good at it,
partly because my voice wasn't right
but mostly because my peculiar
metaphysical stupidity
made it impossible
for me to keep believing
there was somebody listening
when it seemed I was talking   10
only to myself in a room no bigger
than an ordinary bathroom.
I could believe it for a while
and then I'd get somewhat
the same feeling as when you
start to suspect you're the victim
of a practical joke.
                So one part of me
was afraid another part
might blurt out something   20
about myself so terrible
that even I had never until
that moment suspected it.
                This was like the fear
of bridges and other
high places: Will I take off my glasses
and throw them
into the water, although I'm
half-blind without them?
Will I sneak up behind   30
myself and push?

Another thing:
as a reporter
I covered an accident in which a train
ran into a car, killing
three young men, one of whom
was beheaded. The bodies looked
boneless, as such bodies do.
More like mounds of rags.
And inside the wreckage   40
where nobody could get at it
the car radio
was still playing.
                I thought about places
the disc jockey's voice goes
and the things that happen there
and of how impossible it would be for him
to continue if he really knew.

[1974]

What Colour Is Manitoba?

My son, in Grade III or IV
and assigned to make a map,
asked us, what colour is
Manitoba? and refused to believe
it didn't matter, provided
it wasn't the same
as Saskatchewan and Ontario.
I remember his face.
I've seldom observed
such constrained rage   10
except in small children
and university professors.

But it's a common failing,
this excessive faith
in one method of denoting
boundaries. In his atlas
at school, Manitoba was
purple-brown. Similarly,
the road maps indicate
that I live less than   20
five hundred miles
from my birthplace.

There are truer charts.

I'd never once used
a telephone
in the nineteen years
before I left there,
had never eaten a hamburger;
I could milk a cow by hand
or yoke an ox, knew a man who   30
once as a passenger
in a heavily-loaded
stage coach inching up
one side of a very steep
hill in California
had got off to walk
and as a result of this
—the downward slope
being equally precipitous,
the horses being compelled   40
by the weight behind them
to gallop and he having to
run to catch up—
was mistaken by the driver
for a highwayman, and shot:
the scar was still there
after fifty years.
Little else had changed
in our village since
the mid-eighteenth century   50
when Coulon de Villiers
passed through with his troops,
seven years before
he defeated young George
Washington at Fort Necessity.[3]
Scraps of grape-shot worked
their way to the surface
of the earth the way bits
of shrapnel are said to
emerge at last through the skin   60
of an old soldier.

[3] Louis Coulon de Villiers (1710–1757), soldier from New France who defeated Washington's forces at Fort Necessity (in present-day Pennsylvania) during the Seven Years' War.

Add to all this
that it wasn't the same
for everybody, even there.
My family was poor.
Not disadvantaged—curse
that word of the sniffling
middle classes, suggesting
as it does that there's
nothing worse than   70
not being like them.
We were poor—curse that word, too,
as a stroke victim
half-maddened by his inability
to utter a certain phrase
will say "shit" instead
and be understood.

A sociologist,
belonging by definition to
one of the lesser   80
of the ruling sub-castes,
comes from Columbia University
to study a community
in Nova Scotia not very different
from where I was born.
A Tutsi witch doctor among Hutus.[4]
He finds, according to
the New York Times, that
almost everyone he meets is crazy.

It's as if a chemist   90
had analyzed a river
and declared that its water
was an inferior form of fire.

There are secrets I share
with the very old. I know why
we fought in the Boer War[5]
and how in the lumber camps

---

[4] Two ethnic groups in central Africa (Rwanda and Burundi).

[5] The Anglo-Boer War (1899–1902) was fought between the British Empire and the Boer (descendants of the region's first Dutch immigrants) republics in South Africa. Many British imperial colonies, including Canada (its first official dispatch of troops to an overseas war), sent troops in support of Britain.

we cracked the lice between
our thumbnails and it made
a homely sound, was a restful   100
occupation of an evening:
cracking lice, we were
like women knitting.

Altogether apart
from that, I bear tribal
marks, ritual mutilations.
My brothers and sisters
fill the slums of every
city in North America.
(God knows this is no boast.)   110
The poor, whom the Russians
used to call the Dark People,
as if it were in the blood.
I know their footsteps.
We meet each other's eyes.

[1977]

AUSTIN CLARKE ■ (1934–)

Austin Clarke is widely celebrated in Canada for his novels and short fiction about life in Barbados and the experiences of West Indian immigrants in Canada. Born in Barbados in 1934, Clarke immigrated to Canada in 1955 to attend the University of Toronto to study political science. By the early 1960s, having abandoned his university studies and begun working as a freelance broadcaster for the CBC, Clarke turned his attention to writing full time. Many of his works engage with the belief of some West Indian people, living under colonial social structures, that success and prosperity are possible only in North America or England.

Clarke's first two works, *Survivors of the Crossing* (1964) and an early story collection, *Amongst Thistles and Thorns* (1965), are tales of economic hardship and colonial relations in Barbados. In 1967, he published the first novel in his trilogy about Caribbean immigrants in Toronto, *The Meeting Point* (1967), followed a few years later by *Storm of Fortune* (1973) and *The Bigger Light* (1975). This was followed in 1977 by *The Prime Minister,* a novel of political corruption based on Clarke's experience working as general manager of the Caribbean Broadcasting Corporation in Barbados in 1975.

Clarke's Toronto trilogy, like many of his works, deals with the disillusionment of immigrants in Canada who are exposed to exploitation and racial hypocrisy. Clarke's approach is unflinching, providing depictions of encounters of West Indian immigrants and White Canadians that highlight confusion on both sides.

The works are often uncomfortable psychological studies of disappointment and futility told with a characteristic detached and ironic tone. His writing has also been noted for its vivid dialogue, particularly the colloquial speech rhythms of his "WessIndian" characters.

Clarke's most celebrated short story collections are *When He Was Free and Young and He Used to Wear Silks* (1971) and *Nine Men Who Laughed* (1986). "Canadian Experience," taken from the latter collection, recounts the story of a man who is preparing for a job interview. The laughter in the book's title signals how these characters have become resigned to their position as apparent second-class citizens. As Clarke puts it in his Introduction to the book, "These stories were written to destroy the definitions that *others* have used to portray so-called immigrants." "They are laughing," he says, "because they have become accommodating to a hostile society." Laughter becomes a futile weapon against the huge "assault upon personality and character" that the immigrant experiences merely by being identified as "immigrant." The laughter of the characters is not empowering but instead contributes to their inability to help themselves.

Many of Clarke's later works deal with the theme of memory, a topic that is evident in his superb autobiography, *Growing Up Stupid Under the Union Jack* (1980), which tells about his Barbados childhood and the colonial structures of his home society. This book was followed by a novel based on a similar experience, *Proud Empires* (1986). In the 1990s he was acclaimed for two works, *The Origin of Waves* (1997), a novel about two Barbadian men who meet in a Toronto snowstorm and reminisce about their past, and *Pig Tails 'n Breadfruit* (1999), an evocative food memoir in which Clarke's reflections on his past are interspersed with recipes and meditations on the food of his childhood. In more recent years, Clarke garnered wide attention with his astonishing novel *The Polished Hoe* (2002), set in the 1950s on a Caribbean island and staged as a confession to the police of a woman who has killed a plantation manager. The novel won the Giller Prize and a regional Commonwealth Writers Prize. With the publication of this novel, Clarke's work finally began to receive the attention it has long deserved. His most recent novel, *More* (2008), is a powerful indictment of poverty in Canada today. With Dionne Brand, Anita Rau Badami, and Rohinton Mistry, Clarke is one of the most perspicacious and compelling writers about immigrants' experiences in Canada.

Canadian Experience

He passed in front of the oval-shaped looking glass in the hallway on his way out to go to a job interview, his first in five years. His eyes and their reflection made four. He stood looking at himself, laughing, and seeing only a part of his body in the punishing reflection the glass threw back at him. He was cut off at the neck. He laughed again. This time, at the morbidness of his own thoughts. The knot of his tie was shiny with grease. He did not like himself. He was not dressed the way he had hoped to appear, and his image was incorrect. This made him stop laughing.

So he went back upstairs to his rented room on the second floor at the rear of the rooming house. His room was beside the bathroom used by the two other tenants on that floor, and the actress on the third. He wanted to inspect his hair in the better light in the bathroom. But before he reached it, he heard the spikes of a woman's heels clambering down the rear staircase; and as he listened, they landed on the muffling linoleum in the hallway; and before he could move, the bathroom door was shut. He was not laughing now. It was the actress. She was between parts, without money, and she spent more time in the bathroom when she was waiting for auditions than on her parts after she was called.

He unlocked his door and left it slightly open, to wait his turn. He wanted the actress to know he was next in line, but he didn't want her to feel she was welcome. She liked to talk, and talk bad things about her friends, her father and her step-mother, and laugh about her career, for hours.

He had to change his clothes. He thought of what else he had to wear. Suddenly, he heard the heavy downpour of the shower as the water began to rain. So he closed his door.

The heavy ticking of the cheap clock became very loud now. It was the only one he could afford, and he had bought it in Honest Ed's bargain basement nearby. He had got it mainly for its alarm, not for its accuracy of time, which he had to check against the chimes of a rock-and-roll radio station. And he listened to this station against his better musical taste whenever he wanted to be punctual, which was not often. For he had been between jobs a long time.

This morning he had to be punctual. He was going to a job interview. It was on Bay Street in the business district of banks, brokerages and corporations. For all the time he had lived in Toronto, this district had frightened him. He tried to pacify his fear of it now by laughing at himself.

The job he was hoping to get was with a bank. He knew nothing about banks. He was always uncomfortable and impatient whenever he had to go into one. The most he had ever withdrawn was twenty dollars. The most money he had ever deposited at one time was fifteen dollars.

For three months now he had been walking the seven blocks from his rooming house on Major Street to the reference library on Asquith Avenue to sit in the reading room, to watch the women and to peruse the classified advertisements in the pages of the three daily newspapers, searching for a job. The *Star* contained about ten pages of advertisements which the paper called "Employment Opportunities." He was looking for a job, but he was still able to laugh at his plight. The *Sun* had three pages. Sometimes he would see the same "employment opportunities" in this newspaper as in the *Star's* pages, and he would laugh at their stupidity of duplication. He needed a job. And the *Globe & Mail*, which he heard was the best newspaper in the country, carried three pages. He did not like the *Globe & Mail*. There was no laughing matter about its print, which was too small. And it dealt with subjects beyond his understanding and interest, and even if he could smother a laugh about that, he found its small print bad for his deteriorating eyesight; and this made him depressed and bitter. Besides, the "positions" which the *Globe & Mail* advertised were for executives, executive directors, industrial engineers, administrators and managers of quality assurance. He did not know what they meant. But he knew he wanted a job. Any job. His clothes had been in the cleaners for three months. And his diet, which had never been balanced, was becoming even more topsy-turvy with each succeeding month of joblessness.

It was, however, with an irony he himself could not fathom, but about which he smiled, that in the very pages of the *Globe & Mail*, he had seen the advertisement of the position for which he was promised an interview this Monday morning at ten.

His noisy clock, with a silver-painted bell on it—and white face and black luminous numerals of the Roman kind—said it was nine o'clock. His room was still dark.

The *Globe & Mail*'s ad read:

> *We require an energetic junior executive to take a responsible position in our bank. The successful candidate must have a university degree in business or in finance, or the equivalent in business experience. Salary and benefits to be discussed at interview. Reply to the 14th floor, 198 Bay Street.*

He was a man past thirty. But he could not, even at his age, argue about taking this "junior position," because his desperate circumstances were forcing this stern necessity upon him. Junior or senior, he had to take it. And when he got it, he knew it would not be a laughing matter. Necessity would make him bitter, but thankful.

He had only to remember his old refrigerator, which took up one-eighth of the floor space in his room, and which hissed and stuttered whenever he turned on his electric hot plate. The refrigerator contained a box of baking soda, which the talkative actress had told him would kill the smells of food; and on the top shelf, cold water in a half-gallon bottle that had once been full of grapefruit juice; a half-pint carton of homogenized milk, now going bad; his last weiners from Canada Packers, like three children's joyless penises; six hard slices of white bread in soft, sweating plastic wrapping from Wonder Bread, which was printed below the blonde-haired child who persisted in smiling on the package. And three bottles of Molson's beer. In these circumstances of diving subsistence, he knew he had nothing to lose—and nothing to laugh about—concerning the "junior position."

He did not come to this country to attend university. Experience of the world, and his former life at home in Barbados were his only secondary education. He had come here against his father's bitter wishes. But he was not unschooled. He had attended the St Matthias' Elementary School for Boys, Barbados. *For Boys*, he wanted to remember to impress upon his prospective employers, since he was not a believer in the North American practice of having boys going to school with girls. He was a staunch supporter of the British system of public school education. And even though the St Matthias' Elementary School for boys was not, in fact, a public school, it was, nevertheless, a school that was public.[1]

---

[1] In Britain a "public school" refers to what in North America is called a "private school." Here the protagonist assumes the ignorance of his prospective employers and is hoping to pass off St. Matthias' School as a "public school" in the British sense, like the series of exclusive Toronto private schools listed in the next paragraph, even though it is not one.

He laughed at his own cleverness of nuance and logic. Besides, no one in Toronto would know the difference. Toronto has Upper Canada College for boys, Trinity College School for boys, Bishop Strachan School for girls and Havergal College for girls. Boys with boys. And girls with girls. His logic was so ascerbic and sharp, he was already laughing as he heard himself telling them that St Matthias' Elementary School for Boys was a . . .

But he stopped himself in the tracks of his hilarity: "I had better leave out the elementary part and just tell them *St Mathias' School for Boys.*" It was a satisfactory and imaginative rendering of the facts. Bay Street, if not the whole of Canada, he had discovered in his time here, was filled with people of imagination. The actress had been telling him that imagination is something called a euphemism for lies.

But he couldn't take the risk of failure. Failure would breed cynicism. Instead, he had said on his application that he was educated at Harrison College, "a very prestigious college for men in Barbados, and founded in 1783, which produced the leading brains of the leading leaders in books and banking, of the entire West Indies." Had he twisted the facts a little too much? Laughter and reassurance about the imaginative men on Bay Street, liars, as the actress called them, and who became quick millionaires, told him he had not stepped off into fraud. Not yet.

In spite of his lack of formal education, he still considered himself well read. Newspapers, magazines, the *Star* newspaper and *Time* magazine did not escape his daily and weekly scrutiny, even long after he had fallen upon the debris of the country's unemployed, in *decreptitude.* "Decreptitude" was the word he always used to the actress when they talked about their lives, to make her laugh about the apparently irreconcilable differences between her and her own society, and also to impress her that he was not a fool. He had heard the word first on television. And he listened to C.B.C. radio and short-wave broadcasts of the B.B.C. world service, and watched four television news broadcasts each night: two Canadian and two from America. And he never missed *Sixty Minutes* from New York. Except for the three times, consecutive Sundays, when he had lain flat on his back, fed off the public welfare system, on a public ward in the Toronto General Hospital "under observation" for high blood pressure.

"Pressure in my arse!" he told the actress who visited him every day, as he explained his illness.

In the eight years he had spent in this country, he had lain low for the first five, as a non-landed immigrant, in and out of low-paying jobs given specifically to non-landed immigrants, and all the time waiting for amnesty. One year he worked distributing handbills, most of which, because of boredom, he threw into garbage pails when no one was looking, and laughed, until one cold afternoon in February when his supervisor, who did not trust immigrants, carried out a telephone check behind his back, only to discover that none of the householders on the fifteen streets he had been assigned to had ever heard of or had ever seen the brochures advertising *Pete's Pizza Palace, free delivery.* After that mirthless firing, there were three months during which he laboured as a janitor for the Toronto Board of Education—incidentally, his closest touch with higher learning; two months at Eaton's[2] as a night-shift cleaner; then two months at Simpson's as an assistant shipping clerk until the last job, five years ago, held along with Italians, Greeks and Portuguese, cleaning the offices of First Canadian Place, a building with at least fifty floors, made of glass, near Bay Street, where he was heading this morning.

He laughed to himself as he thought of his former circumstances. For he was ready for bigger things. The murmuring refrigerator could not, within reason, be any emptier.

So with the bathroom next door still occupied, he looked at himself, at the way he was dressed. It was nine-fifteen now. His bladder was full. Whenever he had important things on his mind, his bladder filled itself easily, and more unusually heavy, and it made him tense.

He wished the pink shirt was cleaner. He wished the dark brown suit was a black one. He should not wear a yellow tie, but no other ties he had would match the clothes on his back. And he knew through instinct and not through Canadian experience that a job of this importance, "junior executive" in a bank, had to be applied for by a man dressed formally in black.

Laughter, his father had told him many times, a smile at the right moment, melts a woman with even the meanest temperament. He tried this philosophy now, and his attitude changed for the better. He put more Vaseline on his hair to make the part on the left side keener, for he had dressed in the dark. And now that the autumn light was coming through the single glass pane, which he could not reach even standing on a chair and from which he could never see the sidewalk, he could see that the shirt he had thought was slightly soiled was dirty.

The morning was getting older, the time of his appointment was getting closer, the hands of the bargain-basement clock were now at nine thirty-five, and he had only twenty-five minutes left to go; and he had to go badly but couldn't, because the actress was still inside the bathroom, singing a popular song. He could hear the water hitting against the bathtub and could imagine her body soaked in the hot beads of the shower, and he could see the red-faced ugly blackheads painted red, at the bottom of her spine. He had asked her once what they were, and she had told him "cold sores." He thought they had something to do with winter, that they came out in winter. He laughed each time she told him "cold sores." He could see them now, because he had seen them once before. Yesterday, too, for thirty-five minutes counted by his loud, inaccurate, cheap alarm clock, he had heard the torrents of the shower as she washed herself in preparation for an audition.

He had nothing to do now but wait. The shower stopped like a tropical downpour and with a suddenness that jolted him. He opened his door. He listened. Mist floated out of the bathroom door, and he brushed through it as if he were a man seeking passage through thick, white underbrush. And as he got

[2] Eaton's and Simpson's are department stores.

inside and could barely see his way to the toilet bowl, there she was, with one leg on the cover of the bowl which she had painted black, bending down, wiping the smell of the soap from between her legs and then the red, rough dots of bruises on the bottom of her spine, which she insisted were cold sores. When she named them first, he thought she had said "cold stores." He could understand that. "Cold stores," "cold storage"—it was enough to make him laugh.

"Oh, it's you."

He could not move. He did not answer. He could not retreat.

"Close the door and come in."

The mist came back, thick and sudden as fog swallowing him, debilitating him, blinding him, and he lost his vision. But he could see the lines of four ribs on each side of her body, and her spinal cord that ran clear as a wemm, with the dozen or so cold sores, fresh as the evidence from a recent lash.

"I have an audition in an hour, so I'm washing myself clean. You never know what directors're going to ask you to do."

He retreated to his room and closed the door. No mist or even warm sores could confuse him now; and he inspected the clothes he was dressed in, unable to change them, and worried about his interview, refusing all the time to think of the naked actress, and ignored her knocking on his door. Whenever he refused to answer her, she would leave a note on his door in her scratchy, left-handed scrawl.

But this time, when he re-opened his door to leave, she was standing there, and he passed her, wrapped in the large *Holiday Inn* towel she had brought from Sherbrooke and which barely covered the red sores at the bottom of her spine. The two small nipples of her dropped breasts were left bare to his undesiring eyes.

"You're too black to wear brown," she said. He passed her as if she had herpes. "If you don't mind me saying so," she shouted at his back, which moved away from her down the stairs.

This time he did not look at himself in the oval-shaped looking glass in the hall. He just walked out of the house. He wished it was for the last time.

The people at the bus stop are standing like sentries, silent and sullen. They look so sleepy he thinks it could be six o'clock. But a clock in the bank beside the bus stop says ten minutes to ten. He hurries the crowded bus on, with the urging of his anxiety.

The only sound that comes from the larger group of people going down into the subway is the hurrying pounding of heels on the clean, granite steps and the rubbing of hands on the squeaking rails, polished like chrome. More people are coming up out of the subway at greater speed as if they are fleeing the smell of something unwholesome. He can smell only the fumes of the trains. And he wonders if it is his imagination. For he knows that the trains run on electricity. It must be the smell of dust, then. Or the people. Or the perfumes.

He watches a woman's hand as it wipes sleep and excretia from the corners of her eyes. He thinks of the actress, who cleans her face this way.

But it is still September, his month of laughter along the crowded sidewalks, amongst the fallen turning leaves. And the furious memory of growing grass, quicker than the pulse was in summer, is still in the air. There are no lamb's wool, no slaughtered seals, no furs, no coats yet to cover the monotony of women's movement, which he sees like the singlemindedness of sheep, one behind the leader, in single file downwards into the subway and in double file upwards.

He boards a crowded subway car and stands among the sardines of silent, serious people. Where he is, with both hands on a pole, he is surrounded by men dressed in grey and black. Some are darker and richer than others. Some of the women too, are dressed in grey; some better made and better built than others. All the men in this car hold briefcases, either on their laps or between their shoes. And the women carry at least two bags, from one of which they occasionally take small balls of Kleenex.

He has just swayed farther from the steadying pole for moving balance as the train turns, and is standing over a woman cleaning her eyes and her nose with a red fingernail. And, immediately, as his eyes and hers meet, she drops her eyes into the pages of a thick paperback book, as if her turned eyes would obliterate her act.

The second bag he sees some women carrying is larger than a handbag, large enough, he thinks, for rolls of toilet paper and paper towels. The men do not read: they watch the women's legs. And they look over their shoulders, between their shoulders and down into their braless bodies, and their eyes touch the pages of the novels the women are reading; and not certain of the enlightenment and pleasure to be got from this rapid-transit fleeting education, the men reluctantly allow their eyes to wander back to the pages of the *Globe & Mail*, which seem to hold no interest for them. Their eyes roam over the puny print of the stock market quotations, the box scores of the Blue Jays baseball team and the results at Woodbine Race Track.

If his own luck had been really luck—and something to laugh about—the actress told him once, he could win thousands of dollars on a two-dollar bet, as easy as one, two, three. When she told him, "One to win, two to come second and three to come third," he laughed, thinking she was memorizing lines of a play she was auditioning for.

He had been living with so little luck in his life—three months with no money and no hope of any—that he could afford to dream and to laugh as he dreamed, and fill his empty pockets with imagined wealth.

A man beside him shakes out the pages of the *Globe & Mail* to the racing results: *"and in the fifth race yesterday at Woodbine, the first three horses to come in, 1, 2 and 3, paid $15,595.03, ..."*

The jerk of the train stopping pushes him against the metal pole and awakens him from his dreaming. When the doors open, he is at his stop.

The air is cool. He can feel his shirt like wet silk against his body. He pulls the lapels of his jacket together to make himself feel warmer. The sun shines blindingly, but weak, on the tall office buildings that surround him. He is walking in their shadow, as if he is walking in a valley back in Barbados. The buildings look like steel. One facing him, built almost entirely out of glass, shimmers like gold. Its reflection of his body tears him into strides and splatters his suit against four glass panels, and makes him disjointed. It is the building he is going to enter.

The elevator is crowded. The passengers are all looking up at the changing numbers of the floors. He looks up, too. He can hear no breathing. A man shifts his weight from one black alligator shoe to the next. A woman changes her brown leather handbag and her other, larger bag, made of blue parachute material, from her right arm to her left. He reads *Bijoux*, which is printed on it. There is only the humming of the elevator; then the sound of the doors opening; then feet on the polished floor outside; the sound of the doors closing; a deep breath like a sigh of relief or of anticipation for the next floor; then the humming of the next ascent and then silence. The elevator stops on the fourteenth floor. There is no thirteenth. He is at the front, near the door when it opens. Five men and women are beside and behind him. Facing him is glass and chrome and fresh flowers and Persian rugs and women dressed expensively and stylishly in black, with necklaces of pearls. And chewing gum. It is quiet in the office. Deathly quiet. So he stands his ground.

BANK is written on the glass.

"Getting off?" a man beside him asks.

He stands his ground.

The door closes, and he goes up with the five of them and finds himself, gradually, floor by floor, alone, as they slip out one by one. The elevator takes him to the top. The door does not open. And when it starts its descent, he is feeling braver. He remembers the new vigour he felt at the end of three hours with wax and mops and vacuum cleaners with Italians, Greeks and Portuguese, going down the elevator. He will ride it to the bottom.

No one enters, even though it stops two times in quick succession. And then it stops once more, and the door opens, and he is facing the same office with BANK written on the glass, cheerless and frightening, and seeing the same chrome, the rugs and the black and pearls of the women. Just as he moves to step out, the closing door, cut into half, and like two large black hands, comes at him. He gets out of the way just as the blue eyes of one of the women approaching the elevator door to see what he wanted are fixed upon him. Those blue eyes are like ice-water; his are brown and laughing.

" . . . this stop, sir?" is all he gets to hear of the woman's flat voice before the two black palms, like a shutter, have taken her eyes from his view and her words from his hearing.

* * *

"And you didn't even go into the office?"

"I couldn't do it."

"Sometimes when I'm auditioning, I get scared and get butterflies."

"There was so much wealth!"

"Are you a communist? I wish I had money, money and more money. All I think about is money. But here I am in this damn rooming house with a broken shower curtain and a leaky bathtub, trying to be an artist, an actress. Do you think I'll be a dedicated actress because I live in all this shit? When last have I had steak? And a glass of red wine? Or you?"

"I have some weiners."

"Weiners, for Chrissakes!"

Her flat voice and icy manner killed the kindness in his suggestion.

"The people on the subway looked so educated, like everybody was a university graduate. And not one person, man or woman, asked me if I needed directions."

"For Chrissakes! How would they know you don't have Canadian experience?"

"They looked on me and at me and through me, right through me. I was a piece of glass."

"Must have been your brown suit."

"Everybody else was in grey and black."

"I hope I get this part. Just to get my hands on some money and rent a decent place. But what can I do? I even get tired taking showers in a bathroom where the water leaks through the curtain. My whole life is like a shower curtain. That leaks. Oh, the landlady was here. Fifteen minutes after you left. She tells me you have to give up your room on Friday. So I tell her not to worry, that you got a job today. And you didn't even go into the office! She wants you to pay two months this month. But you didn't even face the people!"

"With all that glass and steel and chrome?"

"Do you want me to tell her you're not in? You could always slip out without paying the rent, you know. I've done it lots of times. In Sherbrooke and in Rosedale. God, I nearly broke my ass racing down the metal fire escape, carrying my box of French Canadian plays. Everybody skips out on landlords. Try it. She'll never find you in Toronto! The one in Rosedale hasn't found me yet. And here I am, desperate to be an actress and get the money to move back to Rosedale . . . "

"When she's coming back?"

"Seven."

"She coming in three hours? Are you saying four o'clock, too?"

"You *could* come to my room. I don't have to do the audition. I can skip it. There's a small restaurant on Church Street where a lot of television and radio types eat, and I'm thinking of applying for a waitress job there. It's an artistic restaurant. I'll even slip you a meal if I get the job."

"She said she's coming back at seven?"

"My room is open to you, as I say. Be free. Feel free. Don't you want to be free? Where could you go, anyhow?"

★ ★ ★

In his hands is a glass with a pattern on it that advertises peanut butter. It has dried specks like old saliva round the mouth. He passes his fingers round the mouth of the glass, cleaning it; and when it looks clean and is cloudy from his hand-prints, he pours the first of the three Molson's into it. He sits on his bed. There is no chair in the room. Only his television set, which he sits on when he is not watching *Sixty Minutes* or the American news. His dangling feet can barely touch the floor. On the floor is linoleum with a floral pattern. "Rose of Sharon," the actress had told him. "I was a whiz in Botany at Jarvis Collegiate."

The sun is brighter now. He can smile in this sun and think of home. He is getting warmer, too. A shaft of dust plays within the arrow of September light that comes through the window. It lands at his feet. The light and the particles of dust on the bright leather of his shoes attract his attention for a moment only. He smiles in that moment. And in that moment, his past life fills his heart and shakes his body like a spasm, like a blast of cold air. His attention then strays to the things around him, his possessions, prized so fondly before, and which now seem to be mere encumbrances: the valise he brought from Barbados and carried through so many changes of address in Toronto; heavier always in winter when he changed rooms, when he carried it late at night on his shoulder, although each time that he moved, he had accumulated no more possessions; the two Christmas cards which the actress mailed to him, even though she had been living in the same house, placed open like two tents and which he keeps on top of a wooden kitchen cupboard, used now as his dressing table. "*To George at Xmas*" is written in ball-point, in red, on each, in capital letters; and an unframed colour photograph taken in Barbados, and fading now, showing him with his father and mother and two younger brothers and three sisters: eight, healthy, well-fed Barbadians, squinting because the sun is in their eyes, standing like proprietors in front of a well-preserved plantation house made of coral stone, covered in vines so thick that their spongy greenness strangles the windows and the doors. The name of this house in Barbados is *Edgehill House.* His present residence has no name. It is on a street named Major. It is a rooming house, similar in size, in build and in dirt to the other houses on the street.

He drains the beer from the peanut-butter glass and refills it. He throws the last bottle into the plastic garbage pail, and the rattle of glass and tin is like a drunken cackle. Inside the garbage pail are the classified pages from the *Globe & Mail*, some shrivelled lettuce leaves, an empty milk carton and the caps of beer bottles. He thinks of the woman in the bank's office, dressed in black, with the blue eyes. He thinks of the flowers and the glass in that office and of flowers more violent in colour, growing in wild profusion, untended, round *Edgehill House*, where he was born in a smiling field of comfortable pasture land.

His father never worked for anyone in his whole life, never had to leave the two hundred and eighty acres of green sugar cane and corn to dirty his hands for anyone's money.

"Work on this blasted plantation, boy. Put your hands in the most stinking dirt and cow-dung on this plantation, and it is a hundred times more nobler than working at the most senior position in a country where you wasn't born!"

His father said that almost every day, and more often when his father heard he was leaving for Canada.

"You call yourself a son o' mine? You, a son o' mine? With all this property that I leaving-back for you? You come telling me you going to Canada as a' immigrant? To be a stranger? Where Canada is? What is Canada? They have a Church o' England up there? Canada is no place for you, man. The son of a Barbadian plantation owner? This land was in our family before Canada was even discovered by the blasted Eskimos and the red Indians. Seventeen-something. A.D.! In the year of our Lord, *anno domini*. Who do they worship up there? And you come telling me that you going up there, seeking advancement as a' immigrant? In Canada? Your fortune and your future is *right here!* In this soil. In this mud. In this dirt. 'Pon these two hundred and eighty-something acres o' cane and corn!"

It is six-thirty now. Thirty minutes before the landlady is to arrive. He locks his door. He stands outside in front of it, like a man who has forgotten something inside. There is a red thumb-tack on the door. The actress pins it there whenever she leaves messages that she thinks require urgent replies. Whenever there's a thumb-tack on his door, he thinks of the red cold sores on her back, and it makes him laugh. He does not know why: he just laughs.

He climbs the stairs to go to her room. He can see a red thumb-tack on her door, even before he reaches it. It is similar to the one he has left behind on his own door. She has written his name in red capital letters on a folded piece of lined white paper. He pulls the paper from the tack.

"*I got the waitress job at the restarant.*" He smiles when he sees she has spelled "restaurant" without a "u". She has signed it, "*Pat*".

He did not throw away the balled-up message, even hours afterwards, in all the walking he did that night, until he was standing on the platform of the subway at the Spadina station where he is now.

He looks to his right and then to his left, and there is no one in sight. Across from him, across the clean cement that is divided by a black river of hard dirty steel, are two large billboards. One advocates "pigging-out," and the other tells women about "Light Days, Tampax." Suddenly, into the frame of these two boards rivetted to two steel pillars comes the lone passenger, who stands and waits to take the train going in the other direction.

He does not know why he is in this station and why he has entered on the side for southbound trains.

South is the office building with the glass and the flowers and the women dressed in black and BANK written on the glass. South is Bay Street where no one walks after the Italians and the Greeks and the Portuguese have cleaned the offices and have left to take the subway north to College Street. South is nothing. South is the lake and blackness and cold water that smells of dead fish and screaming children's voices in the short summer, and machines and boats and grease.

The balled-up note from Pat, written on its soiled paper, smelling of the ointment she uses for her cold sores, was in his fist when he first reached this spot where he is standing now. He is standing in the centre of the platform, the same distance from the left end as from the right.

A rumble grows louder. Chains and machinery, iron touching iron, steel rubbing steel, the sound of the approaching train. He can never tell at the first sound of this familiar rumbling, out of a darkened tube, whether it is coming from his left or from his right. He always has to wait longer for the greater roar. Or if it is night-time, watch for the first glare on the tracks.

He thinks the roar is coming from the southbound lines. He feels more at ease for a moment, and braver, and he even laughs, although he doesn't know why. The man on the other side stares at him from his seat on the brown leather, between the two advertising boards, and the man remains querulous with his staring until the train moves northwards.

He is alone again. And more at ease. He moves to the end of the platform, nearest the tube through which the train will emerge, to a spot where he could see it clearly. He wants no surprises. He wants to see it the moment it appears out of the blackness. The blackness that is like the South and the lake. And he wants no one else to see him. He wants to be alone, just as he was alone in the descending elevator in the office building.

How comfortable and safe and brave he had felt travelling and laughing and falling so fast and so free, through the bowels of that glassed-in building!

He hears the rumble. He hears the sound of steel or iron—metal anyhow; and the low screech of the train trying to emerge out of the darkened, curved tube.

He thinks of Pat. So he throws the balled-up note onto the tracks. And that act is her being thrown out of his life, along with her red-corpuscled sores. He sees the note fall. But does not hear it reach the surface of the black river of hard dirty steel below him. He does not hear it reach the tracks. He cannot gauge any distance now. Cannot gauge any face. The paper is very light. Almost without weight. Definitely without purpose and love.

But the train is here. Its lights reflect onto the tracks which now are shining and getting wider as the ugly red engine, like her sores, approaches. He knows that the train is as long as the platform, half of which he has already paced off. The train is here. And just as its lights begin to blind him, he makes his own eyes pierce through that weaker brightness and fixes them on the driver, dressed in a light-brown uniform. He sees the driver's face, the driver's happy eyes and his relief that this is his last trip; and he himself laughs to an empty platform and station that are not listening, and he steps off the platform, just having seen his own eyes, and the driver's, makes four.

[1986]

Few poets are forced to worry about the inconveniences of being an international celebrity. But few writers have been as successful as Leonard Cohen at blending commitments to writing (both poetry and novels) and to music. Born and raised in Montreal, Cohen published his first book of poetry, *Let Us Compare Mythologies,* in the McGill Poetry series under Louis Dudek in 1956 while still an undergraduate at McGill University. His second volume, *The Spice-Box of Earth* (1961), established his reputation in poetry circles both in Canada and abroad. He remained a prolific and extraordinarily influential figure throughout the '60s, publishing several more poetry collections, including *Flowers for Hitler* (1964) and *Parasites of Heaven* (1966), and two novels, both of which are in the New Canadian Library series: *The Favourite Game* (1963) and *Beautiful Losers* (1966). Cohen was awarded a Governor General's Award for *Selected Poems* (1968), which he declined, explaining that "the poems themselves forbid it absolutely." It was during these years that Cohen also established himself as a singer-songwriter. He made his debut at the Newport Folk Festival in 1967 and released his first album that year, *Songs of Leonard Cohen* (1967), which contains several enduring hits, including "Suzanne." The album catapulted him to fame in the folk-music scene that dominated youth culture in the period.

Cohen's writing—as both a poet and a songwriter—is marked by striking, often elaborate imagery, incorporating what Michael Ondaatje calls "a jarring blend of beauty and blood." His work grapples with the crass materialism of the age, when spiritual redemption seemed beyond the individual's reach. Even the idealism of the 1960s is not beyond reproach; the complacency of the period's revolutionary ethos is the subject of critique in "What I'm Doing Here." The poems engage in mythologizations of existential isolation and personal freedom, probing such topics as the elusiveness of spiritual truth, the irresistible promise of sexuality, and the uncertain salvation of human intimacy. At its best, Cohen's poetry explores the intricate connections between these themes, often in terms of a notion of secularized sainthood such as one sees in his poem/song "Suzanne." It revels in the ways that our various impulses, from the coarse to the sublime, are seamlessly interwoven. Religious devotion merges with the prospect of seduction; bittersweet memories of disintegrated relationships are leavened by a renewed promise of self-knowledge. His 1961 poem "The Kite Is a Victim," similar in theme to Irving Layton's "The Birth of Tragedy"(1954) and "The Fertile Muck" (1956), explores these ideas in terms of the turbulent relation of limitation and freedom in the work of art. Some of Cohen's best-known poems explore Jewish themes, in particular his response to the Holocaust, evident in such poems as "The Genius" and "All There Is to Know about Adolph Eichmann."

In much of his work, as in "For E.J.P." (a poem dedicated to the Canadian modernist poet E.J. Pratt) and "How to Speak Poetry," Cohen was plagued by questions about the role of the poet in society, whether art could offer any kind of redemptive potential, and whether, indeed, the cult of celebrity diminished this possibility. Like Layton's, Cohen's public persona is in many ways his greatest work of art. On the run from his beginnings in a wealthy Jewish family in Westmount (his father, who owned a successful clothing store, died when he was nine, leaving Cohen a sizable inheritance in trust), Cohen bought a house on the Greek island of Hydra shortly after his twenty-sixth birthday in 1960, living there for several years while he wrote *Beautiful Losers* and two collections of poetry, *Flowers for Hitler* (1964) and *Parasites of Heaven* (1966). In 1966, at the height of sixties counterculture, Cohen returned to New York, where he had lived very briefly during an aborted graduate student career at Columbia University, this time living in the notorious Chelsea Hotel and mixing with many of the leading cultural figures of his age, from Jack Kerouac, Andy Warhol, and Allen Ginsberg to Bob Dylan, Joni Mitchell, and Joan Baez. If *The Favourite Game* was a talented but in many ways conventional *Bildungsroman,* about a young Montreal man coming of age personally and artistically, *Beautiful Losers* thrived on its shock value. Cohen's publisher, Jack McClelland, wrote to him about the novel: "It's wild and incredible and marvelously well written, and at the same time appalling, shocking, revolting, disgusting, sick and just maybe it's a great novel. I'm damned if I know." Many readers shared McClelland's ambivalence and uncertainty, as well as his more fundamental enthusiasm. If the novel's graphic and unrelenting sexual focus offended some readers as "pornographic," its highly experimental style left others puzzled. Partly owing to these characteristics, it achieved an almost instant notoriety which confirmed Cohen's literary reputation.

Cohen's literary preoccupations revolve around an unwavering interest in the question of what it means to achieve any meaningful form of personal liberation. Poetry such as the work contained in *The Energy of Slaves* (1972) revels in the idea of personal degradation as the only possible basis for emancipation from the burden of modern alienation. Deeply cynical and self-negating, these poems, many of which read more as fragments than as actual poems, turn on the fine line between master and slave, insisting on an aesthetic of self-abnegation as the only possible route to genuine liberation.

Cohen's most recent work, however, is distinguished by an increasingly affirmative turn toward the possibility of religious salvation, not in the reductive terms of any fixed creed or church, but as a fragile sense of an elusive but very real benediction. This may, in part, have something to do with what Cohen himself has described as the recent disappearance of his chronic depression (he credits a combination of the biological effects of aging and the cathartic influence of his rigorously monkish life under the guidance of his Buddhist master Old Roshi). Either way, Cohen's most recent writing is animated by a sense of spiritual renewal that fuses a deeply affirmative mood of celebration with a patient regard for human imperfections.

This insistence on the need to forge a religious faith that does not just tolerate but actively embraces people's frailty and limitations, and the rejection of the fakery of any religious dogma that dismisses these in favour of a more strident tone of social intolerance, are the hallmarks of Cohen's mature work. The turn toward this sort of hopefulness is particularly striking in a writer who had, for so many years, revelled in a series of ironic displace- ments that subordinated the possibility of salvation to a darker fascination with the everyday mythologies that people construct to fill the spiritual void.

A Kite Is a Victim

A kite is a victim you are sure of.
You love it because it pulls
gentle enough to call you master,
strong enough to call you fool;
because it lives
like a desperate trained falcon
in the high sweet air,
and you can always haul it down
to tame it in your drawer.

A kite is a fish you have already caught   10
in a pool where no fish come,
so you play him carefully and long,
and hope he won't give up,
or the wind die down.

A kite is the last poem you've written,
so you give it to the wind,
but you don't let it go
until someone finds you
something else to do.

A kite is a contract of glory   20
that must be made with the sun,
so you make friends with the field
the river and the wind,
then you pray the whole cold night before,
under the travelling cordless moon,
to make you worthy and lyric and pure.

[1961]

The Genius

For you
I will be a ghetto jew
and dance
and put white stockings

on my twisted limbs
and poison wells
across the town

For you
I will be an apostate jew[1]
and tell the Spanish priest   10
of the blood vow
in the Talmud
and where the bones
of the child are hid

For you
I will be a banker jew
and bring to ruin
a proud old hunting king
and end his line

For you   20
I will be a Broadway jew
and cry in theatres
for my mother
and sell bargain goods
beneath the counter

For you
I will be a doctor jew
and search
in all the garbage cans
for foreskins   30
to sew back again

For you
I will be a Dachau jew[2]
and lie down in lime
with twisted limbs
and bloated pain
no mind can understand

[1961]

---

[1] An apostate is one who forsakes his/her religion or principles.

[2] Dachau was a Nazi concentration camp in Germany during the Second World War.

The Only Tourist in Havana
Turns His Thoughts Homeward

Come, my brothers,
let us govern Canada,
let us find our serious heads,
let us dump asbestos on the White House,
let us make the French talk English,
     not only here but everywhere,
let us torture the Senate individually
     until they confess,[3]
let us purge the New Party,
let us encourage the dark races   10
     so they'll be lenient
     when they take over,
let us make the CBC talk English,
let us all lean in one direction
     and float down
     to the coast of Florida,
let us have tourism,
let us flirt with the enemy,
let us smelt pig-iron in our backyards,
let us sell snow   20
     to under-developed nations,
(Is it true one of our national leaders
     was a Roman Catholic?)
let us terrorize Alaska,
let us unite
     Church and State,
let us not take it lying down,
let us have two Governor Generals
     at the same time,
let us have another official language,   30
let us determine what it will be,
let us give a Canada Council Fellowship
     to the most original suggestion,
let us teach sex in the home
     to parents,

[3] A reference to the U.S. Senate Subcommittee, led by Senator Joseph McCarthy, which conducted a series of investigations and public hearings of people accused of so-called "un-American" or "Communist" activities during the 1950s to '70s.

let us threaten to join the U.S.A.
>   and pull out at the last moment,
my brothers, come,
our serious heads are waiting for us somewhere
>   like Gladstone bags[4] abandoned   40
>   after a coup d'état,
let us put them on very quickly,
let us maintain a stony silence
>   on the St. Lawrence Seaway.

Havana
April 1961

[1964]

What I'm Doing Here

I do not know if the world has lied
I have lied
I do not know if the world has conspired against love
I have conspired against love
The atmosphere of torture is no comfort
I have tortured
Even without the mushroom cloud
still I would have hated
Listen
I would have done the same things   10
even if there were no death
I will not be held like a drunkard
under the cold tap of facts
I refuse the universal alibi

Like an empty telephone booth passed at night
and remembered
like mirrors in a movie palace lobby consulted
only on the way out
like a nymphomaniac who binds a thousand
into strange brotherhood   20
I wait
for each one of you to confess

[1964]

---

4 Small leather portmanteau or suitcase with hinged sides.

For E.J.P.[5]

I once believed a single line
    in a Chinese poem could change
        forever how blossoms fell
and that the moon itself climbed on
    the grief of concise weeping men
        to journey over cups of wine
I thought invasions were begun for crows
    to pick at a skeleton
        dynasties sown and spent
to serve the language of a fine lament   10
    I thought governors ended their lives
        as sweetly drunken monks
telling time by rain and candles
    instructed by an insect's pilgrimage
        across the page—all this
so one might send an exile's perfect letter
to an ancient hometown friend

I chose a lonely country
    broke from love
        scorned the fraternity of war   20
I polished my tongue against the pumice moon
    floated my soul in cherry wine
        a perfumed barge for Lords of Memory
to languish on to drink to whisper out
    their store of strength
        as if beyond the mist along the shore
their girls their power still obeyed
    like clocks wound for a thousand years
I waited until my tongue was sore

Brown petals wind like fire around my poems   30
    I aimed them at the stars but
        like rainbows they were bent
before they sawed the world in half
    Who can trace the canyoned paths
        cattle have carved out of time

[5] E.J. Pratt (1882–1964), considered one of Canada's major poets and a forerunner of the modernist movement in Canada (see Section V). Like Cohen, Pratt was also interested in grand questions of human existence and spiritual faith.

wandering from meadowlands to feasts
　　　　Layer after layer of autumn leaves
　　　　　　　　are swept away
Something forgets us perfectly

[1964]

Suzanne Takes You Down

Suzanne takes you down
to her place near the river,
you can hear the boats go by
you can stay the night beside her.
And you know that she's half crazy
but that's why you want to be there
and she feeds you tea and oranges
that come all the way from China.
Just when you mean to tell her
that you have no gifts to give her,　　　　　　　10
she gets you on her wave-length
and she lets the river answer
that you've always been her lover.
　　　　And you want to travel with her,
　　　　you want to travel blind
　　　　and you know that she can trust you
　　　　because you've touched her perfect body
　　　　with your mind

Jesus was a sailor
when he walked upon the water[6]　　　　　　20
and he spent a long time watching
from a lonely wooden tower
and when he knew for certain
only drowning men could see him
he said All men will be sailors then
until the sea shall free them,
but he himself was broken
long before the sky would open,
forsaken, almost human,
he sank beneath your wisdom like a stone.　　　　30
　　　　And you want to travel with him,
　　　　you want to travel blind

[6] A reference to Matthew 14: 23–33 in which Jesus performs a miracle by walking upon the storm-tossed sea to his disciples in their boat. Peter also tries to walk on the water but sinks when he becomes afraid.

and you think maybe you'll trust him
because he touched your perfect body
with his mind.

Suzanne takes your hand
and she leads you to the river,
she is wearing rags and feathers
from Salvation Army counters.
The sun pours down like honey 40
on our lady of the harbour
as she shows you where to look
among the garbage and the flowers,
there are heroes in the seaweed
there are children in the morning,
they are leaning out for love
they will lean that way forever
while Suzanne she holds the mirror.
  And you want to travel with her
  and you want to travel blind 50
  and you're sure that she can find you
  because she's touched her perfect body
  with her mind.

[1966]

How To Speak Poetry

Take the word butterfly. To use this word it is not necessary to make the voice weigh less than an ounce or equip it with small dusty wings. It is not necessary to invent a sunny day or a field of daffodils. It is not necessary to be in love, or to be in love with butterflies. The word butterfly is not a real butterfly. There is the word and there is the butterfly. If you confuse these two items people have the right to laugh at you. Do not make so much of the word. Are you trying to suggest that you love butterflies more perfectly than anyone else, or really understand their nature? The word butterfly is merely data. It is not an opportunity for you to hover, soar, befriend flowers, symbolize beauty and frailty, or in any way impersonate a butterfly. Do not act out words. Never act out words. Never try to leave the floor when you talk about flying. Never close your eyes and jerk your head to one side when you talk about death. Do not fix your burning eyes on me when you speak about love. If you want to impress me when you speak about love put your hand in your pocket or under your dress and play with yourself. If ambition and the hunger for applause have driven you to speak about love you should learn how to do it without disgracing yourself or the material.

 What is the expression which the age demands? The age demands no expression whatever. We have seen photographs of bereaved Asian mothers. We are not interested in the agony of your fumbled organs. There is nothing you can show on your face that can match the horror of this time. Do not even try. You will only hold yourself up to the scorn of those who have felt things deeply. We have seen newsreels of humans in the extremities of pain and dislocation. Everyone knows you are eating well and are even being paid to stand up there. You are playing to people who have experienced a catastrophe. This should make you very quiet. Speak the words, convey the data, step aside. Everyone knows you are in pain. You cannot tell the audience everything you know about love in every line of love you speak. Step aside and they will know what you know because they know it already. You have nothing to teach them. You are not more beautiful than they are. You are not wiser. Do not shout at them. Do not force a dry entry. That is bad sex. If you show the lines of your genitals, then deliver what you promise. And remember that people do not really want an acrobat in bed. What is our need? To be close to the natural man, to be close to the natural woman. Do not pretend that you are a beloved singer with a vast loyal audience which has followed the ups and downs of your life to this very moment. The bombs, flame-throwers, and all the shit have destroyed more than just the trees and villages. They have also destroyed the stage. Did you think that your profession would escape the general destruction? There is no more stage. There are no more footlights. You are among the people. Then be modest. Speak the words, convey the data, step aside. Be by yourself. Be in your own room. Do not put yourself on.

This is an interior landscape. It is inside. It is private. Respect the privacy of the material. These pieces were written in silence. The courage of the play is to speak them. The discipline of the play is not to violate them. Let the audience feel your love of privacy even though there is no privacy. Be good whores. The poem is not a slogan. It cannot advertise you. It cannot promote your reputation for sensitivity. You are not a stud. You are not a killer lady. All this junk about the gangsters of love. You are students of discipline. Do not act out the words. The words die when you act them out, they wither, and we are left with nothing but your ambition.

Speak the words with the exact precision with which you would check out a laundry list. Do not become emotional about the lace blouse. Do not get a hard-on when you say panties. Do not get all shivery just because of the towel. The sheets should not provoke a dreamy expression about the eyes. There is no need to weep into the handkerchief. The socks are not there to remind you of strange and distant voyages. It is just your laundry. It is just your clothes. Don't peep through them. Just wear them.

The poem is nothing but information. It is the Constitution of the inner country. If you declaim it and blow it up with noble intentions then you are no better than the politicians whom you despise. You are just someone waving a flag and making the cheapest appeal to a kind of emotional patriotism. Think of the words as science, not as art. They are a report. You are speaking before a meeting of the Explorers' Club or the National Geographic Society. These people know all the risks of mountain climbing. They honour you by taking this for granted. If you rub their faces in it that is an insult to their hospitality. Tell them about the height of the mountain, the equipment you used, be specific about the surfaces and the time it took to scale it. Do not work the audience for gasps and sighs. If you are worthy of gasps and sighs it will not be from your appreciation of the event, but from theirs. It will be in the statistics and not the trembling of the voice or the cutting of the air with your hands. It will be in the data and the quiet organization of your presence.

Avoid the flourish. Do not be afraid to be weak. Do not be ashamed to be tired. You look good when you're tired. You look like you could go on forever. Now come into my arms. You are the image of my beauty.

[1978]

RUDY WIEBE ■ (1934–)

Rudy Wiebe is widely known for his historical novels about Aboriginal, Métis, Inuit, and Mennonite peoples in Canada. Wiebe's writings are noted for their experimental style, their arresting use of language, and their religious and philosophical complexity, as well as for their postmodern and postcolonial revisioning of heretofore silenced people in Canadian history.

Wiebe's work tends to focus on instances of deep moral crisis, particularly when an individual or community finds itself pitted against the secularized momentum of the surrounding world. A central concern of his work is the upheaval of traditional cultures when challenged by a confrontation from outside, and the subsequent disorientation experienced by individuals as a result of this clash of worldviews. Wiebe's writings, along with those of many other postmodern writers of the late twentieth century including Timothy Findley, Michael Ondaatje, George Bowering, and Robert Kroestch, fall into the category described by Canadian literary theorist Linda Hutcheon as "historiographic metafiction." These texts trouble received understandings of historical

fixity and truth, including the distinction between fact and fiction. As Wiebe put it in his 1980 interview with Shirley Neuman and Robert Kroetsch, "you *should* distrust [history] because when you start looking at the actual stuff from history from a slightly different angle you start seeing so many different stories there than the standard ones we have been given."

Wiebe's method is encapsulated in his 1974 short story, "Where Is the Voice Coming From?" The story is told from the point of view of a narrator determined to relate the "facts" about Almighty Voice, the Cree leader who was hunted down and eventually killed in 1897 by the North West Mounted Police for having stolen a cow. In his 1993 article on the story, Bowering notes that "the narrator naively rejects myth in favour of the scientific approach, and that at the end of the story he represents our national incapacity to understand the spirit of the Native voice." Yet the story ends with a vision of the past that reaches beyond historical reckoning, as an "Almighty Voice" rises out of the landscape as a "wordless cry," untranslatable yet nevertheless audible to anyone willing to hear.

Born into a German-speaking Mennonite family near Fairholme, Saskatchewan, Wiebe had a deeply religious upbringing within the Anabaptist faith. His family, fleeing persecution under the Stalinist regime in the Soviet Union in the 1930s, was part of the last major wave of Mennonite homesteaders to settle the Canadian prairies. Wiebe attended the University of Alberta, from which he received a B.A. in 1956 and an M.A. in 1960. After teaching at Goshen College, Indiana, for a number of years, Wiebe joined the English Department at the University of Alberta in 1967, where he taught English literature and creative writing until his retirement in 1992.

According to Mennonite literary historian Amy Kroeker, the history of the Mennonites has always been one of separation, exile, and a search for a geographic, religious, or cultural "home." Wiebe carries this search into his writing. His first three novels focus on Mennonite communities and explore questions of faith and spirituality in an increasingly materialist age. These include *Peace Shall Destroy Many* (1962), *First and Vital Candle* (1966), and his epic treatment of Mennonite emigration and settlement in *The Blue Mountains of China* (1970).

While his novels are imbued with Christian spirituality, they also explore questions of dogmatism, to the extent that his first novel caused some controversy among the Mennonite community because of its portrayal of hypocritical church leaders. In his work Wiebe tests the foundations of received historical and religious truths, often by using multiple voices and historical documents which attain new meaning when placed in contending contexts. This interest is evident in his novels about western Aboriginal peoples,

particularly in his treatment of their struggle to retain culture and faith in the face of European conquest.

In 1973, Wiebe published his acclaimed historical novel *The Temptations of Big Bear,* for which he received the Governor General's Award. Like other postmodern novels of the period, including Timothy Findley's *The Wars* (1977) and Joy Kogawa's *Obasan* (1981), *The Temptations of Big Bear* uses multiple voices, archival documents, diaries, historical artifacts, newspapers, and firsthand testimony. Wiebe paints a picture of the clash between Native peoples and European settlers during the late nineteenth century, when Aboriginal people were being forced onto reserves by the federal government. As he had done in his Mennonite novels, by recontextualizing historical documents, Wiebe was able to highlight the textualized nature of history, thus producing a postmodern interrogation of received history. Wiebe's innovation in this novel was to re-imagine colonial prairie history from an Aboriginal perspective, namely the viewpoint of Plains Cree Chief Big Bear. Before that time, Big Bear and the other Native leaders had been viewed as rebels and traitors standing in the way of Canadian national progress. In this novel, Big Bear emerges as a visionary who sees the pathos of his people's predicament. Big Bear was one of the last Aboriginal leaders to sign the treaties, and in Wiebe's novel we see him struggling between a commitment to his people and an awareness of the inevitability of their surrender. Big Bear's dilemma, finally, is that the immediate survival of his people requires his capitulation.

Wiebe followed *Big Bear* with a narrative about another Canadian visionary in *The Scorched-Wood People* (1977), which takes as its central characters the figures of Louis Riel and Gabriel Dumont during the Red River (1869–70) and Northwest (1885) rebellions. The novel sets Riel against the materialist and nationalist vision of Canada's first Prime Minister, John A. Macdonald, although its portrayal of its hero is also ambivalent, for in the novel Riel emerges as both prophetic and fanatical. This novel puts Wiebe in the company of many other writers from this period who wrote historical fictions and poems about Riel, including bpNichol's "The Long Weekend of Louis Riel" (1978), included in this section.

In 1994, Wiebe won his second Governor General's Award for *A Discovery of Strangers,* a historical novel about John Franklin's disastrous 1820–22 journey across the barrens to the Arctic Ocean (see Volume I for an excerpt from Franklin's account of this journey). The novel weaves together Native mythology, excerpts from explorers' journals, and certain facts about the expedition. Wiebe also wrote a meditation on the Franklin expedition in *Playing Dead: A Contemplation Concerning the Arctic* (1989). An excerpt from the opening essay from this collection is included here, in which Wiebe considers Franklin's expedition from the perspective of both the Dene/Yellowknife hunters and the French-Canadian *voyageurs,* the men who did most of the heavy labour on the journey.

In 1998, Wiebe collaborated with Yvonne Johnson to write *Stolen Life: The Journey of a Cree Woman.* Johnson, the great-great-granddaughter of Big Bear, contacted Wiebe while she was serving time in prison for murder, asking him to co-write her story. The interweaving of Wiebe's and Johnson's voices throughout the narrative reconstruction of the past using textual documents, taped conversations, and legal records provides a cross-generic example of Wiebe's concern with textuality, language, and "voice." Wiebe's emphasis on the mystical aura of the "voice" or speech of his characters (Big Bear, Almighty Voice, Louis Riel, Robert Hood [in *Discovery of Strangers*]) is echoed in his own resonant rhetorical style. "Where Is the Voice Coming From?" plays on this voicing or "presencing" of an absent figure through its invocation of the spirit of "Almighty Voice" in the land. This theme is also evident in the important collection of essays by and about Wiebe entitled *A Voice in the Land,* edited by W.J. Keith in 1981.

Wiebe's vision is undoubtedly an ethical one, particularly as it concerns his sense of our responsibility toward the past and, by extension, toward the future. In his 1974 essay "On the Trail of Big Bear," he expresses anger at the way Canadians have been deprived of their history: "The stories we tell of our past are by no means merely words: they are meaning and life to us as *people,* as a *particular* people; the stories are there, and if we do not know of them we are simply, like animals, memory ignorant, and the less are we people." This concern links his work with that of fellow prairie writer Robert Kroetsch, whose work (see "Stone Hammer Poem") reveals a similar focus on unearthing a buried past. But unlike Kroetsch, whose radical postmodern perspective posits a "profound distrust of meaning" and an undeniable relativism, Wiebe believes in the "human aspiration to some larger meaning or coherence."

Since 2000, Wiebe has published two important works, *Sweeter Than All the World* (2001), a novel about Mennonite history that many critics consider to be his masterpiece, and his 2006 memoir *Of this earth,* for which he received the Charles Taylor Prize for Literary Nonfiction.

Where Is the Voice Coming From?

The problem is to make the story.

One difficulty of this making may have been excellently stated by Teilhard de Chardin: "We are continually inclined to isolate ourselves from the things and events which surround us . . . as though we were spectators, not elements, in what goes on."[1] Arnold Toynbee does venture, "For all that we know, Reality is the undifferentiated unity of the mystical experience," but that need not here be considered.[2] This story ended long ago; it is one of finite acts, of orders, of elemental feelings and reactions, of obvious legal restrictions and requirements.

Presumably all the parts of the story are themselves available. A difficulty is that they are, as always, available only in bits and pieces. Though the acts themselves seem quite clear, some written reports of the acts contradict each other. As if these acts were, at one time, too well known; as if the original nodule of each particular fact had from somewhere received non-factual accretions; or even more, as if, since the basic facts were so clear perhaps there were a larger number of facts than any one reporter, or several, or even any reporter had ever attempted to record. About facts that are still simply told by this mouth to that ear, of course, even less can be expected.

An affair seventy-five years old should acquire some of the shiny transparency of an old man's skin. It should.

Sometimes it would seem that it would be enough—perhaps more than enough—to hear the names only. The grandfather One Arrow; the mother Spotted Calf; the father Sounding Sky; the wife (wives rather, but only one of them seems to have a name, though their fathers are Napaise, Kapahoo, Old Dust, The Rump)—the one wife named, of all things, Pale Face; the cousin Going-Up-To-Sky; the brother-in-law (again, of all things) Dublin. The names of the police sound very much alike; they all begin with Constable or Corporal or Sergeant, but here and there an Inspector, then a Superintendent and eventually all the resonance of an Assistant Commissioner echoes down. More. Herself: Victoria, by the Grace of God etc., etc., QUEEN, defender of the Faith, etc., etc.; and witness "Our Right Trusty and Right Well-beloved Cousin and Councillor the Right Honorable Sir John Campbell Hamilton-Gordon, Earl of Aberdeen; Viscount Formartine, Baron Haddo, Methlic, Tarves and Kellie, in the Peerage of Scotland; Viscount Gordon of Aberdeen, County of Aberdeen, in the Peerage of the United Kingdom; Baronet of Nova Scotia, Knight Grand Cross of Our Most Distinguished Order of Saint Michael and Saint George, etc., Governor General

---

[1] Pierre Teilhard de Chardin (1881–1955), Jesuit philosopher and author of *The Phenomenon of Man* (1955) (recently translated as *The Human Phenomenon*), who aligned scientific findings with Christian beliefs in identifying a divine evolutionary plan for the cosmos. De Chardin postulated a unitary consciousness of all material and psychic elements that reached backwards and forwards in time.

[2] Arnold Toynbee (1889–1975), English historian and author of the 12-volume *The Study of History* (1934–61), who posited a discernible pattern in the unfolding of world history.

of Canada". And of course himself: in the award proclamation named "Jean-Baptiste" but otherwise known only as Almighty Voice.

But hearing cannot be enough; not even hearing all the thunder of A Proclamation: "Now Hear Ye that a reward of FIVE HUNDRED DOLLARS will be paid to any person or persons who will give such information as will lead ... (etc., etc.) this Twentieth day of April, in the year of Our Lord one thousand eight hundred and ninety-six, and the Fifty-nineth year of Our Reign ... " etc. and etc.

Such hearing cannot be enough. The first item to be seen is the piece of white bone. It is almost triangular, slightly convex—concave actually as it is positioned at this moment with its corners slightly raised—graduating from perhaps a strong eighth to a weak quarter of an inch in thickness, its scattered pore structure varying between larger and smaller on its perhaps polished, certainly shiny surface. Precision is difficult since the glass showcase is at least thirteen inches deep and therefore an eye cannot be brought as close as the minute inspection of such a small, though certainly quite adequate, sample of skull would normally require. Also, because of the position it cannot be determined whether the several hairs, well over a foot long, are still in some manner attached or not.

The seven-pounder cannon can be seen standing almost shyly between the showcase and the interior wall. Officially it is known as a gun, not a cannon, and clearly its bore is not large enough to admit a large man's fist. Even if it can be believed that this gun was used in the 1885 Rebellion and that on the evening of Saturday, May 29, 1897 (while the nine-pounder, now unidentified, was in the process of arriving with the police on the special train from Regina), seven shells (all that were available in Prince Albert at that time) from it were sent shrieking into the poplar bluffs as night fell, clearly such shelling could not and would not disembowel the whole earth. Its carriage is now nicely lacquered, the perhaps oak spokes of its petite wheels (little higher than a knee) have been recently scrapped, puttied and varnished; the brilliant burnish of its brass breeching testifies with what meticulous care charmen and women have used nationally-advertised cleaners and restorers.

Though it can also be seen, even a careless glance reveals that the same concern has not been expended on the one (of two) .44 calibre 1866 model Winchesters apparently found at the last in the pit with Almighty Voice. It also is preserved in a glass case; the number 1536735 is still, though barely, distinguishable on the brass cartridge section just below the brass saddle ring. However, perhaps because the case was imperfectly sealed at one time (though sealed enough not to warrant disturbance now), or because of simple neglect, the rifle is obviously spotted here and there with blotches of rust and the brass itself reveals discolorations almost like mildew. The rifle bore, the three long strands of hair themselves, actually bristle with clots of dust. It may be that this museum cannot afford to be as concerned as the other; conversely, the disfiguration may be something inherent in the items themselves.

The small building which was the police guardroom at Duck Lake, Saskatchewan Territory, in 1895 may also be seen. It had subsequently been moved from its original place and used to house small animals, chickens perhaps, or pigs—such as a woman might be expected to have under her responsibility. It is, of course, now perfectly empty, and clean so that the public may enter with no more discomfort than a bend under the doorway and a heavy encounter with disinfectant. The door-jamb has obviously been replaced; the bar network at one window is, however, said to be original; smooth still, very smooth. The logs inside have been smeared again and again with whitewash, perhaps paint, to an insistent point of identity-defying characterlessness. Within the small rectangular box of these logs not a sound can be heard from the streets of the, probably dead, town.

> Hey Injun you'll get hung for stealing that steer
> Hey Injun for killing that government cow you'll get three weeks on the
> woodpile Hey Injun

RUDY WIEBE

The place named Kinistino seems to have disappeared from the map but the Minnechinass Hills have not. Whether they have ever been on a map is doubtful but they will, of course, not disappear from the landscape as long as the grass grows and the rivers run.[3] Contrary to general report and belief, the Canadian prairies are rarely, if ever, flat and the Minnechinass (spelled five different ways and translated sometimes as "The Outside Hill", sometimes as "Beautiful Bare Hills") are dissimilar from any other of the numberless hills that everywhere block out the prairie horizon. They are bare; poplars lie tattered along their tops, almost black against the straw-pale grass and sharp green against the grey soil of the plowing laid in half-mile rectangular blocks upon their western slopes. Poles holding various wires stick out of the fields, back down the bend of the valley; what was once a farmhouse is weathering into the cultivated earth. The poplar bluff where Almighty Voice made his stand has, of course, disappeared.

The policemen he shot and killed (not the ones he wounded, of course) are easily located. Six miles east, thirty-nine miles north in Prince Alberta, the English Cemetary. Sergeant Colin Campbell Colebrook, North West Mounted Police Registration Number 605, lies presumably under a gravestone there. His name is seventeenth in a very long "list of non-commissioned officers and men who have died in the service since the inception of the force." The date is October 29, 1895, and the cause of death is anonymous: "Shot by escaping Indian prisoner near Prince Albert." At the foot of this grave are two others: Constable John R. Kerr, No. 3040, and Corporal C.H.S. Hockin, No. 3106. Their cause of death on May 28, 1897 is even more anonymous, but the place is relatively precise: "Shot by Indians at Min-etch-inass Hills, Prince Albert District."

The gravestone, if he has one, of the fourth man Almighty Voice killed is more difficult to locate. Mr. Ernest Grundy, postmaster at Duck Lake in 1897,

---

[3] In the treaties that the British government signed with Native peoples in the nineteenth and early twentieth centuries, this phrase was used to demonstrate the supposed permanence of the promise. Wiebe is here quoting it ironically to signal the betrayal of Native peoples and land claims in the story he is relating.

apparently shut his window the afternoon of Friday, May 28, armed himself, rode east twenty miles, participated in the second charge into the bluff at about 6:30 p.m., and on the third sweep of that charge was shot dead at the edge of the pit. It would seem that he thereby contributed substantially not only to the Indians' bullet supply, but his clothing warmed them as well.

The burial place of Dublin and Going-Up-To-Sky is unknown, as is the grave of Almighty Voice. It is said that a Métis named Henry Smith lifted the latter's body from the pit in the bluff and gave it to Spotted Calf. The place of burial is not, of course, of ultimate significance. A gravestone is always less evidence than a triangular piece of skull, provided it is large enough.

Whatever further evidence there is to be gathered may rest on pictures. There are, presumably, almost numberless pictures of the policemen in the case, but the only one with direct bearing is one of Sergeant Colebrook who apparently insisted on advancing to complete an arrest after being warned three times that if he took another step he would be shot. The picture must have been taken before he joined the force; it reveals him a large-eared young man, hair brush-cut and ascot tie, his eyelids slightly drooping, almost hooded under thick brows. Unfortunately a picture of Constable R. C. Dickson, into whose charge Almighty Voice was apparently committed in that guardroom and who after Colebrook's death was convicted of negligence, sentenced to two months hard labour and discharged, does not seem to be available.

There are no pictures to be found of either Dublin (killed early by rifle fire) or Going-Up-To-Sky (killed in the pit), the two teenage boys who gave their ultimate fealty to Almighty Voice. There is, however, one said to be of Almighty Voice, Junior. He may have been born to Pale Face during the year, two hundred and twenty-one days that his father was a fugitive. In the picture he is kneeling before what could be a tent, he wears stripped denim overalls and displays twin babies whose sex cannot be determined from the double-laced dark bonnets they wear. In the supposed picture of Spotted Calf and Sounding Sky, Sounding Sky stands slightly before his wife; he wears a white shirt and a stripped blanket folded over his left shoulder in such a manner that the arm in which he cradles a long rifle cannot be seen. His head is thrown back; the rim of his hat appears as a black half-moon above eyes that are pressed shut in, as it were, profound concentration; above a mouth clenched thin in a downward curve. Spotted Calf wears a long dress, a sweater which could also be a man's dress coat, and a large fringed and embroidered shawl which would appear distinctly Dukhobour in origin if the scroll patterns on it were more irregular. Her head is small and turned slightly towards her husband so as to reveal her right ear. There is what can only be called a quizzical expression on her crumpled face; it may be she does not understand what is happening and that she would have asked a question, perhaps of her husband, perhaps of the photographers, perhaps even of anyone, anywhere in the world if such questioning were possible for an Indian lady.

There is one final picture. That is one of Almighty Voice himself. At least it is purported to be of Almighty Voice himself. In the Royal Canadian Mounted Police

Museum on the Barracks Grounds just off Dewdney Avenue in Regina, Saskatchewan, it lies in the same showcase, as a matter of fact immediately beside, that triangular piece of skull. Both are unequivocally labelled, and it must be assumed that a police force with a world-wide reputation would not label *such* evidence incorrectly. But here emerges an ultimate problem in making the story.

There are two official descriptions of Almighty Voice. The first reads: "Height about five feet, ten inches, slight build, rather good looking, a sharp hooked nose with a remarkably flat point. Has a bullet scar on the left side of his face about 1 1/2 inches long running from near corner of mouth towards ear. The scar cannot be noticed when his face is painted but otherwise is plain. Skin fair for an Indian." The second description is on the Award Proclamation: "About twenty-two years old, five feet ten inches in height, weight about eleven stone, slightly erect, neat small feet and hands; complexion inclined to be fair, w[ith] wavey dark hair to shoulders, large dark eyes, broad forehead, sharp features and parrot nose with flat tip, scar on left cheek running from mouth towards ear, feminine appearance."

So run the descriptions that were, presumably, to identify a well-known fugitive in so precise a manner that an informant could collect five hundred dollars—a considerable sum when a police constable earned between one and two dollars a day. The nexus of the problems appears when these supposed official descriptions are compared to the supposed official picture. The man in the picture is standing on a small rug. The fingers of his left hand touch a curved Victorian settee, behind him a photographer's backdrop of scrolled patterns merges to vaguely paradisiacal trees and perhaps a sky. The moccasins he wears make it impossible to deduce whether his feet are "neat small". He may be five feet, ten inches tall, may weigh eleven stone, he certainly is "rather good looking" and, though it is a frontal view, it may that the point of his long and flaring nose could be "remarkably flat". The photograph is slightly over-illuminated and so the unpainted complexion could be "inclined to be fair"; however, nothing can be seen of a scar, the hair is not wavy and shoulder-length but hangs almost to the waist in two thick straight braids worked through with beads, fur, ribbons and cords. The right hand that holds the corner of the blanket-like coat in position is large and, even in the high illumination, heavily veined. The neck is concealed under coiled beads and the forehead seems more low than "broad".

Perhaps, somehow, these picture details could be reconciled with the official description if the face as a whole were not so devastating.

On a cloth-backed sheet two feet by two and one-half feet in size, under the Great Seal of the Lion and the Unicorn, dignified by the names of the Deputy of the Minister of Justice, the Secretary of State, the Queen herself and all the heaped detail of her "Right Trusty and Right Well Beloved Cousin", this description concludes: "feminine appearance". But the pictures: any face of history, any believed face that the world acknowledges as *man*—Socrates, Jesus, Attila, Genghis Khan, Mahatma Gandhi, Joseph Stalin—no believed face is more *man* than this face. The mouth, the nose, the clenched brows, the eyes—the eyes are large, yes, and dark, but even in this watered-down reproduction of unending reproductions of that original, a steady look into those eyes cannot be endured. It is a face like an axe.

It is now evident that the de Chardin statement quoted at the beginning has relevance only as it proves itself inadequate to explain what has happened. At the same time, the inadequacy of Aristotle's much more famous statement becomes evident: "The true difference [between the historian and the poet] is that one relates what *has* happened, the other what *may* happen."[4] These statements cannot explain the storyteller's activity since, despite the most rigid application of impersonal investigation, the elements of the story have now run me aground. If ever I could, I can no longer pretend to objective, omnipotent disinterestedness. I am no longer *spectator* of what *has* happened or what *may* happen: I am become *element* in what is happening at this very moment.

For it is, of course, I myself who cannot endure the shadows on that paper which are those eyes. It is I who stand beside this broken veranda post where two corner shingles have been torn away, where barbed wire tangles the dead weeds on the edge of this field. The bluff that sheltered Almighty Voice and his two friends has not disappeared from the slope of the Minnechinass, no more than the sound of Constable Dickson's voice in that guardhouse is silent. The sound of his speaking is there even if it has never been recorded in an official report:

> *hey injun you'll get*
> *hung*
> *for stealing that steer*
> *hey injun for killing that government*
> *cow you'll get three*
> *weeks on the woodpile hey injun*

The unknown contradictory words about an unprovable act that move a boy to defiance, an implacable Cree warrior long after the three-hundred-and-fifty-year war is ended, a war already lost the day the Cree watch Cartier hoist his gun ashore at Hochelaga and they begin the long retreat west;[5] these words of incomprehension, of threatened incomprehensible law are there to be heard just as the unmoving tableau of the three-day siege is there to be seen on the slopes of the Minnechinass. Sounding Sky is somewhere not there, under arrest,

4 In *The Poetics* (c. 335 B.C.), Greek philosopher Aristotle outlines the difference between the poet and the historian, maintaining that poetry is more philosophical and hence more important than history because "poetry relates more of the universal, while history relates particulars."

5 Jacques Cartier (1491–1557), French explorer who charted the St. Lawrence River in the 1530s and '40s and described his meeting with the Iroquois people in the region. Cartier is often considered to be the explorer who paved the way for the European conquest and settlement of North America, hence Wiebe's suggestion that the oppression of Aboriginal peoples begins with his arrival. See Volume I for an excerpt from Cartier's *Voyages*, including his description of visiting the village of Hochelaga (Montreal).

but Spotted Calf stands on a shoulder of the Hills a little to the left, her arms upraised to the setting sun. Her mouth is open. A horse rears, riderless, above the scrub willow at the edge of the bluff, smoke puffs, screams tangle in rifle barrage, there are wounds, somewhere. The bluff is so green this spring, it will not burn and the ragged line of seven police and two civilians is staggering through, faces twisted in rage, terror, and rifles sputter. Nothing moves. There is no sound of frogs in the night; twenty-seven policeman and five civilians stand in cordon at thirty-yard intervals and a body also lies in the shelter of a gully. Only a voice rises from the bluff:

> We have fought well
> You have died like braves
> I have worked hard and am hungry
> Give me food

but nothing moves. The bluff lies, a bright green island on the grassy slope surrounded by men hunched forward rigid over their long rifles, men clumped out of rifle-range, thirty-five men dressed as for fall hunting on a sharp spring day, a small gun positioned on a ridge above. A crow is falling out of the sky into the bluff, its feathers sprayed as by an explosion. The first gun and the second gun are in position, the beginning and end of the bristling surround of thirty-five Prince Albert Volunteers, thirteen civilians and fifty-six policemen in position relative to the bluff and relative to the unnumbered whites astride their horses, standing up in their carts, staring and pointing across the valley, in position relative to the bluff and the unnumbered Indians squatting silent along the higher ridges of the Hills, motionless mounds, faceless against the Sunday morning sunlight edging between and over them down along the tree tips, down into the shadows of the bluff. Nothing moves. Beside the second gun the red-coated officer has flung a handful of grass into the motionless air, almost to the rim of the red sun.

And there is a voice. It is an incredible voice that rises from among the young poplars ripped of their spring bark, from among the dead somewhere lying there, out of the arm-deep pit shorter than a man; a voice rises over the exploding smoke and thunder of guns that reel back in their positions, worked over, serviced by the grimed motionless men in bright coats and glinting buttons, a voice so high and clear, so unbelievably high and strong in its unending wordless cry.

The voice of "Gitchie-Manitou Wayo"—interpreted as "voice of the Great Spirit"—that is, The Almighty Voice. His death chant no less incredible in its beauty than in its incomprehensible happiness.

I say "wordless cry" because that is the way it sounds to me. I could be more accurate if I had a reliable interpreter who would make a reliable interpretation. For I do not, of course, understand the Cree myself.

[1974]

From Exercising Reflection

[. . .] John Franklin, aged thirty-three, together with medical doctor and naturalist Dr. John Richardson, thirty-one, midshipmen George Back and Robert Hood, both twenty-two, and ordinary seaman John Hepburn, thirty, sail from Gravesend on May 23, 1819, on board the Hudson's Bay Company ship *Prince of Wales* for York Factory to explore that coast. [. . .]

They are following the traditional fur trade route and they have had no problem with their hired voyageurs (except that their head man drowns on a portage, an occupational hazard one assumes) until they reach Fort Providence on the north shore of Great Slave Lake on July 29, well over a thousand river miles from Cumberland House.[6]

It was here that they must leave the regular trade routes to move north and the voyageurs, who will have to literally carry on their backs all the supplies up over the height of land into the Coppermine basin, begin to voice serious doubts. [. . .]

The weight of canoes and cargo is four tons, all to be heaved over the innumerable rocks and portages of the torturous Yellowknife River by eighteen voyageurs. The officers, as befits the hierarchy of the Royal Navy which informed the expedition throughout, carry only their instruments and personal papers while John Hepburn, quite properly for an ordinary English sailor, has to work and sleep with the voyageurs although he can not even converse with them in their particular French Canadian. The party leaves Great Slave Lake on August 2, preceded by a large flotilla of Indian canoes which even on the initial portages quickly outdistances the English because the women and children also help carry. This convinces Hood that the Indians had very much overestimated the expedition's possible speed.

He is correct. By August 5, after six portages on a single day, they have barely progressed and are already down to the spare provisions of "portable soup." Fishing is unsuccessful and the hunters nowhere in sight; by August 12 they are not halfway up the Yellowknife River and the limping voyageurs are giving "up all hope of relief." They threaten to desert and Franklin, like any good English sea captain, "denounc[ed] the heaviest punishment against the ringleaders."

It is difficult to imagine how the four officers intended to carry out these threats; did they believe the eighteen powerful men would simply bend over a convenient rock to be whipped? Stand by at attention, saluting the Union Jack perhaps while their leaders were being executed by firing squad? Slavery was,

---

[6] Cumberland House was the Hudson Bay Company's first western inland trading post, established by Samuel Hearne in 1774 on the Saskatchewan River. Franklin's expedition was charting the Arctic coastline from the Coppermine River heading eastward. Due to dwindling provisions and harsh weather, the party desperately headed back to their base camp Fort Enterprise, losing numerous men along the way. See Volume I, Section I, for the excerpt from Franklin's version of the journey.

of course, still a standard in the 1820 "civilized" world but Canadian voyageurs were free men, extremely proud of their skills and hired by the job or the season. Fortunately for Franklin, before any punishments had to be attempted "four [Indian] hunters arrived, bringing the flesh of two reindeer [i.e., caribou], and after this period we suffered no more from deficiency of provisions, nor were we [i.e., the officers] again censured for temerity: the Canadians never exercising reflection unless they are hungry." Such a remark from Hood, the gentlest of the officers, pinpoints the English attitude early in the expedition. The voyageurs have literally carried them over two thousand miles into the country, nevertheless they are little more than thoughtless hirelings of burden who, despite their acknowledged excessive burdens, must be kept in place by threat and physical punishment.

By August 20 the torturously moving expedition finally reaches Winter Lake where on the edge of the treeline they intend to build Fort Enterprise and winter over. Hood records that the expedition had moved 1516 miles in the brief summer of 1820 but is still over 300 miles from the Arctic coast. But they are full of hope. It is fortunate for them that the Indian hunters can supply them with plenty of meat [. . .] so that for some months the Canadians do not again need to "exercise reflection."

By October 9 the river is filming with ice, though the lake has been firmly frozen for two weeks. The three buildings of "Fort" Enterprise have been built of logs in the French Canadian post-and-lintel style, the largest being separate quarters and mess for the four officers. They enter again the arctic winter stillness. Within a year young Hood, the most gifted and promising of the officers, will have entered his ultimate stillness. He will not die of overwork and starvation, though he will be on the extremest edge of exactly that. A year later on October 7, 1821, Richardson and Hepburn will be left alone with Hood on the tundra somewhere between the Obstruction Rapids on the Coppermine River and Fort Enterprise; Back and Franklin and those few voyageurs still alive will be struggling ahead through the snow to try to find the Yellowknife Indians who alone can save them all from death by starvation. [. . .]

On October 9 a critical event takes place. Michel Terohaute, the Iroquois voyageur, returns to them from Franklin who is still struggling to get to Fort Enterprise and the hoped-for help from Akaitcho and the Yellowknife people. Michel brings a rabbit and a ptarmigan but, as Richardson writes, he

> complained of cold, and Mr. Hood offered to share his buffalo robe with him at night; I gave him one of the two shirts which I wore, whilst Hepburn, in the warmth of his heart, exclaimed, "How I shall love this man if I find he does not tell lies like the others." . . . after reading the evening service we retired to bed full of hope.

The arctic experience has drastically altered their class behavior: they now share clothes and blankets. Next day Michel, oddly, asks for a hatchet to go hunting; a hunter invariably uses only a gun and a knife. He returns with what he says is the frozen meat of a wolf gored by a caribou; they eat the meat chopped from the carcass, but Richardson becomes convinced that it may be part of the body of one of Franklin's voyageurs frozen farther ahead on the trail to Fort Enterprise. However they dare say nothing since Michel, besides his strange moodiness, is armed and obviously much stronger than they three together. Motionless they wait for help to come, growing steadily weaker. On Sunday, October 20, after the morning service Hepburn is trying to cut willows and Richardson scraping *tripe de roche*[7] off some rocks when they hear Michel quarreling with Hood. A shot goes off. Richardson hurries up fearing Hood in despair has killed himself. His poor friend is most certainly dead, the Bible still in his hand. [. . .]

They must now try to reach Fort Enterprise on their own: the rescue party Franklin promised to send back has not come. Unencumbered by the dying Hood, and cooking pieces of his scraped buffalo robe for food, they set out. Michel always keeps himself armed and between the other two. Finally on the trail on October 23 (fifteen days after Franklin left them behind) the ever-watchful voyageur drops back a little and Richardson reports:

> Hepburn and I were now left together for the first time since Mr. Hood's death, and he acquainted me with several material circumstances which he had observed of Michel's behaviour, and which confirmed me in the opinion that there was no safety for us except in his death, and he [Hepburn] offered to be the instrument of it. I determined, however, as I was thoroughly convinced of the necessity of such a dreadful act, to take the whole responsibility upon myself; and immediately upon Michel's coming up, I put an end to his life by shooting him through the head with a pistol. Had my own life alone been threatened, I would not have purchased it by such a measure; but I considered myself as intrusted also with the protection of Hepburn's, a man, who, by his humane attentions and devotedness, had so endeared himself to me, that I felt more anxiety for his safety than for my own.

At this point of "execution," as Richardson and Franklin both called it (did Richardson in pulling the trigger recall his captain's threat of "the heaviest punishment" against the voyageur complainers?), a review of the expedition's achievement and method will explain what the arctic landscape had perforce done to the usual English standards of conduct. Supported by Indian hunters they had left Fort Enterprise on June 4, 1821, and paddled down the Coppermine River north; by July 19 they at last reached the open ocean. There the Indians left them. [. . .] Meanwhile, facing the ocean encumbered with cakes of ice, Richardson writes that the remaining eleven voyageurs "seem terrified at the idea of a voyage through an icy sea in bark canoes" and indeed one might ask, why should they not

---

[7] Rock lichen.

be? They had only two fragile canoes, one of which a week later was very nearly crushed between two ice floes. [. . .] Nevertheless they did travel; incredibly. By the end of August, after coasting along the Arctic shore for almost six hundred miles, traversing bays of open ocean whose headlands they could not see, the birch-bark is almost falling from the gunwales and Richardson still, amazingly, records:

> The fears of our voyageurs have now entirely mastered their prudence and they are not restrained by the presence of their officers from giving loose to a free and sufficiently rude expression of their feelings.

"Mastered their prudence" indeed! One assumes that Franklin, had he been on board ship, would have keel-hauled them in the face of what they recognized as their imminent death: "They despair of ever seeing home again . . . [they say] any attempt to proceed further [is] little short of madness."

The voyageurs are, of course, deadly right. They know they have been too long on the sea and that the annual caribou migration has left them behind. With the wood and bark of one ruined canoe they cook their last full meal of muskox meat on September 4. The other canoe is destroyed while crossing the Burnside River on September 8. The officers, good seamen all, know the compass course to reach Fort Enterprise and they begin to walk through the sudden and terrifyingly early snow and cold across the tundra. Each voyageur carries a ninety-pound pack; not one of them has any idea what lies in their path and they can eat only what they can find to hunt, daily: if there were some food to carry it would simply increase their enormous burden.

In their path are three unknown and unfordable rivers; they are slivered with ice, but of course the men cannot wait for them to freeze because they have no food. [. . .] The Coppermine River rushing over the double Obstruction Rapids really destroys them. They are stopped there for eleven days, wearing away their last reserves of strength in a desperate search for a means to cross. Finally Pierre St. Germain manages to build a tiny shell out of willows and the oilcloth with which the officers cover their sleeping robes and hauls them all across the vicious river one at a time on a line he strings. By then one of their men, the Inuk translator Junius, has disappeared somewhere never to be seen again. [. . .] The main party trudges on as slowly as the weakest man can move; gradually the men, so long overworked while subsisting mostly on boiled leather and moss, when they can find it, begin to fall behind.

Now Franklin and his party are forced to make certain decisions: everyone is so weak they can barely walk by themselves—they certainly cannot carry the dying. So they do exactly what the Inuit were traditionally forced to do under those circumstances. [. . .]

Franklin faces exactly that situation since his voyageurs, even without a much-reduced pack, can no longer carry their bodies across the endless tundra. But he does not of course shoot those men too weak to keep up, though that might have been a final desperate act of kindness. No. He leaves them behind. Here is a roll call of those men who, on a quest whose purpose none of them could fathom, nevertheless made possible the journey and all the honours Franklin and Richardson and Back were to receive later:

Junius: Inuk translator, canoeman; vanished September 27, 1821, without crossing the Coppermine River.

Mathew Pelonquin: voyageur, unable to keep up, left behind after Obstruction Rapids on October 6.

Registe Vaillant: voyageur, collapsed, left behind some hours later on October 6.

Jean Baptiste Belanger: voyageur, collapsed, left behind October 7.

Ignace Perrault: voyageur, collapsed, left behind October 8.

Antonio Fontano: Italian voyageur, collapsed, left behind October 8. Franklin promised him that, if he survived, he would assist him to return to Italy to see his dying father.

Gabriel Beauparlant: voyageur, collapsed at Round Rock Lake while looking for Indians with Back's party, left behind October 16.

Michel Terohaute: Iroquois voyageur, shot by Richardson on October 23; he lived on either Belanger's or Perrault's frozen flesh and undoubtedly fed some of it to Hood, Richardson and Hepburn.

Joseph Peltier: voyageur, died of malnutrition after the Franklin party reached Fort Enterprise, November 1.

Francois Samandre: voyageur, died of malnutrition at Fort Enterprise, November 2.

Only *Pierre St. Germain*, a Metis and Yellowknife Indian interpreter, the best hunter of all whose skill in somehow fashioning a shell out of oilskins saved the party at the Coppermine River, and the two strongest voyageurs, *Solomon Belanger* and *Joseph Benoit*, survived that dreadful trek.

Four of the five Englishmen, however, survived. It cannot be because they were physically stronger than the Canadians. Whatever food there was was always divided by Hood as long as he lived with scrupulous honesty (he invariably took, writes Franklin, the smallest share for himself), so this pattern of deaths must have come about because the Canadians laboured more, carrying the heavier loads. It would seem that the English officers survive on the Arctic tundra because (a) they leave behind their dying (though they sincerely promise to return with help if they can find it), (b) they eat human flesh (though inadvertently, and horrified at the very thought), and (c) they kill the strongest man in the party because they are afraid he will kill and probably eat them. Later Willard Wentzel, the Northwest Company clerk in charge at Fort Providence, accuses Dr. Richardson of murder, but no investigation is ever made beyond Richardson's report. Yet a hundred years later when two Inuit hunters kill two priests on the lower Coppermine River because they are afraid the priests with their rifles would kill them, those two Inuit men are taken through three years of Canadian judicial systems and courts to be declared guilty of murder. A special law for whites persists in the North.

Lieutenant George Back confesses to Wentzel the next summer (1822) that "to tell the truth, Wentzel, things have taken place which must not be told."

What were these untellable secrets? Richardson presumably tells some of his: he shot and killed Michel Terohaute; he privately writes about perhaps, unknowingly, eating human flesh. Franklin vanishes in 1845 telling nothing of any "secrets." Back himself leads several important Arctic expeditions and dies knighted, an admiral, fifty-seven years later without ever saying anything. [. . .]

[1989]

GEORGE BOWERING ■ (1935–)

Few writers exemplify the postmodern spirit of boisterous irreverence and experimental flair that marked the 1960s and '70s better than George Bowering. An extraordinarily prolific poet, novelist, and critic, Bowering combines a jocular wit with theoretical seriousness, parodic self-reflexivity, and offbeat lyricism.

Since publishing his first poetry collection in 1963 (*Sticks and Stones*), Bowering has gone on to publish over 80 books. Among many honours, he has won two Governor General's Awards: one for poetry (for two books that appeared in 1968 and 1969, *rocky mountain foot* and *The Gangs of Kosmos*) and one for fiction (for *Burning Water* in 1980). Bowering taught English at Simon Fraser University for 30 years, retiring in 2001. The following year, he was made an Officer of the Order of Canada and named the first Poet Laureate of Canada.

Born and raised in Penticton, B.C., Bowering served as an Air Force photographer before attending the University of British Columbia, where he earned a B.A. in history (1960) and an M.A. in English (1963). Along with fellow students Frank Davey, Fred Wah, and Lionel Kearns (all of whom would become major critics and poets), he gravitated to the writing and poetic theories of the leading avant-garde American writers known as the Black Mountain poets:

Robert Duncan, Charles Olson, and Robert Creeley (Creeley served as Bowering's M.A. thesis advisor while working as a visiting professor at UBC).

It was a time of high expectations and bold initiatives. In 1961, Bowering helped to found the influential magazine *TISH,* along with Davey, Wah, Daphne Marlatt (then Daphne Buckle), and others. More than a magazine, *TISH* quickly developed into a major force within the postmodern literary scene. Like the TISH movement itself, Bowering's work was both deeply rooted in British Columbian life and insistently outward-looking, profoundly influenced by the work of American poets William Carlos Williams and Gertrude Stein, and by his contact with Creeley, Olson, and Duncan. His best-known long poem, *Kerrisdale Elegies* (1984), adapted Rainer Maria Rilke's *Duino Elegies* (1923) to a meditative exploration of a Vancouver neighbourhood, naming familiar streets and dwelling fondly on the city's characteristics even as he turned his thoughts to philosophical questions of love and mortality.

Bowering's poetry is widely admired for what poet Robin Blaser called its "restlessness of meaning," which challenges readers to be alert to the process of communication rather than inviting easy or straightforward readings. Like his prose, Bowering's poetry is suffused with a deceptively offhand humour that masks the philosophical rigour of his formal commitments. Rejecting high-flown poetic contrivances such as elaborate metaphors and elevated diction, Bowering's poetry is distinguished by his interest (as he put it) in "making beauty out of very very plain language." Indeed, his writing often challenges the reader with its blend of natural expression, loose form, and deliberately jarring postmodern self-reflexivity. Inserted into the midst of a meditative passage in the eighth "Kerrisdale Elegy," for example, is the comment: "Oh oh, says the anxious reviewer, this poet is not in control of his materials." But for Bowering, these two facets of his poetry—its insistence on plain language and its playful and even sometimes unsettling self-reflexivity—are part of the rebellion against what Bowering, Davey, Wah, Nichol, and their peers rejected as the conventions of "realism." Such self-reflexive strategies enable authors to foreground process and the constructed nature of all writing at the expense of thematic, mimetic, or formal closure. Bowering's "post-realist" and anti-modernist aesthetic is articulated in his various collections of literary criticism, including *The Mask in Place* (1982) and *Craft Slices* (1985).

Like his poetry, Bowering's prose is marked by its avowedly postmodernist love of intertextual allusion, parody, textual innovation, and self-reflexivity, all of which converge in his uncompromising insistence on the artificiality of literature; that is, writing as artifice, or something that needs to be made or wrought in order to exist. Where realist authors frequently tend toward styles that erase their authorial presence in order to foster "a willing suspension of disbelief," Bowering makes his own presence and, even more compelling for him, the vexed question of the relation between himself as author and the unknown reader, one of the central themes of "Staircase Descended," the short story included here from his 2004 collection *standing on richards.*

A Short Sad Book (1977), the poetry-prose novel that established Bowering's reputation as a fiction writer, combined these postmodern preoccupations with his other abiding interest, Canadian history. Its deliberately iconoclastic approach to some of Canada's most fundamental cultural myths anticipated the more fully developed and better remembered treatment of these issues in his popular metafictional novel, *Burning Water* (1980). The novel grew out of a much earlier long poem, *George, Vancouver: A Discovery Poem* (1970). Focused on the efforts of a novelist named "George Bowering" to write a historical novel about the English explorer George Vancouver's mapping of the B.C. coast, *Burning Water* merged his interest in postmodern technique with a historical and political concern for the complicity between Western narrative traditions and the broader cultural and political hierarchies they helped to legitimate.

Bowering's love of parody, like Thomas King's, often manifests itself in what might be called a deconstructive strategy. Novels such as *Caprice* (1987) and *Shoot!* (1994) situate themselves within the time-honoured genre of the dime-store Western in order to unsettle that genre's most entrenched characteristics, challenging their implied social judgments (about women and Aboriginal people, in the case of Westerns) in deliberately subversive ways. Always witty and provocative, Bowering's twin interests in history (both the history of genres and larger national and regional histories) and postmodernism have left an indelible impression on Canadian writing.

Staircase Descended

I opened my eyes or I open my eyes and thought or think it was or is morning. That is a terrible sentence to begin with. I take it back. I open my eyes, usually, and think it might be morning. How do you know? Your, no, my glasses are on the top of the bookcase and so is the clock with its red numerals and they tell the time. But can they be said to tell the time if there is no one in the room who is capable of reading the numerals? That is not the kind of question one, yes that's a good one, one—one wants to ask or even answer first thing in the morning. If it is morning.

One wants to stay in bed, of course, and to hell with the time of day. But one is also predisposed to getting out of bed. For me that is a problem, the first one of the probable day. Here is the problem: when I wake up I am lying on my right side, knees as close to my chest as possible, one hand under the pillow or rather my head because the pillow has fallen to the floor, there is no pillow. The other hand, who knows? It could be pulled up under my chin. My knees as close to my chest as possible. When I was young, I could tuck my knees right up against my chest. No more. But of all the things I cannot make my body do any more, this business with the knees is the least of my troubles. I can lift the knees a lot closer than most men or even women my age, I will wager.

The problem is getting my body out of bed. I do not mean a slacking of the will. I mean that when I wake, nearly blind eyes looking at a red blur of unknown numerals, my body is locked in that position I was so careful to describe just a moment ago. And mind you, I am sick and tired of description. If I go on with this, I might have some difficulty with description. I might not do it. You will not find me throwing around adjectives, in any case. I hate the goddamned slithery unnecessary corruptive willful Anglo-Saxon self-satisfied secondary stylish things. Ha, just a little joke there, you don't mind? To hell with you, too. Just fooling.

Trying to get that body out of that bed. It might help if I described the bed, but I won't. The body is locked in place by a small imperfection low down in the vertebraic column. If the body lies in roughly the same position for a given period of time, as for instance when I am asleep, it is next to impossible to change its attitude. For instance, I cannot induce it to lie on its back and stretch its legs straight toward the so-called foot of the bed. Nor can I swing the legs over the side of the bed, though my body lies on the edge, not the middle of the bed. It is a medium-wide bed. My father died in it, and there was a woman who used to find room for her body beside mine. In those days my body did not lie in the same position all night.

Many people get out of bed by swinging their legs together, rotating on their buttocks, perhaps, and allowing their trunks to be levered to a vertical position as their heels fall to the floor, where there may be cold wood or gritty linoleum or a warm wool carpet. A warm wool carpet. If there were a warm wool carpet in this room, I might sleep on it and avoid this problem of getting out of the bed. But then the problem of rising vertical from the carpet might be even more daunting. I return to the appropriate problem. I wished and I wish that I could rotate and rise, my heels falling on whatever is down there, sometimes it is hard to remember all these things. That is connected to my dislike of description, I am sure. If I find that I cannot remember something that one would never imagine forgetting, anyone's forgetting, one wants to crawl under the covers if he can find them, and go back to sleep, if you can call what I do sleeping.

Not that I don't try the various ways of getting up in the morning. It is impossible, thank goodness, to describe the feeling when one wants to get up but the body will not do it. It is not the same thing as wanting to move your arm when you wake up with your arm asleep over your head. You begin to move your left leg, let us say, and a signal arrives saying that you will soon be in great familiar pain without hope of gaining some movement at its cost. Hopeless. The signal comes from the small place in the lower region of the sacroiliac, you remember that word. It was very popular in radio show jokes in the late forties.

So here is what I do—I could list all the ways I fail every morning, but I cannot summon the energy to try to remember them, and if I miss out a few I will not be proud enough of my list, knowing that you will then think that things are not really as bad as all that. Well, why should I care about that? It is too late now, anyway. Here is what I wind up doing. With extremely small movements I nudge the body closer to the edge of the bed. This nudging is meticulous and painstaking and would seem to be hopeless of success if I had not done it on previous occasions. First I might point the big toe on my top, that is left, foot toward the bookcase and move the foot a bit. Then the lower or right shoulder. Then, with the long bony loose-skinned fingers, damned description, of both hands wrapped around the corner of the edge of the mattress, I manage to bounce the round bony ball of my right hip an inch, or is it a centimetre, over, to the right, that is. You will just have to imagine, if you can summon your faculties better than I can mine, how long this procedure goes on and with what discomfort I must continue it. It makes my body sweat, which is amusing, because my body affords a comparison with the denuded skin of a mature chicken, and one has never seen a chicken perspire, no matter what other discomfiting things one has seen a chicken do. Sweating like that every morning or whenever it is I get out of bed, and, yes, I finally do, I wish momentarily for a shower. Place of potential disaster. Enough, and more.

Enough. If I do not get at it I will never tell you how I get out of bed and thus solve the first problem of the day. And why bother getting up, you ask. I do not get up. After enough edging and pointing and minute hopping with my frozen shut body, I manage to propel myself so far to my right that I achieve the edge and more of the bed. Of course I have not been able to rotate on my hips as we would all like to, but I do turn as I depart the bed, and fall face downward to the floor. There is no stopping me then, not till I come to rest on whatever that surface is. Of course, I always remember if I am jolted enough. It is hardwood, nice dark boards of hardwood. Once they shone, a rich dark brown lateral glint of—no. There is a bang, of course, when I cease falling, and even though I have my hands in position to prevent my face from striking the hardwood, I do land nice and crisp on my knees and elbows, and so the tight grip thus far maintained by the little spot of imperfection in my vertebraic column is slackened just a little. Enough so that in my present position I can begin a careful crawl toward the toilet.

2

Sometimes it is a crawl and sometimes it is more like a creep, a creeping, let us say, to avoid vulgar ambiguity. It would be nice just to stand up and walk or at least hobble to the bathroom, and on the odd occasion I can do just that, if on the route there are enough objects or close enough walls I fall into so that I can support myself on something. There are times when I start by standing up, having pulled myself up the brass leg of the bed, but have to collapse to the hardwood again because the first step or shuffle, let us say, brings a serrated knife blade, this is a fanciful description, you understand, into the small of my back. A small that is the largest thing in my attention at the time. Poor jest, but necessary.

I proceed, embarrassed a little, I mean here is a grown, perhaps, man, on his hands and knees (if it is one of my lucky mornings) crawling out of his bedroom into the hallway and, turning a little to the left, into the bathroom. If you are a man, or if at least a man a little like me, you know that in the morning there is a compulsion you cannot shake. In fact it is often the agent that gets you out of bed in the first place. This is the unnegotiable necessity of passing water. Some people are lucky: they hop out of bed in the morning, perhaps flinging their arms wide of their trunks in a little reminder of elementary-school exercises, and hippity hop to the toilet, where they pull it out and piddle away, great creamy suds rising on the sides of the bowl, a 1950s radio song humming in their heads.

While I am crawling toward the bathroom and then across the bathroom to the convenience, fifteen men in my neighbourhood have done just what I outlined above. I crawl past the sink, along the flank of the bathtub, noticing for the hundredth time that one of its clawed feet has a smear of toothpaste on it, and how did that get there again? It could not, certainly, be the same smear that was there, let us say, last February the twelfth. But there I am then at the device. There is a certain principle at work now—the more movement I am capable of, the more I am capable of movement. It is as though the knot in my back is melting. In an hour or so I will be walking like a normal man or a normal man with a body made of shredded wheat, as I once quipped to Marsha, a woman you will never hear about again. Here I am. But there is no question of waiting until I can perambulate. Not that it is not a temptation. Just let the bladder go, let it unblad, I suppose you could say, and relax. Reeelaaax, says the voice in my left ear. That is where the devil sits when he has time, my mother once said. Enough about her. There will be no resorting to "motivation" in this account.

There I am. There is no question, then, of pointing Percy at the porcelain. I am committed, you might say if this were more serious, this telling, to telling you the details. The truth is that I could stop right here, and I would not mind. You would probably cheer the abandonment. In fact it is unlikely that you have made it this far. If you have, please sign your initials right here:. All right, there I am. I am 186 centimetres in height on the occasions when I can stand up fully. I have never been able to measure the toilet bowl in centimetres, but it is just under fourteen inches in height. All right, I will just tell you and let's forget it. I kneel full of gratitude that I am there and hang poor Percy over the hard white lip. On most occasions he has reached by now the condition of hangability. But there are mornings on which he will not retreat from the condition he was found to be in on my waking. I do not know or have forgotten what those neighbours of mine do on such an occasion, but I can tell you what I do. I can tell you but just this once I do not believe that I will.

Flushed not too far from my embarrassed face, the toilet is finished for now, and glad I am of it. Now there is the sink and perhaps the shower. I would like to take a shower every morning. In fact there was a time a few years back when I did, and not always alone, I can tell you. What a ridiculous image, you say. All right then, you will get urine and atrocious posture instead of soapy euripus. Now I simply hope that by the time I am ready for the shower I can stand up in it. There is nothing gratifying about coming to rest on one's hands and knees in the tub and feeling the hard water against one's back. But first the sink. I always feel a little guilty when it comes to the sink. This guilt reaches, as most do, a long way back, into childhood, when one's mother warned one about putting one's weight on the poor sink. Damn. There is something about a bathroom that allows one's mother to sidle into the discussion, the monologue, yes, I know. But you are here, aren't you, you did sign in, didn't you?

All right, I pull myself up the sink, like a sickly monkey pulling himself up the bars that imprison him while offering him something to ascend. There you go, a simile, I think. You will not, if I have my wits about me, see another of those. Bad enough that I fell into this so-called present tense. No, I made a promise to myself not to spend all my precious time talking about this talking. If it is talking. It looks more like writing to me. There I go. Okay, a short paragraph. I decided on paragraphs, with you in mind. You might remember that.

Up the sink I climbed. (That felt good. Not the climbing. I mean the tense.) (This will get out of hand. I really must stop that sort of thing right now, no matter what attractive thoughts come to mind.) By now I can bear this, the simulacrum of standing while leaning heavily on the basin. I can manage to get the stopper in. I didn't use one for years till I started paying for my own hot water. The taps on. The object is to wash and then debarbarate the face. Now my 186 centimetres give me a new problem, or rather the revisiting of an old problem. I cannot bend to get my face anywhere near the right altitude for laving. I must spread my feet as far apart as possible, rest my bony forearms on the edge of the porcelain, and do the best I can, bobbing my head for a painful half-second, and throwing water and soap toward my cheeks. This goes on. I want to stop but I have to proceed. I want to stop writing or talking or thinking, but you cannot. You cannot stop thinking if you are not a Himalayan anchorite,[1] and what else is there? So, eventually one gets a razor in one's hand and eventually manages to make momentary scrapes at the face. It is a little like reaching for a piece of paper that is just out of reach on the floor on the other side of those monkey bars. If you overextend your shoulder and elbow and wrist for a second before they all snap back into their proper proportions, you can make a little scrape at the whiskers and soap if you have the razor at the correct angle. This is how I shave almost every morning. I have thought of growing a beard but I cannot. I have random hairs on my face, no pattern and certainly no carpet. I used to tell myself that this unmanliness was a sign that I was a forerunner of human beings from the future. I read a lot of science fiction in my youth, and time travel was my favourite narrative device. I was going to say something about that but I cannot remember what it was. Let us say that I have shaved.

Perhaps now I can get into the shower. The main reasons one gets into the shower, or the main reasons I do, are my hair and the cleft between my buttocks. Perhaps I can get into the shower and at least lean against the wall.

3

Now we come to the heart of this story. It is a story, don't you agree? Now we come to what I thought of as the whole of the story. I could probably put this a better way if I started all over again. But then what would you have? Probably a well-rehearsed narrative and therefore something you cannot trust. If you think that is literary theory, think again. There is nothing at all literary here, I the least so.

I am now approaching the bottom of the stairs from above. That is, I am descending. Not at all like the royalty those words might make one think of. I am wearing a pair of slippers so old that I can't remember who gave them to me. One never buys one's own slippers any more than one buys one's own aftershave lotion. They, the slippers, have heels that have been crushed under my own for so long that they would appear to someone who has not yet put on his glasses for the day to be made that way. There are plenty of slippers with no backs to them, you know that. You also know by now that I am for some reason slow to get to this heart of the story I promised or at least mentioned. I am also, I must tell you, since I started on this dressing of the narrator, wearing my ratty old bathrobe, or is it housecoat? It is an item that falls to a level just below my knees and is belted at approximately the waist. That is all. Under this piece of drab phlegm-green terry cloth I am as naked and as attractive as a hog hanging in the cold room at Peerless Packers.

Ah, say you, ablutions done and staircase descended, he is now going to perform the comfortably familiar ritual of the morning newspaper and fresh egg. That is, ah, say you, all this while at the same time saying it looks as if this person is going to force upon me or us a lot more sentences than we need about

---

[1] A hermit or monk who is in seclusion for meditative or religious purposes.

every moment of his waking and God help us perhaps sleeping life. Not so. At least I hope not so: I did not, I will admit, plan on narrating the getting down out of bed and the getting up to the white bowls. How about this: I think that you can depend on my torpor to protect you from a recounting in the familiar present tense of my whole day, one like the next that they are.

No, this is the point at which you encounter not a fresh egg and a minimal daily, but two women at a kitchen table, drinkers of so much coffee that in an hour they will be taking turns at the downstairs toilet, and expenders of more words in that hour than appear in the missing newspaper. It is not really missing, save from this account. Either it is on the front steps where it has been for five hours, or some child, pauper, or dog has made off with it again. If there has been a high wind earlier this morning, its pages will be wet to transparency and wrapped around various bushes or weeds in the yard and the neighbour's yard. The neighbour does not read the newspaper. He is a longhaired youth whose occupation seems to be burglary, judging from the peculiar coming and going of packing cases and trailing electrical cords. But you will not be bothered with him again. I do not even know his name, so I can not even withhold that from you.

So to those two women sitting at the kitchen table, the way women will, sprawling a little, no, that is not quite right, their bodies relaxed so much that they seem to be saying with their easeful slouch that they own the space. No, I will never get that right, so I will drop the attempt. One might as well commit a lot of description, or lay out a row of similes. Anyway, there they are, the two of them, total weight, let us say of 150 kilograms, maybe less. The prettier one is the neighbour lady, but the other one is smarter. She is the one who is related to me by marriage. She thinks that I am gone, and she has her friend persuaded of that illusion. Sometimes it sounds to me as if she thinks that I am dead and gone; other times it seems as if she is convinced that I am just gone, fled, fallen away. Just disappeared from sight. I do not do everything I could do to persuade her otherwise, but I make small attempts in that direction. Why do people call that a direction? Let it stand. I hardly can myself.

They are having one of their usual discussions. This is what the lady of the house says:

"Each thing itself, then, and its essence are one and the same in no merely accidental way, as is evident both from the preceding arguments and because to *know* each thing, at least, is just to know its essence, so that even by the exhibition of instances it becomes clear that both must be one."

To which her visitor responds:

"Ha ha ha ha. You may be right about that and you may be wrong. You could not prove it by me. All I know is that when my old man wants what he wants and I don't want what he wants, essence, well, essence never enters into it. It might have worked differently for you when your old man was around. Might have been essence all over the place. Ha ha ha ha. Far as I know. Ho ho."

Now the woman who lives in this house never condescends to her friends or any stranger. She just assumes that they enjoy the possibility of entering the conversation, when they get the chance to talk, at a level that will be commensurate, is that a usable word here, with the one she is speaking on. So she will continue (ah, the future tense, which no more covers the future than the present tense the present):

"For it has been already shown that the soul of the incarnate deity is often supposed to transmigrate at death into another incarnation; and if this takes place when the death is a natural one, there seems no reason why it should not take place when the death has been brought about by violence. Certainly the idea that the soul of a dying person may be transmitted to his successor is perfectly familiar to primitive peoples."

"I wish I had known that yesterday when I was at the houseplant sale at Corby's," says her fellow coffee-drinker. "That place was full of primitive people yesterday. Oh my!"

At this juncture I decide to try to make my presence known. Luckily, I *have* had a shower this late morning, and that stream of hot, nearly steaming water on the small of my back makes it possible for me to walk, even on a level surface. I generally start with a significant stare at one of the two women. Sometimes the visitor is not there; on that occasion I stare at my close relative, bending my neck down the way a pigeon does when it is contemplating a puddle but wary of a crowd of human feet. Having inaugurated the stare, I lift my left hand to a level with my left nipple, wrist tucked in to trunk, and wiggle the upward pointing fingers a little. When you do that, trying to make each digit independent of the others, the middle finger, the longest, usually refrains from wiggling. Nevertheless, I hope that it *appears* to be wiggling because its neighbours are so doing. I do not want to be thought to be disguising a rude gesture, even with the palm facing the wrong way. Not yet, in any case.

"There is an unmistakable indication in the text of Sophocles' tragedy itself that the legend of Oedipus sprang from some primeval dream-material that had as its content the distressing disturbance of a child's relation to his parents owing to the first stirrings of sexuality."[2]

"Stirrings!" exclaimed the neighbour. "It's too bad you never had any children before he departed. My boys are stirring all the time. I tell you I hate cleaning up their room. And sometimes I don't feel at all safe myself!"

You could not say the word "sexuality" to this woman without rousing her. Even sitting still in her chair, forearms on the table between them, she seemed to experience a sea change. Her body seemed to become more rounded, to make rounded areas of shininess in her print dress. Perspiration made her throat glow, and moisture appeared in the edges of hair over her ear. Her mouth would not

[2] This is a quotation from Sigmund Freud's *The Interpretation of Dreams* (1900). Greek playwright Sophocles is the author of *Oedipus the King*, which tells the tale of a man who inadvertently kills his father and marries his mother. The myth is largely about the impossibility of escaping one's fate, since in trying to evade the tragedy, Oedipus's parents make it happen. The point about primal dream material is a reference to Freud's controversial theory of the Oedipus Complex, which outlines how male children develop an early sexual attraction for their mothers and feelings of competitiveness toward their fathers.

entirely close when it was relieved of its labour of speech. Moisture shone from her front teeth. Her eyes, which before had been simply brown and cool, now glowed as if all at once connected to the electrical power lying patiently in the wires inside the walls between rooms. The palms of her hands were probably wet. The creases at the backs of her knees were likely sticky. She moved her knees a little farther apart, looking, in all likelihood, for air.

How disappointing. I had intended, as you will have gathered, to spare you that sort of thing. The foregoing description should appear thus:

~~You could not say the word "sexuality" to this woman without rousing her. Even sitting still in her chair, forearms on the table between them, she seemed to experience a sea change. Her body seemed to become more rounded, to make rounded areas of shininess in her print dress. Perspiration made her throat glow, and moisture appeared in the edges of hair over her ear. Her mouth would not entirely close when it was relieved of its labour of speech. Moisture shone from her front teeth. Her eyes, which before had been simply brown and cool, now glowed as if all at once connected to the electrical power lying patiently in the wires inside the walls between rooms. The palms of her hands were probably wet. The creases at the backs of her knees were likely sticky. She moved her knees a little farther apart, looking, in all likelihood, for air.~~

You think that you know what you would do in this situation? You have that profound confidence? The universe for you is not a maze with possible beasts at the end of any corridor? I congratulate you on your good fortune, I am without envy. I simply wish to express my joy that there is such a fortunate one among us, and therefore maybe many. Joy is likely too exalted a word. What can I put in its place? I suppose we could agree on satisfaction. All right, my satisfaction. But now you must also allow that it is not for me a simple decision to say or do what I do or did in the above circumstance.

I am not stupid: I know that you are objecting to my silence here. Why, you ask, do I not shout at the women to make them notice and indeed acknowledge my existence and more than that my presence? And while we are at it, why do I not effect another conducting of the senses; that is, why do I or did I not reach out and touch the woman of my choice here? Why not grasp the neighbour lady's thigh or seize a handful of my matrimonial partner's raven hair and pull it, vertically or horizontally about seven centimetres, or to be more certain, fifteen? I do not know whether I will be able to explain this to you. I know that there must be personalities like mine in the world, personalities that have been shaped more or less like mine over all the years of our growing up, albeit like potatoes growing in rocky soil, some of us being compelled to grow around a rock and never to achieve the shape assigned to the potato in the little golden book of west coast gardening. If you happen to be one of those rare but surely extant personalities, you will understand easily why I did not make those auditory or palpatory attempts at communication. In fact it is probable that I would not have to waste breath or ink or whatever I am expending in the explanation. You would intuit and agree, you would find the parallel in or behind your meek heart. For the others, probably the majority of you, I can try the outline of an explanation. Probably anyone, of any personality, will have a layer, a striation of my condition, if condition is an appropriate word here, and I am reluctant to admit it.

All right, for you, the majority, I will try this. If I were to reach out and touch or grab or caress or pull, whether the pretty one or the smart one, and if I could feel the touch and the recipient could not, I would be, ontologically speaking, in trouble. If she could feel it and I could not, I would be filled with doubt at best. If neither of us could feel it—that is, if my hand went right through, say, the upper leg of the woman from down the street, it could mean any number of things. It could mean that we are both goners or creatures of the imagination, and if so, whose? It could mean that I am dreaming, or at least that one of us is, or if that is not stretching likelihood too far, both of us are. It could be that we are both figures in a fiction whose perpetrator is not paying sufficient attention for the moment. It could mean that this is the general rule of things and that my long-held opinion that matter comes to rest against the surface of matter is in error. The possibilities are not endless, but the end is too far away for the amount of energy I have to spare for postulating its place. Suffice it to say that I am aware of many possibilities that I do not want to prove or have proven for me.

It would be a simple thing to attempt a casual, accidental-seeming touch, if there were not other hints of my non-existence, at least as far as these women and the dimension they were in was concerned; and here I go into some sort of past tense again. If they acknowledged me by sight, and were not just ignoring me but unaware of my being, I could touch them without any but the normal fears, a knuckle to the temple or whatever. But then the touch would be unnecessary, as this explanation would be were I speaking or writing to people who could easily understand my attitude. But because these people seemed not to be able to notice me (and this is not just a singular instance, you must remember) by sight, there was a good chance that they would not notice me by touch because the latter was impossible. If not a good chance, at least a chance. As it is, at least till the present time, I would rather try another time to make them notice me by sight, just *in case* they were ignoring me out of spite. I want to hold onto the illusion, if it is an illusion, that I exist, for a while.

There was another possible explanation that I was going to offer, but now I feel that it would take a considerable feat of memory and thought to bring it to the surface of my brain, and I would rather return now to the narrative, if you will agree that that is what I departed from. Besides, the explanation, for those of you who do not resemble me in the most particular of my traits, would be overlong. It is likely that I would lose you, either in the sentences or from the room.

In the meantime, if that is not a silly thing to say at the preface of this resumption, I am in that other room, let us call it a living room—requisite number of furniture items, crooked magazines on one of them, and I can see the brace of women through the extra-wide kitchen door, at least it is the kitchen door from my viewpoint. From theirs it is probably the living room door. It is not really a door, but rather a kind of formality for those who like to know that they are passing between rooms, a kind of minimal archway, really a rounding of the corners, a sort of slight decrease in the distance from wall to wall. Through this thing I will call a door simply for the sake of this narrative, which I persist in misnaming it, I can see the two women and hear their conversation as suggested above. I mean I don't expect you to believe that I have caught a verbatim series of remarks from one particular afternoon—I am using the present tense from time to time, after all. Really I just went and selected some likely passages from books of an unmistakably intellectual bent.

Now what I do is to remove my clothes. I cannot remember what I said I was wearing, so I will rely on you to remember, or to go back and look it up. Let us say that I was wearing pajamas, my ratty old striped blue-and-white ones that I have to hold the pants of up unless I am wearing my old greenish terry cloth robe. Well, let us say, or I will, that I was at the moment in question wearing all that stuff. And my bedroom slippers, the ones, I remember now, with the squashed down heels. I take all these things off. No, I don't. But I undo the belt of my robe, and then I let the pajama bottoms drop. I kick off my bedroom slippers in order to kick off the pajama bottoms that have settled around my feet. Then I can dance.

Here is what the dance looks like. Rather, here is what I imagine the dance to look like; as the dancer I am in no position to observe or reflect on the dance. I hold the skirts of my off-green terry cloth robe in my two hands and lift them sideways, away from my body. Then I contrive to bend my bony legs, knobby, really, they are knobby at the hip, knee, ankle, and foot, bend my knobby legs and kick my feet out sideways. All this time I make certain that I am facing the conversation at the kitchen table. I might describe an arc, little part of a semi-circle, there in the adjoining room, but always with the effect of total angular continuity. I dance and dance. I take a chance and kick my bony heel knobs together. My genitals swing back and forth in opposition to my legs. That is, when my legs are kicking left, my genitals are still swinging right. But enough about them. I don't think that my genitals are any funnier or any more an affront than the rest of my white, hairless, smooth, gravity-formed body.

What do I want? Do I want to test the limits of their ability to pretend that I am not there? Am I by now allowing that I might not exist, at least for them, and enjoying a dare otherwise prevented by childhood training in repression and civility? Why don't I approach, why don't I press the advantage that would be granted by proximity? I believe that I have explained that above, at least for those readers or listeners who would benefit by explanation, that is, understand and even, perhaps, sympathize. Now, wouldn't that be grand? Sympathy. I, even were I not after all a literary figure, as I am sure I am for you, one that you may even have grown tired of, would appreciate and welcome sympathy as quickly as the next fellow. But now I was finding it to be as much as I could handle to try for recognition.

How did my audience, if I may have your indulgence in calling them that for the nonce, react to my terpsichorean[3] antics? After I had exhausted myself, and

---

[3] Relating to dancing.

was sprawled out in what had been her father's favourite easy chair, legs extended in front of me, skirts of my robe falling behind each stringy thigh, this is what I heard them to say:

"Diogenes, another follower of Anaximenes, held that air was the ultimate element of all things, but that nothing could be produced from it without the agency of the divine reason, which permeated it. Anaxagoras was followed by his pupil Archelaus. He, too, asserted that everything in the universe was composed of like particles, which, however, were informed by intelligence. This mind, by causing the conjunction and dissolution of the eternal bodies or particles, was the source of all movements."[4]

"I'd have to think for a while to agree about *all movements*. I got a husband, and you don't know how lucky you are sometimes, and two huge boys, and I can't believe that there is any mind behind their movements, especially when they are coming down the stairs or when they are picking up knives and forks, when I can convince them to use such elementary tools."

I was exhausted. There was nothing more I could do there. I was certainly not going to go into the kitchen to get coffee or a muffin or even a piece of limp broccoli. I did not want to play ghost, because I might start to believe in my own demise. I did not want to touch one of those people. What if I touched one, and she responded in such a way as to show that she had known I was there all the time? One does not like to entertain the notion that one is that little worthy of remark. I would go upstairs, and then I would decide whether to get dressed and go out, thinking of the near impossibility of donning socks, of bending to stick one over a big toe, and if I did go out I would get a cup of coffee and even a lemon-guck-filled Danish pastry. I would go to Daphne's Lunch. Everyone knows me there. They say hello and say my name out loud when I enter the premises. They know enough to let me sit at a banquette even when I am using a table for four, because of my bad back. I am visible there. I do not know the names of any of the waitresses or the regular patrons I see there every time I attend. But we are a community. A community of laggards, perhaps, but a polis.

4

Perhaps you will agree that that scene, with the two talkative women and the dancing geezer, was the heart of this story, given that you have already acceded to the notion that this is a story. What, then, will we call the following? The following scene, perhaps a kind of loosening of the knot we have got ourselves tied in, takes place in Daphne's Lunch, where you will not hear saints and thinkers

[4] Diogenes, Greek philosopher, was one of the founders of the philosophical school known as Cynicism; he made a virtue of poverty in order to teach contempt for human achievements, calling into question social values and institutions. Anaximenes was a philosopher known for his attempts to provide scientific explanations for the world, who taught that air is the source of all things. Anaxagoras was a pre-Socratic Greek philosopher and cosmographer who proposed a unity among all things since initially all things in the Cosmos were combined. He also postulated a governing Mind that guided the principles of the Cosmos. Archelaus was a pupil of Anaxagoras and master of Socrates, who imported the study of natural philosophy to Athens.

discussed all that often. Oh, once in a while I will quote Heraclitus[5] to some hapless toiler for the minimum wage. But in general, philosophy is not broached there. Until today. Or that day. Let us say today.

Today I found myself talking with an old gent who seemed to admire his ability to pick a tea bag out of its cup and suspend it over its home in such a way that the drips of tea will fall into the centre of the red-brown liquid. No, I *find* myself talking with him. I do not know his name, and I do not think that he knows mine. It is in such circumstances that one may find oneself these days. There is a little ambiguity for you, I mean that sentence. But you knew that, didn't you? All right, I will get on with this tale. Nice day. Nice day. Haven't seen such nice weather this time of year in years. Last year we were soaking wet and cold as hell this time of year. This kind of weather is good for your rheumatism. Good for what ails you. You bet. Wouldn't mind being thirty years younger all the same. You bet, I would settle for twenty.

And so on. I know how to tailor my conversation for this crowd. It never strikes me that the guy I am talking with might be tailoring his conversation for this crowd, with me as part of this crowd. Who knows? We may, if we were to meet somewhere else, say one of the conference rooms at the Regency Hotel, have begun a discussion of Anaxagoras and his tradition. Be that as it may, we got onto a discussion of ontology or the like anyway. How we got there from the quite ordinary weather, I do not recall. Or I do not want to write or say it out. Eventually I got most of the lemon guck into my mouth and some on my lap, and was in conversation. I could end this account right here, and not make it any the less inconclusive than it is going to be. You will say that you would have liked to be warned of that at least around page four. Well, here is your chance. You can drop it right now, leave the beanery, browse the bookstore, two blocks east, cross the street, find an uplifting story or a meaningful fiction. Let me suggest the paperback edition of Michael Ondaatje's *Running in the Family*.[6] Even if you don't buy it, you will have avoided the following conversation:

"My wife can't see me."

"You too?"

"She looks right through me."

"They are like that. That is why they are wives."

I let him sip his tea. I allowed the waitress to refill my coffee cup. I had to think about this. How will I relate to this gent who doubtless has a name but one that does not hang in the air between us, a story that will not be instantly convertible into the clichés of figurative language surrounding connubial friction?

"She thinks that I am dead. Or if not that, she is of the opinion that I have in some less mortal way retired from the site of our domicile. She thinks that I am no longer there."

[5] Heraclitus was an influential pre-Socratic Greek philosopher who postulated that the world is in constant change but that there is an underlying order to that change (which he termed *Logos*).

[6] *Running in the Family* (1982), by Michael Ondaatje, is a creative memoir about the author's family in Sri Lanka.

"Sounds just like my wife, bless her departed soul."

Back there, I think, in the heart of the story, I cannot persuade anyone of my existence, much less my propinquity. Now my appearance, in such an habitual location, is unquestioned. I can now not speak the opposite. I can't persuade someone of my absence, my non-being, albeit only in the eyes, or rather out of the eyes and mind of another, or in this case two others, at least.

It strikes me that this gent without the name may think that he is only speaking with a reverie, only imagining this conversation, imagining that there is a coffee-drinking fellow with a bad back with whom he is in conversation. It is late morning. Old bones rest and old brains enjoy their little trips.

"Have a look at me," I say.

People don't, as a rule, like to do that in places like Daphne's. They usually let their eyes flit. To the waitress as she turns her back and carries something to the kitchen hole. To the passing balloon outside the window, a kid has been to a celebrating bank. To the widow at another table. She is smoking a cigarette and reading a small paperback novel placed inside a leatherette cover. But this fellow does look now.

"Am I to look at anything in particular?" he says.

"Can you see a scar on my face?"

He looks.

"Yes I can."

"Where is it?"

"Well, there are two. There is a small one right at your hairline above the middle of your forehead, and there is a slightly longer one that runs from the corner of your mouth down at a 45-degree angle."

It was more like a 30-degree angle, but I let it go.

"Thank you."

All right, I do exist. At least in this circumstance, in this environment, I exist.

"So to you I am visible," I suggest.

"Sure. Unless you are not supposed to be here. If your wife calls, I will say I haven't seen you, if you want."

"No, no. That's not what I mean. She would never phone this place anyway. Nor would she enter it willingly. She goes to well-lit places where they serve little things on croissants for seven dollars."

All right, I have settled the question of whether he is imagining me. There is still the question about whether I have created him. If he is a product of my imagination, there is not all that much currency in his attestation that he can see me as well as talk with me.

It strikes me that I could just rest comfortable, take everything at face value. But it also strikes me that I am not any better off than I was in the living room of my own house, except that here I am enjoying a second cup of coffee. There I was pretty well convinced of my presence; I was propiocepting[7] quite handily,

---

[7] The detection of internal stimuli.

thank you. But others were not reflecting knowledge and awareness of my corporeal entity. Here I receive outside attestation of my being and presence, but I feel the possibility of uncertainty as to whether I have not generated, mentally, of course, the agent of that corroboration.

I should, perhaps, as they say, have stood in bed.

Maybe I did. But no, I cannot accept that. I cannot allow that all that pain of rising for the dubious day was nothing, or for nothing. Or that it will be if I do it. I do not want to spend a life made from now on and who knows how long till now, made entirely of mentation. Of course all you can receive through the agency of this expenditure of words is something that resembles mentation more than it does any more physical and palpable action, if we can speak of action rather than the thing acting as palpable. Maybe I don't even palpate anything any more. Did I just imagine being downstairs and dancing? Am I not now sitting on a reddish banquette at Daphne's, thinking of my hard bed as down that street, up those stairs? Is there anyone reading or hearing this?

[2004]

ALISTAIR MACLEOD ■ (1936–)

The most renowned short story writer of Atlantic Canada, Alistair MacLeod, like Alice Munro, is noted for the fine craftsmanship of his work. Although he has published only two collections of short stories, *The Lost Salt Gift of Blood* (1976) and *As Birds Bring Forth the Sun* (1986)—stories from both collections were gathered together in *The Island* in 2000—MacLeod's reputation for highly symbolic and intricately condensed prose points to the finely wrought nature of his writing.

Most of MacLeod's writings evince a deep connection with the geography and people of Cape Breton. Although he was born in Saskatchewan and grew up in Alberta, the family moved to their ancestral Cape Breton home when he was 10. MacLeod studied at St. Francis Xavier University and the University of New Brunswick (where he wrote an M.A. thesis on Canadian short stories of the 1930s), and eventually garnered a full-time teaching position at the University of Windsor in 1969, where he taught English and creative writing until his retirement in 2000. During these years, MacLeod was fiction editor of the *University of Windsor Review.*

MacLeod's stories tend to focus on fishing or mining communities in the Maritimes, often on characters of Scottish Gaelic heritage. Of particular interest in his work is a concern with the ways the historical and ancestral past infiltrates into the present and influences characters' lives. His stories, often written in the present tense, are marked by what American author Joyce Carol Oates describes as "the urge to memorialize," as characters within the tales, like the author himself, preserve the past in "storied" form. Yet there is also a profound sense of melancholy that pervades his work, a recognition of the inevitability of change. MacLeod's characters are both confined by traditional lifestyles of the past and sustained by communal tradition. This conflict is heightened by the deeply ethical nature of many of his characters. These elements are present, as well, in MacLeod's long-awaited first novel, *No Great Mischief* (1999), which tells the story of generations of the MacDonald family. Members of the youngest generation seek fortune away from Cape Breton but are inevitably tied to the place and their Gaelic ancestors, and are condemned to repeatedly memorialize it. *No Great Mischief* was published to great acclaim and won the prestigious IMPAC Dublin Literary Award.

"The Boat," which Oates describes as "that most appallingly beautiful of stories,"

first published in the *Massachusetts Review* in 1968, won MacLeod international recognition when it was included in *Best American Short Stories* the following year, as was his story "The Lost Salt Gift of Blood" in 1975. The story is an account of a man trapped by traditional expectations, yet it is this circumstance that contributes to his nobility of character. From the narrator's perspective in "present" time, it also charts the uncanny inheritance of his father's trials. Like many of MacLeod's stories, it is a complex psychological drama, a story of the things one does in the name of duty and love.

The Boat

There are times even now, when I awake at four o'clock in the morning with the terrible fear that I have overslept; when I imagine that my father is waiting for me in the room below the darkened stairs or that the shorebound men are tossing pebbles against my window while blowing their hands and stomping their feet impatiently on the frozen steadfast earth. There are times when I am half out of bed and fumbling for socks and mumbling for words before I realize that I am foolishly alone, that no one waits at the base of the stairs and no boat rides restlessly in the waters by the pier.

At such times only the grey corpses on the overflowing ashtray beside my bed bear witness to the extinction of the latest spark and silently await the crushing out of the most recent of their fellows. And then because I am afraid to be alone with death, I dress rapidly, make a great to-do about clearing my throat, turn on both faucets in the sink and proceed to make loud splashing ineffectual noises. Later I go out and walk the mile to the all-night restaurant.

In the winter it is a very cold walk and there are often tears in my eyes when I arrive. The waitress usually gives a sympathetic little shiver and says, "Boy, it must be really cold out there; you got tears in your eyes."

"Yes," I say, "it sure is; it really is."

And then the three or four of us who are always in such places at such times make uninteresting little protective chit-chat until the dawn reluctantly arrives. Then I swallow the coffee which is always bitter and leave with a great busy rush because by that time I have to worry about being late and whether I have a clean shirt and whether my car will start and about all the other countless things one must worry about when he teaches at a great Midwestern university. And I know then that that day will go by as have all the days of the past ten years, for the call and the voices and the shapes and the boat were not really there in the early morning's darkness and I have all kinds of comforting reality to prove it. They are only shadows and echoes, the animals a child's hands make on the wall by lamplight, and the voices from the rain barrel; the cuttings from an old movie made in the black and white of long ago.

I first became conscious of the boat in the same way and at almost the same time that I became aware of the people it supported. My earliest recollection of my father is a view from the floor of gigantic rubber boots and then of being suddenly elevated and having my face pressed against the stubble of his cheek, and of how it tasted of salt and of how he smelled of salt from his red-soled rubber boots to the shaggy whiteness of his hair.

When I was very small, he took me for my first ride in the boat. I rode the half-mile from our house to the wharf on his shoulders and I remember the sound of his rubber boots galumphing along the gravel beach, the tune of the indecent little song he used to sing, and the odour of the salt.

The floor of the boat was permeated with the same odour and in its constancy I was not aware of change. In the harbour we made our little circle and returned. He tied the boat by its painter, fastened the stern to its permanent anchor and lifted me high over his head to the solidity of the wharf. Then he climbed up the little iron ladder that led to the wharf's cap, placed me once more upon his shoulders and galumphed off again.

When we returned to the house everyone made a great fuss over my precocious excursion and asked, "How did you like the boat?" "Were you afraid in the boat?" "Did you cry in the boat?" They repeated "the boat" at the end of all their questions and I knew it must be very important to everyone.

My earliest recollection of my mother is of being alone with her in the mornings while my father was away in the boat. She seemed to be always repairing clothes that were "torn in the boat," preparing food "to be eaten in the boat" or looking for "the boat" through our kitchen window which faced upon the sea. When my father returned about noon, she would ask, "Well, how did things go in the boat today?" It was the first question I remember asking: "Well, how did things go in the boat today?" "Well, how did things go in the boat today?"

The boat in our lives was registered at Port Hawkesbury. She was what Nova Scotians called a Cape Island boat and was designed for the small inshore fishermen who sought the lobsters of the spring and the mackerel of summer and later the cod and haddock and hake. She was thirty-two feet long and nine wide, and was powered by an engine from a Chevrolet truck. She had a marine clutch and a high speed reverse gear and was painted light green with the name *Jenny Lynn* stencilled in black letters on her bow and painted on an oblong plate across her stern. Jenny Lynn had been my mother's maiden name and the boat was called after her as another link in the chain of tradition. Most of the boats that berthed at the wharf bore the names of some female member of their owner's household.

I say this now as if I knew it all then. All at once, all about boat dimensions and engines, and as if on the day of my first childish voyage I noticed the difference between a stencilled name and a painted name. But of course it was not that way at all, for I learned it all very slowly and there was not time enough.

I learned first about our house which was one of about fifty which marched around the horseshoe of our harbour and the wharf which was its heart. Some of them were so close to the water that during a storm the sea spray splashed against their windows while others were built farther along the beach as was the case with ours. The houses and their people, like those of the neighbouring towns and villages, were the result of Ireland's discontent and Scotland's Highland Clearances and America's War of Independence. Impulsive emotional Catholic Celts who could not bear to live with England and shrewd determined Protestant Puritans who, in the years after 1776, could not bear to live without.

The most important room in our house was one of those oblong old-fashioned kitchens heated by a wood- and coal-burning stove. Behind the stove was a box of kindlings and beside it a coal scuttle. A heavy wooden table with leaves that expanded or reduced its dimensions stood in the middle of the floor. There were five wooden homemade chairs which had been chipped and hacked by a variety of knives. Against the east wall, opposite the stove, there was a couch which sagged in the middle and had a cushion for a pillow, and above it a shelf which contained matches, tobacco, pencils, odd fish-hooks, bits of twine, and a tin can filled with bills and receipts. The south wall was dominated by a window which faced the sea and on the north there was a five-foot board which bore a variety of clothes hooks and the burdens of each. Beneath the board there was a jumble of odd footwear, mostly of rubber. There was also, on this wall, a barometer, a map of the marine area and a shelf which held a tiny radio. The kitchen was shared by all of us and was a buffer zone between the immaculate order of ten other rooms and the disruptive chaos of the single room that was my father's.

My mother ran her house as her brothers ran their boats. Everything was clean and spotless and in order. She was tall and dark and powerfully energetic. In later years she reminded me of the women of Thomas Hardy, particularly Eustacia Vye, in a physical way.[1] She fed and clothed a family of seven children, making all of the meals and most of the clothes. She grew miraculous gardens and magnificent flowers and raised broods of hens and ducks. She would walk miles on berry-picking expeditions and hoist her skirts to dig for clams when the tide was low. She was fourteen years younger than my father, whom she had married when she was twenty-six and had been a local beauty for a period of ten years. My mother was of the sea as were all of her people, and her horizons were the very literal ones she scanned with her dark and fearless eyes.

[1] Eustacia Vye is the passionate, dark-haired heroine of British author Thomas Hardy's *The Return of the Native* (1878). Vye yearns to leave the traditional lifestyle of Egdon Heath and marries a man who she mistakenly believes can take her abroad, only to find herself living the very life she had sought to escape. Vye eventually dies by drowning, a possible suicide. While the narrator's mother in this story bears a physical resemblance to Vye, in other respects the two are diametrically opposed; it is the father in the story whose predicament most parallels Vye's.

Between the kitchen clothes rack and barometer, a door opened into my father's bedroom. It was a room of disorder and disarray. It was as if the wind which so often clamoured about the house succeeded in entering this single room and after whipping it into turmoil stole quietly away to renew its knowing laughter from without.

My father's bed was against the south wall. It always looked rumpled and unmade because he lay on top of it more than he slept within any folds it might have had. Beside it, there was a little brown table. An archaic goose-necked reading light, a battered table radio, a mound of wooden matches, one or two packages of tobacco, a deck of cigarette papers and an overflowing ashtray cluttered its surface. The brown larvae of tobacco shreds and the grey flecks of ash covered both the table and the floor beneath it. The once-varnished surface of the table was disfigured by numerous black scars and gashes inflicted by the neglected burning cigarettes of many years. They had tumbled from the ashtray unnoticed and branded their statements permanently and quietly into the wood until the odour of their burning caused the snuffing out of their lives. At the bed's foot there was a single window which looked upon the sea.

Against the adjacent wall there was a battered bureau and beside it there was a closet which held his single ill-fitting serge suit, the two or three white shirts that strangled him and the square black shoes that pinched. When he took off his more friendly clothes, the heavy woollen sweaters, mitts and socks which my mother knitted for him and the woollen and doeskin shirts, he dumped them unceremoniously on a single chair. If a visitor entered the room while he was lying on the bed, he would be told to throw the clothes on the floor and take their place upon the chair.

Magazines and books covered the bureau and competed with the clothes for domination of the chair. They further overburdened the heroic little table and lay on top of the radio. They filled a baffling and unknowable cave beneath the bed, and in the corner by the bureau they spilled from the walls and grew up from the floor.

The magazines were the most conventional: *Time, Newsweek, Life, Maclean's, Family Herald, Reader's Digest*. They were the result of various cut-rate subscriptions or of the gift subscriptions associated with Christmas, "the two whole years for only $3.50."

The books were more varied. There were a few hard-cover magnificents and bygone Book-of-the-Month wonders and some were Christmas or birthday gifts. The majority of them, however, were used paperbacks which came from those second-hand bookstores which advertise in the backs of magazines: "Miscellaneous Used Paperbacks 10¢ Each." At first he sent for them himself, although my mother resented the expense, but in later years they came more and more often from my sisters who had moved to the cities. Especially at first they were very weird and varied. Mickey Spillane and Ernest Haycox vied with Dostoyevsky and Faulkner, and the Penguin Poets edition of Gerard Manley Hopkins arrived in the same box as a little book on sex technique called *Getting the Most Out of Love.*[2] The former had been assiduously annotated by a very fine hand using a very blue-inked fountain pen while the latter had been studied by someone with very large thumbs, the prints of which were still visible in the margins. At the slightest provocation it would open almost automatically to particularly graphic and well-smudged pages.

When he was not in the boat, my father spent most of his time lying on the bed in his socks, the top two buttons of his trousers undone, his discarded shirt on the ever-ready chair and the sleeves of the woollen Stanfield underwear, which he wore both summer and winter, drawn halfway up to his elbows. The pillows propped up the whiteness of his head and the goose-necked lamp illuminated the pages in his hands. The cigarettes smoked and smouldered on the ashtray and on the table and the radio played constantly, sometimes low and sometimes loud. At midnight and at one, two, three and four, one could sometimes hear the radio, his occasional cough, the rustling thud of a completed book being tossed to the corner heap, or the movement necessitated by his sitting on the edge of the bed to roll the thousandth cigarette. He seemed never to sleep, only to doze, and the light shone constantly from his window to the sea.

My mother despised the room and all it stood for and she had stopped sleeping in it after I was born. She despised disorder in rooms and in houses and in hours and in lives, and she had not read a book since high school. There she had read *Ivanhoe* and considered it a colossal waste of time.[3] Still the room remained, like a solid rock of opposition in the sparkling waters of a clear deep harbour, opening off the kitchen where we really lived our lives, with its door always open and its contents visible to all.

The daughters of the room and of the house were very beautiful. They were tall and willowy like my mother, and had her fine facial features set off by the reddish copper-coloured hair that had apparently once been my father's before it turned to white. All of them were very clever in school and helped my mother a great deal about the house. When they were young they sang and were very happy and very nice to me because I was the youngest and the family's only boy.

My father never approved of their playing about the wharf like the other children, and they went there only when my mother sent them on an errand. At such times they almost always overstayed, playing screaming games of tag or hide-and-seek in and about the fishing shanties, the piled traps and tubs of trawl, shouting down to the perch that swam languidly about the wharf's algae-covered

[2] Frank Morrison Spillane (1918–2006), American author of popular crime novels featuring the detective Mike Hammer. Ernest James Haycox (1899–1950), American author of Westerns whose books formed the basis of a number of Hollywood movies. The other authors mentioned here are more high-brow, including Fyodor Dostoevsky (1821–1881), Russian novelist and author of *Crime and Punishment* (1866); William Faulkner (1897–1962), American fiction writer known for his novels set in the American south, including *The Sound and the Fury* (1929); and Gerard Manley Hopkins (1844–1889), English Jesuit poet known for his use of striking imagery and experimental rhythm.

[3] *Ivanhoe* (1819) is a historical and highly romantic novel by Scottish writer Sir Walter Scott (1771–1832) set during the Middle Ages.

piles, or jumping in and out of the boats that tugged gently at their lines. My mother was never uneasy about them at such times, and when her husband criticized her she would say, "Nothing will happen to them there," or "They could be doing worse things in worse places."

By about the ninth or tenth grade my sisters one by one discovered my father's bedroom and then the change would begin. Each would go into the room one morning when he was out. She would go with the ideal hope of imposing order or with the more practical objective of emptying the ashtray, and later she would be found spellbound by the volume in her hand. My mother's reaction was always abrupt, bordering on the angry. "Take your nose out of that trash and come and do your work," she would say, and once I saw her slap my youngest sister so hard that the print of her hand was scarletly emblazoned upon her daughter's cheek while the broken-spined paperback fluttered uselessly to the floor.

Thereafter my mother would launch a campaign against what she had discovered but could not understand. At times although she was not overly religious she would bring in God to bolster her arguments, saying, "In the next world God will see to those who waste their lives reading useless books when they should be about their work." Or without theological aid, "I would like to know how books help anyone to live a life." If my father were in, she would repeat the remarks louder than necessary, and her voice would carry into his room where he lay upon his bed. His usual reaction was to turn up the volume of the radio, although that action in itself betrayed the success of the initial thrust.

Shortly after my sisters began to read the books, they grew restless and lost interest in darning socks and baking bread, and all of them eventually went to work as summer waitresses in the Sea Food Restaurant. The restaurant was run by a big American concern from Boston and catered to the tourists that flooded the area during July and August. My mother despised the whole operation. She said the restaurant was not run by "our people," and "our people" did not eat there, and that it was run by outsiders for outsiders.

"Who are these people anyway?" she would ask, tossing back her dark hair, "and what do they, though they go about with their cameras for a hundred years, know about the way it is here, and what do they care about me and mine, and why should I care about them?"

She was angry that my sisters should even conceive of working in such a place and more angry when my father made no move to prevent it, and she was worried about herself and about her family and about her life. Sometimes she would say softly to her sisters, "I don't know what's the matter with my girls. It seems none of them are interested in any of the right things." And sometimes there would be bitter savage arguments. One afternoon I was coming in with three mackerel I'd been given at the wharf when I heard her say, "Well I hope you'll be satisfied when they come home knocked up and you'll have had your way."

It was the most savage thing I'd ever heard my mother say. Not just the words but the way she said them, and I stood there in the porch afraid to breathe for what seemed like the years from ten to fifteen, feeling the damp moist mackerel with their silver glassy eyes growing clammy against my leg.

Through the angle in the screen door I saw my father who had been walking into his room wheel around on one of his rubber-booted heels and look at her with his blue eyes flashing like clearest ice beneath the snow that was his hair. His usually ruddy face was drawn and grey, reflecting the exhaustion of a man of sixty-five who had been working in those rubber boots for eleven hours on an August day, and for a fleeting moment I wondered what I would do if he killed my mother while I stood there in the porch with those three foolish mackerel in my hand. Then he turned and went into his room and the radio blared forth the next day's weather forecast and I retreated under the noise and returned again, stamping my feet and slamming the door too loudly to signal my approach. My mother was busy at the stove when I came in, and did not raise her head when I threw the mackerel in a pan. As I looked into my father's room, I said, "Well how did things go in the boat today?" and he replied, "Oh not too badly, all things considered." He was lying on his back and lighting the first cigarette and the radio was talking about the Virginia coast.

All of my sisters made good money on tips. They bought my father an electric razor which he tried to use for a while and they took out even more magazine subscriptions. They bought my mother a great many clothes of the type she was very fond of, the wide-brimmed hats and the brocaded dresses, but she locked them all in trunks and refused to wear any of them.

On one August day my sisters prevailed upon my father to take some of their restaurant customers for an afternoon ride in the boat. The tourists with their expensive clothes and cameras and sun glasses awkwardly backed down the iron ladder at the wharf's side to where my father waited below, holding the rocking *Jenny Lynn* in snug against the wharf with one hand on the iron ladder and steadying his descending passengers with the other. They tried to look both prim and wind-blown like the girls in the Pepsi-Cola ads and did the best they could, sitting on the thwarts where the newspapers were spread to cover the splattered blood and fish entrails, crowding to one side so that they were in danger of capsizing the boat, taking the inevitable pictures or merely trailing their fingers through the water of their dreams.

All of them liked my father very much and, after he'd brought them back from their circles in the harbour, they invited him to their rented cabins which were located high on a hill overlooking the village to which they were so alien. He proceeded to get very drunk up there with the beautiful view and the strange company and the abundant liquor, and late in the afternoon he began to sing.

I was just approaching the wharf to deliver my mother's summons when he began, and the familiar yet unfamiliar voice that rolled down from the cabins made me feel as I had never felt before in my young life or perhaps as I had always felt without really knowing it, and I was ashamed yet proud, young yet old and saved yet forever lost, and there was nothing I could do to control my legs which trembled nor my eyes which wept for what they could not tell.

The tourists were equipped with tape recorders and my father sang for more than three hours. His voice boomed down the hill and bounced off the surface of the harbour, which was an unearthly blue on that hot August day, and was then reflected to the wharf and the fishing shanties where it was absorbed amidst the men who were baiting their lines for the next day's haul.

He sang all the old sea chanties which had come across from the old world and by which men like him had pulled ropes for generations, and he sang the East Coast sea songs which celebrated the sealing vessels of Northumberland Strait and the long liners of the Grand Banks, and of Anticosti, Sable Island, Grand Manan, Boston Harbor, Nantucket and Block Island. Gradually he shifted to the seemingly unending Gaelic drinking songs with their twenty or more verses and inevitable refrains, and the men in the shanties smiled at the coarseness of some of the verses and at the thought that the singer's immediate audience did not know what they were applauding nor recording to take back to staid old Boston. Later as the sun was setting he switched to the laments and the wild and haunting Gaelic war songs of those spattered Highland ancestors he had never seen, and when his voice ceased, the savage melancholy of three hundred years seemed to hang over the peaceful harbour and the quiet boats and the men leaning in the doorways of their shanties with their cigarettes glowing in the dusk and the women looking to the sea from their open windows with their children in their arms.

When he came home he threw the money he had earned on the kitchen table as he did with all his earnings but my mother refused to touch it and the next day he went with the rest of the men to bait his trawl in the shanties. The tourists came to the door that evening and my mother met them there and told them that her husband was not in although he was lying on the bed only a few feet away with the radio playing and the cigarette upon his lips. She stood in the doorway until they reluctantly went away.

In the winter they sent him a picture which had been taken on the day of the singing. On the back it said, "To Our Ernest Hemingway" and the "Our" was underlined. There was also an accompanying letter telling how much they had enjoyed themselves, how popular the tape was proving and explaining who Ernest Hemingway was. In a way it almost did look like one of those unshaven, taken-in-Cuba pictures of Hemingway.[4] He looked both massive and incongruous in the setting. His bulky fisherman's clothes were too big for the green and white lawn chair in which he sat, and his rubber boots seemed to take up all of the well-clipped grass square. The beach umbrella jarred with his sunburned face and because he had already been singing for some time, his lips which chapped in the winds of spring and burned in the water glare of summer had already cracked in

[4] Ernest Hemingway (1899–1961), American author known for his direct writing style, who has been romanticized for, among other things, his heavy drinking and love of fishing. Hemingway was an adventurer, who lived in Paris, Spain, and Cuba. *The Old Man and the Sea* (1951), written while he lived in Cuba, tells the story of a fisherman who battles for days with a giant marlin, only to see the fish eaten by sharks before he manages to get it home. In later years, Hemingway suffered from depression, and he committed suicide in his early sixties.

several places, producing tiny flecks of blood at their corners and on the whiteness of his teeth. The bracelets of brass chain which he wore to protect his wrists from chafing seemed abnormally large and his broad leather belt had been slackened and his heavy shirt and underwear were open at the throat revealing an uncultivated wilderness of white chest hair bordering on the semi-controlled stubble of his neck and chin. His blue eyes had looked directly into the camera and his hair was whiter than the two tiny clouds which hung over his left shoulder. The sea was behind him and its immense blue flatness stretched out to touch the arching blueness of the sky. It seemed very far away from him or else he was so much in the foreground that he seemed too big for it.

Each year another of my sisters would read the books and work in the restaurant. Sometimes they would stay out quite late on the hot summer nights and when they came up the stairs my mother would ask them many long and involved questions which they resented and tried to avoid. Before ascending the stairs they would go into my father's room and those of us who waited above could hear them throwing his clothes off the chair before sitting on it or the squeak of the bed as they sat on its edge. Sometimes they would talk to him a long time, the murmur of their voices blending with the music of the radio into a mysterious vapour-like sound which floated softly up the stairs.

I say this again as if it all happened at once and as if all of my sisters were of identical ages and like so many lemmings going into another sea and, again, it was of course not that way at all. Yet go they did, to Boston, to Montreal, to New York with the young men they met during the summers and later married in those far-away cities. The young men were very articulate and handsome and wore fine clothes and drove expensive cars and my sisters, as I said, were very tall and beautiful with their copper-coloured hair and were tired of darning socks and baking bread.

One by one they went. My mother had each of her daughters for fifteen years, then lost them for two and finally forever. None married a fisherman. My mother never accepted any of the young men, for in her eyes they seemed always a combination of the lazy, the effeminate, the dishonest and the unknown. They never seemed to do any physical work and she could not comprehend their luxurious vacations and she did not know whence they came nor who they were. And in the end she did not really care, for they were not of her people and they were not of her sea.

I say this now with a sense of wonder at my own stupidity in thinking I was somehow free and would go on doing well in school and playing and helping in the boat and passing into my early teens while streaks of grey began to appear in my mother's dark hair and my father's rubber boots dragged sometimes on the pebbles of the beach as he trudged home from the wharf. And there were but three of us in the house that had at one time been so loud.

Then during the winter that I was fifteen he seemed to grow old and ill at once. Most of January he lay upon the bed, smoking and reading and listening to the radio while the wind howled about the house and the needle-like snow blistered off the ice-covered harbour and the doors flew out of people's hands if they did not cling to them like death.

In February when the men began overhauling their lobster traps he still did not move, and my mother and I began to knit lobster trap headings in the evenings. The twine was as always very sharp and harsh, and blisters formed upon our thumbs and little paths of blood snaked quietly down between our fingers while the seals that had drifted down from distant Labrador wept and moaned like human children on the ice-floes of the Gulf.

In the daytime my mother's brother who had been my father's partner as long as I could remember also came to work upon the gear. He was a year older than my mother and was tall and dark and the father of twelve children.

By March we were very far behind and although I began to work very hard in the evenings I knew it was not hard enough and that there were but eight weeks left before the opening of the season on May first. And I knew that my mother worried and my uncle was uneasy and that all of our very lives depended on the boat being ready with her gear and two men, by the date of May the first. And I knew then that *David Copperfield* and *The Tempest*[5] and all of those friends I had dearly come to love must really go forever. So I bade them all good-bye.

The night after my first full day at home and after my mother had gone upstairs he called me into his room where I sat upon the chair beside his bed. "You will go back tomorrow," he said simply.

I refused then, saying I had made my decision and was satisfied.

"That is no way to make a decision," he said, "and if you are satisfied I am not. It is best that you go back." I was almost angry then and told him as all children do that I wished he would leave me alone and stop telling me what to do.

He looked at me a long time then, lying there on the same bed on which he had fathered me those sixteen years before, fathered me his only son, out of who knew what emotions when he was already fifty-six and his hair had turned to snow. Then he swung his legs over the edge of the squeaking bed and sat facing me and looked into my own dark eyes with his of crystal blue and placed his hand upon my knee. "I am not telling you to do anything," he said softly, "only asking you."

The next morning I returned to school. As I left, my mother followed me to the porch and said, "I never thought a son of mine would choose useless books over the parents that gave him life."

In the weeks that followed he got up rather miraculously and the gear was ready and the *Jenny Lynn* was freshly painted by the last two weeks of April when the ice began to break up and the lonely screaming gulls returned to haunt the silver herring as they flashed within the sea.

On the first day of May the boats raced out as they had always done, laden down almost to the gunwales with their heavy cargoes of traps. They were

[5] *David Copperfield* (1850), novel by English author Charles Dickens (1812–1870); MacLeod's story later mentions the Peggottys, the good-hearted fishing family in Dickens's novel. *The Tempest* (1611), a play by William Shakespeare (1564–1616) that tells of a shipwreck at sea.

almost like living things as they plunged through the waters of the spring and manoeuvred between the still floating icebergs of crystal-white and emerald green on their way to the traditional grounds that they sought out every May. And those of us who sat that day in the high school on the hill, discussing the water imagery of Tennyson, watched them as they passed back and forth beneath us until by afternoon the piles of traps which had been stacked upon the wharf were no longer visible but were spread about the bottoms of the sea.[6] And the *Jenny Lynn* went too, all day, with my uncle tall and dark, like a latter-day Tashtego[7] standing at the tiller with his legs wide apart and guiding her deftly between the floating pans of ice and my father in the stern standing in the same way with his hands upon the ropes that lashed the cargo to the deck. And at night my mother asked, "Well, how did things go in the boat today?"

And the spring wore on and the summer came and school ended in the third week of June and the lobster season on July first and I wished that the two things I loved so dearly did not exclude each other in a manner that was so blunt and too clear.

At the conclusion of the lobster season my uncle said he had been offered a berth on a deep sea dragger and had decided to accept. We all knew that he was leaving the *Jenny Lynn* forever and that before the next lobster season he would buy a boat of his own. He was expecting another child and would be supporting fifteen people by the next spring and could not chance my father against the family that he loved.

I joined my father then for the trawling season, and he made no protest and my mother was quite happy. Through the summer we baited the tubs of trawl in the afternoon and set them at sunset and revisited them in the darkness of the early morning. The men would come tramping by our house at four A.M. and we would join them and walk with them to the wharf and be on our way before the sun rose out of the ocean where it seemed to spend the night. If I was not up they would toss pebbles to my window and I would be very embarrassed and tumble downstairs to where my father lay fully clothed atop his bed, reading his book and listening to his radio and smoking his cigarette. When I appeared he would swing off his bed and put on his boots and be instantly ready and then we would take the lunches my mother had prepared the night before and walk off toward the sea. He would make no attempt to wake me himself.

It was in many ways a good summer. There were few storms and we were out almost every day and we lost a minimum of gear and seemed to land a maximum of fish and I tanned dark and brown after the manner of my uncles.

My father did not tan—he never tanned—because of his reddish complexion, and the salt water irritated his skin as it had for sixty years. He burned and

[6] Alfred, Lord Tennyson (1809–1862), popular English poet during the Victorian period. The imagery here echoes his 1833 poem "The Lady of Shalott," in which a young woman/artist watches the life of the labourers from her towered window, but when she steps into the scene and into a boat on the river, she dies.

[7] Native American harpooner in Herman Melville's *Moby Dick* (1851).

reburned over and over again and his lips still cracked so that they bled when he smiled, and his arms, especially the left, still broke out into the oozing salt-water boils as they had ever since as a child I had first watched him soaking and bathing them in a variety of ineffectual solutions. The chafe-preventing bracelets of brass linked chain that all the men wore about their wrists in early spring were his the full season and he shaved but painfully and only once a week.

And I saw then, that summer, many things that I had seen all my life as if for the first time and I thought that perhaps my father had never been intended for a fisherman either physically or mentally. At least not in the manner of my uncles; he had never really loved it. And I remembered that, one evening in his room when we were talking about *David Copperfield*, he had said that he had always wanted to go to the university and I had dismissed it then in the way one dismisses his father's saying he would like to be a tight-rope walker, and we had gone on to talk about the Peggottys and how they loved the sea.

And I thought then to myself that there were many things wrong with all of us and all our lives and I wondered why my father, who was himself an only son, had not married before he was forty and then I wondered why he had. I even thought that perhaps he had had to marry my mother and checked the dates on the flyleaf of the Bible where I learned that my oldest sister had been born a prosaic eleven months after the marriage, and I felt myself then very dirty and debased for my lack of faith and for what I had thought and done.

And then there came into my heart a very great love for my father and I thought it was very much braver to spend a life doing what you really do not want rather than selfishly following forever your own dreams and inclinations. And I knew then that I could never leave him alone to suffer the iron-tipped harpoons which my mother would forever hurl into his soul because he was a failure as a husband and a father who had retained none of his own. And I felt that I had been very small in a little secret place within me and that even the completion of high school was for me a silly shallow selfish dream.

So I told him one night very resolutely and very powerfully that I would remain with him as long as he lived and we would fish the sea together. And he made no protest but only smiled through the cigarette smoke that wreathed his bed and replied, "I hope you will remember what you've said."

The room was now so filled with books as to be almost Dickensian, but he would not allow my mother to move or change them and he continued to read them, sometimes two or three a night. They came with great regularity now, and there were more hard covers, sent by my sisters who had gone so long ago and now seemed so distant and so prosperous, and sent also pictures of small red-haired grandchildren with baseball bats and dolls which he placed upon his bureau and which my mother gazed at wistfully when she thought no one would see. Red-haired grandchildren with baseball bats and dolls who would never know the sea in hatred or in love.

And so we fished through the heat of August and into the cooler days of September when the water was so clear we could almost see the bottom and the white mists rose like delicate ghosts in the early morning dawn. And one day my mother said to me, "You have given added years to his life."

And we fished on into October when it began to roughen and we could no longer risk night sets but took our gear out each morning and returned at the first sign of the squalls; and on into November when we lost three tubs of trawl and the clear blue water turned to a sullen grey and the trochoidal waves rolled rough and high and washed across our bows and decks as we ran within their troughs. We wore heavy sweaters now and the awkward rubber slickers and the heavy woollen mitts which soaked and froze into masses of ice that hung from our wrists like the limbs of gigantic monsters until we thawed them against the exhaust pipe's heat. And almost every day we would leave for home before noon, driven by the blasts of the northwest wind, coating our eyebrows with ice and freezing our eyelids closed as we leaned into a visibility that was hardly there, charting our course from the compass and the sea, running with the waves and between them but never confronting their towering might.

And I stood at the tiller now, on these homeward lunges, stood in the place and in the manner of my uncle, turning to look at my father and to shout over the roar of the engine and the slop of the sea to where he stood in the stern, drenched and dripping with the snow and the salt and the spray and his bushy eyebrows caked in ice. But on November twenty-first, when it seemed we might be making the final run of the season, I turned and he was not there and I knew even in that instant that he would never be again.

On November twenty-first the waves of the grey Atlantic are very very high and the waters are very cold and there are no signposts on the surface of the sea. You cannot tell where you have been five minutes before and in the squalls of snow you cannot see. And it takes longer than you would believe to check a boat that has been running before a gale and turn her ever so carefully in a wide and stupid circle, with timbers creaking and straining, back into the face of storm. And you know that it is useless and that your voice does not carry the length of the boat and that even if you knew the original spot, the relentless waves would carry such a burden perhaps a mile or so by the time you could return. And you know also, the final irony, that your father like your uncles and all the men that form your past, cannot swim a stroke.

The lobster beds off the Cape Breton coast are still very rich and now, from May to July, their offerings are packed in crates of ice, and thundered by the gigantic transport trucks, day and night, through New Glasgow, Amherst, Saint John and Bangor and Portland and into Boston where they are tossed still living into boiling pots of water, their final home.

And though the prices are higher and the competition tighter, the grounds to which the *Jenny Lynn* once went remain untouched and unfished as they have for the last ten years. For if there are no signposts on the sea in storm there are certain ones in calm and the lobster bottoms were distributed in calm before any of us can remember and the grounds my father fished were those his father fished before him and there were others before and before and before. Twice the big boats have come from forty and fifty miles, lured by the promise of the grounds, and strewn the bottom with their traps and twice they have returned to find their buoys cut adrift and their gear lost and destroyed. Twice the Fisheries Officer and the Mounted Police have come and asked many long and involved questions and twice they have received no answers from the men leaning in the doors of their shanties and the women standing at their windows with their children in their arms. Twice they have gone away saying: "There are no legal boundaries in the Marine area"; "No one can own the sea"; "Those grounds don't wait for anyone."

But the men and the women, with my mother dark among them, do not care for what they say, for to them the grounds are sacred and they think they wait for me.

It is not an easy thing to know that your mother lives alone on an inadequate insurance policy and that she is too proud to accept any other aid. And that she looks through her lonely window onto the ice of winter and the hot flat calm of summer and the rolling waves of fall. And that she lies awake in the early morning's darkness when the rubber boots of the men scrunch upon the gravel as they pass beside her house on their way down to the wharf. And she knows that the footsteps never stop, because no man goes from her house, and she alone of all the Lynns has neither son nor son-in-law that walks toward the boat that will take him to the sea. And it is not an easy thing to know that your mother looks upon the sea with love and on you with bitterness because the one has been so constant and the other so untrue.

But neither is it easy to know that your father was found on November twenty-eighth, ten miles to the north and wedged between two boulders at the base of the rock-strewn cliffs where he had been hurled and slammed so many many times. His hands were shredded ribbons as were his feet which had lost their boots to the suction of the sea, and his shoulders came apart in our hands when we tried to move him from the rocks. And the fish had eaten his testicles and the gulls had pecked out his eyes and the white-green stubble of his whiskers had continued to grow in death, like the grass on graves, upon the purple, bloated mass that was his face. There was not much left of my father, physically, as he lay there with the brass chains on his wrists and the seaweed in his hair.

[1976]

JOHN NEWLOVE ■ (1938–2003)

In the 1960s, John Newlove was acclaimed as one of the finest poets of his generation. Though his writing career spanned over four decades, Newlove's work voices the sense of intense disillu-sionment that undergirded the euphoria of the 1960s and '70s in North America and lingered in the decades that followed. His poetry expresses an acute yearning, a striving toward meaning that somehow always escapes the searcher's grasp. Jeff Derksen, in his Afterword to Newlove's *A Long Continual Argument* (2007), describes his central theme as one of "obstructed agency." The position of despair, resignation, and self-recrimination that is so characteristic of Newlove's poetry is all the more bitter for the speaker's awareness that he is to blame for bringing about his own isolation. The speakers in Newlove's poems are idealists at heart but must accommodate themselves to not finding what they seek. This theme is clearly evident in "Samuel Hearne in Wintertime," which reimagines Samuel Hearne's journey to the Arctic Ocean (see the excerpt from Hearne's journals in Volume I) from a modern-day perspective and concludes with the evocative and enigmatic description of the Inuit woman who is "dying, never to know."

Newlove was born in Regina, but grew up in rural Saskatchewan, where he was raised by his mother after his father abandoned the family. Some years later, his father, who was an alcoholic, returned, and Newlove was subjected to physical abuse. In the early 1960s, he hitchhiked across Canada and eventually moved to Vancouver, where he lived a welfare existence while reading voluminously at the Vancouver Public Library. Throughout his life, Newlove was plagued by debilitating shyness that impeded his public poetry readings and affected his social relationships. To combat his shyness, Newlove drank excessively in social situations, often resulting in outrageous and troublesome behaviour. He was a prolific writer during the 1960s and early '70s, writing poetry that was finely crafted and praised for its meticulous, flawless diction, condensation of meaning, and precise line breaks. His third poetry collection, *Moving in Alone* (1965), was met with critical acclaim and immediately earned him the reputation of a writer to be watched. It was followed by other important works, including *Black*

Night Window (1968) and *The Cave* (1970). In 1992, he published his selected poems, *Apology for Absence,* a collection that was further expanded and edited by Robert McTavish in 2007 in a collection entitled *A Long Continual Argument.*

In 1970, Newlove moved to Toronto to take up a position as editor for the publishing firm of McClelland and Stewart, where he edited the work of such notable fellow writers as Irving Layton, Leonard Cohen, Rudy Wiebe, and Al Purdy. In 1972, he received the Governor General's Award for *Lies.* Because editing left him insufficient time to write poetry, Newlove quit his publishing job in 1974 and subsequently took on a variety of jobs, as writer-in-residence, freelance editor, letter writer for Prime Minister Pierre Trudeau, and eventually editor for the federal government in Ottawa. Nevertheless, his poetic output dwindled substantially in the late 1980s and 1990s.

While Newlove's poetry is often highlighted for its evocation of the prairie landscape, as is evident in such poems as "Ride Off Any Horizon" and "The Double-Headed Snake," it is an over-simplification to peg him as a prairie poet or, for that matter, as a nationalist poet. His 1970 poem "America" voices the sense of threat of American imperialism that dominated Canadian attitudes in the early 1970s, evident as well in such works from this period as bpNichol's "Statement 10" and Margaret Atwood's "Backdrop Addresses Cowboy." However, nationalist themes are not the predominant concern of Newlove's poetry. His work charts his responses to the turbulent social world of the late twentieth century: its possibilities and, ultimately, its disappointments. The concluding lines from his poem "Remembering Christopher Smart" provide an encapsulation of Newlove's romantic, yet ultimately realistic, despondence: "I see that we all make the world what we want. / Our disappointment lies in the world as it is."

The Double-Headed Snake

Not to lose the feel of the mountains
while still retaining the prairies
is a difficult thing. What's lovely
is whatever makes the adrenalin run;
therefore I count terror and fear among
the greatest beauty. The greatest
beauty is to be alive, forgetting nothing,
although remembrance hurts
like a foolish act, is a foolish act.

Beauty's whatever   10
makes the adrenalin run. Fear
in the mountains at night-time's
not tenuous, it is not the cold
that makes me shiver, civilized man,
white, I remember
the stories of the Indians,
Sis-i-utl, the double-headed snake.[1]

Beauty's what makes
the adrenalin run. Fear at night
on the level plains, with no horizon   20
and the stars too bright, wind bitter
even in June, in winter
the snow harsh and blowing,
is what makes me
shiver, not the cold air alone.

And one beauty cancels another. The plains
seem secure and comfortable
at Crow's Nest Pass;[2] in Saskatchewan
the mountains are comforting
to think of; among   30
the eastwardly diminishing hills
both the flatland and the ridge
seem easy to endure.

[1] A powerful figure of Pacific Northwest peoples, Sisiutl is a two-headed snake with a human head and hands in the middle that could transform itself into a canoe or salmon. According to legend, seeing or touching one could cause illness or death.

[2] Pass through the Rocky Mountains between Alberta and British Columbia.

As one beauty
cancels another, remembrance
is a foolish act, a double-headed snake
striking in both directions, but I
remember plains and mountains, places
I come from, places I adhere and live in.

[1968]

Samuel Hearne in Wintertime³

1.

In this cold room
I remember the smell of manure
on men's heavy clothes as good,
the smell of horses.

It is a romantic world
to readers of journeys
to the Northern Ocean—

especially if their houses are heated
to some degree, Samuel.

Hearne, your camp must have smelled   10
like hell whenever you settled down
for a few days of rest and journal-work:

hell smeared with human manure,
hell half-full of raw hides,
hell of sweat, Indians, stale fat,
meat-hell, fear-hell, hell of cold.

2.

One child is back from the doctor's while
the other one wanders about in dirty pants
and I think of Samuel Hearne and the land—

JOHN NEWLOVE

³ The speaker in this poem is addressing Samuel Hearne (1745–1792), explorer of the Canadian north and author of *A Journey from Prince of Wales's Fort in Hudson's Bay to the Northern Ocean* (1795). In the poem, the speaker aligns his experiences in the present day with those of Hearne on his travels. The poem is sprinkled with allusions to Hearne's account, including the well-known "Eskimo" massacre scene at Bloody Falls (at the mouth of the Coppermine River) in which a dying girl is described as "twining round their spears like an eel" as Hearne tries unsuccessfully to plead for her life (see the excerpt in Volume I).

puffy children coughing as I think,
crying, sick-faced,
vomit stirring in grey blankets
from room to room.

It is Christmastime—
the cold flesh shines.
No praise in merely enduring.

3.
Samuel Hearne did more
in the land (like all the rest

full of rocks and hilly country,
many very extensive tracts of land,
tittimeg, pike and barble,

and the islands:
the islands, many
of them abound

as well as the main
land does
with dwarf woods,

chiefly pine
in some parts intermixed
with larch and birch) than endure.

The Indians killed twelve deer.
It was impossible to describe
the intenseness of the cold.

4.
And, Samuel Hearne,
I have almost begun to talk

as if you wanted to be
gallant, as if you went
through that land for a book—

as if you were not SAM, wanting
to know, to do a job.

5.

There was that Eskimo girl
at Bloody Falls, at your feet

Samuel Hearne, with two spears in her,
you helpless before your helpers,

and she twisted about them like
an eel, dying, never to know.

[1968]

America

Even the dissident ones speak
as members of an Empire, residents
of the centre of the earth. Power
extends from their words
to all the continents and their modesty
is liable for millions. How must it be
to be caught in the Empire, to have
everything you do matter? Even
treason is imperial; the scornful
self-abuse comes from inside the boundaries   10
of the possible. Outside the borders of royalty
the barbarians wait in fear,
finding it hard to know which prince
to believe; trade-goods comfort them,
gadgets of little worth, cars, television,
refrigerators, for which they give iron,
copper, uranium, gold, trees, and water,
worth of all sorts for the things
citizens of Empire take as their due.

In the Empire power speaks from the poorest   20
and culture flourishes. Outside the boundaries
the barbarians imitate styles and send their sons,
the talented hirelings, to learn and to stay;
the sons of their sons will be princes too,
in the Estate where even the unhappy
carry an aura of worldly power; and the lords
of power send out directives
for the rest of the world to obey. If they live
in the Empire, it matters what they say.

[1970]

Gordon Lightfoot is arguably Canada's most renowned folksinger and lyricist, and has been a fixture on the Canadian music and cultural scene for more than 40 years. Born in Orillia, Ontario, Lightfoot began his singing and song-writing career early, when even at the age of 10 he was winning prizes for his performances. Known today for such popular songs as "For Lovin' Me" (1966), "Early Mornin' Rain" (1966), "Did She Mention My Name?" (1968), and "If You Could Read My Mind" (1970), he is also celebrated for his bal-lads on Canadian historical subjects, including "Canadian Railroad Trilogy" (1967) and "The Wreck of the Edmund Fitzgerald" (1976).

His first album was recorded in 1966, entitled simply *Lightfoot!* That year, he was commissioned by the CBC to write a song for Canada's upcoming centennial. The result was "Canadian Railroad Trilogy," which premiered on CBC-TV on New Year's Day 1967 and was broadcast across the country; in the broadcast, the building of the railway was re-enacted by actors as Lightfoot strolled in front playing the song. The song, which celebrates the ordinary workers who laboured and died building the transcontinental CPR in the late nine-teenth century, was later released on his 1967 album, *The Way I Feel.*

His songs have been recorded by many well-known international perform-ers, including Bob Dylan, Elvis Presley, Ian and Sylvia Tyson, Johnny Cash, and Peter, Paul, and Mary. Lightfoot was named to the Order of Canada in 1970 and inducted into the Canadian Music Hall of Fame in 1986.

Canadian Railroad Trilogy

There was a time in this fair land when the railroad did not run
When the wild majestic mountains stood alone against the sun
Long before the white man and long before the wheel
When the green dark forest was too silent to be real

But time has no beginnings and history has no bounds
As to this verdant country they came from all around
They sailed upon her waterways and they walked the forests tall
Built the mines, mills and the factories for the good of us all

And when the young man's fancy was turnin' to the spring
The railroad men grew restless for to hear the hammers ring   10
Their minds were overflowing with the visions of their day
And many a fortune lost and won and many a debt to pay

For they looked in the future and what did they see
They saw an iron road running from the sea to the sea
Bringing the goods to a young growing land
All up from the seaports and into their hands

Look away said they across this mighty land
From the eastern shore to the western strand

Bring in the workers and bring up the rails
We gotta lay down the tracks and tear up the trails   20
Open her heart let the life blood flow
Gotta get on our way 'cause we're moving too slow

Bring in the workers and bring up the rails
We're gonna lay down the tracks and tear up the trails
Open her heart let the life blood flow
Gotta get on our way 'cause we're moving too slow
Get on our way 'cause we're moving too slow

Behind the blue Rockies the sun is declining
The stars they come stealing at the close of the day
Across the wide prairie our loved ones lie sleeping   30
Beyond the dark ocean in a place far away

We are the navvies who work upon the railway
Swinging our hammers in the bright blazing sun
Living on stew and drinking bad whiskey
Bending our backs til the long days are done

We are the navvies who work upon the railway
Swinging our hammers in the bright blazing sun
Laying down track and building the bridges
Bending our backs til the railroad is done

So over the mountains and over the plains   40
Into the muskeg and into the rain
Up the St. Lawrence all the way to Gaspé
Swinging our hammers and drawing our pay
Layin' 'em in and tying them down
Away to the bunkhouse and into the town
A dollar a day and a place for my head
A drink to the living, a toast to the dead

Oh the song of the future has been sung
All the battles have been won
On the mountain tops we stand   50
All the world at our command
We have opened up her soil
With our teardrops and our toil

For there was a time in this fair land when the railroad did not run
When the wild majestic mountains stood alone against the sun
Long before the white man and long before the wheel
When the green dark forest was too silent to be real
When the green dark forest was too silent to be real
And many are the dead men too silent to be real

[1967]

MARGARET ATWOOD ■ (1939–)

"We need to know about here, because here is where we live." So wrote Margaret Atwood in her landmark literary manifesto, *Survival: A Thematic Guide to Canadian Literature,* in 1972. Atwood has contributed to that literature in myriad ways, becoming perhaps the best-known Canadian writer of the twentieth century. Rising to public prominence when, as a relatively unknown poet, she won the Governor General's Award for *The Circle Game* (1966), Atwood has been unstinting in her commitment to the "cause" of Canadian literature. Along with Dennis Lee, she was a central voice in the late 1960s and early '70s promoting the importance of Canadian cultural identity against the sense of inferiority that had come to dominate the Canadian mindset, particularly in comparison to the United States. However, it is not only the politics of Canadian nationalism that has informed Atwood's writing. She has taken on many of the critical political and social issues of the late twentieth and early twenty-first centuries, including women's equality, violence against women, totalitarianism, religious fundamentalism, environmentalism, genetic modification, American cultural imperialism (including the threat of free trade to Canadian cultural independence), consumerism, freedom of speech, and authors' rights. She has also been an active member of Amnesty International

and was one of the founders of The Writers' Union of Canada. Atwood is an enviably multi-talented writer and thinker: a poet, a novelist, a short story writer, a literary critic, a satirist, a children's author, a painter and illustrator, a cultural commentator, and a mentor to generations of Canadian writers.

Atwood was born in Ottawa in 1939, and her family moved to Toronto in 1946. By all accounts, her childhood was unusual, especially for a family in the 1940s. Because her father worked as an entomologist, the family spent every spring, summer, and autumn living in the bush in northern Quebec or Ontario while her father did field research on insects. Atwood thus grew up with a foot in two worlds: the isolated and unsophisticated world of outhouses and log cabins, and the middle-class urban world of 1950s Toronto. This experience gave her a handy "outsider's" perspective on much of the social conformity and materialism of urban life in the 1950s.

From early on, Atwood knew that she wanted to be a writer. Her stated ambition as recorded in her high school yearbook the year she graduated was "to write THE Canadian novel." She graduated with a B.A. in English literature from the University of Toronto in 1961, where she was a student of Northrop Frye and poet Jay Macpherson. It was here that she met Dennis Lee, a fellow aspiring poet with whom she became close friends; both published pieces in the Victoria College student magazine, *Acta Victoriana*. Under Frye's influence, Atwood absorbed a sense of the underlying mythological structure of all stories, a motif that arises throughout her writing, even as late as 2005 when she published her revision of Homer's *Odyssey* in *The Penelopiad.* Her extensive background in English literary genres is evident in her varied body of writing in which she plays with multiple forms: the dystopian novel (*The Handmaid's Tale*), Gothic literature (*Lady Oracle*), science fiction (*Oryx and Crake*), fairy tales (*Bluebeard's Egg* and *The Robber Bride*), and thrillers (*Bodily Harm*).

During her undergraduate years, Atwood also made the acquaintance of poet and playwright James Reaney, poet Gwendolyn MacEwen, and painter Charles Pachter, with whom Atwood still has a close friendship. In 1961 Atwood entered Radcliffe College (part of Harvard University) in Cambridge, Massachusetts, receiving her M.A. in 1962 and beginning a Ph.D. in Victorian literature that same year. However, she began spending more and more time on her creative writing, completing the manuscript of her first novel, *The Edible Woman,* during these years. After winning the Governor General's Award for *The Circle Game*—the youngest writer at that time ever to receive the award—Atwood decided not to complete her Ph.D. Yet without doubt, her experience as an "expatriate" Canadian influenced her perspective, convincing her that Canadian culture was distinct from that of the United States.

From early on, Atwood was an important part of the burgeoning literary and cultural scene in Toronto in the 1960s and '70s, publishing her poetry and articles in many of the little magazines of the day and giving frequent poetry readings alongside the other members of her generation: Lee, MacEwen, Leonard Cohen,

Michael Ondaatje, and George Bowering. After leaving Harvard, she devoted herself to writing, editing, and reviewing, including a stint on the editorial board of House of Anansi Press, for which she edited Michael Ondaatje's poetry sequence *The Collected Works of Billy the Kid* (1970).

Atwood, like many female writers of her generation, was also faced with the problem of defining the role of the woman writer in a milieu of very strong, and in some cases misogynistic, male personalities. Atwood's biographer, Rosemary Sullivan, relates the story of how Irving Layton, threatened by the idea of a talented woman poet invading what he considered traditional male terrain, attempted to undermine Atwood's first poetry reading by reciting his own poems aloud from the back of the room, but Atwood persevered. Many of her writings, including her first book of poems, *Double Persephone* (1961), provide tongue-in-cheek meditations on female stereotypes, while "The Age of Lead" contains a disturbing portrait of female frustration (the "mothers" in the story) in response to the gender restrictions that continued to hold women back even into the 1970s. Her short prose piece "The Female Body," included here, is a piercing yet comic critique of the objectification of women.

Atwood was a prolific writer in the 1960s and '70s, publishing numerous poetry collections, including *The Animals in That Country* (1968), *The Journals of Susanna Moodie* (1970), *Procedures for Underground* (1970), *Power Politics* (1971), *You Are Happy* (1974), and *Two-Headed Poems* (1978). Her poetry is marked by a curiously clinical style mixed with startling, often macabre, imagery. The clash between the deadpan tone and the almost hallucinatory imagery is a trademark of Atwood's work, such as one sees in her Vietnam protest poem, "It is dangerous to read newspapers." These early works are also replete with a good deal of mythological resonance and scientific imagery, the latter emerging from Atwood's interest in biology and evolution. *The Journals of Susanna Moodie* is one of Atwood's best-known collections from this period, lauded for its attempt to resuscitate a forgotten Canadian ancestor. The collection posits Moodie as an archetypal Canadian who, caught between the Old World and the New, embodies the divided nature of the Canadian psyche, or what Atwood in the Afterword to the book terms the "paranoid-schizophrenia" that characterizes Canadian culture. The poems have strangely Gothic undertones, in which the boundaries between self and other, human and animal, civilization and wilderness are fused as Moodie metamorphoses into something different than her original self. They are accompanied by Atwood's eerie illustrations, which invite narratives of their own (see Figure VI-7).

During these years, Atwood also began to establish herself as a novelist, publishing her first novel, *The Edible Woman,* in 1969. This and her subsequent novels, *Surfacing* (1972) and *Lady Oracle* (1976), along with her early poetry, earned Atwood a reputation as a notable feminist writer and social commentator, though her tongue-in-cheek comments also took the Women's Liberation Movement to task for its sometimes myopic intolerance of any but a woman-centred agenda and its "women are better" argument. With Graeme Gibson (her future husband), she became involved in the 1970s movement to establish The Writers' Union of Canada, an organization committed to the legal and financial rights of authors. She was its president in 1981–82. It was also in the 1970s that Atwood published her work of Canadian literary criticism, *Survival* (1972), while working with Lee at Anansi. Not only did the book take issue with the absence of Canadian content in Canadian schools (the book was in part intended as a CanLit primer for high school and college English

teachers), but it proposed a characteristic mode of expression in Canadian literature: that of "survival." This thematic approach undoubtedly emerged out of the period's sense that Canada was under threat both by the reputation of Britain and by the world dominance of the United States, though it also took its lead from Frye's postulation of the "garrison mentality" in Canadian culture (the tendency to cordon oneself off from the perceived threat of the surrounding world—the world of nature, animals, or people who are perceived as "other"). While Atwood has been accused of overly emphasizing Canadians' colonial mentality in this work, it was in fact the opposite effect that Atwood sought, since *Survival* launched a harsh critique of Canadian insecurity. Within the book, Atwood outlined a series of "victim positions" that were identifiable in Canadian literature, concluding with the suggestion that the real test was to discover how to be a "creative non-victim." The book received a great deal of acclaim at the time, but also some censure. Today, Atwood's "survival thesis" is criticized by many Canadian scholars who find the approach overly homogenizing, especially in its exclusion of many non-mainstream voices in Canadian writing. Nevertheless, the manifesto garnered much support for Canadian literature at the time.

In the 1980s and '90s, Atwood's interests extended beyond her emphasis on Canadian national and cultural questions into issues of international human rights and environmentalism. During this period, she became a prominent member of the human rights organization PEN International, acting as president of its Canadian branch from 1984 to 1986. In the 1980s, Atwood published *The Handmaid's Tale* (1985), which not only won the Governor General's Award in Canada, but catapulted Atwood into international prominence. It was the first of her novels to be shortlisted for the prestigious Booker Prize. While the novel is set in a futuristic United States, it is clearly a condemnation of the threat of fundamentalist, and misogynistic, dictatorships worldwide. There is a similar interest in some of Atwood's political poetry from this period, particularly in *True Stories* (1981). Her poem "Footnote to the Amnesty Report on Torture" is unflinching in its commitment to human rights.

Sullivan puts it succinctly when she states, "For Atwood the essential human impulse is to reduce an irrational and threatening environment to a closed circle of orthodoxy. Thus the writer's responsibility is to expose the conventions . . . by which we invent convenient versions of ourselves. She sees modern man as being prey to continual invasions of fear and paranoia . . . yet committed to an anachronistic belief in civilized order that is patently contradicted by the barbarism of the twentieth century." This is certainly true in much of Atwood's writing, including *Bodily Harm* (1981), *The Handmaid's Tale* (1985), *Cat's Eye* (1988), *The Robber Bride* (1993), and *Oryx and Crake* (2003).

Atwood has written about numerous Canadian cultural icons, particularly in her 1995 essay collection *Strange Things* and in the stories in *Wilderness Tips* (1991), which reflect ironically on such Canadian figures as the Group of Seven (in the story "Wilderness Tips") and John Franklin (in the story "The Age of Lead"). In "The Age of Lead," Atwood parallels the hubris of the Franklin expedition with the contemporary world of consumerism and environmental destruction. It opens with a reference to forensic anthropologist Owen Beattie's 1981 exhumation of the bodies of three members of Franklin's expedition, including a sailor named John Torrington (see Figure VI-8). The story maps the explorers' quest for adventure and immortality alongside two contemporary characters, Jane and Vincent.

Atwood's writings often posit a dialogue between past and present, living and dead, demonstrating how the present is integrally constituted by events in the past. This is evident in *The Journals of Susanna Moodie,* but is also clearly apparent in *The Blind Assassin* (2000) and in Atwood's historical novel *Alias Grace* (1996), which focuses on the murder trial of Grace Marks, a nineteenth-century servant who was accused of murdering her employer. In all of her work, Atwood is fascinated by the underside of appearances, particularly by the irony that it is often the mask or the false side of the individual that passes for the truth or reality. This interest also applies to her analysis of societal and political norms that impose a version of truth which is often suspect. Atwood's fascination with the Gothic and the supernatural is part of this interest in unseen or hidden depths. In her 1980 essay "An End to Audience?" Atwood defines writing as "a kind of sooth-saying, a truth-telling. . . . It's also a witnessing. *Come with me,* the writer is saying to the reader. *There is a story I have to tell you, there is something you need to know.*"

This Is a Photograph of Me

It was taken some time ago.
At first it seems to be
a smeared
print: blurred lines and grey flecks
blended with the paper;

then, as you scan
it, you see in the left-hand corner
a thing that is like a branch: part of a tree
(balsam or spruce) emerging
and, to the right, halfway up   10
what ought to be a gentle
slope, a small frame house.

In the background there is a lake,
and beyond that, some low hills.

(The photograph was taken
the day after I drowned.

I am in the lake, in the center
of the picture, just under the surface.

It is difficult to say where
precisely, or to say   20
how large or small I am:
the effect of water
on light is a distortion

but if you look long enough,
eventually
you will be able to see me.)

                                                        [1966]

The City Planners

Cruising these residential Sunday
streets in dry August sunlight:
what offends us is
the sanities:
the houses in pedantic rows, the planted
sanitary trees, assert
levelness of surface like a rebuke
to the dent in our car door.
No shouting here, or
shatter of glass; nothing more abrupt   10
than the rational whine of a power mower
cutting a straight swath in the discouraged grass.

But though the driveways neatly
sidestep hysteria

by being even, the roofs all display
the same slant of avoidance to the hot sky,
certain things;
the smell of spilled oil a faint
sickness lingering in the garages,
a splash of paint on brick surprising as a bruise,   20
a plastic hose poised in a vicious
coil; even the too-fixed stare of the wide windows

give momentary access to
the landscape behind or under
the future cracks in the plaster

when the houses, capsized, will slide
obliquely into the clay seas, gradual as glaciers
that right now nobody notices.

That is where the City Planners
with the insane faces of political conspirators   30
are scattered over unsurveyed
territories, concealed from each other,
each in his own private blizzard;

guessing directions, they sketch
transitory lines rigid as wooden borders
on a wall in the white vanishing air

tracing the panic of suburb
order in a bland madness of snows.

[1966]

It is dangerous to read newspapers

While I was building neat
castles in the sandbox,
the hasty pits were
filling with bulldozed corpses

and as I walked to the school
washed and combed, my feet
stepping on the cracks in the cement
detonated red bombs.

Now I am grownup
and literate, and I sit in my chair   10

as quietly as a fuse

and the jungles are flaming, the underbrush is charged with soldiers,
the names on the difficult
maps go up in smoke.

I am the cause, I am a stockpile of chemical
toys, my body
is a deadly gadget,
I reach out in love, my hands are guns,
my good intentions are completely lethal.   20

Even my
passive eyes transmute
everything I look at to the pocked
black and white of a war photo,
how
can I stop myself

It is dangerous to read newspapers.

Each time I hit a key
on my electric typewriter,
speaking of peaceful trees   30

another village explodes.

                                        [1968]

Footnote to the Amnesty Report on Torture

The torture chamber is not like anything
you would have expected.
No opera set or sexy chains and
leather-goods from the glossy
porno magazines, no thirties horror
dungeon with gauzy cobwebs; nor is it
the bare cold-lighted
chrome space of the future
we think we fear.
More like one of the seedier   10
British Railways stations, with scratched green
walls and spilled tea,

crumpled papers, and a stooped man
who is always cleaning the floor.

It stinks, though; like a hospital,
of antiseptics and sickness,
and, on some days, blood
which smells the same anywhere,
here or at the butcher's.

The man who works here   20
is losing his sense of smell.
He's glad to have this job, because
there are few others.
He isn't a torturer, he only
cleans the floor:
every morning the same vomit,
the same shed teeth, the same
piss and liquid shit, the same panic.

Some have courage, others
don't; those who do what he thinks of   30
as the real work, and who are
bored, since minor bureaucrats
are always bored, tell them
it doesn't matter, who
will ever know they were brave, they might
as well talk now
and get it over.

Some have nothing to say, which also
doesn't matter. Their
warped bodies too, with the torn   40
fingers and ragged tongues, are thrown
over the spiked iron fence onto
the Consul's lawn, along with
the bodies of the children
burned to make their mothers talk.

The man who cleans the floors
is glad it isn't him.
It will be if he ever says
what he knows. He works long hours,
submits to the searches, eats   50
a meal he brings from home, which tastes

of old blood and the sawdust
he cleans the floor with. His wife
is pleased he brings her money
for the food, has been told
not to ask questions.

As he sweeps, he tries
not to listen; he tries
to make himself into a wall,
a thick wall, a wall   60
soft and without echoes. He thinks
of nothing but the walk back
to his hot shed of a house,
of the door
opening and his children
with their unmarked skin and flawless eyes
running to meet him.

He is afraid of
what he might do
if he were told to,   70
he is afraid of the door,

he is afraid, not
of the door but of the door
opening; sometimes, no matter
how hard he tries,
his children are not there.

[1978]

From *The Journals of Susanna Moodie*[1]

Disembarking at Quebec

Is it my clothes, my way of walking,
the things I carry in my hand
—a book, a bag with knitting—
the incongruous pink of my shawl

[1] These linked poems are spoken from the point of view of Susanna Moodie (1803–1885), nineteenth-century British settler in Canada and author of *Roughing It in the Bush* (1852) and *Life in the Clearings* (1853), both of which inspired the events treated in Atwood's rendition. See Volume I for excerpts from Moodie's *Roughing It*, including the chapter "A Visit to Grosse Isle," which forms the background to "Disembarking at Quebec" and "Further Arrivals." In the "Grosse Isle" chapter, Moodie describes her disillusionment upon arriving in Canada, and is struck by the chaos and coarse familiarity of the working-class immigrants at Grosse Isle who are emboldened by their new freedom. See also Figure VI-7 for Atwood's illustration that accompanies this poem.

this space cannot hear

or is it my own lack
of conviction which makes
these vistas of desolation,
long hills, the swamps, the barren sand, the glare
of sun on the bone-white   10
driftlogs, omens of winter,
the moon alien in day-
time a thin refusal

The others leap, shout

                    Freedom!

The moving water will not show me
my reflection.

The rocks ignore.

I am a word
in a foreign language.   20

Further Arrivals

After we had crossed the long illness
that was the ocean, we sailed up-river

On the first island
the immigrants threw off their clothes
and danced like sandflies

We left behind one by one
the cities rotting with cholera,
one by one our civilized
distinctions

and entered a large darkness.   10

It was our own
ignorance we entered.

I have not come out yet

My brain gropes nervous
tentacles in the night, sends out
fears hairy as bears,
demands lamps; or waiting

for my shadowy husband, hears
malice in the trees' whispers.

I need wolf's eyes to see   20
the truth.

I refuse to look in a mirror.

Whether the wilderness is
real or not
depends on who lives there.

Departure from the Bush

I, who had been erased
by fire,[2] was crept in
upon by green
                    (how
lucid a season)

          In time the animals
arrived to inhabit me,

first one
    by one, stealthily
(their habitual traces   10
burnt); then
having marked new boundaries
returning, more
confident, year
by year, two
by two

---

[2] In Chapter 22 of *Roughing It in the Bush* (1852), Moodie describes a fire that destroyed her family's cabin. This poem is inspired by the final chapter of *Roughing It*, "Adieu to the Woods" (see Volume I), in which Moodie relates her ambivalent feelings as they leave their bush homestead for the town of Belleville.

but restless: I was not ready
altogether to be moved into

They could tell I was
too heavy: I might   20
capsize;

I was frightened
by their eyes (green or
amber) glowing out from inside me

I was not completed; at night
I could not see without lanterns.

He wrote, We are leaving. I said
I have no clothes
left I can wear

The snow came. The sleigh was a relief;   30
its track lengthened behind,
pushing me towards the city

and rounding the first hill, I was
(instantaneous)
unlived in: they had gone.

There was something they almost taught me
I came away not having learned.

                                                    [1970]

Dream 2: Brian the Still-Hunter[3]

The man I saw in the forest
used to come to our house
every morning, never said anything;
I learned from the neighbours later
he once tried to cut his throat.

---

[3] Chapter 10 of *Roughing It in the Bush* describes an acquaintance of the Moodies, Brian the Still Hunter, a philosophical man who suffers from depression and loneliness in the Canadian backwoods and hence parallels Moodie's experience. Brian has attempted suicide in the past, and at the end of the chapter, Moodie relates how he eventually killed himself after her departure from the woods. The chapter includes Brian's story about a deer being hunted by a pack of hounds in which he asks, "Is God just to his creatures?" See Volume I for the relevant excerpt from Moodie's chapter.

I found him at the end of the path
sitting on a fallen tree
cleaning his gun.

There was no wind;
around us the leaves rustled.   10

He said to me:
I kill because I have to

but every time I aim, I feel
my skin grow fur
my head heavy with antlers
and during the stretched instant
the bullet glides on its thread of speed
my soul runs innocent as hooves.

Is God just to his creatures?

I die more often than many.   20

He looked up and I saw
the white scar made by the hunting knife
around his neck.

When I woke
I remembered: he has been gone
twenty years and not heard from.

Thoughts from Underground[4]

When I first reached this country
I hated it
and I hated it more each year:

in summer the light a
violent blur, the heat
thick as a swamp,
the green things fiercely
shoving themselves upwards, the
eyelids bitten by insects

[4] This poem is spoken by Moodie in Belleville after she has died. See Figure VI-7 for Atwood's illustration accompanying this poem. *Roughing It in the Bush* includes an account of the family eating squirrel pie, which is alluded to here.

In winter our teeth were brittle   10
with cold. We fed on squirrels.
At night the house cracked.
In the mornings, we thawed
the bad bread over the stove.

Then we were made successful
and I felt I ought to love
this country.
                    I said I loved it
and my mind saw double.

I began to forget myself   20
in the middle
of sentences. Events
were split apart

I fought. I constructed
desperate paragraphs of praise, everyone
ought to love it because

and set them up at intervals

        due to natural resources, native industry, superior
        penitentiaries
        we will all be rich and powerful   30

flat as highway billboards

        who can doubt it, look how
        fast Belleville is growing

(though it is still no place for an english gentleman)

                                                            [1970]

MARGARET ATWOOD

446

From Survival: A Thematic Guide to Canadian Literature

[. . .] [I]n Canada, as Frye suggests, the answer to the question "Who am I?" is at least partly the same as the answer to another question: "Where is here?"[5] "Who am I?" is a question appropriate in countries where the environment, the

---

[5] See the excerpt from Northrop Frye's "Conclusion to *Literary History of Canada*" included in this section.

"here," is already well-defined, so well-defined in fact that it may threaten to overwhelm the individual. [. . .]

But when you are here and don't know where you are because you've misplaced your landmarks or bearings, then you need not be an exile or a madman: you are simply lost. Which returns us to our image of the man in an unknown territory. Canada is an unknown territory for the people who live in it, and I'm not talking about the fact that you may not have taken a trip to the Arctic or to Newfoundland, you may not have explored—as the travel folders have it—This Great Land of Ours. I'm talking about Canada as a state of mind, as the space you inhabit not just with your body but with your head. It's that kind of space in which we find ourselves lost.

What a lost person needs is a map of the territory, with his own position marked on it so he can see where he is in relation to everything else. Literature is not only a mirror; it is also a map, a geography of the mind. Our literature is one such map, if we can learn to read it as *our* literature, as the product of who and where we have been. We need such a map desperately, we need to know about here, because here is where we live. For the members of a country or a culture, shared knowledge of their place, their here, is not a luxury but a necessity. Without that knowledge we will not survive. [. . .]

* * *

I'd like to begin with a sweeping generalization and argue that every country or culture has a single unifying and informing symbol at its core. [. . .] The symbol, then— be it word, phrase, idea, image, or all of these—functions like a system of beliefs (it *is* a system of beliefs, though not always a formal one) which holds the country together and helps the people in it to co-operate for common ends. Possibly the symbol for America is The Frontier, a flexible idea that contains many elements dear to the American heart: it suggests a place that is *new*, where the old order can be discarded (as it was when America was instituted by a crop of disaffected Protestants, and later at the time of the Revolution); a line that is always expanding, taking in or "conquering" ever-fresh virgin territory (be it The West, the rest of the world, outer space, Poverty or The Regions of the Mind); it holds out a hope, never fulfilled but always promised, of Utopia, the perfect human society. [. . .]

The central symbol for Canada—and this is based on numerous instances of its occurrence in both English and French Canadian literature—is undoubtedly Survival, *la Survivance*. Like the Frontier and The Island [England], it is a multi-faceted and adaptable idea. For early explorers and settlers, it meant bare survival in the face of "hostile" elements and/or natives: carving out a place and a way of keeping alive. But the word can also suggest survival of a crisis or disaster, like a hurricane or a wreck, and many Canadian poems have this kind of survival as a theme; what you might call 'grim' survival as opposed to 'bare' survival. For French Canada after the English took over it became cultural survival, hanging on as a people, retaining a religion and a language under an alien government. And in English Canada now while the Americans are taking over it is acquiring a similar meaning. [. . .]

A preoccupation with one's survival is necessarily also a preoccupation with the obstacles to that survival. In earlier writers these obstacles are external—the land, the climate, and so forth. In later writers the obstacles tend to become both harder to identify and more internal; they are no longer obstacles to physical survival but obstacles to what we may call spiritual survival, to life as anything more than a minimally human being. Sometimes fear of these obstacles becomes itself the obstacle, and a character is paralyzed by terror (either of what he thinks is threatening him from the outside, or of elements in his own nature that threaten him from within). It may even be life itself that he fears; and when life becomes a threat to life, you have a moderately vicious circle. [. . .]

* * *

Let us suppose, for the sake of argument, that Canada as a whole is a victim, or an "oppressed minority," or "exploited." Let us suppose in short that Canada is a colony. A partial definition of a colony is that it is a place from which a profit is made, but *not by the people who live there:* the major profit from a colony is made in the centre of the empire. That's what colonies are for, to make money for the "mother country," and that's what—since the days of Rome and, more recently, of the Thirteen Colonies—they have always been for. Of course there are cultural side-effects which are often identified as "the colonial mentality," and it is these which are examined here; but the root cause for them is economic.

If Canada is a collective victim, it should pay some attention to the Basic Victim Positions. [. . .]

The positions are the same whether you are a victimized country, a victimized minority group or a victimized individual.

* * *

Basic Victim Positions

Position One: To deny the fact that you are a victim.

This uses up a lot of energy, as you must spend much time explaining away the obvious, suppressing anger, and pretending that certain visible facts do not exist. The position is usually taken by those in a Victim group who are a little better off than the others in that group. They are afraid to recognize they are victims for fear of losing the privileges they possess, and they are forced to account somehow for the disadvantages suffered by the rest of the people in the group by disparaging them. As in: "*I* made it, therefore it's obvious we aren't victims. The rest are just lazy (or neurotic, or stupid); anyway it's their own fault if they aren't happy, look at all the opportunities available for them!"

If anger is felt by Victims in Position One, it is likely to be directed against one's fellow-victims, particularly those who try to talk about their victimization.

The basic game in Position One is "Deny your Victim-experience."

Position Two: To acknowledge the fact that you are a victim, but to explain this as an act of Fate, the Will of God, the dictates of Biology (in the case of women, for instance), the necessity decreed by History, or Economics, or the Unconscious, or any other large general powerful idea.

In any case, since it is the fault of this large *thing* and not your own fault, you can neither be blamed for your position nor be expected to do anything about it. You can be resigned and long-suffering, or you can kick against the pricks and make a fuss; in the latter case your rebellion will be deemed foolish or evil even by you, and you will expect to lose and be punished, for who can fight Fate (or the Will of God, or Biology)?

Notice that:

1. The explanation *displaces* the cause from the real source of oppression to something else.
2. Because the fake cause is so vast, nebulous and unchangeable, you are permanently excused from changing it, *and also* from deciding how much of your situation (e.g. the climate) is unchangeable, how much can be changed, and how much is caused by habit or tradition or your own need to be a victim.
3. Anger, when present—or scorn, since everyone in the category is defined as inferior—is directed against both fellow-victims and oneself.

The basic game in Position Two is Victor/Victim.

Position Three: To acknowledge the fact that you are a victim but to refuse to accept the assumption that the role is inevitable.

As in: "Look what's being done to me, and it isn't Fate, it isn't the Will of God. Therefore I can stop seeing myself as a *fated* Victim."

To put it differently: you can distinguish between the *role* of Victim (which probably leads you to seek victimization even when there's no call for it), and the *objective experience* that is making you a victim. And you can probably go further and decide how much of the objective experience could be changed if you made the effort.

This is a dynamic position, rather than a static one; from it you can move on to Position Four, but if you become locked into your anger and fail to change your situation, you might well find yourself back in Position Two.

Notice that:

1. In this position the real cause of oppression is for the first time identified.
2. Anger can be directed against the real source of oppression, and energy channelled into constructive action.
3. You can make real decisions about how much of your position can be changed and how much can't (you can't make it stop snowing; you can stop blaming the snow for everything that's wrong).

The basic game of Position Three is repudiating the Victim role.

Position Four: To be a creative non-victim.

Strictly speaking, Position Four is a position not for victims but for those who have never been victims at all, or for ex-victims: those who have been able to move into it from Position Three because the external and/or the internal causes of victimization have been removed. (In an oppressed society, of course, you can't become an ex-victim—insofar as you are connected with your society—until the entire society's position has been changed.)

In Position Four, creative activity of all kinds becomes possible. Energy is no longer being suppressed (as in Position One) or used up for displacement of the cause, or for passing your victimization along to others (Man kicks Child, Child kicks Dog) as in Position Two; nor is it being used for the dynamic anger of Position Three. And you are able to accept your own experience for what it is, rather than having to distort it to make it correspond with others' versions of it (particularly those of your oppressors).

In Position Four, Victor/Victim games are obsolete. You don't even have to concentrate on rejecting the role of Victim, because the role is no longer a temptation for you.

(There may be a Position Five, for mystics; I postulate it but will not explore it here, since mystics do not as a rule write books.)

[1972]

The Age of Lead

The man has been buried for a hundred and fifty years. They dug a hole in the frozen gravel, deep into the permafrost, and put him down there so the wolves couldn't get to him. Or that is the speculation.[6]

When they dug the hole the permafrost was exposed to the air, which was warmer. This made the permafrost melt. But it froze again after the man was covered up, so that when he was brought to the surface he was completely enclosed in ice. They took the lid off the coffin and it was like those maraschino cherries you used to freeze in ice-cube trays for fancy tropical drinks: a vague shape, looming through a solid cloud.

Then they melted the ice and he came to light. He is almost the same as when he was buried. The freezing water has pushed his lips away from his teeth into an astonished snarl, and he's a beige colour, like a gravy stain on linen, instead of pink, but everything is still there. He even has eyeballs, except that they aren't white but the light brown of milky tea. With these tea-stained eyes he regards Jane: an indecipherable gaze, innocent, ferocious, amazed, but

---

[6] The description here and in the subsequent paragraphs is of the exhumed body of John Torrington, one of the sailors from Sir John Franklin's disastrous expedition in 1845 (see Volume I, Section I, for more information on Franklin). The photos were taken by forensic scientist Owen Beattie, whose team exhumed the body to test it for lead poisoning. See Figure VI-8 for the photo described in this story.

contemplative, like a werewolf meditating, caught in a flash of lightning at the exact split second of his tumultuous change.

Jane doesn't watch very much television. She used to watch it more. She used to watch comedy series, in the evenings, and when she was a student at university she would watch afternoon soaps about hospitals and rich people, as a way of procrastinating. For a while, not so long ago, she would watch the evening news, taking in the disasters with her feet tucked up on the chesterfield, a throw rug over her legs, drinking a hot milk and rum to relax before bed. It was all a form of escape.

But what you can see on the television, at whatever time of day, is edging too close to her own life; though in her life, nothing stays put in those tidy compartments, comedy here, seedy romance and sentimental tears there, accidents and violent deaths in thirty-second clips they call *bites,* as if they were chocolate bars. In her life, everything is mixed together. *Laugh, I thought I'd die,* Vincent used to say, a very long time ago, in a voice imitating the banality of mothers; and that's how it's getting to be. So when she flicks on the television these days, she flicks it off again soon enough. Even the commercials, with their surreal dailiness, are beginning to look sinister, to suggest meanings behind themselves, behind their façade of cleanliness, lusciousness, health, power, and speed.

Tonight she leaves the television on, because what she is seeing is so unlike what she usually sees. There is nothing sinister behind this image of the frozen man. It is entirely itself. *What you sees is what you gets,* as Vincent also used to say, crossing his eyes, baring his teeth at one side, pushing his nose into a horror-movie snout. Although it never was, with him.

The man they've dug up and melted was a young man. Or still is: it's difficult to know what tense should be applied to him, he is so insistently present. Despite the distortions caused by the ice and the emaciation of his illness, you can see his youthfulness, the absence of toughening, of wear. According to the dates painted carefully onto his nameplate, he was only twenty years old. His name was John Torrington. He was, or is, a sailor, a seaman. He wasn't an able-bodied seaman though; he was a petty officer, one of those marginally in command. Being in command has little to do with the ableness of the body.

He was one of the first to die. This is why he got a coffin and a metal nameplate, and a deep hole in the permafrost—because they still had the energy, and the piety, for such things that early. There would have been a burial service read over him, and prayers. As time went on and became nebulous and things did not get better, they must have kept the energy for themselves; and also the prayers. The prayers would have ceased to be routine and become desperate, and then hopeless. The later dead ones got cairns of piled stones, and the much later ones not even that. They ended up as bones, and as the soles of boots and the occasional button, sprinkled over the frozen stony treeless relentless ground in a trail heading south.[7] It was like the trails in fairy tales, of bread crumbs or seeds or white stones. But in this case nothing had sprouted or lit up in the moonlight, forming a miraculous pathway to life; no rescuers had followed. It took ten years before anyone knew even the barest beginnings of what had been happening to them.

All of them together were the Franklin Expedition. Jane has seldom paid much attention to history except when it has overlapped with her knowledge of antique furniture and real estate—"19th C. pine harvest table," or "Prime location Georgian centre hall, impeccable reno"—but she knows what the Franklin Expedition was. The two ships with their bad-luck names have been on stamps—the *Terror*, the *Erebus*. Also she took it in school, along with a lot of other doomed expeditions. Not many of those explorers seemed to have come out of it very well. They were always getting scurvy, or lost.

What the Franklin Expedition was looking for was the Northwest Passage, an open seaway across the top of the Arctic, so people, merchants, could get to India from England without going all the way around South America. They wanted to go that way because it would cost less and increase their profits. This was much less exotic than Marco Polo or the headwaters of the Nile;[8] nevertheless, the idea of exploration appealed to her then: to get onto a boat and just go somewhere, somewhere mapless, off into the unknown. To launch yourself into fright; to find things out. There was something daring and noble about it, despite all of the losses and failures, or perhaps because of them. It was like having sex, in high school, in those days before the Pill, even if you took precautions. If you were a girl, that is. If you were a boy, for whom such a risk was fairly minimal, you had to do other things: things with weapons or large amounts of alcohol, or high-speed vehicles, which at her suburban Toronto high school, back then at the beginning of the sixties, meant switchblades, beer, and drag races down the main streets on Saturday nights.

Now, gazing at the television as the lozenge of ice gradually melts and the outline of the young sailor's body clears and sharpens, Jane remembers Vincent, sixteen and with more hair then, quirking one eyebrow and lifting his lip in a mock sneer and saying, "Franklin, my dear, I don't give a damn." He said it loud

---

[7] After Franklin's ships, the *Terror* and the *Erebus*, had been trapped in the ice for the course of two summers, the remaining members of the expedition attempted to walk southwards overland in the hope of being rescued. They pulled with them a lifeboat filled with various objects. Buttons and other items belonging to the Franklin expedition have been found in the Arctic tundra. It took more than 10 years for search parties to piece together the fate of the expedition (see the Franklin headnote in Volume I). When the lifeboat was discovered, it was found pointing in the direction of the ships, suggesting either that the men had been pulling it backwards (and hence evidence of their irrationality), or that they had changed their minds and were retreating back to the ships (see Figure I-10 and the testimony by Tooktoocheer about finding the lifeboat with skeletons, in Volume I).

[8] Marco Polo (1254–1324/25) was a Venetian explorer and trader who published a book describing his travels overland to Cathay (China) in the mid-thirteenth century. The search for the source of the Nile River consumed explorers throughout the eighteenth and nineteenth centuries, and opinion is divided about who discovered its headwaters first, in part because it divides into the Blue Nile (source is Lake Tana) and White Nile (source is Lake Victoria) before the two rivers converge to form the Nile proper.

enough to be heard, but the history teacher ignored him, not knowing what else to do. It was hard for the teachers to keep Vincent in line, because he never seemed to be afraid of anything that might happen to him.

He was hollow-eyed even then; he frequently looked as if he'd been up all night. Even then he resembled a very young old man, or else a dissipated child. The dark circles under his eyes were the ancient part, but when he smiled he had lovely small white teeth, like the magazine ads for baby foods. He made fun of everything, and was adored. He wasn't adored the way other boys were adored, those boys with surly lower lips and greased hair and a studied air of smouldering menace. He was adored like a pet. Not a dog, but a cat. He went where he liked, and nobody owned him. Nobody called him Vince.

Strangely enough, Jane's mother approved of him. She didn't usually approve of the boys Jane went out with. Maybe she approved of him because it was obvious to her that no bad results would follow from Jane's going out with him: no heartaches, no heaviness, nothing burdensome. None of what she called *consequences*. Consequences: the weightiness of the body, the growing flesh hauled around like a bundle, the tiny frill-framed goblin head in the carriage. Babies and marriage, in that order. This was how she understood men and their furtive, fumbling, threatening desires, because Jane herself had been a consequence. She had been a mistake, she had been a war baby. She had been a crime that had needed to be paid for, over and over.

By the time she was sixteen, Jane had heard enough about this to last her several lifetimes. In her mother's account of the way things were, you were young briefly and then you fell. You plummeted downwards like an overripe apple and hit the ground with a squash; you fell, and everything about you fell too. You got fallen arches and a fallen womb, and your hair and teeth fell out. That's what having a baby did to you. It subjected you to the force of gravity.

This is how she remembers her mother, still: in terms of a pendulous, drooping, wilting motion. Her sagging breasts, the downturned lines around her mouth. Jane conjures her up: there she is, as usual, sitting at the kitchen table with a cup of cooling tea, exhausted after her job clerking at Eaton's department store, standing all day behind the jewellery counter with her bum stuffed into a girdle and her swelling feet crammed into the mandatory medium-heeled shoes, smiling her envious, disapproving smile at the spoiled customers who turned up their noses at pieces of glittering junk she herself could never afford to buy. Jane's mother sighs, picks at the canned spaghetti Jane has heated up for her. Silent words waft out of her like stale talcum powder: *What can you expect*, always a statement, never a question. Jane tries at this distance for pity, but comes up with none.

As for Jane's father, he'd run away from home when Jane was five, leaving her mother in the lurch. That's what her mother called it—"running away from home"—as if he'd been an irresponsible child. Money arrived from time to time, but that was the sum total of his contribution to family life. Jane resented him for it, but she didn't blame him. Her mother inspired in almost everyone who encountered her a vicious desire for escape.

Jane and Vincent would sit out in the cramped backyard of Jane's house, which was one of the squinty-windowed little stuccoed wartime bungalows at the bottom of the hill. At the top of the hill were the richer houses, and the richer people: the girls who owned cashmere sweaters, at least one of them, instead of the Orlon and lambswool so familiar to Jane. Vincent lived about halfway up the hill. He still had a father, in theory.

They would sit against the back fence, near the spindly cosmos flowers that passed for a garden, as far away from the house itself as they could get. They would drink gin, decanted by Vincent from his father's liquor hoard and smuggled in an old military pocket flask he'd picked up somewhere. They would imitate their mothers.

"I pinch and I scrape and I work my fingers to the bone, and what thanks do I get?" Vincent would say peevishly. "No help from you, Sonny Boy. You're just like your father. Free as the birds, out all night, do as you like and you don't care one pin about anyone else's feelings. Now take out that garbage."

"It's love that does it to you," Jane would reply, in the resigned, ponderous voice of her mother. "You wait and see, my girl. One of these days you'll come down off your devil-may-care high horse." As Jane said this, and even though she was making fun, she could picture love, with a capital L, descending out of the sky towards her like a huge foot. Her mother's life had been a disaster, but in her own view an inevitable disaster, as in songs and movies. It was Love that was responsible, and in the face of Love, what could be done? Love was like a steamroller. There was no avoiding it, it went over you and you came out flat.

Jane's mother waited, fearfully and uttering warnings, but with a sort of gloating relish, for the same thing to happen to Jane. Every time Jane went out with a new boy her mother inspected him as a potential agent of downfall. She distrusted most of these boys; she distrusted their sulky, pulpy mouths, their eyes half-closed in the up-drifting smoke of their cigarettes, their slow, sauntering manner of talking, their clothing that was too tight, too full: too full of their bodies. They looked this way even when they weren't putting on the sulks and swaggers, when they were trying to appear bright-eyed and industrious and polite for Jane's mother's benefit, saying goodbye at the front door, dressed in their shirts and ties and their pressed heavy-date suits. They couldn't help the way they looked, the way they were. They were helpless; one kiss in a dark corner would reduce them to speechlessness; they were sleepwalkers in their own liquid bodies. Jane, on the other hand, was wide awake.

Jane and Vincent did not exactly go out together. Instead they made fun of going out. When the coast was clear and Jane's mother wasn't home, Vincent would appear at the door with his face painted bright yellow, and Jane would put her bathrobe on back to front and they would order Chinese food and alarm the delivery boy and eat sitting cross-legged on the floor, clumsily, with chopsticks. Or Vincent would turn up in a threadbare thirty-year-old suit and a bowler hat and a cane, and Jane would rummage around in the cupboard for a discarded church-going hat of her mother's, with smashed cloth violets and a veil, and they would go downtown and walk around, making loud remarks about the passers-by, pretending to be old, or poor, or crazy. It was thoughtless and in bad taste, which was what they both liked about it.

Vincent took Jane to the graduation formal, and they picked out her dress together at one of the second-hand clothing shops Vincent frequented, giggling at the shock and admiration they hoped to cause. They hesitated between a flame-red with falling-off sequins and a backless hip-hugging black with a plunge front, and chose the black, to go with Jane's hair. Vincent sent a poisonous-looking lime-green orchid, the colour of her eyes, he said, and Jane painted her eyelids and fingernails to match. Vincent wore white tie and tails, and a top hat, all frayed Sally-Ann issue and ludicrously too large for him. They tangoed around the gymnasium, even though the music was not a tango, under the tissue-paper flowers, cutting a black swath through the sea of pastel tulle, unsmiling, projecting a corny sexual menace, Vincent with Jane's long pearl necklace clenched between his teeth.

The applause was mostly for him, because of the way he was adored. Though mostly by the girls, thinks Jane. But he seemed to be popular enough among the boys as well. Probably he told them dirty jokes, in the proverbial locker room. He knew enough of them.

As he dipped Jane backwards, he dropped the pearls and whispered into her ear, "No belts, no pins, no pads, no chafing." It was from an ad for tampons, but it was also their leitmotif. It was what they both wanted: freedom from the world of mothers, the world of precautions, the world of burdens and fate and heavy female constraints upon the flesh. They wanted a life without consequences. Until recently, they'd managed it.

The scientists have melted the entire length of the young sailor now, at least the upper layer of him. They've been pouring warm water over him, gently and patiently; they don't want to thaw him too abruptly. It's as if John Torrington is asleep and they don't want to startle him.

Now his feet have been revealed. They're bare, and white rather than beige; they look like the feet of someone who's been walking on a cold floor, on a winter day. That is the quality of the light that they reflect: winter sunlight, in early morning. There is something intensely painful to Jane about the absence of socks. They could have left him his socks. But maybe the others needed them. His big toes are tied together with a strip of cloth; the man talking says this was to keep the body tidily packaged for burial, but Jane is not convinced. His arms are tied to his body, his ankles are tied together. You do that when you don't want a person walking around.

This part is almost too much for Jane; it is too reminiscent. She reaches for the channel switcher, but luckily the show (it is only a show, it's only another show) changes to two of the historical experts, analyzing the clothing. There's a close-up of John Torrington's shirt, a simple, high-collared, pin-striped white-and-blue cotton, with mother-of-pearl buttons. The stripes are a printed pattern, rather than a woven one; woven would have been more expensive. The trousers are grey linen.

Ah, thinks Jane. Wardrobe. She feels better: this is something she knows about. She loves the solemnity, the reverence, with which the stripes and buttons are discussed. An interest in the clothing of the present is frivolity, an interest in the clothing of the past is archaeology; a point Vincent would have appreciated.

After high school, Jane and Vincent both got scholarships to university, although Vincent had appeared to study less, and did better. That summer they did everything together. They got summer jobs at the same hamburger heaven, they went to movies together after work, although Vincent never paid for Jane. They still occasionally dressed up in old clothes and pretended to be a weird couple, but it no longer felt careless and filled with absurd invention. It was beginning to occur to them that they might conceivably end up looking like that.

In her first year at university Jane stopped going out with other boys: she needed a part-time job to help pay her way, and that and the schoolwork and Vincent took up all her time. She thought she might be in love with Vincent. She thought that maybe they should make love, to find out. She had never done such a thing, entirely; she had been too afraid of the untrustworthiness of men, of the gravity of love, too afraid of consequences. She thought, however, that she might trust Vincent.

But things didn't go that way. They held hands, but they didn't hug; they hugged, but they didn't pet; they kissed, but they didn't neck. Vincent liked looking at her, but he liked it so much he would never close his eyes. She would close hers and then open them, and there would be Vincent, his own eyes shining in the light from the street-lamp or the moon, peering at her inquisitively as if waiting to see what odd female thing she would do next, for his delighted amusement. Making love with Vincent did not seem altogether possible.

(Later, after she had flung herself into the current of opinion that had swollen to a river by the late sixties, she no longer said "making love"; she said "having sex." But it amounted to the same thing. You had sex, and love got made out of it whether you liked it or not. You woke up in a bed or more likely on a mattress, with an arm around you, and found yourself wondering what it might be like to keep on doing it. At that point Jane would start looking at her watch. She had no intention of being left in any lurches. She would do the leaving herself. And she did.)

Jane and Vincent wandered off to different cities. They wrote each other postcards. Jane did this and that. She ran a co-op food store in Vancouver, did the financial stuff for a diminutive theatre in Montreal, acted as managing editor for a small publisher, ran the publicity for a dance company. She had a head for details and for adding up small sums—having to scrape her way through university had been instructive—and such jobs were often available if you didn't demand much money for doing them. Jane could see no reason to tie herself down, to make any sort of soul-stunting commitment, to anything or anyone. It was the early seventies; the old heavy women's world of girdles and precautions and consequences had been swept away. There were a lot of windows opening, a lot of doors: you could look in, then you could go in, then you could come out again.

She lived with several men, but in each of the apartments there were always cardboard boxes, belonging to her, that she never got around to unpacking; just as well, because it was that much easier to move out. When she got past thirty she decided it might be nice to have a child, some time, later. She tried to figure out a way of doing this without becoming a mother. Her own mother had moved to Florida, and sent rambling, grumbling letters, to which Jane did not often reply.

Jane moved back to Toronto, and found it ten times more interesting than when she'd left it. Vincent was already there. He'd come back from Europe, where he'd been studying film; he'd opened a design studio. He and Jane met for lunch, and it was the same: the same air of conspiracy between them, the same sense of their own potential for outrageousness. They might still have been sitting in Jane's garden, beside the cosmos flowers, drinking forbidden gin and making fun.

Jane found herself moving in Vincent's circles, or were they orbits? Vincent knew a great many people, people of all kinds; some were artists and some wanted to be, and some wanted to know the ones who were. Some had money to begin with, some made money; they all spent it. There was a lot more talk about money, these days, or among these people. Few of them knew how to manage it, and Jane found herself helping them out. She developed a small business among them, handling their money. She would gather it in, put it away safely for them, tell them what they could spend, dole out an allowance. She would note with interest the things they bought, filing their receipted bills: what furniture, what clothing, which *objets*. They were delighted with their money, enchanted with it. It was like milk and cookies for them, after school. Watching them play with their money, Jane felt responsible and indulgent, and a little matronly. She stored her own money carefully away, and eventually bought a townhouse with it.

All this time she was with Vincent, more or less. They'd tried being lovers but had not made a success of it. Vincent had gone along with this scheme because Jane had wanted it, but he was elusive, he would not make declarations. What worked with other men did not work with him: appeals to his protective instincts, pretences at jealousy, requests to remove stuck lids from jars. Sex with him was more like a musical workout. He couldn't take it seriously, and accused her of being too solemn about it. She thought he might be gay, but was afraid to ask him; she dreaded feeling irrelevant to him, excluded. It took them months to get back to normal.

He was older now, they both were. He had thinning temples and a widow's peak, and his bright inquisitive eyes had receded even further into his head. What went on between them continued to look like a courtship, but was not one. He was always bringing her things: a new, peculiar food to eat, a new grotesquerie to see, a new piece of gossip, which he would present to her with a sense of occasion, like a flower. She in her turn appreciated him. It was like a yogic exercise, appreciating Vincent; it was like appreciating an anchovy, or a stone. He was not everyone's taste.

There's a black-and-white print on the television, then another: the nineteenth century's version of itself, in etchings. Sir John Franklin, older and fatter than Jane had supposed; the *Terror* and the *Erebus,* locked fast in the crush of the ice. In the high Arctic, a hundred and fifty years ago, it's the dead of winter. There is no sun at all, no moon; only the rustling northern lights, like electronic music, and the hard little stars.

What did they do for love, on such a ship, at such a time? Furtive solitary gropings, confused and mournful dreams, the sublimation of novels. The usual, among those who have become solitary.

Down in the hold, surrounded by the creaking of the wooden hull and the stale odours of men far too long enclosed, John Torrington lies dying. He must have known it; you can see it on his face. He turns towards Jane his tea-coloured look of puzzled reproach.

Who held his hand, who read to him, who brought him water? Who, if anyone, loved him? And what did they tell him about whatever it was that was killing him? Consumption, brain fever, Original Sin. All those Victorian reasons, which meant nothing and were the wrong ones. But they must have been comforting. If you are dying, you want to know why.

In the eighties, things started to slide. Toronto was not so much fun any more. There were too many people, too many poor people. You could see them begging on the streets, which were clogged with fumes and cars. The cheap artists' studios were torn down or converted to coy and upscale office space; the artists had migrated elsewhere. Whole streets were torn up or knocked down. The air was full of windblown grit.

People were dying. They were dying too early. One of Jane's clients, a man who owned an antique store, died almost overnight of bone cancer. Another, a woman who was an entertainment lawyer, was trying on a dress in a boutique and had a heart attack. She fell over and they called the ambulance, and she was dead on arrival. A theatrical producer died of AIDS, and a photographer; the lover of the photographer shot himself, either out of grief or because he knew he was next. A friend of a friend died of emphysema, another of viral pneumonia, another of hepatitis picked up on a tropical vacation, another of spinal meningitis. It was as if they had been weakened by some mysterious agent, a thing like a colourless gas, scentless and invisible, so that any germ that happened along could invade their bodies, take them over.

Jane began to notice news items of the kind she'd once skimmed over. Maple groves dying of acid rain, hormones in the beef, mercury in the fish, pesticides in the vegetables, poison sprayed on the fruit, God knows what in the drinking water. She subscribed to a bottled spring-water service and felt better for a few weeks, then read in the paper that it wouldn't do her much good, because whatever it was had been seeping into everything. Each time you took a breath, you breathed some of it in. She thought about moving out of the city, then read about toxic dumps, radioactive waste, concealed here and there in the countryside and masked by the lush, deceitful green of waving trees.

Vincent has been dead for less than a year. He was not put into the permafrost or frozen in ice. He went into the Necropolis, the only Toronto cemetery of whose general ambience he approved; he got flower bulbs planted on top of him, by Jane and others. Mostly by Jane. Right now John Torrington, recently thawed after a hundred and fifty years, probably looks better than Vincent.

A week before Vincent's forty-third birthday, Jane went to see him in the hospital. He was in for tests. Like fun he was. He was in for the unspeakable, the unknown. He was in for a mutated virus that didn't even have a name yet. It was creeping up his spine, and when it reached his brain it would kill him. It was not, as they said, responding to treatment. He was in for the duration.

It was white in his room, wintry. He lay packed in ice, for the pain. A white sheet wrapped him, his white thin feet poked out the bottom of it. They were so pale and cold. Jane took one look at him, laid out on ice like a salmon, and began to cry.

"Oh Vincent," she said. "What will I do without you?" This sounded awful. It sounded like Jane and Vincent making fun, of obsolete books, obsolete movies, their obsolete mothers. It also sounded selfish: here she was, worrying about herself and her future, when Vincent was the one who was sick. But it was true. There would be a lot less to do, altogether, without Vincent.

Vincent gazed up at her; the shadows under his eyes were cavernous. "Lighten up," he said, not very loudly, because he could not speak very loudly now. By this time she was sitting down, leaning forward; she was holding one of his hands. It was thin as the claw of a bird. "Who says I'm going to die?" He spent a moment considering this, revised it. "You're right," he said. "They got me. It was the Pod People from outer space. They said, 'All I want is your poddy.'"

Jane cried more. It was worse because he was trying to be funny. "But what *is* it?" she said. "Have they found out yet?"

Vincent smiled his ancient, jaunty smile, his smile of detachment, of amusement. There were his beautiful teeth, juvenile as ever. "Who knows?" he said. "It must have been something I ate."

Jane sat with the tears running down her face. She felt desolate: left behind, stranded. Their mothers had finally caught up to them and been proven right. There were consequences after all; but they were the consequences to things you didn't even know you'd done.

The scientists are back on the screen. They are excited, their earnest mouths are twitching, you could almost call them joyful. They know why John Torrington died; they know, at last, why the Franklin Expedition went so terribly wrong. They've snipped off pieces of John Torrington, a fingernail, a lock of hair, they've run them through machines and come out with the answers.

There is a shot of an old tin can, pulled open to show the seam. It looks like a bomb casing. A finger points: it was the tin cans that did it, a new invention back then, a new technology, the ultimate defence against starvation and scurvy. The Franklin Expedition was excellently provisioned with tin cans, stuffed full of meat and soup and soldered together with lead. The whole expedition got lead-poisoning. Nobody knew it. Nobody could taste it. It invaded their bones, their lungs, their brains, weakening them and confusing their thinking, so that at the end those that had not yet died in the ships set out in an idiotic trek across the stony, icy ground, pulling a lifeboat laden down with toothbrushes, soap, handkerchiefs, and slippers, useless pieces of junk. When they were found ten years later, they were skeletons in tattered coats, lying where they'd collapsed. They'd been heading back towards the ships. It was what they'd been eating that had killed them.

Jane switches off the television and goes into her kitchen—all white, done over the year before last, the outmoded butcher-block counters from the seventies torn out and carted away—to make herself some hot milk and rum. Then she decides against it; she won't sleep anyway. Everything in here looks ownerless. Her toaster oven, so perfect for solo dining, her microwave for the vegetables, her espresso maker—they're sitting around waiting for her departure, for this evening or forever, in order to assume their final, real appearances of purposeless objects adrift in the physical world. They might as well be pieces of an exploded spaceship orbiting the moon.

She thinks about Vincent's apartment, so carefully arranged, filled with the beautiful or deliberately ugly possessions he once loved. She thinks about his closet, with its quirky particular outfits, empty now of his arms and legs. It has all been broken up now, sold, given away.

Increasingly the sidewalk that runs past her house is cluttered with plastic drinking cups, crumpled soft-drink cans, used take-out plates. She picks them up, clears them away, but they appear again overnight, like a trail left by an army on the march or by the fleeing residents of a city under bombardment, discarding the objects that were once thought essential but are now too heavy to carry.

[1991]

The Female Body

'... entirely devoted to the subject of "The Female Body." Knowing how well you have written on this topic ... this capacious topic ...'

—letter from the *Michigan Quarterly Review*

1.

I agree, it's a hot topic. But only one? Look around, there's a wide range. Take my own, for instance.

I get up in the morning. My topic feels like hell. I sprinkle it with water, brush parts of it, rub it with towels, powder it, add lubricant. I dump in the fuel and away goes my topic, my topical topic, my controversial topic, my capacious topic, my limping topic, my nearsighted topic, my topic with back problems, my badly behaved topic, my vulgar topic, my outrageous topic, my ageing topic, my topic that is out of the question and anyway still can't spell, in its oversized coat and worn winter boots, scuttling along the sidewalk as if it were flesh and blood, hunting for what's out there, an avocado, an alderman, an adjective, hungry as ever.

2.

The basic Female Body comes with the following accessories: garter-belt, panty-girdle, crinoline, camisole, bustle, brassiere, stomacher, chemise, virgin zone, spike heels, nose-ring, veil, kid gloves, fishnet stockings, fichu, bandeau, Merry Widow, weepers, chokers, barrettes, bangles, beads, lorgnette, feather boa, basic black, compact, Lycra stretch one-piece with modesty panel, designer peignoir, flannel nightie, lace teddy, bed, head.

3.

The Female Body is made of transparent plastic and lights up when you plug it in. You press a button to illuminate the different systems. The Circulatory System is red, for the heart and arteries, purple for the veins; the Respiratory System is blue, the Lymphatic System is yellow, the Digestive System is green, with liver and kidneys in aqua. The nerves are done in orange and the brain is pink. The skeleton, as you might expect, is white.

The Reproductive System is optional, and can be removed. It comes with or without a miniature embryo. Parental judgement can thereby be exercised. We do not wish to frighten or offend.

4.

He said, I won't have one of those things in the house. It gives a young girl a false notion of beauty, not to mention anatomy. If a real woman was built like that she'd fall on her face.

She said, If we don't let her have one like all the other girls she'll feel singled out. It'll become an issue. She'll long for one and she'll long to turn into one. Repression breeds sublimation. You know that.

He said, It's not just the pointy plastic tits, it's the wardrobes. The wardrobes and that stupid male doll, what's his name, the one with the underwear glued on.

She said, Better to get it over with when she's young. He said, All right but don't let me see it.

She came whizzing down the stairs, thrown like a dart. She was stark naked. Her hair had been chopped off, her head was turned back to front, she was missing some toes and she'd been tattooed all over her body with purple ink, in a scroll-work design. She hit the potted azalea, trembled there for a moment like a botched angel, and fell.

He said, I guess we're safe.

5.

The Female Body has many uses. It's been used as a door-knocker, a bottle-opener, as a clock with a ticking belly, as something to hold up lampshades, as a nutcracker, just squeeze the brass legs together and out comes your nut. It bears torches, lifts victorious wreaths, grows copper wings and raises aloft a ring of neon stars; whole buildings rest on its marble heads.

It sells cars, beer, shaving lotion, cigarettes, hard liquor; it sells diet plans and diamonds, and desire in tiny crystal bottles. Is this the face that launched a thousand products? You bet it is, but don't get any funny big ideas, honey, that smile is a dime a dozen.

It does not merely sell, it is sold. Money flows into this country or that country, flies in, practically crawls in, suitful after suitful, lured by all those hairless pre-teen legs. Listen, you want to reduce the national debt, don't you? Aren't you patriotic? That's the spirit. That's my girl.

She's a natural resource, a renewable one luckily, because those things wear out so quickly. They don't make 'em like they used to. Shoddy goods.

6.

One and one equals another one. Pleasure in the female is not a requirement. Pair-bonding is stronger in geese. We're not talking about love, we're talking about biology. That's how we all got here, daughter.

Snails do it differently. They're hermaphrodites, and work in threes.

7.

Each female body contains a female brain. Handy. Makes things work. Stick pins in it and you get amazing results. Old popular songs. Short circuits. Bad dreams.

Anyway: each of these brains has two halves. They're joined together by a thick cord; neural pathways flow from one to the other, sparkles of electric information washing to and fro. Like light on waves. Like a conversation. How does a woman know? She listens. She listens in.

The male brain, now, that's a different matter. Only a thin connection. Space over here, time over there, music and arithmetic in their own sealed compartments. The right brain doesn't know what the left brain is doing. Good for aiming though, for hitting the target when you pull the trigger. What's the target? Who's the target? Who cares? What matters is hitting it. That's the male brain for you. Objective.

This is why men are so sad, why they feel so cut off, why they think of themselves as orphans cast adrift, footloose and stringless in the deep void. What void? she says. What are you talking about? The void of the Universe, he says, and she says Oh and looks out the window and tries to get a handle on it, but it's no use, there's too much going on, too many rustlings in the leaves, too many voices, so she says, Would you like a cheese sandwich, a piece of cake, a cup of tea? And he grinds his teeth because she doesn't understand, and wanders off, not just alone but Alone, lost in the dark, lost in the skull, searching for the other half, the twin who could complete him.

Then it comes to him: he's lost the Female Body! Look, it shines in the gloom, far ahead, a vision of wholeness, ripeness, like a giant melon, like an apple, like a metaphor for *breast* in a bad sex novel; it shines like a balloon, like a foggy noon, a watery moon, shimmering in its egg of light.

Catch it. Put it in a pumpkin, in a high tower, in a compound, in a chamber, in a house, in a room. Quick, stick a leash on it, a lock, a chain, some pain, settle it down, so it can never get away from you again.

[1992]

DENNIS LEE ■ (1939–)

The name Dennis Lee is intricately connected with the cultural and literary renaissance that took place in Canada during the 1960s and '70s. Lee was a central figure in the active literary scene in Toronto during the period, earning a reputation as a poet, editor, critic, children's writer, anti-Vietnam protester, and all-round promoter of Canadian literature.

Born in Toronto in 1939, Lee attended Victoria College at the University of Toronto, where he met fellow poet Margaret Atwood; together they were involved in numerous theatrical and writing ventures at the university, both publishing pieces in the Victoria College student magazine, *Acta Victoriana.* In 1967, frustrated at the lack of publishing venues for Canadian authors and the conservatism of the publishers that did exist, he founded, with Dave Godfrey, House of Anansi Press (the name comes from an African trickster spider god). At the outset, the editors believed in the integral connection between literature and the world; as part of the 1960s project for social change, they saw the press to be facilitating a sense of empowerment and public responsibility in Canadian readers, a sense that society could be changed by ordinary people. As Lee stated in an interview with Cynthia Gunn in the Montreal

Star in 1969, "Literature is a whole dimension of being a citizen of a country. . . . Without it, you have something less than an adequate society."

Anansi's first publication was Lee's collection *The Kingdom of Absence* (1967). The company operated from the basement of Godfrey's house on Spadina Avenue in Toronto, and when Godfrey left to start up New Press in 1969, Lee became the main editor until 1972. Anansi quickly established itself as the publisher of choice for many Canadian authors, in part due to Lee's devotion and painstaking work as an editor on the manuscripts he accepted. Like many of this generation, Lee considered the cause of Canadian literature to be something of a mission, to acquaint Canadians with their surroundings and history and to give them a sense of pride in their cultural identity. His devotion to promoting Canadian literature led to his encouragement of Margaret Atwood, who had joined the editorial board of Anansi in 1971, to compile a "reader's guide" to Canadian literature that could be used as a sourcebook for Canadian readers and teachers. This significant work was published by Anansi in 1972 under the title *Survival: A Thematic Guide to Canadian Literature.*

Lee's political and social interests took many forms during this period. Between 1967 and 1969, he became involved with Howard Adelman in the planning of Rochdale College, an educational experiment based on cooperative, non-competitive learning and anti-hierarchical organization. Lee was also an active opponent of the Vietnam War. In 1968, Anansi published the notorious *Manual for Draft-Age Immigrants to Canada,* a book that was disseminated throughout Canada and the United States and which had sold more than 55,000 copies by 1970. Lee's support of American draft dodgers extended into weekly counselling sessions in his Toronto home, which sometimes also included offering refugees a place to stay.

According to Lee's account in his 1973 essay "Cadence, Country, Silence," his psychological awakening occurred in 1965 during the early days of the Vietnam War. Taking part in a "teach-in" at the University of Toronto, Lee was shocked to learn not only that the American government had been lying to the people about Vietnam, but that the Canadian media had gone along with it. The experience revealed to him the extent to which Canadians had allowed themselves to become "colonized" by the United States and had lost any clear sense of their "native voice." In his view Canadians had been "silenced" and were unable to express any authentic sense of themselves as a distinct culture and people. In his essay he attempts to diagnose the sense of "dis-ease" that permeated Canadian society in the late 1960s and early '70s. Lee believed that it was George Grant who had most clearly analyzed Canada's colonial condition. Grant's analysis of the deadening influence of American liberal materialism and tech-nologization on Canadian culture struck a chord. For Lee, Grant "enabled us to

say for the first time where we are, who we are—to become articulate."

Lee's long poem *Civil Elegies,* originally published by Anansi in 1968 (and later revised and republished in 1972), attempted to come to terms with this predicament of Canadian inarticulateness. In the poem, the ghosts of overlooked ancestors hover over the city of Toronto (comparable to the ghost of Susanna Moodie in Atwood's 1970 poem sequence *The Journals of Susanna Moodie*), "demanding whether Canada will be." *Civil Elegies and Other Poems* (1972) won the Governor General's Award for poetry.

There is a distinctive quality of reverence and spirituality in Lee's outlook and poetics. His Preface to his 1998 essay collection *Body Music* describes this as an interest in "the kind of reality people once pointed to with terms like 'good,' 'evil,' 'the sacred.' It is not that we have lost contact with such things in our lives, but rather that educated thinking no longer recognized them as having any substance." Lee's quest for "cadence" in writing is connected to his search for an intangible authenticity of expression. The colonial predicament of Canadians in the 1960s, Lee argued, had introduced "obstructions to cadence" which it was the task of his generation to revivify. His subsequent works, including his extended critical essay *Savage Fields* (1977) and his poetry collections *The Death of Harold Ladoo* (1976) and *The Gods* (1978), all deal with this conflict between modernity and authenticity.

After leaving Anansi, Lee worked as an editorial consultant for Macmillan of Canada (1974–79) and for McClelland and Stewart as poetry advisor (1981–84). During these years, he gained a significant reputation as a Canadian children's author. His most famous work is *Alligator Pie* (1974), which won the Canadian Association of Children's Libraries bronze medal for children's literature in 1974. The book had a huge impact on generations of young readers for its invocation of Canadian place-names and historical figures in a series of humorous rhymes. In it Lee explains that he had become tired of the distant world of *Mother Goose* and wanted to provide the Canadian child with rhymes that "play[ed] on things she lived with every day."

Lee's more recent poetry has taken a turn toward more abstract forms. His 1993 *Riffs* contains a series of poems that imitate the improvisational form of jazz to tell of a failing love affair. His more recent works, *Un* (2003) and *Yes/No* (2007), sound an apocalyptic note, evincing what Douglas Barbour in the November 2007 Montreal *Gazette* described as a "cri de coeur for our time."

From Civil Elegies

1

Often I sit in the sun and brooding over the city, always
in airborne shapes among the pollution I hear them, returning;
pouring across the square
in fetid descent, they darken the towers
and the wind-swept place of meeting and whenever
the thick air clogs my breathing it teems with their presence.
Many were born in Canada, and living unlived lives they died
of course but died truncated, stunted, never at
home in native space and not yet
citizens of a human body of kind. And it is Canada   10
that specialized in this deprivation. Therefore the spectres arrive, congregating
in bitter droves, thick in the April sunlight,
accusing us and we are no different, though you would not expect
the furies assembled in hogtown[1] and ring me round, invisible, demanding
what time of our lives we wait for till we shall start to be.
Until they come the wide square stretches out
serene and singly by moments it takes us in, each one for now
a passionate civil man, until it
sends us back to the acres of gutted intentions,
back to the concrete debris, to parking scars and the four-square tiers   20
of squat and righteous lives. And here
once more, I watch the homing furies' arrival.

I sat one morning by the Moore,[2] off to the west
ten yards and saw though diffident my city nailed against the sky
in ordinary glory.

[1] Colloquial name for Toronto.

[2] A statue by British sculptor Henry Moore (1898–1986) entitled *The Archer* is located in front of City Hall (the "two towers" referred to four lines later) in Toronto's Nathan Phillips Square, which is the setting for this section of the poem.

It is not much to ask. A place, a making,
two towers, a teeming, a genesis, a city.
And the men and women moved in their own space,
performing their daily lives, and their presence occurred
in time as it occurred, patricians in   30
muddy York and made their compact together against the gangs of the new.
And as that crumpled before the shambling onset, again the
lives we had not lived in phalanx[3] invisibly staining
the square and vistas, casting back I saw
regeneration twirl its blood and the rebels riding
riderless down Yonge Street, plain men much
goaded by privilege—our other origin, and cried
"Mackenzie knows a word, Mackenzie
knows a meaning!" but it was not true. Eight hundred-odd steely Canadians
turned tail at the cabbage patch when a couple of bullets fizzed   40
and the loyalists, scared skinny by the sound of their own gunfire,
gawked and bolted south to the fort like rabbits,
the rebels for their part bolting north to the pub: the first
spontaneous mutual retreat in the history of warfare.
Canadians, in flight.[4]

Buildings oppress me, and the sky-concealing wires
bunch zigzag through the air. I know
the dead persist in
buildings, by-laws, porticos—the city I live in
is clogged with their presence; they   50
dawdle about in our lives and form a destiny, still
incomplete, still dead weight, still
demanding whether Canada will be.

But the mad bomber, Chartier of Major Street,[5] Chartier
said it: that if a country has no past,
neither is it a country and promptly
blew himself to bits in the parliament john, leaving as civil testament
assorted chunks of prophet, twitching and
bobbing to rest in the flush.
And what can anyone do in this country, baffled and   60

[3] A united front.

[4] This section of the poem contains references to the 1837 rebellion in Upper Canada led by
William Lyon Mackenzie (1795–1861). Mackenzie was the first mayor of the city of Toronto (formerly called York) in 1834 who supported constitutional reform and, ultimately, independence
from Britain. The rebels gathered in Montgomery's Tavern on Yonge Street and marched from
there, but once the troops were fired upon, many of Mackenzie's men deserted.

[5] Paul Chartier, a bomber who tried to blow up the House of Commons in Ottawa in 1966.

making our penance for ancestors, what did they leave us? Indian-swindlers,
stewards of unclaimed earth and rootless what does it matter if they, our
forebears' flesh and bone were often
good men, good men do not matter to history.
And what can we do here now, for at last we have no notion
of what we might have come to be in America, alternative, and how make public
a presence which is not sold out utterly to the modern? utterly? to the
savage inflictions of what is for real, it pays off, it is only
accidentally less than human?

In the city I long for, green trees still   70
asphyxiate. The crowds emerge at five from jobs
that rankle and lag. Heavy developers
pay off aldermen still; the craft of neighbourhood,
its whichway streets and generations
anger the planners, they go on jamming their maps
with asphalt panaceas; single men
still eke out evenings courting, in parks, alone.
A man could spend a lifetime looking for
peace in that city. And the lives give way around him—marriages
founder, the neighhourhoods sag—until   80
the emptiness comes down on him to stay.
But in the city I long for men complete
their origins. Among the tangle of
hydro, hydrants, second mortgages, amid
the itch for new debentures, greater expressways,
in sober alarm they jam their works of progress, asking where in truth
they come from and to whom they must belong.
And thus they clear a space in which
the full desires of those that begot them, great animating desires
that shrank and grew hectic as the land pre-empted their lives   90
might still take root, which eddy now and
drift in the square, being neither alive nor dead.
And the people accept a flawed inheritance
and they give it a place in their midst, forfeiting progress, forfeiting
dollars, forfeiting yankee visions of cities that in time it might grow
whole at last in their lives, they might
belong once more to their forebears, becoming their own men.

To be our own men! in dread to live
the land, our own harsh country, beloved, the prairie, the foothills—
and for me it is lake by rapids by stream-fed lake, threading   100
north through the terminal vistas of black spruce, in a
bitter, cherished land it is farm after

farm in the waste of the continental outcrop—
for me it is Shield but wherever terrain informs our lives and claims us;
and then, no longer haunted by
unlived presence, to live the cities:
to furnish, out of the traffic and smog and the shambles of dead precursors,
a civil habitation that is
human, and our own.

The spectres drift across the square in rows.   110
How empire permeates! And we sit down
in Nathan Phillips Square, among the sun,
as if our lives were real.
Lacunae. Parking lots. Regenerations.
Newsstand euphorics and Revell's sign,[6] that not
one countryman has learned, that
men and women live that
they may make that
life worth dying. Living. Hey,
the dead ones! Gentlemen, generations of   120
acquiescent spectres gawk at the chrome
on American cars on Queen Street, gawk and slump and retreat.
And over the square where I sit, congregating above the Archer
they crowd in a dense baffled throng and the sun does not shine through.

                                                          [1968, rev. 1972]

Alligator Pie

Alligator pie, alligator pie,
If I don't get some I think I'm gonna die.
Give away the green grass, give away the sky,
But don't give away my alligator pie.

Alligator stew, alligator stew,
If I don't get some I don't know what I'll do.
Give away my furry hat, give away my shoe,
But don't give away my alligator stew.

Alligator soup, alligator soup,
If I don't get some I think I'm gonna droop.   10
Give away my hockey-stick, give away my hoop,
But don't give away my alligator soup.

                                                                   [1974]

___

[6] Viljo Revell, the architect who designed Toronto's City Hall.

Cadence

We know a place to be.
It is not the same
for all, yet for each there is
one subcutaneous claiming: the place we belong to,
where our humanness is home.   And it is more an
exquisite taunt than a dwelling, for mostly we scruff along
by scotching the hints and traces—and how should we
honour that place? It is hard enough to get by.
And there are places I love, but when I found the one that owned me
it was nothing I knew. For in my twenties, god help me I
blundered into a—
what? A luminous tumult. Where I went in my body's mind. Not knowing
what that place could be, yet sensing
swivel and carom[7] and thud I called it
cadence, more flex than content and
us in it. Feeling the current
snake through my life like a leghold rumble of *is*.
Though all the words are wrong—the place was
not a "place," nor a "thing," and the going was not in my
"mind" and I didn't "go" there—still,
tumble and source and
vocation, and in that hush and quake of almost-words,
cadence is iffy but utter, preemptive, you
come or you go but you
do not possess it.   It is
given and gift, a daily grace of
what.   And
what I know of being claimed, and home, and thank you,
is drenched with that sojourn.

And it was there I spent myself, day after day, in my thirties, obscurely,
gone now, and it nearly took me apart
to weather the pang transitions,
for when I emerged half out of my tree I was
nowhere, I could not find good
distance with others—craving too hothouse a
union or blah from adrenalin crash and that
herky-jerky to-&-fro
abrades a marriage; I came unstuck; I got frantic I
went to live in career, for I could not honour the stillness
in worship or in words—

---

[7] Ricochet.

what claimed me, unfitted me. And then it deserted me.
Yet when I was present to presence
there was nowhere else to be, and when not
it felt like betrayal.
As tonight it does also.

[1996]

From Cadence, Country, Silence: Writing in Colonial Space

[. . .] What is the relation of cadence and poem?

Michaelangelo said he could sense the figure in the uncut stone; his job was to prune away marble till it emerged. Eskimo sculptors say the same thing. It makes sense to me. Cadence is the medium, the raw stone. Content is already there in the cadence. And writing a poem means cutting away everything in the cadence that isn't that poem. You can't "write" a poem, in fact: you can only help it stand free in the torrent of cadence. Most of my time with a pen is spent giving words, images, bright ideas that are borne along in cadence their permission to stay off the paper. The poem is what remains; it is local cadence minus whatever is extraneous to its shapely articulation. [. . .]

I have been writing of cadence as though one had merely to hear its words and set them down. But that is not true, at least not in my experience. There is a check on one's pen which seems to take hold at the very moment that cadence declares itself. Words arrive, but words have also gone dead.

To get at this complex experience we must begin from the hereness, the local nature of cadence. We never encounter cadence in the abstract; it is insistently here and now. Any man aspires to be at home where he lives, to celebrate communion with men on earth around him, under the sky where he actually lives. And to speak from his own dwelling—however light or strong the inflections of that place—will make his words intelligible to men elsewhere, because authentic. In my case, then, cadence seeks the gestures of being a Canadian human: *mutatis mutandi*, the same is true for anyone here—an Israeli, an American, a Quebecker.

But if we live in space which is radically in question for us, that makes our barest speaking a problem to itself. For voice does issue in part from civil space. And alienation in that space will enter and undercut our writing, make it recoil upon itself, become a problem to itself.

The act of writing "becomes a problem to itself" when it raises a vicious circle; when to write necessarily involves something that seems to make writing impossible. Contradictions in our civil space are one thing that make this happen, and I am struck by the subtle connections people here have drawn between words and their own problematic public space. [. . .]

To explore the obstructions to cadence is, for a Canadian, to explore the nature of colonial space. Here I am particularly concerned with what it does to writing. One can also analyse it economically or politically, or try to act upon it; but at this point I want only to find words for our experience of it. [. . .]

* * *

For a Canadian, our form of civil alienation is not manifested that dramatically in language. The prime fact about my country as a public space is that in the last 25 years it has become an American colony. But we speak the same tongue as our new masters; we are the same colour, the same stock. We know their history better than our own. Thus while our civil inauthenticity has many tangible monuments, from *Time* to Imperial Esso, the way it undercuts our writing is less easy to discern—precisely because there are so few symptomatic literary battle-grounds (comparable to the anglicized French of Quebec) in which the takeover is immediately visible. Nevertheless, many writers here know how the act of writing calls itself radically into question.

I will take the external pressure for granted—the American tidal-wave that inundates us, in the cultural sphere as much as in the economic and political. How maybe 2 per cent of the books on our paperback racks are Canadian, because the American-owned distributors refuse to carry them. How Canadian film-makers have to go to the U.S. to seek distribution arrangements for Canada—where they are commonly turned down, which means the film is usually not made. How almost all our prime TV time is filled with yankee programs. How a number of Alberta schoolchildren were still being taught, recently, that Abraham Lincoln was their country's greatest president. But brushing past these things for now I want to explore how, in a colony, the simple act of writing becomes a problem to itself. [. . .]

* * *

Those of us who stumbled into this kind of problem in the nineteen-sixties—whatever form it took—were suffering the recoil from something Canadians had learned very profoundly in the fifties. To want to see one's life, we had been taught, to see one's own most banal impulses and deeper currents made articulate on paper, in a film, on records—that was ridiculous, uppity. Canadians were by definition people who looked over the fence and through the windows at America, un-self-consciously learning from its movies, comics, magazines and TV shows how to go about being alive. The disdainful amusement I and thousands like me felt for Canadian achievement in any field, especially those of the imagination, was a direct reflection of our self-hatred and sense of inferiority. And while we dismissed American mass culture, we could only separate ourselves from it by soaking up all the elite American culture we could get at. If anyone from another country was around we would outdo ourselves with our knowledge of Mailer and Fiedler and Baldwin,[8] of the beatniks and the hipsters, of—if we were really showing our breadth of mind—the new plays from angry London. And we fell all over ourselves putting down the Canadians. This was between 1955 and 1965. [. . .]

It boggles the imagination now, but that was really what we did—it was how we really *felt*. We weren't pretending, we were desperate. And the idea that these things confirmed our colonialism with a vengeance would have made us laugh our continentalized heads off. We weren't all that clear on colonialism to begin with, but if anybody had colonialism it was our poor countrymen, the Canadians, who in some unspecified way were still in fetters to England. But we weren't colonials; hell, *we* could have held our heads up in New York, if it had occurred to anyone to ask us down. Though it was a bit of a relief that no one ever did.

* * *

My awakening from this astonishing condition was private and extremely confusing. It was touched off by the radical critiques of America that originated in America, especially over Viet Nam; but it ended up going further. From that muddled process I remember one particularly disorienting couple of months in 1965, after a teach-in on Viet Nam held at the University of Toronto (in the fashion of American teach-ins) by a group of first-rate professors and students. It lasted a weekend, and as I read the background material and followed the long, dull speeches in the echoing cavern of Varsity Arena, two things dawned on me. The first was that the American government had been lying about Viet Nam. The second was that the Canadian media, from which I had learnt all I knew about the war, were helping to spread its lies.

I present these discoveries in all the crashing naivete with which they struck me then. Interestingly, while the first revelation shocked me more at the time, it was the second that gnawed at me during the ensuing months. I couldn't get my mind around it. I did not believe that our newspapers or radio and TV stations had been bought off directly by Washington, of course. But if it was not a case of paid corruption, the only reason for co-operating in such a colossal deception—consciously or unconsciously—was that they were colonial media, serving the interests of the imperial rulers. [. . .]

Worse than that, however, was the recognition that the sphere of imperial influence was not confined to the pages of newspapers. It also included my head. And that shook me to the core, because I could not even restrict the brainwashing I began to recognize to the case of Viet Nam. More and more of the ideas I had, my assumptions, even the instinctive path of my feelings well

DENNIS LEE

472

[8] Norman Mailer (1923–2007), American author and journalist whose books include *The Naked and the Dead* (1948), *The American Dream* (1965), and *The Executioner's Song* (1979); Leslie Fiedler (1917–2003), American literary critic known for his book *Love and Death in the American Novel* (1960); and James Baldwin (1924–1987), American writer and civil rights activist, author of *Notes of a Native Son* (1955).

before they jelled into notions, seemed to have come north from the States unexamined. [. . .] After ten years of continentalizing my ass, what had I accomplished? . . . I was a colonial.

It was during the period when my system began to rebel against our spineless existence in this colonial space—by 1967, say—that I began to find literary words impossible. I read far less, I stopped going to Stratford, I squirmed in front of TV. And nothing I wrote felt real. I didn't know why. [. . .]

Writing had become a full-fledged problem to itself; it had grown into a search for authenticity, but all it could manage to be was a symptom of inauthenticity. I couldn't put my finger on what was inauthentic, but I could feel it with every nerve-end in my body. [. . .] So for four years I shut up.

* * *

Though I hope not to over-dramatize this, it was when I read a series of essays by the philosopher George Grant that I started to comprehend what we had been living inside. [. . .]

Grant's analysis of "Canadian Fate and Imperialism," which I read in *Canadian Dimension,* was the first that made any contact whatsoever with my tenuous sense of living here—the first that seemed to be speaking the words of our civil condition. My whole system had been coiling in on itself for want of them. As subsequent pieces appeared (they eventually came out as *Technology and Empire*),[9] I realised that somehow it had happened: a man who knew this paralysing condition first-hand was nevertheless using words authentically, from the very centre of everything that had tied my tongue. [. . .]

One central perception was that, in refusing the American dream, our Loyalist forebears (the British Americans who came north after 1776)[10] were groping to reaffirm a classical European tradition, one which embodies a very different sense of public space. By contrast with the liberal assumptions that gave birth to the United States, it taught that reverence for what is is more deeply human than conquest of what is. That men are subject to sterner civil necessities than liberty or the pursuit of happiness—that they must respond, as best they can, to the demands of the good. [. . .] And while our ancestors were often mediocre or muddling, convictions like these demonstrably did underlie many of their attitudes to law, the land, indigenous peoples and Europe. Their refusal of America issued, in part, from disagreement with the early Americans about what it meant to be a human being.

What the Loyalists were refusing was the doctrine of essential human freedom, which in an argument of inspired simplicity Grant sees as the point of generation of technological civilization. That doctrine led to a view of everything

---

[9] House of Anansi Press published Grant's *Technology and Empire* in 1969 under the editorial guidance of Lee; the book includes the essay "Canadian Fate and Imperialism" which had so influenced Lee in 1967. See the excerpt from Grant's *Lament for a Nation* in this section.

[10] After the American Revolution (1775–1783), many American colonists who remained loyal to Britain ("Loyalists") settled in Canada. (See the introduction to Volume 1, Section II, for more details.)

but one's own will—the new continent, native peoples, other nations, outer space, one's own body—as raw material, to be manipulated and remade according to the hungers of one's nervous system and the demands of one's technology. But not only did this view of an unlimited human freedom seem arrogant and suicidal; it also seemed inaccurate, wrong, a piece of self-deception. For we are not radically free, in simple fact, and to act as if we were is to behave with lethal naivete. What is more, trying to force everything around us to conform to our own wills is just not the best use of what freedom we do have. [. . .]

I found the account of being alive that Grant saw in the classic tradition far less self-indulgent than the liberal version that achieved its zenith in America— far closer to the way things are. And suddenly there were terms in which to recognize that, as we began to criticize our new masters during the sixties, we were not just wanting to be better Americans than the Americans, to dream their dream more humanely. Our dissent went as deep as it did because, obscurely, we did not want to be American at all. Their dream was wrong. [. . .]

But Grant is scarcely an apostle of public joy. His next perception virtually cancels his reclamation of space to be in. By now, he says, we have replaced our forebears' tentative, dissenting North American space with a wholehearted and colonial American space. The sellout of Canada which has been consummated over the last few decades does not just involve real estate or corporate takeovers, nor who will put the marionettes in Ottawa through their dance. It replaces one human space with another.

For the political and military rule of the United States, and the economic rule of its corporations, are merely the surface expression of modernity in the West. That modernity is also inward. It shapes the expression of our bodies' impulses, the way we build cities, what we do in our spare time. [. . .]

Grant declares that to dissent from liberal modernity is necessarily to fall silent, for we now have no terms in which to speak that do not issue from the space we are trying to speak against. [. . .]

What is most implacable about this modern despair, Grant holds, is that it cannot get outside itself. Any statement of ideals by which we might bring our plight into perspective turns out to be either a hollow appeal to things we no longer have access to, or (more commonly) a restatement of the very liberal ideals that got us into the fix in the first place. [. . .]

I do not expect to spend my life agreeing with George Grant. But, in my experience at least, the sombre Canadian has enabled us to say for the first time where we are, who we are—to become articulate. That first gift of speech is a staggering achievement. And in trying to comprehend the deeper ways in which writing is a problem to itself in Canada, I can start nowhere but with Grant.

* * *

Grant showed me that we have been colonized, not just by American corporations and governments, but by the assumptions and reflexes of the liberalism they embody. And this inward colonisation is a serious thing; it means that we are now ex-Canadians—or to put it at its most recklessly hopeful, that we are not-yet-Canadians. What does that do to a writer who wants to work from his roots?

In *Survival*,[11] Margaret Atwood suggests an alarming answer: much of our literature, she says, is an involuntary symptom or projection of colonial experience. The dominant themes of Canadian writing have been death, failure of nerve, and the experience of being victimized by forces beyond our control. Heroes lose, personal relations go awry, animals, Indians and immigrants are mowed down with such knee-jerk regularity that we have clearly moved past candour to compulsiveness.

Why do Canadian writers return to the lot of the victim with such dreary zest? Atwood's explanation is tempting: the species "Canadian human" has felt itself to be powerless and threatened from the beginning, and as a result the collective author "Canada" projects itself time and again as a victim.

But I wonder whether there isn't more to it. The colonial writer does not have words of his own. Is it not possible that he projects his own condition of voicelessness into whatever he creates? that he articulates his own powerlessness, in the face of alien words, by seeking out fresh tales of victims? Over and above Atwood's account of it, perhaps the colonial imagination is driven to recreate, again and again, the experience of writing in colonial space.

We are getting close to the centre of the tangle. [. . .]

The words I knew said Britain, and they said America, but they did not say my home. They were always and only about someone else's life. All the rich structures of language were present, but the currents that animated them were not home to the people who used the language here. [. . .]

The first necessity for the colonial writer—so runs the conventional wisdom—is to start writing of what he knows. His imagination must come home. But that first necessity is not enough. For if you are Canadian, home is a place that is not home to you—it is even less your home than the imperial centre you used to dream about. Or to say what I really know best, the *words* of home are silent. And to write a jolly ode to harvests in Saskatchewan, or set an American murder mystery in Newfoundland, is no answer at all. Try to speak the words of your home and you will discover—if you are a colonial—that you do not know them. [. . .]

But perhaps—and here was the breakthrough—perhaps our job was not to fake a space of our own and write it up, but rather to find words for our spacelessness. Perhaps that *was* home. This dawned on me gradually. Instead of pushing against the grain of an external, uncharged language, perhaps we should finally come to writing *with* that grain. [. . .]

---

[11] *Survival: A Thematic Guide to Canadian Literature* (1972) is Atwood's critical study of Canadian literature, which she produced for House of Anansi Press with Lee's encouragement; see the excerpt from *Survival* in this section.

Where I lived, a whole swarm of inarticulate meanings lunged, clawed, drifted, eddied, sprawled in half grasped disarray beneath the tidy meaning which the simplest word had brought with it from England and the States. "City": once you learned to accept the blurry, featureless character of that word—responding to it as a Canadian word, with its absence of native connotation—you were dimly savaged by the live, inchoate meanings trying to surface through it. The whole tangle and sisyphean problematic of people's existing here, from the time of the *coureurs de bois* to the present day, came struggling to be included in the word "city." Cooped up beneath the familiar surface of the word as we use it ("city" as London, as New York, as Los Angeles)—and cooped up further down still, beneath the blank and blur you heard when you sought some received indigenous meaning for the word— listening all the way down, you began to overhear the strands and communal lives of millions of people who went their particular ways here, whose roots and lives and legacy come together in the cities we live in. Edmonton, Toronto, Montreal, Halifax: "city" meant something still unspoken, but rampant with held-in energy. Hearing it was like watching the contours of an unexpected continent gradually declare themselves through the familiar lawns and faces of your block.

Though that again is hindsight: all of it. You heard an energy, and those lives were part of it. Under the surface alienation and the second-level blur of our words there was a living barrage of meaning: private, civil, religious—unclassifiable finally, but there, and seamless, and pressing to be spoken. And I *felt* that press of meaning: I had no idea what it was, but I could feel it teeming towards words. I called it cadence. [. . .]

[1973]

MARIA CAMPBELL ■ (1940–)

Many critics have argued that the publication of Maria Campbell's 1973 autobiography, *Halfbreed,* initiated the birth of modern Aboriginal literature in Canada. The book was a searing wake-up call to Native and non-Native Canadians alike, for its painful depiction of the dislocation and oppression of Métis and Aboriginal peoples in Canada. Because the book was one of the first accounts of contemporary Aboriginal women's experiences to be written by a Native author, it became an important text in raising the consciousness of Indigenous people across the country, and helped catalyze a resurgence in Aboriginal activism and cultural pride. The book has had a major impact on Aboriginal and non-Aboriginal readers alike. Literary critic Janice Acoose contends that "many contemporary Indigenous women . . . look to Maria Campbell's text as the one which encouraged them to speak out, name their oppressors, and re-claim their selves."

Campbell was born in Park Valley, near Prince Albert in northern Saskatchewan, in a "road allowance"

Métis community (because the Métis had been run off their traditional lands, they were forced to build their homes on federally owned sections of land on the edge of roadways). At the age of 12, she had to quit school after her mother's death to look after her seven siblings. In an attempt to keep the family together, she married a White man when she was only 15. Her husband was violent and abusive, and he eventually called social services to have her brothers and sisters put into foster homes. After the couple separated in Vancouver, Campbell turned to a life of drug abuse, alcoholism, and prostitution (an experience she relates in detail in *Halfbreed*). It took years for her to rehabilitate herself, largely through the strong and positive example of her great-grandmother Cheechum (the niece of Gabriel Dumont). After suffering a nervous breakdown, Campbell became determined to heal herself and do something for her community. She became involved in numerous Native activist organizations and gradually began writing *Halfbreed* as a way of healing the pain of her early years.

Campbell has written several plays and children's books, including *Little Badger and the Fire Spirit* (1977) and *Riel's People* (1978). In the early 1980s she became involved in a project with Theatre Passe Muraille to workshop a theatrical version of her life story. The play that emerged from the process, and the account of its tortured production as Campbell and her co-writer Linda Griffiths struggled to write the play together, is printed in *The Book of Jessica: A Theatrical Transformation* (1989). The play premiered in Toronto in 1986 and won the Dora Mavor Moore Award. In 1995 Campbell published *Stories of the Road Allowance People* (1995), which contains her translations of a series of Cree-Mitchif oral stories into the colloquial English spoken by western Métis communities. The story included here, "Jacob," is taken from this collection.

During the 1980s and '90s, Campbell worked as a director and writer on various films for the CBC and National Film Board, winning an Aboriginal Achievement Award in 1996. She currently teaches Native studies at the University of Saskatchewan in Saskatoon, and is also an active community worker.

Jacob

Mistupuch he was my granmudder.
He come from Muskeg
dat was before he was a reservation.
My granmudder he was about twenty-eight when he
marry my granfawder.
Dat was real ole for a woman to marry in dem days
But he was an Indian doctor
I guess dats why he wait so long.

Ooh he was a good doctor too
All the peoples dey say dat about him.   10

He doctor everybody dat come to him
an he birt all dah babies too.
Jus about everybody my age
my granmudder he birt dem.

He marry my granfawder around 1890.
Dat old man he come to him for doctoring
and when he get better
he never leave him again.

Dey get married dah Indian way
an after dat my granfawder   20
he help him with all hees doctoring.
Dats dah way he use to be a long time ago.
If dah woman he work
den dah man he help him an if dah man he work
dah woman he help.
You never heerd peoples fighting over whose job he was
dey all know what dey got to do to stay alive.

My granfawder his name he was Kannap
but dah whitemans dey call him Jim Boy
so hees Indian name he gets los.   30
Dats why we don know who his peoples dey are.
We los lots of our relations like dat.
Dey get dah whitemans name
den no body
he knows who his peoples dey are anymore.

Sometimes me
I tink dats dah reason why we have such a hard time
us peoples.
Our roots dey gets broken so many times.
Hees hard to be strong you know   40
when you don got far to look back for help.

Dah whitemans
he can look back tousands of years
cause him
he write everything down.
But us peoples
we use dah membering
an we pass it on by telling stories an singing songs.
Sometimes we even dance dah membering.

But all dis trouble you know   50
he start after we get dah new names
cause wit dah new names
he come a new language an a new way of living.
Once a long time ago
I could 'ave told you dah story of my granfawder Kannap
an all his peoples but no more.
All I can tell you now
is about Jim Boy
an hees story hees not very ole.

Well my granmudder Mistupuch   60
he never gets a whitemans name an him
he knowed lots of stories.
Dat ole lady
he even knowed dah songs.
He always use to tell me
one about an ole man call Jacob.

Dat old man you know
he don live to far from here.
Well hees gone now
but dis story he was about him when he was alive.   70

Jacob him
he gets one of dem new names when dey put him in dah
residential schoool.
He was a jus small boy when he go
an he don come home for twelve years.

Twelve years!
Dats a long time to be gone from your peoples.
He can come home you know
cause dah school he was damn near two hundred miles
away.   80
His Mommy and Daddy dey can go and see him
cause deres no roads in dem days
an dah Indians dey don gots many horses
'specially to travel dat far.

Dats true you know
not many peoples in dem days dey have horses.
Its only in dah comic books an dah picture shows dey
gots lots of horses.
He was never like dat in dah real life.

Well Jacob him   90
he stay in dat school all dem years an when he come
home he was a man.
While he was gone
his Mommy and Daddy dey die so he gots nobody.
An on top of dat
nobody he knowed him cause he gots a new name.
My granmudder
he say dat ole man he have a hell of time.
No body he can understand dat
unless he happen to him.   100

Dem peoples dat go away to dem schools
an come back you know dey really suffer.
No matter how many stories we tell
we'll never be able to tell
what dem schools dey done to dah peoples
an all dere relations.

Well anyways
Jacob he was jus plain pitiful
He can talk his own language
He don know how to live in dah bush.   110
Its a good ting da peoples dey was kine
cause dey help him dah very bes dey can.
Well a couple of summers later
he meet dis girl
an dey gets married.

Dat girl he was kine
an real smart too.
He teach Jacob how to make an Indian living.
Dey have a good life togedder an after a few years
dey have a boy.   120
Not long after dat
dey raise two little girls dat was orphans.

Jacob and his wife dey was good peoples
Boat of dem dey was hard working
an all dah peoples
dey respec dem an dey come to Jacob for advice.

But dah good times dey was too good to las
cause one day

dah Preeses
dey comes to dah village with dah policemans.   130
Dey come to take dah kids to dah school.

When dey get to Jacob hees house
he tell dem dey can take his kids.
Dah Prees he tell him
he have to lets dem go cause dats the law.
Well dah Prees
he have a big book
an dat book he gots dah names
of all dah kids
an who dey belongs to.   140

He open dat book an ask Jacob for his name
an den he look it up.
"Jacob" he say
"you know better you went to dah school an you know
dah edjication hees important."

My granmudder Mistupuch
he say Jacob he tell that Prees
"Yes I go to dah school
an dats why I don wan my kids to go.
All dere is in dat place is suffering."   150

Dah Prees he wasn happy about dat
an he say to Jacob
"But the peoples dey have to suffer Jacob
cause dah Jesus he suffer."

"But dah Jesus he never lose his language an
hees peoples" Jacob tell him.
"He stay home in hees own land and he do hees
suffering."

Well da Prees him
he gets mad   160
an he tell him its a sin to tink like dat
an hees gonna end up in purgatory for dem kind of
words.

But Jacob he don care
cause far as hees concern

purgatory
he can be worse den the hell he live with trying to
learn hees language and hees Indian ways.

He tell dat Prees
he don even know who his people dey are.   170
"Dah Jesus he knowed his Mommy and Daddy"
Jacob he tell him
"and he always knowed who his people dey are."

Well
dah Prees he tell him
if he wans to know who hees peoples dey are
he can tell him dat
an he open in dah book again.

"Your Dad hees Indian name he was Awchak"
dah prees he say   180
"I tink dat means Star in your language.
He never gets a new name cause he never become a
Christian."

Jacob he tell my granmudder
dat when da Prees he say hees Dad hees name
his wife he start to cry real hard.

"Jacob someday you'll tank the God we done dis."
dah Prees he tell him
an dey start loading up dah kids on dah big wagons.
All dah kids dey was crying an screaming   190
An dah mudders
dey was chasing dah wagons.

Dah ole womans
dey was all singing dah det song
an none of the mans
dey can do anyting.
Dey can
cause the policemans dey gots guns.

When dah wagons dey was all gone
Jacob he look for hees wife but he can find him no   200
place.
An ole woman he see him an he call to him

"Pay api noosim"
"Come an sit down my granchild I mus talk to you.
Hees hard for me to tell you dis but dat Prees
hees book he bring us bad news today.
He tell you dat Awchak he was your Daddy.
My granchild
Awchak he was your wife's Daddy too."

Jacob he tell my granmudder   210
he can cry when he hear dat.
He can even hurt inside.
Dat night he go looking
an he fine hees wife in dah bush
Dat woman he kill hisself.

Jacob he say
dah ole womans
dey stay wit him for a long time
an dey sing healing songs an dey try to help him
But he say he can feel nutting.   220
Maybe if he did
he would have done dah same ting.

For many years Jacob he was like dat
just dead inside.

Dah peoples dey try to talk wit him
but it was no use.
Hees kids dey growed up
an dey come home an live wit him.
"I made dem suffer" he tell my granmudder.
"Dem kids dey try so hard to help me."   230

Den one day
his daughter he get married an he have a baby.
He bring it to Jacob to see.
Jacob he say
he look at dat lil baby
an he start to cry and he can stop.
He say he cry for himself an his wife
an den he cry for his Mommy and Daddy.
When he was done
he sing dah healing songs dah ole womans   240
dey sing to him a long time ago.

Well you know
Jacob he die when he was an ole ole man.
An all hees life
he write in a big book
dah Indian names of all dah Mommies and Daddies.
An beside dem
he write dah old names and
dah new names of all dere kids.

An for dah res of hees life   250
he fight dah government to build schools on the
reservation.
"The good God he wouldn of make babies come
from Mommies and Daddies"
he use to say
"if he didn want dem to stay home
an learn dere language
an dere Indian ways."

You know
dat ole man was right.   260
No body he can do dat.
Take all dah babies away. Hees jus not right.
Long time ago
dah old peoples dey use to do dah naming
an dey do dah teaching too.

If dah parents dey have troubles
den dah aunties and dah uncles
or somebody in dah family
he help out till dah parents dey gets dere life work
out.   270
But no one
no one
he ever take dah babies away from dere peoples.

You know my ole granmudder
Mistupuch
he have lots of stories about people like Jacob.
Good ole peoples
dat work hard so tings will be better for us.
We should never forget dem ole peoples.

[1995]

Daphne Marlatt is one of the major Canadian postmodern writers of the late twentieth century. Her work exemplifies many of the cultural and political movements that animated this period: an interest in the perspective of marginalized communities, a self-reflexive interrogation of dominant histories and the processes of recording history, and an exploration of feminist and lesbian poetics. Her writing is equally notable for its experimental richness and lyrical immediacy, its theoretical sophistication and political commitment, its interest in broad historical processes and deeply personal intensity.

These strengths are exemplified by the technical range which distinguished two early long poems, *Frames of a Story* (1968) and *leaf/leaf/s* (1969). Where the former adapted Hans Christian Anderson's "The Snow Queen" into an autobiographical narrative written in a long-line style that would become an enduring characteristic of her work, *leaf/leaf/s*, written in lines of single words and syllables, highlighted the allure of the most basic elements of language itself. If the long line would remain a central aspect of her writing, the question of the nature of language, at the level of phoneme and syntax, would emerge as a major element of Marlatt's interest in a poetics which reflected her developing feminist and lesbian commitments. Drawing on the work of French feminist theorists such as Julia Kristeva, Luce Irigaray, and Hélène Cixous, who argued that women had access to a particular relation to language that lay outside of the more authoritarian and rigidly structured "phallogocentrism" that characterized a male relation to language, Marlatt aligned herself with Cixous's ideal of *écriture féminine*. According to this theory, women (and some men), by virtue of their different biological natures, are able to tap into a more fluid relation to language. Kristeva defines this as a semiotic rather than a symbolic relation to language, a style that is marked by transgressive *jouissance* or playfulness which celebrates loosened syntax and the free play of meaning.

Marlatt (née Daphne Buckle) was born in Australia to English parents who had been evacuated from Malaya in advance of the Japanese occupation; she moved with her family to Malaysia when she was three years old, and then to North Vancouver when she was nine. She became one of the editors of *TISH* while studying English at the University of British Columbia, before pursuing a master's degree in comparative literature at the University of Indiana.

Marlatt has published extensively and with great acclaim in a range of genres, including two novels, *Ana Historic* (1988) and *Taken* (1996); 14 books of poetry, including *Vancouver poems* (1972), *Steveston* (1974), *How hug a stone* (1983), *Touch to my tongue* (1984), and *Salvage* (1991); a travel memoir of Mexico, *Zócalo* (1977); and two works of non-fiction, *Steveston Recollected: A Japanese-Canadian History* (1975) and *Opening Doors: Vancouver's East End* (1980), both of which stem from her work with the British Columbia Archives oral history project. She has also played an active role in Canadian publishing, serving as editor of the *Capilano Review* from 1973 to 1976, co-editing the prose magazine *Periodics* from 1977 to 1981, and helping to launch in 1984 the feminist editorial collective and bilingual journal *Tessera,* for which she was a founding co-editor alongside Barbara Godard, Kathy Mezei, and Gail Scott. The *Tessera* collective aimed to disseminate the theories and techniques of Quebec women writers throughout the Canadian writing community.

Social and psychic landscapes have always been deeply entwined in Marlatt's verse. If *Vancouver poems* was distinguished by the highly subjective vision that animates its encounter with the city, her major work of this period, *Steveston,* fused this sense of narrative intimacy with an archival interest in the past and present of a Japanese-Canadian fish-cannery town near Vancouver. The book is supplemented with evocative photographs by Robert Minden that tell a story in parallel to the poetic texts. The sense of ebb and flow of the Fraser River, and the aura of a period that is soon to die out, are evoked in Marlatt's distinctive free-associative, long lines.

In the 1980s, Marlatt's politics and poetry were transformed by her public commitment to lesbian writing and politics. This new focus remained infused with her extraordinary artistic and intellectual range. The long-poem/journal *How hug a stone* held her mother's marriage up to a critical examination, while the following year's *Touch to my tongue* combined an intensely personal series of lesbian love poems with a critical essay, "musing with mothertongue," which explored ideas about the sexual politics of language espoused by French feminists such as Kristeva. As part of a commitment to feminist modes of scholarship, Marlatt has collaborated on numerous occasions with poet Betsy Warland, as well as with other feminist writers such as Lee Maracle and Nicole Brossard.

Although Marlatt's work has remained deeply self-reflexive, focusing on her own evolving consciousness as an historical artefact in itself, her interests bear eloquent witness to the pressures of her age. Her experimental novel, *Ana Historic,* attempts to conjure the lives of generations of women who have been deleted from Vancouver's official history. Its interspersing of poetic fragments amidst a meandering narrative and her highly stylized poetic prose situate Marlatt's text alongside other historical metafictions of the period such as those by Michael Ondaatje. Her 1991 work *Salvage* registered her own complicity in the process of historical erasure by presenting readers with a series of texts she had deleted from *Steveston* a decade earlier, which would have given the earlier book a more feminist emphasis had they been included at the time. In 1996, she published a second novel, *Taken,* which traced the history of her mother's life in Malaya during the Japanese invasion. Simultaneously introspective and historically rooted, technically ambitious and deeply personal, Marlatt's work develops a shrewd meditation on the vexed relations between different forms of desire and absence in a poetic world that is marked by the shaping influence of language, on the one hand, and the historical power of the West Coast on the other.

From Steveston[1]

Steveston as you find it:

multiplicity simply there: the physical matter of the place (what matters) meaning, don't get theoretical now, the cannery.

[1] Steveston is a fishing village near Vancouver at the mouth of the Fraser River, originally established as a salmon canning centre in the late nineteenth century. The working community was made up of a large number of Japanese Canadians.

It's been raining, or it's wet. Shines everywhere a slick on the surface of
things wet gumboots walk over, fish heads & other remnants of sub/ or
marine life, brought up from under. Reduced to the status of things hands
lop the fins off, behead, tail, tossed, this matter that doesn't matter,
into a vat or more correctly box the forklifts will move, where they swim,
flat of eye—deathless that meaningless stare, "fisheye" (is it only
dead we recognize them?) in a crimson sauce of their own blood.   10

                                                                      We orient
always toward the head, & eyes (eyes) as knowing, & knowing us, or what we do.
But these, this, is "harvest". These are the subhuman facets of life we the
town (& all that is urban, urbane, our glittering table service, our white
wine, the sauces we pickle it with, or ourselves), live off. These torsos.
& we throw the heads away. Or a truck passes by, loaded with offal for what
we also raise to kill, mink up the valley.

                                                       That's not it. It's wet,
& there's a fish smell. There's a subhuman, sub/marine aura to things. The
cavernous "fresh fish" shed filled with water, with wet bodies of dead fish,   20
in thousands, wet aprons & gloves of warm bodies whose hands expertly trim,
cut, fillet, pack these bodies reduced to non-bodies, nonsensate food *these*
bodies ache from, feet in gumboots on wet cement, arms moving, hands, cold
blowing in from open doors facing the river, whose ears dull from, the insensate noise of machinery, of forklifts, of grinding & washing, of conveyor
belt. Put on an extra sweater, wear long underwear against the damp that
creeps up from this asphalt, from this death that must be kept cool, fresh.

             "DISINFECT YOUR GLOVES BEFORE RESUMING WORK."

That no other corpus work within it. Kept at the freshest, at the very point of
mutable life, diverting, into death. To be steamed in cans, or baked, frozen in   30
fillets, packaged sterile for the bacteria of living bodies to assimilate. break
down. Pacific Ocean flesh.

No, that's not it. There's a dailiness these lives revolve around, also immersed.
Shifts, from seven to four or otherwise. Half an hour for lunch. & a long
paperwrapt & tied form outside the lunchroom, keeping cool. 'til shift's
end & the fridge, supper, bed. "my life," etc.

                                     "You leave 2 minutes after 4,
& not before, you understand? Two minutes after." Two minutes, as if that,
together with the sardine cans for ashtray, made all the difference. Which is,
simply, as two Japanese women sit, relaxing with their fifteen minute coffee   40
out of thermos, more likely hot soup, one rearranges the chrysanthemums, red &

yellow, she placed in an empty can on their table this morning when the day
began. Or more directly how in "fresh fish" the lunchrooms, men's & women's,
face over an expanse of roof with flowerboxes even, river & the delta, Ladner,
space. & remain spacious, time turned calendar of kimona'd beauty, kneeling,
on the wall. While in the cannery close to wharfedge they face north,
backed by old wooden lockers to the door: DO NOT SPIT IN THE GARBAGE. USE THE
TOILETS. & here they flood in together, giggling, rummaging thru bags,
eating grapes, girlish even ("I've worked here 20 years") under severe
green kerchief like Italian peasants, except that they are mostly Japanese,
plunked under a delicate mobile of Japanese ribbon fish in their gumboots   50
& socks. Break, from routine, with the ease of tired bodies laughing,
for what? "It's life." *Their* life?

                          Or how the plant packs their lives, chopping
off the hours, contains *them* as it contains first aid, toilets, beds, the
vestige of a self-contained life in this small house back of the carpentry
shed, where two woodburners are littered with pots & hot plates, & the table
still bears its current pattern of dominoes. Where a nude on the wall glints
kittenish at one of the two small rooms inside, each with iron bed. Some
sleeping place between shifts? Dark. Housing wet dreams, pale beside the
clank of forklift, supply truck, welding shed.   60

It's a mis-step, this quiet gap on everyone else's shift, when you're off,
when accidental gravel rattles loud on the wooden walk. wan sun. coffee,
gone cold. There's a surface skin of the familiar, familial. Running into
shadow, where old socks, someone else's intimate things, call up the fishy
odour of cunt, of lamp black in the old days you could hear them screwing
behind their door (cardboard), & even the kitchen still exists to pull you
back in, to smallness, a smell of coal, the aura of oil, of what comes up
from under, sleeping—nets, wet still from riverbottom, & the fish.

This darker seam that slips underneath the coppery gleam of all those cans stacked
flat after flat, waiting transfer. Men. & Women. Empty familiar lunchroom,   70
& the dream, pounding with the pound of machinery under mountains of empty packer
pens at night, the endless (white) stream of flesh passing under the knives,
To be given up, gone, in a great bleeding jet, into that other (working) world.

                                              [1974]

prairie

in this land the rivers carve furrows and canyons as sudden to the eye as if earth
opened up its miles and miles of rolling range, highway running to its evercom-
ing horizon, days of it, light picking flowers. your blackeyed susans are here, my
coral weed in brilliant patches, and always that grass frayed feathery by the

season, late, and wild canada geese in the last field. i imagine your blue eye gathering these as we go, only you are not here and the parched flat opens up: badlands and hoodoos and that river with dangerous currents you cannot swim, TREACHEROUS BANK, sandstone caving in: and there she goes, Persephone[2] caught in a whirlwind the underside churns up, the otherwise of where we are, cruising earth's surface, gazing on it, grazing, like those 70 million year old dinosaurs, the whole herd browsing the shore of Bearpaw Sea[3] which ran all the way in up here, like Florida, she said, came in from the desert region they were hungry for grass (or flowers) when something like a flashflood caught them, their bones, all these years later, laid out in a whirlpool formation i cannot see (that as the metaphor) up there on the farthest hoodoo, those bright colours she keeps stressing, the guy in the red shirt, metal flashing, is not Hades but only the latest technician in a long line of measurers. and earth? i have seen her open up to let love in, let loose a flood, and fold again, so that even my fingers could not find their way through all that bush, all that common day rolling unbroken.

[1984]

hidden ground

lost without you, though sun accompanies me, though moon and the maps say always i am on the right track, the Trans-Canada heading east—everything in me longs to turn around, go back to you, to (that gap), afraid i'm lost, afraid i've driven out of our territory we found (we inhabit together), not *terra firma*, not dry land, owned, along the highway, cleared for use, but that other, lowlying, moist and undefined, hidden ground, wild and running everywhere along the outer edges. lost, *losti,* lust-y one, who calls my untamed answering one to sally forth, finding alternate names, finding the child provoked, invoked, lost daughter, other mother and lover, waxing tree, waist i love, water author sounding the dark edge of the words we come to, augur- ess, issa, lithesome, *lilaiesthai,* yearning for you, and like a branch some hidden spring pulls toward our ground, i grow unafraid increasing ("lust of the earth or of the plant"), *lasati,* (she) yearns and plays, letting the yearning play it out, playing it over, every haystack, every passing hill, that tongue our bodies utter, woman tongue, speaking in and of and for each other.

[1984]

---

[2] Persephone, the daughter of Zeus and Demeter (goddess of the harvest and fertility), was abducted by Hades who burst through the earth while she was picking flowers in a field and took her to the underworld. In order to appease Demeter, Zeus arranged for Persephone to be returned to the earth if she had eaten nothing while in Hades; because she had eaten some pomegranate seeds, Persephone was only allowed to return for a portion of each year. When she and Demeter are together, the earth flourishes in spring and summer; when she returns to Hades, Demeter mourns and winter begins.

[3] The Bearpaw Sea extended from the Arctic Circle to the Gulf of Mexico, a warm sea that was teeming with life and now abounds with well-preserved fossils and some dinosaur remains. Hoodoos are tall pillars of soft rock that protrude upwards in arid plains and in the badlands.

musing with mothertongue

DAPHNE MARLATT

the beginning: language, a living body we enter at birth, sustains and contains us. it does not stand in place of anything else, it does not replace the bodies around us. placental, our flat land, our sea, it is both place (where we are situated) and body (that contains us), that body of language we speak, our mothertongue. it bears us as we are born in it, into cognition.

language is first of all for us a body of sound. leaving the water of the mother's womb with its one dominant sound, we are born into this other body whose multiple sounds bathe our ears from the moment of our arrival. we learn the sounds before we learn what they say: a child will speak baby-talk in pitch patterns that accurately imitate the sentence patterns of her mothertongue. an adult who cannot read or write will speak his mothertongue without being able to say what a particular morpheme or even word in a phrase means. we learn nursery rhymes without understanding what they refer to. we repeat skipping songs significant for their rhythms. gradually we learn how the sounds of our language are active as meaning, and then we go on learning for the rest of our lives what the words are actually saying.

in poetry, which has evolved out of chant and song, in rhyming and tone-leading, whether they occur in prose or poetry, sound will initiate thought by a process of association. words call each other up, evoke each other, provoke each other, nudge each other into utterance. we know from dreams and schizophrenic speech how deeply association works in our psyches, a form of thought that is not rational but erotic because it works by attraction. a drawing, a pulling toward. a "liking." Germanic līk-, body form; like, same.

like the atomic particles of our bodies, phonemes and syllables gravitate toward each other. they attract each other in movements we call assonance, euphony, alliteration, rhyme. they are drawn together and echo each other in rhythms we identify as feet—lines run on, phrases patter like speaking feet. on a macroscopic level, words evoke each other in movements we know as puns and figures of speech. (these endless similes, this continuing fascination with making one out of two, a new one, a simultitude.) meaning moves us deepest the more of the whole field it puts together, and so we get sense where it borders on nonsense ("what is the sense of it all?") as what we sense our way into. the sentence. ("life.") making our multiplicity whole and even intelligible by the end-point. intelligible: logos there in the gathering hand, the reading eye.

hidden in the etymology and usage of so much of our vocabulary for verbal communication (contact, sharing) is a link with the body's physicality: matter (the import of what you say) and matter and by extension mother; language and tongue; to utter and outer (give birth again); a part of speech and a part of the body; pregnant with meaning; to mouth (speak) and the mouth with which we also eat and make love; sense (meaning) and that with which we sense the world; to relate (a story) and to relate to somebody, related (carried back) with its connection with bearing (a child); intimate and to intimate; vulva and voluble; even sentence, which comes from a verb meaning to feel.

like the mother's body, language is larger than us and carries us along with it. it bears us, it births us, insofar as we bear with it. if we are poets we spend our lives discovering not just what *we* have to say but what language is saying as it carries us with it. in etymology we discover a history of verbal relations (a family tree, if you will) that has preceded us and given us the world we live in. the given, the immediately presented, as at birth—a given name a given world. we know language structures our world, and in a crucial sense we cannot see what we cannot verbalize, as the work of Whorf[4] and ethnolinguistics has pointed out to us. here we are truly contained within the body of our mothertongue. and even the physicists, chafing at these limits, say that the glimpse physics now gives us of the nature of the universe cannot be conveyed in a language based on the absolute difference between a noun and a verb. poetry has been demonstrating this for some time.

if we are women poets, writers, speakers, we also take issue with the given, hearing the discrepancy between what our patriarchally-loaded language bears (can bear) of our experience and the difference from it our experience bears out— how it misrepresents, even miscarries, and so leaves unsaid what we actually experience. can a pregnant woman be said to be "master" of the gestation process she finds herself within—is that her relationship to it?[5] are women included in the statement "God appearing as man"? (has God ever appeared as a woman?) can a woman ever say she is "lady of all she surveys," or could others ever say of her she "ladies it over them"?

so many terms for dominance in English are tied up with male experiencing, masculine hierarchies and differences (exclusion), patriarchal holdings with their legalities. where are the poems that celebrate the soft letting-go the flow of menstrual blood is as it leaves her body? how can the standard sentence structure of English with its linear authority, subject through verb to object,

---

4 Benjamin Whorf (1897–1941), American linguist who proposed that language affected cognition and perception.

5 [Marlatt's note: see Julia Kristeva, *Desire in Language*, p. 238.] Julia Kristeva (1941–), Bulgarian-French feminist and psychoanalytic theorist, is a clear influence on Marlatt's aesthetic. In *Desire in Language* (1969) and other works Kristeva distinguishes between semiotic (bodily, primal, pre-linguistic) and symbolic relations to language and experience, the former of which are more easily accessed by women

convey the wisdom of endlessly repeating and not exactly repeated cycles her body knows? or the mutuality her body shares embracing other bodies, children, friends, animals, all those she customarily holds and is held by? how can the separate nouns "mother" and "baby" convey the fusion, bleeding womb-infant mouth, she experiences in those first days of feeding? what syntax can carry the turning herself inside out in love when she is both sucking mouth and hot gush on her lover's tongue?

Julia Kristeva says: "If it is true that every national language has its own dream language and unconscious, then each of the sexes—a division so much more archaic and fundamental than the one into languages—would have its own unconscious wherein the biological and social program of the species would be ciphered in confrontation with language, exposed to its influence, but independent from it."[6] i link this with the call so many feminist writers in Quebec have issued for a language that returns us to the body, a woman's body and the largely unverbalized, presyntactic, postlexical field it knows. postlexical in that, as Mary Daly[7] shows, with intelligence (that gathering hand) certain words (dandelion sparks) seed themselves back to original and originally-related meanings. this is a field where words mutually attract each other, fused by connection, enthused (inspired) into variation (puns, word play, rime at all levels), fertile in proliferation (offspring, rooting back to *al-*, seed syllable to grow, and leafing forward into *alma*, nourishing, a woman's given name, soul, inhabitant.)

inhabitant of language, not master, not even mistress, this new woman writer (Alma, say) in having is had, is held by it, what she is given to say, in giving it away is given herself, on that double edge where she has always lived, between the already spoken and the unspeakable, sense and non-sense. only now she writes it, risking nonsense, chaotic language leafings, unspeakable breaches of usage, intuitive leaps. inside language she leaps for joy, shoving out the walls of taboo and propriety, kicking syntax, discovering life in old roots.

language thus speaking (i.e., inhabited) relates us, "takes us back" to where we are, as it relates us to the world in a living body of verbal relations. articulation: seeing the connections (and the thighbone, and the hipbone, etc.). putting the living body of language together means putting the world together, the world we live in: an act of composition, an act of birthing, us, uttered and outered there in it.

[1984]

[6] [Marlatt's note: *Desire in Language*, p. 241.]
[7] Mary Daly (1928–), American radical feminist, author of *Beyond God the Father* (1973) and *Gyn/Ecology* (1978).

DAPHNE MARLATT

492

Few Canadian authors are more widely recognized both nationally and internationally than Michael Ondaatje. In 2007, he matched Hugh MacLennan's record of five Governor General's Awards — twice for poetry, for *The Collected Works of Billy the Kid* (1970) and *There's a Trick with a Knife I'm Learning to Do* (1979); and three times for fiction, for *The English Patient* (1987), *Anil's Ghost* (2000), and *Divisadero* (2007). Ondaatje also won the Giller Prize (for *Anil's Ghost*), the Booker Prize (for *The English Patient*), and the Prix Medicis, as well as various other national and international awards. A movie version of *The English Patient* won nine Academy Awards including Best Picture. Ondaatje was named to the Order of Canada in 1988.

Born in Sri Lanka in 1943, he immigrated with his mother, brother, and sister to England in 1954, and then to Canada in 1962. After attending Bishop's University, and then receiving his B.A. from the University of Toronto and his M.A. from Queen's University in Kingston, Ondaatje joined the English Department at Glendon College, York University, in 1971. Although he has spent most of his adult life in Toronto, he has also lived in Bellrock, Ontario (the setting of "Pig Glass" and the opening section of *In the Skin of a Lion* [1987]), and Bowen Island, B.C. Ondaatje has been influential not only as a distinguished poet and novelist, but also as a committed member of the Canadian literary community, through his involvement with Coach House Press, and journals such as *Quarry* and *Brick.* Ondaatje has also edited several influential anthologies, including *The Long Poem Anthology* (1979) and *From Ink Lake: Canadian Stories* (1990).

Since the publication of his poetry collection *Dainty Monsters* in 1967, Ondaatje has flourished in a number of genres, from poetry to novels to texts which blur the boundaries between these genres, and, to a lesser extent, as a film-maker. His poetry ensemble *The Collected Works of Billy the Kid: Left Handed Poems* (1970) moulded poetry into a form whose narrative possibilities seemed almost novelistic (even as it defies the narrative containment offered by a "collected works" since it contains blank spaces and unattributed voices). Similarly, his first novel, *Coming Through Slaughter* (1976), insistently undermined its own form in ways that read more like poetry than prose. Together, these works place Ondaatje at the forefront of postmodern experimental writing in Canada in the 1970s. The self-reflexive metafictionality and genre-blurring that characterize these works had an enormous impact on subsequent writing in Canada in the decades that followed.

Much of Ondaatje's early work probed the connections between different forms of social and psychic violence, focusing on the brutalized world of outlaw heroes, self-destructive geniuses, or traumatized survivors: from the legendary American outlaw William H. Bonney, who was better known as Billy the Kid, to the New Orleans cornetist Buddy Bolden, to the protagonist of *the man with seven toes* (1969), an anonymous white woman who spends a period of time living with a group of Australian Aboriginal people before being rescued. These early works use a radically fragmented style that fuses Ondaatje's interest in the broken lives of many of these characters with a haunting capacity to make details resonate. In doing so, they invest the violence associated with these various characters with an aesthetic allure. But this fascination with different forms of violence is itself offset by the compassion with which these books explore the fragility of human consciousness and the fine line many of these characters straddle between devotion and betrayal.

Running in the Family (1982) marked a crucial turning point for Ondaatje, while still sharing his earlier works' fascination with the unstable but suggestive connections between fiction and history. A memoir that deals with Ondaatje's return to Sri Lanka, *Running in the Family* relates the extraordinary history of his family's colonial extravagance and debauchery (also the subject of his 1973 poem about his parents, "Letters & Other Worlds"). "In Sri Lanka," Ondaatje writes, "a well-told lie is worth a thousand facts." Its account of the tragic life of his charismatic but alcoholic father, whom he barely knew, recalls his previous books' interest in the compelling but flawed lives of people such as Bolden and Bonney, but this is offset by two very different developments. On the one hand, as a family memoir *Running in the Family* marked a new sense of personal immediacy; on the other hand, it represented a turn outwards to broader social and political considerations that were bound up with a postcolonial interest in the human consequences of geopolitical dynamics. Ondaatje's interest in Sri Lanka returned in a far more directly political way in *Anil's Ghost* (2000), which tells the story of Anil Tissera, a woman who emigrates from Sri Lanka to the United States only to return as part of a U.N. human rights investigation during Sri Lanka's bloody civil war.

Ondaatje's interest in non-mainstream histories manifested itself again in his highly successful metafictional novel about the building of Toronto in the early twentieth century, *In the Skin of a Lion*. While making use of actual historical events (such as the building of the Bloor Street Viaduct and the R.C. Harris water treatment plant), the novel glimpses behind the received accounts of Canadian history and the limited accounts in historical documentation to explore the experience of the people who have been left out of standard histories. It juxtaposes the marginal existence of the immigrant communities of Macedonians, Italians, and Finns, for instance, whose labour built these landmarks, with the easy familiarity of the city they constructed. Like much of his most recent work, *In the Skin of a Lion* was experimental in form, less in terms of the fusion of poetry and prose which distinguished his earlier works than in its highly textured and metaphorical style and its disruption of linear, homogeneous perspectives.

Ondaatje's Booker Prize-winning novel, *The English Patient* (1992), centres on the intertwined lives of four very different characters who, having been thrown together by forces beyond their control, live out the end of the Second World War in a bombed-out Italian villa: a badly burned man whose mysterious identity is at the core of the novel's investigation of the power and price of national affiliations; Hana, a Canadian nurse who first appeared as a young girl in *In the Skin of a Lion;* Kip, an Indian soldier who specializes in bomb disposal; and Caravaggio, the thief from *In the Skin of a Lion.* Set in the very different worlds of an Italian villa and the North African desert, the novel circles around the burn victim, whose identity has been erased, and anticipates the power with which the skeleton in

Anil's Ghost stands as a challenge to the brutalities of patriotic violence. The scorched figure at the centre of *The English Patient* is emblematic of a life beyond national identity at the epicentre of one of history's greatest nationalist collisions. It thus renews Ondaatje's early interest in evoking the enigmatic quality of the broken lives of his protagonists, an interest continued in *Divisadero,* but now in terms of a more thoughtful exploration of the human cost of personal and familial conflict.

The widely noted poetic quality of Ondaatje's prose style is no accident. Ondaatje has published several books of poetry, from early work such as *Dainty Monsters* (1967) and *Rat Jelly* (1973) to more recent collections such as *Secular Love* (1984) and *Handwriting* (1998). Poet-critic Frank Davey has noted Ondaatje's "thoroughly disconcerting talent for presenting the ordinary in an extraordinary way." As Ondaatje writes in his 1998 poem "Buried 2," "the deeper levels of the self" are deliberately juxtaposed with the "landscapes of daily life," an approach that is beautifully evoked in "To a Sad Daughter." The uncompromising honesty of his poems is balanced against their theatricality, a technique that one sees in his playful yet poignant "Translations of My Postcards" or in the ambiguous allegory of poetic workmanship in "Spider Blues." Animated by his unmistakable blend of ironic wit and intimacy, Ondaatje's poems read like elegiac tapestries of indefinable loss, fragile redemption, lyrical immediacy, and formal elegance.

White Dwarfs[1]

This is for people who disappear
for those who descend into the code
and make their room a fridge for Superman
—who exhaust costume and bones that could perform flight,
who shave their moral so raw
they can tear themselves through the eye of a needle
this is for those people
that hover and hover
and die in the ether peripheries

There is my fear   10
of no words   of
falling without words
over and over   of
mouthing the silence

[1] White dwarfs are stars that glow with a faint light because they are no longer generating energy. Their light comes from the emission of stored heat, not from nuclear fusion, since they have already exhausted their source of fuel.

Why do I love most
among my heroes those
who sail to that perfect edge
where there is no social fuel
Release of sandbags
to understand their altitude—   20

        that silence of the third cross[2]
        3rd man hung so high and lonely
        we dont hear him say
        say his pain, say his unbrotherhood
        What has he to do with the smell of ladies
        can they eat off his skeleton of pain?

The Gurkhas in Malaya
cut the tongues of mules
so they were silent beasts of burden
in enemy territories   30
after such cruelty what could they speak of anyway
And Dashiell Hammett[3] in success
suffered conversation and moved
to the perfect white between the words

This white that can grow
is fridge, bed,
is an egg—most beautiful
when unbroken, where
what we cannot see is growing
in all the colours we cannot see   40

there are those burned out stars
who implode into silence
after parading in the sky
after such choreography what would they wish to speak of   anyway

                                         [1973]

[2] Luke 23: 32–43 tells of two thieves who were crucified alongside Christ. One rebuked him, the other acknowledged his divinity and asked for forgiveness; as a result, one was damned (the "third cross"), the other saved.

[3] Dashiell Hammett (1894–1961), American left-wing civil rights activist and author of hard-boiled detective novels such as *The Maltese Falcon* (1930). After 1934, Hammett stopped writing and published almost nothing for the last 27 years of his life. Hammett was involved in a remarkable court case in 1951, coming under scrutiny by Senator Joseph McCarthy and the House Un-American Activities Committee, in which he refused to testify against people convicted of helping suspected Communists; he invoked the Fifth Amendment and was charged with contempt of court and imprisoned.

Letters & Other Worlds

'for there was no more darkness for him and, no doubt
like Adam before the fall, he could see in the dark'[4]

My father's body was a globe of fear
His body was a town we never knew
He hid that he had been where we were going
His letters were a room he seldom lived in
In them the logic of his love could grow

My father's body was a town of fear
He was the only witness to its fear dance
He hid where he had been that we might lose him
His letters were a room his body scared

He came to death with his mind drowning.   10
On the last day he enclosed himself
in a room with two bottles of gin, later
fell the length of his body
so that brain blood moved
to new compartments
that never knew the wash of fluid
and he died in minutes of a new equilibrium.

His early life was a terrifying comedy
and my mother divorced him again and again.
He would rush into tunnels magnetized   20
by the white eye of trains
and once, gaining instant fame,
managed to stop a Perahara[5] in Ceylon
—the whole procession of elephants dancers
local dignitaries—by falling
dead drunk onto the street.

As a semi-official, and semi-white at that,
the act was seen as a crucial
turning point in the Home Rule Movement
and led to Ceylon's independence in 1948.[6]   30

---

[4] Quotation from French surrealist playwright Alfred Jarry (1873–1907), a notorious alcoholic and drinker of absinthe.

[5] An annual Sri Lankan parade and festival that includes decorated elephants and dancers.

[6] Ceylon, renamed Sri Lanka in 1972, achieved independence from British rule in 1948.

(My mother had done her share too—
her driving so bad
she was stoned by villagers
whenever her car was recognized)

For 14 years of marriage
each of them claimed he or she
was the injured party.
Once on the Colombo docks
saying goodbye to a recently married couple
my father, jealous   40
at my mother's articulate emotion,
dove into the waters of the harbour
and swam after the ship waving farewell.
My mother pretending no affiliation
mingled with the crowd back to the hotel.

Once again he made the papers
though this time my mother
with a note to the editor
corrected the report—saying he was drunk
rather than broken hearted at the parting of friends.   50
The married couple received both editions
of *The Ceylon Times* when their ship reached Aden.

And then in his last years
he was the silent drinker,
the man who once a week
disappeared into his room with bottles
and stayed there until he was drunk
and until he was sober.

There speeches, head dreams, apologies,
the gentle letters, were composed.   60
With the clarity of architects
he would write of the row of blue flowers
his new wife had planted,
the plans for electricity in the house,
how my half-sister fell near a snake
and it had awakened and not touched her.
Letters in a clear hand of the most complete empathy
his heart widening and widening and widening
to all manner of change in his children and friends
while he himself edged   70

into the terrible acute hatred
of his own privacy
till he balanced and fell
the length of his body
the blood screaming in
the empty reservoir of bones
the blood searching in his head without metaphor

[1973]

King Kong meets Wallace Stevens[7]

Take two photographs—
Wallace Stevens and King Kong
(Is it significant that I eat bananas as I write this?)

Stevens is portly, benign, a white brush cut
striped tie. Businessman but
for the dark thick hands, the naked brain
the thought in him.

Kong is staggering
lost in New York streets again
a spawn of annoyed cars at his toes.   10
The mind is nowhere.
Fingers are plastic, electric under the skin.
He's at the call of Metro-Goldwyn-Mayer.

Meanwhile W. S. in his suit
is thinking chaos is thinking fences.
In his head the seeds of fresh pain
his exorcising,
the bellow of locked blood.

The hands drain from his jacket,
pose in the murderer's shadow.   20

[1973]

[7] Wallace Stevens (1879–1955), Pulitzer Prize-winning American modernist poet who worked much of his life as an insurance agent (hence the "striped suit" and "brush cut" mentioned here). His philosophical poetry is often concerned with the relationship between reality and the imagination, namely how the imagination imposes order on the world to make sense of it. King Kong is the giant ape in the 1933 Hollywood movie of the same name that terrorized the city of New York.

Spider Blues

'Well I made them laugh, I wish 1 could make them cry.'
                                                David McFadden[8]

My wife has a smell that spiders go for.
At night they descend saliva roads
down to her dreaming body.
They are magnetized by her breath's rhythm,
leave their own constructions
for succulent travel across her face and shoulder.
My own devious nightmares
are struck to death by her shrieks.

About the spiders.
Having once tried to play piano   10
and unable to keep both hands
segregated in their intent
I admire the spider, his control classic,
his eight legs finicky,
making lines out of the juice in his abdomen.
A kind of writer I suppose.
He thinks a path and travels
the emptiness that was there
leaves his bridge behind
looking back saying Jeez   20
did I do that?
and uses his ending
to swivel to new regions
where the raw of feelings exist.

Spiders like poets are obsessed with power.
They write their murderous art which sleeps
like stars in the corner of rooms,
a mouth to catch audiences
weak   broken   sick

And spider comes to fly, says   30
Love me I can kill you, love me
my intelligence has run rings about you
love me, I kill you for the clarity that
comes when roads I make are being made
love me, antisocial, lovely.

[8] David McFadden (1940–), Canadian poet and fiction writer.

And fly says, O no
no your analogies are slipping
no I choose who I die with
you spider poets are all the same
you in your close vanity of making,   40
you minor drag, your saliva stars always
soaking up the liquid from our atmosphere.
And the spider in his loathing
crucifies his victims in his spit
making them the art he cannot be.

So. The ending we must arrive at.
                              ok folks.
Nightmare for my wife and me:

It was a large white room
and the spiders had thrown   50
their scaffolds off the floor
onto four walls and the ceiling.
They had surpassed themselves this time
and with the white roads
their eight legs built with speed
they carried her up—her whole body
into the dreaming air so gently
she did not wake or scream.
What a scene. So many trails
the room was a shattered pane of glass.   60
Everybody clapped, all the flies.
They came and gasped, all
everybody cried at the beauty
ALL
except the working black architects
and the lady locked in their dream   their theme

                                                       [1973]

Pig Glass

Bonjour.   This is pig glass
a piece of cloudy sea

nosed out of the earth by swine
and smoothed into pebble
run it across your cheek
it will not cut you

and this is my hand   a language
which was buried for years   touch it
against your stomach

           The pig glass   10
I thought
was the buried eye of Portland Township[9]
slow faded history
waiting to be grunted up
There is no past until you breathe
on such green glass
                  rub it
over your stomach and cheek

The Meeks family used this section
years ago to bury tin   20
crockery forks dog tags
and each morning
pigs ease up that ocean
redeeming it again
into the possibilities of rust
one morning I found a whole axle
another day a hand crank
but this is pig glass
tested with narrow teeth
and let lie. The morning's green present.   30
Portland Township jewelry.

There is the band from the ankle of a pigeon
a weathered bill from the Bellrock Cheese Factory
letters in 1925 to a dead mother I
disturbed in the room above the tractor shed.
Journals of family love
servitude to farm weather
a work glove in a cardboard box
creased flat and hard like a flower.

A bottle thrown   40
by loggers out of a wagon
past midnight

[9] Portland Township is in Frontenac County, in eastern Ontario. Ondaatje spent the summers in the 1970s living at Blue Roof Farm outside of the hamlet of Bellrock in Portland Township. The Meeks, referred to later in the poem, are an old local family who lived on the farm before the Ondaatjes. In "Pig Glass," Ondaatje, like Robert Kroetsch in "Stone Hammer Poem," digs through the layers of local history.

explodes against rock.
This green fragment had behind it
The *booomm* when glass
tears free of its smoothness

now once more smooth as knuckle
a tooth on my tongue.
Comfort that bites through skin
hides in the dark afternoon of my pocket.   50
Snake shade.
Determined histories of glass.

[1979]

The Cinnamon Peeler

If I were a cinnamon peeler
I would ride your bed
and leave the yellow bark dust
on your pillow.

Your breasts and shoulders would reek
you could never walk through markets
without the profession of my fingers
floating over you. The blind would
stumble certain of whom they approached
though you might bathe   10
under rain gutters, monsoon.

Here on the upper thigh
at this smooth pasture
neighbour to your hair
or the crease
that cuts your back. This ankle.
You will be known among strangers
as the cinnamon peeler's wife.

I could hardly glance at you
before marriage   20
never touch you
—your keen nosed mother, your rough brothers.
I buried my hands
in saffron, disguised them
over smoking tar,
helped the honey gatherers . . .

When we swam once
I touched you in water
and our bodies remained free,
you could hold me and be blind of smell.   30
You climbed the bank and said

                     this is how you touch other women
the grass cutter's wife, the lime burner's daughter.
And you searched your arms
for the missing perfume
                      and knew
               what good is it
to be the lime burner's daughter
left with no trace
as if not spoken to in the act of love   40
as if wounded without the pleasure of a scar.

You touched
your belly to my hands
in the dry air and said
I am the cinnamon
peeler's wife. Smell me.

[1982]

To a Sad Daughter

All night long the hockey pictures
gaze down at you
sleeping in your tracksuit.
Belligerent goalies are your ideal.
Threats of being traded
cuts and wounds
—all this pleases you.
O my god! you say at breakfast
reading the sports page over the Alpen[10]
as another player breaks his ankle   10
or assaults the coach.

When I thought of daughters
I wasn't expecting this
but I like this more.
I like all your faults

---

[10] A type of cereal.

even your purple moods
when you retreat from everyone
to sit in bed under a quilt.
And when I say 'like'
I mean of course 'love'   20
but that embarrasses you.
You who feel superior to black and white movies
(coaxed for hours to see *Casablanca*)
though you were moved
by *Creature from the Black Lagoon*.

One day I'll come swimming
beside your ship or someone will
and if you hear the siren
listen to it. For if you close your ears
only nothing happens. You will never change.[11]   30

I don't care if you risk
your life to angry goalies
creatures with webbed feet.
You can enter their caves and castles
their glass laboratories. Just
don't be fooled by anyone but yourself.

This is the first lecture I've given you.
You're 'sweet sixteen' you said.
I'd rather be your closest friend
than your father. I'm not good at advice   40
you know that, but ride
the ceremonies
until they grow dark.

Sometimes you are so busy
discovering your friends
I ache with a loss
—but that is greed.
And sometimes I've gone
into *my* purple world
and lost you.   50

---

[11] Allusion to the scene in Homer's *Odyssey* in which Odysseus passes an island inhabited by Sirens (mermaids) who lure ships onto the rocks with their song. Odysseus orders his sailors to plug their ears with wax and tie him to the mast with his ears unstopped so that he can hear the song but not endanger the ship.

One afternoon I stepped
into your room. You were sitting
at the desk where I now write this.
Forsythia outside the window
and sun spilled over you
like a thick yellow miracle
as if another planet
was coaxing you out of the house
—all those possible worlds!—
and you, meanwhile, busy with mathematics.   60

I cannot look at forsythia now
without loss, or joy for you.
You step delicately
into the wild world
and your real prize will be
the frantic search.
Want everything. If you break
break going out not in.
How you live your life I don't care
but I'll sell my arms for you,   70
hold your secrets forever.

If I speak of death
which you fear now, greatly,
it is without answers,
except that each
one we know is
in our blood.
Don't recall graves.
Memory is permanent.
Remember the afternoon's   80
yellow suburban annunciation.
Your goalie
in his frightening mask
dreams perhaps
of gentleness.

                                        [1984]

Translations of my Postcards

the peacock means order
the fighting kangaroos mean madness
the oasis means I have struck water

positioning of the stamp—the despot's head
horizontal, or 'mounted policemen,'
mean political danger

the false date means I
am not where I should be

when I speak of the weather
I mean business   10

a blank postcard says
I am in the wilderness

[1984]

---

bpNICHOL ■ (1944–1988)

The idealistic spirit of youthful abandon and revolutionary iconoclasm that animated so much of 1960s counter-culture found its literary manifestation in many writers' determination to shatter what they regarded as the conservatism of traditional literary form. This experimental ethos distinguished the work of a range of writers, but few were as bold or as determined in their efforts to shake language free of its inherited constraints as bpNichol. It was not that Nichol was pursuing a unique vision—his own richly collaborative spirit would have bristled at the idea. But his efforts to forge a poetic style that centred on the creative force of language as an end in itself, rather than approaching writing as a set of references to other things (the standard idea of the role of language), were exceptional for their uncompromising boldness, their extraordinary variety, and the love of life which they embodied. The impact of Nichol's achievements was recognized in his selection for the Governor General's Award in 1970 and, less officially, in Michael Ondaatje's film about Nichol, entitled *Sons of Captain Poetry,* which appeared in the same year.

Born in Vancouver in 1944, Barrie Phillip Nichol grew up in British Columbia, Manitoba, and Ontario, before returning to Vancouver in 1960, where he earned his elementary teaching certificate from the University of British Columbia three years later. After a short-lived career teaching grade four in Port Coquitlam, B.C., Nichol gained public acclaim for his concrete poems, which approached writing more as visual sculpture than as linear narrative. For Nichol, concrete poetry offered an aesthetic means of situating his work at "that point where language and/or the image blur together into the inbetween & become concrete objects to be understood as such." Concrete poetry's ability to exploit the sensory and spatial qualities of print infused it with a visceral immediacy which aligned it with Nichol's underlying desire to have "as many perceptual systems available to you as possible." In a kind of literary manifesto in *Open Letter* in 1966, Nichol bristled at Frank Davey's insistence that "visual poetry is 'irrelevant to what I know as poetry. For me poetry is of language, & language is still sound.'" For Nichol, the very idea that language could be so easily quarantined from the sensory realm of the visual smacked of an arbitrary and unwarranted exclusion, a denial of one crucial aspect of our relationship to words.

Although he died at age 43 in 1988, his short career was marked by an extraordinarily rich variety of literary forms and preoccupations, from relatively traditional lyrics to book-length poems to visual poems which ranged from spatialized play with words and letters to photo montages and comic strips. Many of his works thrived on an enigmatic and elusive quality which made them difficult to conceptualize in the terms traditionally used to define a writer's literary corpus. They ranged from simple sheets of paper or small books to silkscreen prints. Some were sent through the mail as greeting cards. One, a short booklet entitled *Cold Mountain* (1966), contained instructions for folding the book and burning it. *Journeying and the Returns* (1967), writes Roy MacSkimming, "incorporated a small, perfect-bound book along with other 'poem objects' inside a blue and lavender cardboard case. . . . The case held printed samples of Nichol's playful concrete poems in various shapes, sizes, and media. These included an animated thumb-flip poem the size of a matchbox, a cutaway poem giving directions for its own destruction by fire, and *Borders,* a 45-rpm disk of Nichol chanting his sound poetry." According to Victor Coleman, one of the early employees at Coach House Press, the book received "appreciable attention in the mainstream literary press" but also "garnered remarks such as 'You call this a book?'" Nichol also published an essay collection, *Craft Dinner* (1978), purely visual texts such as *still water* (1970) and *ABC: The Aleph Beth Book* (1971), and several children's books. In the mid-1980s, he collaborated with Dennis Lee on the TV children's series *Fraggle Rock.* Much of Nichol's work was jovially upbeat, a celebration of life's anarchic potential, but his writing was also charged with a much darker awareness of the ultimate limits of human communication and of humanity's capacity for violence. His most ambitious

work, *The Martyrology,* which appeared in six volumes beginning in 1967 (the final volumes appeared posthumously), turned on a central tension between its preoccupation with saints and an underlying sense of existential despair.

The philosophical commitments that informed Nichol's gravitation to the disruptive appeal of concrete poetry manifested themselves in his interest in sound poetry. Sound poetry shared concrete poetry's emphasis on what Nichol called the "kinetic use of language," but its performative context offered him an even greater communicative vitality. Nichol had been experimenting with sound poetry from the mid-1960s, but in 1970 he joined forces with three other poets, Steve McCaffery, Paul Dutton, and Rafael Barreto-Rivera, to form the Four Horsemen. Four Horsemen performances offered their audiences freewheeling blends of raucous improvisation and highly orchestrated forms of textual interplay, anarchic sounds, and elaborate rhetorical structures. Featuring shrieks, squawks, and grunts, Four Horsemen performances incorporated jarring blends of poignant lyricism and broad self-parody. At their core, these performances thrived on an anarchic sense of the expressive potential of language as pure sound, a fully embodied celebration of the physicality of all acts of communication. In doing so, these performances celebrated yet "another kind of relationship between words," as Nichol had insisted in his letter to Davey about visual poetry.

Nichol worked equally hard to reshape the map of contemporary literary production. He founded Ganglia Press in 1965 and the grOnk series of pamphlets in 1969, joined Coach House Press in 1974 as an unpaid volunteer though he quickly became a central editorial presence, and in the early 1980s helped found the small writers' co-operative Underwhich Editions. These efforts to participate in reshaping the cultural landscape through practical interventions into the world of publishing reflected Nichol's widely noted spirit of personal generosity, but they were also consistent with the broader philosophical ideals that grounded his literary efforts.

Nichol's experiments with language were never wholly ends in themselves; his poetic efforts were manifestations of an underlying fascination with the promise of all acts of communication. In a manifesto entitled "statement, november 1966," Nichol explained that for him, the promise of linguistic "diversification" lay in the hope "of finding as many exits as possible from the self (language/communication exits) in order to form as many entrances as possible for the other." For Nichol, as for so many writers in this period, this orientation to the other was part of a much broader cultural revolution that had the potential to overturn deeply ingrained systems of psychic and political repression. As Nichol puts it, "[T]here is a new humanism afoot that will one day touch the world to its core." This "new humanism" revealed itself in strikingly practical ways, from his sustained involvement with the lay therapy foundation Therafields, with which he worked as a therapist and administrator from 1967 until it was dismantled in 1983, to his efforts as a teacher of creative writing, to his support for small presses long after his own canonized status had ceased to force him to do so.

From *still water*

sea sea sea you sea sea sea me sea sea sea

fisheyes

----

moon

owl

tree   tree   tree   shadowy

blob
pɭop

[1970]

The Long Weekend of Louis Riel

FRIDAY
louis riel liked back bacon & eggs easy over   nothing's as
easy as it seems tho   when the waitress cracked the eggs
open louis came to his guns blazing   like dissolution
like the fingers of his hand coming apart as he squeezed the
trigger
                        this made breakfast the most difficult meal of the
day   lunch was simpler   two poached eggs & toast
with a mug of coffee   he never ate supper never ate after
four in the afternoon spent his time planning freedom the triumph   10
of the metis over the whiteman

SATURDAY
louis felt depressed   when he got up he sat down & wrote a
letter to the english   there was no use waiting for a reply

        it came   hey gabriel[1] look at this shouted louis a letter
from those crazy english   they both laughed & went off to
have breakfast
                        that morning there was no bacon to fry
        its those damn englishers said gabriel those damn white-
men theyre sitting up in all night diners staging a food blockade   20
        louis was watching the waitress's hands as she flipped the
pancakes spun the pizza dough kneaded the rising bread & didnt
hear him   its as canadian as genocide thot gabriel

---

[1] Gabriel Dumont (1837–1906), leader of the Métis army alongside Louis Riel (1844–1885)
during the Northwest Rebellion of 1885. See Volume I, Section III, for more information
about Riel.

bpNICHOL

510

SUNDAY

the white boys were hanging around the local bar feeling guilty
looking for someone to put it on   man its the blacks said
billie its what weve done to the blacks   hell said george
what about the japanese   but johnny said naw its what
weve done to the indians

                              outside in the rain louis was dying   30
          its always these damn white boys writing my story these
same stupid fuckers that put me down try to make a myth out of
me   they sit at counters scribbling their plays on napkins
their poems on their sleeves & never see me[2]

                                        hell said george
its the perfect image the perfect metaphor   he's a symbol
said johnny   but he's dead thot billie but didn't say it out
loud   theyre crazy these white boys said louis riel

MONDAY

they killed louis riel & by monday they were feeling guilty   40
maybe we shouldn't have done it said the mounties as they sat
down to breakfast   louis rolled over in his grave & sighed
          its not enough they take your life away with a gun they
have to take it away with their pens   in the distance he could
hear the writers scratching louder & louder   i'm getting sick
of being dished up again & again like so many slabs of back
bacon he said   i don't think we should've done it said the
mounties again reaching for the toast & marmalade   louis
clawed his way thru the rotting wood of his coffin & struggled up
thru the damp clay onto the ground   they can write down   50
all they want now he said they'll never find me   the mounties were eating with their mouths open & couldn't hear him
louis dusted the dirt off his rotting flesh & began walking
when he came to gabriel's grave he tapped on the tombstone &
said come on gabriel its time we were leaving & the two of them
walked off into the sunset like a kodachrome postcard from the
hudson bay

                                                  [1978]

[2] In the 1960s and '70s, Louis Riel formed the subject of numerous poems and plays, including
John Coulter's plays *The Crime of Louis Riel* (1966) and *The Trial of Louis Riel* (1967). See footnote 4
of the Introduction to Section VI for a list of some of these; see also Volume I, Section III, for an
excerpt from Riel's address to the jury during his trial in 1885.

landscape: 1

for thomas a. clark

alongthehorizongrewanunbrokenlineoftrees

[1985]

Blues

```
      l  e
      o e
     love
     o evol
  love o
     evol
     e o
     e  l
```

[1967]

statement, november 1966

now that we have reached the point where people have finally come to see that language means communication and that communication does not just mean language, we have come up against the problem, the actual fact, of diversification, of finding as many exits as possible from the self (language/communication exits) in order to form as many entrances as possible for the other.

the other is the loved one and the other is the key, often the reason for the need/desire to communicate. how can the poet reach out and touch you physically as say the sculptor does by caressing you with objects you caress? only if he drops the barriers. if his need is to touch you physically he creates a poem/object for you to touch and is not a sculptor for he is still moved by the language and sculpts with words. the poet who paints or sculpts is different from the painter who writes. he comes at his art from an entirely different angle and brings to it different concerns and yet similar ones. but he is a poet always.

this is not a barrier. there are no barriers in art. where there are barriers the art is made small by them. but this is to say no matter where he moves or which "field" he chooses to work in, he is always a poet and his creations can always be looked upon as poems.

there is a new humanism afoot that will one day touch the world to its core. traditional poetry is only one of the means by which to reach out and touch the other. the other is emerging as the necessary prerequisite for dialogues with the self that clarify the soul & heart and deepen the ability to love. i place myself there, with them, whoever they are, wherever they are, who seek to reach themselves and the other thru the poem by as many exits and entrances as are possible.

[1966]

TOM WAYMAN ■ (1945–)

Tom Wayman is a poet and essayist whose work is known for its ironic edge and left-wing perspective. Though born in Ontario, Wayman grew up in Prince Rupert, British Columbia. He earned his B.A. at the University of British Columbia and M.A. at the University of California in the late 1960s, and became involved in the radical student movements of the time. After university, he held a number of teaching and manual labour jobs, and was one of the founders and teachers at the Kootenay School of Writing in Vancouver in the mid-1980s. His first poetry collection was entitled *Waiting for Wayman* (1973), and it has been followed by many more, including *The Astonishing Weight of the Dead* (1994), which contains his beautiful lyrical series "The Politics of the House" commemorating everyday objects in the home, and *My Father's Cup* (2002), a collection initiated by the death of his father.

One of Wayman's pervading interests is the life of ordinary working people, a topic that he believes is a notable absence in Canadian writing. As he puts it in his Introduction to his selected poems, *Did I Miss Anything?* (1993), "I believe that to try to articulate the human story without depicting the core of daily existence is a tragic mistake. . . . [O]ur literature mostly has ignored [this] and focussed instead on the unlikely lives of those whose day-to-day existence apparently is not governed by concerns of work or money: the rich, killers, outlaws, or fantastic representations of people. . . ." In keeping with this interest, he has published two essay collections, *Inside Job* (1983) and *A Country Not Considered: Canada, Culture, Work* (1993), as well as his own poetry collection, *Free Time: Industrial Poems* (1977). He has also edited a number of poetry collections on this topic, including *A Government Job at Last* (1976), *Going for Coffee* (1981), and *PaperWork* (1991). This interest in the average person's experience, informed by his left-wing politics, echoes the writings of Earle Birney and Dorothy Livesay a generation earlier, as well as the work of Al Purdy, all of whom are distinct influences on Wayman's writing. In this work, Wayman also wants to revive the mode of realism in

Canadian writing, a genre which he believes had been relegated to the realm of "low art" in literary circles (as, for example, in the theoretical essays of George Bowering). His essay "The Limits of Realism," published in *Inside Job,* contains a full explanation of his approach.

The speaker in many of Wayman's poems, often referred to in the third person as "Wayman," is characteristically distanced and ironic. This voice is evident in his 1981 collection, *The Nobel Prize Acceptance Speech* (1981), as well as in Wayman's immensely popular poem "Did I Miss Anything?," in which a teacher imagines his response to the perennial student question. Very recently, Wayman has turned his attention to fiction, publishing a collection of short stories, *Boundary Country,* and a series of novellas, *A Vain Thing,* in 2007. He currently teaches in the English Department at the University of Calgary.

TOM WAYMAN

Did I Miss Anything?

Question frequently asked by
students after missing a class

Nothing. When we realized you weren't here
we sat with our hands folded on our desks
in silence, for the full two hours

>Everything. I gave an exam worth
>40 percent of the grade for this term
>and assigned some reading due today
>on which I'm about to hand out a quiz
>worth 50 per cent   10

Nothing. None of the content of this course
has value or meaning
Take as many days off as you like:
any activities we undertake as a class
I assure you will not matter either to you or me
and are without purpose

>Everything. A few minutes after we began last time
>a shaft of light descended and an angel
>or other heavenly being appeared
>and revealed to us what each woman or man must do   20
>to attain divine wisdom in this life and
>the hereafter
>This is the last time the class will meet
>before we disperse to bring this good news to all people
>on earth

Nothing. When you are not present
how could something significant occur?

　　Everything. Contained in this classroom
　　is a microcosm of human existence
　　assembled for you to query and examine and ponder　　30
　　This is not the only place such an opportunity has been
　　　　gathered

but it was one place

And you weren't here

　　　　　　　　　　　　　　　　　　　　　　　　　　[1993]

STAN ROGERS ■ (1949–1983)

Stan Rogers is one of Canada's most celebrated songwriters and folksingers. Born in Hamilton, Ontario, in November 1949, he is often associated with Nova Scotia, where Rogers had extended family in Canso and where he spent his childhood summers. His music tells of the working lives of ordinary Canadians: fishermen, sailors, miners, farmers, husbands and wives. His national reputation was solidified with the release of *Fogarty's Cove* (1976), which contains some of his most famous songs, including "Barrett's Privateers" and "The *Mary Ellen Carter.*"

　　Rogers wrote many of his own songs and adapted traditional pieces, setting them all to his rich baritone voice. Along with *Fogarty's Cove,* one of his most popular albums is *Northwest Passage* (1981), whose title song is reproduced here. This haunting piece mythologizes the explorers who sought the fabled Northwest Passage in Canada's north, memorializing Sir John Franklin in particular, whose disappearance in the Arctic in the 1840s has long been a source of fascination for Canadians. The "long-forgotten lonely cairn of stones" mentioned here refers to a cairn that was discovered in 1859 by Francis Leopold McClintock's expedition on King William Island, which contained a document describing Franklin's death and the crew's abandonment of the ships. In this song, the speaker aligns himself with these explorers as he travels westward along the Trans-Canada Highway, similarly seeking escape and adventure. This song constitutes part of the rich tradition of Canadian literary texts about Franklin, from Franklin's own journal about his voyages, to the testimonies of numerous Inuit people who encountered Franklin's dying men, to the nineteenth-century ballad "Lady Franklin's Lament" (see Volume I for all of these), and finally to the pieces by Rudy Wiebe and Margaret Atwood included in this volume. At the age of 33, when he was at the height of his fame, Rogers suffered an untimely and tragic death: returning from a music festival in the United States, he was killed in an airplane fire. His ashes were scattered in the Atlantic Ocean off the coast of Nova Scotia. When CBC Radio host Peter Gzowski asked Canadians to pick an alternative national anthem, "Northwest Passage" was their top choice.

Northwest Passage

Chorus:
Ah, for just one time I would take the Northwest Passage
To find the hand of Franklin reaching for the Beaufort Sea;
Tracing one warm line through a land so wild and savage
And make a Northwest Passage to the sea.

Westward from the Davis Strait 'tis there 'twas said to lie
The sea route to the Orient for which so many died;
Seeking gold and glory, leaving weathered, broken bones
And a long-forgotten lonely cairn of stones.

Three centuries thereafter, I take passage overland   10
In the footsteps of brave Kelso,[1] where his "sea of flowers" began
Watching cities rise before me, then behind me sink again
This tardiest explorer, driving hard across the plain.

And through the night, behind the wheel, the mileage clicking west
I think upon Mackenzie, David Thompson and the rest[2]
Who cracked the mountain ramparts and did show a path for me
To race the roaring Fraser to the sea.

How then am I so different from the first men through this way?
Like them, I left a settled life, I threw it all away.
To seek a Northwest Passage at the call of many men
To find there but the road back home again.   20

[1981]

---

[1] A reference to Henry Kelsey (1667?–1724), an English explorer and trader apprenticed to the Hudson's Bay Company in 1684, who was commissioned to explore the prairies in response to the competition posed by French traders. He is best known for the journal he kept during his 1690–92 journey. In a 1982 interview, Rogers admitted that he had been unsure of Kelsey's name and had guessed Kelso while recording the song.

[2] Alexander Mackenzie (1763/64–1820), North West Company trader who explored the Canadian northwest and charted the Mackenzie River. David Thompson (1770–1857), renowned cartographer of the Canadian northwest who charted the Columbia River. Both explorers made their way across the Rockies (hence "crack[ing] the mountain ramparts"), but neither managed to chart the full extent of the important Fraser River, which was traced in 1808 by Simon Fraser (1776–1862).

Contemporary Canada, 1985–Present

Introduction: The Local, the National, and the Global

Some days, the wall that separates us from the future / is too thin.
—Jan Zwicky, "Poppies" (1998)

IN THE FINAL DECADES OF THE OLD MILLENNIUM and the first years of the new, Canada's sense of identity has undergone a sea change. Because of the combined forces of globalization, diasporic migration, and technological development, the commitment to a singular Canadian identity is being replaced by an appreciation of the heterogeneity of the nation. However, many of the issues that dominated the 1960s and 1970s in Canada—nationalism, feminism, First Nations self-government, Quebec sovereignty, sexual rights, civil rights, protection for Canadian culture, and historical revisionism—are still prominent today, albeit in different forms. They have been joined by increased concerns about globalization, including reservations about the excessive power of multinational corporations undermining democratically elected governments, increases in North/South economic disparities and continued East/West aggression, and expanding notions of citizenship. Linked to this are growing fears about terrorism and its after-effects, including limitations on civil liberties and the prevalence of religious fundamentalism. The most pressing global issue may be the urgent crisis-state of the environment, which brings with it concerns about pollution and toxic waste, global warming, exploitation of natural resources, and human and animal rights. Many of these topics transcend borders and are not limited to specific territorial considerations. They are not only Canadian issues, but issues that affect people on local, national, and global levels everywhere.

Following the September 11, 2001, bombings of the World Trade Center in New York and the Pentagon in Washington, when almost 3,000 civilians hailing from 80 countries died in a single day of terrorist attacks, United States President George W. Bush declared a "war on terror." Three days later Canadian Prime Minister Jean Chrétien publicly reacted in horror to the attacks and pledged Canada's support to the American Ambassador to Canada: "We reel before the blunt and terrible reality of the evil we have just witnessed.... Do not despair. You are not alone. We are with you. The whole world is with you" (Gruending 287). Chrétien's condolence speech shows Canada as part of an international community. However, Canada subsequently refused to support the 2003 American-led invasion of Iraq because it lacked United Nations Security Council sanction. In a speech a month after the bombings, former president of the National Action Committee on the Status of Women (NAC) Sunera Thobani spoke openly, and contentiously, about her fears of condoning the American "war on terror." She pointed to the history of American foreign policy as a motivation for the attacks: "Living in a period of escalating global interaction now on every front, on every level, we have to recognize that this level and this particular phase of globalization is rooted ... in the colonization of Aboriginal peoples and Third World people all over the world.... From Chile to El Salvador, to Nicaragua to Iraq, the path of U.S. foreign policy is soaked in blood" (Gruending 289). The statements of Thobani and Chrétien highlight distinct aspects of "escalating global interaction" in today's world, contemporaneously and historically.

Over the past 25 years, the world has been plagued by both civil and multinational wars in Iraq, Northern Ireland, Lebanon, Bosnia, Rwanda, Afghanistan, Ethiopia, Haiti, Chechnya, Darfur, Guatemala, Pakistan, Chile, Israel, Palestine, and many other countries. However, these years also witnessed the fall of the Iron Curtain and the end of the Cold War (1989), the Nuclear Non-Proliferation Treaty (1968; rev. 1995), the first democratic elections in South Africa (1994), the Ottawa Treaty banning landmines (1998), the establishment of an International Criminal Court (2001), and peace treaties negotiated in Northern Ireland, Bosnia and Herzegovina, and Guatemala, among others. With peacekeeping missions that have drawn criticism in Somalia, Rwanda, Bosnia, and Afghanistan, Canada's role as a peacekeeper came under scrutiny during this time as well. Historian Robert Bothwell suggests that the nature of war in the past few years has changed the nature of peacekeeping. When danger is internal (as was the case with ethnic conflicts in Somalia, Bosnia, and Rwanda) rather than international, peacekeeping shifts from focusing on national sovereignty to attempting to preserve and respect human rights within the nation (520). Still, some critics see Canada's peacekeeping role as an intrusive one that involves the imposition of Canadian values on vulnerable peoples.

Contemporary politicians debating Canada's role as peacekeeper in Afghanistan, regardless of their stance on the debate, repeatedly appeal to "Canadian values." This, of course, leads to the question of what such values might be, as the Liberals, Conservatives, New Democrats, and Bloc Québécois articulate these values differently. Literary and cultural texts often give clues to national values, preferences, and priorities. How do we know what national values are? To what degree are they constructions? And if they are constructions, does this diminish their value, or add to the element of free choice involved in establishing such values? Do national values differ from local communal values? What effects do these values and assumptions have on the ways individuals experience their place in society? How do they affect Canadian foreign policy and/or policies at home (environmental, social, educational, cultural)? Many intellectuals and artists in this period have looked beyond the borders of the nation to consider Canada's role as a "global citizen." In the opening years of the new millennium, even at a time when the very concept of "the nation" is being reformulated, there is a sense of urgency in studying the culture of Canada as we ask, What is Canada's role in the international public sphere? This larger question is complemented by others: Has national sovereignty become more or less important in a "globalized" world? To what extent can "difference" be accepted if it involves a direct conflict with certain cherished national values, even things that have been identified as fundamental human rights? What is the line between freedom of expression and censorship when it involves such things as hate speech? What is the relationship between individual rights and communal rights, and are there instances where the latter might override the former? Should art be linked to or separated from politics?

Smaro Kamboureli argues that "literature functions as a sphere of public debates, but is never fully harmonized with them, thus registering the limits of cultural knowledge and politics" (*Trans.Can.Lit* viii). Canadian literature and criticism during this period addressed questions of "appropriation of voice," systemic racism, and the need to move beyond a homogeneous nationalism in favour of more ethnic, regional, gender, and class diversity. More recently, these discussions have expanded to consider the role of institutions, citizenship, belonging, diasporic movement, migration, community formations, ecology and the environment, human rights, and transnationalism. In response to the commodifications and imperialisms of globalization, a key focus in this period is on what globalization theorist Jeff Derksen terms an "engaged poetics" or a way of gaining agency for the global citizen through cultural and social interventions. With an increase in interdisciplinary approaches to literature and a move toward a global framework, Canadian writers and artists, as well as teachers and students, over the past few decades have engaged with the nation in a profoundly new way. In cultural theorist Diana Brydon's terms, this new direction necessitates overturning the myth of the "national dream" in favour of imagining Canada within a "planetary" context ("Metamorphoses"16).

From Free Trade to Oka to Nunavut

Domestically, some key political issues and events stand out over the past 25 years—each highlighting the connections between shifting Canadian values and Canada's evolving role in the world. They also raise important questions about the relationship between politics and art, and between the artist and society. Some of the issues that link politics and art revolve around Quebec sovereignty, First Nations rights and land claims, and international trade initiatives. Further, in this period there were passionate debates in the House of Commons (and in the public sphere) about legalizing same-sex marriage; implementing a gun registry; racial profiling; fighting AIDS and SARS; reorganizing the health care system; and acknowledging the need for redress for historical injustices committed by past governments of Canada. This is a truncated list of the kinds of domestic issues that dominated the media during this period.

The debate that arose in 1988 around the tariff and trade management agreement between Canada and the United States, known as the Free Trade Agreement,[1] highlighted the ongoing division between protectionism and internationalism. In the fiery 25 October televised election debate, anti-free trade Liberal leader John Turner attacked Progressive Conservative Prime Minister Brian Mulroney with the indictment, "I happen to believe that you have sold us out," to which Mulroney replied, "You do not have a monopoly on patriotism" (Gruending 232). Turner's charge against free trade was based on a fear that it would threaten the very independence of Canada: "We built a country east and west and north. We built it on an infrastructure that deliberately resisted the continental pressure of the United States. For 120 years we've done it. With one signature of a pen, you've reversed that, thrown us into the north-south influence of the United States and will reduce us, I am sure, to a colony of the United States because when the economic levers go, the political independence is sure to follow" (Gruending 233). The tenor of the debate bore remarkable echoes with similar issues that had been discussed during the period following Confederation in the late nineteenth century and again at the time of the Massey Report in the 1950s: fears of being subsumed into the United States, fears of being culturally and economically isolated. As in the previous debates, Canadian artists were engaged participants, playing active public roles on both sides of the free trade issue. Two significant advertisements appeared in the 19 November 1988 *Globe and Mail*. In one, artists against free trade (Gordon Lightfoot, Robertson Davies, Adrienne Clarkson, and 36 other signatories) stated: "[T]he Mulroney-Reagan Trade Deal . . . will irrevocably damage the Canada we care about" (qtd. in Davey 10). Evincing an emotional attachment to the nation, this group insisted on the links between economic, political, and cultural sovereignty. In many ways the anti-free trade camp was invoking the cultural nationalist arguments of the 1960s and '70s, such

---

[1] In 1988, it was called the Canada-U.S. Free Trade Agreement. In 1994, with the addition of Mexico, it became known as the North American Free Trade Agreement (NAFTA).

as the arguments for cultural sovereignty laid out in Margaret Atwood's *Survival* (1972) and Dennis Lee's "Cadence, Country, Silence" (1973). The group of artists and writers in favour of the agreement (including Mordecai Richler, Ken Danby, Robert Fulford, and 59 other signatories) wrote: "There is no threat to our national identity anywhere in the Agreement. Nor is there a threat to any form of Canadian cultural expression. As artists and writers we reject the suggestion that our ability to create depends upon the denial of economic opportunities to our fellow citizens. What we make is to be seen and read by the whole world. The spirit of protectionism is the enemy of art and thought" (qtd. in Davey 12). By "rejecting a materialist analysis of artistic activity," Frank Davey argues that the pro-free trade signatories share an open competition theory of art. In looking for the "open playing field" of internationalism, then, the pro-free trade artists signalled their belief in universal aesthetics rising above national borders; while the anti-free trade artists, and politicians, held on to the need to protect Canada as a nation. In this pitting of aesthetics against nationalism, one can see traces of A.J.M. Smith's categorization of "native" and "cosmopolitan" art from 1943. It also connects with the notorious "CanCon" requirements that were imposed on Canadian broadcasters in the late 1960s by the Canadian Radio-television and Telecommunications Commission (CRTC).

The free trade debate took place in the midst of another important discussion about the fate of Canada. After the patriation of the Constitution in 1982, Quebec remained outside the Canadian "constitutional family" because it felt that the new Constitution would hamper its ability to preserve and promote Quebec's distinct culture. Mulroney's Progressive Conservative Party formed a majority government in 1984 with a promise to bring Quebec back into the constitutional fold. Negotiations culminated in an agreement to amend the Constitution, dubbed the Meech Lake Accord. "Meech" addressed Quebec's principal demands, including a recognition of Quebec as a "distinct society." However, the importance of the changes meant that all provincial legislatures had to vote in favour of the amendments. In 1990, near the end of the three-year limit for this approval, the process unravelled, with a committee recommending more changes and a schedule for future rounds of negotiation on other constitutional matters. Many Canadians, especially First Nations people, agreed with Newfoundland Premier Clyde Wells when he objected that the process for constitutional reform was faulty because decisions were made between the 11 first ministers in secrecy behind closed doors, rather than through public consultation. Ultimately, Elijah Harper, a Cree chief and member of the Manitoba Legislative Assembly, insisted on a full debate in the Manitoba legislature, effectively killing the Accord by making it impossible for Manitoba to ratify it before the deadline. The eagle feather Harper held up to stall ratification became a symbol of peaceful resistance.

The sense of rejection in Quebec was reinforced by the formation in 1990 of the Bloc Québécois, a federal separatist party, by former Conservative cabinet minister Lucien Bouchard; it was seen by the Mulroney government as an urgent threat to national unity. Almost immediately, Mulroney took steps to generate another proposal, but one that emerged from a much more inclusive process of public consultation. The result was the Charlottetown Accord, which included most of what was in the Meech Lake Accord, plus a broader definition of Canada—the "Canada Clause"—to appear in section 1 of the Constitution, a clearer role for Aboriginal peoples in future amendments, and reform of the Senate. Most importantly, it was to be approved by all Canadians in a referendum in October 1992. Despite support by the major political parties, a majority of Canadians found something to object to. The Charlottetown Accord referendum result was 54.3% for the No side, with a clear rejection in Quebec and the four western provinces.

Many commentators concluded that the constitutional demands of Quebec and the west were irreconcilable. Quebeckers came within a whisker of making this final in the 1995 Quebec referendum. As in 1980, Quebeckers had a choice: to remain in Canada or begin negotiations to become a sovereign nation. In the final hours of the campaign, with busloads of non-Quebeckers (who could not vote in the referendum) travelling to Montreal to show their support of Quebec within Canada, Chrétien made a passionate plea for patriotism (see Figure VII-2). He asked Quebeckers: "Do you really want to turn your back on Canada? Does Canada deserve that?" and "Have you found one reason, one good reason, to destroy Canada?" (Televised Address to Canadians, 25 October 1995). Playing on a love of the country and the economic consequences for Quebec if it chose to separate, Chrétien's words were only barely successful. The final vote was 50.58% in favour of Quebec remaining part of Canada. No federal government since 1993 has made a serious attempt to restart constitutional negotiations.

Quebec was not the only constituency that wanted reform during this period. Frustration with the slow progress of land claim negotiations and self-government agreements led some First Nations people to take more vigorous political action in a number of contexts. The most prominent manifestation of this frustration occurred in the summer of 1990 when Mohawk residents of the Kanesatake reserve near Oka, Quebec, set up a blockade to prevent the extension of a golf course into "The Pines," land they claimed as a traditional burial ground (see Figure VII-1). The "Oka Crisis" standoff lasted nearly three months and claimed the life of a Sûreté du Québec officer. Mohawk Warriors,[2] wearing army fatigues, bandanas, and balaclavas, stood up first to Quebec police officers and subsequently to members of the Canadian Forces (deployed by the federal government to take down the barricades). For one tense summer—78 days of confrontations and negotiations—members of the community of Kanesatake decided to "take a stand against people taking their land" (kanesetake.com). Despite high tension between Canadian soldiers and

---

[2] According to Taiaiake Alfred and Lana Lowe in "Warrior Societies" (2005): "Contrary to the militaristic and soldierly associations of the term in European languages—and in common usage—the word translated from indigenous languages as 'warrior' generally has deep and spiritual meaning. This deeper sense is exemplified, to use one example, in the English-Kanienkeha translation *rotiskenhrakete*, which literally means, carrying the burden of peace" (6).

the Mohawk people, what could have been a bloodbath was averted by both sides. Other, similar standoffs between police/government and Aboriginal groups at Ipperwash, Ontario (where protester Dudley George was shot and killed by an Ontario Provincial Police officer); Caledonia, Ontario; Burnt Church, New Brunswick; and Gustafson Lake, B.C., are clear reminders that many First Nations people are still fighting the legacy of the Indian Act and are getting impatient with the pace of change.

The word "Oka" has come to stand for the conflicts over land rights and land use in Canada. Such conflicts ultimately go back hundreds of years and concern the interpretation of treaties, property law, and historical negotiations. "Oka" has also become a rallying cry for Native self-determination. Lenore Keeshig-Tobias's essay "After Oka—How Has Canada Changed?" calls Oka an event "to be reckoned with" (Moses and Goldie 258). Similarly, Beth Cuthand's poem "Post-Oka Kinda Woman" positions Oka as a turning point from which Native people have emerged proud and powerful, ready to claim an active place in contemporary society yet not willing to settle for less than their due. Cuthand's "Post-Oka" woman rejects the "victimization, reparation/degradation, assimilation" that are part of the "plight of Native Peoples" (262). She is an audacious figure who combines contemporary material culture ("drives a Toyota, reads bestsellers") with traditional practices ("Sings old songs, gathers herbs") (262–63). Many First Nations writers have expressed "post-Oka" positions of discomfort with the pace of negotiations and have written forceful works of protest and assertions of identity, particularly in the 1990s. Armand Garnet Ruffo argues in his essay "Why Native Literature?" that it is necessary to "come to some understanding of the position in which many Native writers see themselves in relation to their work, their people and Canadian society at large" (663). They are, according to Ruffo, "a people under siege . . . who write literature as a call for liberation, survival and beyond to affirmation" (663, 664). Okanagan writer Jeannette Armstrong's essay in this anthology speaks to such a need for empowerment through writing. Part of this recognition of Aboriginal perspectives has involved seeing Canada in historical terms and acknowledging its status as a "settler-invader society," a history that has had long-lasting ramifications for the descendants of those whose land was invaded. In keeping with this project, many contemporary non-Indigenous scholars and writers have engaged with critic Len Findlay's call to "always indigenize," or to carefully consider the colonial frameworks of contemporary institutional structures.[3]

---

[3] Literary and cultural works have been potent venues for Indigenous authors to pursue these expressions of affirmation. In an era when all publishers in Canada are battling for survival, the success of three Indigenous-centred presses marks their significance in the cultural field for many contemporary artists: Theytus Books (1980) and Kegedonce Press (1993) are operated by Native publishers for Native writers. Pemmican Publications (1990) is dedicated to Métis writers and subjects. Other active writers, storytellers, and artists of this period are Cree playwright and novelist Tomson Highway, Cherokee/Greek writer and academic Thomas King, Anishinaabe poet Marie Annharte Baker and playwright Drew Hayden Taylor, Inuit poet and artist Alootook Ipellie, Delaware poet and playwright Daniel David Moses, Haisla-Heiltsuk writer Eden Robinson, Salish and Cree author Lee Maracle, Cree poet Louise Bernice Halfe, Métis artist Rosalie Favell, and Métis poets Marilyn Dumont and Gregory Scofield, among many others.

The post-1985 period has also seen significant movement with land claims settlements. For example, the Nisga'a Treaty was negotiated in the 1980s and '90s between the Nisga'a people, the B.C. government, and the government of Canada. Under the treaty, the Nisga'a own approximately 2,000 square kilometres of land, an amount that greatly exceeds the small reserve allocated by the colonial government. Chief Dr. Joseph Gosnell, president of the Tribal Council of the Nisga'a, made the following "Address from the Bar of the House" in the B.C. legislature, 2 December 1998, citing the Treaty as an example of how a modern society can correct the errors of the past. The speech provides a counterpoint to the words of previous generations, such as those of Deskaheh in his last radio address arguing the necessity of settling land claims (see Volume I, Section IV):

> It's a triumph because under the treaty, we will no longer be wards of the state, no longer beggars in our own land. . . . We will once again govern ourselves by our own institutions but within the context of Canadian law. . . . The treaty proves beyond all doubt that negotiations—not lawsuits, not blockades, not violence—are the most effective, honourable way to resolve aboriginal issues in this country. It's a triumph, I believe, that signals the end of the Indian Act, the end of more than a century of humiliation, degradation and despair for the Nisga'a nation. (Hansard 10859–10860)

Gosnell's speech is not only about triumph. He also painstakingly outlines the distant and recent history of treaty negotiations, pointing specifically to the Supreme Court of Canada's decision in 1973, the Calder case, that Aboriginal title existed prior to Confederation. This, he reminds us, initiated the modern-day process of land claims negotiations. The Nisga'a Treaty was passed into law in the spring of 2000.

Another important change to the Canadian political landscape came in 1999 with the creation of the Territory of Nunavut (ᓄᓇᕗᑦ) (the Inuktitut word for "our land") as a result of the Nunavut Land Claims Agreement (initiated in 1973). Often cited as a success story of contemporary government-Indigenous relations, Nunavut abounds with optimism in its public documents. According to the Government of Nunavut website, "[G]overnment, business and day-to-day life are shaped by Inuit *Qaujimajatuqangit*, the traditional knowledge, values and wisdom of Nunavut's founding people," drawing attention to the fact that of its 29,500 residents, 85% of the population is Inuit. Premier Paul Okalik speaks in particularly optimistic terms of the expectation of significant development in the North over the next decades, making the links between cultural and economic prosperity clear, but he also expresses a desire for more territorial control of natural resources.

The development of natural resource industries has long been a contentious subject in Canada. Since the turn of the millennium, environmental issues and the fear of the effects of global warming have led to the "greening" of public discourse. However, federal and provincial environmental review processes have sometimes clashed. The decline in fisheries stocks (leading to the Atlantic cod moratorium), worries over the softwood lumber dispute, concerns over large-scale hydroelectric projects, problems of provincial and federal oil and gas revenue sharing, and uncertainty in agriculture all illustrate the significance of resource management and the interconnections between government regulations, the state of the environment, and the economy. Former American vice-president Al Gore's 2006 film *An Inconvenient Truth*, Karsten Heuer's film and book *Being Caribou* (2005), and David Suzuki's ongoing voice, including that in *The Sacred Balance* (with Amanda McConnell, 1997) and *Tree: A Life* (with Wayne Grady, 2004), have had a massive impact on drawing the public's attention to the existence of global warming. Once again we are reminded of the need to move beyond borders on this topic. Environmentalists argue that Canada must act in concert with nations around the world to address the most pressing environmental issues: greenhouse gas emissions, climate change, energy use, food production and food sovereignty, the banning of toxic substances, and the protection of water, forests, and oceans. As part of this move to "think globally, act locally," there has also been a trend toward embracing the local in food (with Alisa Smith and J.B. MacKinnon's "100-mile diet") and locally produced products in order to lesser each person's "ecological footprint" (a term coined by Canadian geographer William Rees).

In fiction, Chef Jeremy Papier, the protagonist of Timothy Taylor's novel *Stanley Park* (2001), exemplifies this trend back to the local, as The emphasizes his preference for locally grown ingredients and his desire to try "to remind people of something. Of what the soil under their feet has to offer. Of a time when they would have known only the food that their own soil could offer" (23). The increase in environmental awareness has led in cultural terms to a resurgence in writing about nature. Though reminiscent of the prevalence of nature writing in the late nineteenth century and again in the 1970s, the approach now differs considerably. There is no longer an inward-looking Romantic "back-to-the-earth" philosophy. The concern now is about what happens after nature has been changed irreparably as a result of human intervention/disturbance, as in Don McKay's poem "Après Chainsaw" and his essay "Baler Twine." McKay, Tim Lilburn, Roo Borson, Christopher Dewdney, Adam Dickinson, Robert Bringhurst, and Rita Wong, among many others, are contemporary poets who engage with nature in ways that re-imagine humans' place in, and responsibility toward, the nonhuman world. Literary critics have responded to these and other authors, contributing to the growth of a field known as "ecocriticism," an interdisciplinary approach that foregrounds environmental (and ecological) concerns by considering the interconnections between nature and its human inhabitants, between social, cultural, and environmental actions. While in many ways extensions of, and responses to, such works as Atwood's *Survival*, D.G. Jones' *Butterfly on Rock*, and Dennis Lee's *Savage Fields*, more recent studies announce their place within an ongoing tradition of ecocritical research.[4] A linked area of study that has developed over the past few decades is that of ecofeminism: a social and

[4] These newer works include D.M.R. Bentley's *The Gay]Grey Moose: Essays on the Ecologies and Mythologies of Canadian Poetry, 1690–1990* (1992), W.H. New's *Land Sliding: Imagining Space, Presence, and Power in Canadian Writing* (1997), Diana Relke's *Greenwor(l)ds: Ecocritical Readings of Canadian Women's Poetry* (1999), and Laurie Ricou's *Salal: Listening for the Northwest Understory* (2007).

political movement that attempts to unite environmentalism and feminism. Identifying a relationship between the oppression of women and the degradation of nature, ecofeminists emphasize connections between sexism, power imbalances, and the domination of the natural world.

Alongside Canadian engagements with nature and the environment, Canadian multiculturalism—often phrased in terms of a cultural "mosaic"— has come to be one of the first things people, both in Canada and abroad, highlight as definitive of Canadian identity. The multiculturalism policy was introduced by Prime Minister Pierre Trudeau's Liberal government in October of 1971 (see the introduction to Section VI and the headnote to the Multiculturalism Act in this section), and the subsequent act of law was passed in 1988. "Official multiculturalism" has drawn substantial criticism from those arguing that it is a good policy in principle but that the practice falls short. The criticisms tend to focus on the faulty idealism of the government programs and what is viewed as too great an emphasis on what cultural and legal theorist Stanley Fish has called "boutique multiculturalism." Sociologist-poet Himani Bannerji describes multiculturalism as "management through racialization" (9), while Toronto cultural theorist Rinaldo Walcott critiques multiculturalism by arguing that it "reduces cultures to their basic denomination, which turns them into folklore" (*Rude* 43). Short stories such as Austin Clarke's "Canadian Experience" and Rohinton Mistry's humorous allegory of non-assimilation, "Squatter," both included in this anthology, contain explicit critiques of the policy for its commitment to cultural issues at the expense of social and economic ones. Neil Bissoondath's *Selling Illusions: The Cult of Multiculturalism in Canada* (1994) was one of the most notorious denunciations of multiculturalism during this period (see the excerpt included here). In it, Bissoondath argues that multiculturalism has had a divisive influence and has fostered intolerance between Canadians of different backgrounds. More recently, in their book *Selling Diversity* (2002), political scientists Yasmeen Abu-Laban and Christina Gabriel argue that the Canadian government uses multiculturalism as a selling feature of Canada in the current global market. Multiculturalism, they claim, is not an ideal but a marketing tool for global trade and international big business, as well as a convenient means of promoting an idealized version of Canada internationally. A very different approach comes from political philosopher Charles Taylor, who discusses multiculturalism as the recognition of the equal value of different cultures (see the excerpt from his essay "The Politics of Recognition").

Those who support multiculturalism as an effective tool for minority groups tend to focus on the programs themselves. Acknowledging the criticism of official multiculturalism from artistic communities, George Elliott Clarke concedes that "multiculturalism in Canada may have been promulgated as a means of trying to gloss over issues of race, language, and class; but I think that writers and artists in Canada have been able to take advantage of the policy, and to continue to promote it as a means of getting their works out to the public as well as a means of establishing their cultural presences within their work" (102). He advocates working around the system. It is clear that the multicultural policy (specifically the funding linked to the Writing and Publications Program) has been a significant factor in the development of a diverse Canadian literature over the past decades.

Tracing the Shifts in Literary Production, Criticism, and Theory

In the late 1980s and early 1990s, literary criticism in Canada, as elsewhere, showed the influence of many international developments in literary and cultural theory. This era is often referred to in terms of the "deconstructive turn," an allusion to some of the major philosophical developments of this period that sought to interrogate inherited histories and philosophical belief systems. Many of these philosophers and critics were writing in the 1960s, but it took some time before their ideas filtered into the critical mainstream (and, in some cases, before they were translated into English). Theoretical approaches such as poststructuralism, deconstruction, feminism, queer theory, Marxism, psychoanalysis, postmodernism, new historicism, postcolonialism, and diaspora theory became dominant, and hotly debated, modes of literary analysis.[5] Two innovative collections of Canadian literary criticism, *Future Indicative: Literary Theory and Canadian Literature* (1987) and *Canada: Theoretical Discourse* (1994), demonstrated some of the shifts in Canadian literary studies. Literary criticism in Canada pointed in two, sometimes overlapping, directions: deconstructive readings of textual play and allusion (whether it be Marxist, psychoanalytic, deconstructive, or feminist), and interpretations overtly concerned with issues of social awareness, history, and ethics (critical race theory, postcolonialism, feminism, gender studies). Both of these groups demonstrated a break from the thematic criticism of the 1970s (see Section VI) in that they rejected the quest for coherence that motivated the thematic approach in favour of models that aimed to read for "contradiction" (to use Heather Murray's phrase from her 1987 essay "Reading for Contradiction in the Literature of Colonial Space").

Since 1985, the study of Canadian literature has developed in four interwoven ways. First, the literature itself has developed along the lines of the demographic shifts in Canada. In the 2006 census, 16.2% of Canadians identified themselves as

---

[5] Such texts as Michel Foucault's *The Order of Things* (1970), Hayden White's *Metahistory* (1973) and *Tropics of Discourse* (1978), Jacques Derrida's *Of Grammatology* (1976) and *Writing and Difference* (1978), Jacques Lacan's *Écrits* (1977), Terry Eagleton's *Marxism and Literary Criticism* (1976), Edward Said's *Orientalism* (1978) and *Culture and Imperialism* (1993), Fredric Jameson's *The Political Unconscious* (1981) and *Postmodernism, or The Cultural Logic of Late Capitalism* (1991), bell hooks's *Ain't I a Woman?* (1981), Mikhail Bakhtin's *The Dialogic Imagination* (1981), Benedict Anderson's *Imagined Communities* (1983), Jean-François Lyotard's *The Postmodern Condition* (1984), Luce Irigaray's *This Sex Which Is Not One* (1985), Stephen Greenblatt's *Shakespearean Negotiations* (1988), Homi Bhabha's *Nation and Narration* (1990) and *The Location of Culture* (1994), and Judith Butler's *Gender Trouble* (1990) had an enormous influence on the study of English literature worldwide. The dates in this list refer to the first English translation.

"visible minorities," with the largest groups being South Asian Canadian and Chinese Canadian. This is an increase of almost 10% since the 1986 census (from 6.3%). With an increase in immigration from Africa, South Asia, the Caribbean, South America, and Asia, there has been both a desire for opening up the Canadian literary canon and an expansion of the people and texts identified as Canadian, as well as the beginning of a critical mass of theorists, critics, and teachers who were immigrants themselves and who have added to literary debates about Canadian writing from multiple perspectives. In this period there has been a sense of urgency among many critics and writers about the need for pluralizing the concept of "Canadianness." Writers born outside Canada such as Michael Ondaatje, Rohinton Mistry, Anita Rau Badami, M.G. Vassanji, Thomas King, Carol Shields, and Dionne Brand have become as central to the Canadian canon—and the business of "CanLit"—as writers born in Canada like Margaret Atwood, Alice Munro, Nino Ricci, Tomson Highway, Wayne Johnston, and Miriam Toews.

Second, there has been a noticeable increase in interest in the after-effects of colonialism in Canada, especially with the growing awareness of the legacies of Canada's invader-settler history. Many contemporary Canadian writers have explored this history in literary form; such texts as Highway's *Kiss of the Fur Queen*, John Steffler's *The Afterlife of George Cartwright*, Margaret Sweatman's *When Alice Lay Down with Peter*, Jane Urquhart's *Away*, and Michael Crummey's *River Thieves* are a few examples. Third, though not unconnected to the second, there has been renewed interest in historical research as it applies to Canadian writing, an interest influenced by the approach known as New Historicism, especially the work of such notable American critics as Stephen Greenblatt and Hayden White. In Canada, critics such as Heather Murray, D.M.R. Bentley, Tracy Ware, Nick Mount, and Carole Gerson have made important contributions that tease out the complexities of precise historical moments in Canada's past, including the major three-volume *History of the Book in Canada* initiative.

Fourth, many people currently working in the Canadian literary community are committed to the integration of literary studies and community activism. Smaro Kamboureli reminds us of "how history, ideology, method, pedagogy, capital economies, cultural capital, institutional and social structures, community, citizenship, advocacy, racialization, indigeneity, diaspora, and globalization are all intricately related to CanLit and its complex, often tortuous, trajectories" (*Trans.Can.Lit* xv). Writer-critics such as Roy Miki, Daphne Marlatt, Fred Wah, Rita Wong, Lisa Robertson, Dionne Brand, Larissa Lai, Jeff Derksen, Erín Moure, Ashok Mathur, and David Chariandy, among many others, have combined activism and artistic intervention in various forms of proactive public involvement. Wong's poetry collection *forage* (2007), for example, engages with issues of ecological crisis and global politics, while Moure's *O Cidadán* (2002), like Yann Martel's novel *The Life of Pi* (2001), explores the notion of a global citizenship.

The rise in literary theory has had a clear impact on discussions of canonization, the question of which literary works come to be validated over time and why. These debates were raging in England and the United States during the 1980s and '90s because there, too, people were wondering if the canon replicated a limited sense of aesthetic value that served certain interests. A central question in these debates was whether there was such a thing as "literary excellence" and by what standards that could be judged. For Robert Lecker in "The Canonization of Canadian Literature" (1990), nationalist imperatives informed an institutionally constructed canon that held a "conservative, yet profound desire for unity, community, coherence, authority, [and] place" (671). Critics such as Frank Davey, Lorraine Weir, Barbara Godard, Imre Szeman, Arun Mukherjee, and Terry Goldie highlighted their increasing unease with categorizing Canadian literature into a singular recognizable national canon. One of the main calls for the opening up of the canon came from those writers and critics who saw Canadian literature as either patriarchal or racially and ethnically exclusive, or both. The silencing these critics were worried about was not so much the silencing of experimental genres that Lecker argued against, but rather the silencing of women and ethnic minorities.

In keeping with these kinds of inquiries, there has been substantial work done by scholars, activists, and artists in this period to address issues of sexuality, violence against women,[6] unequal labour markets, and normative gender expectations in contemporary discussions of Canadian literature. Further, sexuality and homosexuality, links between gender and ethnic communities, regional affiliation and gender, performance and the body, have all become major issues in literary and critical texts. Studies such as Smaro Kamboureli's *A Mazing Space* (1986), Lorraine McMullen's *Re(Dis)covering Our Foremothers* (1990), and Peter Dickinson's *Here Is Queer* (1999) give some sense of the wide range of feminist- and gender-based work being done in the field of Canadian literature. Further, periodicals such as *Tessera* (begun in order to publish the theoretical and experimental writing of Québécois and English-Canadian feminist writers) and *Fireweed*, and book publishers like Women's Press and Gynergy Press, have shown a continued commitment to feminist scholarship in Canada. One key publisher during this period was Press Gang, a feminist collective active from 1970 to 2002 that published important work by SKY Lee, Ivan E. Coyote, Daphne Marlatt, Betsy Warland, and Rita Wong, among other important activist women writers of the period.

---

[6] A misogynist event that shocked the nation during this period was the "Montreal Massacre" of 6 December 1989, when 14 women, mostly engineering students at Montreal's École Polytechnique, were killed by a 25-year-old man who targeted most of them precisely because they were women in a non-traditional field. Soon, mourning for the murdered women turned into recognition of and outrage about violence against women. December 6 remains an annual day of remembrance and acknowledgement of abuse in Canada.

During this time, the gender issues central to the 1960s and '70s women's movement, what has been described as "White liberal feminism," came under censure when some women were critiqued for speaking for all women regardless of racial or class positioning. This in turn led to another kind of call for the opening of the Canadian literary canon to include voices of racial and ethnic minorities as well as women's voices. Accordingly, the national identity that dominated the 1960s and '70s (formed around ideas of Canadian identity based on endurance, survival, isolation, and victimization) was displaced in the 1980s and then again in the 1990s by concerns over who is included and excluded in such conceptions of the nation. By this point it was no longer perceived as philosophically responsible (or economically tenable) to exclude the contributions of some Canadian writers (because of where they were born or whether or not they wrote about Canadian places and characters) in an attempt to create a cohesive vision of a national imaginary.

While Canadian cultural nationalism in a literary sense began as a means of distinguishing a specifically Canadian artistic ethos in an emergent culture (a move beyond "derivative mediocrity," as F.R. Scott and A.J.M. Smith had described it in 1928), its entrenchment by the 1970s meant that it needed to be updated to reflect the realities of contemporary Canadian demographics and artistic production. Literary theory followed suit and postcolonial criticism emerged, first in concert with the study of Canada in the framework of "World Literature Written in English" or Commonwealth studies, and subsequently with critical race theory and theories of diaspora. A postcolonial approach—with its focus on colonial legacies, hybridity, marginalization, language, cultural politics, and power inequities—is evident in a number of important literary and critical works that situate postcolonial discourse in a Canadian framework.[7]

Postcolonial criticism emerged out of the identity politics and "discourse analysis" of the previous decades (most obviously, Edward Said's untangling of the colonialist language of "orientalism" in his 1978 book of that title). This emphasis on discourse (language representation systems) and semiotics (symbolic representation systems) informed the textual analysis of much feminist, Marxist, and postcolonial theory of this period, both in Canada and elsewhere. Of particular concern has been an exploration of the intricate ways that knowledge and power are mutually constituted, a phenomenon that formed the central tenet of the work of French theorist Michel Foucault.

---

[7] See, for example, Leslie Monkman's *A Native Heritage* (1981), Terry Goldie's *Fear and Temptation* (1989), Sylvia Söderlind's *Margin/Alias* (1991), Julia Emberley's *Thresholds of Difference* (1993) and *Defamiliarizing the Aboriginal* (2007), Christl Verduyn's *Literary Pluralities* (1998), Arun Mukherjee's *Postcolonialism: My Living* (1998), Jonathan Kertzer's *Worrying the Nation* (1998), Roy Miki's *Broken Entries* (1998), Smaro Kamboureli's *Scandalous Bodies* (2000), Helen Hoy's *How Should I Read These?* (2001), Renée Hulan's *Northern Experience and the Myths of Canadian Culture* (2002), Laura Moss's *Is Canada Postcolonial?* (2003), Jennifer Henderson's *Settler Feminism and Race Making in Canada* (2003), and Cynthia Sugars's *Unhomely States* (2004) and *Home-Work* (2004).

Interrogations of the ways the "nation" had been used to police and order certain systems of knowledge, and to render only particular stories or histories acceptable, has been central in current discussions of Canadian writing. If in a global context an important postcolonial move had been to "write back" to the British Empire, in Canada this took the form of "writing back" to the nation and validating the numerous voices that had not been allowed to contribute to national identity-making (voices of women, gays and lesbians, Aboriginal peoples, and immigrant communities). Thus, in the 1980s and 1990s, the emphasis on national identification that was characteristic of the 1970s shifted toward an increased focus on discrete elements of personal identity: race, ethnicity, gender, sexuality, class, and region. The strategic emphasis on one or two of these elements as central to identity formation led in part to the emergence of distinct branches of literary analysis (queer theory, disability studies, and diaspora theory, for instance). It also resulted in the demand by various groups for state recognition and the redress of histories of oppression. Art joined forces with political activism, carrying the axiom "the personal is political" into literary, cultural, and historical debates.

The Appropriation of Voice Debate and the "Writing Thru Race" Conference

In the late 1980s and early 1990s, one of the central critical discussions in public discourse amongst writers and critics concerned the issue of "appropriation of voice." Linked in larger theoretical terms to Gayatri Chakravorty Spivak's groundbreaking essay "Can the Subaltern Speak?" (1988), the question emerged in Canada of whether it was acceptable for a non-Indigenous person to write from an Indigenous perspective. The debate arose when some writers, such as Lenore Keeshig-Tobias (in a *Globe and Mail* article of 26 January 1990), urged non-Native authors to "stop stealing Native stories." In response to Farley Mowat's many depictions of the Arctic and W.P. Kinsella's stories about the "Hobbema Indian Reserve," for instance, some Aboriginal writers argued that it was time for Native authors to have a chance to "tell their own stories" for themselves. Keeshig-Tobias contextualizes the debate in terms of the larger framework of Indigenous peoples' rights in Canada: "With native people struggling for justice with land claims and in education, what makes Canadians think they have equality in the film industry? In publishing? With agencies that make arts grants? In the arts themselves?" M. NourbeSe Philip usefully defines appropriation "to mean the abuse of power by one group in exploiting indiscriminately, *for their own economic advantage*, the cultural resources of other groups" and concludes that the "real issue in Canada is the systemic racism in the publishing industry" (qtd. in "Voice" 15). Arguing for a kind of affirmative action in order to achieve such systemic equality, some people declared that it was time for those who had long been in positions of cultural power to step aside and let minority writers speak for themselves as a matter of cultural survival. This position was responded to by those who cried that artistic freedom was being curtailed and that limiting Native stories to Native writers (or minority stories to minority writers, more generally) was a form of censorship. Rather than thinking of these two positions as oppositional, it is perhaps more useful to think of individual responses lying on a continuum of responses to the very difficult juggling of artistic production and cultural responsibility.

The continuum spans many positions articulated in a key article published in *Books in Canada* (Jan/ Feb 1991) entitled "Whose Voice *Is* It, Anyway?" that places at stake "questions of imaginative freedom and authorial responsibility central to the development of a truly multicultural national literature." In this article, a number of writers articulate their positions:

> George Bowering: James Baldwin's *Giovanni's Room* . . . was the first novel openly about homosexual life that I had ever read. . . . It did not strike me as anything but interesting that the author was Black while the main characters were white. (11)

> Daniel David Moses: Native people should tell Native stories. Why has such a simple statement been the cause of controversy? (15)

> M.G. Vassanji: How easy it is to cry 'Censorship!' or 'Art is universal!' and then sit back smugly—and safely. Many people . . . surely agree that it cannot be divorced from histories of oppression—colonialism, slavery, even genocide. There are many peoples whose stories have not been told while stories of those who dominated them have been stuffed down their throats ad nauseam. (16–17)

One of the most vocal opponents of the charge of appropriation of voice was author Timothy Findley. His 28 March 1992 letter to the *Globe and Mail* aligns the anti-appropriation argument with fascism. As he points out, he had frequently written in "voices" not his own: a murderer's (*The Last of the Crazy People*), a cat's (*Not Wanted on the Voyage*), a woman's (*The Telling of Lies, Headhunter, The Piano Man's Daughter*). In Findley's view, such strictures on artistic freedom were part of the authoritarian program that he had spent his life trying to oppose. While the debate is no longer as heated as it was in the 1990s, the question of how to balance artistic freedom and political responsibility to subject matter is still very prominent.

Alongside the "appropriation of voice" debate, one moment stands out as pivotal in the development of more diverse and racially aware literature in Canada. In 1994 "Writing Thru Race: A Conference for First Nations Writers and Writers of Colour" was a controversial national writers' conference sponsored by The Writers' Union of Canada and chaired by poet-critic Roy Miki. Designed to be a safe space to discuss issues of race and racism in Canadian literature and literary production, it confronted topics such as unfair publishing practices and the presence of systemic racism in academic and non-academic book reviews. The conference was to have daytime events open only to "writers of colour" and First Nations writers, and evening sessions open to the general public.

The massive debate sparked by the decision of the organizers to have separate cultural spaces at "Writing Thru Race" was unprecedented in the development of literature and culture in Canada. Responses ranged from full support of the notion of separate spaces, based on a feminist principle of empowerment through strategic consolidation, to vehement criticism of the conference. The controversy centred on the fact that public funding had been used to support a conference that was viewed by some as discriminatory. The government responded to the controversy by withdrawing its support from the conference. In turn, the Writers' Union was outraged by what it saw as the government's failure to stand by its policy of multiculturalism and its commitment to affirmative action as defended in the Charter of Rights. The conference went ahead with emergency funds raised by those who supported the event.

Historiographic Metafiction and Narrating the Nation

One of the prevalent trends in fiction in the post-1985 period has been the narrating of history in fictionalized forms. In *The Canadian Postmodern* (1988), Linda Hutcheon focused on the way in which Canadian literature proliferates with works of fiction that retell historical events in a self-reflexive, and questioning, manner. Such fascination with historical fiction has been identified by Hutcheon as a characteristic Canadian genre. "Historiographic metafiction" is Hutcheon's term for this trend in Canadian postmodern writing (with "historiography" referring to the act of narrativizing factual events into stories and "metafiction" indicating the self-referential nature of writing fiction about the processes of writing, reading, and interpreting fiction [13–14]). This genre of writing seeks to call into question official versions of history, destabilize power structures, and adhere to the postmodern notion of maintaining an "incredulity toward metanarratives," as Jean-François Lyotard put it.

In the 1970s and early '80s there had already been an interest in revising accepted historical narratives (including national metanarratives); this approach is evident in works such as Rudy Wiebe's novel *The Temptations of Big Bear* (1973), Timothy Findley's *The Wars* (1977), and Joy Kogawa's *Obasan* (1981), which "wrote back" to received histories by telling stories from marginalized perspectives. In recent years, however, there has been a marked resurgence of historical fiction in Canada, especially novels that look back to the foundational periods of Canadian history.[8] A genre related to historiographic metafiction is the generational novel, which tells stories of real and fictional families—effectively expanding conceptions of Canadian

[8] For example, Brian Moore's *Black Robe* (1985), Daphne Marlatt's *Ana Historic* (1988), John Steffler's *The Afterlife of George Cartwright* (1992), Bernice Morgan's *Random Passage* (1992), Jane Urquhart's *Away* (1993), Rudy Wiebe's *A Discovery of Strangers* (1994), Margaret Atwood's *Alias Grace* (1996), Guy Vanderhaeghe's *The Englishman's Boy* (1996), Wayne Johnston's *The Colony of Unrequited Dreams* (1998), Fred Stenson's *The Trade* (2000), Michael Crummey's *River Thieves* (2001), Margaret Sweatman's *When Alice Lay Down with Peter* (2001), George Elliott Clarke's *George & Rue* (2005), Lawrence Hill's *The Book of Negroes* (2007), Alice Munro's *The View from Castle Rock* (2006), and Roy MacSkimming's *Macdonald* (2007) fall into this category.

history and "identity" by following the stories of multiple generations in Canada.[9] Dionne Brand's *What We All Long For* (2005) illustrates the sentiments of the Canadian children of immigrants well: "They all . . . felt as if they inhabited two countries—their parents' and their own—when they sat dutifully at their kitchen tables being regaled with how life used to be 'back home'" (20). The culturally diverse community of characters in Brand's novel explores the nature of identity, longing, and belonging as contemporary history is narrated in terms of multi-generational family stories rather than national epics.

In a different framework, over this period there have also been a number of notable oral history projects that record non-fictional stories that do not normally figure as part of official versions of history and community narratives. The publication of Harry Robinson's *Write It on Your Heart* (1989) marks a significant moment in the retelling of history during this period. The book is a compilation of stories told by Okanagan storyteller Harry Robinson to an academic named Wendy Wickwire. Their collaboration created a written text that reflects the oral nature of Robinson's stories. The storyteller was keenly interested in preserving the stories of the past because "it was the one way to leave his people with [a] testament to their past" (15). Wickwire notes how she searched for a "presentation style to capture the nuance of the oral tradition—the emphasis on certain phrases, intentional repetition, and dramatic rhythms and pauses" (16) and settled on a form that visually resembles poetry rather than the more conventional method of transcribing stories in prose form. The book is an example of what critic Susan Gingell calls "textualizing orality," or presenting oral stories in written form by trying to mimic the cadence, form, and syntax of the spoken words. In an interview with CBC Radio host Peter Gzowski, writer Thomas King is vocal in his gratitude to Robinson:

> I couldn't believe the power and the skill with which Robinson could work up a story—in English: they weren't translated, they were simply transcribed— and how well he understood the power of the oral voice in a written piece . . . I could see what he had done and how he worked it and I began to try to adapt it to my own fiction. It was inspirational—I don't use that word very often, because I think it's so badly misused—but I remember sitting in my office, just sort of sweating, reading this stuff: it was so good. (72)

King is not alone in being influenced by Robinson's eloquent stories. The textualizing of Indigenous oral traditions has become a key element of contemporary Native literatures.

---

[9] Mordecai Richler's *Solomon Gursky Was Here* (1989), SKY Lee's *Disappearing Moon Café* (1990), Nino Ricci's *Lives of the Saints* (1990), Wayson Choy's *The Jade Peony* (1995), Fred Wah's *Diamond Grill* (1996), Janice Kulyk Keefer's *Honey and Ashes* (1998), Lawrence Hill's *Any Known Blood* (1997), David Macfarlane's *The Danger Tree* (2000), Aimée Laberge's *Where the River Narrows* (2003), Anita Rau Badami's *Can You Hear the Nightbird Call?* (2006), and David Chariandy's *Soucouyant* (2007) tell the stories of multiple generations of families in Canada.

Performance poets take the presentation of the oral and the written in another direction. Foremost in contemporary Canadian "spoken word" poetry are people like Christian Bök, Shane Koyczan, rob mclennan, and Sheri-D Wilson. Dub poetry, spoken word over reggae rhythms, is another fundamental element of the contemporary Canadian poetry scene. Dub poetry originated in Jamaica and England in the late 1970s, though Toronto now has the second most active dub poetry community in the world, led by the dynamic Dub Poets Collective: Lillian Allen (*Psychic Unrest*, 1999), Afua Cooper (*Worlds of Fire: In Motion*, 2006), Clifton Joseph (*Metropolitan Blues*, 1983), and d'bi.young.anitafrika (*rivers . . . and other blackness . . . between us*, 2008), among them. Allen in particular is at the forefront of spoken word poetry in Canada, having issued her first recording, *Dub Poet: The Poetry of Lillian Allen*, in 1983 and having won a Juno Award for *Revolutionary Tea Party* in 1986. Dub is concerned with social and political justice, is anchored firmly in a strong sense of history underscored by a communal sensibility, and is focused on racial, and sometimes gender, equality. Dub poets will often appear on stage with musical accompaniment composed specifically for the poems. Wayde Compton is another poet who joins technology and "black Englishes" as he overlays turntable recordings of his own poetry with live performances of his work. He focuses on how "elements of ancient, non-literate, vestigial African culture [can] be blended directly into textual poetry, and both [can] be blended back into hip hop" as a way to "carry orality forward" through the "manipulation of received sound and received culture" (8).

Many contemporary writers play with language in order to articulate cultural distinctiveness. Writers such as Maria Campbell, George Elliott Clarke, Marilyn Dumont, Dionne Brand, M. NourbeSe Philip, and Rohinton Mistry, to name some of the writers included in this anthology, manipulate language to reflect both context and culture. In *The Empire Writes Back* (1989), postcolonial theorists W.D. Ashcroft, Gareth Griffiths, and Helen Tiffin show how writers undermine the hegemony of Received Standard English through two strategies: "abrogation," or the "refusal of the categories of the imperial culture, its aesthetic, its illusory standard of a normative or 'correct' usage, and its assumption of a traditional and fixed meaning 'inscribed' in words" (38); and "appropriation," or the "process by which the language is taken and made to bear the burden of one's own cultural experience" (38–39). Such processes include refusing to gloss untranslated words, the fusion of linguistic structures of two distinct languages, and the use of local idiom and vernacular speech. This assertion of identity through language reinforces poet Derek Walcott's notion that "no language is neutral." In the Canadian context, it has been important for First Nations and minority writers to assert cultural and political sovereignty through abrogated language usage.

The (International) Roles of Canadian Literature

Timothy Taylor's novel *Stanley Park* contains a powerful critique of unthinking celebrations of consumerized (and consumable) globalization. When one of the characters describes Jeremy Papier's restaurant as "International Groove," Jeremy is quick to object:

> "We're more than that," Jeremy said. . . . "We're beyond international. Beyond globalized. We aren't the restaurant of *all* places—Europe and Africa, Asia and the Americas. This is *not* fusion. We are the restaurant of *no* place. We belong to no soil, no cuisine, to no people, to no culinary morality. We belong only to those who can reach us and understand us and afford us. Gerriamo's is post-national. . . . Post-National Groove Food." (365)

When Jeremy is compelled by his financial backer, the owner of a multinational coffee chain, to adhere to market forces and create Gerriamo's, a restaurant geared to trends rather than based on beliefs, he cooks one of the most memorable (and subversive) meals in Canadian writing: raccoon, dandelion greens, rock doves, and squirrel from Vancouver's Stanley Park. Taylor's sharp satire on the popular desire for fusion food and culture serves up anti-globalization on a plate. Taylor satirizes the unthinking trendiness of post-nationalism in an era of increased globalization and points out what is lost in "no place."

Economic globalization arises out of the unfettered growth of markets and transnational corporations, the abolition of trade barriers, and the dismantling of special interest groups (Bothwell 523). In *Many Globalizations*, Peter Berger outlines its contradictions: "For some, it implies the promise of an international civil society, conducive to a new era of peace and democratization. For others, it implies the threat of an American economic and political hegemony, with its cultural consequence being a homogenized world resembling a sort of metastasized Disneyland" (2). Clearly in the latter camp, massive anti-globalization protests in Seattle in 1999 and Quebec City in 2001, among other locations around the globe, saw protesters argue that multinational corporations often held more power than democratically elected governments. They also strongly criticized the poor working conditions and low wages of employees of corporations in Third World countries that bolstered artificially low prices in the First World. In the spirit of Marshall McLuhan's *Understanding Media* (1964), Naomi Klein's wildly popular journalistic manifesto *No Logo* (2000) and Joel Bakan's *The Corporation* (2004) stand out as key texts in highlighting what they see as the problems of globalization, the failings of a neo-liberal agenda, and the pathology of corporations. While Klein and Bakan are both Canadian, their work has purchase in contemporary left-wing America as well.

As part of the context of the globalization of culture, the Canadian government is eager to capitalize on the popularity and economic success of Canadian literature and other arts abroad. An online publication of the Department of Foreign Affairs entitled "Canada World View: As Others See Us," packages the arts as integral components of "Canada's global brand" because "Canada's credibility in the cultural arena strengthens all aspects of our country's international relations" ("World"). The image of Canada branded for export is one of "quirky" individuality and transcultural harmony. In short, through its art and literature,

Canada is being branded as "culturally progressive" and such progress helps in the country's international relations as well as in the business of marketing culture.

Canadian literature has never been produced in a national vacuum. Canadian writers have been keenly informed about international literary and cultural movements for centuries, and many moved to the United States, France, and England for part of their careers. However, although Canadian writers have long viewed themselves as part of international movements—as was true of the post-Confederation poets, the modernists, and the 1960s/70s generation—international audiences have not always reciprocated. Over the last three decades a wider range of Canadian writing has reached a broader audience and become more and more internationally celebrated. No one was surprised when Alice Munro, Margaret Atwood, and Michael Ondaatje were among the 15 authors on the shortlist for the 2007 Man Booker International Prize—the literary honour recognizing a fiction writer's entire body of work. These three writers had been garnering international attention for years. To be placed in the company of the best writers in the world—writers such as Chinua Achebe, the winner of the 2007 prize, Salman Rushdie, Peter Carey, Ian McEwan, and Doris Lessing—is not unusual for contemporary Canadian writers. It is not too long ago, however, that such a feat would have been considered impossible and would have elicited a chuckle from literary elites. The international reception of Canadian literature has changed dramatically in the wake of the success of works by Munro, Atwood, Ondaatje, Carol Shields, Rohinton Mistry, Anne Michaels, and Yann Martel, among others.[10] These novelists have won international prizes such as the Booker/Man Booker, the Commonwealth Writers' Prize, the Orange Prize, and the International IMPAC Dublin Award, as well as Canadian prizes such as the Governor General's Award and the Giller Prize. Some books, such as Ondaatje's *The English Patient*, have been made into Academy Award-winning films, and others have been showcased on Oprah Winfrey's television book club. These authors are joined in international recognition and book sales by Douglas Coupland—who popularized the term "Generation X" in his 1991 novel of that title and who has remained ahead of the curve with such novels as *All Families Are Psychotic* (2001) and *jPod* (2006)—and William Gibson, who coined the term "cyberspace" in his 1984 science fiction novel *Neuromancer*. Besides Gibson, younger writers of speculative fiction are also thriving on the international stage. The work of Candas Jane Dorsey, Robert Charles Wilson, and Nalo Hopkinson sits alongside science fiction and fantasy by Robert J. Sawyer, Sean Stewart, and Guy Gavriel Kay in global markets.

---

[10] See Munro's *Open Secrets* (1994) and *The View from Castle Rock* (2006); Atwood's *The Blind Assassin* (2000) and *Oryx and Crake* (2003); Ondaatje's *The English Patient* (1992) and *Divisadero* (2007); Carol Shields's *The Stone Diaries* (1993) and *Larry's Party* (1997); Rohinton Mistry's *A Fine Balance* (1995) and *Family Matters* (2002); Anne Michaels's *Fugitive Pieces* (1998); and Yann Martel's *The Life of Pi* (2001), among others that have won international awards.

Canada's global brand sells in domestic markets as well. The popularity of Canadian literature within Canada is clearly evident in the number of weeks Canadian books now spend on the bestseller lists and the success of cultural events such as CBC Radio's annual literary book contest "Canada Reads." The show has tapped into the increasing recognition of Canadian literature locally and the growing popularity of Canadian literature globally. Running annually since 2002, the success of the week-long book club mirrors the rise in popularity of book clubs in Canada and around the world. Five celebrity panellists each champion a book that they think Canadians should read. The success of the radio program illustrates the degree to which Canadian literature has become a part of public discourse. Not long ago it would have been unimaginable to sell more than 80,000 copies of a Canadian novel within Canada in a single year (as was the case after Ondaatje's *In the Skin of a Lion* won the "Canada Reads" competition in 2002) or to have thousands of people vote (online) for a single novel as the People's Champion (as was the case with Mistry's *A Fine Balance* in 2002). Certainly, the "Canada Reads" contest has helped to solidify a popular understanding of the quantity and quality of works of Canadian literature. It is also important in the way it has helped the expansion of a public readership and recirculated works of Canadian literature in the popular limelight (Paul Quarrington's 1988 novel *King Leary* was out of print before writer and Rheostatics singer Dave Bidini nominated it for the 2008 "Canada Reads," which it won). The "Canada Reads" canon is an eclectic mixture of books from an eclectic mixture of writers. It is one, among many, examples of the pluralization of the Canadian literary canon that has been occurring since the 1970s.

Now, well into the twenty-first century, literature can help track the shifting conceptualizations of Canada and its constituent parts. Diana Brydon reminds us of the "need to rethink Canadian literature beyond older forms of nationalism and internationalism, and toward multiscaled visions of place— local, regional, national, and global—each imbricated within the other. Writers and critics are rethinking relations of place, space, and non-place in ways that complicate understandings of where and how the nation fits. They are not transcending nation but resituating it" (*Trans.Can.Lit* 14–15). This, it seems, is the continued mandate for the next period of Canadian letters.

FIGURE VII-1 Oka, Quebec, 1 September 1990
This photograph from the "Oka Crisis" captures a faceoff between Pte. Patrick Cloutier, a Canadian Forces perimeter sentry, and Mohawk Warrior Brad Larocque, a University of Saskatchewan economics student. Over 78 days of confrontation and negotiation in the tense summer of 1990, Mohawks guarded a blockade set up to prevent the extension of a golf course into land they claimed as a traditional burial ground. Mohawk Warriors—wearing army fatigues, bandanas, and balaclavas—stood up first to Quebec police officers and subsequently to members of the Canadian Forces (deployed by the federal government to take down the barricades). Despite the tension and intractability of the Canadian soldiers and the Mohawk people, captured in this image, what could have been a bloodbath was averted by both sides.

Source: CP PHOTO/Shaney Komulainen

FIGURE VII-2 "We love you/Pas cette fois-ci, j'ai mal à la tête! ('Not right now, I have a headache!')" (1995)

This political cartoon by Serge Chapleau appeared in the run-up to the fall 1995 Quebec referendum. The referendum question asked if Quebec should secede from Canada and "become sovereign, after having made a formal offer to Canada for a new economic and political partnership" or remain within the federation. Because non-Quebeckers couldn't vote, they resorted to other measures to show solidarity for keeping Quebec within Canada. In the last days of the campaign, the federalists organized a "we love you" rally in Montreal. Busloads of Canadians went to Montreal to declare their support of the province. In this cartoon, the show of "love" by Canada is satirically met with the classic cold shoulder. The margin of victory for the No side was minuscule: 50.56% voting "No" to separation from Canada and 49.44% voting "Yes" to beginning negotiations for sovereignty.

Source: "We love you!/Not right now, I have a headache!"; Serge Chapleau,
1995, 20th century; M998.51.207; © McCord Museum

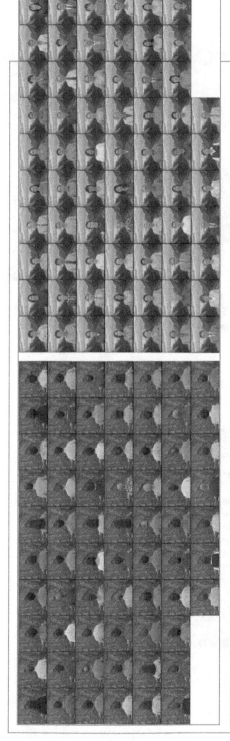

FIGURE VII-3 *A Group of Sixty-Seven* (framed C-print, 1996), Jin-Me Yoon (1960–)

In the 134 frames of her 1996 installation entitled *A Group of Sixty-Seven*, Vancouver artist Jin-Me Yoon updates and populates Canadian landscape portraiture. In one compilation of 67 frames, 67 figures stand with their backs to the audience looking at a detail of Emily Carr's painting *Old Time Coast Village*. In the collage presented here, 67 people of Korean heritage pose in front of Lawren Harris's 1924 painting *Maligne Lake, Jasper Park*. Playing with the name of Harris's "Group of Seven" art movement and the significance of the 1967 centenary as a moment of national self-articulation (including Expo 67), the installation is a powerful reconfiguration of the Canadian landscape to include the heterogeneity of Canadians. The installation subverts the expectations of conventional landscape art as it draws on now iconic images to comment on contemporary Canadianicity.

Source: Jin-me Yoon, *A Group of Sixty Seven*, 1996; chromogenic print; Collection of the Vancouver Art Gallery Acquisition Fund, VAG 97.2 a-eeeee; Photo: Trevor Mills, Vancouver Art Gallery

FIGURES FOR SECTION VII

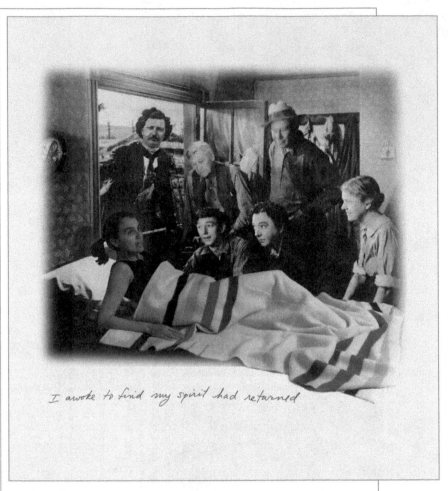

I awoke to find my spirit had returned

FIGURE VII-4 "*I awoke to find my spirit had returned*" **(giclée print, 1999),**
Rosalie Favell (1958–)
This image, from Rosalie Favell's *Plain(s) Warrior Artist* series, now in the Winnipeg Art
Gallery, is an adaptation of a scene from the film *The Wizard of Oz* (1939). In her work, Favell
digitally manipulates images from Métis history, mass media, and family albums. Here the
Dorothy character (in colour), a self-portrait of Favell, looks up from under a colourful
Hudson's Bay trading blanket (with the recognizable HBC stripes), while the family (film characters depicted in black-and-white) huddled around the bed are joined by Métis leader Louis
Riel looking in through the window in the spot where the wizard stands in the original *Wizard
of Oz* scene. The caption alludes to Riel's purported statement that Native people would rise
to prominence 100 years after his death. The photo has an uncanny effect as it is unclear
whether the black-and-white figures are benevolent or malign; the expression on the
woman's face highlights this ambiguity. The mix of colour and black-and-white plays on the
overlayering of dream and reality that is prevalent in the film, making it unclear which portion
of the photo, if any, is "real." Favell turns this iconic Hollywood image into a commentary on
Métis history, while also ironizing it, by drawing on the parodic conjunction of the figures in
"Kansas" and the Canadian prairies.

Source: Rosalie Favell, *I awoke to find my spirit had returned*, from the series
Plain(s) Warrior Artist, 1999; giclée print on paper 118.5 × 87.0 cm

FIGURE VII-5 Thomas King as the Lone Ranger (photograph, 2001), Thomas King (1943–)

This photograph of Thomas King seated beside a drum, in front of a movie poster for *Navajo*, wearing a bolo tie, a cowboy hat, and a Lone Ranger mask is a cheeky self-portrait. King summons various props of Indigeneity and humorously subverts the expectations that accompany the mask of the famous hero of "Cowboy and Indian" westerns. Ironically, the Lone Ranger was accompanied by an Aboriginal sidekick (Kemosabe), who in the original film series gives the Lone Ranger his legendary identity and fashions his mask; here, it is the Aboriginal person who assumes the more empowered position of the Lone Ranger. King also parodies the long tradition of anthropological photographers like Edward Curtis, who, as King says in his "Artist's Statement," in the nineteenth century "took along boxes of Indian para-phernalia (blankets, wigs, etc.) in case he ran into Indians who didn't look Indian enough." One in a series of photographs taken by King of Native artists donning the Lone Ranger mask, it begs the viewer to consider the relationship between the Cowboy and the "Indian" and to wonder who is really behind the costume. This satrical use of the Lone Ranger iconography also occurs in King's 1993 novel, *Green Grass, Running Water*.

Source: Thomas King

The Canadian Multiculturalism Act was passed in Parliament in 1988 under Prime Minister Brian Mulroney's government, enshrining multiculturalism in Canadian law. However, the concept was actually brought into the public domain 17 years before. On 8 October 1971, Prime Minister Pierre Elliott Trudeau introduced the multiculturalism policy in Parliament. It was unanimously supported by all political parties. In his introduction of the policy to the House of Commons, Trudeau famously announced: "Although there are two official languages, there is no official culture, nor does any ethnic group take precedence over any other." So multiculturalism within a bilingual framework was born.

The policy was meant to address the concerns of the "third" order of Canadians who were not of English or French origin (or Native—because Aboriginal affairs were treated under the auspices of the Indian Act, multiculturalism did not include Indigenous Canadians in 1971), and to preserve "the cultural freedom of Canadian citizens and landed immigrants." The effect in 1971 was to distance Canada from its colonial roots. The multiculturalism policy was said, by some critics, to have come out of Trudeau's desire to downplay the power of Quebec as a nation within Canada by making it just one of many ethnic communities. The government argued that it promoted the new approach to national identity through the (limited) financial support of "ethnocultural programs" as a way to increase all Canadians' sense of belonging.

Since the introduction of the policy in 1971, multiculturalism has been embraced by many Canadians as a distinctive part of English-Canadian identity. It has also been sharply criticized as overly idealistic, with some calling it superficial state sponsorship of cultural pluralism. Certainly it is part of the reality of Canadian demographics: in the 2006 census, more than 200 different ethnic origins were reported, and 11 ethnic origins passed the one-million population mark. Interestingly, the largest group enumerated by the census consisted of just over 10 million people who identified their ethnic ancestry as Canadian, either alone or with other origins.

In recent years, government support of multiculturalism has shifted from cultural issues to social ones. The priorities of the government's multiculturalism program were stated in 2005 as 1) fostering cross-cultural understanding; 2) combatting racism and discrimination; 3) promoting civic participation; and 4) making Canadian institutions more reflective of Canadian diversity. The long-term strategic objective of official multiculturalism at present is to have "Canadians living in an inclusive society built on intercultural understanding and citizen participation." Official multiculturalism has inspired much debate (see the introduction to this section for additional details), including such diverse commentaries as Neil Bissoondath's *Selling Illusions* (1994) and philosopher Charles Taylor's "The Politics of Recognition" (1992), as well as Austin Clarke's short story "Canadian Experience" (1986), Rohinton Mistry's "Squatter" (1987), and Fred Wah's *Diamond Grill* (1996).

From The Canadian Multiculturalism Act, 1988

An Act for the preservation and enhancement of multiculturalism in Canada

MULTICULTURALISM POLICY OF CANADA

3. (1) It is hereby declared to be the policy of the Government of Canada to

   (a) recognize and promote the understanding that multiculturalism reflects the cultural and racial diversity of Canadian society and acknowledges the freedom of all members of Canadian society to preserve, enhance and share their cultural heritage;

   (b) recognize and promote the understanding that multiculturalism is a fundamental characteristic of the Canadian heritage and identity and that it provides an invaluable resource in the shaping of Canada's future;

   (c) promote the full and equitable participation of individuals and communities of all origins in the continuing evolution and shaping of all aspects of Canadian society and assist them in the elimination of any barrier to that participation;

   (d) recognize the existence of communities whose members share a common origin and their historic contribution to Canadian society, and enhance their development;

   (e) ensure that all individuals receive equal treatment and equal protection under the law, while respecting and valuing their diversity;

   (f) encourage and assist the social, cultural, economic and political institutions of Canada to be both respectful and inclusive of Canada's multicultural character;

   (g) promote the understanding and creativity that arise from the interaction between individuals and communities of different origins;

   (h) foster the recognition and appreciation of the diverse cultures of Canadian society and promote the reflection and the evolving expressions of those cultures;

   (i) preserve and enhance the use of languages other than English and French, while strengthening the status and use of the official languages of Canada; and

   (j) advance multiculturalism throughout Canada in harmony with the national commitment to the official languages of Canada. [. . .]

[1988]

CHARLES TAYLOR ■ (1931–)

Political philosopher and noted public intellectual Charles Taylor is known for his communitarian critique of liberal theory's understanding of the "self." Educated at McGill University and Oxford, Taylor combines Anglo-American and continental philosophies to address problems in epistemology, ethics, language, multiculturalism, religion and secularism, and most recently, the "reasonable accommodation" debate in Quebec. In *Sources of the Self: The Making of the Modern Identity* (1989), he emphasizes the significance of social and communal institutions to the development of individual identity, arguing that moral questions must be understood as informed by particular communities' norms and practices. Speaking from within the context of Quebec, Taylor has been a strong advocate of both cross-cultural understanding and federalism (he ran unsuccessfully for a seat in Parliament for the NDP four times, most famously losing to Pierre Trudeau in 1965).

In his influential article "The Politics of Recognition" (1992), Taylor's inquiry into multiculturalism hinges on the notion that identity is shaped by recognition or, more damagingly, the absence of recognition of cultural distinctiveness. Drawing on arguments about Quebec's status as a "distinct society," Taylor criticizes the dominance of a narrowly rights-based liberalism (or "difference-blind liberalism"). According to Taylor, such liberalism is inhospitable to difference in that it is suspicious of collective goals and insists on uniformity in the application of rules defining rights. Such suspicion means that this kind of liberalism cannot "accommodate what members of distinct societies really aspire to, survival." Taylor argues that many societies contain more than one cultural community that wants to survive, and are thus multicultural. He posits that nonrecognition or misrecognition of distinction is a form of oppression that can lead to real harm, when what is actually required is an acknowledgement of another's worth. Presenting a midway point between what he maintains is the homogenizing demand for equal worth on one hand and "self-immurement within ethnocentric standards," on the other, Taylor suggests the need for a

willingness to be open to comparative cultural studies. He also advocates a fusion of horizons of meaning (one's background of social and dialogical relations with others) that might grow out of recognizing the qualitative contrast between cultures. Taylor's position has sparked a range of responses from such notable philosophers as Kwame Anthony Appiah, Michael Walzer, Amy Gutman, and, particularly, Canadian philosopher of multiculturalism Will Kymlicka. His work has had an impact on discussions of multiculturalism around the world and has been translated into Spanish, Dutch, Italian, German, French, Japanese, and Turkish.

Drawing on his previous work on multiculturalism, Taylor joined sociologist and historian Gérard Bouchard in 2007–08 to lead the Commission de consultation sur les pratiques d'accommodement reliées aux différences culturelles (known as the Bouchard-Taylor Commission), holding public hearings investigating Quebec's current position on the "reasonable accommodation" of minorities and immigrants. The Commission spent a year interviewing Quebeckers on their views about immigration and the importance of, and the best method for, the protection of cultural and religious communities. It concluded that "interculturalism" is preferable to multiculturalism in Quebec because, it argues, the Canadian multiculturalism model is not well suited to conditions in the Quebec context. The Commission identified four reasons for this: "a) anxiety over language is not an important factor in English Canada; b) minority insecurity is not found there; c) there is no longer a majority ethnic group in Canada (citizens of British origin account for 34% of the population, while citizens of French-Canadian origin make up a strong majority of the population in Québec, i.e., roughly 77%); d) it follows that in English Canada, there is less concern for the preservation of a founding cultural tradition than for national cohesion." In short, the Commission concluded, old and new Quebeckers share the responsibility to adapt to each other's fundamental values. The philosophical basis of multiculturalism in Canada continues to be under scrutiny in Quebec and the rest of Canada.

From The Politics of Recognition

A number of strands in contemporary politics turn on the need, sometimes the demand, for *recognition*. The need, it can be argued, is one of the driving forces behind nationalist movements in politics. And the demand comes to the fore in a number of ways in today's politics, on behalf of minority or "subaltern" groups, in some forms of feminism and in what is today called the politics of "multiculturalism."

The demand for recognition in these latter cases is given urgency by the supposed links between recognition and identity, where this latter term designates something like a person's understanding of who they are, of their fundamental defining characteristics as a human being. The thesis is that our identity is partly shaped by recognition or its absence, often by the *mis*recognition of others, and so a person or group of people can suffer real damage, real distortion, if the people or society around them mirror back to them a confining or demeaning or contemptible picture of themselves. Nonrecognition or misrecognition can inflict harm, can be a form of oppression, imprisoning someone in a false, distorted, and reduced mode of being.

Thus some feminists have argued that women in patriarchal societies have been induced to adopt a depreciatory image of themselves. They have internalized a picture of their own inferiority, so that even when some of the objective obstacles to their advancement fall away, they may be incapable of taking advantage of the new opportunities. And beyond this, they are condemned to suffer the pain of low self-esteem. [. . .] Recently, a similar point has been made in relation to indigenous and colonized people in general. It is held that since 1492 Europeans have projected an image of such people as somehow inferior, "uncivilized," and through the force of conquest have often been able to impose this image on the conquered. The figure of Caliban[1] has been held to epitomize this crushing portrait of contempt of New World aboriginals.

Within these perspectives, misrecognition shows not just a lack of due respect. It can inflict a grievous wound, saddling its victims with a crippling

---

[1] In William Shakespeare's *The Tempest* (1611), Caliban is the character indigenous to the island that the European characters are cast upon in a shipwreck and is turned into their slave. In the play he is meant to be the savage Other to the figures of European civilization, but he has been recuperated in the past decades as a symbol of imperial subjugation. As such, Caliban has also been held up to show the subversive potential of language in the colonial encounter when he vituperatively remarks to his "master" Prospero, "You taught me language, and my profit on't is, I know how to curse." However, he does not gain power beyond the curse and thus demonstrates the limitations of speech.

self-hatred. Due recognition is not just a courtesy we owe people. It is a vital human need. [...]

The importance of recognition is now universally acknowledged in one form or another; on an intimate plane, we are all aware of how identity can be formed or malformed through the course of our contact with significant others. On the social plane, we have a continuing politics of equal recognition. Both planes have been shaped by the growing ideal of authenticity, and recognition plays an essential role in the culture that has arisen around this ideal.

On the intimate level, we can see how much an original identity needs and is vulnerable to the recognition given or withheld by significant others. It is not surprising that in the culture of authenticity, relationships are seen as the key loci of self-discovery and self-affirmation. Love relationships are not just important because of the general emphasis in modern culture on the fulfillments of ordinary needs. They are also crucial because they are the crucibles of inwardly generated identity.

On the social plane, the understanding that identities are formed in open dialogue, unshaped by a predefined social script, has made the politics of equal recognition more central and stressful. It has, in fact, considerably raised the stakes. Equal recognition is not just the appropriate mode for a healthy democratic society. Its refusal can inflict damage on those who are denied it, according to a widespread modern view, as I indicated at the outset. The projection of an inferior or demeaning image on another can actually distort and oppress, to the extent that the image is internalized. Not only contemporary feminism but also race relations and discussions of multiculturalism are undergirded by the premise that the withholding of recognition can be a form of oppression. [...]

And so the discourse of recognition has become familiar to us, on two levels: First, in the intimate sphere, where we understand the formation of identity and the self as taking place in a continuing dialogue and struggle with significant others. And then in the public sphere, where a politics of equal recognition has come to play a bigger and bigger role. Certain feminist theories have tried to show the links between the two spheres.

I want to concentrate here on the public sphere, and try to work out what a politics of equal recognition has meant and could mean.

In fact, it has come to mean two rather different things, connected, respectively, with the two major changes I have been describing.[2] With the move from honor to

---

[2] Taylor argues that there are two changes that make the modern preoccupation with identity and recognition inevitable: honour and dignity. He uses honour "in the *ancien régime* sense in which it is intrinsically linked to inequalities" whereby for some to attain honour, it is essential that others must lack it. In the Canadian context, Taylor explains the concept in terms of public awards such as the Order of Canada, an award that has significance because of its rarity. Conversely, dignity is meant to be shared by every human being and the term is now used in a universalist and egalitarian sense. What drives this notion of dignity is the view that in a democratic society, everyone should be entitled to share in "human dignity" and "citizen dignity." Taylor uses the example of the decline of titles in front of surnames to indicate class positioning. He explains that forms of equal recognition are essential to democratic society: using "Mr." or "Ms." is more democratic than using "Lord" and "Lady" on one hand, or simply a surname (indicating lower class status than the speaker), on the other.

dignity has come a politics of universalism, emphasizing the equal dignity of all citizens, and the content of this politics has been the equalization of rights and entitlements. What is to be avoided at all costs is the existence of "first-class" and "second-class" citizens. Naturally, the actual detailed measures justified by this principle have varied greatly, and have often been controversial. For some, equalization has affected only civil rights and voting rights; for others, it has extended into the socioeconomic sphere. People who are systematically handicapped by poverty from making the most of their citizenship rights are deemed on this view to have been relegated to second-class status, necessitating remedial action through equalization. But through all the differences of interpretation, the principle of equal citizenship has come to be universally accepted. Every position, no matter how reactionary, is now defended under the colors of this principle. Its greatest, most recent victory was won by the civil rights movement of the 1960s in the United States. It is worth noting that even the adversaries of extending voting rights to blacks in the southern states found some pretext consistent with universalism, such as "tests" to be administered to would-be voters at the time of registration.

By contrast, the second change, the development of the modern notion of identity, has given rise to a politics of difference. There is, of course, a universalist basis to this as well, making for the overlap and confusion between the two. *Everyone* should be recognized for his or her unique identity. But recognition here means something else. With the politics of equal dignity, what is established is meant to be universally the same, an identical basket of rights and immunities; with the politics of difference, what we are asked to recognize is the unique identity of this individual or group, their distinctness from everyone else. The idea is that it is precisely this distinctness that has been ignored, glossed over, assimilated to a dominant or majority identity. And this assimilation is the cardinal sin against the ideal of authenticity.

Now underlying the demand is a principle of universal equality. The politics of difference is full of denunciations of discrimination and refusals of second-class citizenship. This gives the principle of universal equality a point of entry within the politics of dignity. But once inside, as it were, its demands are hard to assimilate to that politics. For it asks that we give acknowledgment and status to something that is not universally shared. Or, otherwise put, we give due acknowledgment only to what is universally present—everyone has an identity—through recognizing what is peculiar to each. The universal demand powers an acknowledgment of specificity. [. . .]

Similar conflicts arise today around the politics of difference. Where the politics of universal dignity fought for forms of nondiscrimination that were quite "blind" to the ways in which citizens differ, the politics of difference often redefines nondiscrimination as requiring that we make these distinctions the basis of differential treatment. So members of aboriginal bands will get certain rights and powers not enjoyed by other Canadians, if the demands for native self-government are finally agreed on, and certain minorities will get the right to exclude others in order to preserve their cultural integrity, and so on. [. . .]

These two modes of politics, then, both based on the notion of equal respect, come into conflict. For one, the principle of equal respect requires that we treat people in a difference-blind fashion. The fundamental intuition that humans command this respect focuses on what is the same in all. For the other, we have to recognize and even foster particularity. The reproach the first makes to the second is just that it violates the principle of nondiscrimination. The reproach the second makes to the first is that it negates identity by forcing people into a homogeneous mold that is untrue to them. This would be bad enough if the mold were itself neutral—nobody's mold in particular. But the complaint generally goes further. The claim is that the supposedly neutral set of difference-blind principles of the politics of equal dignity is in fact a reflection of one hegemonic culture. As it turns out, then, only the minority or suppressed cultures are being forced to take alien form. Consequently, the supposedly fair and difference-blind society is not only inhuman (because suppressing identities) but also, in a subtle and unconscious way, itself highly discriminatory.

[. . .] The issue came to the fore because of the adoption in 1982 of the Canadian Charter of Rights, which aligned our political system in this regard with the American one in having a schedule of rights offering a basis for judicial review of legislation at all levels of government. The question had to arise how to relate this schedule to the claims for distinctness put forward by French Canadians, and particularly Quebeckers, on the one hand, and aboriginal peoples on the other. Here what was at stake was the desire of these peoples for survival, and their consequent demand for certain forms of autonomy in their self-government, as well as the ability to adopt certain kinds of legislation deemed necessary for survival.

For instance, Quebec has passed a number of laws in the field of language. One regulates who can send their children to English-language schools (not francophones or immigrants); another requires that businesses with more than fifty employees be run in French; a third outlaws commercial signage in any language other than French. In other words, restrictions have been placed on Quebeckers by their government, in the name of their collective goal of survival, which in other Canadian communities might easily be disallowed by virtue of the Charter.[3] The fundamental question was: Is this variation acceptable or not? [. . .]

This brings us to the issue of multiculturalism as it is often debated today, which has a lot to do with the imposition of some cultures on others, and with the assumed superiority that powers this imposition. [. . .]

---

[3] Taylor's note: The Supreme Court of Canada did strike down one of these provisions, the one forbidding commercial signage in languages other than French. But in their judgment the justices agreed that it would have been quite reasonable to demand that all signs be in French, even though accompanied by another language. In other words, it was permissible in their view for Quebec to outlaw unilingual English signs. The need to protect and promote the French language in the Quebec context would have justified it.

Recognition of equal value was not what was at stake—at least in a strong sense—in the preceding section [about Quebec]. There it was a question of whether cultural survival will be acknowledged as a legitimate goal, whether collective ends will be allowed as legitimate considerations in judicial review, or for other purposes of major social policy. The demand there was that we let cultures defend themselves, within reasonable bounds. But the further demand we are looking at here is that we all *recognize* the equal value of different cultures; that we not only let them survive, but acknowledge their *worth*. [. . .]

There must be something midway between the inauthentic and homogenizing demand for recognition of equal worth, on the one hand, and the self-immurement within ethnocentric standards, on the other. There are other cultures, and we have to live together more and more, both on a world scale and commingled in each individual society.

What there is is the presumption of equal worth I described above: a stance we take in embarking on the study of the other. Perhaps we don't need to ask whether it's something that others can demand from us as a right. We might simply ask whether this is the way we ought to approach others. [. . .]

There is perhaps after all a moral issue here. We only need a sense of our own limited part in the whole human story to accept the presumption. It is only arrogance, or some analogous moral failing, that can deprive us of this. But what the presumption requires of us is not peremptory and inauthentic judgments of equal value, but a willingness to be open to comparative cultural study of the kind that must displace our horizons in the resulting fusions. What it requires above all is an admission that we are very far away from that ultimate horizon from which the relative worth of different cultures might be evident. This would mean breaking with an illusion that still holds many "multiculturalists"—as well as their most bitter opponents—in its grip.

[1992]

CAROL SHIELDS ■ (1935–2003)

Upon publication, Carol Shields's novel *The Stone Diaries* (1993) won enthusiastic praise, not the least of which came in a review in the *New York Times*: "The Stone Diaries reminds us again why literature matters." Such praise was not always the case. At the beginning of her writing career, Shields was often overlooked, criticized, or, worse, patronized, for writing about the daily lives of women. Shields once remarked that she was initially compelled to write stories, in the mid-1970s, because she couldn't find any novels about the women she knew or about women's friendships and inner lives. As a woman who "elected a writing life," Shields was interested in "writing away the invisibility of women's lives, looking at writing as an act of redemption." Like that of Margaret Laurence, Bronwen Wallace, Rohinton Mistry, and Alice Munro, Shields's work explores the practice of everyday life and uncovers stories that lie within the ordinary worlds of regular people. More often than not, Shields's characters are intimately drawn figures who move through the day with a naked vulnerability. Shields's first four novels—*Small Ceremonies* (1976); *The Box Garden* (1977); *Happenstance* (1980); and *A Fairly Conventional Woman* (1982)—are "quite traditional" in form, as Shields puts it. With *Swann: A Mystery* (1987), a satire of the world of academic criticism, her novels become more unconventional, and playful, particularly in narrative perspective. With her final three novels—*The Stone Diaries, Larry's Party* (1997), and *Unless* (2002)—Shields reached a wide popular audience and garnered international acclaim (winning the Pulitzer Prize, the Governor General's Award, and the Orange Prize).

Shields's fiction often shares with poetic imagism a focus on precise, concentrated images and an emphasis on clearing away the clutter in language. Her stories regularly emerge from a single image, provocatively stated—a man carrying a mango in his left hand, a woman buying her daughter a scarf, or a bank teller fantasizing about an empty baby stroller. In her essay "Narrative Hunger and the Overflowing Cupboard," Shields argues that we all search for stories everywhere. She asks us to think of the small narrative in the grade-school arithmetic problem (Mary Brown buys four pounds of cheese at five dollars a pound) that "leaves us tugging at a narrative thread—who is this Mary Brown, and what will she do with that cheese? What of her wider life, her passions and disappointments?"

Working through the "inaccessible stories of others," Shields published, in addition to poetry and drama, nine novels, three collections of stories, and two works of literary criticism (on the nineteenth-century settler Susanna Moodie and on English writer Jane

Austen). "Weather," published in *Dressing Up for the Carnival* (2000), is one of that collection's "what if" stories (what if meteorologists went on strike, what if Roman ruins were found in southern Manitoba, what if the letter "I" was missing from all the words in a story about a missing "I" on a typewriter). Shields expands the "what if" premise to show human consequences.

Born in Oak Park, Illinois, Shields attended Nathaniel Hawthorne Public School and Ralph Waldo Emerson Public School (both named after canonical American writers) and so, she says, it took her some time to displace the notion that important writers were the bearded men pictured in the school hallways, who were safely dead. While on a student exchange from Hanover College at the University of Exeter, she met her future husband Donald Shields. After she graduated from Hanover with a B.A., they were married and she immigrated to Canada, his homeland. Together the couple had five children. While the family lived in Ottawa, Shields obtained an M.A. from the University of Ottawa with a thesis on Moodie. She later taught in that department. The family finally settled in Winnipeg when Donald Shields took up a position in the Faculty of Engineering at the University of Manitoba. In the years that followed, Shields raised her family and began to write in earnest. She also held the positions of lecturer and professor at the University of Manitoba, working alongside writer-critics Robert Kroetsch, Dennis Cooley, and David Arnason. In 1997 she took up the post of Chancellor at the University of Winnipeg. In her honour, the City of Winnipeg established the Carol Shields Winnipeg Book Award, which was given out for the first time in 2000. After retiring to Victoria in 2000, Shields died of breast cancer in 2003.

Weather

My husband came home from work in a bad mood. There'd been a sudden downpour as he was driving in the direction of our village, and the rain, as usual, found its way into the distributor of his ancient car. Twice he'd had to stop at the side of the road, raise the hood, and apply a rag to the distributor cap.

His shirt was soaked by the time he came muttering up the back steps into the house, and his hair, what remains of it, was plastered to his head, exaggerating his already petulant look. To make matters worse, he'd heard on the car radio that the National Association of Meteorologists was going on strike the following day.

I cheered him up as best I could and fed him a hot meal even though it was the height of summer, his favourite braised lamb chops with mint sauce, the mint coming fresh from our own garden, that wild strip running along the side of the garage. "Never mind about the strike," I said, "it'll only last a day or two."

How wrong I was!

We kept tuned to the radio as the hours passed, but learned little more. Heated discussions were taking place, that was all we were told. For some reason these talks were kept highly secret. Conducted behind closed doors. Hush-hush.

"They're stuck on wages, I bet," my husband said. "This world of ours is getting greedier every year."

He likes to think he is above ordinary greed and materialistic longing, and he is. The neighbours are forever trading in their lawn mowers for bigger and better models, or investing in swimming pools, which he believes are pretentious and foolish, though I myself would be happy to think about installing a small concrete pool next to the porch, a glint of turquoise water meeting my eye as I glance out the window in the early morning; even a goldfish pond would give a kind of pleasure.

He cares nothing about such luxuries. He has his job at the plant nursery, his decent-though-troublesome car, his paid-for house, his vegetable garden, and he has a glassed-in porch from which he can watch the side-yard trees as they bend in the wind, a sight that never fails to rouse his spirits. I think— indeed he confided this to me in one of our rare tender moments—that he likes to imagine the immensity of the trees' root systems, plunging downward beneath the surface of the complacent lawn, then branching sideways, and adding foot by fibrous foot to a complex network of tentacles that grab at the earth's clumped particles, securely anchoring the great oaks and maples, never mind how rambunctious the wind gets, never mind the weather warnings. Roots, he said to me the evening we had this strange conversation, perform the job they're designed to do, no more, no less. They don't take time off for coffee and a smoke, and they don't bellyache about remuneration. (You need to understand that my husband is the sort of man who appreciates a high degree of application and tenacity. He wishes that his fellow human beings were just as dutiful and as focused in their day-to-day lives as he himself is.)

The first twenty-four hours of the strike stretched to forty-eight and then seventy-two. My own opinion was that the meteorologists were holding out for a better pension plan. Retirement and pensions are all everyone talks about these days, though I'm frightened of retirement myself, my husband's retirement that is. What will he do with himself, a man with his ever-present tide of irascibility? "It's probably working conditions they're quibbling about," my husband barked. His own work conditions suit him perfectly, since he is an outdoors man by nature. I sometimes sense, but then I have known him for a long time, that he can barely distinguish between where his body stops and the elements begin—though he does, as I say, hate getting soaked in the rain.

The first week of the strike affected us both. There was talk about arbitration but, as is often the case, it came to nothing. Meanwhile without weather, we struggled against frustration and boredom. I had never before thought about deprivation on this scale, but I soon discovered that one day is exactly like the next, hour after hour of featureless, tensionless air. We were suddenly without seasonal zest, without hourly variation, without surprise and complaint, dislocated in time and space. There was nothing to press upon the skin, nothing for the body to exert itself against, nothing that satisfied. The idea of umbrellas was suddenly laughable (though we didn't laugh, at least I don't remember laughing). And there was no thought of drawing the living-room blinds against the sun.

The garden more or less disowned its responsibilities. The row of tomato plants—Mexican Ecstasy was what we were trying out this year—bore well enough, though the tomatoes themselves refused to ripen. Ripeness requires long periods of bright, warm light, as everyone knows, but for the duration of the strike we were stuck in a bland width of greyness with day after day of neither heat nor cold. "At least we don't have to worry about frost," my husband grumbled in one of his reasonable moments, but his forehead was warped with anger, and his patience further tried by yet another extension of the strike. Deadlocked, they said on the eleven o'clock news; the two sides still miles apart.

A neighbour—he owns one of those satellite dishes and is therefore able to tune in to five hundred news sources—told us the government was thinking of calling in the troops. What good would that do? I thought. "What good would that do?" my husband said loudly. He'd gone off his food by now. Nothing I put on the table seemed right, not my special potato salad, not even my New Orleans gumbo. Winter fare, summer fare, it didn't matter. The cherry vanilla ice cream we like so much withheld its flavour during this weatherless period, as did my spiced beef stew and dumplings. Our own green beans from the garden, needless to say, shrivelled before we could pick them.

Like children, we were uncertain as to how to clothe ourselves in the morning. Longs or shorts? Wool or cotton? Denim or polyester? My green short-sleeved rayon dress that I'm quite fond of—and so too is my husband, if I can read his eyes—seemed inappropriate, out of place, too loaded with interseasonal deliberation. As for his own work shirts, should he put on the plaid flannel or the boxy open-weave? How were we to decide, and what did it matter anyway? This lack of mattering smarted like a deerfly's sting. I found it impossible to look directly at my husband during those early morning decisions.

Something that surprised me was how much I missed the heft of daily barometric reassurance, and this was particularly curious since all my life the humidity index has felt obscurely threatening, informing us in a firm, masculine radio voice that we were either too wet or too dry for our own good. For our health and happiness. For the continuation of the planet. No one ever indicated we might reach a perfect state of humidity/dryness balance, and perhaps there is no such thing. But to be *unsituated* in terms of moisture, without either dampness or aridity to serve as a guide, is to be nowhere. The skin of my inner thighs was suddenly in a state of ignorance, not knowing how to react. My breasts itched, but the itch could not be relieved by scratching or by the application of calamine lotion. I mentioned to my husband a rustic barometer I remembered from childhood, a mechanism consisting of a tiny wooden house with two doors. When the humidity was high and rain imminent, the right-hand door opened and a little lean boy-doll, mild-faced and costumed in Alpine dress, appeared. When it was dry, a smiling little girl swung into view, promising sunshine.

My husband, his elbows on the kitchen table, listened. His nicely trimmed beard twitched and vibrated, and I thought for a minute he was about to ask a question, raising a point that, in fact, had just occurred to me: Why should the little boy signify rain and the girl sunshine? Did humidity and dryness possess such specific and biologically assigned qualities, each of which could be measured and interpreted?

But all he said was, "You never told me that before."

"You never asked me," I said, exasperated.

The strike was into its third week, and I found myself impatient with the dulling and rounding of each twenty-four-hour segment, marked by a pencil check on the calendar and nothing else. Our lives have always been uncertain owing to my husband's disposition, and mine too perhaps, but at least we'd had the alternating rhythm of light and darkness to provide continuity.

To live frictionlessly in the world is to understand the real grief of empty space. Nostalgically I recalled the fluting of air currents in the late afternoon hours, hissing against the backyard shrubs and the fetid place where we stashed the garbage cans. And the interlace of heat and coolness on my cheeks as I carried home my sacks of groceries. I wondered if my husband remembered how, only days ago, the wind used to slide against the west side of the porch, arriving in chunks or else splinters, and how it rattled the glass in the window frames, serving up for us a nervous, silvery sort of evening music that produced, simultaneously, a sense of worry and of consolation.

I felt an urge to voice such thoughts aloud, but, as usual, was uncertain in my husband's presence. To speak of propulsive sunshine and solemn shade, and the jolts of expectation that hang between the two, would be to violate a code of intimacy we had long since established.

What I remember most from that painful, weatherless period is the sky's mute bulk of stillness. Day after day it continued in its building up—pressureless, provisional, and, most heartbreaking of all, exhibiting a cloudlessness that was unrelieved. Clouds. After a month I began to think that perhaps clouds were something I had only imagined. How could anything exist as lovely and as whimsical as these masses of whipped cream that transformed themselves an hour later into bright rapturous streamers of scratched air?

I dreamed one night of a tower of cloud rising in the vivid setting sun, its fringed edges painted the deep-fried gold of apple fritters, and, at the centre, shading inward with a sly, modulated subtlety, the dense pewtery purple that announces a storm either approaching or receding, it didn't matter which. By morning I was sobbing into my pillow, but my husband, who had risen earlier, was not there to offer comfort.

We woke and slept. My husband's job was cancelled for the duration of the strike, and so we were thrown more and more together. We tended to bump into each other around the house, getting on each other's nerves, and one day I discovered him on the porch staring out at the vacant air; he was stooped and looked older than he is, and on impulse I laced my hands around the bulk of his back, pressing the side of my face against his shirt.

Later that same day we heard the news about the settlement of the strike. It seemed the meteorologists had wanted nothing all along but the public's appreciation and gratitude, and this now had been unanimously promised and even written into their contract.

My husband and I slept in each other's arms that night, and it was shortly after midnight when we were stirred out of profound unconsciousness by a breeze loosened in the elms and carried to us through the mesh of the house's various window screens.

Then, after an hour or so, drifting in and out of wakefulness, we heard, or perhaps imagined, the ballet-slipper sound of raindrops on the garage roof. A bank of coolness and damp arrived together at first dawn, and entered the valved darkness of our lungs, mine and his.

I touched his mouth with my thumb then, rubbing it back and forth. We held on to each other tightly during those minutes, feeling the essence of weather blow through us, thinking the same thoughts, and I remembered that thing which, for stretches of dull time, I tend to forget. That despite everything, the two of us have learned the trick of inhabiting parallel weather systems, of making for ourselves—and no one else—snowstorms in August, of bringing into view the air of autumn, whenever we wish, the icy pain at the bottom of every breath, and then arriving at the gateway of illogical, heat-enhanced January, and imagining the April wind on my face, and his too, which is no louder nor more damaging than a dozen friendly bees, so that we have curiosity enough to rise and begin another day.

[2000]

FRED WAH ■ (1939–)

Fred Wah tells much of his own story in his poetic "biotext" *Diamond Grill* (1996), a literary exploration of his family history. The book, which centres on the family's Chinese restaurant named Diamond Grill in Nelson, B.C., mixes family anecdotes and memories with social criticism, theories of ethnicity, and a poignant analysis of systemic racism.

Born in Swift Current, Saskatchewan, Wah is the son of a Chinese-Canadian father and a Swedish-Canadian mother. While studying music and English literature at the University of British Columbia in the early 1960s, Wah became one of the founding members of the poetry group TISH. With Frank Davey, George Bowering, Daphne Marlatt, Jamie Reid, David Bromige, and others, he helped inaugurate a West Coast school of experimental poetry that rebelled against what it saw as the conservatism of the modernist poets (who had in turn rebelled against the generation before them). In 1978, at David Thompson University Centre in Nelson (an undergraduate fine arts college that later became the Kootenay School of Writing, or KSW, in Vancouver), Wah developed and coordinated a writing program until 1982. During this time, he also co-founded *Writing*. In 1984, Wah and Davey established *SwiftCurrent,* the world's first literary e-journal. At the vanguard of Canadian

poetry for over five decades, Wah has also been editorially involved with the literary magazines *Open Letter* and *West Coast Line*. After years spent teaching in the Creative Writing Program at the University of Calgary, Wah is now professor emeritus. With his wife, writer-critic Pauline Butling, Wah is still active in the West Coast writing community.

Wah's first collection *Lardeau* (1965) has been followed by 17 others, including the concrete poetry in *Pictograms from the Interior of B.C.* (1975), the Governor General's Award-winning formally experimental poems in *Waiting for Saskatchewan* (1985), the critically acclaimed *Alley Alley Home Free* (1992), and his recent book of poetic responses to photographic images, *Sentenced to Light* (2008). After 20 years of writing, it was in *Breathin' My Name with a Sigh* (1981) that Wah began to "confront [his] racialized past," as he terms it. Influenced by the increasing attention to race in 1980s Canada (in part brought about by the Japanese-Canadian redress movement and the related publication of Joy Kogawa's novel *Obasan,* as well as the larger contextual framework of the passing of multiculturalism into law), Wah's *Waiting for Saskatchewan* is a series of poems that explore his mixed-race identity.

In *Diamond Grill,* Wah continues the stories of his multiracial family in a series of linked prose-poems. The volume hijacks the possibility of applying ready-made generic categories (of life-writing, autobiography, fiction, or the long poem). The mixture of genres mirrors the mixing of cultures, histories, and languages detailed in the text. Keeping in mind Wah's training in jazz music and his commitment to the notion of the combined musicality and physicality of language and breath, it is fruitful to approach *Diamond Grill* as you might approach music, noting the cumulative effect of its cadence and rhythm. Wah presents narrative growth as a process of open-ended accretion: compiling stories on top of stories. Narrative builds through the layering of intertextual references, nostalgic reminiscences, painful memories, verbal maps, and glimpses into the present. Integrating contemporary theories of hybridity, place, and language into his thinking about poetry and form, Wah engages in the "compound composition" of what he calls "RE-poetics": re-cuperating, re-furbishing, re-writing, re-peating, re-iterating, and re-mixing with an emphasis on the way the prefix "re-does" the meaning of the verb.

Wah's focus on hybridity in *Diamond Grill* (on being "ChineseHYPHENCanadian") is further theorized in his collection of critical essays *Faking It: Poetics and Hybridity* (2000). In his essay "Half-Bred Poetics," for instance, Wah puts it like this: "The site of this poetics for me, and many other multi-racial and multi-cultural writers, is the hyphen, that marked (or unmarked) space that both binds and divides." In the 1950s Canada of Wah's youth, the hyphen in "Chinese-Canadian" was non-existent and people were forced to choose to be either Canadian or Chinese. This was a problem for someone who "felt neither and both." He reminds his readers that he is among many people who have grown up "living in the hyphen" in Canada. Wah views this "hyphen poetics" as a recognition of the ambivalence that is in permanent flux and transition, like the constantly swinging restaurant door in the excerpts included here (which functions as a metaphor of hyphenation). He notes that one of the main goals of "hyphen poetics" is to identify with this ambivalent, hybrid subjectivity, while maintaining the sense of conflict and fluidity on which it is based.

From Diamond Grill

IN THE DIAMOND, AT THE END OF A

long green vinyl aisle between booths of chrome, Naugahyde, and Formica, are two large swinging wooden doors, each with a round hatch of face-sized window. Those kitchen doors can be kicked with such a slap they're heard all the way up to the soda fountain. On the other side of the doors, hardly audible to the customers, echoes a jargon of curses, jokes, and cryptic orders. Stack a hots! Half a dozen fry! Hot beef san! Fingers and tongues all over the place jibe and swear You mucka high!—Thloong you! And outside, running through and around the town, the creeks flow down to the lake with, maybe, a spring thaw. And the prairie sun over the mountains to the east, over my family's shoulders. The journal journey tilts tight-fisted through the gutter of the book, avoiding a place to start—or end. Maps don't have beginnings, just edges. Some frayed and hazy margin of possibility, absence, gap. Shouts in the kitchen. Fish an! Side a fries! Over easy! On brown! I pick up an order and turn, back through the doors, whap! My foot registers more than its own imprint, starts to read the stain of memory.

Thus: a kind of heterocellular[1] recovery reverberates through the busy body, from the foot against that kitchen door on up the leg into the torso and hands, eyes thinking straight ahead, looking through doors and languages, skin recalling its own reconnaissance, cooked into the steamy food, replayed in the folds of elsewhere, always far away, tunneling through the centre of the earth, mouth saying can't forget, mouth saying what I want to know can feed me, what I don't can bleed me.

YET LANGUAGELESS, MOUTH ALWAYS
A GAUZE, WORDS LOCKED

behind tongue, stopped in and out, what's she saying, what's she want, why's she mad, this woman-silence stuck, struck, stopped—there and back, English and Chinese churning ocean, her languages caught in that loving angry rip tide of children and coercive tradition and authority. Yet.

Grampa Wah's marriage to Florence Trimble is a surprise to most of the other Chinamen in the cafes around southern Saskatchewan, but not to his wife back in China. Kwan Chung-keong comes to Canada in 1892, returns to his small village in Hoiping County in 1900, and stays just long enough to marry a girl from his village and father two daughters and a son. When he returns to Canada in 1904 he has to leave his family behind because the head tax has, in his absence, been raised to five hundred dollars (two years' Canadian wages).[2] He realizes he'll never be able to get his family over here so, against the grain for Chinamen, he marries a white woman (Scots-Irish from Trafalgar, Ontario), the cashier in his cafe. They have three boys and four girls and he never goes back to China again.

I don't know how Grampa Wah talks her into it (maybe he doesn't) but somehow Florence lets two of her children be sent off to China as recompense in some patriarchal deal her husband has with his Chinese wife. He rationalizes to her the Confucian idea that a tree may grow as tall as it likes but its leaves will always return to the ground. Harumph, she thinks, but to no avail.

Fred[3] and his older sister Ethel are suddenly one day in July 1916 taken to the train station in Swift Current, their train and boat tickets and identities pinned to their coats in an envelope. My grandfather had intended to send number one son but when departure day arrives Uncle Buster goes into hiding. Grampa grabs the next male in line, four-year-old Fred, and, because he is so young, nine-year-old Ethel as well, to look after him. He has the word of the conductor that the children will be delivered safely to the boat in Vancouver and from there the connections all the way to Canton have been arranged. Fred, Kwan Foo-lee, and Ethel, Kwan An-wa, spend the next eighteen years, before returning to Canada, being raised by their Chinese step-mother alongside two half-sisters and a half-brother.

---

[1] Composed of cells of different kinds.

[2] The Chinese Immigration Act of 1885 imposed a "head tax" on all Chinese immigrants to Canada at the sum of $50. In 1901, it was raised to $100 and in 1903 to $500. See Volume I, Section III, for excerpts from the Act.

[3] The poet's father.

Yet, in the face of this patrimonial horse-trading it is the women who turn it around for my father and Aunty Ethel. Back in Canada my grandmother, a deeply religious lady, applies years of Salvation Army morality to her heathen husband to bring her children home. But he is a gambler and, despite his wife's sadness and Christian outrage, he keeps gambling away the money that she scrapes aside for the kids' return passage.

Meanwhile, the remittance money being sent from Canada to the Chinese wife starts to dwindle when the depression hits. She feels the pinch of supporting these two half-ghosts and, besides, she reasons with my grandfather, young Foo-lee is getting dangerously attracted to the opium crowd. As a small landholder she sells some land to help buy his way back to Canada.

Aunty Ethel's situation is different. She is forced to wait while, back in Canada, Fred convinces his father to arrange a marriage for her with a Chinaman in Moose Jaw. She doesn't get back to Canada until a year later, 1935.[4]

Yet the oceans of women migrant-tongued words in a double-bind of bossy love and wary double-talk forced to ride the waves of rebellion and obedience through a silence that shutters numb the traffic between eye and mouth and slaps across the face of family, yet these women forced to spit, out of bound-up feet and torsoed hips made-up yarns and foreign scripts unlucky colours zippered lips—yet, to spit, when possible, in the face of the father the son the holy ticket safety-pinned to his lapel—the pileup of twisted curtains intimate ink pious pages partial pronouns translated letters shore-to-shore Pacific jetsam pretending love forgotten history braided gender half-breed loneliness naive voices degraded miscourse racist myths talking gods fact and fiction remembered faces different brothers sisters misery tucked margins whisper zero crisscross noisy mothers absent fathers high muckamuck[5] husbands competing wives bilingual I's their unheard sighs, their yet still-floating lives.

THOSE DOORS TAKE QUITE
A BEATING. BRASS

sheet nailed across the bottom. *Whap!* What a way to announce your presence. You kind of explode, going through one door onto the customers, through the other onto the cooks. It's so nifty when I discover how they work: you're supposed to go through only on the right-hand side and that's how you don't get hit not looking when someone steamrollers through the other door at full clip with a load of dirty dishes or food spread out along their hands and arms. *Boom!* You'd think the glass portholes'd fall out of the doors, but they're built to take it. Inch-and-a-half varnished fir plywood with big spring hinges. When I first start working in the cafe

---

[4] Later in *Diamond Grill*, Wah revisits the 89-year-old Ethel and writes about her "life's outrage" as she "shows the anger she's carried all these years . . . for a languagelessness impossible to overcome for a woman, thus for the imposed interruptions and silences of a life so totally intended by others that she can only outlive them all."

[5] Variant on "high mucky muck," a Chinook word that refers to an important or powerful person.

I love to wallop that brass as hard as I can. But my dad warns me early to not make such a noise because that disturbs the customers, so I come up with a way of placing my heel close to the bottom and then rocking the foot forward to squeeze the door open in a silent rush of air as I come through on the fly. But when we get real busy, like at lunchtime, all the waiters and waitresses, including my dad, will let loose in the shape and cacophony of busy-ness, the kicker of desire hidden in the isochronous[6] torso, a necessary dance, a vital percussion, a critical persuasion, a playful permission fast and loud, *WhapBamBoom!*—feels so good.

MY SISTER SAYS TOMATO BEEF
IS ENOUGH TO

make her go back to eating meat. This is a really good gingery winter dish, particularly as a leftover when you get home late from playing hockey and it's still warm on top of the stove.

Use nine to ten small tomatoes or a forty-eight ounce can, stewed or whole. Stir-fry strips of beef with about a thumb of sliced ginger, one or two cloves of crushed garlic, a chopped onion, and a ladle full of soy sauce. Add tomatoes, one tsp. sugar, a little salt, and simmer to boil down a bit to stew-like consistency. Add some diced celery about ten minutes before serving. Spoon over top of rice and pick out pungent chunks of ginger and hide under bowl.

IN NELSON MY FATHER JOINS
THE LIONS CLUB,

one of those service clubs like the Rotary Club, Gyros, and Junior Chamber of Commerce.[7] And that's what most of the clubs are for, business connections, working on community projects, and having some fun. Most of the clubs meet at the Hume Hotel for lunch or dinner once a week and each meeting is full of shenanigans, like having to pay a fine for not wearing a tie and things like that. My dad really enjoys the Lions Club and works hard on projects, like coaching Little League baseball and putting on the mid-summer bonspiel pancake breakfast on Baker Street. I think what he likes most, though, is the kidding around, the high jinks.

I think a lot of his kidding around is in order to hide his embarrassment at not knowing English as well as he'd like to. His only schooling in English he picks up during six months in Cabri, Saskatchewan, just north of Swift Current. His father sends him there to work in a small cafe soon after he returns from China. And then one of his sisters, Hanna, helps him out with reading and writing a bit during those first years back with his English-speaking family. Whatever else he learns about English he picks up from working in the cafe.

---

[6] Taking place (vibrating) in the same time, or at the same intervals of time.

[7] For a satirical portrait of such clubs, see Stephen Leacock's 1912 story "The Marine Excursion of the Knights of Pythias" in Volume I, Section IV.

When he joins the Lions Club and has to give an initiation speech, he gets my mother to help him write something up. She says he's very nervous about this event; worried that he might flub it, make a fool of himself, the only Chinaman at an all-white dinner meeting. But there he is, with his little speech on a piece of paper in front of all these Baker Street nickel millionaires in the Hume Hotel dining room, thanking these guys for inviting him to join their club, thanking them for making Nelson such a wonderful place to live and raise his family, and then thanking them for this meal with the wonderful *sloup*. We always kid around at home when he says *sloup* and he laughs and, we suspect, even says it that way intentionally just to horse around with us. But here such a slip just turns him copper red (the colour you get when you mix yellow with either embarrassment or liquor). So when he hears himself say *sloup* for soup he stops suddenly and looks out at the expected embarrassed and patronizing smiles from the crowd. Then he does what he has learned to do so well in such instances, he turns it into a joke, a kind of self put-down that he knows these white guys like to hear: he bluffs that Chinamen call soup *sloup* because, as you all know, the Chinese make their soup from the slop water they wash their underwear and socks in, and besides, it's just like when you hear me eating my soup, Chinamen like to slurp and make a lot of noise. That's a compliment to the cook!

So he fakes it, and I guess I pick up on that sense of faking it from him, that English can be faked. But I quickly learn that when you fake language you see, as well, how everything else is a fake.

I'M JUST A BABY, MAYBE
SIX MONTHS (.5%)

old. One of my aunts is holding me on her knee. Sitting on the ground in front of us are her two daughters, 50% Scottish. Another aunt, the one who grew up in China with my father, sits on the step with her first two children around her. They are 75% Chinese. There is another little 75% girl cousin, the daughter of another 50% aunt who married a 100% full-blooded Chinaman (full-blooded, from China even). At the back of the black-and-white photograph is my oldest boy cousin; he's 25% Chinese. His mother married a Scot from North Battleford and his sisters married Italians from Trail. So there, spread out on the stoop of a house in Swift Current, Saskatchewan, we have our own little western Canadian multicultural stock exchange.

We all grew up together, in Swift Current, Calgary, Trail, Nelson and Vancouver (27% of John A's nation[8]) and only get together now every three years (33%) for a family reunion, to which between 70% and 80% of us show up. Out of fifteen cousins only one (6.6%) married a 100% pure Chinese.

[8] A reference to Canada's first Prime Minister, John A. Macdonald.

The return on these racialized investments has produced colourful dividends and yielded an annual growth rate that now parallels blue-chip stocks like Kodak and Fuji, though current global market forces indicate that such stocks, by their volatile nature, will be highly speculative and risky. Unexpected developments (like Immigration Acts) could knock estimates for a loop. Always take future projections with either a grain of salt or better still a dash of soy.

ANOTHER CHIP ON MY SHOULDER
IS THE APPROPRIATION

of the immigrant identity. I see it all over the place. Even one of the country's best-known writers has said We are all immigrants to this place even if we were born here.[9] Can't these people from *central* leave anything to itself? Why deny the immigrant his or her real world? Why be in such a rush to dilute? Those of us who have already been genetically diluted need our own space to figure it out. I don't want to be inducted into someone else's story, or project. Particularly one that would reduce and usurp my family's residue of ghost values to another status quo. Sorry, but I'm just not interested in this collective enterprise erected from the sacrosanct great railway imagination dedicated to harvesting a dominant white cultural landscape. There's a whole forest of us out here who don't like clear-cut, suspect the mechanical purity of righteous, clear, shining, Homelite Americas,[10] chainsaws whining, just across the valley.

No way I'll let these chips fall where they may.

[1996]

[9] A reference to Margaret Atwood's Afterword to *The Journals of Susanna Moodie* (1970). The full passage is: "We are all immigrants to this place even if we were born here: the country is too big for anyone to inhabit completely, and in the parts unknown to us we move in fear, exiles and invaders. This country is something that must be chosen—it is so easy to leave— and if we do choose it we are still choosing a violent duality." See the excerpts from *The Journals of Susanna Moodie* in Section VI.

[10] Home Electric Lighting Company produced power generators.

PATRICK LANE ■ (1939–)

Patrick Lane, along with such poets as Milton Acorn and Alden Nowlan, is known for the unflinching honesty with which he portrays the struggles of everyday working people. Having produced over two dozen collections of poetry, he has won numerous literary prizes, including the Governor General's Award for *Poems, New and Selected* (1978), the Canadian Authors Association Award, the Dorothy Livesay Prize for *Too Spare, Too Fierce* (1995), and two National Magazine Awards. In 2007, he was awarded the first Lieutenant Governor's Award for Literary Excellence for his lifetime contribution to literature in British Columbia.

Lane was born in Nelson and raised in Vernon in the B.C. interior. His experience in an extraordinary range of jobs—truck driver, boxcar loader, carpenter, clerk at a number of sawmills, office manager, accountant—has contributed to the diverse subject matter and settings of his poems. In 1965 Lane moved to Vancouver to become part of the burgeoning poetry scene there, co-founding with Seymour Mayne and bill bissett Very Stone House, a small publishing firm dedicated to new poetic voices. In 1968 he moved to South America to pursue his writing, returning to B.C. two years later. While working as writer-in-residence at the University of Manitoba in 1978, Lane met the poet Lorna Crozier. They were later married and have since collaborated on several projects.

Having established himself as one of Canada's leading poets, Lane has been a writer-in-residence at a number of universities, in Canada and abroad, including the University of Victoria from 1991 to 2004. Now retired from institutional positions, Lane and Crozier, who live in a small community outside of Victoria, remain active in Canadian poetry. With Crozier, Lane co-edited the landmark collections of contemporary poetry *Breathing Fire* (1995) and *Breathing Fire 2: Canada's New Poets* (2004), as well as a collection of essays on the power of addiction, *Addicted: Notes from the Belly of the Beast* (2001).

Lane's early collections such as *Letters from the Savage Mind* (1966) and *Mountain Oysters* (1971) challenge readers' complacencies by providing vignettes about the sorts of brutalized lives that often go unnoticed in mainstream society. His early poems underscore the hardships that afflict people in thankless and exploitative jobs, or in sexual and family relations.

Many of these accounts of personal suffering and violation trace the connection between processes of social injustice and the more intimate forms of barbarity that result. Abused animals often figure in these poems as appalling but eloquent expressions of innocent suffering in a hostile world, but they are just as often invoked as predatorial examples of the fundamentally hostile nature of life.

In recent years, Lane's focus has become increasingly introspective, though no less honest. His 1990 collection, *Winter,* thrives on a feeling of personal intimacy with the environment, and works like a series of riddles, embracing "[t]he generosity of snow, the way it forgives / transgression, filling in the many betrayals," as he declares in the book's opening lines, but never in a way that betrays the memories of those earlier chronicles of desperation. *Mortal Remains* (1991) wrestles with Lane's memories of the premature death of his brother and the murder of his father in the 1960s, while his most recent collection, *Last Water Song* (2007), is a series of elegies dedicated to writer acquaintances who have died, including such figures as Al Purdy, Irving Layton, and Earle Birney. His 2004 memoir, *There Is a Season* (published in the United States as *What the Stones Remember*), turns his poetic gaze on his own struggle with alcoholism and drug addiction, but balances this tale of despair and fragile hope with an evocative account of the endless forms of beauty that he finds in his garden; his work in his half-acre garden, he suggests, is what saved him. Throughout his work, Lane's graphic descriptions of suffering gain much of their power by handling emotionally dramatic material in understated ways, mixing moral outrage with genuine compassion, and lyrical insight with social realities.

Winter 1

The generosity of snow, the way it forgives
transgression, filling in the many betrayals
and leaving the world
exactly as it was. Imagine a man
walking endlessly and finding his tracks,
knowing he has gone in a circle. Imagine
his disappointment. See how he strikes out again
in a new direction, hoping this way
will lead him out. Imagine how much
happier he will be this time with the wind   10
all around him, the wind filling in his tracks.

He is thinking of that man,
of what keeps him going.
The thought of snow,
small white grains sifting
into the holes where his feet went,
filling things in,
leaving no room for despair.

Winter 4

He is thinking of the end of Oedipus,[1]
not the beginning, not the part
where Oedipus chooses by giving the answer
to the beast at the crossroads. No,
it is the end he likes. The part
just after he puts out his eyes
and stands, suddenly
in that certain darkness, decided.

It is not a story of winter
but of the sun, the ceaseless   10
perfection of the desert in Africa.

How different it would be
had it taken place here, he thinks.
Here the critical moment

---

[1] *Oedipus Rex* is the title of a play by the Greek playwright Sophocles. Early in the play, we learn that Oedipus, now King of Thebes, once answered the riddle of the Sphinx that had been terrorizing the land. As a result he is allowed to marry Queen Jocasta, only to find out many years later that she is his mother. In horror at having committed incest and murdered his father, Oedipus puts out his eyes and has himself cast out of the city into exile.

would be putting the eyes back
in their sockets, that first shock
exactly the same as in the other story
only the beginning would have
to be different, all the roles
reversed.   20

Winter 7

It is the bare bone of winter
he holds in his hand, a wisp of ice
slender as a fifteenth century Spanish knife
fashioned in Cordova. A woman's knife
to be hidden in a sleeve when meeting
a false lover. It is delicately curved,
a small floating rib, just right
to slip into the heart as they embrace.
He looks at the thing in his hand
as it transforms itself, changing,   10
melting into a thin pool of water. He is
almost afraid to return it to its element.

Winter 8

The second riddle is more difficult.
The answer to the first riddle was *snow*.
Not the soft snow of early winter, but
the coarse granular snow that sweeps
with the wind in the blizzards of January.
The kind that leaves the skin
scored with myriad tiny cuts.
The answer to the second riddle
could be *snow* as well. He
repeats the enigma to himself,   10
pondering the last couplet:

The absence of colour
is the colour of blue.

For a moment he wonders if the answer is *love*.
Perhaps it is *ice*.
Or it could be *cold*, that simple word
for which there are a thousand meanings,
all of them correct.

[1990]

Don McKay's poetry is for the birds— literally. An avid birdwatcher, McKay writes poems that abound with avian creatures that fly through a rapidly eroding wilderness. In McKay's work, birding is a metaphor for the poetic process, and, also, birds are celebrated for being birds. As poet-critic Méira Cook claims, "[T]he bird itself, that hollow boned creature . . . lends itself to an openformed [sic] lyricism in which poems gather flight paths, locate tensile rhythms, stretch time and contract space." In *Birding, or desire* (1983), McKay's lyrics engage with ornithology but also ironically undercut the poet- persona's human presence in the natu- ral space. Critic Travis Mason notes that McKay's poems often acknowledge a literary tradition that pays homage to birdsong while challenging the anthro- pocentric thrust of such a tradition. Like Anne Carson's poem "Audubon," McKay's poetry explores the construc- tions of nature as art. In *Another Gravity* (2000), McKay entitles poems after the basic elements of flight: "Lift," "Drag," and "Load." The recognition of terror in the exhausted white-throated sparrow in "Load" is emblematic of McKay's empathetic encounters with nature as the speaker refuses his own desire to tame the animal.

His work is pivotally concerned with dwindling ecologies as he uses scientific taxonomies to investigate ani- mals, the environment, geology, and life, in a kind of "wilderness poetics." McKay's recent poetic engagements with geology in *Strike/Slip* (2006) come out of his "astonishment" at the immutability of stone. "Quartz Crystal," taken from this collection, is a profound meditation on human insignificance (in the grand scale of time) and awe (in the face of ancient geological traces). In its preoccupation with con- necting the speaker's present with an ancient past, McKay's poem bears interesting connections with Robert Kroetsch's "Stone Hammer Poem" (see Section VI). In this poetry, McKay con- templates crystals, magma, and rock formations to rethink human under- standings of land, space, and time.

McKay emerged alongside Jan Zwicky, Tim Lilburn, and Robert Bringhurst in the 1980s and '90s as an ecologically focused poet determined to redefine what being a nature poet means today. Bringhurst aligns poetry and nature in his essay "Poetry and Thinking" when he writes that "poetry is what I start to hear when I concede the world's ability to manage and under- stand itself. It is the language of the world: something humans overhear if they are willing to pay attention." McKay echoes Bringhurst's call to listen in "Baler Twine," first published in *Poetry and Knowing* (1995), a collection of essays edited by Lilburn, and reprinted in McKay's own *Vis à Vis: Field Notes on Poetry & Wilderness* (2001). His comments on the necessity of the nature writer to "enact" anthro- pocentrism can be compared with Charles G.D. Roberts's essay "The Animal Story," included in Volume I. Roberts's anthropomorphism, in which he adopts a kind of romanticized "realism," is different from McKay's notion of acknowledging "wilderness" (or the radical otherness of nature), as he outlines it here. For McKay, it is the otherness of nature that renders it of supreme importance to human beings, who glimpse therein a sense of their integral connection to something beyond rational determination.

McKay continues his ruminations on the poetics of place in *Deactivated West 100* (2005) in the midst of the reclaimed wilderness of southern Vancouver Island. The aggressive logging of the area has also led him to consider the history and politics of forestry in his poetry (including technological advances like the Shay locomotive and the Stihl chainsaw).

The winner of two Governor General's Awards for poetry (for the 1991 collection *Night Field: Poems* and for *Another Gravity*), McKay was born in Owen Sound, Ontario. He was educated at Bishop's University, the University of Western Ontario, and the University of Wales, where he received his Ph.D. in 1971 (and came under the influence of Dylan Thomas's poetry, on which he has published several critical studies). Besides writing poetry, watching birds, and walking trails, McKay worked for almost three decades as a creative writing teacher at the UWO and the University of New Brunswick, as well as at the Banff Centre and Sage Hill. He has also served as an editor with Brick Books since 1978 and, while at UNB, as the editor of *The Fiddlehead* (1991–96), one of Canada's oldest and most influential literary journals. In his essay "The Shell of the Tortoise," McKay pronounces, equivocally, on the role of the artist as listener: "[I]n practice a poet fumbles about, rummages (remember your grandfather in his workshop), having been smitten by a frisson or hunch, trying to get a handle on it by listening through language." He ends with an exhortation to listen to poetry: "[I]t is as though language, which is—so we think—all mouth, were trying to grow ears."

Close-Up on a Sharp-Shinned Hawk

Concentrate upon her attributes:
the accipiter's[1] short
roundish wings, streaked breast, talons fine
and slender as the x-ray of a baby's hand.
The eyes (yellow in this hatchling
later deepening to orange then
blood red) can spot
a sparrow at four hundred metres and impose
silence like an overwhelming noise
to which you must not listen.   10

Suddenly, if you're not careful, everything
goes celluloid and slow
and threatens to burn through and you
must focus quickly on the simple metal band around her leg
by which she's married to our need to know.

[1983]

---

[1] *Accipiter*, genus of the family *Accipitridae*, the goshawks and sparrowhawks.

Song for the Song of the Wood Thrush

For the following few seconds, while the ear
inhales the evening
only the offhand is acceptable. Poetry
clatters. The old contraption pumping
iambs in my chest is going to take a break
and sing a little something. What? Not much. There's
a sorrow that's so old and silver it's no longer
sorry. There's a place
between desire and memory, some back porch
we can neither wish for nor recall.   10

[1997]

Load

We think this
the fate of mammals—to bear, be born,
be burden, to carry our own bones
as far as we can and know the force that earths us
intimately. Sometimes, while I was reading,
Sam would bestow one large paw on my foot,
as if to support my body
while its mind was absent—mute
commiseration, load to load, a message
like the velvet heaviness which comes   10
to carry you deliciously
asleep.
        One morning
on the beach at Point Pelee,[2] I met
a White-throated Sparrow so exhausted from the flight
across Lake Erie it just huddled in itself
as I crouched a few yards off.
I was thinking of the muscles in that grey-white breast,
pectoralis major powering each downstroke,
pectoralis minor with its rope-and-pulley tendon   20
reaching through the shoulder to the
top side of the humerus to haul it up again;
of the sternum with the extra keel it has evolved to
anchor all that effort, of the dark wind

---

[2] Southernmost point in Canada, in southwestern Ontario, and an important bird observation area, located at the point where two migration routes meet and hence a stopover area for many bird species.

and the white curl on the waves below, the slow dawn
and the thickening shoreline.
                            I wanted
very much to stroke it, and recalling
several terrors of my brief
and trivial existence, didn't.   30

                                                        [2000]

Sometimes a Voice (1)

Sometimes a voice—have you heard this?—
wants not to be voice any longer, wants something
whispering between the words, some
rumour of its former life. Sometimes, even
in the midst of making sense or conversation, it will
hearken back to breath, or even farther,
to the wind, and recognize itself
as troubled air, a flight path still
looking for its bird.   10
                        I'm thinking of us up there
shingling the boathouse roof. That job is all
off balance—squat, hammer, body skewed
against the incline, heft the bundle,
daub the tar, squat. Talking,
as we always talked, about not living
past the age of thirty with its
labyrinthine perils: getting hooked,
steady job, kids, business suit. Fuck that. The roof
sloped upward like a take-off ramp   20
waiting for Evel Knievel,[3] pointing into open sky. Beyond it
twenty feet or so of concrete wharf before
the blue-black water of the lake. Danny said
that he could make it, easy. We said
never. He said case of beer, put up
or shut up. We said
asshole. Frank said first he should go get our beer
because he wasn't going to get it paralysed or dead.
Everybody got up, taking this excuse
to stretch and smoke and pace the roof   30
from eaves to peak, discussing gravity

DON MCKAY

---

[3] Evel Knievel (1938–2007) was an American daredevil and stuntman known for riding his motorcycle
over large obstacles (cars, cliffs, canyons).

and Steve McQueen,[4] who never used a stunt man, Danny's
life expectancy, and whether that should be a case
of Export or O'Keefe's.[5] We knew what this was—
ongoing argument to fray
the tedium of work akin to filter vs. plain,
stick shift vs. automatic, condom vs.
pulling out in time.[6] We flicked our butts toward the lake
and got back to the job. And then, amid the squat,
hammer, heft, no one saw him go. Suddenly he   40
wasn't there, just his boots
with his hammer stuck inside one like a heavy-headed
flower. Back then it was bizarre that,
after all that banter, he should be so silent,
so inward with it just to
run off into sky. Later I thought,
cool. Still later I think it makes sense his voice should
sink back into breath and breath
devote itself to taking in whatever air
might have to say on that short flight between the roof   50
and the rest of his natural life.

[2000]

Après Chainsaw

Everything listening at me:
the stumps oozing resin, the birdsong
bouncing off my head like sonar,
the bludgeoned air with its fading
after-echoes. I think of people
herded to a square, staring
at the man on the platform.
Whatever I say now
will be strictly interpreted
and parsed. Is this the way it works,   10
locking you, stunned, in the imperative,
making a weapon of each tool?
Why can't we just bury innocence instead of
wrecking it over and over, as if
it could never die
enough?

---

[4] American actor (1930–1980), known for his counterculture and anti-hero roles in films like *The Magnificent Seven* (1960) and *The Great Escape* (1963). He was also an avid motorcycle rider thought to have done his own stunts.

[5] Brands of beer.

[6] Decisions to be made with cigarettes, cars, and sex.

What I want to say is
somewhere a man steps
softly into a hemlock-and-fir-fringed
pause. Heart full.   20
Head empty. His lost path
scrawls away behind him. A blue
dragonfly with double wings zags, hovers,
zags. A flicker he can't see
yucks its ghost laugh
into the thin slant light.

[2006]

Quartz Crystal

It rests among the other stones on my desk—small chunks of granite, wafers of schist and slate[7]—but it has clearly arrived from another dimension. While the others call, in the various dialects of gravity, to my fingers, the quartz crystal is poised to take off and return to its native aether.[8] Some act of pure attention—Bach's D Minor concerto[9] for instance—was hit by a sudden cold snap and fell, like hail, into the present. Here it lives in exile, a bit of locked Pythagorean[10] air amid the pleasant clutter of my study: simple, naked, perilously perfect.

Just the same, I can pick it up, I can number its faces, I can hold its slim hexagonal columns in my fingers like empty pencils. Who do I think I am, with my little dish of stones, my ballpoint pen, my shelf of books full of notions, that I should own this specimen of earth's own artifice, this form before mind or math, its axes reaching back to the Proterozoic, its transparence the Zen before all Zen?[11] It becomes clear that I must destroy my watch, that false professor of time, and free its tiny slave.[12] No problem—a few taps with a piece of Leech River schist and the deed is done. But more is required. What? Off with my clothes; how else but naked should we approach the first of symmetries? Still

[7] Types of hornblendic rocks whose component minerals are arranged in a roughly parallel manner.

[8] Also "ether," the upper regions of space.

[9] A reference to a classical concerto by German composer Johann Sebastian Bach (1685–1750).

[10] Pythagoras of Samos, Greek philosopher and mathematician, famous for the Pythagorean theorem, the equation that charts the relation of the three sides of a right triangle (and, through related formulae, the sides of other triangles). The description here alludes to the mathematical perfection and simplicity of the crystal formation.

[11] "Proterozoic" refers to a time between about 2.5 billion and 542 million years ago when the earliest forms of life are believed to have evolved. "Zen" refers to a school of Buddhism that emphasizes meditation and calmness.

[12] Many watches run on quartz batteries.

insufficient, I can tell, although I can also feel waves of dismay radiating from my reference books, their mute embarrassment on my behalf. It is just the sort of thing they feared might happen when the first stones moved into the neighbourhood.

What next? Unfortunately, it appears I must set aside my fingers and thumbs, those tricky manipulators who have so busily converted rock to stone, who perpetrated the pyramids and silicon valley: go clasp yourselves in the dark until you learn to sit still and attend. More?

> I give up baseball, with its derivative threes
> and dreams of diamond.
> I forswear the elegant pairs and numbered runs
> of minuet and cribbage.
> I renounce the fugue. Dialectic,
> I bid you adieu. And you,
> my little poems, don't imagine I can't hear you
> plotting under your covers, hoping to avoid
> your imminent depublication.[13]

While the crystal floats like a lotus on my palm, bending the light from a dying star to dance upon my coffee cup this fine bright Cenozoic[14] morning.

[2006]

From "Baler Twine: thoughts on ravens, home, and nature poetry"

[. . .] Having recently moved to New Brunswick from Southwestern Ontario, I have more opportunity to observe ravens on a regular basis. And in the last few months, for some reason, I have found myself taking drives and walks with raven-watching as an agenda. Why? Perhaps it's all this reading and ruminating I've been doing about the place of our species among others—and the other. Is this mental space priming me to seek out contact with one of the few other creatures I can imagine speaking to me? I mean, this is an itch, an intuition, not a sacred quest or totem animal rite. Anyhow, I was driving a bit south of Gagetown along the Saint John River, where there are lots of high places to park and scan the low-lying interval land (areas which are under water during the spring flood) for large passerines.[15] It was mid-January, quite cold, and clear. Saw a couple of ravens, far off, who were buzzing and bugging one another—romantically? (I imagine a raven relationship, which lasts a lifetime, involves a certain amount of teasing.) Saw some Snow Buntings,[16] lifting off from roadside gravel like an old black and white eight-millimeter movie,

---

[13] Here the speaker is rejecting various forms of "artificial," man-made patterning.

[14] The Cenozoic era encompasses the last 65.5 million years.

[15] A type of perching bird of the order *Passeriformes.*

[16] A bird of the passerine order, with a grey-black body and bright white patches on its wings.

flickering over a fence into a field. Then, on my way back home, I got my best look at a raven. It was hung up by the roadside at the entrance to a lane, a piece of baler twine[17] around one leg, wings spread. There was a huge shot-gun hole in its back just above the tail, which was missing altogether.

What do you think I should make of this? It won't do to be sentimental here. But this doesn't fall into an ethic of hunting; nor can it be understood from the rational-cum-aesthetic perspective of someone like Audubon,[18] who would shoot individuals of a species in order to have tractable models. Even without the myths which attend this creature, even discounting "the sacred" and setting aside the ancient mariner,[19] this seems very bad. Shooting the raven was one thing: we all know, each of us, that sinister delight in casual brutality and long-distance death. Displaying it was another—controlling its death, as well as taking its life. Displaying it declares that the appropriation is total. A dead body seeks to rejoin the elements; this one is required to function as a sign, a human category—a sign which says simply "we can do this." The raven's being, in Martin Heidegger's terms,[20] was not just used, but used up.

So I cut it down. Its wings were large and eloquent, and not like anything I could think of, certainly not like blown-away umbrellas.[21] The feathers, including the lavish neck-flounce, were still very glossy and fine. Its eyes were sphincters of nothing. And where did I get that notion that black was "merely" the absence of color?

Now I'd like to freeze me there, standing by the road with a dead raven on a piece of baler twine, wondering what to do with it, while we consider some of the reading and reflection I mentioned. We might think of this as climbing a ladder of o's into a thought-balloon above my head, where a small flock of issues awaits. To reduce the cacophony, I'll try voicing these one at a time, but let's keep in mind that this is not a necessary or logical progression.

Matériel

What happened to the raven is I think an example of one pole of our relations to material existence, which I have come to call "matériel." In its limited sense matériel

[17] Thread or string twisted to form a rope used to tie up bales of hay.

[18] John James Audubon (1785–1851), naturalist and painter, famous for his immense work *The Birds of America* (1827–1838). See also Anne Carson's poem "Audubon."

[19] The raven is a sacred animal in many First Nations cultures, often associated with an ambivalent trickster figure. Earlier in the essay, McKay locates the raven in Haida legends of the trickster. The ancient mariner is an allusion to Samuel T. Coleridge's (1772–1834) poem "The Rime of the Ancient Mariner" (1798), in which the killing of an albatross—a bird of good luck—leads to a series of unfortunate events at sea for the narrator and his shipmates, and a life of penance forever after for the man who kills the bird.

[20] The author of *Being and Time* (1927), Martin Heidegger (1889–1976) was a German philosopher concerned with the study of being (ontology).

[21] Earlier in the essay, McKay recalls how the previous winter he mistook two ravens at his bird feeder for a blown-away umbrella, covering the feeder completely.

is military equipment; in a slightly larger sense it is any equipment owned by an institution. But I'm taking the term to apply even more widely to any instance of second-order appropriation, where the first appropriation is the making of tools, or the address to things in the mode of utility, the mind-set which Heidegger calls "standing reserve." To make things into tools in the first place, we remove them from autonomous existence and conscript them as servants, determining their immediate futures. To make tools into matériel we engage in a further appropriation. This second appropriation of matter may be the colonization of its death, as in the case of the raven, the nuclear test site, the corpse hung on a gibbet or public crucifixion.[22] On the other hand, matérielization could be a denial of death altogether, as in the case of things made permanent and denied access to decomposition, their return to elements. We inflict our rage for immortality on things, marooning them on static islands; and then, frequently enough, we condemn them as pollutants. Why are the fixed smiles on Barbie Dolls and Fisher Price toys so pathetic?

Wilderness

By "wilderness" I want to mean, not just a set of endangered spaces, but the capacity of all things to elude the mind's appropriations. That tools retain a vestige of wilderness is especially evident when we think of their existence in time and eventual graduation from utility: breakdown. To what *degree* do we own our houses, hammers, dogs? Beyond that line lies wilderness. We probably experience its presence most often in the negative as dry rot in the basement, a splintered handle, or shit on the carpet. But there is also the sudden angle of perception, the phenomenal surprise which constitutes the sharpened moments of *haiku* and imagism.[23] The coat hanger asks a question; the armchair is suddenly crouched: in such defamiliarizations, often arranged by art, we encounter the momentary circumvention of the mind's categories to glimpse some thing's autonomy—its rawness, its *duende*, its alien being.[24] [...]

Poetic Attention and the Aeolian Harp

[...] The first indicator of one's status as nature poet is that one does not invoke language right off when talking about poetry, but acknowledges some extra-linguistic condition as the poem's input, output, or both. A second indicator may be actual content, front lawn to back country, but this, if one uses my peculiar notion of wilderness, becomes a dubious signal, since the poet may be

---

[22] The gibbet was originally synonymous with the gallows, but in later use the term signified an upright post with projecting arm from which the bodies of criminals were hung in chains or irons after execution.

[23] Two literary modes that crystallize expression into briefly expressed and immediate images. "Defamiliarization" is a literary term that refers to a writer's ability to render everyday objects or experiences "visible" in a new way, to make them "unfamiliar."

[24] *Duende*, Spanish expression for a goblin or sprite, but also used to refer to an uncanny awareness of essence, psychic or emotional inspiration, or what might be called "soul" in the case of a work of art.

focused on the wilderness in a car, a coat hanger, or even language itself, as much as Kluane Park.[25] (She might, in point of fact, be focused on Kluane Park as a tool.) My own reasons for failing to postmodernize are merely empirical: before, under, and through the wonderful terrible wrestling with words and music there is a state of mind which I'm calling "poetic attention." I'm calling it that, though even as I name it I can feel the falsity (and in some way the transgression) of nomination: it's a sort of readiness, a species of longing which is without the desire to possess, and it does not really wish to be talked about. To me, this is a form of knowing which counters the "primordial grasp" in homemaking, and celebrates the wilderness of the other;[26] it gives ontological applause. Even after linguistic composition has begun, and the air is thick with the problematics of reference, this kind of knowing remains in touch with perception. The nature poet may (should, in fact) resort to the field guide or library, but will keep coming, back, figuratively speaking, to the trail—to the grain of the experience, the particular angle of expression in a face, and O.K., to the raven on the baler twine.

There is, for this nature poet, at any rate, an important distinction between poetic attention and romantic inspiration. The romantic poet (or tourist, for that matter) desires to be spoken *to*, inspired by the other, so that perception travels into language (or slide show) without a palpable break. The paradigm for this ideal relation is the aeolian harp,[27] which is simply the larynx of natural phenomena, "Sensations sweet / felt in the blood, and felt along the heart / And passing even into my purer mind."[28] Or it may be that poetry itself is seen as natural, as in Neruda's

> And it was at that age ... Poetry
> arrived in search of me. I don't know,
> I don't know where it came from, from
> winter or a river.[29]

Wonderful: we want to believe this graceful act of personification and animism; why should it not be true, as music, or as fairytale is? Aeolian harpism relieves us of our loneliness as a species, reconnects us to the natural world, restores a coherent reality. It also, not incidentally, converts natural

---

[25] A national park in the Yukon known for its spectacular mountains, icefields, and valleys.

[26] Earlier in the essay, McKay has discussed French philosopher Emmanuel Levinas's (1906–1995) notion of the other, namely how the self is constituted in relation to the other. According to Levinas, through the "primordial grasp" (the hand), the self gains knowledge and internalizes or possesses the other.

[27] Æolian harp: a stringed instrument adapted to produce musical sounds on exposure to a current of air.

[28] A passage from English poet William Wordsworth's (1770–1850) "Lines written a few miles above Tintern Abbey." The poem is often cited as one of the finest examples of English Romanticism.

[29] The opening lines from "Poetry" (1964) by Nobel Prize-winning Chilean poet Pablo Neruda (1904–1973).

energy into imaginative power, so that Romanticism, which begins in the contemplation of nature, ends in the celebration of the creative imagination in and for itself. No wonder it is so compelling, whether we find it in Wordsworth, Neruda, or Levertov:[30] it speaks directly to a deep and almost irresistible desire for unity. But poetic attention is based on a recognition and a valuing of the other's wilderness; it leads to a work which is not a *vestige* of the other, but a *translation* of it.

Objection and Response

Enter the ambassador from post-structural theory.[31] "Well, this is all very well, Mr. Nature Poet, standing by the roadside, outfitted no doubt by L.L. Bean, happily twirling your dead raven, but it's a fact that you're going to crash into language in about .05 seconds, and that your perception is already saturated with it. This parade of perceptual innocence is simply a new twist on the old notion of romantic inspiration, designed to sneak a transcendental signified back into the game. Before you ever came upon the dead raven your head was filled with myths and soft ecology, a whole library of assumptions about the 'natural' world [. . .]. The individual who stands and stares at the dead raven or live warbler, ontologically applauding, is always already made of linguistic and cultural categories, loosely strung together, in your case, with the mental equivalent of baler twine. The nature poet, like anyone else, is 'locked in a tower of words' as Dylan Thomas puts it;[32] imagining otherwise is romantic mysticism. Need I go on?"

Putting aside for the moment the question of whether non-linguistic experience is possible (whether there may be an element of wilderness in perception), let me acknowledge the force of this objection. Given the unique relation of language to our species, how can our perception, as well as our writing, *not* be a restructuring of the world?[. . .] Being language, it cannot avoid the primordial grasp, but this occurs simultaneously with the extended palm, the openness in knowing that I've been calling poetic attention. And that experience suggests strongly that, although it cannot be spoken, radical otherness exists. In fact, nature poetry should not be taken to be *avoiding* anthropocentrism, but to be enacting it, thoughtfully. It performs the translation which is at the heart of being human, the simultaneous grasp and gift of home-making. And the persistence of poetic attention during the act of composition is akin to the translator's attention to the original, all the while she performs upon it a delicate and dangerous

---

[30] Denise Levertov (1923–1997), British-born American poet known for her anti-war poetry and engagement with her social and political environment.

[31] Poststructuralism is a mid- to late-twentieth-century literary theoretical approach that argues at its basis that reality is mediated through language; in other words, that there is no "transcendental signified" or absolute truth outside of language and culture systems.

[32] Welsh poet Dylan Thomas (1914–1953) writes in his poem, "Especially when the October wind" (1934), "Shut, too, in a tower of words, I mark / On the horizon walking like the trees / The wordy shapes of women, and the rows / Of the star-gestured children in the park."

transformation. Our epistemological dilemma is not resolved, as by aeolian harpism, but ritualized and explored.

The ambassador from post-structuralism has also done us a service by pointing out that the step-by-step model of perception-translation is too simple and naive. Language *is* already there in poetic attention; like an athlete at her limit, language is experiencing its speechlessness and the consequent need to stretch *itself* to be adequate to this form of knowing. Part of the excitement inside this species of meditative act is linguistic; it's the excitement of a tool which has hatched the illicit desire to behave like an animal.

One word more on post-structural thought: in its problematization of terms like "nature" and "natural" (that is, in their reduction to disguised categories of language and culture) it provides a salutary check on romantic innocence, a positive reminder of the fact of the frame. But—and here I indulge in intuition based on tone and style—its skepticism nurtures its excess, secretly worships a nihilistic impulse as surely as Romanticism worshiped the creative imagination in the guise of nature. It is, no less than Romanticism, an ideology, a politics, and an erotics, despite protestations to the contrary. In the realm of ideas, as in human relations, we do well to suspect any basic drive that presents itself simply as method or a form of rationalism. That is, to be blunt, it is as dangerous to act as though we were not a part of nature as it is to act as though we were not a part of culture; and the intellectual and political distortions produced by these contrary ideologies are greatly to be feared.[. . .]

[1995]

THOMAS KING ■ (1943–)

As the narrator of Thomas King's 1993 novel *Green Grass, Running Water* puts it, "There are no truths . . . only stories." A playful interrogation of dominant narratives characterizes all of King's work. A noted author, critic, photographer, radio personality, satirist, and professor, King consistently uses humour to combat stereotypes about Native people in North America. In his novels and story collections—*Medicine River* (1989), *One Good Story, That One* (1993), *Green Grass, Running Water* (1993), *Truth and Bright Water* (1999), and *A Short History of Indians in Canada* (2005)—King explores the

ways "stories" can be used as a source of both subjugation and pride. In the past few years, King has taken a new turn in his fiction, publishing detective stories under the pseudonym Hartley GoodWeather, about a Cherokee photographer-turned-detective who lives in the fictional town of Chinook and solves mysteries (*Dreadful Water Shows Up* [2002] and *Red Power Murders* [2006]).

King characterizes himself as a "serious writer. Tragedy is my topic. Comedy is my strategy." In *The Truth About Stories* (2003), the published version of the Massey Lectures that he delivered at the University of Toronto, King quotes the Anishinaabe storyteller Basil Johnston when he describes the role of comedy and laughter in stories by Native people: "It is precisely because our tribal stories are comical and evoke laughter that they have never been taken seriously outside the tribe. But behind and beneath the comic characters and the comic situations exists the real meaning of the story . . . what the tribe understood about human growth and development." King's writing is satiric: with broad strokes he debunks both non-Native and Native misconceptions and misreadings of Aboriginal people's lives.

King was born in northern California to a Cherokee father and a mother of Greek and German heritage. Since earning his Ph.D. in English literature and American studies at the University of Utah in 1986, King has worked at the University of Minnesota, the University of Lethbridge, and the University of Guelph, where he currently teaches Native literature and creative writing. As an academic, King edited *All My Relations: An Anthology of Contemporary Canadian Native Fiction* (1990) and, with his wife, Helen Hoy, co-edited *The Native in Literature* (1987), a collection of critical essays on representations of Indigenous people in Canadian writing. This interest complements King's "pan-Indian" approach, which has allowed him to broaden his political critique.

Retelling stories from multiple perspectives, King targets the cultural icons of patriarchal settler society by criticizing materialism, capitalism, and neo-imperialism. King's writing is often postmodern and irreverent in its approach, containing dialogues between storytellers and audiences, between postcolonial theories and Indigenous modes of narration, and

between traditional stories and popular culture. Influenced by Aboriginal storytelling traditions, particularly the works of Okanagan storyteller Harry Robinson, King's stories recreate the sense of oral storytelling in written form—or to use critic Susan Gingell's phrase, they "textualize orality."

In *Green Grass, Running Water,* King engages with the myth of Canada as an empty wilderness, and the subsequent stereotypes about "Indians" propagated by European explorers and settlers, Hollywood movies, and Westerns. One of the pivotal moments in the novel is when the ending of a popular Western film is revised so that the "Indians" win and kill John Wayne. The novel highlights the fact that First Nations people have often been constructed in Western narratives as commodities or have been romanticized (see the writings by Grey Owl in Section V and Armand Ruffo's Grey Owl poems in this section). Introduced in *Green Grass* is the Dead Dog Café, a tourist trap that capitalizes on the appetite of non-Native tourists for the consumption of stereotypes about Indigenous peoples; this became the source of the title for King's immensely popular CBC Radio comedy, *The Dead Dog Café Comedy Hour* (1997–2000). This satirical upending of stereotypes is evident in King's series of portrait photographs, in which he photographed Aboriginal artists wearing Lone Ranger masks (see Figure VII-5 for King's self-portrait in a mask).

While King has been criticized for glossing over the "serious" issues of Aboriginal people's lives in the United States and Canada instead of creating realistic portraits of the everyday problems of racism, alcoholism, suicide, and poverty, he argues that he is presenting a working portrait of those often depicted as oppressed and downtrodden. King responds to such criticism in an interview with Jeffrey Canton, arguing that in his work he "wanted to emphasize that the range of 'Indian' is not as narrow as many people try to make it." He also avoids writing "issue-dominated" fiction and so his characters are not drawn according to type, or as political mouthpieces; indeed, they often defy both stereo-type and polemic. In *Medicine River,* for instance, one of the central characters, Louise Heavyman, is an accountant and single mother by choice—not by accident and not as a feminist manoeuvre. In the naming of Louise's daughter "South Wing," after the area in the hospital in which the child is born, we can see the humour with which King combines "Indian" and non-Native symbolism.

King's third novel, *Truth and Bright Water,* is a coming-of-age tragedy set in twin towns that straddle the American-Canadian border. Like King's other work, the novel engages with the artificiality of the border for North American Native people, many of whom do not recognize the divide as a legitimate one. His short story "Borders," from *One Good Story, That One,* concerns a Blackfoot woman who refuses to declare herself as either Canadian or American when crossing the border in her car. King employs his characteristic comic strategy to comment on the right to self-determination as the protagonist's mother declares her "citizenship" as Blackfoot in a quiet political act of self-identification.

Borders

When I was twelve, maybe thirteen, my mother announced that we were going to go to Salt Lake City to visit my sister who had left the reserve, moved across the line, and found a job. Laetitia had not left home with my mother's blessing, but over time my mother had come to be proud of the fact that Laetitia had done all of this on her own.

"She did real good," my mother would say.

Then there were the fine points to Laetitia's going. She had not, as my mother liked to tell Mrs. Manyfingers, gone floating after some man like a balloon on a string. She hadn't snuck out of the house, either, and gone to Vancouver or Edmonton or Toronto to chase rainbows down alleys. And she hadn't been pregnant.

"She did real good."

I was seven or eight when Laetitia left home. She was seventeen. Our father was from Rocky Boy on the American side.[1]

"Dad's American," Laetitia told my mother, "so I can go and come as I please."

"Send us a postcard."

---

[1] The Rocky Boy Indian Reservation, of the Chippewa Cree Tribe, in northern Montana, 65 kilometres south of the Canadian border.

Laetitia packed her things, and we headed for the border. Just outside of Milk River, Laetitia told us to watch for the water tower.

"Over the next rise. It's the first thing you see."

"We got a water tower on the reserve," my mother said. "There's a big one in Lethbridge, too."

"You'll be able to see the tops of the flagpoles, too. That's where the border is."

When we got to Coutts,[2] my mother stopped at the convenience store and bought her and Laetitia a cup of coffee. I got an Orange Crush.

"This is real lousy coffee."

"You're just angry because I want to see the world."

"It's the water. From here on down, they got lousy water."

"I can catch the bus from Sweetgrass. You don't have to lift a finger."

"You're going to have to buy your water in bottles if you want good coffee."

There was an old wooden building about a block away, with a tall sign in the yard that said "Museum." Most of the roof had been blown away. Mom told me to go and see when the place was open. There were boards over the windows and doors. You could tell that the place was closed, and I told Mom so, but she said to go and check anyway. Mom and Laetitia stayed by the car. Neither one of them moved. I sat down on the steps of the museum and watched them, and I don't know that they ever said anything to each other. Finally, Laetitia got her bag out of the trunk and gave Mom a hug.

I wandered back to the car. The wind had come up, and it blew Laetitia's hair across her face. Mom reached out and pulled the strands out of Laetitia's eyes, and Laetitia let her.

"You can still see the mountain from here," my mother told Laetitia in Blackfoot.

"Lots of mountains in Salt Lake," Laetitia told her in English.

"The place is closed," I said. "Just like I told you."

Laetitia tucked her hair into her jacket and dragged her bag down the road to the brick building with the American flag flapping on a pole. When she got to where the guards were waiting, she turned, put the bag down, and waved to us. We waved back. Then my mother turned the car around, and we came home.

We got postcards from Laetitia regular, and, if she wasn't spreading jelly on the truth, she was happy. She found a good job and rented an apartment with a pool.

"And she can't even swim," my mother told Mrs. Manyfingers.

Most of the postcards said we should come down and see the city, but whenever I mentioned this, my mother would stiffen up.

So I was surprised when she bought two new tires for the car and put on her blue dress with the green and yellow flowers. I had to dress up, too, for my mother did not want us crossing the border looking like Americans. We made

---

[2] Coutts, Alberta, and Sweetgrass, Montana, straddle the Canada-U.S. border.

sandwiches and put them in a big box with pop and potato chips and some apples and bananas and a big jar of water.

"But we can stop at one of those restaurants, too, right?"

"We maybe should take some blankets in case you get sleepy."

"But we can stop at one of those restaurants, too, right?"

The border was actually two towns, though neither one was big enough to amount to anything. Coutts was on the Canadian side and consisted of the convenience store and gas station, the museum that was closed and boarded up, and a motel. Sweetgrass was on the American side, but all you could see was an overpass that arched across the highway and disappeared into the prairies. Just hearing the names of these towns, you would expect that Sweetgrass, which is a nice name and sounds like it is related to other places such as Medicine Hat and Moose Jaw and Kicking Horse Pass, would be on the Canadian side, and that Coutts, which sounds abrupt and rude, would be on the American side. But this was not the case.

Between the two borders was a duty-free shop where you could buy cigarettes and liquor and flags. Stuff like that.

We left the reserve in the morning and drove until we got to Coutts.

"Last time we stopped here," my mother said, "you had an Orange Crush. You remember that?"

"Sure," I said. "That was when Laetitia took off."

"You want another Orange Crush?"

"That means we're not going to stop at a restaurant, right?"

My mother got a coffee at the convenience store, and we stood around and watched the prairies move in the sunlight. Then we climbed back in the car. My mother straightened the dress across her thighs, leaned against the wheel, and drove all the way to the border in first gear, slowly, as if she were trying to see through a bad storm or riding high on black ice.

The border guard was an old guy. As he walked to the car, he swayed from side to side, his feet set wide apart, the holster on his hip pitching up and down. He leaned into the window, looked into the back seat, and looked at my mother and me.

"Morning, ma'am."

"Good morning."

"Where you heading?"

"Salt Lake City."

"Purpose of your visit?"

"Visit my daughter."

"Citizenship?"

"Blackfoot," my mother told him.

"Ma'am?"

"Blackfoot," my mother repeated.

"Canadian?"

"Blackfoot."

It would have been easier if my mother had just said "Canadian" and been done with it, but I could see she wasn't going to do that. The guard wasn't angry or anything. He smiled and looked towards the building. Then he turned back and nodded.

"Morning, ma'am."

"Good morning."

"Any firearms or tobacco?"

"No."

"Citizenship?"

"Blackfoot."

He told us to sit in the car and wait, and we did. In about five minutes, another guard came out with the first man. They were talking as they came, both men swaying back and forth like two cowboys headed for a bar or a gunfight.

"Morning, ma'am."

"Good morning."

"Cecil tells me you and the boy are Blackfoot."

"That's right."

"Now, I know that we got Blackfeet on the American side and the Canadians got Blackfeet on their side.[3] Just so we can keep our records straight, what side do you come from?"

I knew exactly what my mother was going to say, and I could have told them if they had asked me.

"Canadian side or American side?" asked the guard.

"Blackfoot side," she said.

It didn't take them long to lose their sense of humor, I can tell you that. The one guard stopped smiling altogether and told us to park our car at the side of the building and come in.

We sat on a wood bench for about an hour before anyone came over to talk to us. This time it was a woman. She had a gun, too.

"Hi," she said. "I'm Inspector Pratt. I understand there is a little misunderstanding."

"I'm going to visit my daughter in Salt Lake City," my mother told her. "We don't have any guns or beer."

"It's a legal technicality, that's all."

"My daughter's Blackfoot, too."

The woman opened a briefcase and took out a couple of forms and began to write on one of them. "Everyone who crosses our border has to declare their citizenship. Even Americans. It helps us keep track of the visitors we get from the various countries."

[3] The Blackfoot Confederacy consists of four distinct nations, three in southern Alberta and the fourth in northwestern Montana: the Blackfoot/Siksika Nation, the Blood/Kainai Nation, the Peigan/Pikuni Nation, and the Blackfeet Tribe.

She went on like that for maybe fifteen minutes, and a lot of the stuff she told us was interesting.

"I can understand how you feel about having to tell us your citizenship, and here's what I'll do. You tell me, and I won't put it down on the form. No-one will know but you and me."

Her gun was silver. There were several chips in the wood handle and the name "Stella" was scratched into the metal butt.

We were in the border office for about four hours, and we talked to almost everyone there. One of the men bought me a Coke. My mother brought a couple of sandwiches in from the car. I offered part of mine to Stella, but she said she wasn't hungry.

I told Stella that we were Blackfoot and Canadian, but she said that that didn't count cause I was a minor. In the end, she told us that if my mother didn't declare her citizenship, we would have to go back to where we came from. My mother stood up and thanked Stella for her time. Then we got back in the car and drove to the Canadian border, which was only about a hundred yards away.

I was disappointed. I hadn't seen Laetitia for a long time, and I had never been to Salt Lake City. When she was still at home, Laetitia would go on and on about Salt Lake City. She had never been there, but her boyfriend Lester Tallbull had spent a year in Salt Lake at a technical school.

"It's a great place," Lester would say. "Nothing but blondes in the whole state."

Whenever he said that, Laetitia would slug him on his shoulder hard enough to make him flinch. He had some brochures on Salt Lake and some maps, and every so often the two of them would spread them out on the table.

"That's the temple. It's right downtown. You got to have a pass to get in."

"Charlotte says anyone can go in and look around."

"When was Charlotte in Salt Lake? Just when the hell was Charlotte in Salt Lake?"

"Last year."

"This is Liberty Park. It's got a zoo. There's good skiing in the mountains."

"Got all the skiing we can use," my mother would say. "People come from all over the world to ski at Banff. Cardston's got a temple, if you like those kinds of things."

"Oh, this one is real big," Lester would say. "They got armed guards and everything."

"Not what Charlotte says."

"'What does she know?"

Lester and Laetitia broke up, but I guess the idea of Salt Lake stuck in her mind.

The Canadian border guard was a young woman, and she seemed happy to see us. "Hi," she said. "You folks sure have a great day for a trip. Where are you coming from?"

"Standoff."

"Is that in Montana?"

"No."

"Where are you going?"

"Standoff."

The woman's name was Carol and I don't guess she was any older than Laetitia. "Wow, you both Canadians?"

"Blackfoot."

"Really? I have a friend I went to school with who is Blackfoot. Do you know Mike Harley?"

"No."

"He went to school in Lethbridge, but he's really from Browning."

It was a nice conversation and there were no cars behind us, so there was no rush.

"You're not bringing any liquor back, are you?"

"No."

"Any cigarettes or plants or stuff like that?"

"No."

"Citizenship?"

"Blackfoot."

"I know," said the woman, "and I'd be proud of being Blackfoot if I were Blackfoot. But you have to be American or Canadian."

When Laetitia and Lester broke up, Lester took his brochures and maps with him, so Laetitia wrote to someone in Salt Lake City, and, about a month later, she got a big envelope of stuff. We sat at the table and opened up all the brochures, and Laetitia read each one out loud.

"Salt Lake City is the gateway to some of the world's most magnificent skiing.

"Salt Lake City is the home of one of the newest professional basketball franchises, the Utah Jazz.

"The Great Salt Lake is one of the natural wonders of the world."

It was kind of exciting seeing all those color brochures on the table and listening to Laetitia read all about how Salt Lake City was one of the best places in the entire world.

"That Salt Lake City place sounds too good to be true," my mother told her.

"It has everything."

"We got everything right here."

"It's boring here."

"People in Salt Lake City are probably sending away for brochures of Calgary and Lethbridge and Pincher Creek right now."

In the end, my mother would say that maybe Laetitia should go to Salt Lake City, and Laetitia would say that maybe she would.

We parked the car to the side of the building and Carol led us into a small room on the second floor. I found a comfortable spot on the couch and flipped through some back issues of *Saturday Night* and *Alberta Report*.[4]

When I woke up, my mother was just coming out of another office. She didn't say a word to me. I followed her down the stairs and out to the car. I thought we were going home, but she turned the car around and drove back towards the American border, which made me think we were going to visit Laetitia in Salt Lake City after all. Instead she pulled into the parking lot of the duty-free store and stopped.

"We going to see Laetitia?"

"No."

"We going home?"

Pride is a good thing to have, you know. Laetitia had a lot of pride, and so did my mother. I figured that someday, I'd have it, too.

"So where are we going?"

Most of that day, we wandered around the duty-free store, which wasn't very large. The manager had a name tag with a tiny American flag on one side and a tiny Canadian flag on the other. His name was Mel. Towards evening, he began suggesting that we should be on our way. I told him we had nowhere to go, that neither the Americans nor the Canadians would let us in. He laughed at that and told us that we should buy something or leave.

The car was not very comfortable, but we did have all that food and it was April, so even if it did snow as it sometimes does on the prairies, we wouldn't freeze. The next morning my mother drove to the American border.

It was a different guard this time, but the questions were the same. We didn't spend as much time in the office as we had the day before. By noon, we were back at the Canadian border. By two we were back in the duty-free shop parking lot.

The second night in the car was not as much fun as the first, but my mother seemed in good spirits, and, all in all, it was as much an adventure as an inconvenience. There wasn't much food left and that was a problem, but we had lots of water as there was a faucet at the side of the duty-free shop.

One Sunday, Laetitia and I were watching television. Mom was over at Mrs. Manyfingers's. Right in the middle of the program, Laetitia turned off the set and said she was going to Salt Lake City, that life around here was too boring. I had wanted to see the rest of the program and really didn't care if Laetitia went to Salt Lake City or not. When Mom got home, I told her what Laetitia had said.

What surprised me was how angry Laetitia got when she found out that I had told Mom.

[4] Two Canadian magazines. "Borders" was first published in *Saturday Night,* December 1991.

"You got a big mouth."

"That's what you said."

"'What I said is none of your business."

"I didn't say anything."

"Well, I'm going for sure, now."

That weekend, Laetitia packed her bags, and we drove her to the border.

Mel turned out to be friendly. When he closed up for the night and found us still parked in the lot, he came over and asked us if our car was broken down or something. My mother thanked him for his concern and told him that we were fine, that things would get straightened out in the morning.

"You're kidding," said Mel. "You'd think they could handle the simple things."

"We got some apples and a banana," I said, "but we're all out of ham sandwiches."

"You know, you read about these things, but you just don't believe it. You just don't believe it."

"Hamburgers would be even better because they got more stuff for energy."

My mother slept in the back seat. I slept in the front because I was smaller and could lie under the steering wheel. Late that night, I heard my mother open the car door. I found her sitting on her blanket leaning against the bumper of the car.

"You see all those stars," she said. "When I was a little girl, my grandmother used to take me and my sisters out on the prairies and tell us stories about all the stars."

"Do you think Mel is going to bring us any hamburgers?"

"Every one of those stars has a story. You see that bunch of stars over there that look like a fish?"

"He didn't say no."

"Coyote went fishing, one day. That's how it all started." We sat out under the stars that night, and my mother told me all sorts of stories. She was serious about it, too. She'd tell them slow, repeating parts as she went, as if she expected me to remember each one.

Early the next morning, the television vans began to arrive, and guys in suits and women in dresses came trotting over to us, dragging microphones and cameras and lights behind them. One of the vans had a table set up with orange juice and sandwiches and fruit. It was for the crew, but when I told them we hadn't eaten for a while, a really skinny blonde woman told us we could eat as much as we wanted.

They mostly talked to my mother. Every so often one of the reporters would come over and ask me questions about how it felt to be an Indian without a country. I told them we had a nice house on the reserve and that my cousins had a couple of horses we rode when we went fishing. Some of the television people went over to the American border, and then they went to the Canadian border.

Around noon, a good-looking guy in a dark blue suit and an orange tie with little ducks on it drove up in a fancy car. He talked to my mother for a while, and, after they were done talking, my mother called me over, and we got into our car. Just as my mother started the engine, Mel came over and gave us a bag of peanut brittle and told us that justice was a damn hard thing to get, but that we shouldn't give up.

I would have preferred lemon drops, but it was nice of Mel anyway.

"Where are we going now?"

"Going to visit Laetitia."

The guard who came out to our car was all smiles. The television lights were so bright they hurt my eyes, and, if you tried to look through the windshield in certain directions, you couldn't see a thing.

"Morning, ma'am."

"Good morning."

"Where you heading?"

"Salt Lake City."

"Purpose of your visit?"

"Visit my daughter."

"Any tobacco, liquor, or firearms?"

"Don't smoke."

"Any plants or fruit?"

"Not any more."

"Citizenship?"

"Blackfoot."

The guard rocked back on his heels and jammed his thumbs into his gun belt. "Thank you," he said, his fingers patting the butt of the revolver. "Have a pleasant trip."

My mother rolled the car forward, and the television people had to scramble out of the way. They ran alongside the car as we pulled away from the border, and, when they couldn't run any farther, they stood in the middle of the highway and waved and waved and waved.

We got to Salt Lake City the next day. Laetitia was happy to see us, and, that first night, she took us out to a restaurant that made really good soups. The list of pies took up a whole page. I had cherry. Mom had chocolate. Laetitia said that she saw us on television the night before and, during the meal, she had us tell her the story over and over again.

Laetitia took us everywhere. We went to a fancy ski resort. We went to the temple. We got to go shopping in a couple of large malls, but they weren't as large as the one in Edmonton, and Mom said so.

After a week or so, I got bored and wasn't at all sad when my mother said we should be heading back home. Laetitia wanted us to stay longer, but Mom said no, that she had things to do back home and that, next time, Laetitia should come up and visit. Laetitia said she was thinking about moving back, and Mom told her to do as she pleased, and Laetitia said that she would.

On the way home, we stopped at the duty-free shop, and my mother gave Mel a green hat that said "Salt Lake" across the front. Mel was a funny guy. He took the hat and blew his nose and told my mother that she was an inspiration to us all. He gave us some more peanut brittle and came out into the parking lot and waved at us all the way to the Canadian border.

It was almost evening when we left Coutts. I watched the border through the rear window until all you could see were the tops of the flagpoles and the blue water tower, and then they rolled over a hill and disappeared.

[1993]

M. NOURBESE PHILIP ■ (1947–)

M. NourbeSe Philip (who has also published under the names Marlene Philip and Marlene Nourbese Philip) is a poet, playwright, fiction writer, community activist, and lawyer. Her work sustains a focus on language, the body, history, colonialism, memory, and longing. In her essay "The Absence of Writing or How I Almost Became a Spy" (1989/97), Philip concentrates on the ability of language to alter the way a community perceives itself and its collective consciousness. If language is the site of power, then it is the responsibility of the artist to harness that language and rework images to better reflect the real struggles of subjugated peoples. For Philip, born in Tobago and growing up in Trinidad, "English" was imbued with an imperialist ideology that, as she explains, was "not only experientially foreign, but also etymologically hostile and expressive of the non-being of the African." Her poetry seizes language, resists its structures, and makes it new. In "A Genealogy of Resistance" (1997), Philip articulates the poet's desire to embrace through language "a genealogy of bodies. Of ghosts. Of the silenced. Whose voices can still be heard. If you listen closely enough. Of resistance."

Philip's route to poetry was not direct. She recalls that in school in Trinidad, writing did not figure among the occupations a middle-class student might pursue, so she did not consider it as a career path early on. In 1965 she won a scholarship for achieving first place in a Caribbean-wide examination at the high school level. It helped send her to the University of the West Indies, where she earned a B.Sc. (Econ.) in 1968. She continued on to the University of Western Ontario to complete a Master's degree in political science (1970) and earn a degree in law (1973). During the seven years she practised law (at Parkdale Community Services and then in a partnership), Philip published two books of poetry, *Thorns* (1980) and *Salmon Courage* (1983). Following the publication of her second volume, she left law to write full time (although she continued to work occasionally for Ontario Legal Aid). Over the past three decades, while writing, she has also taught at the University of Toronto and the Ontario College of Art and Design and has been awarded the "Rebel with a Cause" Award by the Elizabeth Fry Society.

Philip's first work of fiction, *Harriet's Daughter* (1988), is the story of a Black girl growing up in Toronto. It is about the intersections of friendship, self-image, ethics, and migration. This teenage *Bildungsroman* was conceived as something of a corrective for the absence of Black characters in Canadian children's literature. After the esteemed publisher of the African Writers Series, Heinemann, published it in England, a Canadian edition was issued by the Women's Press. Proving the Canadian publishers wrong who had originally rejected it on the grounds that it might not appeal to a wide audience, the novel met with critical success (winning the Canadian Children's Book Centre's Choice Award) and is now used in high school curricula in Canada, Great Britain, and the Caribbean.

Distinguishing loosely between genres, Phillip writes, "[F]iction is about telling lies, but you must be scathingly honest in telling those lies. Poetry is about truth telling, but you need the lie—the artifice of the form to tell those truths." Philip's third poetry book, *She Tries Her Tongue, Her Silence Softly Breaks* (1989) was awarded the Casa de las Américas Prize for Literature while still in manuscript form. In "The Habit Of: Poetry, Rats and Cats," Philip reasons, "I set out to destroy the lyric voice, the singularity of the lyric voice, and found that poetry had split. Metamorphosed. Into a multiplicity of voices—the polyvocular. In opposition to the univocal lyric voice." Comparing poststructuralist thought and L=A=N=G=U=A=G=E poetry (with prominent sound patterning, unusual diction, and experimental play with

language) with Philip's work, poet-critic George Elliott Clarke points out that in "Discourse on the Logic of Language," Philip "cascades verse sideways down the left-hand margins of the page, conjoins verse and prose, mocks grammars and primers, and throws into jeopardy any attempt to read the poem in a standard linear fashion." The poem actively counters the concept of universal truth in the polyphony and multiplicity of its poetic fragments. Philip counters the edicts of colonial authorities and the discourse of nineteenth-century neurology, with the actions of the new mother and the forbidden language of the mother tongue. Philip herself suggests that multiple readers should read the poem out loud at the same time in order to hear the poem's competing voices.

Philip's language is muscular, kinetically joining the body and the word, as she writes in "Genealogy": "[T]he body—tongues, penises, the brain, the skin, the ribcage, breasts—the black body erupting into the work." Her poem "Meditations on the Declension of Beauty by the Girl with the Flying Cheek-bones" further illustrates the conjunction of the body and language. As critic Maureen Moynagh argues, "[T]he use of repetition with variation to suggest grammatical declension here becomes incantatory, an affirmation of identity and beauty achieved in language," but the precariousness of the speaker's beauty is highlighted in the slippage between affirmation and denial, and between the interrogative and the declarative. Philip's poetry can be compared to that of Dionne Brand and Jeannette Armstrong, both of whom engage with the cultural politics of language, and with Daphne Marlatt's feminist poetics in "musing with mothertongue" (1984) and Margaret Atwood's prose poem "The Female Body" (1992).

Following *She Tries Her Tongue,* Philip was a resident at the Banff School of the Arts and won a Guggenheim Fellowship in Poetry that allowed her to complete her next poetic work, *Looking for Livingstone* (1991), a volume that reworks Dr. David Livingstone's journeys in Africa through the eyes of The Traveller, a woman who searches for what Philip calls the "echoes in the silence of another language that was obliterated." In addition to her poetic work, Philip is an active member of PEN International and the Writers' Union. Some of her opinion pieces on the way racism operates in Canadian cultural institutions were collected in *Frontiers* (1992). Among them is the pragmatic article from the 6 March 1990 *Toronto Star,* "Why Multiculturalism Can't End Racism," where she concludes that "multiculturalism as we know it, has no answers for the problems of racism, or white supremacy— unless it is combined with a clearly articulated policy of anti-racism." She ends the article by arguing that understanding the ideological lineage of a racist belief system is fundamental to any debate about multiculturalism.

Meditations on the Declension of Beauty by the Girl with the Flying Cheek-bones

If not   If not   If
Not
If not in yours
           In whose
In whose language
Am I
If not in yours
           In whose
In whose language
Am I   I am   10
           If not in yours
In whose
           Am I
(if not in yours)
           I am yours
In whose language
             Am I not
Am I not   I am yours
If not in yours
If not in yours   20

        In whose
In whose language
            Am I . . .

Girl with the flying cheek-bones:
She is
I am
Woman with the behind that drives men mad
And if not in yours
Where is the woman with a nose broad
As her strength   30
If not in yours
In whose language
Is the man with the full-moon lips
Carrying the midnight of colour
Split by the stars—a smile
If not in yours

        In whose

In whose language
           Am I
           Am I not   40
           Am I   I am yours
           Am I not   I am yours
           Am I   I am

If not in yours
        In whose
In whose language
           Am I
If not in yours
           Beautiful

                                      [1989]

Discourse on the Logic
of Language

English
is my mother tongue.
A mother tongue is not
not a foreign lan lan lang
language
l/anguish
  anguish
—a foreign anguish.

English is
my father tongue.
A father tongue is
a foreign language,
therefore English is
a foreign language
not a mother tongue.

What is my mother
tongue
my mammy tongue
my mummy tongue
my momsy tongue
my modder tongue
my ma tongue?

I have no mother
tongue
no mother to tongue
no tongue to mother
to mother
tongue
me

I must therefore be tongue
dumb
dumb-tongued
dub-tongued
damn dumb
tongue

WHEN IT WAS BORN, THE MOTHER HELD HER NEWBORN CHILD CLOSE: SHE BEGAN THEN TO LICK IT ALL OVER. THE CHILD WHIMPERED A LITTLE, BUT AS THE MOTHER'S TONGUE MOVED FASTER AND STRONGER OVER ITS BODY, IT GREW SILENT—THE MOTHER TURNING IT THIS WAY AND THAT UNDER HER TONGUE, UNTIL SHE HAD TONGUED IT CLEAN OF THE CREAMY WHITE SUBSTANCE COVERING ITS BODY.

EDICT I

*Every owner of slaves
shall, wherever possible,
ensure that his slaves
belong to as many
ethno-linguistic groups
as possible. If they can-
not speak to each other,
they cannot then foment
rebellion and revolution.*

Those parts of the brain chiefly responsible for speech are named after two learned nineteenth century doctors, the eponymous Doctors Wernicke and Broca respectively.

Dr. Broca believed the size of the brain determined intelligence; he devoted much of his time to 'proving' that white males of the Caucasian race had larger brains than, and where therefore superior to, women, Blacks and other peoples of colour.

Understanding and recognition of the spoken word takes place in Wernicke's area—the left temporal lobe, situated next to the auditory cortex; from there relevant information passes to Broca's area—situated in the left frontal cortex—which then forms the response and passes it on to the motor cortex. The motor cortex controls the muscles of speech.[1]

[1] Broca's area, named after the nineteenth-century French physician Paul Broca (1824–1880), is the section of the brain identified with speech and language processing. Wernicke's area, named after German neurologist Carl Wernicke (1848–1905), is the part of the brain involved in the comprehension of spoken language. Broca also developed the science of craniometry, the precise measurement of human skulls. Stephen Jay Gould undertook an analysis of the racist conclusions that have emerged as a result of Broca's findings in *The Mismeasure of Man* (1981).

but I have
a dumb tongue
tongue dumb
father tongue
and english is
my mother tongue
is
my father tongue
is a foreign lan lan lang
language
l/anguish
  anguish
a foreign anguish
is english—
another tongue
my mother
    mammy
    mummy
    moder
    mater
    macer
    moder
tongue
mothertongue

tongue mother
tongue me
mothertongue me
mother me
touch me
with the tongue of your
lan lan lang
language
l/anguish
  anguish
english
is a foreign anguish

EDICT II

*Every slave caught
speaking his native lan-
guage shall be severely
punished. Where neces-
sary, removal of the
tongue is recommended.
The offending organ,
when removed, should be
hung on high in a cen-
tral place, so that all
may see and tremble.*

THE MOTHER THEN PUT HER FINGERS INTO HER CHILD'S MOUTH—GENTLY FORCING IT OPEN; SHE TOUCHES HER TONGUE TO THE CHILD'S TONGUE, AND HOLDING THE TINY MOUTH OPEN, SHE BLOWS INTO IT—HARD. SHE WAS BLOWING WORDS—HER WORDS, HER MOTHER'S WORDS, THOSE OF HER MOTHER'S MOTHER, AND ALL THEIR MOTHERS BEFORE—INTO HER DAUGHTER'S MOUTH.

A tapering, blunt-tipped, muscular, soft and fleshy organ describes
(a) the penis.
(b) the tongue.
(c) neither of the above.
(d) both of the above.

In man the tongue is
(a) the principal organ of taste.
(b) the principal organ of articulate speech.
(c) the principal organ of oppression and exploitation.
(d) all of the above.

The tongue
(a) is an interwoven bundle of striated muscle running in three planes.
(b) is fixed to the jawbone.
(c) has an outer covering of a mucous membrane covered with papillae.
(d) contains ten thousand taste buds, none of which is sensitive to the taste of foreign words.

Air is forced out of the lungs up the throat to the larynx where it causes the vocal cords to vibrate and create sound. The metamorphosis from sound to intelligible word requires
(a) the lip, tongue and jaw all working together.
(b) a mother tongue.
(c) the overseer's whip.
(d) all of the above or none.

[1989]

JEANNETTE ARMSTRONG ■ (1948–)

Throughout her life, Jeannette Armstrong, of the Okanagan Nation, has advocated Indigenous knowledge, self-determination, creativity, and leadership among First Nations peoples. In 2003 her pivotal role in Indigenous cultural and political affairs was recognized when she received the Buffet Award for Indigenous Leadership. Since 1989, Armstrong has been involved in the En'owkin Centre (an Indigenous cultural, educational, and creative arts post-secondary institution located in Penticton, B.C.), where she teaches creative writing and serves as executive director. Armstrong has also served on a range of boards of organizations invested in studying the environment, globalization, Indigenous governance, and justice (through groups like the Center for Ecoliteracy in Berkeley, California), been an international observer to the Continental Coordinating Commission of Indigenous Peoples and Organizations, and served on the Canadian Commission for UNESCO.

In addition to her community leadership, Armstrong is an important writer. In the artist's statement for the selection of her own poetry in the anthology she co-edited with Lally Grauer,

Native Poetry in Canada (2001), Armstrong writes: "The purpose of my writing has always been to tell a better story than is being told about us. To give that to the people and to the next generations." Her landmark novel *Slash* (1985), for instance, offers a counterpoint to White cultural and political dominance in Canada, replacing it with the affirmation of traditional Indigenous practices and the possibility of reasonable self-determination. Her books, like her activism, span a range of subjects and genres: children's books; non-fiction work with architect Douglas Cardinal on the process of collaboration, *The Native Creative Process* (1991); an edited collection of essays, *Looking at the Words of Our People: First Nations Analysis of Literature* (1993); poetry, *Breath Tracks* (1991), from which "History Lesson" is drawn; and fiction, *Whispering in Shadows* (2000). Armstrong puts her creative work in context: "Through my language I understand I am being spoken to, I'm not the one speaking. The words are coming from many tongues and mouths of Okanagan people and the land around them. I am a listener to the language's stories, and when my words form I am merely retelling the same stories in different patterns." Like her other work, "The Disempowerment of First North American Native Peoples and Empowerment Through Their Writing" focuses not only on the problems faced by contemporary Indigenous peoples, but also on modes of empowerment and creative solutions. In keeping with Armstrong's focus on being part of a community of Indigenous artists, this talk was first published alongside the work of other prominent Native writers and thinkers such as Lee Maracle, Armand Garnet Ruffo, Annharte, and Kateri Damm in *Gatherings: The En'owkin Journal of First North American Peoples, Survival Issue* (1990).

History Lesson

Out of the belly of Christopher's ship[1]
a mob bursts
Running in all directions
Pulling furs off animals
Shooting buffalo
Shooting each other
left and right

Father mean well
waves his makeshift wand
forgives saucer-eyed Indians   10

Red coated knights
gallop across the prairie

---

[1] Christopher Columbus (1451–1506), the European explorer who is often heralded as the "discoverer" of the Americas, which he asserted was the East Coast of Asia (the "Indies"), in 1492. Columbus's treatment of Indigenous peoples on the islands in the West Indies, which included acts of kidnapping, enslavement, and extermination, is now well known. The poem proceeds from this early event of colonization and moves forward in history to the Canadian fur trade and the British settlement of the Canadian prairies (red-coated knights being a reference to the North West Mounted Police).

to get their men
and to build a new world

Pioneers and traders
bring gifts
Smallpox, Seagrams[2]
and rice krispies

Civilization has reached
the promised land   20

Between the snap crackle pop
of smoke stacks
and multicolored rivers
swelling with flower powered zee
are farmers sowing skulls and bones
and miners
pulling from gaping holes
green paper faces
of a smiling English lady

The colossi   30
in which they trust
while burying
breathing forests and fields
beneath concrete and steel
stand shaking fists
waiting to mutilate
whole civilizations
ten generations at a blow

Somewhere among the remains
of skinless animals   40
is the termination
to a long journey
and unholy search
for the power
glimpsed in a garden
forever closed
forever lost

[1991]

---

[2] Seagrams is a long-standing Canadian distilling company; the reference here is to the brand of whiskey. Rice Krispies in the next line is a type of breakfast cereal whose advertising for years has used the phrase "snap crackle pop."

The Disempowerment of First North American Native Peoples and Empowerment Through Their Writing[3]

In order to address the specifics of Native people's writing and empowerment, I must first present my view on the disempowerment of first North American Nations.

Without recounting various historical versions of *how* it happened, I would like to refer only to *what* happened here.

Indigenous peoples in North America were rendered powerless and subjugated to totalitarian domination by foreign peoples, after they were welcomed as guests and their numbers were allowed to grow to the point of domination through aggression.

Once total subjective control was achieved over my peoples through various coercive measures and the direct removal of political, social, and religious freedoms accomplished, the colonization process began.

In North America this has been to systemically enforce manifest destiny or the so-called "White Man's burden" to civilize.[4] In the 498 years of contact in The Americas,[5] the thrust of this bloody sword has been to hack out the spirit of all the beautiful cultures encountered, leaving in its wake a death toll unrivalled in recorded history. This is what happened and what continues to happen.

There is no word other than totalitarianism which adequately describes the methods used to achieve the condition of my people today. Our people were not given choices. Our children, for generations, were seized from our communities and homes and placed in indoctrination camps until our language, our religion, our customs, our values, and our societal structures almost disappeared. This was the residential school experience.

Arising out of the siege conditions of this nightmare time, what is commonly referred to as the "social problems" of Native peoples emerged. Homes and communities, without children, had nothing to work for, or live for. Children returned to communities and families as adults, without the necessary skills for parenting, for Native life style, or self-sufficiency on their land base, deteriorated into despair. With the loss of cohesive cultural relevance with their own peoples and a distorted view of the non-Native culture from the

---

[3] This paper was prepared for the Saskatchewan Writers Guild 1990 Annual Conference, for a panel discussion entitled "Empowering Aboriginal Writers."

[4] "The White Man's Burden" (1899) is the title of a poem by English poet and novelist Rudyard Kipling (1865–1936), in which imperialism is portrayed as a "burden" or duty that Western nations must carry in order to bring civilization around the world; it is often used as a phrase to describe the ways racism is couched as philanthropy in imperialist rhetoric. "Manifest destiny" refers to the expansionist belief in the nineteenth-century United States that Americans were predestined to settle the continent from the Atlantic to the Pacific.

[5] In other words, the time span between 1492 (Christopher Columbus's arrival in the Americas) and 1990.

clergy who ran the residential schools, an almost total disorientation and loss of identity occurred. The disintegration of family and community and nation was inevitable, originating with the individual's internalized pain. Increasing death statistics from suicide, violence, alcohol and drug abuse, and other poverty-centred physical diseases, can leave no doubt about the question of totalitarianism and genocide.

You writers from the dominating culture have the freedom of imagination. You keep reminding us of this. Is there anyone here who dares to imagine what those children suffered at the hands of their so-called "guardians" in those schools. You are writers, imagine it on yourselves and your children. Imagine you and your children and imagine how they would be treated by those who abhorred and detested you, all, as savages without any rights.

Imagine at what cost to you psychologically, to acquiesce and attempt to speak, dress, eat, and worship, like your oppressors, simply out of a need to be treated humanly. Imagine attempting to assimilate so that your children will not suffer what you have, and imagine finding that assimilationist measures are not meant to include you but to destroy all remnants of your culture. Imagine finding that even when you emulate every cultural process from customs to values you are still excluded, despised and ridiculed because you are Native.

Imagine finding out that the dominating culture will not tolerate any real cultural participation and that cultural supremacy forms the basis of the government process and that systemic racism is a tool to maintain their kind of totalitarianism. And all the while, imagine that this is presented under the guise of "equal rights" and under the banner of banishing bigotry on an individual basis through law.

Imagine yourselves in this condition and imagine the writer of that dominating culture berating you for speaking out about appropriation of cultural voice and using the words "freedom of speech" to condone further systemic violence,[6] in the form of entertainment literature about *your* culture and *your* values and all the while, yourself being disempowered and rendered voiceless through such "freedoms".

Imagine how you as writers from the dominant society might turn over some of the rocks in your own garden for examination. Imagine in your literature courageously questioning and examining the values that allow the dehumanizing of peoples through domination and the dispassionate nature of the racism inherent in perpetuating such practices. Imagine writing in honesty, free of the romantic bias about the courageous "pioneering spirit" of colonialist practice and imperialist process. Imagine interpreting for us *your own people's* thinking toward us, instead of interpreting for us, our thinking, our lives and our stories. We wish to know, and you need to understand, why it is that you want to

[6] Armstrong is referring to the "appropriation of voice" debate that was raging in the late 1980s and early '90s. The argument was that authors of non-Aboriginal origin should not be writing in the "voice" of Indigenous characters or using Indigenous cultures' stories for their own purposes. See the introduction to this section for more discussion of the debate.

own our stories, our art, our beautiful crafts, our ceremonies, but you do not appreciate or wish to recognize that these things of beauty arise out of the beauty of our people.

Imagine these realities on yourselves in honesty and let me know how you imagine that you might approach empowerment of yourselves in such a situation. Better yet, do not dare speak to me of "Freedom of Voice", "Equal Rights", "Democracy", or "Human Rights" until this totalitarianistic approach has been changed by yourselves as writers and shapers of philosophical direction. Imagine a world where domination is not possible because all cultures are valued.

To the Native writers here, my words are meant as empowerment to you. In my quest for empowerment of my people through writing, there are two things of which I must steadfastly remind myself.

The first is that the reality I see is the reality for the majority of Native people and that although severe and sometimes irreparable damage has been wrought, healing can take place through cultural affirmation. I have found immense strength and beauty in my people.

The dispelling of lies and the telling of what really happened until *everyone*, including our own people understands that this condition did not happen through choice or some cultural defect on our part, is important. Equally important is the affirmation of the true beauty of our people whose fundamental co-operative values resonated pacifism and predisposed our cultures as vulnerable to the reprehensible value systems which promote domination and aggression.

The second thing I must remind myself of is that the dominating culture's reality is that it seeks to affirm itself continuously and must be taught that *numbers* are not the basis of democracy, *people* are, *each one* being important. It must be pushed, in Canada, to understand and accept that this country is multi-racial and multi-cultural now, and the meaning of that. I must remind myself constantly of the complacency that makes these conditions possible, and that if I am to bridge into that complacency that I will be met with hostility from the majority, but, that those whose thoughts I have provoked may become our greatest allies in speaking to their own. It is this promotion of an ideal which will produce the courage to shake off centuries of imperialist thought and make possible the relearning of co-operation and sharing, in place of domination.

Our task as Native writers is twofold. To examine the past and culturally affirm toward a new vision for all our people in the future, arising out of the powerful and positive support structures that are inherent in the principles of co-operation.

We, as Native people, through continuously resisting cultural imperialism and seeking means toward teaching co-operative relationships, provide an integral mechanism for solutions currently needed in this country.

We must see ourselves as undefeatably pro-active in a positive sense and realize that negative activism actually serves the purpose of the cultural imperialism practised on our people. Lies need clarification, truth needs to be stated, and resistance to oppression needs to be stated, without furthering division and participation in the same racist measures. This is the challenge that we rise to. Do not make the commonly made error that it is a people that we abhor, be clear that it is systems and processors which we must attack. Be clear that change to those systems will be promoted by people who can perceive intelligent and non-threatening alternatives. Understand that these alternatives will be presented only through discourse and dialogue flowing outward from us, for now, because we are the stakeholders. We need the system to change. Those in the system can and will remain complacent until moved to think, and to understand how critical change is needed at this time for us all. Many already know and are willing to listen.

The responsibility of the Native writer is tremendous in light of these times in which world over, solutions are being sought to address the failed assimilationist measures originating out of conquest, oppression and exploitation, whether under the socialist or capitalist banner. We as writers can show how support for Lithuanian independence and support for South African Black equality becomes farcical in the glare of the Constitutional position to First Nations here in Canada, who seek nothing more than co-operative sovereign relationships guaranteed in the principles of treaty making. No one will desire or choose to hear these truths unless they are voiced clearly to people who have no way to know that there are good alternatives and that instead of losing control we can all grow powerful together.

Finally, I believe in the basic goodness of the majority of people. I rely on the common human desire to be guilt free and fulfilled, to triumph, towards attainment of our full potential as wonderful, thinking beings at the forward edge of the Creator's expression of beauty.

I believe in the strength and rightness in the values of my people and know that those principles of peace and co-operation, in practice, are natural and survival-driven mechanisms which transcend violence and aggression. I see the destructive paths that have led us to this time in history, when all life on this planet is in peril, and know that there *must* be change. I believe that the principles of co-operation are a sacred trust and the plan and the intent of the Creator and therefore shall endure.

[1990]

PIER GIORGIO DI CICCO ■ (1949–)

Pier Giorgio Di Cicco has been at the forefront of Italian-Canadian writing, the Toronto poetry explosion of the 1970s, and the more recent reassessment of religion in a global age of secularity. For literary historian Joseph Pivato, Italian-Canadian literature as a recognizable category of writing came into existence in 1975 when Di Cicco realized that there was a critical mass of Italian-Canadian poets in Canada. This realization culminated in his publication of the first Canadian anthology of writers of Italian heritage, *Roman Candles: An Anthology of Poems by Seventeen Italo-Canadian Poets* (1978). In the Introduction to

Roman Candles, Di Cicco outlines how he searched for the contributors in the nationalist climate of the mid-1970s: "I found isolated gestures by isolated poets, isolated mainly by the condition of nationalism prevalent in Canada in the last 10 years. However pluralistic the landscape seemed to be to sociologists, the sheer force of Canadianism had been enough to intimidate all but the older 'unofficial-language' writers." In that same landmark year for Italian-Canadian studies, Frank Paci published his bestselling *The Italians* (1978). Di Cicco followed with his first major literary success, *The Tough Romance,* in 1979. Over the next decades, these writers were joined by Mary Di Michele, Mary Melfi, Maria Ardizzi, Caterina Edwards, Pasquale Verdecchio, George Amabile, Marco Micone, and perhaps most famously, Nino Ricci, author of the Governor General's Award-winning *Lives of the Saints* (1990), in the burgeoning field of Italian-Canadian literature. Also in 1978 Antonio D'Alfonso founded Guernica Editions, the pre-eminent Italian-Canadian-American press that publishes work in English, French, and Italian. Di Michele asserts that "in opening a space in English-language poetry for experience and feeling born in Italian, Pier Giorgio Di Cicco changed my life . . . as well as Canadian literature's landscape." Di Cicco's early poetry joined the physical and emotional spaces of Italy and Canada (as in the beautiful poem "Arezzo-Toronto"), employed unglossed Italian words, and followed Italian literary traditions.

Born in Arezzo, Italy, Di Cicco immigrated to Montreal with his family when he was three, moved to Toronto a few years later, and lived in Baltimore for nine years after that. In 1967, he returned to Toronto to take a B.A. in literature. Over the next two decades Di Cicco was firmly entrenched in the burgeoning Toronto poetry scene, often reading at the Harbourfront Reading series and fraternizing with the poets of the day: Al Purdy, Joe Rosenblatt, Irving Layton, Gwendolyn MacEwen, Dennis Lee, and Margaret Atwood, among many others. Burnt out by poetry (in 13 years publishing 10 books, including the 1982 volume *Flying Deeper into the Century,* and three chapbooks), he turned to the sanctity of the Marylake Monastery, taking his vows as an Augustinian monk shortly after *Virgin Science* was published in 1986. Over the next 15 years, Di Cicco was on a self-imposed hiatus from poetry. After four years he again shifted trajectories and began to train for the Catholic priesthood. In 1993 he was ordained, and he now serves in the parish of King City, north of Toronto. It wasn't until 2001 that he returned to the world of poetry with a new collection entitled *Living in Paradise.*

There are a serenity and an acceptance in Di Cicco's recent writing that were absent in his earlier work. Unlike the devout poems of Margaret Avison, the poetry Di Cicco composed after he entered the priesthood is spare in reference to religion. Still, these poems—such as "Fraters," published in *The Honeymoon Wilderness* (2002), and "God as Moths," published in *The Dark Time of Angels* (2003)—explore questions of spirituality and faith. While the monks in "Fraters" are rendered as ordinary humans, the moths are imbued with a transcendent spirituality. Francesco Loriggio, editor of *The Last Effort of Dreams: Essays on the Poetry of Pier Giorgio Di Cicco* (2007), reasons that in Di Cicco's poetry, God is a paradoxical figure who is both ubiquitous and absent, unfathomable and approachable; in short, a rather human God. As well as being a poet and a priest, Di Cicco is curator of the Toronto Humanities Project, a teacher at the University of Toronto, and a consultant on issues of global aesthetics.

God as Moths

PIER GIORGIO DI CICCO

1

I will not kill this one.
he is large and hides
and comes out of shadows,
big as a pet;
he is neither worm nor butterfly,
he is a mystery thing looking for light,
like me.
he is my brother,
I will let in and out.
I hurt him inadvertently,   10
and he springs back to life.

2

this one clung to the night window,
spread like a cross,
a cross resting.

he brought a tiny saviour through the dark.
he is a breath against my face.
he waits.
the kitchen light; false light, or daylight,
it does not matter, he is not fussy.
I should be happy in my ignorant life.   20

3

the smaller ones flit in and out.
I no sooner open the door than they follow
me in, companions, careful doves,
lost souls of those who loved me.
they wait at the houselight for me,
to see what I have been up to.
hushed, so hushed.
like the mute hand of Him
on my shoulder.

4

now He is telling me   30
by His wing on sin

and wayward,
so gentle, this awesome
perpetrator of sea and pole,
He deigns a little finger
on the obtrusive dark,
like a child carried across
the battlefield,
He sends a motherly feather,
He sends a sliver of my conscience.   40
He is in the room with me.
the mighty into the hapless,
in no found thing,
but moth.

5

one day I put my face to
the bark of a tree, and heard
my blood shoots, heard earth stirring
in its taps, the water that must come
when I am drained of love.
pale and drawn from the surface planet,   50
tired as the old tree, I kissed my brethren,
the beaten, weathered, who had been standing in
the cold all winter long,
and I heard the tap roots, a gurgle,
something saved, like spring.

moth too, is saved of me.
the silence of my soul,
spared of me,
like memory
of the good I am.   60

6

and now one comes,
a sheen on its wings. this one different from
all the others; a silver sheen,
that is not like a crown
nor the hope I make of dumb things,
but like
leaves in the rush of wind,
what tracks me to Him.

so many angel messengers.
all with his kiss on my nape.
so many eyes on Him,
all with my desire.

70

[2003]

ANNE CARSON ■ (1950–)

Any discussion of Anne Carson's work should ideally have multiple beginnings. Carson is a poet, classical scholar, essayist, and translator venerated by such writers as Alice Munro, Susan Sontag (who called her an anti-bourgeois icon), and a great number of the contemporary literati in New York and London. She is, according to Michael Ondaatje, "the most exciting poet writing in English today." Carson's deeply philosophical and allusive poetry has garnered such exalted praise because of its erosion of conventional boundaries: it integrates both modern and classical references within new generic forms that fuse poetic expression with essayistic style. Carson's poetry has won numerous lucrative awards, including the Pushcart Prize (1997), a Guggenheim Fellowship (1998), and the Griffin Poetry Prize (2001). Because of the sheer volume of awards she has received, mainly in the United States, there is also a sizable group of critics who maintain that her reputation is "ludicrously over-inflated" (Roger Kimball, managing editor of the *New Criterion,* for instance), arguing that her diction is either impenetrable with classical references or lightweight in its use of conversational language.

Because Carson shies away from literary celebrity, the only biographical detail that appears on her dust jackets is that she lives in Canada. Born in Toronto in 1950, Carson graduated from the University of Toronto with a B.A., M.A., and Ph.D. in classics. While a professor of Greek and Latin at McGill University, Carson issued a translation from ancient Greek of the lyric poet Sappho, *If Not, Winter: Fragments of Sappho* (2002). She has also published a series of strikingly diverse poetic works that include *Eros the Bittersweet* (1986); *Goddesses and Wise Women* (1992); *Short Talks* (1992); *Glass, Irony and God* (1995); *Autobiography of Red* (1998); *Men in the Off Hours* (2000); *The Beauty of the Husband* (2001); and *Decreation* (2005).

The judges' citation for the Griffin Prize for *Men in the Off Hours* reads: "Anne Carson continues to redefine what a book of poetry can be; this ambitious collection ranges from quatrains studded with uncanny images . . . to musing verse essays, personal laments, rigorous classical scholarship, and meditations on artists' lives, caught in the carnage of history. All are burnished by Carson's dialectical imagination, and her quizzical, stricken moral sense." It is just such an eclectic imagination that informs all of Carson's work. Her poetry also makes reference to numerous literary figures: Emily Dickinson, Gertrude Stein, Sigmund Freud, Virginia Woolf, Sappho, and Simone Weil, to name a few of a dozen characters who inhabit her texts and surface time and again—sometimes in conversation with each other, sometimes conversing with the poetic voice herself. Carson's use of these writers and their words goes beyond simple acts of reference. Instead, they are embedded in the poems as a polyphony of voices.

Carson's work juxtaposes images to combine philosophical ideas, emotional intensity, and realistic vignettes. Marijke Emeis notes that "when the mind reads Carson, the heart reads along. The reason is in the sweat of suffering, in the erotic, bleeding pain that emanates from her lines." Indeed, Carson's poetry never steers away from descriptions of internalized suffering, evident in the two poems about her father included here. Her long poem "The Glass Essay" weaves together the story of a woman, her failed lover, her mother, romantic humiliation, a kitchen table, visions she calls "nudes," and a memorable and moving portrait of Emily Brontë cleaning the carpet and thinking poetic thoughts to her unnamed "Thou." Carson's "short talks," the series of prose poems excerpted here, touch on affairs of the heart, everyday life, and philosophic beliefs in snapshot form. In her introduction to *Short Talks,* Carson writes that her words work to "construct an instant of nature gradually, without the boredom of story. I emphasize this. I will do anything to avoid boredom. It is the task of a lifetime. You can never know enough, never work enough, never use the infinitives and participles oddly enough, never impede the movement harshly enough, never leave the mind quickly enough."

Short Talk on Sunday Dinner with Father

Are you going to put that chair back where it belongs or just leave it there looking like a uterus? (Our balcony is a breezy June balcony). Are you going to let your face distorted by warring desires pour down on us all through the meal or tidy yourself so we can at least enjoy our dessert? (We weight down the corners of everything on the table with little solid silver laws). Are you going to nick your throat open on those woodpecker scalps as you do every Sunday night or just sit quietly while Laetitia plays her clarinet for us? (My father, who smokes a brand of cigar called *Dimanche Eternel,* uses them as ashtrays.)

Short Talk on My Task

My task is to carry secret burdens for the world. People watch curiously. Yesterday morning at sunrise for example, you could have seen me on the breakwall carrying gauze. I also carry untimely ideas and sins in general or any faulty action that has been lowered together with you into this hour. Trust me. The trotting animal can restore red hearts to red.

Short Talk on Major and Minor

Major things are wind, evil, a good fighting horse, prepositions, inexhaustible love, the way people choose their king. Minor things include dirt, the names of schools of philosophy, mood and not having a mood, the correct time. There are more major things than minor things overall, yet there are more minor things than I have written here, but it is disheartening to list them. When I think of you reading this I do not want you to be taken captive, separated by a wire mesh lined with glass from your life itself, like some Elektra.[1]

[1992]

Father's Old Blue Cardigan

Now it hangs on the back of the kitchen chair
where I always sit, as it did
on the back of the kitchen chair where he always sat.

I put it on whenever I come in,
as he did, stamping
the snow from his boots.

I put it on and sit in the dark.
He would not have done this.
Coldness comes paring down from the moonbone in the sky.

His laws were a secret.   10
But I remember the moment at which I knew
he was going mad inside his laws.

He was standing at the turn of the driveway when I arrived.
He had on the blue cardigan with the buttons done up all the way to the top.
Not only because it was a hot July afternoon

but the look on his face—
as a small child who has been dressed by some aunt early in the morning
for a long trip

on cold trains and windy platforms
will sit very straight at the edge of his seat   20
while the shadows like long fingers

over the haystacks that sweep past
keep shocking him
because he is riding backwards.

[2000]

---

[1] There are various stories about Electra, but in most versions Electra is the sister of Orestes who helps her brother plot revenge against their mother Clytemnestra, who betrayed their father Agamemnon while he was away at the Trojan War. Together, they murder their mother in retaliation for their mother's murder of Agamemnon. Carson herself has translated three of the plays dealing with this subject: Sophocles's *Electra*, Euripedes's *The Oresteia*, and Aeschylus's *Agamemnon*.

ANNE CARSON

608

Audubon

Audubon perfected a new way of drawing birds that he called his.[2]
On the bottom of each watercolor he put "drawn from nature"
which meant he shot the birds

and took them home to stuff and paint them.
Because he hated the unvarying shapes
of traditional taxidermy

he built flexible armatures of bent wire and wood
on which he arranged bird skin and feathers—
or sometimes

whole eviscerated birds—   10
in animated poses.
Not only his wiring but his lighting was new.

Audubon colors dive in through your retina
like a searchlight
roving shadowlessly up and down the brain

until you turn away.
And you do turn away.
There is nothing to see.

You can look at these true shapes all day and not see the bird.
Audubon understands light as an absence of darkness,   20
truth as an absence of unknowing.

It is the opposite of a peaceful day in Hokusai.[3]
Imagine if Hokusai had shot and wired 219 lions
and then forbade his brush to paint shadow.

---

[2] John James Audubon (1785–1851), famous naturalist and painter, whose opus *The Birds of America* (1827–1838) has been widely distributed and republished around the world. Audubon's prime claim to originality was that he drew detailed renditions of actual bird specimens, which, as the poem notes, he wired into particular positions and placed into mini-dramatic "scenes." Audubon engaged in an overt self-fashioning of his persona, obscuring his Haitian origins and presenting himself as an American frontiersman (not dissimilar to the biographical masquerades of Grey Owl and Frederick Philip Grove). The irony of Audubon's career is that he is now celebrated as the great conservationist even though he killed thousands of specimens for his paintings. Canadian novelist Katherine Govier's 2002 novel *Creation* weaves a fictionalized story of Audubon's career, art, and various deceptions.

[3] Katsushika Hokusai (1760–1849), Japanese painter and printmaker, famous for his *Thirty-Six Views of Mount Fuji*. Hokusai shifted the traditional focus in Japanese painting from courtly figures to depictions of landscape and animals. Late in life, Hokusai began drawing a lion each day, completing over 200 paintings of lions.

"We are what we make ourselves," Audubon told his wife
when they were courting.
In the salons of Paris and Edinburgh

where he went to sell his new style
this Haitian-born Frenchman
lit himself   30

as a noble rustic American
wired in the cloudless poses of the Great Naturalist.
They loved him

for the "frenzy and ecstasy"
of true American facts, especially
in the second (more affordable) octavo edition (*Birds of America,* 1844).

[2000]

ROHINTON MISTRY ■ (1952–)

From his first published work, Rohinton Mistry has proven himself to be a master storyteller. His writing has garnered significant critical praise and a loyal readership. Since winning the Governor General's Award for his first novel, *Such a Long Journey* (1991), receiving the Giller Prize for *A Fine Balance* (1995), and making the Booker Prize shortlist for his first two novels as well as for his third, *Family Matters* (2002), Mistry has developed a reputation as one of the finest writers in English today. While Mistry's work follows in the tradition of Indian social realists such as Raja Rao, Mulk Raj Anand, and R. K. Narayan, who use the form of realism to examine the ramifications of the social problems of the day, it also shares characteristics with nineteenth-century English writer Charles Dickens and such twentieth-century Canadians as Margaret Laurence and Carol Shields. Some critics have even spoken of his work as containing magic-realist elements, in the vein of Salman Rushdie. In all his work, Mistry elegantly leads his characters through seemingly ordinary situations in Bombay (now Mumbai) and Toronto, defamiliarizing, and often exaggerating, these situations so that they achieve an almost epic aura.

Mistry was born and raised in a Parsi (Zoroastrian) community in Bombay. According to his literary biographer Martin Genetsch, as a teenager growing up in India, Mistry spoke English, Hindi, and Gujarati, and learned to play the guitar and the harmonica so he could be in a folk band that performed songs by Bob Dylan and Leonard Cohen. After completing a B.Sc. at the University of Bombay, Mistry moved to Toronto to join his fiancée, Freny Elavia, who was studying to become a teacher. The couple were married in 1975 and settled in Brampton, Ontario. For the next decade Mistry worked at the Canadian Imperial Bank of Commerce, attended the University of Toronto part time (earning a B.A. in literature), and began to write fiction. By

1985, on the strength of a short story contest prize (and the praise of judge Mavis Gallant), Mistry left his job at the bank to write full time. The result was his Governor General's Award-nominated book *Tales from Firozsha Baag* (1987), from which "Squatter" is taken, a collection of stories centred on the inhabitants of a Bombay apartment complex named Firozsha Baag.

A number of the stories in *Tales from Firozsha Baag* engage humorously with immigration as Mistry satirizes official multiculturalism and critiques the desire for complete, uncomplicated assimilation. Like the characters in Hanif Kureishi's stories set in England, Rushdie's novels set in India, England, and America, and Jhumpa Lahiri's fiction set in the United States, Sarosh/Sid in "Squatter" is part of the South Asian diaspora. The term "diaspora" is Greek for "dispersion" and is associated with groups of people who share cultural and historical features in a new land, retain a connection to a place of origin, and make a "home" in a new context. It is essential to note that all diasporas are differentiated, heterogeneous, contested groups that are always shifting and in process. In writing that engages with diasporic communities there is often a conflict over the notion of "home," as an imagined or remembered space, and a question of whether what is permissible (culturally and historically) in one home is permissible and desirable in another. In "Squatter," Mistry gently satirizes diasporic longing and discussions of home, family, migration, displacement, and belonging as Sarosh/Sid sets himself the impossible challenge of total assimilation. In doing so, Mistry, who is highly resistant to demands that he become a spokesperson for multicultural issues, subverts the more conventional immigration narratives of people struggling against the land, elements, and inhospitable strangers. The framed story, told by Nariman to the boys of Firozsha Baag, takes the form of an amusing oral "tall tale," yet it is also self-reflexive: embedded within it are hints at its own literary method, and, by extension, instructions in how it is to be read.

Squatter

Whenever Nariman Hansotia returned in the evening from the Cawasji Framji Memorial Library in a good mood the signs were plainly evident.

First, he parked his 1932 Mercedes-Benz (he called it the apple of his eye) outside A Block, directly in front of his ground-floor veranda window, and beeped the horn three long times. It annoyed Rustomji who also had a ground-floor flat in A Block. Ever since he had defied Nariman in the matter of painting the exterior of the building, Rustomji was convinced that nothing the old coot did was untainted by the thought of vengeance and harassment, his retirement pastime.

But the beeping was merely Nariman's signal to let Hirabai inside know that though he was back he would not step indoors for a while. Then he raised the hood, whistling "Rose Marie,"[1] and leaned his tall frame over the engine. He

---

[1] A song from the 1924 operetta, released in 1936 as the Hollywood film *Rose Marie* starring Nelson Eddy and Jeanette MacDonald (set in Quebec). It has become famous in cultural discussions as an example of Hollywood's misrepresentation of Canada.

checked the oil, wiped here and there with a rag, tightened the radiator cap, and lowered the hood. Finally, he polished the Mercedes star and let the whistling modulate into the march from *The Bridge On The River Kwai*.[2] The boys playing in the compound knew that Nariman was ready now to tell a story. They started to gather round.

"*Sahibji*, Nariman Uncle," someone said tentatively and Nariman nodded, careful not to lose his whistle, his bulbous nose flaring slightly. The pursed lips had temporarily raised and reshaped his Clark Gable[3] moustache. More boys walked up. One called out, "How about a story, Nariman Uncle?" at which point Nariman's eyes began to twinkle, and he imparted increased energy to the polishing. The cry was taken up by others, "Yes, yes, Nariman Uncle, a story!" He swung into a final verse of the march. Then the lips relinquished the whistle, the Clark Gable moustache descended. The rag was put away, and he began.

"You boys know the great cricketers: Contractor, Polly Umrigar, and recently, the young chap, Farokh Engineer. Cricket *aficionados*, that's what you all are." Nariman liked to use new words, especially big ones, in the stories he told, believing it was his duty to expose young minds to as shimmering and varied a vocabulary as possible; if they could not spend their days at the Cawasji Framji Memorial Library then he, at least, could carry bits of the library out to them.

The boys nodded; the names of the cricketers were familiar.

"But does any one know about Savukshaw, the greatest of them all?" They shook their heads in unison.

"This, then, is the story about Savukshaw, how he saved the Indian team from a humiliating defeat when they were touring in England." Nariman sat on the steps of A Block. The few diehards who had continued with their games could not resist any longer when they saw the gathering circle, and ran up to listen. They asked their neighbours in whispers what the story was about, and were told: Savukshaw the greatest cricketer. The whispering died down and Nariman began.

"The Indian team was to play the indomitable MCC[4] as part of its tour of England. Contractor was our captain. Now the MCC being the strongest team they had to face, Contractor was almost certain of defeat. To add to Contractor's troubles, one of his star batsmen, Nadkarni, had caught influenza early in the tour, and would definitely not be well enough to play against the MCC. By the way, does anyone know what those letters stand for? You, Kersi, you wanted to be a cricketer once."

Kersi shook his head. None of the boys knew, even though they had heard the MCC mentioned in radio commentaries, because the full name was hardly ever used.

---

[2] 1957 Hollywood film *The Bridge on the River Kwai*, directed by David Lean.

[3] Hollywood star of such notable films as *Gone with the Wind* (1939) and *Mutiny on the Bounty* (1935), known for his good looks and thin moustache.

[4] Marylebone Cricket Club, founded in 1787, plays at Lord's Cricket Ground in London, England, affectionately known as the home of cricket.

Then Jehangir Bulsara spoke up, or Bulsara Bookworm, as the boys called him. The name given by Pesi *paadmaroo*[5] had stuck even though it was now more than four years since Pesi had been sent away to boarding-school, and over two years since the death of Dr Mody.[6] Jehangir was still unliked by the boys in the Baag, though they had come to accept his aloofness and respect his knowledge and intellect. They were not surprised that he knew the answer to Nariman's question: "Marylebone Cricket Club."

"Absolutely correct," said Nariman, and continued with the story. "The MCC won the toss and elected to bat. They scored four hundred and ninety-seven runs in the first inning before our spinners could get them out. Early in the second day's play our team was dismissed for one hundred and nine runs, and the extra who had taken Nadkarni's place was injured by a vicious bumper that opened a gash on his forehead." Nariman indicated the spot and the length of the gash on his furrowed brow. "Contractor's worst fears were coming true. The MCC waived their own second inning and gave the Indian team a follow-on, wanting to inflict an inning's defeat. And this time he had to use the second extra. The second extra was a certain Savukshaw."

The younger boys listened attentively; some of them, like the two sons of the chartered accountant in B Block, had only recently been deemed old enough by their parents to come out and play in the compound, and had not received any exposure to Nariman's stories. But the others like Jehangir, Kersi, and Viraf were familiar with Nariman's technique.

Once, Jehangir had overheard them discussing Nariman's stories, and he could not help expressing his opinion: that unpredictability was the brush he used to paint his tales with, and ambiguity the palette he mixed his colours in. The others looked at him with admiration. Then Viraf asked what exactly he meant by that. Jehangir said that Nariman sometimes told a funny incident in a very serious way, or expressed a significant matter in a light and playful manner. And these were only two rough divisions, in between were lots of subtle gradations of tone and texture. Which, then, was the funny story and which the serious? Their opinions were divided, but ultimately, said Jehangir, it was up to the listener to decide.

"So," continued Nariman, "Contractor first sent out his two regular openers, convinced that it was all hopeless. But after five wickets were lost for just another thirty-eight runs, out came Savukshaw the extra. Nothing mattered any more."

The street lights outside the compound came on, illuminating the iron gate where the watchman stood. It was a load off the watchman's mind when Nariman told a story. It meant an early end to the hectic vigil during which he had to ensure that none of the children ran out on the main road, or tried to jump over the wall. For although keeping out riff-raff was his duty, keeping in the boys was as important if he wanted to retain the job.

---

[5] Pesi is a brutish child and bully from C Block known for his spitting talents and his ability to break wind in a manner that sounds like a question or an exclamation.

[6] Dr Burjor Mody is the stamp-collecting neighbour who becomes Jehangir's friend and mentor in "The Collectors," earlier in *Tales*. He is also the father of Pesi.

"The first ball Savukshaw faced was wide outside the off stump. He just lifted his bat and ignored it. But with what style! What panache! As if to say, come on, you blighters, play some polished cricket. The next ball was also wide, but not as much as the first. It missed the off stump narrowly. Again Savukshaw lifted his bat, boredom written all over him. Everyone was now watching closely. The bowler was annoyed by Savukshaw's arrogance, and the third delivery was a vicious fast pitch, right down on the middle stump.

"Savukshaw was ready, quick as lightning. No one even saw the stroke of his bat, but the ball went like a bullet towards square leg.

"Fielding at square leg was a giant of a fellow, about six feet seven, weighing two hundred and fifty pounds, a veritable Brobdingnagian,[7] with arms like branches and hands like a pair of huge *sapaat,* the kind that Dr Mody used to wear, you remember what big feet Dr Mody had." Jehangir was the only one who did; he nodded. "Just to see him standing there was scary. Not one ball had got past him, and he had taken some great catches. Savukshaw purposely aimed his shot right at him. But he was as quick as Savukshaw, and stuck out his huge *sapaat* of a hand to stop the ball. What do you think happened then, boys?"

The older boys knew what Nariman wanted to hear at this point. They asked, "What happened, Nariman Uncle, what happened?" Satisfied, Nariman continued.

"A howl is what happened. A howl from the giant fielder, a howl that rang through the entire stadium, that soared like the cry of a banshee right up to the cheapest seats in the furthest, highest corners, a howl that echoed from the scoreboard and into the pavilion, into the kitchen, startling the chap inside who was preparing tea and scones for after the match, who spilled boiling water all over himself and was severely hurt. But not nearly as bad as the giant fielder at square leg. Never at any English stadium was a howl heard like that one, not in the whole history of cricket. And why do you think he was howling, boys?"

The chorus asked, "Why, Nariman Uncle, why?"

"Because of Savukshaw's bullet-like shot, of course. The hand he had reached out to stop it, he now held up for all to see, and *dhur-dhur, dhur-dhur* the blood was gushing like a fountain in an Italian piazza, like a burst water-main from the Vihar-Powai reservoir, dripping onto his shirt and his white pants, and sprinkling the green grass, and only because he was such a giant of a fellow could he suffer so much blood loss and not faint. But even he could not last forever; eventually, he felt dizzy, and was helped off the field. And where do you think the ball was, boys, that Savukshaw had smacked so hard?"

And the chorus rang out again on the now dark steps of A Block:

"Where, Nariman Uncle, where?"

"Past the boundary line, of course. Lying near the fence. Rent asunder. Into two perfect leather hemispheres. All the stitches had ripped, and some of the insides had spilled out. So the umpires sent for a new one, and the game

---

[7] A reference to the giants of Brobdingnag, a fictional land in *Gulliver's Travels* (1726) by English writer Jonathan Swift (1667–1745).

resumed. Now none of the fielders dared to touch any ball that Savukshaw hit. Every shot went to the boundary, all the way for four runs. Single-handedly, Savukshaw wiped out the deficit, and had it not been for loss of time due to rain, he would have taken the Indian team to a thumping victory against the MCC. As it was, the match ended in a draw."

Nariman was pleased with the awed faces of the youngest ones around him. Kersi and Viraf were grinning away and whispering something. From one of the flats the smell of frying fish swam out to explore the night air, and tickled Nariman's nostrils. He sniffed appreciatively, aware that it was in his good wife Hirabai's pan that the frying was taking place. This morning, he had seen the pomfret she had purchased at the door, waiting to be cleaned, its mouth open and eyes wide, like the eyes of some of these youngsters. It was time to wind up the story.

"The MCC will not forget the number of new balls they had to produce that day because of Savukshaw's deadly strokes. Their annual ball budget was thrown badly out of balance. Any other bat would have cracked under the strain, but Savukshaw's was seasoned with a special combination of oils, a secret formula given to him by a *sadhu* who had seen him one day playing cricket when he was a small boy. But Savukshaw used to say his real secret was practice, lots of practice, that was the advice he gave to any young lad who wanted to play cricket."

The story was now clearly finished, but none of the boys showed any sign of dispersing. "Tell us about more matches that Savukshaw played in," they said.

"More nothing. This was his greatest match. Anyway, he did not play cricket for long because soon after the match against the MCC he became a champion bicyclist, the fastest human on two wheels. And later, a pole-vaulter—when he glided over on his pole, so graceful, it was like watching a bird in flight. But he gave that up, too, and became a hunter, the mightiest hunter ever known, absolutely fearless, and so skilful, with a gun he could have, from the third floor of A Block, shaved the whisker of a cat in the backyard of C Block."

"Tell us about that," they said, "about Savukshaw the hunter!"

The fat ayah, Jaakaylee, arrived to take the chartered accountant's two children home. But they refused to go without hearing about Savukshaw the hunter. When she scolded them and things became a little hysterical, some other boys tried to resurrect the ghost she had once seen: "Ayah *bhoot!* Ayah *bhoot!*" Nariman raised a finger in warning—that subject was still taboo in Firozsha Baag; none of the adults was in a hurry to relive the wild and rampageous days that Pesi *paadmaroo* had ushered in, once upon a time, with the *bhoot* games.[8]

Jaakaylee sat down, unwilling to return without the children, and whispered to Nariman to make it short. The smell of frying fish which had tickled Nariman's nostrils ventured into and awakened his stomach. But the story of Savukshaw the hunter was one he had wanted to tell for a long time.

---

[8] A reference to "The Ghost of Firozsha Baag," another story in the collection.

"Savukshaw always went hunting alone, he preferred it that way. There are many incidents in the life of Savukshaw the hunter, but the one I am telling you about involves a terrifying situation. Terrifying for us, of course; Savukshaw was never terrified of anything. What happened was, one night he set up camp, started a fire and warmed up his bowl of chicken-*dhansaak*."

The frying fish had precipitated famishment upon Nariman, and the subject of chicken-*dhansaak* suited him well. His own mouth watering, he elaborated: "Mrs Savukshaw was as famous for her *dhansaak* as Mr was for hunting. She used to put in tamarind and brinjal, coriander and cumin, cloves and cinnamon, and dozens of other spices no one knows about. Women used to come from miles around to stand outside her window while she cooked it, to enjoy the fragrance and try to penetrate her secret, hoping to identify the ingredients as the aroma floated out, layer by layer, growing more complex and delicious. But always, the delectable fragrance enveloped the women and they just surrendered to the ecstasy, forgetting what they had come for. Mrs Savukshaw's secret was safe."

Jaakaylee motioned to Nariman to hurry up, it was past the children's dinner-time. He continued: "The aroma of savoury spices soon filled the night air in the jungle, and when the *dhansaak* was piping hot he started to eat, his rifle beside him. But as soon as he lifted the first morsel to his lips, a tiger's eyes flashed in the bushes! Not twelve feet from him! He emerged licking his chops! What do you think happened then, boys?"

"What, what, Nariman Uncle?"

Before he could tell them, the door of his flat opened. Hirabai put her head out and said, "*Chaalo ni*, Nariman, it's time. Then if it gets cold you won't like it."

That decided the matter. To let Hirabai's fried fish, crisp on the outside, yet tender and juicy inside, marinated in turmeric and cayenne—to let that get cold would be something that *Khoedaiji* above would not easily forgive. "Sorry boys, have to go. Next time about Savukshaw and the tiger."

There were some groans of disappointment. They hoped Nariman's good spirits would extend into the morrow when he returned from the Memorial Library or the story would get cold.

But a whole week elapsed before Nariman again parked the apple of his eye outside his ground-floor flat and beeped the horn three times. When he had raised the hood, checked the oil, polished the star and swung into the "Colonel Bogie March,"[9] the boys began drifting towards A Block.

Some of them recalled the incomplete story of Savukshaw and the tiger, but they knew better than to remind him. It was never wise to prompt Nariman until he had dropped the first hint himself, or things would turn out badly.

Nariman inspected the faces: the two who stood at the back, always looking superior and wise, were missing. So was the quiet Bulsara boy, the intelligent one. "Call Kersi, Viraf, and Jehangir," he said, "I want them to listen to today's story."

[9] Whistled in *The Bridge on the River Kwai*.

Jehangir was sitting alone on the stone steps of C Block. The others were chatting by the compound gate with the watchman. Someone went to fetch them.

"Sorry to disturb your conference, boys, and your meditation, Jehangir," Nariman said facetiously, "but I thought you would like to hear this story. Especially since some of you are planning to go abroad."

This was not strictly accurate, but Kersi and Viraf did talk a lot about America and Canada. Kersi had started writing to universities there since his final high-school year, and had also sent letters of inquiry to the Canadian High Commission in New Delhi and to the U.S. Consulate at Breach Candy. But so far he had not made any progress. He and Viraf replied with as much sarcasm as their unripe years allowed, "Oh yes, next week, just have to pack our bags."

"Riiiight," drawled Nariman. Although he spoke perfect English, this was the one word with which he allowed himself sometimes to take liberties, indulging in a broadness of vowel more American than anything else. "But before we go on with today's story, what did you learn about Savukshaw, from last week's story?"

"That he was a very talented man," said someone.

"What else?"

"He was also a very lucky man, to have so many talents," said Viraf.

"Yes, but what else?"

There was silence for a few moments. Then Jehangir said, timidly: "He was a man searching for happiness, by trying all kinds of different things."

"Exactly! And he never found it. He kept looking for new experiences, and though he was very successful at everything he attempted, it did not bring him happiness. Remember this, success alone does not bring happiness. Nor does failure have to bring unhappiness. Keep it in mind when you listen to today's story."

A chant started somewhere in the back: "We-want-a-story! We-want-a-story!"

"Riiiight," said Nariman. "Now, everyone remembers Vera and Dolly, daughters of Najamai from C Block." There were whistles and hoots; Viraf nudged Kersi with his elbow, who was smiling wistfully. Nariman held up his hand: "Now now, boys, behave yourselves. Those two girls went abroad for studies many years ago, and never came back. They settled there happily.

"And like them, a fellow called Sarosh also went abroad, to Toronto, but did not find happiness there. This story is about him. You probably don't know him, he does not live in Firozsha Baag, though he is related to someone who does."

"Who? Who?"

"Curiosity killed the cat," said Nariman, running a finger over each branch of his moustache, "and what's important is the tale. So let us continue. This Sarosh began calling himself Sid after living in Toronto for a few months, but in our story he will be Sarosh and nothing but Sarosh, for that is his proper Parsi name. Besides, that was his own stipulation when he entrusted me with the sad but instructive chronicle of his recent life." Nariman polished his glasses with his handkerchief, put them on again, and began.

"At the point where our story commences, Sarosh had been living in Toronto for ten years. We find him depressed and miserable, perched on top of the toilet, crouching on his haunches, feet planted firmly for balance upon the white plastic oval of the toilet seat.

"Daily for a decade had Sarosh suffered this position. Morning after morning, he had no choice but to climb up and simulate the squat of our Indian latrines. If he sat down, no amount of exertion could produce success.

"At first, this inability was no more than mildly incommodious. As time went by, however, the frustrated attempts caused him grave anxiety. And when the failure stretched unbroken over ten years, it began to torment and haunt all his waking hours."

Some of the boys struggled hard to keep straight faces. They suspected that Nariman was not telling just a funny story, because if he intended them to laugh there was always some unmistakable way to let them know. Only the thought of displeasing Nariman and prematurely terminating the story kept their paroxysms of mirth from bursting forth unchecked.

Nariman continued: "You see, ten years was the time Sarosh had set himself to achieve complete adaptation to the new country. But how could he claim adaptation with any honesty if the acceptable catharsis continually failed to favour him? Obtaining his new citizenship had not helped either. He remained dependent on the old way, and this unalterable fact, strengthened afresh every morning of his life in the new country, suffocated him.

"The ten-year time limit was more an accident than anything else. But it hung over him with the awesome presence and sharpness of a guillotine. Careless words, boys, careless words in a moment of lightheartedness, as is so often the case with us all, had led to it.

"Ten years before, Sarosh had returned triumphantly to Bombay after fulfilling the immigration requirements of the Canadian High Commission in New Delhi. News of his imminent departure spread amongst relatives and friends. A farewell party was organized. In fact, it was given by his relatives in Firozsha Baag. Most of you will be too young to remember it, but it was a very loud party, went on till late in the night. Very lengthy and heated arguments took place, which is not the thing to do at a party. It started like this: Sarosh was told by some what a smart decision he had made, that his whole life would change for the better; others said he was making a mistake, emigration was all wrong, but if he wanted to be unhappy that was his business, they wished him well.

"By and by, after substantial amounts of Scotch and soda and rum and Coke had disappeared, a fierce debate started between the two groups. To this day Sarosh does not know what made him raise his glass and announce: 'My dear family, my dear friends, if I do not become completely Canadian in exactly ten years from the time I land there, then I will come back. I promise. So please, no more arguments. Enjoy the party.' His words were greeted with cheers and shouts of hear! hear! They told him never to fear embarrassment; there was no shame if he decided to return to the country of his birth.

"But shortly, his poor worried mother pulled him aside. She led him to the back room and withdrew her worn and aged prayer book from her purse, saying, 'I want you to place your hand upon the *Avesta* and swear that you will keep that promise.'

"He told her not to be silly, that it was just a joke. But she insisted: '*Kassum khà*—on the *Avesta*. One last thing for your mother. Who knows when you will see me again?' and her voice grew tremulous as it always did when she turned deeply emotional. Sarosh complied, and the prayer book was returned to her purse.

"His mother continued: 'It is better to live in want among your family and your friends, who love you and care for you, than to be unhappy surrounded by vacuum cleaners and dishwashers and big shiny motor cars.' She hugged him. Then they joined the celebration in progress.

"And Sarosh's careless words spoken at the party gradually forged themselves into a commitment as much to himself as to his mother and the others. It stayed with him all his years in the new land, reminding him every morning of what must happen at the end of the tenth, as it reminded him now while he descended from his perch."

Jehangir wished the titters and chortles around him would settle down, he found them annoying. When Nariman structured his sentences so carefully and chose his words with extreme care as he was doing now, Jehangir found it most pleasurable to listen. Sometimes, he remembered certain words Nariman had used, or combinations of words, and repeated them to himself, enjoying again the beauty of their sounds when he went for his walks to the Hanging Gardens or was sitting alone on the stone steps of C Block. Mumbling to himself did nothing to mitigate the isolation which the other boys in the Baag had dropped around him like a heavy cloak, but he had grown used to all that by now.

Nariman continued: "In his own apartment Sarosh squatted barefoot. Elsewhere, if he had to go with his shoes on, he would carefully cover the seat with toilet paper before climbing up. He learnt to do this after the first time, when his shoes had left telltale footprints on the seat. He had had to clean it with a wet paper towel. Luckily, no one had seen him.

"But there was not much he could keep secret about his ways. The world of washrooms is private and at the same time very public. The absence of feet below the stall door, the smell of faeces, the rustle of paper, glimpses caught through the narrow crack between stall door and jamb—all these added up to only one thing: a foreign presence in the stall, not doing things in the conventional way. And if the one outside could receive the fetor of Sarosh's business wafting through the door, poor unhappy Sarosh too could detect something malodorous in the air: the presence of xenophobia and hostility."

What a feast, thought Jehangir, what a feast of words! This would be the finest story Nariman had ever told, he just knew it.

"But Sarosh did not give up trying. Each morning he seated himself to push and grunt, grunt and push, squirming and writhing unavailingly on the white plastic oval. Exhausted, he then hopped up, expert at balancing now, and completed the movement quite effortlessly.

"The long morning hours in the washroom created new difficulties. He was late going to work on several occasions, and one such day, the supervisor called him in: 'Here's your time-sheet for this month. You've been late eleven times. What's the problem?'"

Here, Nariman stopped because his neighbour Rustomji's door creaked open. Rustomji peered out, scowling, and muttered: "*Saala* loafers, sitting all evening outside people's houses, making a nuisance, and being encouraged by grownups at that."

He stood there a moment longer, fingering the greying chest hair that was easily accessible through his *sudra,* then went inside. The boys immediately took up a soft and low chant: "Rustomji-the-curmudgeon! Rustomji-the-curmudgeon!"

Nariman held up his hand disapprovingly. But secretly, he was pleased that the name was still popular, the name he had given Rustomji when the latter had refused to pay his share for painting the building. "Quiet, quiet!" said he. "Do you want me to continue or not?"

"Yes, yes!" The chanting died away, and Nariman resumed the story.

"So Sarosh was told by his supervisor that he was coming late to work too often. What could poor Sarosh say?"

"What, Nariman Uncle?" rose the refrain.

"Nothing, of course. The supervisor, noting his silence, continued: 'If it keeps up, the consequences could be serious as far as your career is concerned.'

"Sarosh decided to speak. He said embarrassedly, 'It's a different kind of problem. I . . . I don't know how to explain . . . it's an immigration-related problem.'

"Now this supervisor must have had experience with other immigrants, because right away he told Sarosh, 'No problem. Just contact your Immigrant Aid Society. They should be able to help you. Every ethnic group has one: Vietnamese, Chinese—I'm certain that one exists for Indians. If you need time off to go there, no problem. That can be arranged, no problem. As long as you do something about your lateness, there's no problem.' That's the way they talk over there, nothing is ever a problem.

"So Sarosh thanked him and went to his desk. For the umpteenth time he bitterly rued his oversight. Could fate have plotted it, concealing the western toilet behind that shroud of anxieties which had appeared out of nowhere to beset him just before he left India? After all, he had readied himself meticulously for the new life. Even for the great, merciless Canadian cold he had heard so much about. How could he have overlooked preparation for the western toilet with its matutinal[10] demands unless fate had conspired? In Bombay, you know that offices of foreign businesses offer both options in their bathrooms. So do all hotels with three stars or more. By practising in familiar surroundings, Sarosh was convinced he could have mastered a seated evacuation before departure.

---

[10] Of or occurring in the morning.

"But perhaps there was something in what the supervisor said. Sarosh found a telephone number for the Indian Immigrant Aid Society and made an appointment. That afternoon, he met Mrs Maha-Lepate[11] at the Society's office."

Kersi and Viraf looked at each other and smiled. Nariman Uncle had a nerve, there was more *lepate* in his own stories than anywhere else.

"Mrs Maha-Lepate was very understanding, and made Sarosh feel at ease despite the very personal nature of his problem. She said, 'Yes, we get many referrals. There was a man here last month who couldn't eat Wonder Bread—it made him throw up.'

"By the way, boys, Wonder Bread is a Canadian bread which all happy families eat to be happy in the same way; the unhappy families are unhappy in their own fashion by eating other brands." Jehangir was the only one who understood, and murmured: "Tolstoy," at Nariman's little joke.[12] Nariman noticed it, pleased. He continued.

"Mrs Maha-Lepate told Sarosh about that case: 'Our immigrant specialist, Dr No-Ilaaz, recommended that the patient eat cake instead.[13] He explained that Wonder Bread caused vomiting because the digestive system was used to Indian bread only, made with Indian flour in the village he came from. However, since his system was unfamiliar with cake, Canadian or otherwise, it did not react but was digested as a newfound food. In this way he got used to Canadian flour first in cake form. Just yesterday we received a report from Dr No-Ilaaz. The patient successfully ate his first slice of whole-wheat Wonder Bread with no ill effects. The ultimate goal is pure white Wonder Bread.'

"Like a polite Parsi boy, Sarosh said, 'That's very interesting.' The garrulous Mrs Maha-Lepate was about to continue, and he tried to interject: 'But I—' but Mrs Maha-Lepate was too quick for him: 'Oh, there are so many interesting cases I could tell you about. Like the woman from Sri Lanka—referred to us because they don't have their own Society—who could not drink the water here. Dr No-Ilaaz said it was due to the different mineral content. So he started her on Coca-Cola and then began diluting it with water, bit by bit. Six weeks later she took her first sip of unadulterated Canadian water and managed to keep it down.'

"Sarosh could not halt Mrs Maha-Lepate as she launched from one case history into another: 'Right now, Dr No-Ilaaz is working on a very unusual case. Involves a whole Pakistani family. Ever since immigrating to Canada, none of them can swallow. They choke on their own saliva, and have to spit constantly. But we are confident that Dr No-Ilaaz will find a remedy. He has never been

[11] Mrs Maha-Lepate's name roughly translates as Big Yarn Spinner.

[12] A reworking of the famous opening sentence of Russian novelist Leo Tolstoy's (1828–1910) epic story of doomed love *Anna Karenina* (1877): "Happy families are all alike; each unhappy family is unhappy in its own way."

[13] A reference to the supposed words uttered by the Queen of France, Marie Antoinette, when the peasants were protesting that they had no bread to eat: "Let them eat cake." The expression has come to signify the ignorance and callousness of the elites toward ordinary people.

stumped by any immigrant problem. Besides, we have an information network with other third-world Immigrant Aid Societies. We all seem to share a history of similar maladies, and regularly compare notes. Some of us thought these problems were linked to retention of original citizenship. But this was a false lead.'

"Sarosh, out of his own experience, vigorously nodded agreement. By now he was truly fascinated by Mrs Maha-Lepate's wealth of information. Reluctantly, he interrupted: 'But will Dr No-Ilaaz be able to solve my problem?'

" 'I have every confidence that he will,' replied Mrs Maha-Lepate in great earnest. 'And if he has no remedy for you right away, he will be delighted to start working on one. He loves to take up new projects.' "

Nariman halted to blow his nose, and a clear shrill voice travelled the night air of the Firozsha Baag compound from C Block to where the boys had collected around Nariman in A Block: "Jehangoo! O Jehangoo! Eight o'clock! Upstairs now!"

Jehangir stared at his feet in embarrassment. Nariman looked at his watch and said, "Yes, it's eight." But Jehangir did not move, so he continued.

"Mrs Maha-Lepate was able to arrange an appointment while Sarosh waited, and he went directly to the doctor's office. What he had heard so far sounded quite promising. Then he cautioned himself not to get overly optimistic, that was the worst mistake he could make. But along the way to the doctor's, he could not help thinking what a lovely city Toronto was. It was the same way he had felt when he first saw it ten years ago, before all the joy had dissolved in the acid of his anxieties."

Once again that shrill voice travelled through the clear night: "*Arré* Jehangoo! *Muà*, do I have to come down and drag you upstairs!"

Jehangir's mortification was now complete. Nariman made it easy for him, though: "The first part of the story is over. Second part continues tomorrow. Same time, same place." The boys were surprised, Nariman did not make such commitments. But never before had he told such a long story. They began drifting back to their homes.

As Jehangir strode hurriedly to C Block, falsettos and piercing shrieks followed him in the darkness: "*Arré* Jehangoo! *Muà* Jehangoo! Bulsara Bookworm! Eight o'clock Jehangoo!" Shaking his head, Nariman went indoors to Hirabai.

Next evening, the story punctually resumed when Nariman took his place on the topmost step of A Block: "You remember that we left Sarosh on his way to see the Immigrant Aid Society's doctor. Well, Dr No-Ilaaz listened patiently to Sarosh's concerns, then said, 'As a matter of fact, there is a remedy which is so new even the IAS does not know about it. Not even that Mrs Maha-Lepate who knows it all,' he added drolly, twirling his stethoscope like a stunted lasso. He slipped it on around his neck before continuing: 'It involves a minor operation which was developed with financial assistance from the Multicultural Department. A small device, *Crappus Non Interruptus*, or CNI as we call it, is implanted in the bowel. The device is controlled by an external handheld transmitter similar to the ones used for automatic garage door-openers—you may have seen them in hardware stores.'"

Nariman noticed that most of the boys wore puzzled looks and realized he had to make some things clearer. "The Multicultural Department is a Canadian invention. It is supposed to ensure that ethnic cultures are able to flourish, so that Canadian society will consist of a mosaic of cultures—that's their favourite word, mosaic—instead of one uniform mix, like the American melting pot. If you ask me, mosaic and melting pot are both nonsense, and ethnic is a polite way of saying bloody foreigner. But anyway, you understand Multicultural Department? Good. So Sarosh nodded, and Dr No-Ilaaz went on: 'You can encode the handheld transmitter with a personal ten-digit code. Then all you do is position yourself on the toilet seat and activate your transmitter. Just like a garage door, your bowel will open without pushing or grunting.'"

There was some snickering in the audience, and Nariman raised his eyebrows, whereupon they covered up their mouths with their hands. "The doctor asked Sarosh if he had any questions. Sarosh thought for a moment, then asked if it required any maintenance.

"Dr No-Ilaaz replied: 'CNI is semi-permanent and operates on solar energy. Which means you would have to make it a point to get some sun periodically, or it would cease and lead to constipation. However, you don't have to strip for a tan. Exposing ten percent of your skin surface once a week during summer will let the device store sufficient energy for year-round operation.'

"Sarosh's next question was: 'Is there any hope that someday the bowels can work on their own, without operating the device?' at which Dr No-Ilaaz grimly shook his head: 'I'm afraid not. You must think very, very carefully before making a decision. Once CNI is implanted, you can never pass a motion in the natural way—neither sitting nor squatting.'

"He stopped to allow Sarosh time to think it over, then continued: 'And you must understand what that means. You will never be able to live a normal life again. You will be permanently different from your family and friends because of this basic internal modification. In fact, in this country or that, it will set you apart from your fellow countrymen. So you must consider the whole thing most carefully.'

"Dr No-Ilaaz paused, toyed with his stethoscope, shuffled some papers on his desk, then resumed: 'There are other dangers you should know about. Just as a garage door can be accidentally opened by a neighbour's transmitter on the same frequency, CNI can also be activated by someone with similar apparatus.' To ease the tension he attempted a quick laugh and said, 'Very embarrassing, eh, if it happened at the wrong place and time. Mind you, the risk is not so great at present, because the chances of finding yourself within a fifty-foot radius of another transmitter on the same frequency are infinitesimal. But what about the future? What if CNI becomes very popular? Sufficient permutations may not be available for transmitter frequencies and you could be sharing the code with others. Then the risk of accidents becomes greater.'"

Something landed with a loud thud in the yard behind A Block, making Nariman startle. Immediately, a yowling and screeching and caterwauling went up from the stray cats there, and the *kuchrawalli*'s dog started barking. Some of the boys went around the side of A Block to peer over the fence into the backyard. But the commotion soon died down of its own accord. The boys returned and, once again, Nariman's voice was the only sound to be heard.

"By now, Sarosh was on the verge of deciding against the operation. Dr No-Ilaaz observed this and was pleased. He took pride in being able to dissuade his patients from following the very remedies which he first so painstakingly described. True to his name, Dr No-Ilaaz believed no remedy is the best remedy, rather than prescribing this-mycin and that-mycin for every little ailment. So he continued: 'And what about our sons and daughters? And the quality of their lives? We still don't know the long-term effects of CNI. Some researchers speculate that it could generate a genetic deficiency, that the offspring of a CNI parent would also require CNI. On the other hand, they could be perfectly healthy toilet seat-users, without any congenital defects. We just don't know at this stage.'

"Sarosh rose from his chair: 'Thank you very much for your time, Dr No-Ilaaz. But I don't think I want to take such a drastic step. As you suggest, I will think it over very carefully.'

"'Good, good,' said Dr No-Ilaaz, 'I was hoping you would say that. There is one more thing. The operation is extremely expensive, and is not covered by the province's Health Insurance Plan. Many immigrant groups are lobbying to obtain coverage for special immigration-related health problems. If they succeed, then good for you.'

"Sarosh left Dr No-Ilaaz's office with his mind made up. Time was running out. There had been a time when it was perfectly natural to squat. Now it seemed a grotesquely aberrant thing to do. Wherever he went he was reminded of the ignominy of his way. If he could not be westernized in all respects, he was nothing but a failure in this land—a failure not just in the washrooms of the nation but everywhere. He knew what he must do if he was to be true to himself and to the decade-old commitment. So what do you think Sarosh did next?"

"What, Nariman Uncle?"

"He went to the travel agent specializing in tickets to India. He bought a fully refundable ticket to Bombay for the day when he would complete exactly ten immigrant years—if he succeeded even once before that day dawned, he would cancel the booking.

"The travel agent asked sympathetically, 'Trouble at home?' His name was Mr Rawaana, and he was from Bombay too.

"'No,' said Sarosh, 'trouble in Toronto.'

"'That's a shame,' said Mr Rawaana. 'I don't want to poke my nose into your business, but in my line of work I meet so many people who are going back to their homeland because of problems here. Sometimes I forget I'm a travel agent, that my interest is to convince them to travel. Instead, I tell them: don't give up,

God is great, stay and try again. It's bad for my profits but gives me a different, a spiritual kind of satisfaction when I succeed. And I succeed about half the time. Which means,' he added with a wry laugh, 'I could double my profits if I minded my own business.'

"After the lengthy sessions with Mrs Maha-Lepate and Dr No-Ilaaz, Sarosh felt he had listened to enough advice and kind words. Much as he disliked doing it, he had to hurt Mr Rawaana's feelings and leave his predicament undiscussed: 'I'm sorry, but I'm in a hurry. Will you be able to look after the booking?'

"'Well, okay,' said Mr Rawaana, a trifle crestfallen; he did not relish the travel business as much as he did counselling immigrants. 'Hope you solve your problem. I will be happy to refund your fare, believe me.'

"Sarosh hurried home. With only four weeks to departure, every spare minute, every possible method had to be concentrated on a final attempt at adaptation.

"He tried laxatives, crunching down the tablets with a prayer that these would assist the sitting position. Changing brands did not help, and neither did various types of suppositories. He spent long stretches on the toilet seat each morning. The supervisor continued to reprimand him for tardiness. To make matters worse, Sarosh left his desk every time he felt the slightest urge, hoping: maybe this time.

"The working hours expended in the washroom were noted with unflagging vigilance by the supervisor. More counselling sessions followed. Sarosh refused to extinguish his last hope, and the supervisor punctiliously recorded 'No Improvement' in his daily log. Finally, Sarosh was fired. It would soon have been time to resign in any case, and he could not care less.

"Now whole days went by seated on the toilet, and he stubbornly refused to relieve himself the other way. The doorbell would ring only to be ignored. The telephone went unanswered. Sometimes, he would awake suddenly in the dark hours before dawn and rush to the washroom like a madman."

Without warning, Rustomji flung open his door and stormed: "Ridiculous nonsense this is becoming! Two days in a row, whole Firozsha Baag gathers here! This is not Chaupatty beach, this is not a squatters' colony, this is a building, people want to live here in peace and quiet!" Then just as suddenly, he stamped inside and slammed the door. Right on cue, Nariman continued, before the boys could say anything.

"Time for meals was the only time Sarosh allowed himself off the seat. Even in his desperation he remembered that if he did not eat well, he was doomed— the downward pressure on his gut was essential if there was to be any chance of success.

"But the ineluctable day of departure dawned, with grey skies and the scent of rain, while success remained out of sight. At the airport Sarosh checked in and went to the dreary lounge. Out of sheer habit he started towards the washroom. Then he realized the hopelessness of it and returned to the cold, clammy plastic of the lounge seats. Airport seats are the same almost anywhere in the world.

"The boarding announcement was made, and Sarosh was the first to step onto the plane. The skies were darker now. Out of the window he saw a flash of lightning fork through the clouds. For some reason, everything he'd learned years ago in St Xavier's about sheet lightning and forked lightning went through his mind. He wished it would change to sheet, there was something sinister and unpropitious about forked lightning."

Kersi, absorbedly listening, began cracking his knuckles quite unconsciously. His childhood habit still persisted. Jehangir frowned at the disturbance, and Viraf nudged Kersi to stop it.

"Sarosh fastened his seat-belt and attempted to turn his thoughts towards the long journey home: to the questions he would be expected to answer, the sympathy and criticism that would be thrust upon him. But what remained uppermost in his mind was the present moment—him in the plane, dark skies lowering, lightning on the horizon—irrevocably spelling out: defeat.

"But wait. Something else was happening now. A tiny rumble. Inside him. Or was it his imagination? Was it really thunder outside which, in his present disoriented state, he was internalizing? No, there it was again. He had to go.

"He reached the washroom, and almost immediately the sign flashed to 'Please return to seat and fasten seat-belts.' Sarosh debated whether to squat and finish the business quickly, abandoning the perfunctory seated attempt. But the plane started to move and that decided him; it would be difficult now to balance while squatting.

"He pushed. The plane continued to move. He pushed again, trembling with the effort. The seat-belt sign flashed quicker and brighter now. The plane moved faster and faster. And Sarosh pushed hard, harder than he had ever pushed before, harder than in all his ten years of trying in the new land. And the memories of Bombay, the immigration interview in New Delhi, the farewell party, his mother's tattered prayer book, all these, of their own accord, emerged from beyond the region of the ten years to push with him and give him newfound strength."

Nariman paused and cleared his throat. Dusk was falling, and the frequency of B.E.S.T.[14] buses plying the main road outside Firozsha Baag had dropped. Bats began to fly madly from one end of the compound to the other, silent shadows engaged in endless laps over the buildings.

"With a thunderous clap the rain started to fall. Sarosh felt a splash under him. Could it really be? He glanced down to make certain. Yes, it was. He had succeeded!

"But was it already too late? The plane waited at its assigned position on the runway, jet engines at full thrust. Rain was falling in torrents and takeoff could be delayed. Perhaps even now they would allow him to cancel his flight, to disembark. He lurched out of the constricting cubicle.

[14] Public bus service: "Bombay Electric Supply & Transport."

"A stewardess hurried towards him: 'Excuse me, sir, but you must return to your seat immediately and fasten your belt.'

" 'You don't understand!' Sarosh shouted excitedly. 'I must get off the plane! Everything is all right, I don't have to go anymore . . . '

" 'That's impossible, sir!' said the stewardess, aghast. 'No one can leave now. Takeoff procedures are in progress!' The wild look in his sleepless eyes, and the dark rings around them scared her. She beckoned for help.

"Sarosh continued to argue, and a steward and the chief stewardess hurried over: 'What seems to be the problem, sir? You *must* resume your seat. We are authorized, if necessary, to forcibly restrain you, sir.'

"The plane began to move again, and suddenly Sarosh felt all the urgency leaving him. His feverish mind, the product of nightmarish days and torturous nights, was filled again with the calm which had fled a decade ago, and he spoke softly now: 'That . . . that will not be necessary . . . it's okay, I understand.' He readily returned to his seat.

"As the aircraft sped down the runway, Sarosh's first reaction was one of joy. The process of adaptation was complete. But later, he could not help wondering if success came before or after the ten-year limit had expired. And since he had already passed through the customs and security check, was he really an immigrant in every sense of the word at the moment of achievement?

"But such questions were merely academic. Or were they? He could not decide. If he returned, what would it be like? Ten years ago, the immigration officer who had stamped his passport had said, 'Welcome to Canada.' It was one of Sarosh's dearest memories, and thinking of it, he fell asleep.

"The plane was flying above the rainclouds. Sunshine streamed into the cabin. A few raindrops were still clinging miraculously to the windows, reminders of what was happening below. They sparkled as the sunlight caught them."

Some of the boys made as if to leave, thinking the story was finally over. Clearly, they had not found this one as interesting as the others Nariman had told. What dolts, thought Jehangir, they cannot recognize a masterpiece when they hear one. Nariman motioned with his hand for silence.

"But our story does not end there. There was a welcome-home party for Sarosh a few days after he arrived in Bombay. It was not in Firozsha Baag this time because his relatives in the Baag had a serious sickness in the house. But I was invited to it anyway. Sarosh's family and friends were considerate enough to wait till the jet lag had worked its way out of his system. They wanted him to really enjoy this one.

"Drinks began to flow freely again in his honour: Scotch and soda, rum and Coke, brandy. Sarosh noticed that during his absence all the brand names had changed—the labels were different and unfamiliar. Even for the mixes. Instead of Coke there was Thums-Up, and he remembered reading in the papers about Coca-Cola being kicked out by the Indian Government for refusing to reveal their secret formula.

"People slapped him on the back and shook his hand vigorously, over and over, right through the evening. They said: 'Telling the truth, you made the right decision, look how happy your mother is to live to see this day;' or they asked: 'Well, bossy what changed your mind?' Sarosh smiled and nodded his way through it all, passing around Canadian currency at the insistence of some of the curious ones who, egged on by his mother, also pestered him to display his Canadian passport and citizenship card. She had been badgering him since his arrival to tell her the real reason: 'Saachoo kahé, what brought you back?' and was hoping that tonight, among his friends, he might raise his glass and reveal something. But she remained disappointed.

"Weeks went by and Sarosh found himself desperately searching for his old place in the pattern of life he had vacated ten years ago. Friends who had organized the welcome-home party gradually disappeared. He went walking in the evenings along Marine Drive, by the sea-wall, where the old crowd used to congregate. But the people who sat on the parapet while waves crashed behind their backs were strangers. The tetrapods[15] were still there, staunchly protecting the reclaimed land from the fury of the sea. He had watched as a kid when cranes had lowered these cement and concrete hulks of respectable grey into the water. They were grimy black now, and from their angularities rose the distinct stench of human excrement. The old pattern was never found by Sarosh; he searched in vain. Patterns of life are selfish and unforgiving.

"Then one day, as I was driving past Marine Drive, I saw someone sitting alone. He looked familiar, so I stopped. For a moment I did not recognize Sarosh, so forlorn and woebegone was his countenance. I parked the apple of my eye and went to him, saying, 'Hullo, Sid, what are you doing here on your lonesome?' And he said, 'No no! No more Sid, please, that name reminds me of all my troubles.' Then, on the parapet at Marine Drive, he told me his unhappy and wretched tale, with the waves battering away at the tetrapods, and around us the hawkers screaming about coconut-water and sugar-cane juice and paan.

"When he finished, he said that he had related to me the whole sad saga because he knew how I told stories to boys in the Baag, and he wanted me to tell this one, especially to those who were planning to go abroad. 'Tell them,' said Sarosh, 'that the world can be a bewildering place, and dreams and ambitions are often paths to the most pernicious of traps.' As he spoke, I could see that Sarosh was somewhere far away, perhaps in New Delhi at his immigration interview, seeing himself as he was then, with what he thought was a life of hope and promise stretching endlessly before him. Poor Sarosh. Then he was back beside me on the parapet.

" 'I pray you, in your stories,' said Sarosh, his old sense of humour returning as he deepened his voice for his favourite Othello lines"—and here, Nariman produced a basso profundo of his own—" 'When you shall these unlucky deeds relate, speak of me as I am; nothing extenuate, nor set down aught in malice: tell

[15] Concrete structures used to impede erosion of the coastline.

them that in Toronto once there lived a Parsi boy as best as he could. Set you down this; and say, besides, that for some it was good and for some it was bad, but for me life in the land of milk and honey was just a pain in the posterior.'"[16]

And now, Nariman allowed his low-pitched rumbles to turn into chuckles. The boys broke into cheers and loud applause and cries of "Encore!" and "More!" Finally, Nariman had to silence them by pointing warningly at Rustomji-the-curmudgeon's door.

While Kersi and Viraf were joking and wondering what to make of it all, Jehangir edged forward and told Nariman this was the best story he had ever told. Nariman patted his shoulder and smiled. Jehangir left, wondering if Nariman would have been as popular if Dr Mody was still alive. Probably, since the two were liked for different reasons: Dr Mody used to be constantly jovial, whereas Nariman had his periodic story-telling urges.

Now the group of boys who had really enjoyed the Savukshaw story during the previous week spoke up. Capitalizing on Nariman's extraordinarily good mood, they began clamouring for more Savukshaw: "Nariman Uncle, tell the one about Savukshaw the hunter, the one you had started that day."

"What hunter? I don't know which one you mean." He refused to be reminded of it, and got up to leave. But there was loud protest, and the boys started chanting, "We-want-Savukshaw! We-want-Savukshaw!"

Nariman looked fearfully towards Rustomji's door and held up his hands placatingly: "All right, all right! Next time it will be Savukshaw again. Savukshaw the artist. The story of the Parsi Picasso."

[1987]

---

[16] An adaptation of lines spoken by Othello just before he stabs himself in the final scene of William Shakespeare's play *Othello: The Moor of Venice* (1604).

DIONNE BRAND ■ (1953–)

A poet, novelist, essayist, public intellectual, community activist, and oral historian, Dionne Brand does not adhere to strict genre categories in her writing but fluidly blends poetry, prose, and political commitment. Her work explores the intricacies of postcolonial women's identities and places them firmly in the context of African diasporic history. Brand's writing explores what she calls "the blood stained bind of race and sex" as it addresses history, women's love for women, the legacies of slavery, and the physical embodiments of pain. Using a line borrowed from Nobel Prize-winning poet Derek Walcott's *Midsummer* (1984) for the title of her celebrated collection *No Language Is Neutral* (1990), Brand emphasizes that language is imbued with ideology. She suggests ways to write against language, because, as she argues in an interview with Beverley Daurio, "Standard English" was imposed through imperialism and the oppression of women. As such, language carries the history of enslavement for Brand—"a morphology of rolling chain and copper gong" as "falsettos of whip and air / rudiment this grammar." The language of Brand's writing is seldom Standard English with a capital E; rather, her writing echoes with the sounds, cadences, syntaxes, and vernaculars of Trinidad and of Toronto. She engages histories of sexual and racial oppression head-on, within her own fluid aesthetic that evinces joy, sadness, and beauty.

Born in Guayguayare, Trinidad, and raised in San Fernando, Brand moved to Toronto in 1970. She earned a B.A. from the University of Toronto in 1975 and an M.A. in 1989. Although she began a Ph.D. in education, she left the program to work in the community and to write creatively. In the Introduction to her work in a collaborative collection of poems for children entitled *A Caribbean Dozen* (1994), Brand explains the origins of her desire to write: "[I]n the Sixties when I was in elementary and high schools, none of the books we studied were about Black people's lives; they were about Europeans, mostly the British. But I felt that Black people's experiences were as important and as valuable, and needed to be written down and read about. This is why I became a writer." This dearth in representation, echoed as well by M. NourbeSe Philip, led Brand to publish her first children's book, *Earth Magic* (1980), alongside poetry and prose, and to become heavily involved in community work.

Brand recalls arriving in Canada in 1970: "I was only seventeen but I already knew that to live freely in the world as a Black woman I would have to involve myself in political action as well as writing." Her involvement in Black and feminist communities over the years is reflected in her documentary film work, her involvement with the Immigrant Women's Centre, the Black Youth Hotline, and the Toronto Board of

Education, as well as in her non-fictional study of Black working women (the 1991 oral history *No Burden to Carry: Narratives of Black Working Women in Ontario, 1920s–1950s*) and of racism, *Rivers Have Sources, Trees Have Roots: Speaking of Racism* (1986), co-authored with Krisantha Sri Bhaggiyadatta. Much of Brand's writing emerges from her position as a social and cultural critic, evident in her non-fictional essays, compiled in *Bread out of stone: recollections, sex, recognitions, race, dreaming, and politics* (1994), and in her genre-crossing *A Map to the Door of No Return* (2001). Besides her community and creative work, Brand also teaches literature and creative writing at the University of Guelph (where she holds a University Research Chair).

In literary circles, Brand first gained recognition for her poetry. Her first volume, *'Fore Day Morning* (1978), concentrates on memories of childhood in Trinidad; *Primitive Offensive* (1982) tracks the origins of the African diaspora; *Winter Epigrams and Epigrams to Ernesto Cardenal in Defense of Claudia* (1983) traces the racism and sexism endured by Black Canadians with wit and irony; and *Chronicles of the Hostile Sun* (1984) powerfully engages with the revolution in Grenada during the American invasion. With the publication of *No Language Is Neutral* (1990), *Land to Light On* (1997), *thirsty* (2002), and *Inventory* (2006), Brand has risen to the forefront of contemporary Canadian poetry. Thrice nominated, Brand won the Governor General's Award in 1997, and was nominated for the Griffin Award in 2002.

Brand ends *Bread out of stone* with a meditation on writing: "Poetry is here, just *here*. Something wrestling with how we live, something dangerous, something honest." Such honesty is evident in the love poem "hard against the soul: I," where the speaker entwines her love for a woman with her love of the ocean and the earth, and in the enduring image of the 115-year-old woman in the photograph at the core of "Blues Spiritual for Mammy Prater." The long poem *Inventory*—segments II and VI (of VII) are included here—continues Brand's indictment of American cultural and political hegemony so central to *Chronicles of the Hostile Sun*. Now, however, she also exhibits deep empathy for individual Americans victimized by disaster and circumstance as well as contempt for what she calls "the militant consumption of everything" that leaves boys with "fast food breath." Brand takes inventory of the early years of this new century and calls the "toxic genealogy" of the time sharply into account. *Inventory* is, as critic Diana Brydon puts it, "a poem that conveys the emotional impact of globalization as an intensely intimate experience."

Also distinguished for her fiction, Brand has published three novels and one collection of short stories (*Sans Souci* in 1988). *In Another Place, Not Here* (1996) explores the connections between sexuality and the Caribbean diaspora. In so doing, Brand links lesbian and feminist consciousnesses with anti-racist, anti-colonial politics in both Caribbean and Caribbean-diasporic spaces. *At the Full and Change of the Moon* (1999) spans 1820 to 1990 and investigates the legacies of slavery and domination, continuing Brand's emphasis on probing the legacies of history. Her most recent novel, *What We All Long For* (2005), perfectly articulates the turn-of-the-millennium zeitgeist. It links an interracial circle of friends "born in the city from people born elsewhere," who join in "unspoken collaboration on distancing themselves as far as possible from the unreasonableness, the ignorance, the secrets, and the madness of their parents." Writer-critic David Chariandy points to the significance of this book's articulation of intergenerational conflicts about enculturation, and emphasizes the novel's distinctions between immigrant parents and their Canadian children who refuse to inherit their parents' ethnic legacies. He concludes, "In our post 9/11 affective economy of terror and distrust, we desperately require . . . more radical representations of human connection and compassion, even as we continue to challenge the old and newly emerging social hierarchies." With this novel and the poems in *Inventory,* Brand is moving in just such a radical direction.

hard against the soul: I

this is you girl, this cut of road up
to blanchicheuse, this every turn a piece
of blue and earth carrying on, beating, rock and
ocean this wearing away, smoothing the insides
pearl of shell and coral

this is you girl, this is you all sides of me
hill road and dip through the coconut at manzanilla
this sea breeze shaped forest of sand and lanky palm

[1] Blanchicheuse, Manzanilla, and La Fillet[t]e Bay are the names of beaches in Trinidad.

this wanting to fall, hanging, greening
quenching the road   10

this is you girl, even though you never see it
the drop before timberline, that daub of black shine
sea on bush smoke land, that pulse of the heart
that stretches up to maracas, la fillete bay never know
you but you make it wash up from the rocks

this is you girl, that bit of lagoon, alligator
long abandoned, this stone of my youngness
hesitating to walk right, turning to Schoener's road
turning to duenne[2] and spirit, to the sea wall and sea
breaking hard against things, turning to burning reason   20

this is you girl, this is the poem no woman
ever write for a woman because she 'fraid to touch
this river boiling like a woman in she sleep
that smell of fresh thighs and warm sweat
sheets of her like the mitan rolling into the atlantic

this is you girl, something never waning or forgetting
something hard against the soul
this is where you make sense, that the sight becomes
tender, the night air human, the dull silence full
chattering, volcanoes cease, and to be awake is   30
more lovely than dreams

                                                        [1990]

Blues Spiritual for Mammy Prater

On looking at 'the photograph of Mammy Prater an ex-slave,
115 years old when her photograph was taken'

she waited for her century to turn
she waited until she was one hundred and fifteen
years old to take a photograph
to take a photograph and to put those eyes in it
she waited until the technique of photography was
suitably developed
to make sure the picture would be clear

---

[2] In Trinidadian folklore, a duenne is the spirit of a child who died before baptism and who thus
roams the forest looking for other children to entice away.

DIONNE BRAND

to make sure no crude daguerreotype[3] would lose
her image
would lose her lines and most of all her eyes   10
and her hands
she knew the patience of one hundred and fifteen years
she knew that if she had the patience,
to avoid killing a white man
that I would see this photograph
she waited until it suited her
to take this photograph and to put those eyes in it.

in the hundred and fifteen years which it took her to
wait for this photograph she perfected this pose
she sculpted it over a shoulder of pain,   20
a thing like despair which she never called
this name for she would not have lasted
the fields, the ones she ploughed
on the days that she was a mule, left
their etching on the gait of her legs
deliberately and unintentionally
she waited, not always silently, not always patiently,
for this self portrait
by the time she sat in her black dress, white collar,
white handkerchief, her feet had turned to marble,   30
her heart burnished red,
and her eyes.

she waited one hundred and fifteen years
until the science of photography passed tin and
talbotype[4] for a surface sensitive enough
to hold her eyes
she took care not to lose the signs
to write in those eyes what her fingers could not script
a pact of blood across a century, a decade and more
she knew then that it would be me who would find   40
her will, her meticulous account, her eyes,
her days when waiting for this photograph
was all that kept her sane
she planned it down to the day,

[3] Daguerrotype was an early photographic process first used by Daguerre of Paris in 1839. The impression was taken upon a silver plate that was sensitized by iodine and then developed with exposure to mercury.

[4] Patented by W.H. Fox Talbot in 1841, the talbotype was a process of photographing onto sensitized paper.

the light,
the superfluous photographer
her breasts,
her hands
this moment of
my turning the leaves of a book,   50
noticing, her eyes.

[1990]

From Inventory

II

Observed over Miami,[5] the city, an orange slick blister,
the houses, stiff-haired organisms clamped to the earth,
engorged with oil and wheat,
rubber and metals,
the total contents of the brain, the electrical
regions of the atmosphere, water

coming north, reeling, a neurosis of hinged
clouds,
bodies thicken, flesh

out in immodest health,   10
six boys, fast food on their breath,
luscious paper bags, the perfume of grilled offal,[6]
troughlike cartons of cola,
a gorgon[7] luxury of electronics, backward caps,
bulbous clothing, easy hearts

lines of visitors are fingerprinted,
eye-scanned,[8] grow murderous,
then there's the business of thoughts
who can glean with any certainty,
the guards, blued and leathered, multiply   20
to stop them,

[5] Miami, Florida, is a hub of migration and a centre of consumption in this poem.

[6] Offal, the edible trimmings of an animal's carcass when it is cut up. *Larousse Gastronomique* lists offal as red (heart, liver, tongue, kidneys) or white (bone marrow, sweetbreads, feet, or head); it is not the food of the wealthy.

[7] In Greek mythology Gorgons, including Medusa, are female monsters with snakes for hair, whose look turns the beholder into stone. Here the reference is to electrical cords resembling snakes.

[8] Heightened security at the American borders, with fingerprint identification and eye scans introduced in recent years.

palimpsests[9] of old borders, the sea's graph on the skin,
the dead giveaway of tongues,
soon, soon, the implants to discern lies

from the way a body moves

there's that already

she felt ill, wanted
to murder the six boys, the guards,
the dreamless shipwrecked
burning their beautiful eyes in the patient queue   30

Let's go to the republic of home,
let's forget all this then, this victorious procession,
these blenching queues,
this timeless march of nails in shoeless feet[10]

what people will take and give,
the passive lines, the passive guards,
if passivity can be inchoate[11] self-loathing

all around, and creeping

self-righteous, let's say it, fascism,
how else to say, border,   40
and the militant consumption of everything,
the encampment of the airport, the eagerness
to be all the same, to mince biographies
to some exact phrases, some
exact and toxic genealogy

VI

It's August now, the light is deeper,
the sky explosive with rains,
a turning, turning the body of the world
toward a darkness, a sleep, no,
sleep would be forgiving

---

[9] A text that has been over-written or layered. Here it refers to the layers of history one carries.
[10] Reference to the agony of Christ's crucifixion.
[11] The beginning of, or incipient, self-loathing.

last night, late August,
Katrina's[12] wet wing flapped, dishevelled
against the windows like great damp feathers,
she brushed the alleyways, the storm shutters,
I felt the city she had carried away,   10
drowned and stranded New Orleans,
anyway, she was finished,
a ruffed foot, a quilled skirt trailing off

like what billions of rainless universes do we kill
just stepping through air, what failing cultures
submerge under a breath

word on the street is that God sent Katrina
as a lesson in destruction,
lucky I'm not any kind of believer,
a taxi driver told me this, then the hairdresser,   20
then the old Italian ladies who peddle Jesus

when I tell them I'm an atheist they see
an opportunity for conversion

they want some single story, the story of my life,
I say this big world is the story, I don't have any other,
they offer me the immured peace
of Christianity,
and an address in Pennsylvania to send money,
they always win, these soothing ladies,
I haven't the courage to tell them we're fucked,   30
and they, unfortunately, will have a reason for that

though the birds of the world know this,[13]
the banded pitta, the mangrove pitta, the bulbul,
the iora, the red-naped and scarlet-rumped

trogon, the fire-tufted barbet, flame back, philentoma,
the rufous-throated wren babbler, I tell them,

---

[12] Hurricane Katrina hit the southern coast of the United States in August 2005 with devastating effects for Louisiana, Mississippi, and Texas. New Orleans, Louisiana, was particularly hard hit when the levees, ostensibly built to withhold flood waters, were breached and 80% of the city was flooded. The U.S. Department of Health and Human Services reports that "more then 1,800 people lost their lives, and more then $81 billion in damages occurred." Many people link a recent increase in such meteorological disasters with global warming; some Christians see them as signs of the impending apocalypse.

[13] In the next three stanzas, Brand inventories tropical birds indigenous to the Caribbean, Malaysia, Thailand, India, and Indonesia, among other Southern regions.

they, the birds feel this, the wingbeat,
the feathered work of greed,
this shorn planet,
the hoary-throated barwing, the greater adjutant,[14]   40
the crake, the alliterative blue-bearded bee-eater,
it's clear to them,
they all must set a fire to the earth,
you see, they're saying, what would it be without birds,
what if we spread extinction, transform blood
to other tender fluids

listen to all the laughing thrushes,[15]
striated, white throated, orange headed, all
the plain backed, blackened, chestnut, cocoa,
summoning oblivions, raining disasters   50

after all, how many vows of death or endless death
for endless peace have I heard from the wingless,
the flightless? The gulls, the owls, the grouses

the stalks, the larks, the finches have had it too,
with sightlessness, such clarity,
the scientists
are intent on dreamy financial answers,
but I know the suicidal skill of insurrection,
self-slaughter hunched in veins, the skull's
fever, the tissues' elations,   60
I too am waiting for the flutter of another century,
treading water near that meagre strip of land,
stooping there, the noise even closer

[2006]

[14] An officer in an army who assists the commanding officer.
[15] The birds listed here are from the northern hemisphere and around the globe.

NEIL BISSOONDATH ▪ (1955–)

A novelist, short story writer, essayist, and teacher, Neil Bissoondath has never shied away from controversy. Over the years he has written about personal strife and political violence in novels about war, insurgency, disability, immigration, place, memory, and family. In fictional and real locations (including Trinidad, Japan, and Canada), Bissoondath's writing is more concerned with the intricacies of individuality than with the politics of identity.

Born in Trinidad, Bissoondath is the nephew of the 2001 Nobel Prize winner

V.S. Naipaul and of the writer Shiva Naipaul. However, he claims no attachment to the country he left at the age of 18. "My sense of my heritage," he says in an interview with Celia Sankar, "has little to do with superficial things such as food, dance or music, but more with the story of my parents, grandparents and great-grandparents, of the struggle these people had to endure in order to rise out of poverty." He does not want to be read as a diasporic writer or a Caribbean writer, but as a Canadian writer. Bissoondath attended St. Mary's College in Port of Spain before immigrating to Canada in 1973. After studying French, Russian, and Spanish literature at York University (where he received his B.A. in 1977), he taught at a language school in Toronto and began writing short stories. Bissoondath continues to write fiction in English and essays in both English and French. He lives in Quebec City and teaches at the Université Laval.

The short stories in Bissoondath's first book, *Digging Up the Mountains* (1985), engage with migration, dislocation, cultural alienation, memory, and domestic upheaval. These themes are carried into his next story collection, *On the Eve of Uncertain Tomorrows* (1990). His novel *A Casual Brutality* (1988) traces the story of a Canadian-trained doctor from a fictional, politically unstable Caribbean country who returns to his place of birth only to be struck by the violence of war. *The Worlds Within Her* (1998), the story of a Canadian woman who returns to her homeland, Trinidad, to scatter her mother's ashes, was a finalist for the Governor General's Award. His 2002 novel *Doing the Heart Good,* which won the Hugh MacLennan Award, takes on a different subject, focusing on a 70-year-old anglophone Montrealer who finds himself obliged to live with his daughter and her bilingual family.

In 1994 Bissoondath published his most controversial work to date, a treatise on multiculturalism entitled *Selling Illusions: The Cult of Multiculturalism in Canada* (1994, rev. 2002). In this non-fiction work, Bissoondath criticizes official multiculturalism for emphasizing differences rather than similarities amongst the country's various ethnic groups. He declares the government's version of multiculturalism, or "ethnicity as public policy," to be a forum for encouraging exoticism and fostering "social divisiveness." He further asks whether immigrants want to retain ties to the lands they have left and if they should be forced to be regarded as ethnic subjects first and foremost. When *Selling Illusions* was published in 1994, it became a national phenomenon. Its arguments were taken up in newspaper editorials and on current affairs shows across the country. Swimming against the current of public opinion, Bissoondath has held fast to his position. This book is central to discussions of the history of multiculturalism and reflects the debates about culture and ethnicity in early-1990s Canada.

From Selling Illusions

Ethnicity

Divisiveness is a dangerous playmate, and few playgrounds offer greater scope for divisiveness than that of ethnicity. The walls are high, ready-made, as solid as obsession. Guard towers can be built, redoubts that allow defence and a distant view into the land of the other. Like all walls, they can be either accepted as integral to life or breached—dismantled brick by brick—as restrictive to it. How to view those walls, how or even if to deal with them, is a decision each individual must make.

For society at large, though, ethnicity and its walls must be barriers to nothing. No opportunity must be denied, no recognition withheld, no advancement refused. Neither, however, must ethnicity be claimed as grounds for opportunity, recognition or advancement. Tempting though it may be, a multicultural society can ill afford the use of past discrimination as justification for future recrimination. It is essential, in such a society, that discrimination be permissible only on the basis of knowledge and ability. To do otherwise—to discriminate, for instance, against white males as a class because of transgressions by other white males in the past—is to employ the simplistic eye-for-an-eye, tooth-for-a-tooth philosophy implicit in arguments supportive of capital punishment. There is an element of class vengeance to it, an element of self-righteousness, that offers victims or their descendants the opportunity to strike back. It is like arguing that the victims of torture must be allowed to torture their torturers. Redress is important, but the nature of that redress is even more so, for it sets the tone for the future. Yesterday cannot be changed, but tomorrow is yet to be shaped, and ways must be found to avoid creating resentments today that might lead to upheavals tomorrow. As Nelson Mandela has made clear, a peaceful and prosperous future for a multi-racial South Africa cannot be secured through punitive action for the wrongs of the past; it can be attained only through the full recognition of human dignity implicit in the acceptance of equality.[1]

Economic and social imbalance cannot be redressed overnight. Only revolution can effect so radical a change, and if there is a lesson to be learned from the history of the twentieth century it is that revolutionary change is illusory: it merely changes oppressors and the nature of oppression. True and lasting change, then, cannot be imposed; it must come slowly, growing with experience, from within.

The comment was once made that racism is as Canadian as maple syrup. History provides us with ample proof of that. But perspective requires the notation that racism is also as American as apple pie, as French as croissants, as Indian as curry, as Jamaican as Akee, as Russian as vodka . . . It's an item on every nation's menu. Racism, an aspect of human virulence, is exclusive to no race, no country, no culture, no civilization. This is not to excuse it. Murder and rape, too, are international, multicultural, innate to the darker side of the

---

[1] Nelson Mandela (1918–) is a former South African dissident who was imprisoned for 27 years for organizing the African National Congress (ANC) to fight the racist laws of South African apartheid. Mandela became the first democratically elected President of South Africa following the free election of 1994, and advocated peaceful reconciliation rather than violent confrontation with former government leaders.

human experience. But an orderly and civil society requires that the inevitable rage evoked not blind us to the larger context. [. . .]

True racism is based, more often than not, on wilful ignorance and an acceptance of and comfort with stereotype. We like to think, in this country, that our multicultural mosaic will help nudge us into a greater openness. But multiculturalism as we know it indulges in stereotype, depends on it for a dash of colour and the flash of dance—and that in itself is not a bad thing. But such an approach fails to address the most basic questions people have about each other: Do those men doing the Dragon Dance really all belong to secret criminal societies? Do those women dressed in saris really coddle cockroaches for luck? Do those people in dreadlocks all smoke marijuana and live on welfare in between criminal acts? Such questions do not seem to be the concern of multiculturalism in Canada. Far easier is indulgence in the superficial and the exhibitionistic.

Community response to racism, while important, must also be measured, responsible. We must beware the self-appointed activists who seem to pop up in the media at every given opportunity, spouting the rhetoric of retribution, mining distress for personal, political and professional gain. We must beware those who depend on conflict for their sense of self: the non-whites who need to feel themselves victims of racism, the whites who need to feel themselves purveyors of it. We must be certain that in addressing the problem we do not end up creating it. I do not know if the Miss Black Canada Beauty Pageant still exists, but it is my fervent hope that it does not. Not only are beauty contests in themselves offensive, a racially segregated one is even more so. What would public reaction be, I wonder, if every year television offered a broadcast of a Miss White Canada Beauty Pageant? There are community-service awards given exclusively to blacks: would we be comfortable with such awards given exclusively to whites? If we accept a racially exclusive conference for non-white writers, should we not also accept one for white writers?[2] Quebec offers the Association of Black Nurses, the Association of Black Artists, the Congress of Black Jurists. Replace Black with White and watch the dancing visions of apartheid.[3] It is inescapable that racism for one is racism for the other.

It is vital, also, that we beware of abusing the word itself. Let us be certain that we apply it only when it is merited. Doing so not only avoids a harmful backlash but also ensures that we do not empty the word of meaning, that we do not constantly cry wolf by seeing racism as rampant and systemic, and so drain

[2] A reference to the "Writing Thru Race" Conference held in Vancouver in 1994. See the introduction to this section for a full discussion of the event.

[3] Apartheid was a White supremacist ideology of the governing National Party in South Africa from 1948 to 1994, although the official term was no longer used in the final years, which based government segregationist policies on the notion of racial purity and legislated highly preferential treatment to White South Africans.

it of emotional potency. "Racism" remains a dirty word in Canada. It must be kept that way.

The Tolerant Society

In a radio interview, the novelist Robertson Davies[4] once spoke of the difference between two words that are often—and erroneously—used interchangeably: acceptance and tolerance.

Acceptance, he pointed out, requires true understanding, recognition over time that the obvious difference—the accent, the skin colour, the crossed eyes, the large nose—are mere decoration on the person beneath. It is a meeting of peoples that delves under the surface to a knowledge of the full humanity of the other.

Tolerance, on the other hand, is far more fragile, for it requires not knowledge but wilful ignorance, a purposeful turning away from the accent, the skin colour, the crossed eyes, the large nose. It is a shrug of indifference that entails more than a hint of condescension.

The pose of tolerance is seductive, for it requires no effort; it is benign in that it allows others to get on with their lives free of interference—and also free of a helping hand. The problem, of course, is that tolerance—based as it is on ignorance—can, with changing circumstances, give way to a perception of threat. And such a perception is all that is required to cause a defensive reaction to kick in—or to lash out. Already in this country, we are seeing the emergence of reaction from those who feel themselves and their past, their beliefs and their contribution to the country, to be under assault. People who are "put up with" in the good times assume aspects of usurpers in the bad. Notions of purity—both cultural and racial—come to the forefront as the sense of self diminishes under the assault of unemployment, homelessness, a growing sense of helplessness.

This tolerance can very quickly metamorphose into virulent defensiveness, rejecting the different, alienating the new. Understanding, in contrast, requires effort, a far more difficult proposition, but may lead to acceptance and, for the newcomers, a sense of belonging. Multiculturalism, with its emphasis on the easy and the superficial, fosters the former while ignoring the latter.

Canada has long prided itself on being a tolerant society, but tolerance is clearly insufficient in the building of a cohesive society. A far greater goal to strive for would be an *accepting* society. Multiculturalism seems to offer at best provisional acceptance, and it is with some difficulty that one insists on being a full—and not just an associate—member of society. Just as the newcomer must decide how best to accommodate himself or herself to the society, so the society

---

[4] Canadian novelist (1913–1995), author of *Fifth Business* (1970) and outspoken cultural commentator. See Section VI.

must in turn decide how it will accommodate itself to the newcomer. Multiculturalism has served neither interest; it has heightened our differences rather than diminished them; it has preached tolerance rather than encouraging acceptance; and it is leading us into a divisiveness so entrenched that we face a future of multiple solitudes with no central notion to bind us. [. . .]

[1994]

Marilyn Dumont has written numerous poems and essays honouring her Métis background, yet she is also interested in the ways she finds herself straddling two worlds (traditional and urban), two languages (Cree and English), and two cultures (Aboriginal and Western). Throughout her poetry and nonfiction, Dumont confronts the restrictive definitions that have been imposed on Native people, both outside their communities and within them.

Born in Olds, Alberta, Dumont attended the University of British Columbia, where she earned an M.A. in fine arts. After a career in film and video production, Dumont turned to poetry. When her first collection of poems, *A Really Good Brown Girl* (1996), was published, it was marketed first as the work of a descendant of the famous military leader of the Northwest Rebellion, Gabriel Dumont, and second as a work of art by a gifted poet. To her frustration, Native and non-Native readers alike focused on her Native "authenticity" and her bloodline. In her essay "Popular Images of Nativeness" (1993), Dumont summarizes the paralyzing expectations that are placed on Native writers: "If you are old, you are supposed to write legends, that is, stories that were passed down to you from your elders. If you are young, you are expected to relate stories about foster homes, street life and loss of culture and if you

are in the middle, you are supposed to write about alcoholism or residential school." She continues: "[S]omehow throughout all this, you are supposed to infuse everything you write with symbols of the native world view." Echoes of this statement can be heard in comments by writers such as Eden Robinson and Rohinton Mistry, who resist being ethnically labelled before being read artistically.

Dumont's tongue-in-cheek poem "Circle the Wagons" plays on the demand that Native authors incorporate imagery of circles into their writing: mother earth, the circle, the trickster, and the number four. However, Dumont also asks, "What if you are an urban Indian?" Do you feign the significance of the recognizable symbols so you are identified and marketed with the "authentic voice" of a Native artist? Even positive images may be harmful if they rely on a static and singular notion of Native culture. They deny Native people's presence in the here and now as equal participants in society, politics, and economics and fail to take seriously the present-day concerns of Native communities about land claims, self-government, poverty, violence against women, and suicide.

In her poems, Dumont "writes back" to the ways in which Métis identity has been constructed through the colonizer's language and representation, literally doing so in the "Letter" to Canada's first prime minister in which she ironically quotes from F.R. Scott's poem "Laurentian Shield" (see Section V). The poems are also haunted by the silenced voices of children, daughters, mothers, and victims of violence. It is fruitful to compare Dumont's concentration on the connection between control of language and (dis)empowerment with that of Jeannette Armstrong, M. NourbeSe Philip, and Dionne Brand.

In *green girl dreams Mountains* (2001) and the 2007 collection *that tongued belonging,* from which "my life, a sweet berry" is taken, Dumont's poems still "hover over the sweet nectar of identity," as she puts it, as she focuses on women's issues and perspectives. Over the course of her career, Dumont has been writer-in-residence and instructor at several universities across Canada, including Athabasca University in Edmonton, where she currently lives.

The White Judges

We lived in an old schoolhouse, one large room that my father converted into two storeys with a plank staircase leading to the second floor. A single window on the south wall created a space that was dimly lit even at midday. All nine kids and the occasional friend slept upstairs like cadets in rows of shared double beds, ate downstairs in the kitchen near the gas stove and watched TV near the airtight heater in the adjacent room. Our floors were worn linoleum and scatter rugs, our walls high and bare except for the family photos whose frames were crowded with siblings waiting to come of age, marry or leave. At supper eleven of us would stare down a pot of moose stew, bannock and tea, while outside the white judges sat encircling our house.

And they waited to judge

waited till we ate tripe[1]
watched us inhale its wild vapour
sliced and steaming on our plates,
watched us welcome it into our being,
sink our teeth into its rubbery texture
chew and roll each wet and tentacled piece
swallow its gamey juices
until we had become it and it had become us.

Or waited till the cardboard boxes   10
were anonymously dropped at our door, spilling with clothes
waited till we ran swiftly away from the windows and doors
to the farthest room for fear of being seen

[1] Stomach tissue of an animal.

and dared one another to
'open it'
'no you open it'
'no you'
someone would open it
cautiously pulling out a shirt
that would be tried on   20
then passed around till somebody claimed it by fit
then sixteen or eighteen hands would be pulling out
skirts, pants, jackets, dresses from a box transformed now
into the Sears catalogue.

Or the white judges would wait till twilight
and my father and older brothers
would drag a bloodstained canvas
heavy with meat from the truck onto our lawn, and
my mother would lift and lay it in place
like a dead relative,   30
praying, coaxing and thanking it
then she'd cut the thick hair and skin back
till it lay in folds beside it like carpet

carving off firm chunks
until the marble bone shone out of the red-blue flesh
long into the truck-headlight-night she'd carve
talking in Cree to my father and in English to my brothers
long into the dark their voices talking us to sleep
while our bellies rested in the meat days ahead.

Or wait till the guitars came out   40
and the furniture was pushed up against the walls
and we'd polish the linoleum with our dancing
till our socks had holes.

Or wait till a fight broke out
and the night would settle in our bones
and we'd ache with shame
for having heard or spoken
that which sits at the edge of our light side
that which comes but we wished it hadn't
like 'settlement' relatives who would arrive at Christmas and   50
leave at Easter.

[1996]

Letter to Sir John A. Macdonald[2]

Dear John: I'm still here and halfbreed,
after all these years
you're dead, funny thing,
that railway you wanted so badly,
there was talk a year ago
of shutting it down
and part of it was shut down,
the dayliner at least,
'from sea to shining sea,'
and you know, John,   10
after all that shuffling us around to suit the settlers,
we're still here and Metis.

We're still here
after Meech Lake and
one no-good-for-nothin-Indian
holdin-up-the-train,[3]
stalling the 'Cabin syllables / Nouns of settlement,
/ ... steel syntax [and] / The long sentence of its exploitation'[4]
and John, that goddamned railroad never made this a great nation,
cause the railway shut down   20
and this country is still quarreling over unity,
and Riel is dead
but he just keeps coming back
in all the Bill Wilsons[5] yet to speak out of turn or favour
because you know as well as I
that we were railroaded
by some steel tracks that didn't last
and some settlers who wouldn't settle
and it's funny we're still here and callin ourselves halfbreed.

[1996]

[2] John A. Macdonald (1815–1891), first prime minister of Canada after Confederation in 1867. The transcontinental railway which ran across the prairies and through traditional Métis land was one of the main projects of Macdonald's career. The building of the railway and settlement of the prairies with European settlers resulted in the Métis communities being pushed off their land. "From sea to sea" is the official motto of Canada. See the introduction to Volume I, Section III, for a more extended account of this period.

[3] The Meech Lake Accord was a constitutional amendment agreement put together by Prime Minister Brian Mulroney in 1987 in an attempt to have Quebec ratify the Constitution Act, 1982. Aboriginal people opposed the Accord because they had not been consulted in the negotiations. Manitoba MLA Elijah Harper (1949–) blocked the Accord in the legislature in 1990, bringing about its downfall. See the introduction to this section for a more in-depth discussion.

[4] Quotation from F.R. Scott's poem "Laurentian Shield" (see Section V).

[5] Bill Wilson (1944–), Native activist and hereditary chief, and strong advocate for Aboriginal rights and self-government.

Circle the Wagons[6]

There it is again, the circle, that goddamned circle, as if we thought in circles, judged things on the merit of their circularity, as if all we ate was bologna and bannock, drank Tetley tea, so many times 'we are' the circle, the medicine wheel, the moon, the womb, and sacred hoops, you'd think we were one big tribe, is there nothing more than the circle in the deep structure of native literature? Are my eyes circles yet? Yet I feel compelled to incorporate something circular into the text, plot, or narrative structure because if it's linear then that proves that I'm a ghost and that native culture really has vanished and what is all this fuss about appropriation anyway? Are my eyes round yet? There are times when I feel that if I don't have a circle or the number four[7] or legend in my poetry, I am lost, just a fading urban Indian caught in all the trappings of Doc Martens,[8] cappuccinos and foreign films but there it is again orbiting, lunar, hoops encompassing your thoughts and canonizing mine, there it is again, circle the wagons. . . .

[1996]

my life, a sweet berry

I go make friends with this place   where I see   both a single strand of grass   bent white in spring and my own soundless sliver of a life   recalled in the lodge-pole's slender sway   stirring the sky   bluer than suede   the wind's mouth warm and smelling of pine   rehearsing summer   imaging itself
the sound of swift water

this first generous day of sun   began forty years ago   when I picked wild strawberries with my mother who took a rare break from the stifling cook shack only to have me stick a berry up my nose   cutting short her only afternoon of leisure   unable to loosen it I whimpered   then wailed back to camp scrappy as a cat given a bath   I embattled her with my stick arms and legs and she with tweezers crouched ready   pushed my skinny twigs away and aimed for the centre of my face   my head thrashing on the cook shack table mimicking strangulation   my mother with manual precision   gripped the attacking

---

[6] An allusion to the ways European settlers traveling across the prairies would gather their wagons into a circle to defend against an attack by "Indians" (a popular scene in many Hollywood Westerns).

[7] A reference to the four sacred cardinal directions and colours on the Medicine Wheel which work together to create a balanced whole.

[8] A line of British footwear and other clothing accessories, usually referring to the distinctive leather shoe or boot considered to be "hip" in urban centres.

berry   spared me suffocation by edible pulpy mass   and now as I am filled with the
song-rush of memory   and the seduction of nostalgia or worse
the conventions of my genre   to reconstruct my past as a sweet berry
I am rescued from conceit   and this time   it's not my mother   but my
own hand   and that damn honest germ of recall

[2007]

Armand Garnet Ruffo, a writer of Ojibway and European heritage, has been widely celebrated for work that situates Aboriginal cultural identity within larger social and historical contexts. A poet, essayist, playwright, filmmaker, and professor, Ruffo probes the intersections of national history and personal narrative. As he puts it in his influential essay, "Why Native Literature?" (1999), "As the tradition of Native spirituality is inherent in the literature . . . so, too, is the tradition of addressing historical, secular concerns." It is therefore fitting that his first collection of poetry, *Opening in the Sky* (1994), is named after his great-great grandfather, who met and negotiated a treaty with poet and Indian Affairs administrator Duncan Campbell Scott at the turn of the last century (see Volume I). Ruffo's "Poem for Duncan Campbell Scott" imagines one of these meetings from the perspective of the Aboriginal people Scott encountered.

In 1996, Ruffo published *Grey Owl: The Mystery of Archie Belaney.* The book comprises a series of linked poems that follow the life of Archibald Belaney, the famous "Indian" imposter, from his childhood in Hastings, England, to the exposure of his real identity after his death (see the Grey Owl selection and the story by Morley Callaghan in Section V). Ruffo draws on a family connection with Belaney, who was befriended by his great-grandparents and great-uncle (Annie, Alex, and Jim Espaniel), alongside personal anecdotes, archival research, textual citation from Belaney's own notebooks, photographs, and poetic imaginings. The poems do not criticize Grey Owl's appropriation of identity, but rather carefully engage with the complexities of the man, his motivations, and his relationships. Ruffo makes it clear that the Native people in northern Ontario were not duped by Grey Owl's adopted identity, but many accepted him because he helped support the causes of Indigenous people and politics. As the poems progress, the "story" of Grey Owl begins to assume a life of its own, imposing on Belaney an identity that appears out of his control. The portrait that emerges of Grey Owl reveals the contradictions of the man: an Englishman with a romantic notion of Aboriginality who lied about his identity so his concerns about the diminishing wilderness would be heard. The collection addresses the question that underlies any study of Grey Owl: did the laudable purpose justify the egregious misrepresentation? More than that, the book explores the performed nature of identity, as all people find themselves adopting and acting out various versions of themselves.

In the past decade, Ruffo has gained a wide readership for his creative and critical work. His third volume of poetry, *At Geronimo's Grave* (2001), won the Archibald Lampman Poetry Award. As well as writing poetry, Ruffo has produced several films and plays, including "A Windigo Tale" and a dramatic adaptation of his Grey Owl poems. His films include *A Wolf I Consider Myself,* which features his grandmother's narration of a traditional Ojibway oral poem. The collection of essays on Aboriginal literature that Ruffo edited, *(Ad)Dressing Our Words: Aboriginal Perspectives on Aboriginal Literatures* (2001), explores linguistic, national, gender, and sexual differences within Aboriginal traditions of storytelling and cultural expression.

Educated at the University of Ottawa (B.A.) and the University of Windsor (M.A.), where he studied with writer Alistair MacLeod (see Section VI), Ruffo has taught at both the Banff Centre for the Arts and the En'owkin Centre in Penticton, B.C. He now teaches Aboriginal literature and creative writing at Carleton University.

Poem for Duncan Campbell Scott

(Canadian poet who "had a long and distinguished career in
the Department of Indian Affairs, retiring in 1932."
The Penguin Book of Canadian Verse)

Who is this black coat and tie?
Christian severity etched in the lines
he draws from his mouth. Clearly a noble man
who believes in work and mission. See
how he rises from the red velvet chair,
rises out of the boat with the two Union Jacks
fluttering like birds of prey
and makes his way towards our tents.
This man looks as if he could walk on water
and for our benefit probably would,   10
if he could.

He says he comes from Ottawa way, Odawa country,
comes to talk treaty and annuity and destiny,
to make the inevitable less painful,
bearing gifts that must be had.
Notice how he speaks aloud and forthright:
    This or Nothing.
    Beware! Without title to the land
    under the Crown you have no legal right
    to be here.   20
Speaks as though what has been long decided wasn't.
As though he wasn't merely carrying out his duty

to God and King. But sincerely felt.
Some whisper this man lives in a house of many rooms,
has a cook and a maid and even a gardener
to cut his grass and water his flowers.
Some don't care, they don't like the look of him.
They say he asks many questions but
doesn't wait to listen. Asks
much about yesterday, little about today
and acts as if he knows tomorrow.
Others don't like the way he's always busy writing
stuff in the notebook he carries. Him,
he calls it poetry
and says it will make us who are doomed
live forever.

[1994]

From Grey Owl: The Mystery of Archie Belaney

Archie Belaney, 1899

From St. Mary's Terrace you can see the ocean,
dream the real world, America, like the books say,
out there far beyond Hastings beach
where the candy-striped cabins
are rolled out on their wooden wheels,
and a procession of people take turns changing
into their blooming bathing suits,
bathers tiptoeing at the water's edge.
It makes me want to laugh.

Laugh out loud at the crowd gathered along the boardwalk
staring at the brave few who manage to make it in.
You should see them, parasols and all.
The ladies look like they're going to church
where everyone will be sure to see them,
long dresses and fancy feathered hats,
and the men, they're wearing ties and dark jackets,
imagine, in this heat.

And when it rains, with the wind lashing the trees,
thunder and lightning waking the sky,
then they make sure to lock themselves indoors

like little mice snug in their nests.
While I take to the window and down the drainpipe,
and over to a neighbours' house where I settle in the yard
and hoot and howl ever so faintly
but loud enough to make them stir in their beds.

Why don't I go down to the beach?
Because I'd rather go to Saint Helen's Woods.
There I can make camp beside the creek
and practice with my knife or my rifle,
track whatever animals I spot.   30
I can pretend that I'm savage and free
and not trapped amongst strangers too afraid to get wet.
Why don't I go to the beach? Because when I finally do,
it will be to board one of those ships
and never return.

Indian

Country Life wants a book
and you've agreed to give them one,
but the writing doesn't come.

So you force yourself
by solemn oath
to remain seated,
leave only when you must,
to check on the beaver,
chop wood,
fix something to eat.   10

You even erect a table beside the bunk
so you can reach at all hours,
jot down an idea,
            a word
                an image.
And still nothing.

Inspiration
that's what you need,
so you turn to drink and before you know it
you've got an empty bottle of vanilla extract   20
hanging from a cord around your neck
like some kind of broken charm.

Your mind a forest fire
blazing out of control.

And nothing fits.

Grey Owl?
Wa-Sha-Quon-Asin?
Archibald Stansfeld Belaney?[1]
Whiteman? Redman?
Who's speaking? You yell   30
as you now break your pledge and stand and rush
to the mirror and make your Indian face.
Who are you speaking as? Who are you
speaking for? You rip the noose
from your neck and fling it into the corner.

Outside in newborn snow,
without any thought of where you're going
but aware you must go,
you strap on your snowshoes and move
across the lake. Until embraced   40
by pure night,
you stop to catch your breath,
and become aware.
You've nearly lost sight
of your cabin. Even your tracks.

Around you pines sway in their untouched whiteness;
above, the sky dances the dead;
below, its shadow, the lake swims alive.
This is what it's all about.
Why worry about who you are   50
when you already know
you are but a moment
of this harmony, little
more than a snowflake of it.

What you must do is simply act, and be.
Return to the cabin, move
towards the light,
the wind calls as it chills you through
and fills your lungs
with voice.   60

[1] These three names represent the three personae of Belaney.

Archie Belaney, 1930–31

The current is faster than I expect.
Suddenly my articles break into demand.
Letters of congratulations come flying
in from across Britain and the United States
(few from Canada which I find disconcerting).
Strangers want to visit me.
Reporters want to interview me.
They announce that I'm the first
to promote conservation:
the beaver,   10
the forests, the
Indian
way of life.

I begin by signing my name Grey Owl,
and saying I was adopted by the Ojibway,
and that for 15 years I spoke nothing but Indian;
then, before I know it, I have Apache blood.
Finally I'm calling myself an Indian writer.

Fast, it all happens so fast.
At first I'm hesitant.   20
I'm unsure of the name, the sound of it.
(Although, do I not prefer traveling at night?
Did I not hoot like an owl in Bisco?)
I think of the risk, those who know me.
There are Belaneys in Brandon.
My wife Angele in Temagami—
who knew me when I still carried an accent—
not to mention all those folks in northern Ontario.

But the thrust of self-promotion is upon me,
and head first into it, I hear myself   30
convincing myself that nobody's going to listen
to an immigrant ex-trapper from England,
promote an indigenous philosophy for Canada.
And if this is the only way
to get Canadians to listen,
then I'll do it, and more
if I have to. I'll be
what I have to be.
Without hesitation.

Romantic

James Fenimore Cooper,[2]
why, yes, I've read him.
   Last of the Mohicans
   Deerslayer etc. etc.
Fine books. Fine books indeed.

Certainly they're romanticized,
but then, it's all part of the game,
isn't it? To give the public
what it wants,
& expects.   10

I say if they want romance
           give it to them.
If they expect beads and braids
           give it to them.
Butter the facts.
Spread it thick.
The point is
to get the message
across,
isn't it?   20

Grey Owl, 1938

5th Avenue, people rushing from buildings and noise rushing
from traffic, much too much, locked and trying to break free,
to continue on my way, but held fast.

Faker, the man taunts. Faker, he says again, and I try
to ignore him and his venomous mouth, his peeled-back eyes,

---

[2] American writer James Fenimore Cooper (1789–1851) is best known for his series of novels, *The Leather-Stocking Tales*, which includes *The Last of the Mohicans: A Narrative of 1757* (1826) and *The Deerslayer* (1841). Cooper justified his highly romanticized, implausible, and unrealistic treatment of American Indians in his books in his own Introduction to *The Last of the Mohicans*. The protaganist of Cooper's novel is a White character named Nathaniel Bumppo, who was adopted by Aboriginal people and assumed a Native identity. This explains Grey Owl's tentative admission of his knowledge of these books.

while pedestrians stop to watch the commotion,
gather and shove,
and before I know it I'm breathing in his steam.

Come clean, he spits, and I try to push him away.
But where? The crowd surges and he pushes back, and I find   10
myself tethered between bodies. And that's when I react
and reach for my trusty knife and hear Yvonne say No,
the same moment my American agent, Colston, gasps
and grabs my arm to pull me away. Another time, another place,
he wouldn't have been able to stop me so easily.

I'm surprised by my own weakness and, like Colston, I curse
under my breath, but not the troublemaker we've left behind,
rather myself for being stuck here in this no man's land,
useless, worn-out, dead on my feet. Which makes me mad as hell
because I can't die, not here, not yet.   20

Afterwards Colston paces the room, rubs his hands nervously,
wipes his brow with his hanky. You can't do that, he says.
You just can't make a scene like that. Maybe in England
but not here in America. You've got to remember, on this side
of the Atlantic there are people—law biding, upstanding
citizens—who still believe the only good Indian is a dead one.
I'm not saying everybody, but there are some for sure. They hear
your "Tree" story about paleface soldiers and ruthless suppression
of the American Indian, certainly they get riled. You're bound
to get a few hotheads after you.   30

As for the press, sure they're on your side right now, but
don't kid yourself, that could change overnight. You know what
they'll do if they get a taste of something they don't like.
Spit you out. That's what. You could say goodbye
to your lecture tour, if not your career as a writer.
They'd either paint you to look like a sullen, dangerous,
savage who should be locked up or a fork-tongued charlatan
with something to hide, and who doesn't have something to hide?

It's your choice, Chief. But remember, right now you're an idol,
and with the kind of money you're making you can afford   40
to turn the other cheek.

[1996]

The work of poet-philosopher-musician Jan Zwicky can be compared in aesthetic and philosophical intensity to that of Margaret Avison, Anne Carson, Tim Lilburn, and P.K. Page. Although her poetry is difficult, it rewards careful reading. In their citation for her Governor General's Award-winning *Songs for Relinquishing the Earth* (1998), the judges note how Zwicky grounds her "elegant metaphysical and aesthetic insights in the physicality of the natural world and our own sensual natures." The poems included here, originally published in this collection, illustrate a lyric engagement with the physical world through a philosophical lens. In "Being, Polyphony, Lyric" (1998), an open letter to poet Robert Bringhurst written the year *Songs* was published, Zwicky observes that "a lyric mind is one for which the world lives as a complex, intricately structured, mortal & resonant whole." These poems ring with a philosophical musicality that attempts to examine the constituent notes of the whole.

Born in Calgary, Zwicky studied philosophy at the University of Calgary (B.A.) and the University of Toronto, where she earned an M.A. and Ph.D with a dissertation on "A Theory of Ineffability" (1982). Her indebtedness to the work of Austrian philosopher Ludwig Wittgenstein is evident throughout her oeuvre, but particularly in her second collection of poetry, *Wittgenstein Elegies* (1986). Inspired by the Foreword to Wittgenstein's *Philosophical Remarks* (1975), where he defends the spirit of true philosophical inquiry over the power of analytical philosophy, Zwicky reshapes his ideas poetically by creating a voice for him and several of his interlocutors. In her subsequent work *Lyric Philosophy* (1992), Zwicky "attempts to write the poetics for *Wittgenstein Elegies*." The work is unusual in format: on the recto pages, Zwicky presents the words of other poets (Don McKay, Lilburn, William Blake, and many others), as well as those of musicians and philosophers. On the verso pages, she presents her own musings on domesticity (by which she means something in the natural world that is "still explicit—burnished, polished, like bands of agate in rock"), the environment, and lyric poetry. The two sides of the page, according to Zwicky, exist somewhere between counterpoint and harmony.

In *The New Room* (1989) and *Songs for Relinquishing the Earth,* Zwicky turns from the explicit convergence of philosophy and poetry to more concrete lyrics anchored in a concern over ecology and material existence. *Thirty-seven Small Songs & Thirteen Silences* (2005) carries Zwicky's focus on the lyric forward. The songs in this collection are odes, addresses, and apostrophes to household objects, emotions, seasons, landscapes, sounds, and silence. Her collections *Wisdom & Metaphor* (2003) and *Robinson's Crossing* (2004) both received Governor General's Award nominations (in nonfiction and poetry categories, respectively, in the same year) and reiterated her focus on domesticity, ecology, and the lyric. The poems in *Robinson's Crossing* stem from the historical place in Alberta where the railway ends, and European settlers arriving in the northern part of the province had to cross the Pembina River and advance by wagon or on foot. In these poems Zwicky rethinks her family's attachment to place and history, sometimes with great humour: "[F]amily legend has it that she stood there / in the open doorway of the shack / and said, / "You told me, Ernest, / it had windows and a floor."

Zwicky taught both philosophy and creative writing at the University of New Brunswick before moving to Victoria to join the Philosophy Department at the University of Victoria in 1996. Zwicky continues to write and explore the ways lyric poetry can address contemporary environmental crises.

Open Strings[1]

E, laser of the ear, ear's
vinegar, bagpipes
in a tux, the sky's blue, pointed;

A, youngest of the four, cocksure
and vulnerable, the white kid
on the basketball team—immature,
ambitious, charming,
indispensable; apprenticed
to desire;

D is the tailor   10
who sewed the note "I shall always love you"
into the hem of the village belle's wedding dress,
a note not discovered until ten years later in New York
where, poor and abandoned, she was ripping up the skirt
for curtains, and he came,
and he married her;

G, cathedral of the breastbone,
oak-light, earth;

it's air they offer us,
but not the cool draught of their half-brothers   20
the harmonics, no,

---

[1] The open string notes in this poem refer to the four strings of a violin.

a bigger wind, the body
snapped out like a towel, air
like the sky above the foothills,
like the desire to drown,
a place of worship,
a laying down of arms.
                       Open strings
are ambassadors from the republic of silence.
They are the name of that moment when you realize   30
clearly, for the first time,
you will die.   After illness,
the first startled breath.

[1998]

Poppies

Some days, the wall that separates us from the future
is too thin. Standing in my mother's garden
by the bed of poppies on the northwest slope, wind
in the trees and the five-mile sky billowing over us,
I am caught again by their colour: water-colour,
sheer, like ice or silk, or, we imagine,
freedom. Their petals on the ground
collect in drifts, explosions
of arterial light.
                   Or perhaps it's that we are   10
that membrane, an instant thick, days
shine right through us as we charge around,
looking for some explanation in what hasn't happened yet
or what will never happen again. Like last night at dinner:
glancing up at the picture, the one that's always hung there,
the sudden clear presentiment that I would live
to walk into that dining room someday, after
the last death, and find it
waiting for me, the entire past
dangling from a finishing nail.   20

Poppies, what can they teach us?
The windshot light fills them
and they are blind.

[1998]

George Elliott Clarke has emerged as a major figure in contemporary Canadian literature, particularly through his creative and critical contributions to the literary history of African-Canadian writing in Canada. Clarke's widely varied oeuvre contains poetry, prose, librettos, plays, and critical studies. A seventh-generation Canadian of African-American and Mi'kmaq descent, Clarke coined the term "Africadian" (merging *African* and *Acadian*) to signify "Black Nova Scotia, an African-American-founded 'nation' which has flourished for more than two centuries." His work traces the aesthetics of blackness in Canada. In his anthology *Eyeing the North Star: Directions in African-Canadian Literature* (1997), Clarke writes, "*[R]ace, per se,* is not everything for African Canadians. No, it is the struggle against *erasure* that is everything." Part of Clarke's academic project is to raise awareness of the rich history of Black cultures in Canada, specifically (but not limited to) Nova Scotia. To this end he has published an important collection of essays, *Odysseys Home: Mapping African-Canadian Literature* (2002) (which includes an excellent bibliography of African-Canadian writing), and edited two anthologies of Black Canadian literature, *Fire on the Water: An Anthology of Black Nova Scotian Writing* (1992) and *Eyeing the North Star.*

In his work, Clarke expands the parameters of conventional definitions of "literature" to include the letters, poems, anecdotes, stories, and reminiscences of Black Loyalists who landed in Nova Scotia after the American Revolution (see Boston King in Volume I). He identifies John Marrant as the first African-Canadian author with the 1785 publication of *Narrative of the Lord's Dealings with John Marrant, a Black.* He vehemently argues against the notion projected by some literary scholars that African-Canadian writing really began in the 1960s with changes in immigration policy and an influx of immigrants from the Caribbean. What began for Clarke as a corrective to the predominantly White literary history of Canada and the repression of Black voices from the national register has transformed into an exploration of the depth of African-Canadian writing within the national framework. In the Introduction to *Eyeing the North Star,* Clarke argues that African-Canadian literature encompasses "[t]he King James scriptures melded with East Coast spirituals, New Orleans jazz, Bajan calypso, and Nigerian jit-jive . . . . A discourse diced with Motown slang, Caribbean creole, approximated Queen's English, gilt Haitian French, Canuck neologisms, and African patois." West Coast poet-critic Wayde Compton followed Clarke's lead when he edited the anthology *Bluesprint: Black British Columbian Literature and Orature* (2001), and critic Karina Vernon has worked extensively with the literary and cultural archives of Black Albertans.

Clarke sharply criticizes the academic "tendency to overcompensate" for historical wrongs and omissions by praising the work of a writer because of who s/he is rather than what s/he has written. In his 2000 essay "Harris, Philip, Brand: Three Authors in Search of Literate Criticism," Clarke insists that criticism is never innocent and argues against the solidarity criticism that emerges out of "our uncritical guilt and our sycophantic quest for absolution at any cost"; he urges us to read for poetics (structures, styles, influences) rather than politics, or for the literal connections between theoretical *poesis* and political *praxis*. In an interview with poet Anne Compton, Clarke outlines his desire to combine an Africadian perspective on Canadian history and politics with a personal vision that attempts to assert "certain aesthetic/political viewpoints combating the hegemony of the standard aesthetic/political viewpoints."

Born in Windsor Plains, Nova Scotia, Clarke attended the University of Waterloo (where he helped found the Creative Writers' Collective), earning a B.A. in 1984. *Saltwater Spirituals and Deeper Blues* (1983), a volume of poems prompted by his research on Nova Scotian history, was published shortly before he graduated. After his B.A., Clarke spent a year as a social worker in the Annapolis Valley and then four more years as an aide to a member of Parliament in Ottawa, also earning an M.A. in English from Dalhousie University during this time (1989). The book that catapulted him onto the national stage, *Whylah Falls* (1990), was published the following year while he was working on his doctorate at Queen's University (Ph.D., 1993).

Whylah Falls is a poetic retelling of the 1985 murder of a Black man in Weymouth Falls, N.S., and the acquittal of the White man accused of killing him, but Clarke is not fundamentally a narrative poet. He combines characteristics of classic epic poetry and formal genres like the sonnet with the cadence of music and the language of love and violence. From this collection, "Rose Vinegar" and "Blank Sonnet" beautifully illustrate Clarke's dramatic

aesthetic. *Whylah Falls* won the Archibald Lampman Award for Poetry and, over a decade after its publication, had a resurgence in popularity when it was runner-up to Michael Ondaatje's *In the Skin of a Lion* in the inaugural CBC Radio "Canada Reads" contest (2002). Clarke also reworked the poems into a play in 1997.

Clarke's experience teaching at Duke University in Durham, North Carolina (1994–99), allowed him to compare American and Canadian contexts of artistic production and historical engagement. In his 2001 poetry collection *Blue,* written while living in North Carolina, Clarke quotes Irving Layton in the epigraph to the book: "[G]ood poems should rage like a fire / Burning all things, burning them with great splendour," and extends Layton's metaphor by addressing poets who "immolate themselves in the inferno of witnessing." Clarke's incendiary engagement with the poetry community includes work dedicated to Canadian writers such as Dionne Brand and Austin Clarke, who sometimes hold critical and creative perspectives different from his own.

When Gaspereau Press released an exquisite limited edition of Clarke's *Execution Poems: The Black Acadian Tragedy of "George and Rue"* (2000), it sold out in a month. The trade edition (2001) went on to win the Governor General's Award for poetry. The poems follow the story of Clarke's cousins who killed a taxi driver and were hanged for the offence in 1948. In 2005, Clarke published his first novel, *George & Rue,* expanding on the work of *Execution Poems.*

Given his close attention to the musicality of language, it is not surprising that Clarke has also composed librettos for opera, *Beatrice Chancy* (1999) (with music composed by

James Rolfe) and *Trudeau: Long March & Shining Path* (2007) (music composed by D.D. Jackson); as well as *Québécité: A Jazz Fantasia in Three Cantos* (2003). The list of awards Clarke has received is impressive in its range, including the Portia White Prize for Excellence in the Arts, the Pierre Trudeau Fellowship Prize, the Martin Luther King Jr. Achievement Award, the Order of Nova Scotia, the Order of Canada, and a number of honorary doctorates. In 2000, Clarke moved to Toronto to take up his current position as a professor of literature at the University of Toronto.

From Whylah Falls
Rose Vinegar

In his indefatigable delirium of love, Xavier wires rugosa rose blossoms to Shelley.[1] Deluded by his quixotic romanticism,[2] he cannot yet appreciate the practical necessities of friendship. But, Shelley trusts in reason; thus, though she admires the blossoms for their truthfulness to themselves, she does not hesitate to distill a delicate and immortal vinegar from what she considers the ephemeral petals of X's desire. An ornament becomes an investment. She fills a cup with the fresh rose petals; then, stripping off their heels, (the white part), she pours the petals into a quart sealer and adds two cups of white vinegar. Then, she seals the jar and places it on the sunny livingroom windowsill for sixteen days, seven hours, and nine minutes. When the vinegar is ready, she strains it through a sieve and then pours it back into the bottle.

Rose vinegar. It's especially good on salads.

Blank Sonnet

The air smells of rhubarb, occasional
Roses, or first birth of blossoms, a fresh,
Undulant hurt, so body snaps and curls
Like flower. I step through snow as thin as script,
Watch white stars spin dizzy as drunks, and yearn
To sleep beneath a patchwork quilt of rum.
I want the slow, sure collapse of language
Washed out by alcohol. Lovely Shelley,

---

[1] In *Whylah Falls,* Shelley is the practical foil to the romantic poet Xavier. Throughout the text, Clarke presents the two voices contrapuntally so that cumulatively, the poems mimic a "call and response" between the lovers. A rugosa rose is a hardy shrub rose, distinguished by dark green, wrinkled leaves and large orange-red hips.

[2] Quixotic romanticism refers to the exaggerated chivalry and romance characteristic of the hero of Miguel de Cervantes's (1547–1616) novel *Don Quixote* (Part I, 1605; Part II, 1615).

I have no use for measured, cadenced verse
If you won't read. Icarus-like,[3] I'll fall   10
Against this page of snow, tumble blackly
Across vision to drown in the white sea
That closes every poem—the white reverse
That cancels the blackness of each image.

[1990]

Bio: Black Baptist/Bastard

for Dionne Brand[4]

History fell upon us like the lash—
Lacerating. Black Baptists[5] wept out prayers—
Passion—to hector tar into nectar,
To harvest undeniable honey,
But our weak eyes were stooped by white faces,
We sank, stupefied by white capital.
We chewed breaded blasphemy in our pews,
Then gulped *Welch's* grape juice,[6] bile, and venom,
While alabaster Christ carped like a cop,
His lips apocalypsing our asses.   10
Slavery was dead, wasn't it? But blood
Crusted on our rusty-smelling sermons,
A taint of blood for saint-plush lips. How could
We look at the Atlantic and not cry,
"*Eli, Eli, lama sabachthani?*"[7] We knew
The terror of evacuated faith.

---

[3] In the Greek myth of Daedalus and Icarus, a father and son trapped on the island of Crete try to escape by making wings out of wax. Daedalus warns Icarus not to fly too close to the sun or his wings will melt. Intoxicated by flight, Icarus flies higher and higher until the wax melts and he tumbles to his death in the sea below.

[4] Dionne Brand (1953–), poet, novelist, and activist. See the selection of her work in this anthology. Clarke writes both in her honour and as a way of engaging in an ongoing dialogue between the poets about the significance of Black history in Canada. In this poem, Clarke historicizes the community of Black Nova Scotians, elucidating the links between the institutions of religion and racism and thus demonstrating the long history of racial oppression and community identification of African Canadians in the Maritimes.

[5] Many African Nova Scotians belong to the African United Baptist Association of Nova Scotia, established in 1853.

[6] Used instead of wine at Mass.

[7] The words of Jesus on the cross, translated as "My God, my God, why hast thou forsaken me?"

The air swerves cold with such calamity.
I chronicle a dark, pockmarked epoch,
Map a province where trains gnaw their way home,
Blackened mummies pitch, gutted by gypsum,   20
Frail Baptists fall, their crotches worm-eaten:
Debris escalates when black ice sleets in.
I come from Windsor Plains, a wine-stained poet,
Expecting to imbibe William Williams'
Rain in the galvanized pail by the well.[8]
Well, as a child, I spread blackstrap[9] on bread
Between bitter dollops of the Bible.
I had to. I was guilty. I had spied
My sun-skinned mother's glaring skin. (I eyed,
Damningly, her glimmering, mixed-race breasts.)   30
Enough snow has fallen without license.
A *Putsch*[10] arrests my heart. My life's naked.
Listen closely: I am trying to cry.
That's my condemned blood on the page.

[2001]

Antiphony[11]

for Austin C. Clarke

Those chalk-poisoned black men who watched gypsum[12]
Choke off roses could not, would not, have known
Teacher-chalked glories of Wordsworth or Yeats,

---

[8] William Carlos Williams (1883–1963), American imagist poet famous for his poem "The Red Wheelbarrow" (1923), in which he provides very specific visual images of a wheelbarrow in the rain: "so much depends / upon / a red wheel / barrow / glazed with rain / water / beside the white / chickens."

[9] Blackstrap molasses.

[10] An insurrection, a counter-revolutionary movement, or a coup.

[11] Antiphony refers to the response of one voice to another in a choir or in a musical piece. In literary terms, it refers to the presentation of a point and its counterpoint, or a response to another speaker. Austin Clarke (1934–), author of *The Polished Hoe* (2002), is a prominent African-Canadian writer. Clarke has written extensively about being a student in the British colonial education system in Barbados in his memoir *Growing Up Stupid Under the Union Jack* (1980), so George Elliott Clarke's poem responds with a Canadian example of this kind of educational colonialism. See Austin Clarke's story "Canadian Experience" in Section VI.

[12] Windsor, N.S., is home to the Fundy Gypsum mining company where gypsum rock is mined to be used in drywall, plaster, fertilizer, and blackboard chalk. Using an antiphonal method, Clarke juxtaposes the chalk used in schoolrooms with the experiences of the miners.

Or how a boy could kneel before Hopkins,
Chanting him and Herrick (heretic cleric),[13]
In a sorry Baptist-beleaguered field,
All crows and regret, miles and decades late,
Mumbling cavalier love where hogs were hacked.

How could wracked miners've moaned the heavy,
Gorgeous hurt of those epics that spurned   10
Their shouts, their salvos of pain and rough joy,
Bloodying damned Nova Scotia?

So I craved to hear Milton hollered out,
Yelled with handclaps and tin spoons played on thighs,
And the brawl of white, murderous gypsum—
Bawled at last in Luddite[14] language bursting
Spellers, wrecking letters,
Bashing grammar into gravel. Why not?

Our British literature was just dust—
A mob of beetles chewing torn-up books,   20
Royally churning Chaucer into dung.
Tragedy was our slavery. Look-it:
Shakespeare came down to us as *Black Horse* beer—
The only good thing Empire ever made.[15]

[2001]

MIRIAM TOEWS

---

[13] Poets whose work forms part of the English literary canon and whose poems were regularly taught in colonial classrooms: William Wordsworth (1770–1850), W.B. Yeats (1865–1939), Gerard Manley Hopkins (1844–1889), and Robert Herrick (1591–1674). While Hopkins wrote beautifully experimental devotional poetry (celebrating the originality or "inscape" of each of God's creatures), Herrick was a cleric better known for his erotic verse than for his devotional writing. Later in the poem, the speaker refers to John Milton (1608–1674), author of *Paradise Lost* (1667), and Geoffrey Chaucer (1343–1400), author of *The Canterbury Tales* (1387–1400).

[14] One who opposes new technology, based on the band of English merchants who set out to destroy manufacturing machinery in the early nineteenth century.

[15] Black Horse Beer, a Molson Canadian product that is brewed only in Newfoundland; it is a beer that many Atlantic Canadians feel an attachment to.

MIRIAM TOEWS ▪ (1964–)

When Miriam Toews's novel *A Complicated Kindness* (2004) won the CBC Radio "Canada Reads" contest in 2006, it narrowly beat out Al Purdy's selected poems. The reason, according to the judges, was that Canadians were yearning for humour mixed with a strong sense of place (notwithstanding the applicability of this statement to Purdy's poetry). Judge John K. Samson, poet and lead singer of the Winnipeg band the Weakerthans, put it simply: "I can smell the place. I know that place." Such veracity of place is remarkable, given that the setting of the novel is the fictional town of East Village, Manitoba. Toews points the microscope at institutions of the Mennonite faith, and at the destructive elements of what she regards as religious fundamentalism in general, at the same time as she shows the hope, love, forgiveness, and tolerance that can come with faith. As in her other books, *Summer of My Amazing Luck* (1996), *A Boy of Good Breeding* (1998), and *Swing Low: A Life* (2000), Toews's writing is anchored in Manitoban life and landscape.

Like Margaret Laurence and Alice Munro with their portraits of the suffocating nature of small-town life for a teenager, *A Complicated Kindness* is a *Künstlerroman,* or a portrait of an artist as a young woman, told from the perspective of a 16-year-old girl. The novel combines comedy and the self-reflexive narration of history ("historiographic metafiction"), as the protagonist Nomi Nickel provides an account of her community: "[I]magine the least well-adjusted kid in your school starting a breakaway clique of people whose manifesto includes a ban on the media, dancing, smoking, temperate climates, movies, drinking, rock and roll, having sex for fun, swimming, make-up, jewelry, playing pool, going to cities, or staying up past nine o'clock. That was Menno all over." As in *A Complicated Kindness*, in her most recent book, *The Flying Troutmans* (2008), Toews once again explores psychological depression and family bonds, but this time in a road-trip story framework.

Born in Steinbach, Manitoba, the town on which she modelled East Village, Toews is herself Mennonite. When Rudy Wiebe's novel *Peace Shall Destroy Many* (1962) was published, it was considered to be an exposé of the life of the Mennonite community and was viewed by some Mennonites as offensive because it aired dirty laundry to those outside the community. Toews's novel, written two decades later, was received with somewhat more enthusiasm within the community, although its critics saw it, too, as offensive. Other Mennonite poets such as D Brandt and Patrick Friesen, and writers such as Armin Wiebe, have also explored the complexity of being Mennonite, or "in the world but not of the world."

Toews completed a B.A. in film studies from the University of Manitoba (studying with Robert Kroetsch and Carol Shields) and a Bachelor of Journalism degree from the University of King's College in Halifax, Nova Scotia. In addition to writing fiction, Toews works as a freelance journalist for magazines, newspapers, and radio.

"Blueprints" was originally part of a collection entitled *Paper Placemats* (2004), a public art project by J&L Books (edited by Paul Maliszewski) that was distributed free to participating diners across America. Ten stories and 30 photographs combined to make a bound volume of 40 paper placemats that could be ripped out and used. The result was that patrons of diners across America had an unexpected encounter with a work of art. Contributors were asked to submit work that had to do with "place," fitting both for a "placemat" and for Toews's work. The project allowed its audience to connect on a level that challenged traditional methods of artistic interaction and prompted readers to consider the format of the story as well as its content. In "Blueprints," Toews's treatment of a suburban house that is displaced, replaced, and possibly misplaced is both humorous and poignant in its affectionate treatment of the shifting nature of domestic relations, landscape, and home.

Blueprints

When I was twelve my house was taken away to the countryside on the back of a truck, and I haven't seen it since.

I've wanted to, though, and I think about it a lot, but nobody knows where it is . . .

C'mon Mel, my mom said before they took the house away, put up a fight at least.

Mel was my dad, and he didn't like to fight. He liked to read books about people who had accomplished big things in their lives and he liked to make our yard beautiful with flowers. When they carted off our house he couldn't bear to think about it. It was the house he'd built himself when he was twenty-one, freshly married to my mom and filled with hope still.

The man who owned the car dealership next door was to blame. After years of pressuring my dad, he finally bought our house and had it removed. He wanted to expand his parking lot.

My dad didn't want to know where they were taking it.

He stood on the curb in his suit and tie and watched the house get smaller and smaller. Then he walked two blocks over to our new house and stayed in his bedroom for one month, in the dark.

I'm older now, I've got kids, I live in the city, forty miles west of the town where I grew up, I'm halfway through my life probably, my dad's dead—he killed himself, not to sound blunt about something awful like that, but it happened—and I'm thinking a lot these days about when I was a kid in that house.

The other day I was talking to my mom about nothing really—we were just chatting—and she asked me what I was doing that evening, and I told her I was going to a bowling fundraiser at the Billy Mosienko Lanes in the north end.[1]

Billy Mosienko! She says.

And I say, Yeah, and she asks me if I know who he is, and I say no, and she says, Well, Billy Mosienko was a famous hockey player for the Chicago Blackhawks, and in the 1950s he set a record by scoring three goals in twenty-one seconds against the New York Rangers. And he's from here, Winnipeg. And that record has never been broken.

I said, Wow, okay, and then she asked me if she or my dad had ever told me that it was Billy Mosienko who gave my dad the blueprints for the house that was hauled away. You mean, I asked her, I spent my first twelve years in a house that was an exact replica of Billy Mosienko's? Yes, she said.

She and my dad were seventeen years old and dating, and my dad had a job driving into the city delivering eggs. He always passed this house with a big

---

[1] Billy Mosienko was a player for the Chicago Blackhawks in the NHL who came from Winnipeg. After retiring from hockey, he returned to Winnipeg where he ran the Billy Mosienko bowling alley.

picture window and a long brick planter. He really liked that planter, so one day he took my mom with him to the city to point out the house to her and to ask her if she could be happy in a house like that and raise a family and all that stuff, and she said, Yes, of course, and so right then my dad stops the truck, and they go and knock on the door of this house, and who answers their knock but Billy Mosienko.

He gave them a tour of the whole place, including his trophy room (which, in my dad's version of the house, was my bedroom and never housed one trophy) and then, after that, Mosienko gave my dad his blueprints and told him and my mom to have a wonderful life together and good luck.

My dad brought the blueprints back to his small town and built a house "fit for a hero," but things didn't work out as nicely for him as they did for Mosienko. Years later when Mosienko was inducted into the Hockey Hall of Fame, my dad was halfway through spending a year in total silence. Still, we did have plenty of good times there, and the flowers my dad planted every spring in that long brick planter—that was the only distinguishing feature of the house—were beautiful, they really were.

I asked my mom exactly where in the city Mosienko's house had been, but she couldn't remember. Darn it, she said, Mel would know.

Recently I happened to mention to my friend Glenn that I was feeling kind of obsessed with finding my old house. I told him about the Billy Mosienko connection, and he listened to me and nodded and then about a week later he phoned me up and told me that he and his brother Charlie had done a little research and found out that Mosienko had lived at 889 Cathedral Avenue, in the north end, which is about a twenty-minute drive from where I live.

I got into my van right then and drove to Cathedral, and as I got closer and closer to 889 I slowed down, because I so wanted the house to look like mine, and I was thinking about my dad driving down that same street and being seventeen and so eager and optimistic, this young, fun-loving guy telling people how he was building a house just like Billy Mosienko's, and then there it was, the dream house with the long brick planter in the front.

And sure enough, it was exactly the same as the one my dad had built. Same front door, same giant pine tree in the back yard. Same rosy color paint, even the same white pillar things holding up the roof that hung over the planter. I could almost see my dad moving back and forth along the planter with his old watering can. I pulled over and parked and noticed a man and his young son staring at me from the other side of the street and started feeling a bit self-conscious.

When I got home I called my mom and told her I'd seen Mosienko's house. That's good, she said. She laughed. I asked her, Are you sure you don't know where ours went? Who knows, she said. A field somewhere. Maybe southeast of here, maybe west.

[2004]

According to Michael Crummey, "[P]oetry is the one place I can, honestly and with something approaching clarity, acknowledge my love for family, for friends and lovers, for the world I live in." This engagement with family—"where everything starts and finishes"—is well conveyed in his poem "What's Lost."

Crummey is a Newfoundland poet and novelist whose work echoes with the sounds of generations of Newfoundlanders. His writing powerfully evokes a sense of connection with place and across time. The poems from *Hard Light* (1998), including "Newfoundland Sealing Disaster" and "What's Lost," and what he calls the "little story" of "Bread," are preoccupied with his own family history, particularly his father's work in the Labrador fishery.

According to poet and novelist John Steffler, "Crummey approaches characters not as isolated individuals but as beings whose identities are inseparable from their landscape and culture; and culture for him is inseparable from the work people do, inseparable from the tools and routines they have devised to exploit the resources and ward off the dangers in the place where they live." An economical writer, Crummey is able to condense entire lives, as in "Bread," into small narrative spaces. He is also a prolific writer: his early volumes *Arguments with Gravity* (1996) and *Hard Light* (1998) were followed by a book of stories, *Flesh and Blood* (1998); a novel, *River Thieves* (2001); two more collections of poems, *Emergency Roadside Assistance* (2001) and *Salvage* (2002); and another novel, *The Wreckage* (2005). Most of his writing is concerned with the history and culture of Newfoundland, especially with the disappearance and seeming irretrievability of an entire way of life. As Crummey put

it in an interview with Herb Wyile, "It has become clear to me . . . that loss in all its forms is what I'm interested in—personal loss, cultural loss." Still, Crummey points to this emphasis in his work with a sense of irony in the opening poem of *Salvage: "Sad Book Ahead. / Poems about Loss / Next 100 pgs."*

Born in Buchans, Newfoundland, Crummey grew up in the interior of the province and in Wabush, Labrador. After attending Memorial University for his B.A. (1987), Crummey pursued graduate work at Queen's University (where he earned his M.A. in 1988) but later left the Ph.D. program. Crummey's most discussed work is his historical novel, *River Thieves,* set in nineteenth-century Newfoundland when the British settlers were beginning to realize that the Aboriginal peoples of the island were on the brink of extinction. The novel centres on the capture of a Beothuk woman, Demasduit (or Mary March), who was to be trained to become a translator and mediator between the British and the Beothuk. Crummey provides an anguished meditation on the historical and psychological complexities surrounding the event, telling the story from the perspective of a group of settlers who must come to terms with their complicity in exterminating an entire people.

Crummey's preoccupation with the recuperation of buried histories echoes many of the concerns of earlier writers such as Al Purdy, Rudy Wiebe, and Robert Kroetsch. In addition, his poems can be fruitfully read beside other Atlantic-Canadian treatments of the haunting disjunction between past and present, works such as E.J. Pratt's poem "Newfoundland" (see Section V) and Alistair MacLeod's story "The Boat" (see Section VI).

Bread

I was twenty years younger than my husband, his first wife dead in childbirth. I agreed to marry him because he was a good fisherman, because he had his own house and he was willing to take in my mother and father when the time came. It was a practical decision and he wasn't expecting more than that. Two people should never say the word love before they've eaten a sack of flour together, he told me.

The night we married I hiked my night dress around my thighs and shut my eyes so tight I saw stars. Afterwards I went outside and I was sick, throwing up over the fence. He came out the door behind me and put his hand to the small of my back. It happens your first time, he said. It'll get better.

I got pregnant right away and then he left for the Labrador. I dug the garden, watched my belly swell like a seed in water. Baked bread, bottled bakeapples for the winter store, cut the meadow grass for hay. After a month alone I even started to miss him a little.

The baby came early, a few weeks after my husband arrived home in September. We had the minister up to the house for the baptism the next day, Angus Maclean we named him, and we buried him in the graveyard in the Burnt Woods a week later. I remember he started crying at the table the morning of the funeral and I held his face against my belly until he stopped, his head in my hands about the size of the child before it was born. I don't know why sharing a grief will make you love someone.

I was pregnant again by November. I baked a loaf of bread and brought it to the table, still steaming from the oven. Set it on his plate whole and stood there looking at him. That's the last of that bag of flour, I told him. And he smiled at me and didn't say anything for a minute. I'll pick up another today, he said finally.

And that's how we left it for a while.

[1998]

What's Lost

The Labrador coastline is a spill of islands,
salt-shaker tumble of stone,
a cartographer's nightmare—
on the coastal boat 50 years ago
the third mate marked his location after dark
by the outline of a headland against the stars,
the sweetly acrid smell of bakeapples blowing off
a stretch of bog to port or starboard,
navigating without map or compass
where hidden shoals shadow the islands   10
like the noise of hammers echoed across a valley.

The largest are home to harbours and coves,
a fringe of clapboard houses

threaded by dirt road,
grey-fenced cemeteries sinking
unevenly into mossy grass.
Even those too small to be found on the map
once carried a name in someone's mind,
a splinter of local history—
a boat wracked up in a gale of wind, 20
the roof-wrecked remains of a stage house
hunkered in the lee.

Most of what I want him to remember
lies among those islands, among the maze
of granite rippling north a thousand miles,
and what he remembers is all I have a claim to.
My father nods toward the coastline,
to the bald stone shoals almost as old as light—
That was 50 years ago, he says,
as a warning, wanting me to understand 30
that what's forgotten is lost
and most of this he cannot even recall
forgetting

[1998]

Newfoundland Sealing Disaster[1]

Sent to the ice after white coats,
rough outfit slung on coiled rope belts,
they stooped to the slaughter: gaffed pups,[2]
slit them free of their spotless pelts.

The storm came on unexpected.
Stripped clean of bearings, the watch struck
for the waiting ship and missed it.
Hovelled in darkness two nights then,

bent blindly to the sleet's raw work,
bodies muffled close for shelter, 10
stepping in circles like blinkered mules.
The wind jerking like a halter.

---

[1] In March 1914, 132 sealers from the SS *Newfoundland*, upon orders from their captain, were sent out into an incoming blizzard and became stranded on the ice floes for two days. An attempt to return to the ship proved futile and more than two-thirds of the men died. Some men became delirious and walked off the ice into the water.

[2] Seal pups.

Minds turned by the cold, lured by small
comforts their stubborn hearts rehearsed,
men walked off ice floes to the arms
of phantom children, wives; of fires

laid in imaginary hearths.
Some surrendered movement and fell,
moulting warmth flensed from their faces
as the night and bitter wind doled out   20

their final, pitiful wages.

                                                                              [1998]

CHRISTIAN BÖK ■ (1966–)

"Eunoia," meaning "beautiful thinking," is the shortest word in English to employ all five vowels. Christian Bök's Griffin Award-winning volume of poetry *Eunoia* (2001) is a "lipogram," or a "constraint-based" form of writing in which each chapter restricts itself to the use of a single vowel. Over the course of seven years, working by hand rather than with a computer program, Bök sorted all the single-vowel words in English into topical categories and arranged them like a jigsaw puzzle into five chapter-long narratives. In the end, according to Bök, each chapter contains at least 98% of the words in the vowel's lexicon. In his essay "The New Ennui," which concludes the collection, Bök notes the thematic parallels between chapters: "All chapters must allude to the art of writing. All chapters must describe a culinary banquet, a prurient debauch, a pastoral tableau and a nautical voyage." In the process, as the book tells us, each vowel develops a personality: A is courtly, E is elegiac, I is lyrical, O is jocular, and U is obscene. In an interview with poet Charles Bernstein at the University of Pennsylvania, Bök argues that he is committed to invention and experimentation in poetry in order to,

as he says, "indulge in a completely exploratory adventure through language itself." In recognition of the significance of sound in this work, Coach House Press released a recording of Bök performing *Eunoia* on CD to accompany the print version of the text.

Having worked with poets such as Paul Dutton, Steve McCaffery, Darren Wershler-Henry (who edited *Eunoia*), and Christopher Dewdney, Bök is best known for his work in experimental sound poetry. Born Christian Book in Toronto, the poet has also published *Crystallography* (1994) and *Pataphysics: The Poetics of an Imaginary Science* (2002) to wide acclaim. In his recent short manifesto "Virtually Nontoxic," Bök asks, "[H]as not the act of writing simply become another chemically engineered experience, in which we manufacture a complex polymer by stringing together syllables instead of molecules?" He suggests instead that "we need a lingual variety of gelignite or plastique—the kind of incendiary literature, written only by misfits, who have grown up, still dizzy from the fumes, after having melted a platoon of plastic armymen with a match."

Beyond writing and performing poetry, Bök has also created artificial languages for Gene Rodenberry's *Earth: Final Conflict* and Peter Benchley's *Amazon,* and placed conceptual artworks in galleries internationally. Having completed his B.A. and M.A. at Carleton University and his Ph.D. at York University, Bök is now a professor of experimental poetics, Canadian literature, and literary theory at the University of Calgary.

From Eunoia
Chapter I

for Dick Higgins

Writing is inhibiting. Sighing, I sit, scribbling in ink this pidgin script. I sing with nihilistic witticism, disciplining signs with trifling gimmicks—impish hijinks which highlight stick sigils.[1] Isn't it glib? Isn't it chic? I fit childish insights within rigid limits, writing shtick which might instill priggish misgivings in critics blind with hindsight. I dismiss nitpicking criticism which flirts with philistinism. I bitch; I kibitz—griping whilst criticizing dimwits, sniping whilst indicting nitwits, dismissing simplistic thinking, in which philippic wit is still illicit.   10

Pilgrims, digging in shifts, dig till midnight in mining pits, chipping flint with picks, drilling schist with drills, striking it rich mining zinc. Irish firms, hiring micks whilst firing Brits, bring in smiths with mining skills: kilnwrights grilling brick in brickkilns, millwrights grinding grist in gristmills. Irish tinsmiths, fiddling with widgits, fix this rig, driving its drills which spin whirring drillbits. I pitch in, fixing things. I rig this winch with its wiring; I fit this drill with its piping. I   20 dig this ditch, filling bins with dirt, piling it high, sifting it, till I find bright prisms twinkling with glitz.

Hiking in British districts, I picnic in virgin firths, grinning in mirth with misfit whims, smiling if I find birch twigs, smirking if I find mint sprigs. Midspring brings with it singing birds, six kinds (finch, siskin, ibis, tit, pipit, swift), whistling shrill chirps, trilling *chirr chirr* in high pitch. Kingbirds flit in gliding flight, skimming limpid springs, dipping wingtips in rills which brim with living things: krill, shrimp, brill —   30

[1] Magical symbol, sometimes used to summon spirits.

fish with gilt fins, which swim in flitting zigs. Might Virgil[2] find bliss implicit in this primitivism? Might I mimic him in print if I find his writings inspiring?

Fishing till twilight, I sit, drifting in this birch skiff, jigging kingfish with jigs, bringing in fish which nip this bright string (its vivid glint bristling with stick pins). Whilst I slit this fish in its gills, knifing it, slicing it, killing it with skill, shipwrights might trim this jib, swinging it right, hitching it tight, riding brisk winds which pitch this skiff, tipping it, tilting it, till this ship   40 in crisis flips. Rigging rips. Christ, this ship is sinking. Diving in, I swim, fighting this frigid swirl, kicking, kicking, swimming in it till I sight high cliffs, rising, indistinct in thick mists, lit with lightning.

Lightning blinks, striking things in its midst with blinding light. Whirlwinds whirl; driftwinds drift. Spindrift is spinning in thrilling whirligigs. Which blind spirit is whining in this whistling din? Is it this grim lich, which is writhing in its pit, lifting its lid with whitish limbs, rising, vivific, with ill will in   50 its mind, victimizing kids timid with fright? If it is — which blind witch is midwifing its misbirth, binding this hissing djinni with witching spiritism? Is it this thin, sickish girl, twitching in fits, whilst writing things in spirit-writing? If it isn't—it is I; it is I . . .

Lightning flicks its riding whip, blitzing this night with bright schisms. Sick with phthisis[3] in this drizzling mist, I limp, sniffling, spitting bilic spit, itching livid skin (skin which is tingling with stinging pinpricks). I find this frigid drisk dispiriting; still, I fight   60 its chilling windchill. I climb cliffs, flinching with skittish instincts. I might slip. I might twist this infirm wrist, crippling it, wincing whilst I bind it in its splint, cringing whilst I gird it in its sling; still, I risk climbing, sticking with it, striving till I find this rift, in which I might fit, hiding in it till winds diminish.

Minds grim with nihilism still find first light inspiring. Mild pink in tint, its shining twilight brings bright

[2] Virgil (70–19 BCE), classical Roman poet, author of the *Eclogues*, a series of pastoral poems, and the epic poem about the founding of Rome, the *Aeneid*.

[3] Another name for tuberculosis or consumption.

tidings which lift sinking spirits. With firm will, I finish
climbing, hiking till I find this inviting inn, in which
I might sit, dining. I thirst. I bid girls bring stiff drinks
—gin fizz which I might sip whilst finishing this rich
dish, nibbling its tidbits: ribs with wings in chili, figs
with kiwis in icing. I swig citric drinks with vim, tip-
pling kirsch, imbibing it till, giggling, I flirt with girlish virgins in miniskirts: *wink, wink*. I miss living
in sin, pinching thighs, kissing lips pink with lipstick.

Slick pimps, bribing civic kingpins, distill gin in stills,
spiking drinks with illicit pills which might bring bliss.
Whiz kids in silk-knit shirts script films in which
slim girls might strip, jiggling tits, wiggling hips, in-
citing wild shindigs. Twin siblings in bikinis might kiss
rich bigwigs, giving this prim prig his wish, whipping
him, tickling him, licking his limp dick till, rigid,
his prick spills its jism. Shit! This ticklish victim is
trifling with kink. Sick minds, thriving in kinship
with pigs, might find insipid thrills in this filth. This
flick irks critics. It is swinish; it is piggish. It stinks.

Thinking within strict limits is stifling. Whilst Viking
knights fight griffins, I skirmish with this riddling
sphinx (this sigil—I). I print lists, filing things (kin with
kin, ilk with ilk), inscribing this distinct sign, listing
things in which its imprint is intrinsic. I find its missing links, divining its implicit tricks. I find it whilst
skindiving in Fiji; I find it whilst picnicking in Linz. I
find it in Inniskillin; I find it in Mississippi. I find it
whilst skiing in Minsk. (Is this intimism civilizing if
Klimt limns it, if Liszt lilts it?)[4] I sigh; I lisp. I finish writing this writ, signing it, kind sir: NIHIL DICIT, FINI.[5]

[2001]

---

[4] Gustav Klimt (1862–1918), Austrian painter of the Art Nouveau school known particularly for his
erotic subjects; Franz Liszt (1811–1886), nineteenth-century Hungarian pianist and composer.

[5] Latin, "he says nothing, the end." "Nihil dicit" is also a legal phrase to refer to a judgment that is
brought against a defendant who refuses to answer charges laid against him.

EDEN ROBINSON ■ (1968–)

"Six crows sit in our greengage tree.
Half-awake, I hear them speak to me in
Haisla." So begins Eden Robinson's
novel *Monkey Beach* (2000), which fol-
lows the story of a teenager (named
Lisamarie after Elvis Presley's daughter)
who searches for her brother, a cham-
pion swimmer, lost in the waters off the
Queen Charlotte Islands in British
Columbia. This Northern Gothic novel

provoked writer Anita Rau Badami to declare that reading the book was like "discover[ing] a haunted world . . . where the spirit world is as real as the human."

The daughter of a Haisla father and a Heiltsuk mother, Robinson brings both traditions into her writing, alongside a score of popular cultural influences. She credits her uncle Gordon Robinson—whom she cites as the first Haisla writer to be published (*Tales of Kitamaat,* 1956)—as an influence on her but also notes how he was criticized by some members of the community for writing down oral stories. She also frequently cites the influence of American horror writer Stephen King (whose books she read compulsively between the ages of 10 and 14 when she began writing stories), as well as films by Canadian director David Cronenberg and edgy music videos. With characteristic humour, Robinson says, "I was born on the same day as Edgar Allan Poe and Dolly Parton: January 19. I am absolutely certain that this affects my writing in some way."

Robinson has been sharply critical of the problems of thematic, political, and even generic expectations that arise in response to her Aboriginal heritage. In a *Quill and Quire* profile that appeared after her first collection of stories, *Traplines* (1996), was published, she states that "people assumed I couldn't write anything that wasn't native because I'm native." In keeping with this concern, Robinson often does not identify the cultural or racial heritage of her characters, leaving readers to question their assumptions about what constitutes particular "racialized" identities. Much of her writing focuses on the world of teenagers, pop culture, and violence; as she acknowledges, "I'm fascinated with serial killers, psychopaths, and sociopaths." The dark, gritty side of the lives of psychologically disturbed people is abundantly present in the stories collected in *Traplines,* including "Dogs in Winter." Yet the ostensible subject matter of the story, a girl struggling with her mother's violent actions, is underwritten by a black humour that is disarming, as when the mother chases down and "scalps" a dog that has lunged at her daughter. The anaesthetized tone and casual violence of the stories renders them quietly horrific, particularly as readers find themselves amused in the midst of the intense horror.

The book was hugely successful for a debut short story collection. Picked up by publishers in seven countries, it was awarded the Winifred Holtby Prize for the best first work of fiction in the Commonwealth. Robinson's second novel, *Blood Sports* (2006), continues her interest in violent themes, building on the story "Contact Sports" that first appeared in *Traplines.* Robinson studied creative writing at the University of Victoria (B.A.) and the University of British Columbia (M.F.A.), and worked at a series of "McJobs" (to use her term) in Vancouver before achieving success in her writing. She has recently returned to live and write in Kitimaat, B.C., where she was raised.

Dogs in Winter

Aunt Genna's poodle, Picnic, greeted people by humping their legs. He had an incredible grip. A new postman once dragged Picnic six blocks. Picnic bumped and ground as they went; the postman swore and whacked at the poodle with his mailbag.

Picnic humped the wrong leg, however, when he burst out of our lilac bushes and attached himself to one of Officer Wilkenson's calves. I was lounging on the porch swing, watching hummingbirds buzz around the feeder. On that quiet, lazy summer afternoon, traffic on the nearby highway was pleasantly muted.

"Whose fucking dog is this?" A man's yell broke the silence.

I sat up. A policeman was trying to pry Picnic off his leg. Picnic was going at it steady as a jackhammer.

"Frank! Get this thing off me!" the policeman said to his partner, who was unhelpfully snapping Polaroids.

The policeman lifted his leg and shook it hard. Picnic hopped off and attacked the other leg. The officer gave Picnic a kick that would have disabled a lesser dog. Not Picnic. I brought them the broom from the porch, but not even a sharp rap with a broom handle could quell Picnic's passion.

"Oh my," Aunt Genna said, arriving on the porch with a tray of lemonade. She had rushed inside when she saw the police officers coming because she wanted to get refreshments. I didn't know it at the time, but they kept returning to ask if Mama had contacted me since her jailbreak. I just thought they really liked Aunt Genna's cookies. She was always hospitable, the very picture of a grand Victorian lady, with her hair up in a big salt-and-pepper bun on top of her head. The lace on her dress fluttered as she put the tray down and rushed to the walkway where the policemen stood.

"Is—this—your—dog?" the policeman hissed.

"Why, yes, Officer Wilkenson." She knelt to help them pry Picnic from the policeman's foot. "I'm so sorry. Are you hurt?"

"Can you just hold it for a moment?" Officer Wilkenson's partner said to Aunt Genna, holding up his Polaroid. "I want to get you all in."

There is a lake I go to in my dreams. Mama took me there when I got my period for the first time.

In the dream, she and I are sitting on the shore playing kazoos. Mama has a blue kazoo; mine is pink. We play something classical. Crickets are chirping. The sun is rising slowly over the mountains. The lake is cool and dark and flat as glass.

A moose crashes through the underbrush. It lumbers to the edge of the lake, then raises its head and bellows.

Mama puts her kazoo down quietly. She reaches behind her and pulls a shotgun from the duffle bag. She hands me the gun. We have trained for this moment. I steady the gun on my shoulder, take aim, then gently squeeze the trigger.

The sound of the shot explodes in my ear. A hole appears between the moose's eyes. I don't know what I expected, maybe the moose's head to explode like a dropped pumpkin, but not the tidy red hole. The moose collapses forward, headfirst into the water.

"Let's get breakfast," Mama says.

Wearing my blue dress, I walk calmly into the lake. The pebbles on the shore are all rose quartz, round and smooth as Ping-Pong balls. As I go deeper into the lake, my dress floats up around me. When I am in up to my waist, I see the moose surfacing. It rises out of the water, its coat dripping, its eyes filled with dirt. It towers over me, whispering, mud dribbling from its mouth like saliva. I lean toward it, but no matter how hard I try, I can never understand what the moose is saying.

Paul and Janet are the parents I've always wanted. Sometimes I feel like I've stepped into a storybook or into a TV set. The day we were introduced, I don't know what the counselors had told them, but they were trying not to look apprehensive. Janet was wearing a navy dress with a white Peter Pan collar. Light makeup, pearls, white shoes. Her blond hair was bobbed and tucked behind her ears. She looked like the elementary school teacher that she was. Paul had on stiff, clean jeans and an expensive-looking shirt.

"Hello, Lisa," Janet said, tentatively holding out her hands.

I stayed where I was. At thirteen, I felt gawky and awkward in clothes that didn't quite fit me and weren't in fashion. Paul and Janet looked like a couple out of a Disney movie. I couldn't believe my luck. I didn't trust it. "Are you my new parents?"

Janet nodded.

We went to McDonald's and I had a Happy Meal. It was my first time at a McDonald's. Mama didn't like restaurants of any kind. The Happy Meal came with a free toy—a plastic Garfield riding a motor scooter. I still have it on my bookshelf.

Paul and Janet talked cautiously about my new school, my room, meeting their parents. I couldn't get over how perfect they looked, how normal they seemed. I didn't want to say anything to them about Mama. If I did, they might send me back like a defective toaster.

The first time I saw Aunt Genna, the sun was high and blinding. She came out to the porch with lemonade and told her poodle Picnic to leave me alone. Picnic jumped up on me, licking my face when I bent to pet him. I ran across the yard, squealing and half afraid, half delighted. Aunt Genna tucked her dogs up with quilts embroidered with their names. She served them breakfast and dinner on porcelain plates. Aunt Genna took me in when Mama went to jail that first time, took me in like another stray dog, embroidered my pillow with my name, served me lemonade and cookies in miniature tea sets. One of her dogs—Jenjen, Coco, or Picnic—was always following her. Although she was born in Bended River, Manitoba, she liked to believe she was an English lady.

We had tea parties every Sunday after church. Aunt Genna brought out her plastic dishes and sat the dogs on cushions. Jenjen and Coco loved teatime. I would serve them doggie biscuits from plates decorated with blue bears and red balloons. Picnic didn't like to sit at the table and would whine until Aunt Genna let him go to his hallway chair.

Since I wasn't allowed to have real tea, Aunt Genna filled the silver teapot with grape juice.

"How are you today, Lady Lisa?" she would ask, in her best English accent.

"Oh, I am quite fine," I would say. "And yourself?"

"Quite well, except that I have gout."

"Oh, how awful! Is it very painful?"

"It makes my nose itchy."

"Would you like a scone?"

"I'd adore one."

It was at one of these tea parties that I first asked about my parents. Jenjen was gnawing at her biscuit, spreading crumbs on the table. Coco and Picnic were howling. I poured grape juice for both of us, then said, "Are my parents dead?"

"No," Aunt Genna said. "They are in Africa."

I put down my cup and crawled into Aunt Genna's lap. "What are they doing in Africa?"

"They are both doctors and great explorers. They wanted so very much to take you with them, but there are too many snakes and tigers in Africa. They were afraid you'd be eaten."

"But why did they go?"

"They went because they were needed there. There are very few doctors in Africa, you see, and every single one counts."

"But why did they go?"

"Lady Lisa," Aunt Genna said, kissing the top of my head. "My Lady Lisa, they didn't want to leave you. Your mother cried and cried when they took you out of her arms. Oh, how she cried. She was so very sad."

"Then why did she go?"

"She had no choice. Duty called. She was called to Africa."

"Was my father called too?"

"Yes. Your mother took him with her. They went together."

"When are they coming back?"

"Not for a long, long time."

I put my arms around her and cried.

"But I will always be here for you," she said, patting my back. "I will always be here, my Lady Lisa."

Aunt Genna told me other things. She told me there were monsters and bogeymen in the world, but all you had to do was be a good girl and they wouldn't get you. I always believed Aunt Genna until Mama killed her.

Janet liked these weird art movies that never made it to the Rupert theaters. She was always renting stuff with subtitles, dark lighting, talking heads, and bad special effects. This one was called *Street Angel*, and I secretly hoped it would have some sex, but when the movie opened in a squalid hut, I wondered if Janet would believe me if I said I wanted to do homework. For the first few minutes nothing happened, except this grimy, skinny kid scrounged through garbage heaps for food. In the background there were all these dogs getting kicked and shot and run over. Then the kid was in an alley and it began to snow. I stayed very still, not really paying attention to the end, my mind stuck on the scene where this old dog collapsed and the rest of the pack circled, sniffing its body. A skinny brown mutt nipped at the old dog's leg. The dog growled deep in its throat and staggered to its feet. I knew what was coming. I knew and I couldn't stop watching. The mutt ripped into its stomach. The scene went on and on until the dog stopped yelping and jerking on the ground, its eyes flat as the mutt dragged its intestines away from the feeding frenzy. The boy kicked the pack aside and stood over the body. He picked up a cigarette butt and stuck it in the dead dog's mouth.

I saw Mama on a talk show one day.

She was hooked in from her cell via satellite. Another woman, one who had murdered her mother and her grandmother, sat in front of the studio audience, handcuffed to the chair. Next to her was a girl who had drowned her baby in a toilet, thinking it had been sent to her by the devil.

Mama wore no makeup. Her hair was pulled back and gray streaks showed through the brown. She looked wan. Sometimes, when she gestured, I could see the belly shackle that bound her wrists to her waist.

The talk-show host gave the microphone to a man from the audience who asked, "When was the first time you killed?"

For a long time Mama said nothing. She stared straight into the camera, as if she could see the audience.

"I lost my virginity when I was twenty-seven," Mama said. "That wasn't the question," the talk-show host said impatiently.

Mama smiled, as if they hadn't got the punch line. "I know what the question was." I shut the TV off.

How old was I the first time I saw Mama kill? I can't remember. I was small. Not tall enough to see over our neighbor's fence. Our neighbor, Mr. Watley, built a fence to keep kids from raiding his apple orchard. It was flat cedar planks all the way round to the back, where he'd put up chicken wire. When the fence didn't keep them out, he bought a Pit Bull, a squat black-and-brown dog with bowlegs.

I had to pass Mr. Watley's house on the way home from school. I could hear the dog pacing me, panting loud. Once, I stopped by the fence to see what would happen. The dog growled long and low. The hair stood up on the back of my neck and on my arms and legs.

"Who's there?" Mr. Watley called out. "Sic 'em, Ginger."

Ginger hit the fence. It wobbled and creaked. I shrieked and ran home.

After that I walked home on the other side of the street, but I could still hear Ginger. I could hear her when she growled. I could sense her pacing me.

None of the kids liked to play at my house. No one wanted to go near Ginger.

A carload of teenagers drove by Mr. Watley's house the morning Mama killed. They hung out the windows, and one of them came up and pounded on the fence until Ginger howled in frustration. When Mr. Watley opened his door, they threw beer bottles. He swore at them. I heard him from my bedroom. Down in the yard, Ginger kept ramming into the fence. She'd run up to it and try to jump and hit it. The fence shuddered.

"Stay away from that man," Mama said to me before I left for school. "He's crazy."

All day long at school I'd been dreading the walk home. I waited on the other side of the street, just before Mr. Watley's house. My thermos rattled in my lunch box as my hands shook.

Ginger barked.

I waited until I saw Mama peeking out the kitchen. I felt a bit safer, but not much. I ran. Maybe it was stupid, but I wanted to be inside. I wanted to be with Mama. I remember looking both ways before crossing the street, the way I'd been taught. I ran across the street with my thermos clunking against the apple that I hadn't eaten and hadn't been able to trade. Running, reaching our lawn, and thinking, I'm safe, like playing tag and getting to a safety zone where you can't be touched. I remember the sound of wood breaking and I turned.

Ginger bounded toward me and I couldn't move, I just couldn't move. She stopped two feet away and snarled and I couldn't make any muscle in my body move. Ginger's teeth were very white and her lips were pulled back way up over her gums.

I found my voice and I screamed.

The dog leapt and I banged my lunch box against the side of her head and her jaws snapped shut on my wrist. There was no pain, but I screamed again when I saw the blood. I dropped the lunch box and Ginger let go because Mama was running toward us. Mama was coming and she was shrieking.

It was as unreal then as it is now. Mama and Ginger running toward each other. They ran in slow motion, like lovers bounding across a sunlit field. Mama's arm pulled back before they met and years later I would be in art class and see a picture of a peasant woman in a field with a curved knife, a scythe, cutting wheat. Her pose, the lines of her body would be so like Mama's that I would leave the class, run down the hallway to the bathroom, and heave until I vomited.

Mama slid the knife across Ginger's scalp, lopping off the skin above her eyebrows. Ginger yelped. Mama brought her knife up and down. Ginger squealed, snapped her jaws at Mama, and crawled backward. Up and down. Mama's rapt face. Up and down. The blood making patterns on her dress like the ink blots on a Rorschach test.[1]

_____

[1] The Rorschach Inkblot test, developed in 1921, has been used by psychologists (most popularly in the 1950s) to see how patients project emotions or thoughts when asked to describe what they see in ambiguous patterns of inkblots on a page.

The moose's short neck makes her unsuited for grazing; consequently, she is a browser. Her preference runs to willow, fir, aspen, and birch, as well as the aquatic plants found at the bottoms of lakes. The moose is quite able to defend herself; even grizzly bears and wolf packs think twice before attempting to kill the largest member of the deer family. Much of the moose's time is spent in the water. She is an excellent swimmer, easily covering fifteen or twenty miles. She is a powerful traveler on land, too, trotting uphill or jumping fallen branches for hour after hour.

During the rutting season, her mate, the bull moose, is one of the most dangerous animals, frenzied enough to inflict death or dismemberment on those who stand between him and her and incapable of distinguishing between friend and enemy.

A man and a woman came into our backyard. The woman knelt beside me as I lay back in my lawn chair feeling the drizzle on my face. She touched my hand and said, "Your mother's been asking for you."

Her hair and skin were tinged blue by the diffused light through her umbrella. She showed me a card. I didn't bother reading it, knew just by looking at her perfectly groomed face that she was someone's hound dog.

"Janet's in the house," I said, deciding to play dense. It never worked.

Her hand squeezed my arm. "Your real mother."

I wondered what she did when she wasn't trying to convince people to visit serial killers in jail. Sometimes they were writers or tabloid reporters, grad students, the merely morbid, or even a couple of psychics. I wondered why they always came in pairs, and what her partner was thinking as he stood behind her, silent. Only the sleaziest ones came after me like this, not asking Paul or Janet's permission, waiting for a time when I was alone.

Mama kept sending these people to talk to me, to persuade me to come visit her. I suspected that what she really wanted was a good look at my face so she'd know whom to come after if she ever got out.

"She misses you."

I turned my face up to the sky. "Tell her I miss Aunt Genna."

"You don't really want me to tell her that, do you?"

I closed my eyes. "You're taping this, aren't you?"

"Lisa," the woman held onto my arm when I tried to sit up. "Lisa, listen— it would only take a day, just one day out of your life. She only wants to see you—"

I jerked my arm away and ran for the house just as Janet came out.

"Who are they?"

The man and the woman were already leaving. They could try all they liked. I wasn't ready to see Mama and maybe never would be. But I didn't want any questions either. "Just Jehovah's Witnesses."

I saw the woman waiting outside school the next day but pretended not to notice her. Eventually she went away.

I was fourteen when I first tried to commit suicide. I remember it clearly because it was New Year's Eve. Paul and Janet were at a costume ball and thought I was with a friend. Paul was a pirate and Janet was a princess.

They drove me to my friend's house. Paul put his eye patch on his chin so it wouldn't bother him while he drove. I sat in the back, at peace with myself. In my mind I was seeing my foster parents at my funeral, standing grief-stricken at the open casket, gazing down at my calm face.

When they let me off, I walked back home. I brought all Janet's Midol[2] and all Paul's stomach pills upstairs to my bedroom, where I had already stashed two bottles of aspirin. I went back down to get three bottles of ginger ale and a large plastic tumbler.

Then I wrote a poem for Paul and Janet. It was three pages long. At the time it seemed epic and moving, but now I squirm when I think about it. I'm glad I didn't die. What a horrible piece of writing to be remembered by. It was something out of a soap opera: "My Darling Parents, I must leave / I know you will, but you must not grieve" sort of thing. I guess it wouldn't have been so bad if I hadn't made everything rhyme.

I emptied the aspirin into a cereal bowl. Deciding to get it all over with at once, I stuffed a handful into my mouth. God, the taste. Dusty, bitter aspirin crunched in my mouth like hard-shelled bugs. My gag reflex took over, and I lost about twenty aspirin on my quilt. I chugalugged three cups of ginger ale to get the taste out of my mouth, then went more slowly and swallowed the pills one by one.

After the twenty-sixth aspirin, I stopped counting and concentrated on not throwing up. I didn't have enough money to get more, and I didn't want to waste anything. When I got to the bottom of the cereal bowl, I'd had enough. I'd also run out of ginger ale. Bile was leaking into my mouth. Much later, I discovered that overdosing on aspirin is one of the worst ways to go. Aspirin is toxic, but the amount needed to kill a grown adult is so high that the stomach usually bursts before toxicity kicks in.

My last moments on earth. I didn't know what to do with them. Nothing seemed appropriate. I lay on my bed and read *People* magazine. Farrah was seeing Ryan O'Neal.[3] Some model was suing Elvis's estate for palimony. Disco was dying. A Virginia woman was selling Belgian-chocolate-covered caramel apples at twelve dollars apiece to stars who said they had never tasted anything so wonderful.

At midnight I heard the fireworks but was too tired to get out of bed. I drifted into sleep, my ears ringing so loud I could barely hear the party at our neighbor's house next door.

Some time during the night, I crawled to the bathroom at the end of the hall and vomited thin strings of yellow bile into the toilet.

[2] Mild medication used for menstrual cramps.

[3] Farrah Fawcett, star of the 1970s cult TV show *Charlie's Angels*. Ryan O'Neal, Hollywood actor, starred in *Love Story* (1970) and *Paper Moon* (1973).

All the next week I wished I had died. My stomach could hold nothing down. Janet thought it was a stomach flu and got me a bottle of extra-strength Tylenol and some Pepto-Bismol. To this day, I can't stand the taste of ginger ale.

By some strange quirk of fate, Mama came for me not long after the SPCA took Picnic away. People had complained about Picnic's affectionate behavior, and when Officer Wilkenson got involved, it was the end.

Aunt Genna was weeping quietly upstairs in her bedroom when the doorbell rang. She was always telling me not to let strangers in, so when I saw the woman waiting on the steps, I just stared at her.

"Auntie's busy," I said.

The woman's face was smooth and pale. "Lisa," she said. "Don't you remember me, baby?"

I backed away, shaking my head.

"Come here, baby, let me look at you," she said, crouching down. "You've gotten so big. You remember how I used to sing to you? 'A-hunting we will go'? Remember?"

Her brown eyes were familiar. Her dark blond hair was highlighted by streaks that shone in the sunlight.

"Aunt Genna doesn't like me talking to strangers," I said.

Her face set in a grim expression and I knew who she was. She stood. "Where is your aunt?"

"Upstairs," I said.

"Let me go talk to her. You wait right here, baby. When I come back, maybe we'll go shopping. We can get some cotton candy. It used to be your favorite, didn't it? Would you like that?"

I nodded.

"Stay right here," the woman said as she walked by me, her blue summer dress swishing. "Right here, baby."

Her high heels clicked neatly as she went upstairs. I sat in the hallway, on Picnic's high-backed chair. It still smelled of him, salty, like seaweed.

Something thunked upstairs. I heard a dragging sound. Then the shower started. After endless minutes, the door to the bathroom creaked open. Mama's high heels clicked across the floor again.

"I'm back!" Mama said cheerfully, bouncing down the stairs. "Your aunt says we can go shopping if you want. She's taking a bath." Mama leaned down and whispered, "She wants to be alone."

She had my backpack over one shoulder. I jumped down from the chair. Mama held out her hand. I hesitated.

"Coming?" she said.

"I have to be back tonight," I said. "I'm going to Jimmy's birthday party."

"Well then," she said. "Let's go buy him a present."

She led me to her car. It was bright blue and she let me sit up front. I couldn't see over the dashboard because she made me wear a seat belt. Aunt Genna's house shrank as we drove away. I remember wondering if we were going to get another dog now that Picnic was gone. I remember looking down at Mama's shoes and seeing little red flecks sprayed across the tips like a splatter paint I'd done in kindergarten. I remember Mama giving me a bad-tasting orange juice, and then I remember nothing.

"Yuck," I said. "I'm not touching it."

"No problem," Amanda said. "I'll do it."

Amanda was everyone's favorite lab partner because she'd do absolutely anything, no matter how gross. We looked down at the body of a dead fetal pig that Amanda had chosen from the vat of formaldehyde. We were supposed to find its heart.

"Oh, God," I said, as Amanda made the first cut.

For a moment, I was by the lake and Mama was smearing blood on my cheeks.

"Now you're a real woman," she said. Goose bumps crawled up my back.

"I don't know how you can do that," I said to Amanda.

"Well, you put the knife flat against the skin. Then you press. Then you cut. It's very simple. Want to try?"

I shook my head and crossed my arms over my chest.

"Chickenshit," Amanda said.

"Better than being a ghoul," I said.

"Just my luck to get stuck with a wimp," she muttered loud enough for me to hear as she poked around the pig's jellied innards, looking for a small purple lump.

I sat on my lab stool feeling stupid while Amanda hunched over the pig. Not all the chopping and dismemberment in the world could make her queasy. Mama would have liked her. She straightened up then and shoved the scalpel in my face, expecting me to take it from her.

At that moment, I saw the scars on her wrists. When she noticed me staring, she pulled her sleeve down to cover them.

"I slipped," she said defensively. "And cut myself."

We faced each other, oblivious to the murmur of the class around us.

"Don't you say anything," she said.

Instead of answering, I unbuttoned the cuff of my blouse and rolled it up my arm. I turned my hand over so the palm was up.

The second time I tried to commit suicide was when I was fifteen, a year after my attempt with the aspirin. This time I had done my homework. I knew exactly what I was going to do.

I bought a straight-edged razor.

Janet and Paul were off to the theater. I waved them goodbye cheerfully as they raced through the rain to the car.

I closed the front door and listened to the house. Then I marched upstairs and put on my bikini. I ran a bath, putting in Sea Foam bubble bath and mango bath oil. I stepped into the tub, then lay back slowly, letting the water envelop me as I watched the bathroom fill with steam.

The razor was cold in my hands, cold as a doctor's stethoscope. I held it underwater to warm it up. Flexed my arms a few times. Inhaled several deep breaths. Shut the water off. It dripped. There was no way I could die with the tap dripping, so I fiddled with that for a few minutes.

Got out of the tub. Took a painkiller. Got back in the tub. Placed the razor in the crook of my elbow. Hands shaking. Pushed it down. It sank into my skin, the tip disappearing. I felt nothing at first. I pulled the razor toward my wrist, but halfway down my forearm the cut began to burn. I yanked the razor away.

Blood welled in the cut. Little beads of blood. I hadn't gone very deep, just enough for the skin to gape open slightly. Not enough to reach a vein or an artery.

I was shaking so hard the bubbles in the tub were rippling. The wound felt like a huge paper cut. I clutched it, dropping the razor in the tub.

"I can do it," I said, groping for the razor.

I put it back in the same place and pushed deeper. A thin stream of blood slithered across my arm and dripped into the tub. It burned, it burned.

Paul and Janet came home and found me in front of the TV watching Jimmy Stewart in *It's a Wonderful Life*. It always makes me cry. So there I was, bawling as Paul and Janet came through the door. They sat on either side of the armchair and they hugged me.

"What is it, honey?" Paul kissed my forehead.

"No, really, I'm okay. It's nothing." I said.

"You sure? You don't look okay," Janet said.

I rested my head on her knees, making her dress wet. Paul and Janet said they wanted to know everything about me, but there were things that made them cringe. What would they do if I said, "I'm afraid Mama will find me and kill me"?

"I'm such a marshmallow. I even cry at B.C. telephone commercials," is what I said.

Paul leaned over and smoothed my hair away from my face. "You know we love you, don't you, Pumpkin?"

He smelled of Old Spice and I felt like I was in a commercial. Everything would be perfect, I thought, if only Canada had the death penalty.

In a tiny, grungy antique store in Masset on the Queen Charlotte Islands I found the moose. Paul and Janet had brought me with them to a business convention. Since the finer points of Q-Base accounting bored me silly, I left the hotel and wandered into the store.

Nature pictures and small portraits of sad-eyed Indian children cluttered the wall. The hunchbacked owner followed me everywhere I went, saying nothing. Not even hello. I was about to leave when I saw the moose.

"How much is that?" I asked, reaching for it.

"Don't touch," he grunted at me.

"How much?" I said.

"Twenty."

I handed him the twenty dollars, grabbed the picture, and left.

"What on earth is that?" Janet asked when I got back. She was at the mirror, clipping on earrings.

"Oh, nothing. Just a picture."

"Really? I didn't know you were interested in art. Let me see."

"It's just a tacky tourist picture. I'll show it to you later."

"Here," Janet said, taking the package from my hands and unwrapping it.

"Careful." I said.

"Yes, yes." Janet's mouth fell open and she dropped the picture onto the bed. "Oh my God, that's disgusting! Why on earth did you buy it? Take it back."

I picked up the picture and hugged it to my chest. She tried to pry it from me, but I clung to it tightly. Paul came in and Janet said, "Paul, get that disgusting thing out of here!"

She made me show it to him and he laughed. "Looks very Dali,"[4] he said.

"It's obscene."

"This from the woman who likes Pepsi in her milk."

"Paul, I'm serious," she hissed.

"Let her keep it," Paul said. "What harm can it do?"

Later I heard him whisper to her, "Jan, for God's sake, you're overreacting. Drop it, all right? All right?"

I still have it, hanging in my bathroom. Except for the moose lying on its side, giving birth to a human baby, it's a lovely picture. There are bright red cardinals in the fir trees, and the sun is beaming down on the lake in the left-hand corner. If you squint your eyes and look in the trees, you can see a woman in a blue dress holding a drawn bow.

Amanda's house was the kind I'd always wanted to live in. Lace curtains over the gabled windows, handmade rugs on the hardwood floors, soft floral chairs, and dark-red cherry furniture polished to a gleam.

"You like it?" Amanda said, throwing her coat onto the brass coat stand. "I'll trade you. You live in my house and I'll live in yours."

"I'd kill to live here," I said.

---

[4] Spanish artist Salvador Dalí (1904–1989) was known for his surreal art combining grotesque and violent images with depictions of everyday objects.

Amanda scratched her head and looked at the living room as if it were a dump. "I'd kill to get out."

I followed her up the stairs to a large, airy room done in pale pink and white. I squealed, I really did, when I saw her canopied bed. Amanda wore a pained expression.

"Isn't it revolting?"

"I love it!"

"You do?"

"It's gorgeous!"

She tossed her backpack into a corner chair. I flopped down on the bed. Amanda had tacked a large poster to the underside of her canopy—a naked man with a whip coming out of his butt like a tail.

"It's the only place Mother let me put it," she explained. "Cute, huh?"

Downstairs, a bass guitar thumped. A man shrieked some words, but I couldn't make them out. Another guitar screeched, then a heavy, pulsating drumbeat vibrated the floor. Then it stopped.

"Matthew," Amanda said.

"Matthew?"

"My brother."

Amanda's mother called us to dinner. Matthew was already heading out the door, wearing a kilt and white body makeup. His hair was dyed black and stood up like the spikes on a blowfish. When his mother wasn't looking, he snatched a tiny butter knife with a pearl handle and put it down his kilt. He saw me watching him and winked as he left.

"So where do your real parents come from?" Amanda's mother said, pouring more wine into cut crystal glasses.

There were only the four of us. We sat close together at one end of a long table. My face flushed. I was feeling tipsy.

"Africa," I said.

Amanda's mother raised an elegant eyebrow.

"They were killed in an uprising."

She still looked disbelieving.

"They were missionaries," I added. I took a deep drink. "Doctors."

"You don't say."

"Mother," Amanda said. "Leave her alone."

We were silent as the maid brought in a large white ceramic tureen. As she lifted the lid, the sweet, familiar smell of venison filled the room. I stared at my plate after she placed it in front of me.

"Use the fork on the outside, dear," Amanda's mother said helpfully.

But I was down by the lake. Mama was so proud of me. "Now you're a woman," she said. She handed me the heart after she wiped the blood onto my cheeks with her knife. I held it, not knowing what to do. It was as warm as a kitten.

"I think you'd better eat something," Amanda said.

"Maybe we should take that glass, dear."

The water in the lake was cool and dark and flat as glass. The bones sank to the bottom after we'd sucked the marrow. Mama's wet hair was flattened to her skull. She pried a tooth from the moose and gave it to me. I used to wear it around my neck.

"I'm afraid," I said. "She has a pattern, even if no one else can see it."

"Your stew is getting cold," Amanda's mother said.

The coppery taste of raw blood filled my mouth. "I will not be her," I said. "I will break the pattern."

Then I sprayed sour red wine across the crisp handwoven tablecloth that had been handed down to Amanda's mother from her mother and her mother's mother before that.

After a long, shimmering silence, Amanda's mother said, "I have a Persian carpet in the living room. Perhaps you'd like to shit on it." Then she stood, put her napkin on the table, and left.

"Lisa," Amanda said, clapping her hand on my shoulder. "You can come over for dinner anytime you want."

Mama loved to camp in the summer. She would wake me early, and we'd sit outside our tent and listen. My favorite place was in Banff. We camped by a turquoise lake. Mama made bacon and eggs and pancakes over a small fire. Everything tasted delicious. When we were in Banff, Mama was happy. She whistled all the time, even when she was going to the bathroom. Her cheeks were apple-red and dimpled up when she smiled. We hiked for hours, seeing other people only from a distance.

"Imagine there's no one else on earth," she said once as she closed her eyes and opened her arms to embrace the mountains. "Oh, just imagine it."

When we broke camp, we'd travel until Mama felt the need to stop and settle down for a while. Then we would rent an apartment, Mama would find work, and I would go to school. I hated that part of it. I was always behind. I never knew anybody, and just as I started to make friends, Mama would decide it was time to leave. There was no arguing with her. The few times I tried, she gave me this look, strange and distant.

I was eleven when we went through the Badlands of Alberta, and while I was dozing in the back, the car hit a bump and Mama's scrapbook fell out of her backpack.

I opened it. I was on the second page when Mama slammed on the brakes, reached back, and slapped me.

"Didn't I tell you never to touch that? Didn't I? Give it to me now. Now, before you're in even bigger trouble."

Mama used the scrapbook to start our fire that night, but it was too late. I had seen the clippings, I had seen the headlines, and I was beginning to remember.

That night I dreamed of Aunt Genna showering in blood. Mama held me until I stopped trembling.

"Rock of ages, cleft for me," Mama sang softly, as she cradled me back and forth. "Let me hide myself in thee."[5]

I closed my eyes and pretended to sleep. Mama squeezed herself into the sleeping bag with me and zipped us up. I waited for her to say something about the scrapbook. As the night crawled by, I became afraid that she would never mention it, that I would wait and wait for something to happen. The waiting would be worse, far worse, than anything Mama could do to me.

Amanda and Matthew had a game called Take It. The first time I played, we were behind a black van in the school parking lot. They stood beside me as I rubbed a patch of skin on my calf with sandpaper until I started to bleed. The trick to this game is to be extremely high or just not give a shit.

Amanda squeezed lemon juice onto my calf. I looked straight into her eyes. "Thank you," I said.

Matthew pulled a glue stick out of his schoolbag and smeared it on my calf. "Thank you," I said.

Back to Amanda, who had been poking around in the bald patch of earth by the parking lot and had come back with a hairy spider as large as a quarter. It wriggled in her hands. Fuck, I thought. Oh, fuck.

She tilted her hands toward my calf. The spider struggled against falling, its long, thin legs scrabbling against her palm, trying to grab something.

Long before it touched me, I knew I'd lost. I yanked my leg back so that the spider tickled the inside of my leg as it fell, missing the mess on my calf completely. I brought my foot up and squashed it before anyone thought of picking it up again.

When I was twelve, I took the Polaroid picture Officer Wilkenson had given me to a police station in Vancouver.

In the picture, Aunt Genna and Officer Wilkenson are both blurs, but there is a little brown-haired girl in the foreground clutching a broom handle and squinting into the camera.

I showed the Polaroid to a man behind a desk. "That's my Aunt Genna," I said. "My mama killed her, but she's not in the picture."

He glanced at the picture, then at me. "We're very busy," he said. "Sit down." He waved me toward a chair. "Crazies," he muttered as I turned away. "All day long I got nuts walking in off the street."

After a while a policewoman took me to another room, where a grave-looking man in a navy-blue suit asked a lot of questions. He had a flat, nasal voice.

"So this is you, right? And you say this is Officer Wilkenson?"

He made a few calls. It all took a long time, but he was getting more and more excited. Then someone else came in and they made me say it all over again.

[5] A Christian hymn, dating from the 1700s, which continues "Let the water and the blood, / From Thy riven side which flowed, / Be of sin the double cure; / Save from wrath and make me pure."

"I already told you. That's Aunt Genna. Yes," I said, "that's the officer. And that's me."

"Holy smokaroonies," said the navy-blue suit. "We've got her."

The third time I tried to commit suicide, I found out where Paul kept his small automatic at work. It was supposed to be protection against robbers, but it wasn't loaded and I had a hard time finding the ammunition. When he was busy with an order, I put the gun in my purse.

This time I was going to get it right.

I remember it was a Wednesday. The sky was clear and there was no moon. I didn't want to mess up Paul and Janet's house, so I was going to do it at Lookout Point, where I could watch the waves and listen to the ocean.

I left no note. Couldn't think of anything to say, really. Nothing I could explain. There was already a queer deadness to my body as I walked up the road trying to hitch a ride. This time was the last time.

Cars passed me. I didn't care. I was willing to be benevolent. They didn't know. How ironic, I thought, when Matthew pulled over and powered down his windows.

"Where to?"

"You going anywhere near Lookout?"

"I am now."

I opened the door and got in. He was surprisingly low-key for Matthew. He had on a purple muscle shirt and black studded shorts.

"Going to a party?"

"Yeah," I said. "Me and a few old friends." Something British was on the radio. We drove, not saying anything until we came to the turnoff.

"You were supposed to go left," I said.

Matthew said nothing.

"We're going the wrong way," I said.

"Yeah?"

"Yeah. Lookout's that way."

"Yeah?"

"Matthew, quit fucking around."

"Ooh. Nasty language."

"Matthew, stop the car."

"Scared?"

"Shitting my pants. Pull over."

"You know," he said casually. "I could do anything to you out here and no one would ever know."

"I think you'd better stop the car before we both do something we might regret."

"Are you scared now?"

"Pull the car over, Matthew."

"Babe, call me Matt."

"You are making a big mistake," I said.

"Shitting my pants," he said.

I unbuttoned my purse. Felt around until the smooth handle of the gun slid into my palm. The deadness was gone now, and I felt electrified. Every nerve in my body sang.

Matthew opened his mouth, but I shut him up by slowly leveling the gun at his stomach.

"You could try to slap this out of my hand, but I'd probably end up blowing your nuts off. Do you know what dumdum bullets are, asshole?"[6]

He nodded, his eyes fixed on the windshield.

"Didn't I tell you to stop the car?" I clicked off the safety. Matthew pulled over to the embankment. The radio played "Mr. Sandman."[7] A semi rumbled past, throwing up dust that blew around us like a faint fog.

He lifted his finger and put it in the barrel of the gun.

"Bang," he said.

Mama would never have hesitated. She'd have enjoyed killing him.

I had waited too long. Matthew popped his finger out of the barrel. I put the gun back in my purse. He closed his eyes, rested his head on the steering wheel. The horn let out a long wail.

I can't kill, I decided then. That is the difference. I can betray, but I can't kill. Mama would say that betrayal is worse.

A long time ago in Bended River, Manitoba, six people were reported missing:

Daniel Smenderson, 32,	last seen going out to the nearby 7-Eleven for cigarettes
Angela Iyttenier, 18,	hitchhiking
Geraldine Aksword, 89,	on her way to a curling match
Joseph Rykman, 45,	taking a lunch break at the construction site where he worked
Peter Brendenhaust, 56,	from the St. Paul Mission Home for the Homeless
Calvin Colnier, 62,	also from the St. Paul Mission

After a snowstorm cut off power to three different subsections near Bended River, a police officer, investigating complaints of a foul smell, went to 978 West Junction Road. A little girl greeted him at the door in her nightgown. The house was hot. He could smell wood smoke from the fireplace in the living room. Chopped wood was piled to the ceiling. As he stomped the snow off his boots, he asked if her parents were home. She said her daddy was in the basement.

---

[6] Bullets that expand on impact.

[7] Song by Pat Ballard recorded by the Chordettes in 1954 in which the speaker asks "Mr. Sandman" to bring her a perfect lover.

"Where's your mommy?" he asked.

"Gone," she said.

"How long have you been here on your own?"

She didn't answer.

"Do you know where your mommy went?" he asked.

"A-hunting we will go," the little girl sang. "A-hunting we will go. Heigh-ho the derry-oh, a-hunting we will go."

He took her hand, but she wouldn't go down to the basement with him.

"Mama says it's bad."

"How come?"

"Daddy's down there."

As he opened the door, the reek grew stronger. Covering his mouth with a handkerchief, he took a deep breath and flicked the light switch, but it didn't work. He went back to his car, radioed for backup, and was refused. The other officer on the Bended River police force was on lunch break. So he got his flashlight, then descended.

And found nothing. The smell seemed to be coming from everywhere. Nauseated, he called out, asking if anyone was down there.

The basement had neatly tiled floors. Everything sparkled under the flashlight's beam. Faintly, beneath the overpowering stench, he could smell something antiseptic, like the hospitals used. There was a large, thick butcher's block with a marble counter against the wall in the center room.

"It smelled something like rotten steaks," he told friends later. "But more like the smell my wife gets when she has her period."

There were only three rooms in the basement. A bathroom, a storeroom, and the center room with the marble counter. After checking them all twice, he noticed that the butcher's block was hinged. He heaved and strained but couldn't lift it. His fingers, though, felt a small button on one of the drawers. What did he have to lose? He pressed it.

The countertop popped up an inch. He tried to move it again and managed to slide it open. Beneath the butcher's block was a freezer. It was making no sound, no humming or purring. It was dead. The stench intensified and he thought he was going to faint.

He reached down and lifted the lid. For a moment, the skinned carcasses inside the freezer looked to him like deer or calves. Then he saw the arms and legs, sealed in extra-large plastic bags piled high.

Three days later, Moreen Lisa Rutford was charged with seven counts of murder. The bodies were identified only with difficulty, as they had no heads or fingers and Moreen refused to cooperate. The easiest to identify was David Jonah Rutford, Moreen's husband, who was missing only his heart.

Death should have a handmaiden: her pale, pale skin should be crossed with scars. Her hair should be light brown with blond streaks. Maybe her dress should only be splattered artistically with blood, like the well-placed smudge of dirt on a movie heroine's face after she's battled bad guys and saved the world. Maybe her dress should be turquoise.

She should walk beside a dark, flat lake.

In the morning, with rain hissing and rippling the lake's gray surface, a moose should rise slowly from the water, its eyes blind, its mouth dripping mud and whispering secrets.

She should raise a shotgun and kill it.

Mama wore her best dress to go calling. She sat me at the kitchen table and we ate pizza, Hawaiian, my favorite. She was cheerful that morning and I was happy because Daddy was gone so they hadn't argued. The house, for once, was quiet and peaceful.

She said, "I'm going to have to leave you alone for a bit, honey. Can you take care of yourself? Just for a little while?"

I nodded. "Yup."

"I made you some lunch. And some dinner, just in case I take too long. You know how to pour cereal, don't you?"

"Yup."

"Don't let anyone in," she said. "Don't go out. You just watch TV and Mama will be back before you know it. I got you some comics."

"Yay!" I said.

And I never saw her again until she came to get me at Aunt Genna's.

She kissed me all over my face and gave me a big hug before she left. Then she hefted her backpack onto one shoulder and pulled her baseball cap low over her face.

I watched her bounce down the walkway to the car, wave once, and drive away, smiling and happy and lethal.

[1996]

RITA WONG ■ (1968–)

Rita Wong combines concerns about social justice, racial inequality, environmental destruction, and genetic modification with rich poetic experimentation and a love of language. Wong's first collection of poetry, *monkeypuzzle* (1998), engages questions of family, childhood, racism, and historical injustice. These poems, set around the family grocery store, loosely follow a first-person narrator who negotiates between being a "wannabe bad girl & good chinese girl"

(as she puts it in "Crush"). In an interview with Larissa Lai, Wong cites as catalysts for her work, "Generations and generations of Chinese women struggling and working. A patriarchal family structure. Wars. Famines. Migration. So much upheaval reverberating down my bones. They have instilled into me an attention to larger societal forces and a passion for justice, for sustainable communities."

In her recent collection *forage* (2007), Wong explores how ecological crises result from the injustices of the international political landscape and questions the relationship between writing and other forms of social action. In this collection, which won the Dorothy Livesay Poetry Prize awarded to the best collection of poetry by a resident of British Columbia, Wong has created what poet-critic George Elliott Clarke terms "a formidable fusion" of marginalia, quotations from academic works, Chinese words, and photos that situate the poems in social and political context. In an interview with poet rob maclennan, Wong outlines one of her central concerns: "I want to understand what it means to act ethically in a globalized world," and asks the guiding question: "How do I reconcile my intent (to work toward peace and social justice) with my consumption patterns as a citizen in North America?" The poems in forage, in particular, provide a significant commentary on contemporary ecological crises and global politics. In "nervous organism," Wong frames her words with those of Northrop Frye from Anatomy of Criticism (1957). Similarly, in "canola queasy," she surrounds her words with a passage from Mae-wan Ho's book Genetic Engineering (2000). Wong is part of a community of writers committed to combining social justice and artistic experimentation in Canada today. Born in Calgary, Wong trained as an archivist at the University of British Columbia and as a literary scholar at the University of Calgary (B.A.), University of Alberta (M.A.), and Simon Fraser University (Ph.D.). She currently lives and writes in Vancouver, teaches at the Emily Carr Institute of Art and Design, and is active in a number of community initiatives.

nervous organism

jellyfish potato/ jellypo fishtato/ glow in the pork toys/ nab your crisco while it's genetically cloudy boys/ science lab in my esophagus/ what big beakers you have sir/ all the better to mutate you with my po monster/ po little jelly-kneed demonstrator/ throws flounder-crossed tomatoes / hafta nasty nafta through mexico, california, oregon, washington, canada/ hothoused experiment nestled beside basketballs of lettuce, avocado bullets/ industrial food defeats nutrition/ immune systems attrition/ soil vampires call/ shiny aisles all touch and no contact/ jellypish for tato smack/ your science experiment snack yields slugfish arteries brain murmurs tumour precipitation whack

[handwritten marginalia surrounding the poem] "Some philosophers who assume that all meaning is descriptive meaning tell us that, as a poem does not describe things, referential, it must be a description of emotion. According to this, the literal core of poetry... would be a cri de coeur, to use the elegant expression, the direct statement of a nervous organism confronted with something that seems to demand an emotional response, like a dog howling at the moon." —Northrop Frye

In April 1997 Monsanto pulled two varieties of genetically engineered canola seeds from the Canadian market after testing revealed that at least one of the patented herbicide-tolerant transgenic varieties contained an 'unexpected' gene. This was after 60,000 bags of the seeds had already been sold throughout Western Canada." – Mee-Kwan Ho

canola queasy

vulture capital hovers over dinner tables, covers hospitals a
sorrowful shade of canola, what gradient decline in the stuck
market, what terminal severity in that twenty-year monopoly
culled the patent regime, its refrain of greed, false prophets
hawk oily platitudes in rapacity as they engineer despair in
those brilliant but foolish yellow genetically stacked prairie
crops. how to converse with the willfully profitable stuck in
their monetary monologue? head-on collisions create more
energy but who gets obliterated? despite misgivings i blurt,
don't shoot the messy angels with your cell-arranging blasts,
don't document their properties in order to pimp them.
the time for business-as-usual died with the first colonial
casualty. reclaim the long now. hey bloated monstrosity:
transcribe your ethics first or your protein mass shall turn
protean mess and be auctioned off in the stacked market and
so you can reap endless cussed stunts.

---

*Dedicated to Percy Schmeiser, the Saskatchewan farmer harassed
and sued by Monsanto because genetically engineered canola blew
into his fields.*

MADELEINE THIEN ■ (1974–)

Rarely has a single story in Canada become canonized as quickly as Madeleine Thien's "Simple Recipes," but the story evokes the intergenerational conflicts of the first decade of this century so well, and is written with such grace, that it has become central to the recent literary history of the country. A graduate of the University of British Columbia Creative Writing Program (M.F.A.), Thien published her short story collection *Simple Recipes* in 2001. It won both the Ethel Wilson Fiction Prize and the City of Vancouver Book Award, and became a Regional Finalist for the Commonwealth Writers Prize for Best First Book. On its strength, Thien also won the Canadian Authors Association Award for most promising Canadian writer under the age of 30.

Thien is the daughter of immigrants from Malaysia who came to Vancouver shortly before she was born. Her early writing deals with the experiences of immigration and the bonds that unite families and tear them apart. In an interview with Alden Mudge, she articulates her perspective: "I think my interest was always in families and immigration, in what kinds of lives people lived then let go of in order to immigrate, the way they remake themselves, the divides between parents and children in those kinds of families." Rather than focusing on racial politics, she maintains that "what binds my characters together, regardless of their background, is that they have so many similar questions."

Her first novel, *Certainty* (2006), also met with critical acclaim, winning the Books in Canada First Novel Award. The novel, an exploration of an unexplained death in wartime Malaysia, follows Gail Lim, a producer of radio documentaries in present-day Vancouver, who finds herself haunted by events in her parents' past in war-torn Asia. It takes its title from writer and politician Michael Ignatieff's book *The Needs of Strangers* (1984): "We could face the worst if we simply renounced our yearning for certainty. But who among us is capable of that renunciation?" This question applies equally well to the narrator's quandary at the conclusion of "Simple Recipes." Thien currently lives and writes in Quebec City.

Simple Recipes

There is a simple recipe for making rice. My father taught it to me when I was a child. Back then, I used to sit up on the kitchen counter watching him, how he sifted the grains in his hands, sure and quick, removing pieces of dirt or sand, tiny imperfections. He swirled his hands through the water and it turned cloudy. When he scrubbed the grains clean, the sound was as big as a field of insects. Over and over, my father rinsed the rice, drained the water, then filled the pot again.

The instructions are simple. Once the washing is done, you measure the water this way—by resting the tip of your index finger on the surface of the rice. The water should reach the bend of your first knuckle. My father did not need instructions or measuring cups. He closed his eyes and felt for the waterline.

Sometimes I still dream my father, his bare feet flat against the floor, standing in the middle of the kitchen. He wears old buttoned shirts and faded sweatpants drawn at the waist. Surrounded by the gloss of the kitchen counters, the sharp angles of the stove, the fridge, the shiny sink, he looks out of place. This memory of him is so strong, sometimes it stuns me, the detail with which I can see it.

Every night before dinner, my father would perform this ritual—rinsing and draining, then setting the pot in the cooker. When I was older, he passed this task on to me but I never did it with the same care. I went through the motions, splashing the water around, jabbing my finger down to measure the water level. Some nights the rice was a mushy gruel. I worried that I could not do so simple a task right. "Sorry," I would say to the table, my voice soft and embarrassed. In answer, my father would keep eating, pushing the rice into his mouth as if he never expected anything different, as if he noticed no difference between what he did so well and I so poorly. He would eat every last mouthful, his chopsticks walking quickly across the plate. Then he would rise, whistling, and clear the table, every motion so clean and sure, I would be convinced by him that all was well in the world.

***

My father is standing in the middle of the kitchen. In his right hand he holds a plastic bag filled with water. Caught inside the bag is a live fish.

The fish is barely breathing, though its mouth opens and closes. I reach up and touch it through the plastic bag, trailing my fingers along the gills, the soft, muscled body, pushing my finger overtop the eyeball. The fish looks straight at me, flopping sluggishly from side to side.

My father fills the kitchen sink. In one swift motion he overturns the bag and the fish comes sailing out with the water. It curls and jumps. We watch it closely, me on my tiptoes, chin propped up on the counter. The fish is the length of my arm from wrist to elbow. It floats in place, brushing up against the sides of the sink.

I keep watch over the fish while my father begins the preparations for dinner. The fish folds its body, trying to turn or swim, the water nudging overtop. Though I ripple tiny circles around it with my fingers, the fish stays still, bobbing side-to-side in the cold water.

For many hours at a time, it was just the two of us. While my mother worked and my older brother played outside, my father and I sat on the couch, flipping channels. He loved cooking shows. We watched *Wok with Yan,*[1] my father passing judgement on Yan's methods. I was enthralled when Yan transformed orange peels into swans. My father sniffed. "I can do that," he said. "You don't have to be a genius to do that." He placed a sprig of green onion in water and showed me how it bloomed like a flower. "I know many tricks like this," he said. "Much more than Yan."

Still, my father made careful notes when Yan demonstrated Peking Duck. He chuckled heartily at Yan's punning. "Take a wok on the wild side!" Yan said, pointing his spatula at the camera.

"Ha ha!" my father laughed, his shoulders shaking. "*Wok* on the wild side!"

In the mornings, my father took me to school. At three o'clock, when we came home again, I would rattle off everything I learned that day. "The brachiosaurus," I informed him, "eats only soft vegetables."

My father nodded. "That is like me. Let me see your forehead." We stopped and faced each other in the road. "You have a high forehead," he said, leaning down to take a closer look. "All smart people do."

I walked proudly, stretching my legs to match his steps. I was overjoyed when my feet kept time with his, right, then left, then right, and we walked like a single unit. My father was the man of tricks, who sat for an hour mining a watermelon with a circular spoon, who carved the rind into a castle.

My father was born in Malaysia and he and my mother immigrated to Canada several years before I was born, first settling in Montreal, then finally in

[1] *Wok with Yan* was a Canadian TV show (1980–1995) starring Hong Kong-born chef Stephen Yan, who was famous less for his stir-fries than for his word play, his aprons that punned on the word *wok* (Don't Wok the Boat; Keep on Wokking in the Free World; Wokkey Night in Canada), and his constant flow of one-liners.

Vancouver. While I was born into the persistence of the Vancouver rain, my father was born in the wash of a monsoon country. When I was young, my parents tried to teach me their language but it never came easily to me. My father ran his thumb gently over my mouth, his face kind, as if trying to see what it was that made me different.

My brother was born in Malaysia but when he immigrated with my parents to Canada the language left him. Or he forgot it, or he refused it, which is also common, and this made my father angry. "How can a child forget a language?" he would ask my mother. "It is because the child is lazy. Because the child chooses not to remember." When he was twelve years old, my brother stayed away in the afternoons. He drummed the soccer ball up and down the back alley, returning home only at dinner time. During the day, my mother worked as a sales clerk at the Woodward's store downtown, in the building with the red revolving W on top.

In our house, the ceilings were yellowed with grease. Even the air was heavy with it. I remember that I loved the weight of it, the air that was dense with the smell of countless meals cooked in a tiny kitchen, all those good smells jostling for space.

The fish in the sink is dying slowly. It has a glossy sheen to it, as if its skin is made of shining minerals. I want to prod it with both hands, its body tense against the pressure of my fingers. If I hold it tightly, I imagine I will be able to feel its fluttering heart. Instead, I lock eyes with the fish. *You're feeling verrrry sleepy,* I tell it. *You're getting verrrry tired.*

Beside me, my father chops green onions quickly. He uses a cleaver that he says is older than I am by many years. The blade of the knife rolls forward and backward, loops of green onion gathering in a pyramid beside my father's wrist. When he is done, he rolls his sleeve back from his right hand, reaches in through the water and pulls the plug.

The fish in the sink floats and we watch it in silence. The water level falls beneath its gills, beneath its belly. It drains and leaves the sink dry. The fish is lying on its side, mouth open and its body heaving. It leaps sideways and hits the sink. Then up again. It curls and snaps, lunging for its own tail. The fish sails into the air, dropping hard. It twitches violently.

My father reaches in with his bare hands. He lifts the fish out by the tail and lays it gently on the counter. While holding it steady with one hand, he hits the head with the flat of the cleaver. The fish falls still, and he begins to clean it.

***

In my apartment, I keep the walls scrubbed clean. I open the windows and turn the fan on whenever I prepare a meal. My father bought me a rice cooker when I first moved into my own apartment, but I use it so rarely it stays in the back of the cupboard, the cord wrapped neatly around its belly. I have no longing for the meals themselves, but I miss the way we sat down together, our bodies leaning hungrily forward while my father, the magician, unveiled plate after plate. We laughed and ate, white steam fogging my mother's glasses until she had to take them off and lay them on the table. Eyes closed, she would eat, crunchy vegetables gripped in her chopsticks, the most vivid green.

***

My brother comes into the kitchen and his body is covered with dirt. He leaves a thin trail of it behind as he walks. The soccer ball, muddy from outside, is encircled in one arm. Brushing past my father, his face is tense.

Beside me, my mother sprinkles garlic onto the fish. She lets me slide one hand underneath the fish's head, cradling it, then bending it backwards so that she can fill the fish's insides with ginger. Very carefully, I turn the fish over. It is firm and slippery, and beaded with tiny, sharp scales.

At the stove, my father picks up an old teapot. It is full of oil and he pours the oil into the wok. It falls in a thin ribbon. After a moment, when the oil begins crackling, he lifts the fish up and drops it down into the wok. He adds water and the smoke billows up. The sound of the fish frying is like tires on gravel, a sound so loud it drowns out all other noises. Then my father steps out from the smoke. "Spoon out the rice," he says as he lifts me down from the counter.

My brother comes back into the room, his hands muddy and his knees the colour of dusty brick. His soccer shorts flutter against the backs of his legs. Sitting down, he makes an angry face. My father ignores him.

Inside the cooker, the rice is flat like a pie. I push the spoon in, turning the rice over, and the steam shoots up in a hot mist and condenses on my skin. While my father moves his arms delicately over the stove, I begin dishing the rice out: first for my father, then my mother, then my brother, then myself. Behind me the fish is cooking quickly. In a crockery pot, my father steams cauliflower, stirring it round and round.

My brother kicks at a table leg.

"What's the matter?" my father asks.

He is quiet for a moment, then he says, "Why do we have to eat fish?"

"You don't like it?"

My brother crosses his arms against his chest. I see the dirt lining his arms, dark and hardened. I imagine chipping it off his body with a small spoon.

"I don't like the eyeball there. It looks sick."

My mother tuts. Her nametag is still clipped to her blouse. It says *Woodward's*, and then, *Sales Clerk*. "Enough," she says, hanging her purse on the back of the chair. "Go wash your hands and get ready for supper."

My brother glares, just for a moment. Then he begins picking at the dirt on his arms. I bring plates of rice to the table. The dirt flies off his skin, speckling the tablecloth. "Stop it," I say crossly.

"*Stop it*," he says, mimicking me.

"Hey!" My father hits his spoon against the counter. It *pings*, high-pitched. He points at my brother. "No fighting in this house."

My brother looks at the floor, mumbles something, and then shuffles away from the table. As he moves farther away, he begins to stamp his feet.

Shaking her head, my mother takes her jacket off. It slides from her shoulders. She says something to my father in the language I can't understand. He merely shrugs his shoulders. And then he replies, and I think his words are so familiar, as if they are words I should know, as if maybe I did know them once but then I forgot them. The language that they speak is full of soft vowels, words running together so that I can't make out the gaps where they pause for breath.

My mother told me once about guilt. Her own guilt she held in the palm of her hands, like an offering. But your guilt is different, she said. You do not need to hold on to it. Imagine this, she said, her hands running along my forehead, then up into my hair. Imagine, she said. Picture it, and what do you see?

A bruise on the skin, wide and black.

A bruise, she said. Concentrate on it. Right now, it's a bruise. But if you concentrate, you can shrink it, compress it to the size of a pinpoint. And then, if you want to, if you see it, you can blow it off your body like a speck of dirt.

She moved her hands along my forehead.

I tried to picture what she said. I pictured blowing it away like so much nothing, just these little pieces that didn't mean anything, this complicity that I could magically walk away from. She made me believe in the strength of my own thoughts, as if I could make appear what had never existed. Or turn it around. Flip it over so many times you just lose sight of it, you lose the tail end and the whole thing disappears into smoke.

My father pushes at the fish with the edge of his spoon. Underneath, the meat is white and the juice runs down along the side. He lifts a piece and lowers it carefully onto my plate.

Once more, his spoon breaks skin. Gingerly, my father lifts another piece and moves it towards my brother.

"I don't want it," my brother says.

My father's hand wavers. "Try it," he says, smiling. "Take a wok on the wild side."

"No."

My father sighs and places the piece on my mother's plate. We eat in silence, scraping our spoons across the dishes. My parents use chopsticks, lifting their bowls and motioning the food into their mouths. The smell of food fills the room.

Savouring each mouthful, my father eats slowly, head tuned to the flavours in his mouth. My mother takes her glasses off, the lenses fogged, and lays them on the table. She eats with her head bowed down, as if in prayer.

Lifting a stem of cauliflower to his lips, my brother sighs deeply. He chews, and then his face changes. I have a sudden picture of him drowning, his hair waving like grass. He coughs, spitting the mouthful back onto his plate. Another cough. He reaches for his throat, choking.

My father slams his chopsticks down on the table. In a single movement, he reaches across, grabbing my brother by the shoulder. "I have tried," he is saying. "I don't know what kind of son you are. To be so ungrateful." His other hand sweeps by me and bruises into my brother's face.

My mother flinches. My brother's face is red and his mouth is open. His eyes are wet.

Still coughing, he grabs a fork, tines aimed at my father, and then in an unthinking moment, he heaves it at him. It strikes my father in the chest and drops.

"I hate you! You're just an asshole, you're just a fucking asshole chink!" My brother holds his plate in his hands. He smashes it down and his food scatters across the table. He is coughing and spitting. "I wish you weren't my father! I wish you were dead."

My father's hand falls again. This time pounding downwards. I close my eyes. All I can hear is someone screaming. There is a loud voice. I stand awkwardly, my hands covering my eyes.

"Go to your room," my father says, his voice shaking.

And I think he is talking to me so I remove my hands.

But he is looking at my brother. And my brother is looking at him, his small chest heaving.

A few minutes later, my mother begins clearing the table, face weary as she scrapes the dishes one by one over the garbage.

I move away from my chair, past my mother, onto the carpet and up the stairs.

Outside my brother's bedroom, I crouch against the wall. When I step forward and look, I see my father holding the bamboo pole between his hands. The pole is smooth. The long grains, fine as hair, are pulled together, at intervals, jointed. My brother is lying on the floor, as if thrown down and dragged there. My father raises the pole into the air.

I want to cry out. I want to move into the room between them, but I can't.

It is like a tree falling, beginning to move, a slow arc through the air.

The bamboo drops silently. It rips the skin on my brother's back. I cannot hear any sound. A line of blood edges quickly across his body.

The pole rises and again comes down. I am afraid of bones breaking.

My father lifts his arms once more.

On the floor, my brother cries into the carpet, pawing at the ground. His knees folded into his chest, the crown of his head burrowing down. His back is hunched over and I can see his spine, little bumps on his skin.

The bamboo smashes into bone and the scene in my mind bursts into a million white pieces.

My mother picks me up off the floor, pulling me across the hall, into my bedroom, into bed. Everything is wet, the sheets, my hands, her body, my face, and she soothes me with words I cannot understand because all I can hear is screaming. She rubs her cool hands against my forehead. "Stop," she says. "Please stop," but I feel loose, deranged, as if everything in the known world is ending right here.

In the morning, I wake up to the sound of oil in the pan and the smell of French toast. I can hear my mother bustling around, putting dishes in the cupboards.

No one says anything when my brother doesn't come down for breakfast. My father piles French toast and syrup onto a plate and my mother pours a glass of milk. She takes everything upstairs to my brother's bedroom.

As always, I follow my father around the kitchen. I track his footprints, follow behind him and hide in the shadow of his body. Every so often, he reaches down and ruffles my hair with his hands. We cast a spell, I think. The way we move in circles, how he cooks without thinking because this is the task that comes to him effortlessly. He smiles down at me, but when he does this, it somehow breaks the spell. My father stands in place, hands dropping to his sides as if he has forgotten what he was doing mid-motion. On the walls, the paint is peeling and the floor, unswept in days, leaves little pieces of dirt stuck to our feet.

My persistence, I think, my unadulterated love, confuse him. With each passing day, he knows I will find it harder to ignore what I can't comprehend, that I will be unable to separate one part of him from another. The unconditional quality of my love for him will not last forever, just as my brother's did not. My father stands in the middle of the kitchen, unsure. Eventually, my mother comes downstairs again and puts her arms around him and holds him, whispering something to him, words that to me are meaningless and incomprehensible. But she offers them to him, sound after sound, in a language that was stolen from some other place, until he drops his head and remembers where he is.

Later on, I lean against the door frame upstairs and listen to the sound of a metal fork scraping against a dish. My mother is already there, her voice rising and falling. She is moving the fork across the plate, offering my brother pieces of French toast.

I move towards the bed, the carpet scratchy, until I can touch the wooden bedframe with my hands. My mother is seated there, and I go to her, reaching my fingers out to the buttons on her cuff and twisting them over to catch the light.

"Are you eating?" I ask my brother.

He starts to cry. I look at him, his face half hidden in the blankets.

"Try and eat," my mother says softly.

He only cries harder but there isn't any sound. The pattern of sunlight on his blanket moves with his body. His hair is pasted down with sweat and his head moves forward and backward like an old man's.

At some point I know my father is standing at the entrance of the room but I cannot turn to look at him. I want to stay where I am, facing the wall. I'm afraid that if I turn around and go to him, I will be complicit, accepting a portion of guilt, no matter how small that piece. I do not know how to prevent this from happening again, though now I know, in the end, it will break us apart. This violence will turn all my love to shame and grief. So I stand there, not looking at him or my brother. Even my father, the magician, who can make something beautiful out of nothing, he just stands and watches.

A face changes over time, it becomes clearer. In my father's face, I have seen everything pass. Anger that has stripped it of anything recognizable, so that it is only a face of bones and skin. And then, at other times, so much pain that it is unbearable, his face so full of grief it might dissolve. How to reconcile all that I know of him and still love him? For a long time, I thought it was not possible. When I was a child, I did not love my father because he was complicated, because he was human, because he needed me to. A child does not know yet how to love a person that way.

How simple it should be. Warm water running over, the feel of the grains between my hands, the sound of it like stones running along the pavement. My father would rinse the rice over and over, sifting it between his fingertips, searching for the impurities, pulling them out. A speck, barely visible, resting on the tip of his finger.

If there were some recourse, I would take it. A cupful of grains in my open hand, a smoothing out, finding the impurities, then removing them piece by piece. And then, to be satisfied with what remains.

Somewhere in my memory, a fish in the sink is dying slowly. My father and I watch as the water runs down.

[2001]

MOLSON CANADA

In 1994 Molson Breweries launched its "I AM CANADIAN" ad campaign, which reached its height in the now famous "Rant" advertisement that aired on national television and in movie theatres across the country in March 2000. The "Rant" features an average "Joe Canadian," dressed in jeans and lumberjack shirt, who reluctantly steps up to a solitary microphone and proceeds to list the various things that distinguish Canadians from Americans. His monologue builds to a crescendo, a "rant," as images relating to his monologue are flashed on an immense screen behind him. The "Rant" culminates in Joe's final assertion—"My name is Joe. And I am Canadian!"—and concludes with him mumbling "thank you" and sheepishly walking off the stage. The words I AM CANADIAN, in the font of the product being marketed, replace Joe on the screen and are superimposed on a glass being filled with Molson Canadian beer. The ad quickly became a national rallying cry, inspiring often satiric imitation and citation across the country. The actor who played Joe was hired to perform the skit live at hockey games, fundraising events, and at selected Canada Day venues that year. The approach was successful because it was able to tap into an ambivalent nationalist subtext that informs many assertions of Canadian culture and identity. Making use of such characteristically Canadian approaches as self-deprecating irony, cultural inferiority, and reluctant patriotism (through Joe's reluctance to be ranting in the first place), the ad also performs a version of national skepticism, for even as it promotes Canadian national identity, it dramatizes the very things that Canada *is not* on the screen behind Joe, thereby solidifying the association of Canada with these images. The ad also made use of the long-standing strategy, dating back to the eighteenth century, of defining Canadian identity against the United States. The text of the "Rant" invokes various elements of Canada's colonial history (fur traders, lumberjacks, the "North") and was spoken to the score of the British imperialist anthem *The Land of Hope and Glory*. It managed to strike a chord in the Canadian psyche, recalling the popular success of two earlier beer-swigging Canadians, Bob and Doug McKenzie, from the 1980s (see Figure VI-9).

I AM CANADIAN

Hey.
I'm not a lumberjack,
or a fur trader . . .
and I don't live in an igloo
or eat blubber, or own a dogsled . . .
and I don't know Jimmy, Sally or Suzy from Canada,
although I'm certain they're really, really nice.

I have a Prime Minister,
not a President.
I speak English and French,   10
NOT American.
and I pronounce it ABOUT,
NOT A BOOT.

I can proudly sew my country's flag on my backpack.
I believe in peace keeping, NOT policing.
DIVERSITY, NOT assimilation,
AND THAT THE BEAVER IS A TRULY PROUD AND NOBLE ANIMAL.
A TOQUE IS A HAT,
A CHESTERFIELD IS A COUCH,
AND IT IS PRONOUCED 'ZED' NOT 'ZEE', 'ZED'!   20

CANADA IS THE SECOND LARGEST LANDMASS!
THE FIRST NATION OF HOCKEY!
AND THE BEST PART OF NORTH AMERICA!
MY NAME IS JOE!
AND I AM CANADIAN!

Thank you.

[2000]

bibliography

V. Modernist Period

Primary Texts

Avison, Margaret. *Always Now: The Collected Poems.* Vols. 1–3. Erin, ON: Porcupine's Quill, 2003–05.

—. *Not Yet but Still.* London, ON: Brick, 1997.

—. *Selected Poems.* Toronto: Oxford UP, 1991.

—. *Winter Sun.* London: Routledge, Kegan Paul, 1960.

Birney, Earle. *Collected Poems.* Toronto: McClelland, 1975.

—. "Mainly About Books." CBC Radio Broadcast. 2 Mar. 1949.

—. "The Earle Birney Homepage." Accessed May 2007. <http://www.cariboo.bc.ca/ae/e_birney/home.htm>.

—. "Preface." *Ghost in the Wheels.* Toronto: McClelland, 1977. 9–11.

—. *Selected Poems: 1940–1966.* Toronto: McClelland, 1966.

—. *Twentieth Century Canadian Poetry.* Toronto: Ryerson, 1953.

Callaghan, Morley. "Loppy Phelan's Double Shoot." *The Lost and Found Stories of Morley Callaghan.* Toronto: Lester & Orpen Dennys, 1985. 18–32.

—. *That Summer in Paris: Memories of Tangled Friendships with Hemingway, Fitzgerald, and Some Others.* Toronto: Macmillan, 1963; rpt. Toronto: Stoddart, 1992.

Canada. *Royal Commission on National Development in the Arts, Letters, and Sciences.* Report. Ottawa: King's Printer, 1951.

Carr, Emily. "Ucluelet." *Klee Wyck.* Toronto: Oxford UP, 1941. 3–17.

—. "Modern and Indian Art of the West Coast." *Supplement to the McGill News* 10 (June 1929): 20.

Grey Owl. *A Book of Grey Owl: Pages from the Writings of WA-SHA-QUON-ASIN.* 1938. Ed. E.E. Reynolds. London: Peter Davies, 1960.

—. "Letter to William Arthur Deacon, 10 May 1935." *Dear Bill: The Correspondence of William Arthur Deacon.* Ed. John Lennox and Michèle Lacombe. Toronto: U of Toronto P, 1988. 162–66.

—. *Pilgrims of the Wild.* London: Peter Davies, 1935. 24–30.

Grove, Frederick Philip. "Canadians Old and New." *Maclean's* 41.6 (1928): 55–56.

—. "Dawn and Diamonds." *Over Prairie Trails.* Toronto: McClelland, 1922. 81–104.

Harris, Lawren. "The Group of Seven in Canadian History." *Canadian Historical Society, Report of the Annual Meeting Held at Victoria and Vancouver June 16–19, 1948.* Ed. R.A. Preston. Toronto: U of Toronto P, 1948. 28–38.

—. "A New Artistic Expression." CBC broadcast. 9 Apr. 1954. Accessed 10 Oct. 2007. <http://archives.cbc.ca/IDC-1-68-754-4626/arts_entertainment/group_of_seven/clip1>.

—. "Revelation of Art in Canada." *Canadian Theosophist* 15 July 1926: 85–88.

Kitagawa, Muriel. *This Is My Own: Letters to Wes & Other Writings on Japanese Canadians, 1941–1948.* Ed. Roy Miki. Vancouver: Talonbooks, 1985. 89–91, 114–118.

Klein, A.M. "A Modest Proposal." *Canadian Jewish Chronicle* 14 July 1939; rpt. *A.M. Klein Beyond Sambation: Selected Essays and Editorials, 1928–1955.* Ed. M.W. Steinberg and Usher Caplan. Toronto: U of Toronto P, 1982. 56–57.

—. *The Collected Poems of A.M. Klein.* Ed. Miriam Waddington. Toronto: McGraw-Hill Ryerson, 1974.

—. *Hath not a Jew . . .* Toronto: Ryerson, 1940.

—. *The Rocking Chair and Other Poems.* Toronto: Ryerson, 1948.

Layton, Irving. *Collected Poems.* Toronto: McClelland, 1971.

—. *A Red Carpet for the Sun.* Toronto: McClelland, 1959.

LePan, Douglas. *Far Voyages.* Toronto: McClelland, 1990.

—. *Weathering It: Complete Poems, 1948–1987.* Toronto: McClelland, 1987.

Livesay, Dorothy. *Collected Poems: The Two Seasons.* Toronto: McGraw-Hill Ryerson, 1972.

—. *The Documentaries.* Toronto: Ryerson, 1968.

—. "A Putting Down of Roots." *CV/II* 1 (1975): 2.

—. "Proletarianitis in Canada." *Right Hand, Left Hand.* Erin, ON: Press Porcepic, 1977. 230–32.

—. *Selected Poems: 1926–1956.* Ed. Desmond Pacey. Toronto: Ryerson, 1957.

—. "Writers Have a Big Part in Making New World." *Saturday Night* Apr. 1947: 17.

Macleish, Archibald. *Streets in the Moon.* Boston: Houghton Mifflin, 1926.

MacLennan, Hugh. "Boy Meets Girl in Winnipeg and Who Cares?" *Scotchman's Return and Other Essays.* Toronto: Macmillan, 1960. 113–24.

—. "Literature in a New Country." *Scotchman's Return and Other Essays.* Toronto: Macmillan, 1960. 137–41.

—. *On Being a Maritime Writer.* Sackville, NB: Mt. Allison UP, 1984.

—. *Thirty & Three.* Toronto: Macmillan, 1954.

—. *Two Solitudes.* Toronto: Collins, 1945.

—. *The Watch That Ends the Night.* New York: Scribners, 1959.

Page, P.K. *As Ten, As Twenty.* Toronto: Ryerson, 1946.

—. *Brazilian Journal.* Toronto: Lester & Orpen Dennys, 1988.

—. "Canadian Poetry 1942." *Preview* 8 (Oct. 1942): 8–9.

—. *Hologram: A Book of Glosas.* London, ON: Brick, 1994.

—. *P.K. Page: Poems Selected and New.* Toronto: Anansi, 1967.

—. "Traveller, Conjuror, Journeyman." *Canadian Literature* 46 (1970): 35–40.

Pratt, E.J. *The Complete Letters of E.J. Pratt: A Hypertext Edition.* Ed. David Pitt and Elizabeth Popham. Accessed 22 June 2008. <http://www.trentu.ca/faulty/pratt/letters/frletters.html>.

—. *The Complete Poems of E.J. Pratt: A Hypertext Edition.* Ed. Sandra Djwa and Zailig Pollock. Accessed 22 June 2008. <http://www.trentu.ca/faculty/pratt/poems/texts/174/fr174.html>.

—. *Collected Poems.* Toronto: Macmillan, 1944.

—. *Towards the Last Spike.* Toronto: Macmillan, 1952.

Ross, Sinclair. "The Painted Door." *Queen's Quarterly* XLVI (1939): 145–69.

Salverson, Laura Goodman. "Those Child Transgressions." *Confessions of an Immigrant's Daughter.* London: Faber, 1939; rpt. with introd. Peter Stich. Toronto: U of Toronto P, 1981. 103–08.

Scott, F.R. *Events and Signals.* Toronto: Ryerson, 1945.

—. Notebook of Minutes from *Preview* Meeting. Montreal. 13 March 1944. F.R. Scott fonds. National Library Archives, Ottawa. MG 30 D211 vol. 87.

—. "A Note on Canadian Colonialism." *Preview* (1943): 5.

—. *F.R. Scott: Selected Poems.* Toronto: Oxford UP, 1966.

—, and A.J.M. Smith, eds. *The Blasted Pine.* Toronto: Macmillan, 1957.

Smith, A.J.M. "A Rejected Preface." *Towards a View of Canadian Letters: Selected Critical Essays, 1928–1971.* Vancouver: U of British Columbia P, 1973. 170–73; rpt. *New Provinces: Poems of Several Authors.* Ed. Michael Gnarowski. Toronto: U of Toronto P, 1976. 144–49.

—, ed. *The Book of Canadian Poetry.* Toronto: Gage, 1943.

—. *The Complete Poems of A.J.M. Smith.* Ed. Brian Trehearne. London: Canadian Poetry Press, 2007.

—. "Contemporary Poetry." *The McGill Fortnightly Review* 2.4 (15 Dec. 1926): 31–32.

—, ed. *The Oxford Book of Canadian Verse in English and French.* Toronto: Oxford UP, 1960.

—. *Poems: New and Collected.* Toronto: Oxford UP, 1967.

—. "Some Letters of A.M. Klein to A.J.M. Smith 1941–1951." *A.M. Klein Symposium.* Ed. Seymour Mayne. Ottawa: U of Ottawa P, 1975. 1–13.

—. "Wanted – Canadian Criticism." *Canadian Forum* 8 (1927–28): n.p.

—, and F.R. Scott. *New Provinces: Poems of Several Authors.* Toronto: Macmillan, 1936.

Underhill, Frank. "Notes on the Massey Report." *Canadian Forum* Aug. 1951: 100–02.

Secondary Texts

Abella, Irving, and Harold Troper. *None Is Too Many: Canada and the Jews of Europe, 1933–1948.* Toronto: Lester & Orpen Dennys, 1982.

Adams, Mary Louise. "Margin Notes: Reading Lesbianism as Obscenity in a Cold War Courtroom." *Love, Hate, and Fear in Canada's Cold War.* Ed. Richard Cavell. Toronto: U of Toronto P, 2004. 135–58.

Anahareo. *Devil in Deerskins: My Life with Grey Owl.* Toronto: New Press, 1972.

Barton, John, and Billeh Nickerson. *Seminal: The Anthology of Canada's Gay Male Poets.* Vancouver: Arsenal Pulp, 2007.

Beardsley, Doug, and Rosemary Sullian. "An Interview with Dorothy Livesay." Accessed April 2007. <http://www.uwo.ca/english/canadianpoetry/cpjrn/vol03/sullivan.htm>.

Berland, Jody. "Marginal Notes on Cultural Studies in Canada." *University of Toronto Quarterly* 64.4 (1995): 514–25.

Billinghurst, Jane. *Grey Owl: The Many Faces of Archie Belaney.* Vancouver: Greystone, 1999.

Bliss, Michael, ed. "XXVIII: 1 Louis St. Laurent Proposes an Atlantic Alliance, 1948." *Canadian History in Documents, 1763–1966.* Toronto: Ryerson, 1966. 320–22.

—, ed. "XXVIII: 3 Lester B. Pearson on Canadian Foreign Policy in the 1950s." *Canadian History in Documents, 1763–1966.* Toronto: Ryerson, 1966. 325–26.

Boire, Gary. *Morley Callaghan and His Works.* Toronto: General, 1990.

Bordo, Jonathan. "Jack Pine – Wilderness Sublime or the Erasure of the Aboriginal Presence from the Canadian Landscape." *Journal of Canadian Studies* 27.4 (1992–93): 98–128.

Bothwell, Robert. *The Penguin History of Canada.* Toronto: Penguin, 2006.

Broadus, Edmund, and Eleanor Broadus. *A Book of Canadian Prose and Verse.* Toronto: Macmillan, 1934.

Brown. E.K. *On Canadian Poetry.* Toronto: Ryerson, 1943.

—. "Our Neglect of Our Literature." *The Civil Service Review* 17.3 (Sept. 1944): 306, 308.

Calder, Alison. "Sinclair Ross." *The Literary Encyclopedia.* 30 June 2002. Accessed 23 May 2008. <http://www.litencyc.com/php/speople.php?rec=true&UID=4928>.

Caplan, Usher. *Like One That Dreamed: A Portrait of A.M. Klein.* Toronto: McGraw-Hill Ryerson, 1982.

Cavell, Richard. "Introduction: The Cultural Production of Canada's Cold War." *Love, Hate, and Fear in Canada's Cold War.* Ed. Richard Cavell. Toronto: U of Toronto P, 2004. 3–34.

Compton, Anne. *A.J.M. Smith: Canadian Metaphysical.* Toronto: ECW, 1994.

Darling, Michael. *A. J. M. Smith and His Works.* Toronto: ECW, 1990.

—. "A.J.M. Smith (1902–80)." *ECW's Biographical Guide to Canadian Poets.* Toronto: ECW, 1993. 93–98.

Davey, Frank. "Canadian Canons." *Critical Inquiry* 16 (1990): 672–81.

Davies, Robertson. "Literature in a Country without a Mythology." *The Merry Heart: Selections 1980–1995.* New York: Viking, 1997. 40–63.

Di Michele, Mary. "Stuffing the World in at Your Eyes: Margaret Avison and the Poetics of Seeing and Believing" *Jacket* 29 (April 2006). Accessed 3 July 2007. <http://jacketmagazine.com/30/dimichele-avison.html>.

Dudek, Louis, and Michael Gnarowski, eds. *The Making of Modern Poetry in Canada.* Toronto, Ryerson Press, 1967.

Dudek, Louis, Irving Layton, and Raymond Souster. *Cerberus: Poems.* Toronto: Contact, 1952.

Dupuis, Katie. "The Way We Were." *Chatelaine* 81.5 (2008): 321–52.

Djwa, Sandra. "The *Canadian Forum:* Literary Catalyst." *Studies in Canadian Literature* 1.1 (1976): 7–25.

Eaman, Ross. "Founding of the CBC." *The Canadian Encyclopedia.* Accessed 14 Sept. 2007. <http://www.thecanadianencyclopedia.com/index.cfm?PgNm=TCE&Params=A1SEC817660>.

"Elizabeth Bagshaw." Library and Archives Canada. Accessed 16 July 2008. <http://www.collection-scanada.gc.ca/women/002026-296-e.html>.

Friskney, Janet, B. *New Canadian Library: The Ross-McClelland Years 1952–1978.* Toronto: U of Toronto P, 2007.

Frye, Northrop. "Conclusion." *Literary History of Canada.* Ed. Carl. F. Klinck. Toronto: U of Toronto P, 1965. 821–49.

—. *Divisions on a Ground: Essays on Canadian Culture.* Ed. James Polk. Toronto: Anansi, 1982.

Gammel, Irene. *Baroness Elsa. Gender, Dada, and Everyday Modernity: A Cultural Biography.* Cambridge: MIT Press, 2002.

Gerson, Carol. "The Canon Between the Wars: Field Notes of a Feminist Literary Archaeologist." *Canadian Canons.* Ed. Robert Lecker. Toronto: U of Toronto P, 1991. 46–56.

Gingell, Susan, ed. *E.J. Pratt on His Life and Poetry.* Toronto: U of Toronto P, 1983.

Gitlin, Todd. *The Sixties: Years of Hope, Days of Rage.* Rev. ed. New York: Bantam, 1993.

Gnarowski, Michael, ed. "Introduction." *New Provinces: Poems of Several Authors.* Toronto: U of Toronto P, 1976. vii–xxxii.

—, ed. "Introduction." *A.J.M. Smith: Selected Writings.* Toronto: Dundurn, 2006. 13–28.

Grey, Julius, and John Gill. "Citizenship." *The Canadian Encyclopedia.* Accessed 24 Sept. 2007. <http://thecanadianencyclopedia.com/index.cfm?PgNm=TCE&Params=A1ARTA0001634>.

Groening, Laura. "Malcolm Ross and the New Canadian Library: Making It Real or Making a Difference?" *Studies in Canadian Literature* 25.1 (2000): 95–110.

Gruending, Dennis. *Great Canadian Speeches.* Toronto: Fitzhenry & Whiteside, 2004.

Harlequin Enterprises. "About Harlequin." Accessed 10 Apr. 2008. <http://www.eharlequin.com>.

Harrington, Lyn. *Syllables of Recorded Time: The Story of the Canadian Authors Association 1921–1981.* Toronto: Simon & Pierre, 1981.

Hill, Colin. "Frederick Philip Grove." *The Literary Encyclopedia.* Accessed 4 June 2007. <http://www.litencyc.com/php/speople.php?rec=true&UID=1901>.

Hjartarson, Paul, and Tracy Kulba, eds. *The Politics of Cultural Mediation: Baroness Elsa von Freytag-Loringhoven and Felix Paul Greve.* Edmonton: U of Alberta P, 2003.

Housser, F.B. *A Canadian Art Movement: The Story of the Group of Seven.* Toronto: Macmillan, 1926; rpt. 1974.

Howarth, Dorothy. "New Province Tomorrow: Hope, Sorrow Blend on Confederation Eve." *Telegram* 31 Mar. 1949: 1, 3.

Irvine, Dean, ed. *Archive for Our Times: Previously Uncollected and Unpublished Poems of Dorothy Livesay.* Vancouver: Arsenal Pulp, 1998.

—, ed. *The Canadian Modernists Meet.* Ottawa: U of Ottawa P, 2005.

Jackson, A.Y. *A Painter's Country: Autobiography.* Toronto: Clarke, Irwin, 1958.

Kattan, Naïm. *A. M. Klein: Poet and Prophet.* Trans. Edward Baxter. Montreal: XYZ, 2001.

Keith, W.J. *Canadian Literature in English.* London: Longman, 1985.

—. *Canadian Literature in English.* 2 vols. Erin, ON: Porcupine's Quill, 2006.

—. "Morley Callaghan and the Test of Time." *Books in Canada.* Sept. 2005. Accessed 12 Mar. 2007. <http://www.booksincanada.com>.

Kelly, Peggy. "Anthologies and the Canonization Process: A Case Study of the English-Canadian Literary Field, 1920–1950." *Studies in Canadian Literature* 25.1 (2000): 73–94.

Kennedy, Leo. "Direction for Canadian Poets." 1936. *The McGill Movement: A.J.M. Smith, F.R. Scott and Leo Kennedy.* Ed. Peter Stevens. Toronto: Ryerson, 1969. 11–19.

Kertzer, J.M. "The Wounded Eye: The Poetry of Douglas Le Pan." *Studies in Canadian Literature* 6.1 (1981): 5–23.

Kröller, Eva-Marie, ed. *The Cambridge Companion to Canadian Literature.* New York: Cambridge UP, 2004.

Lecker, Robert. "The Canonization of Canadian Literature: An Inquiry into Value." *Critical Inquiry* 16.3 (1990): 656–71.

—. *Making It Real: The Canonization of English-Canadian Literature.* Toronto: Anansi, 1995.

Ley, Robert, ed. "Nazi Conspiracy and Aggression: Volume IV, Document No. 1708-PS." *The Avalon Project at Yale Law School.* Accessed 19 Feb. 2008. <http://www.yale.edu/lawweb/avalon/imt/document/nca_vol4/1708-ps.htm>.

Lismer, Arthur. "The West Wind." *McMaster Monthly* 43 (1934): 163–64.

Machardy, Carolyn. "An Inquiry into the Success of Tom Thomson's 'The West Wind.'" *University of Toronto Quarterly* 68.3 (1999): 768–89.

Martens, Klaus. *F.P. Grove in Europe and Canada: Translated Lives.* Edmonton: U of Alberta P, 2001.

Mayne, Semour, ed. *The A. M. Klein Symposium.* Ottawa: U of Ottawa P, 1975.

McCullagh, Joan. *Alan Crawley and Contemporary Verse.* Vancouver: UBC Press. U of British Columbia P, 1976.

McLuhan, Marshall. *Understanding Media.* Toronto: New American, 1964.

McNeilly, Kevin. "Toward a Poetics of Dislocation: Elizabeth Bishop and P.K. Page Writing Brazil." *Studies in Canadian Literature* 23.2 (1998): 85–108.

Moray, Gerta. *Unsettling Encounters: First Nations Imagery in the Art of Emily Carr.* Vancouver: U of British Columbia P, 2006.

Morley, Patricia. *As Though Life Mattered: Leo Kennedy's Story.* Montreal-Kingston: McGill-Queen's, 1994.

Murray, Joan. *The Best of the Group of Seven.* Toronto: McClelland, 1984.

National Association of Japanese Canadians. "World War II." Accessed 28 July 2007. <http://www.najc.ca/thenandnow/experiencec_firstorder.php>.

New, W.H., ed. *Dictionary of Literary Biography Volume 68: Canadian Writers, 1920–1959 First Series.* Detroit: Gale, 1988.

—. "A Geography of 'Snow': Reading Notes." *Studies in Canadian Literature* 23.1 (1998): 53–74.

—. *A History of Canadian Literature.* 2nd ed. Montreal: McGill-Queen's UP, 2003.

"Newfoundland Confederation." Library and Archives Canada. Accessed 7 Oct. 2007. <http://www.collection-scanada.gc.ca/confederation/023001-2230-e.html>.

Neijmann, Daisy. "Laura Goodman Salverson." *The Literary Encyclopedia.* Accessed 21 Sept. 2007. <http://www.litencyc.com/php/speople.php?rec=true&UID=3923>.

Niewyk, Donald L. and Francis Nicosia. *The Columbia Guide to the Holocaust.* New York: Columbia UP, 2000.

Norris, Ken. "The Beginnings of Canadian Modernism." *Canadian Poetry* 11 (1982): 56–66.

Pacey, Desmond: "At Last—A Canadian Literature." *Cambridge Review* 2 Dec. 1938: 146–47.

—. *Creative Writing in Canada.* Toronto: Ryerson, 1961.

—. *Frederick Philip Grove.* Toronto: Ryerson, 1970.

—. *Our Literary Heritage.* Toronto: McGraw-Hill Ryerson, 1982.

—. *Ten Canadian Poets: A Group of Biographical and Critical Essays.* Toronto: Ryerson, 1958.

Pevere, Geoff, and Greig Dymond. *Mondo Canuck.* Toronto: Prentice Hall, 1996.

Polk, James. *Wilderness Writers.* Toronto/Vancouver: Clarke, Irwin, 1972.

Purdy, Al. "The Man Who Killed David." *Weekend Magazine* Dec. 1974. Accessed 12 Apr. 2007. <http://www.cariboo.bc.ca/ae/e_birney/english/level3/level/doc00702.htm>.

Precosky, Don. "*Preview*: An Introduction and Index." Accessed Mar. 2007. <http://www.uwo.ca/english/canadianpoetry/cpjrn/vol08/precosky.htm>.

—. "Seven Myths about Canadian Literature." *Studies in Canadian Literature* 11.1 (1986): 86–95.

Ricou, Laurie. *Vertical Man, Horizontal World: Man and Landscape in Canadian Prairie Fiction.* Vancouver: U of British Columbia P, 1973.

Roberts, Charles G.D. "A Note on Modernism." *Open House.* Ed. William Arthur Deacon and Wilfred Reeves. Ottawa: Graphic, 1931. 19–25.

Ross, Malcolm, ed. *The Arts in Canada: A Stock-taking at Mid-Century.* Toronto: Macmillan, 1958.

—, ed. *Our Sense of Identity: A Book of Canadian Essays.* Toronto: Ryerson, 1954.

Royal Commission on Spy Activities in Canada, by the Honourable Mr. Justice Robert Taschereau and the Honourable Mr. Justice R.L. Kellock. Ottawa: Edmond Cloutier, Printer to the King's Most Excellent Majesty, 1946.

Shadbolt, Doris. *Emily Carr.* Vancouver: Douglas & McIntyre, 1990.

Smith, Donald B. *From the Land of Shadows: The Making of Grey Owl.* Vancouver: Greystone-Douglas, 1999.

Spender, Stephen. "The Making of a Poem." *Partisan Review* XIII (1946): 294–308.

Spettigue, Douglas O. *FPG: The European Years.* Ottawa: Oberon, 1973.

—. "The Grove Enigma Resolved." *Queen's Quarterly* 79 (1972): 1–2.

Statistics Canada. National Income and Expenditure Accounts, Volume 1, The Annual Estimates, 1926–1974. Catalogue 13-531.

Steinberg, M.W. "A.M. Klein as Journalist." *Canadian Literature* 83 (1979): 21–30.

Stevens, Peter, ed. *The McGill Movement: A.J.M. Smith, F. R. Scott and Leo Kennedy.* Critical Views on Canadian Writers Series. Toronto: Ryerson, 1969.

Stevenson, Lionel. *Appraisals of Canadian Literature.* Toronto: Macmillan, 1926.

Stich, K.P. "F.P. Grove's Language of Choice." *Journal of Commonwealth Literature* 14 (1979): 9–17.

Stouck, David. *As for Sinclair Ross.* Toronto: U of Toronto P, 2005.

—. *Ethel Wilson: A Critical Biography.* Toronto: U of Toronto P, 2003.

Struthers, James. "Great Depression." *The Canadian Encyclopedia.* Accessed 15 Sept. 2007.<http://www.thecanadianencyclopedia.com/index.cfm?PgNm=TCE&Params=A1ARTA0003425>.

Sutherland, John. "Literary Colonialism." *First Statement* 2.4 (Feb. 1944): 3.

—, ed. *Other Canadians: An Anthology of the New Poetry in Canada, 1940–1946.* Montreal: First Statement Press, 1947.

Thomas, Clara. "A Conversation about Literature: An Interview with Margaret Laurence and Irving Layton." *Journal of Canadian Fiction* 1.1 (1972): 65–69.

—, and John Lennox. *William Arthur Deacon: A Canadian Literary Life.* Toronto: U of Toronto P, 1982.

Thompson, Eric. "Prairie Mosaic: The Immigrant Novel in the Canadian West." *Studies in Canadian Literature* 5.2 (1980): 236–59.

Trehearne, Brian. *The Montreal Forties: Modernist Poetry in Transition.* Toronto: U of Toronto P, 1999.

Troper, Harold. "Becoming an Immigrant City: A History of Immigration into Toronto since the Second World War." *The World in a City.* Ed. Paul Anisef and Michael Lanphier. Toronto: U of Toronto P, 2003. 19–92.

Veterans Affairs Canada. "Canada and the Second World War 1939–1945." Accessed Sept. 22, 2007. <http://www.vacacc.gc.ca/remembers/sub.cfm?source=history/secondwar/canada2/intro>.

Waddington, Miriam. *A. M. Klein.* Toronto: Copp Clark, 1970.

Watson, Albert Durrant, and Lorne Pierce, eds. *Our Canadian Literature.* Toronto: Ryerson, 1922.

Whitaker, Reg, and Steve Hewitt. *Canada and the Cold War.* Toronto: Lorimer, 2003.

Willmott, Glenn. *Unreal Country: Modernity in the Canadian Novel in English.* Montreal: McGill-Queen's UP, 2002.

Wilson, Edmund. *O Canada: An American's Notes on Canadian Culture.* New York: Octagon, 1976.

VI. Contemporary Canada, 1960–1985

Primary Texts

Atwood, Margaret. *The Animals in That Country.* Toronto: Oxford UP, 1968.

—. *The Circle Game.* Toronto: Anansi, 1966.

—. "Dissecting the Way a Writer Works." Interview with Graeme Gibson. 1972. *Margaret Atwood: Conversations.* Ed. Earl G. Ingersoll. Willowdale, ON: Firefly, 1990. 3–19.

—. "Foreword." *Beyond Remembering: The Collected Poems of Al Purdy.* Ed. Al Purdy and Sam Solecki. Madeira Park: Harbour, 2000.

—. *Good Bones.* Toronto: Coach House, 1992.

—. "How Do I Get Out of Here?: The Poetry of John Newlove." 1973. *Second Words: Selected Critical Prose.* Toronto: Anansi, 1982. 114–28.

—. *The Journals of Susanna Moodie.* Toronto: Oxford UP, 1970.

—. "Nationalism, Limbo and the Canadian Club." *Second Words: Selected Critical Prose.* Toronto: Anansi, 1982. 83–89. [Orig. *Saturday Night* Jan. 1971.]

—. "Power and Non-Power." Interview with Marilyn Snell. *The Power to Bend Spoons: Interviews with Canadian Novelists.* Ed. Beverley Daurio. Toronto: Mercury Press, 1998. 20–24.

—. *Survival: A Thematic Guide to Canadian Literature.* Toronto: Anansi, 1972.

—. *Two-Headed Poems.* Toronto: Oxford UP, 1978.

—. *Wilderness Tips.* Toronto: McClelland, 1991.

Bowering, George. *George Bowering Selected: Poems 1961–1992.* Ed. Roy Miki. Toronto: McClelland, 1993.

—. *rocky mountain foot: a lyric, a memoir.* Toronto: McClelland, 1968.

—. *A Short Sad Book.* Vancouver: Talonbooks, 1977.

—. *standing on richards.* Toronto: Viking, 2004.

Campbell, Maria. *Stories of the Road Allowance People.* Trans. Maria Campbell. Penticton: Theytus, 1995.

Clarke, Austin. *Nine Men Who Laughed.* Markham, ON: Penguin, 1986.

Cohen, Leonard. *Death of a Lady's Man.* Toronto: McClelland, 1978.

—. *Flowers for Hitler.* Toronto: McClelland, 1964.

—. *Let Us Compare Mythologies.* Toronto: McClelland, 1956.

—. *Parasites of Heaven.* Toronto: McClelland, 1966.

—. *The Spice-Box of Earth.* Toronto: McClelland, 1961.

Davies, Robertson. "The Bizarre and Passionate Life of the Canadian People." Interview with Donald Cameron. *Conversations with Canadian Novelists: Part One.* Ed. Donald Cameron. Toronto: Macmillan, 1973. 30–48.

—. "The Canada of Myth and Reality." *One Half of Robertson Davies: Provocative Pronouncements on a Wide Range of Topics.* Toronto: Macmillan, 1977. 271–86.

—. *High Spirits: A Collection of Ghost Stories.* Harmondsworth: Penguin, 1982.

—. "What May Canada Expect from Her Writers?" *One Half of Robertson Davies: Provocative Pronouncements on a Wide Range of Topics.* 1972. Toronto: Macmillan, 1977. 135–42.

Frye, Northrop. *The Bush Garden: Essays on the Canadian Imagination.* Toronto: Anansi, 1971.

Gallant, Mavis. *Home Truths: Selected Canadian Stories.* Toronto: Macmillan, 1981.

George, Chief Dan. "Lament for a Nation." *Native Poetry in Canada: A Contemporary Anthology.* Ed. Jeannette C. Armstrong and Lally Grauer. Peterborough, ON: Broadview, 2001. 2–3.

Grant, George. *Lament for a Nation: The Defeat of Canadian Nationalism.* 1965. Ottawa: Carleton UP, 1991.

Kroetsch, Robert. "Disunity as Unity: A Canadian Strategy." *The Lovely Treachery of Words: Essays Selected and New.* Toronto: Oxford UP, 1989. 21–33.

—. "On Being an Alberta Writer." *Open Letter* (1983): 69–80.

—. *Seed Catalogue.* Winnipeg: Turnstone, 1977.

—. *The Stone Hammer Poems: 1960–1975.* Lantzville, BC: oolichan, 1976.

Laurence, Margaret. *A Bird in the House.* London: Macmillan, 1970.

—. "A Conversation about Literature: An Interview with Margaret Laurence and Irving Layton." *Journal of Canadian Fiction* 1.1 (1972): 65–69.

—. "A Conversation with Margaret Laurence." With Robert Kroetsch. *Creation.* Ed. Robert Kroetsch. Toronto: new press, 1970. 53–63.

—. *Dance on the Earth: A Memoir.* Toronto: McClelland, 1989.

—. *The Diviners.* Toronto: McClelland, 1974.

—. "Ivory Tower or Grassroots?: The Novelist as Socio-Political Being." *A Political Art: Essays and Images in Honour of George Woodcock.* Ed. W.H. New. Vancouver: U of British Columbia P, 1978. 15–25.

—. *Margaret Laurence-Al Purdy: A Friendship in Letters.* Ed. John Lennox. Toronto: McClelland, 1993.

—. "A Place to Stand On." 1970. *Heart of a Stranger.* Toronto: McClelland, 1976. 13–18.

—. *A Very Large Soul: Selected Letters from Margaret Laurence to Canadian Writers.* Ed. J.A. Wainwright. Dunvegan, ON: Cormorant, 1995.

—. "Where the World Began." 1972. *Heart of a Stranger.* Toronto: McClelland, 1976. 213–19.

Lee, Dennis. *Alligator Pie.* Toronto: Key Porter, 1974.

—. "Cadence, Country, Silence: Writing in Colonial Space." *Unhomely States: Theorizing English-Canadian Postcolonialism.* Ed. Cynthia Sugars. Peterborough, ON: Broadview, 2004. 43–60. [Orig. published in *Open Letter* 2.6 (1973): 34–53 and *Boundary* 2 3.1 (1974): 151–68.]

—. *Civil Elegies and Other Poems.* Toronto: Anansi, 1972. [Rev. version; orig. 1968.]

—. *Nightwatch: New & Selected Poems 1968–1996.* Toronto: McClelland, 1996.

MacLeod, Alistair. *The Lost Salt Gift of Blood.* Toronto: McClelland, 1976.

Marlatt, Daphne. *Steveston.* Vancouver: Talonbooks, 1974.

—. *Touch to My Tongue.* Edmonton: Longspoon, 1984.

Munro, Alice. "Everything Here Is Touchable and Mysterious." *Weekend Magazine* 11 May 1974: 33.

—. *Friend of My Youth.* Toronto: McClelland, 1990.

—. "What Is Real?" *Making It New: Contemporary Canadian Stories.* Ed. John Metcalf. Toronto: Methuen, 1982. 223–26.

Newlove, John. *Black Night Window.* Toronto: McClelland, 1968.

—. *The Cave.* Toronto: McClelland, 1970.

—. *A Long Continual Argument: The Selected Poems of John Newlove.* Ed. Robert McTavish. Ottawa: Chaudière, 2007.

Nowlan, Alden. *An Exchange of Gifts: Poems New and Selected.* Toronto: Irwin, 1985.

—. *I'm a Stranger Here Myself.* Toronto: Clarke, Irwin, 1974.

—. *The Mysterious Naked Man.* Toronto: Clarke, Irwin, 1969.

—. *Smoked Glass.* Toronto: Clarke, Irwin, 1977.

—. *The Things Which Are.* Toronto: Contact, 1962.

Nichol, bp. *The Alphabet Game: a bpNichol reader.* Ed. Darren Wershler-Henry and Lori Emerson. Toronto: Coach House, 2007.

—. "Letter to the Editor, *Open Letter.*" *meanwhile: the critical writings of bpNichol.* Ed. Roy Miki. Vancouver: Talonbooks, 2002. 16–17.

—. "statement, november 1966." *meanwhile: the critical writings of bpNichol.* Ed. Roy Miki. Vancouver: Talonbooks, 2002. 18.

—. *still water.* Vancouver: Talonbooks, 1970.

—. *Zygal: A Book of Mysteries and Translations.* Toronto: Coach House, 1985.

Ondaatje, Michael. *The Cinnamon Peeler*. New York: Knopf, 1989.

—. *The Collected Works of Billy the Kid: Left Handed Poems*. Toronto: Anansi, 1970.

—. *Leonard Cohen*. Toronto: McClelland, 1970.

—. *Rat Jelly*. Toronto: Coach House, 1973.

—. *Secular Love*. Toronto: Coach House, 1984.

Purdy, Al. *The Cariboo Horses*. Toronto: McClelland, 1965.

—. *The Collected Poems of Al Purdy*. Ed. Russell Brown. Toronto: McClelland, 1986.

—. *Naked With Summer in Your Mouth*. Toronto: McClelland, 1994.

—, ed. *The New Romans: Candid Canadian Opinions of the U.S.* New York: St. Martin's, 1968.

—. *North of Summer: Poems from Baffin Island*. Toronto: McClelland, 1967.

—. *Piling Blood*. Toronto: McClelland, 1984.

—. *Reaching for the Beaufort Sea: An Autobiography*. Ed. Alex Widen. Madeira Park: Harbour, 1993.

—. *The Stone Bird*. Toronto: McClelland, 1981.

—. *Wild Grape Wine*. Toronto: McClelland, 1968.

Wiebe, Rudy. "On the Trail of Big Bear." *A Voice in the Land: Essays By and About Rudy Wiebe*. Ed. W.J. Keith. Edmonton: NeWest, 1981. 132–41.

—. *Playing Dead: A Contemplation Concerning the Arctic*. Edmonton: NeWest, 1989.

—. "Unearthing Language: An Interview with Rudy Wiebe and Robert Kroetsch." With Shirley Neuman. *A Voice in the Land: Essays By and About Rudy Wiebe*. Ed. W.J. Keith. Edmonton: NeWest, 1981. 226–47.

—. *Where Is the Voice Coming From?* Toronto: McClelland, 1974.

Secondary Texts

Acoose, Janice. "Post *Halfbreed*: Indigenous Writers as Authors of Their Own Realities." *Looking at the Words of Our People: First Nations Analysis of Literature*. Ed. Jeannette Armstrong. Penticton: Theytus, 1993. 29–44.

—. "*Halfbreed*: A Revisiting of Maria Campbell's Text from an Indigenous Perspective." *Looking at the Words of Our People: First Nations Analysis of Literature*. Ed. Jeannette Armstrong. Penticton: Theytus, 1993. 137–50.

"Assembly of First Nations: The Story." Assembly of First Nations. Accessed 7 March 2008. <http://www.afn.ca/article.asp?id=59>

Barbour, Douglas. "Some Notes about a Long Relationship with the Coach House." *Open Letter* 8 (1997): 16–22.

Beattie, Owen, and John Geiger. *Frozen in Time: Unlocking the Secrets of the Franklin Expedition*. Saskatoon: Western Producer Prairie Books, 1987.

Birney, Earle. "Can. Lit." *Ice Cod Bell or Stone*. Toronto: McClelland, 1962. 18.

Blaser, Robin. "George Bowering's Plain Song." *Particular Accidents: Selected Poems*. Ed. Robin Blaser. Vancouver: Talonbooks, 1980. 9–28.

Bowering, George. "Wiebe and Bail: re making the story." *Journal of the South Pacific Association for Commonwealth Literature and Language Studies* (SPAN) 36 (1933). Accessed 5 Dec. 2007. <http://wwwmcc.murdoch.edu.au/ReadingRoom/litserv/SPAN/36/Bowering.html>

Bolster, Stephanie. "Surviving Survival." *Northern Poetry Review* 2006. Accessed 29 April 2008. <http://www.northernpoetryreview.com/articles/stephanie-bolster/surviving-survival.html>

Butling, Pauline, and Susan Rudy. *Writing in Our Time: Canada's Radical Poetries in English (1957–2003)*. Waterloo: Wilfrid Laurier UP, 2005.

Cameron, David. *Taking Stock: Canadian Studies in the Nineties*. Montreal: Association for Canadian Studies, 1996.

Cameron, Elspeth. Introduction. *Multiculturalism & Immigration in Canada*. Ed. Elspeth Cameron. Toronto: Canadian Scholars' Press, 2004. xv–xxiv.

Cardinal, Harold. *The Unjust Society: The Tragedy of Canada's Indians*. Edmonton: Hurtig, 1969.

—. *The Rebirth of Canada's Indians*. Edmonton: Hurtig, 1977.

Christian, William. *George Grant: A Biography*. Toronto: U of Toronto P, 1993.

—, and Sheila Grant, eds. *The George Grant Reader*. Toronto: U of Toronto P, 1998.

Cogswell, Fred. "Alden Nowlan as Regional Atavist." *Encounters and Explorations: Canadian Writers and European Critics*. Eds. Franz K. Stanzel and Waldemar Zacharasiewicz. Würzburg, Germany: Königshausen und Neumann, 1986. 37–55.

Cohen, Matt. *Typing: A Life in 26 Keys*. Toronto: Vintage, 2001.

Coleman, Victor. "The Coach House Press: The First Decade. An Emotional Memoir." *Open Letter* 8 (1997): 26–35.

Crean, S.M. *Who's Afraid of Canadian Culture?* Don Mills: General Publishing, 1976.

Davey, Frank. *From There to Here: A Guide to English-Canadian Literature since 1960: Our Nature-Our Voices II*. Erin, ON: Press Porcepic, 1974.

—. *Introducing Tish: The Writing Life*. Ed. C.H. Gervais. Coatsworth, ON: Black Moss, 1976.

Derksen, Jeff. "'These Things Form Poems When I Allow It': After John Newlove." *A Long Continual Argument: The Selected Poems of John Newlove*. Ed. Robert McTavish. Ottawa: Chaudière, 2007. 237–45.

Fetherling, Douglas. *Travels By Night: A Memoir of the Sixties*. Toronto: Lester, 1994.

Fogel, Stan. "CanLit and Class(room) Struggle." *Studies in Canadian Literature* 25.2 (2000): 145–58.

Fulford, Robert. "The New Anti-Americanism." *Saturday Night* 85.5 (May 1970): 11.

—. *This Was Expo*. Toronto: McClelland, 1968.

Gitlin, Todd. *The Sixties: Years of Hope, Days of Rage*. Rev. ed. New York: Bantam, 1993.

Gunn, Cynthia. "The House of Anansi." *The Montreal Star* 9 Aug. 1969: 6.

Gray, Charlotte, ed. *Canada: A Portrait in Letters, 1800–2000*. Toronto: Doubleday, 2003.

Hodgetts, A.B. *What Culture? What Heritage?: A Study of Civic Education in Canada*. Curriculum Series 5. Toronto: OISE, 1968.

Howells, Coral Ann. *Alice Munro*. Manchester: Manchester UP, 1998.

Huggan, Graham. *The Postcolonial Exotic: Marketing the Margins*. London: Routledge, 2001.

Hutcheon, Linda, and Marion Richmond, eds. *Other Solitudes: Canadian Multicultural Fictions*. Toronto: Oxford UP, 1990.

Kalman Naves, Elaine. *Robert Weaver: Godfather of Canadian Writing*. Montreal: Vehicule, 2008.

Keith, W.J. *Canadian Literature in English.* 2 vols. Rev. ed. Erin, ON: Porcupine's Quill, 2006.

King, James. *The Life of Margaret Laurence.* Toronto: Knopf, 1997.

Kroeker, Amy. "A 'Place' Through Language: Postcolonial Implications of Mennonite/s Writing in Western Canada." *Is Canada Postcolonial?: Unsettling Canadian Literature.* Ed. Laura Moss. Waterloo: Wilfrid Laurier UP, 2003. 238–51.

Lee, Dennis. "Grant's Impasse: Beholdenness and the Silence of Reason." *Body Music: Essays.* Toronto: Anansi, 1998. 129–60.

—. "The Poetry of Al Purdy: An Afterword." *The Collected Poems of Al Purdy.* Ed. Russell Brown. Toronto: McClelland, 1986. 371–91.

—. "Running and Dwelling: Homage to Al Purdy." *Saturday Night* July 1972: 14–16.

Lyotard, Jean-François. *The Postmodern Condition: A Report on Knowledge.* Trans. Geoff Bennington and Brian Massumi. Introd. Fredric Jameson. Minneapolis: U of Minnesota P, 1984.

MacSkimming, Roy. *The Perilous Trade: Publishing Canada's Writers.* Toronto: McClelland, 2003.

Metcalf, John. "A Collector's Notes on the House of Anansi." *Notes & Queries.* Accessed 5 Jan. 2008. <http://www.anansi.ca/assets/ACollector_sNotesontheHouseofAnansi.pdf >.

Moore, Christopher. "The Writers' Union of Canada, 1973–2007." Accessed 20 Feb. 2008. <http://www.writersunion.ca/au_history.asp>.

Moss, John. *Patterns of Isolation in English Canadian Fiction.* Toronto: McClelland, 1974.

—. *A Reader's Guide to the Canadian Novel.* Toronto: McClelland, 1981.

Oates, Joyce Carol. Afterword. *The Lost Salt Gift of Blood,* by Alistair MacLeod. Toronto: McClelland, 1989. 157–60.

Porter, John. *The Vertical Mosaic: An Analysis of Social Class and Power in Canada.* Toronto: U of Toronto P, 1965.

Powers, Lyall. *Alien Heart: The Life and Work of Margaret Laurence.* Winnipeg: U of Manitoba P, 2003.

Richards, David Adams. "I Went to Meet Alden Nowlan . . ." *Globe and Mail* 21 June 2003: R1, R5.

Richler, Mordecai. *Home Sweet Home: My Canadian Album.* Toronto: McClelland, 1985.

Rimstead, Roxanne. *Remnants of Nation: On Poverty Narratives by Women.* Toronto: U of Toronto P, 2001.

Skelton Grant, Judith. *Robertson Davies: Man of Myth.* New York: Viking, 1994.

Solecki, Sam. *The Last Canadian Poet: An Essay on Al Purdy.* Toronto: U of Toronto P, 1999.

Stegner, Wallace. *Wolf Willow: A History, a Story, and a Memory of the Last Plains Frontier.* 1962. Harmondsworth: Penguin, 1990.

Sullivan, Rosemary. *The Red Shoes: Margaret Atwood Starting Out.* Toronto: HarperFlamingo, 1998.

Symons, T.H.B. *The Symons Report.* Toronto: Book and Periodical Development Council, 1978.

Trigger, Bruce G. *Natives and Newcomers: Canada's 'Heroic Age' Reconsidered.* Kingston and Montreal: McGill-Queen's UP, 1985.

Turner, Chris. "On Strawberry Hill: BC's Draft Dodgers and the 1960s, Revisited." *The Walrus* Sept 2007: 68–73.

Vallières, Pierre. *Nègres blancs d'Amérique.* Montreal: Editions Parti pris, 1968.

York, Lorraine. *Literary Celebrity in Canada.* Toronto: U of Toronto P, 2007.

VII. Contemporary Canada, 1985–Present

Primary Texts

Armstrong, Jeannette. *Breath Tracks.* Stratford/Vancouver: Williams-Wallace/Theytus, 1991.

—. "The Disempowerment of First North American Native Peoples and Empowerment Through Their Writing." *Gatherings* 1.1 (1990): 142–46.

—, and Lally Grauer, eds. *Native Poetry in Canada.* Peterborough, ON: Broadview, 2001.

Bissoondath, Neil. *Selling Illusions: The Cult of Multiculturalism in Canada.* Toronto: Penguin, 1994.

Bök, Christian. *Eunoia.* Toronto: Coach House, 2001.

—. "Studio 111 Conversation with Christian Bök and Penn students." Accessed 12 Apr. 2008. <http://www.writing.upenn.edu/pennsound/x/Bok.html>.

—. "Virtually Nontoxic." *West Coast Line* 40.4 (2007): 58–60.

Brand, Dionne. *Bread Out of Stone.* Toronto: Coach House, 1994.

—. *Inventory.* Toronto: McClelland, 2006.

—. *No Language Is Neutral.* Toronto: Coach House, 1990.

—. *What We All Long For.* Toronto: Vintage, 2005.

Act for the Preservation and Enhancement of Multiculturalism in Canada Bill C-93. The Canadian Multiculturalism Act (1985/88). Government of Canada. Accessed 16 Aug. 2007. <http://www.canadianheritage.gc.ca/progs/multi/policy/act_e.cfm>.

Carson, Anne. *Men in the Off Hours.* Toronto: Knopf, 2000.

—. *Short Talks.* London, ON: Brick, 1992.

Clarke, George Elliott. "1933." E-mail to Laura Moss. 25 July 2008.

—. *Blue.* Vancouver: Polestar, 2001.

—, ed. *Eyeing the North Star: Directions in African-Canadian Literature.* Toronto: McClelland, 1997.

—. "Harris, Philip, Brand: Three Authors in Search of Literate Criticism." *Journal of Canadian Studies* 35.1 (Spring 2000): 161–89.

—. *Whylah Falls.* Vancouver: Polestar, 1990.

Crummey, Michael. *Hard Light.* London, ON: Brick, 1998.

—. "The Living Haunt the Dead: Michael Crummey." Interview with Herb Wyile. *Speaking in the Past Tense: Canadian Novelists on Writing Historical Fiction.* Ed. Herb Wyile. Waterloo: Wilfrid Laurier UP, 2007. 295–319.

—. *Salvage.* Toronto: McClelland, 2002.

—. "Speaking Terms: A Rebuttal." Canadian Poetry. Accessed 20 May 2008. <http://www.library.utoronto.ca/canpoetry/crummey/write.htm>.

Di Cicco, Pier Giorgio. *The Dark Time of Angels.* Toronto: Mansfield, 2003.

—. *The Honeymoon Wilderness*. Toronto: Mansfield, 2002.

—, ed. *Roman Candles: An Anthology of Poems by Seventeen Italo-Canadian Poets*. Toronto: Hounslow, 1978.

—. *Virgin Science: Hunting Holistic Paradigms*. Toronto: McClelland, 1986.

Dumont, Marilyn. "Popular Images of Nativeness." *Looking at the Words of Our People: First Nations Analysis of Literature*. Ed. Jeannette Armstrong. Penticton, BC: Theytus, 1993. 45–50.

—. *A Really Good Brown Girl*. London, ON: Brick, 1996.

—. *that tongued belonging*. Wiarton, ON: Kegedonce, 2007.

King, Thomas. "Coyote Lives: Thomas King." Interview with Jeffrey Canton. *The Power to Bend Spoons: Interviews with Canadian Novelists*. Ed. Beverley Daurio. Toronto: Mercury Press, 1998. 90–97.

—. "Godzilla vs. Post-Colonial." *World Literature Written in English* 30.2 (Autumn 1990): 10–16.

—. *Green Grass, Running Water*. Toronto: HarperCollins, 1993.

—. *One Good Story, That One*. Toronto: HarperCollins, 1993.

—. "Peter Gzowski Interviews Thomas King on *Green Grass, Running Water*." *Canadian Literature* 161/162 (1999): 65–76.

—. *The Truth about Stories*. Minneapolis: U of Minneapolis P, 2005.

King, Thomas, and Helen Hoy, eds. *The Native in Literature*. Oakville, ON: ECW, 1987.

Lane, Patrick. *Winter*. Regina: Coteau, 1990.

McKay, Don. *Another Gravity*. Toronto: McClelland, 2000.

—. *Apparatus*. Toronto: McClelland, 1997.

—. "Baler Twine: Thoughts on Ravens, Home, and Nature Poetry." *Poetry and Knowing*. Ed. Tim Lilburn. Kingston, ON: Quarry, 1995. Rpt. in *Vis à Vis: Field Notes on Poetry and Wilderness*. Wolfville, NS: Gaspereau, 2001.

—. *Birding, or desire*. Toronto: McClelland, 1983.

—. "The Shell of the Tortoise." Ed. Méira Cook. *Field Marks: The Poetry of Don McKay*. Waterloo: Wilfrid Laurier UP. 2006. 49–56.

—. *Strike/Slip*. Toronto: McClelland, 2006.

Mistry, Rohinton. *Tales from Firozsha Baag*. Markham: Penguin, 1987.

Philip, M. NourbeSe. "The Absence of Writing or How I Almost Became a Spy." *A Genealogy of Resistance*. Toronto: Mercury, 1997. 41–57.

—. "The Habit of: Poetry, Rats and Cats." *A Genealogy of Resistance*. Toronto: Mercury, 1997. 113–19.

—. *She Tries Her Tongue, Her Silence Softly Breaks*. Charlottetown: Ragweed Press, 1989.

—. "Why Multiculturalism Can't End Racism." *Toronto Star* 6 Mar. 1990: A21.

Robinson, Eden. *Monkey Beach*. Toronto: Knopf, 2001.

—. *Traplines*. Toronto: Knopf, 1996.

Ruffo, Armand Garnet. *Grey Owl: The Mystery of Archie Belaney*. Regina: Coteau, 1996.

—. *Opening in the Sky*. Penticton, BC: Theytus, 1994.

—. "Why Native Literature?" *American Indian Quarterly* 21. 4. (Autumn 1997): 663–73.

Shields, Carol. *Dressing Up for the Carnival*. Toronto: Random House, 2000.

—. "A View from the Edge of the Edge." *Carol Shields and the Extra-Ordinary*. Ed. Marta Dvorák and Manina Jones. Montreal & Kingston: McGill-Queens UP, 2007. 17–29.

—. "Narrative Hunger and the Overflowing Cupboard." *Carol Shields, Narrative Hunger, and the Possibilities of Fiction*. Ed. Edward Eden and Dee Goertz. Toronto: U of Toronto P, 2003. 19–36.

Taylor, Charles. "The Politics of Recognition." *Multiculturalism and "The Politics of Recognition."* Ed. Amy Gutmann. Princeton: Princeton UP, 1992. 25–74.

Thein, Madeleine. *Simple Recipes*. Toronto: McClelland, 2001.

Toews, Miriam. "Blueprints." *Paper Placemats*. Ed. Paul Maliszewski. Atlanta, GA: J&L, 2007.

—. *A Complicated Kindness*. Toronto: Vintage, 2005.

Wah, Fred. *Diamond Grill*. Edmonton: NeWest, 1996.

—. "Half-Bred Poetics." *Faking It: Poetics and Hybridity*. Edmonton: NeWest, 2000. 71–96.

—. "Re-Mixed: The Compound Composition of Diamond Grill." *Diamond Grill*. 10th Anniversary ed. Edmonton: NeWest, 2006. 177–89.

Wong, Rita. *forage*. Robert's Creek, BC: Harbour, 2007.

—. *monkeypuzzle*. Vancouver: Press Gang, 1998.

Zwicky, Jan. "Being, Polyphony, Lyric: An Open Letter to Robert Bringhurst." *Canadian Literature* 156 (Spring 1998): 181–84.

—. *Lyric Philosophy*. Toronto: U of Toronto P, 1992.

—. *Robinson's Crossing*. London, ON: Brick, 2004.

—. *Songs for Relinquishing the Earth*. London, ON: Brick, 1998.

Secondary Texts

Abu-Laban, Yasmeen, and Christina Gabriel. *Selling Diversity: Immigration, Multiculturalism, Employment Equity and Globalization*. Peterborough, ON: Broadview, 2002.

Alfred, Taiaiake. *Heeding the Voices of our Ancestors: Kahnawake Mohawk Politics and the Rise of Native Nationalism*. Toronto: Oxford UP, 1995.

—, and Lana Lowe. "Warrior Societies in Contemporary Indigenous Communities: A Background Paper prepared for the Ipperwash Inquiry." May 2005. Accessed 15 Mar.2008. <http://intercontinental-cry.org/warrior-societies-in-contemporary-indigenous-communities/>.

Ashcroft, W.D., Gareth Griffiths, and Helen Tiffin. *The Empire Writes Back*. New York: Routledge, 1989.

Atwood, Margaret, ed. *Story of a Nation: Defining Moments in Our History*. Toronto: Doubleday, 2001.

Bannerji, Himani. "Multiculturalism Is Anti-anti-racism." *Kinesis* (Feb. 1997): 8–9.

Berger, Peter L. "Introduction: The Cultural Dynamics of Globalization." *Many Globalizations: Cultural Diversity in the Contemporary World*. Ed. Peter L. Berger and Samuel Huntington. Oxford: Oxford UP, 2003. 1–16.

Bothwell, Robert. *The Penguin History of Canada*. Toronto: Penguin, 2006.

Bringhurst, Robert. "Poetry and Thinking." *Thinking and Singing: Poetry and the Practice of Philosophy*. Ed. Tim Lilburn. Toronto: Cormorant, 2002. 155–72.

Brown, Russell. "The Practice and Theory of Canadian Thematic Criticism: A Reconsideration." *University of Toronto Quarterly* 70.2 (Spring 2001): 653–89.

Brydon, Diana. "Metamorphoses of a Discipline: Rethinking Canadian Literature within Institutional Contexts." Kamboureli and Miki 1–16.

—. "A Word about the Poem." BookLounge.ca. Accessed 18 July 2008. <http://www.mcclelland.com/catalog/display.pperl?isbn=9780771016622>.

Canadian Heritage. "Moving Forward: Healing Canada's Relationship with Iits Aboriginal Peoples." Accessed Feb. 2008. <http://www.pch.gc.ca/progs/multi/respect_e.cfm#forward>.

Canadian Museum of Civilization. Accessed 26 Feb. 2008. <http://www.pch.gc.ca/special/dcforum/info-bg/05_e.cfm>.

Chariandy, David. "Book Review: *What We All Long For.*" *New Dawn: The Journal of Black Canadian Studies* 1.1 (Spring 2006): 103–09.

Compton, Wayde. "The Reinventing Wheel: On Blending the Poetry of Cultures through Hip Hop Turntablism." *HorizonZero* Issue 8: Remix. Accessed 20 Aug. 2007. <http://www.horizonzero.ca/textsite/remix.php?is=8&file=7&tlang=0>.

Cook, Méira. *Field Marks: The Poetry of Don McKay.* Waterloo: Wilfrid Laurier UP, 2006.

Cooper, James Fenimore. "Introduction." *The Last of the Mohicans: A Narrative of 1757.* New York: Hurd and Houghton, 1876. v–viii.

Cuthand, Beth. "Post-Oka Kinda Woman." *Gatherings V: "Celebrating the Circle": Recognizing Women and Children in Restoring the Balance.* Ed. Beth Cuthand and William George. Penticton, BC: Theytus, 1994. 262–63.

Davidson, Arnold E., Priscilla L. Walton, and Jennifer Andrews. *Border Crossings: Thomas King's Cultural Inversions.* Toronto: U of Toronto P, 2003.

Davey, Frank. "Canadian Canons." *Critical Inquiry* 16 (1990): 672–81.

—. *Post-National Arguments: The Politics of the Anglophone-Canadian Novel since 1967.* Toronto: U of Toronto P, 1997.

Di Michele, Mary. "Living Inside the Poem." Loriggio 1–10.

Dudek, Debra. "George Elliott Clarke." Riegel 50–55.

Dvořák, Marta, and Manina Jones, eds. *Carol Shields and the Extra-Ordinary.* Montreal and Kingston: McGill-Queen's UP, 2007.

Ede, Amatoritsero. "Predicting the Past: Interview with Armand Garnet Ruffo." *Sentinel Poetry (Online)* 48 (Nov. 2006). Accessed 6 June 2008. <http://www.sentinelpoetry.org.uk/1106/frontpage.html>.

Emeis, Marijke. "Anne Carson." *Poetry International Web.* Accessed 18 July 2008. <http://international.poetry-internationalweb.org/piw_cms/cms/cms_module/index.php?obj_id=403>.

Findlay, Len. "Always Indigenize! The Radical Humanities in the Postcolonial Canadian University." *ARIEL* 31.1 (2000): 307–26.

Fish, Stanley. "Boutique Multiculturalism: Or, Why Liberals Are Incapable of Thinking about Hate Speech." *Critical Inquiry* 23: 2 (1997): 378–95.

Foreign Affairs and International Trade Canada. "Canada World View/As Others See Us." Accessed Sept. 2004. <http://www.dfait-maeci.gc.ca/canada-magazine/issue22/04-title-en.asp>.

Francis, Daniel. *The Imaginary Indian: The Image of the Indian in Canadian Culture.* Vancouver: Arsenal Pulp, 1992.

Gadsby, Meredith M. "'I Suck Coarse Salt': Caribbean Women Writers in Canada and the Politics of Transcendence." *Modern Fiction Studies* 44.1 (1998): 144–63.

Gagnon, Monika Kin, and Scott Toguri McFarlane. "The Capacity of Cultural Difference." Minster's Forum on Diversity and Culture, 22 April 2003.

Genetsch, Martin. "Rohinton Mistry." Riegel 187–91.

Gingell, Susan. "Textualizing Orature & Orality." *Essays on Canadian Writing* 83.1 (Fall 2004): 1–18.

Gruending, Dennis. *Great Canadian Speeches.* Toronto: Fitzhenry & Whiteside, 2004.

Griffiths, Rudyard. "Preface." *Story of a Nation: Defining Moments in Our History.* Ed. Margaret Atwood. Toronto: Doubleday, 2001. vii–x.

Halfe, Louise Bernice. *Bear Bones & Feathers.* Regina: Coteau, 1994.

Huggan, Graham, and Winfried Siemerling. "U.S./Canadian Writers' Perspectives on the Multiculturalism Debate: A Roundtable Discussion at Harvard University." *Canadian Literature* 164 (Spring 2000): 82–111.

Hutcheon, Linda. *The Canadian Postmodern.* Toronto: Oxford UP, 1988.

Kamboureli, Smaro, ed. *Making a Difference: Canadian Multicultural Literature.* Toronto: Oxford UP, 1996; rev. ed. 2006.

Kamboureli, Smaro, and Roy Miki, eds. *Trans.Can.Lit: Resituating the Study of Canadian Literature.* Waterloo: Wilfrid Laurier UP, 2007.

Keeshig-Tobias, Lenore. "After Oka—How Has Canada Changed?" Moses and Goldie 234–35.

—. "Stop Stealing Native Stories." *Globe and Mail* 26 Jan. 1990: A7.

Kootenay School of Writing. "KSW Chronology, 1978–1996." Accessed 22 May 2008. <http://www.kswnet.org/fire/ksw-docs-targetpage.cfm?showannouncement=KSW-CHRONOLOGY-detailed.htm&announceID=57>.

Lackenbauer, P. Whitney. "Carrying the Burden of Peace: The Mohawks, the Canadian Forces, and the Oka Crisis." *Journal of Military and Strategic Studies* 10.2. (Winter 2008): 1–41. Accessed 13 Mar. 2008. <http://www.jmss.org/2008/winter/articles/lackenbauer.pdf>.

Lai, Larissa. "Interview with Rita Wong, 1999." Accessed 14 May 2008. <http://www.eciad.ca/~amathur/writers/rita-int.html>.

Lecker, Robert. "The Canonization of Canadian Literature: An Inquiry into Value." *Critical Inquiry* 16.3 (Spring, 1990): 656–71.

—. *Making It Real: The Canonization of English-Canadian Literature.* Toronto: Anansi, 1995.

Libin, Mark. "Non-Generic Brands." *Canadian Literature* 163 (Winter 1999): 204–06.

Loriggio, Francesco, ed. *The Last Effort of Dreams: Essays on the Poetry of Pier Giorgio Di Cicco.* Waterloo: Wilfrid Laurier UP, 2007.

maclennan, rob. "12 or 20 questions: with Marilyn Dumont, October 1, 2007." Accessed 29 May 2008. <http://12or20questions.blogspot.com/2007/10/12-or-20-questions-with-marilyn-dumont.html>.

—. "12 or 20 questions: with Rita Wong, January 5, 2008." Accessed 14 May 2008. <http://12or20ques-tions.blogspot.com/2008/01/12-or-20-questions-with-rita-wong.html>.

Mason, Travis. "Ornithology of Desire: Birding in the Ecotone and the Poetry of Don McKay." Diss. University of British Columbia, 2007.

Methot, Suzanne. "Spirits in the Material World: Eden Robinson." *Quill & Quire* (Jan. 2000). Accessed 12 June 2008. <http://www.quillandquire.com/authors/profile.cfm?article_id=1656>.

Miki, Roy. "Can I See Your ID?: Writing in the 'Race' Codes That Bind." *West Coast Line* 24 (Winter 1997–98): 85–94.

—. *Broken Entries: Race, Subjectivity, Writing.* Toronto: Mercury, 1998.

Monkman, Leslie. *A Native Heritage: Images of the Indian in English-Canadian Literature.* Toronto: U Toronto P, 1981.

Moses, Daniel David, and Terry Goldie, eds. *An Anthology of Canadian Native Literature in English.* 3rd ed. Don Mills, ON: Oxford UP, 2005.

Moss, Laura. "Can Rohinton Mistry's Realism Rescue the Novel?" *Postcolonizing the Commonwealth: Studies in Literature and Culture.* Ed. Rowland Smith. Waterloo: Wilfrid Laurier UP, 2000. 157–65.

—, ed. *Is Canada Postcolonial? Unsettling Canadian Literature.* Waterloo: Wilfrid Laurier UP, 2003.

Moynagh, Maureen. "M. NourbeSe Philip." Riegel 198–205.

Mudge, Alden. "Conversation with Madeleine Thien." *Waterbridge Review.* Accessed 5 June 2008. <http://www.waterbridgereview.org/062007/cnv_thien.php>.

Mulroney, Brian. "Redress for Japanese Canadians." Speech in Parliament, September 22, 1988. Accessed 27 Feb. 2008. <http://www.najc.ca/thenandnow/renewal6a.php>.

Murray, Heather. "Reading for Contradiction in the Literature of Colonial Space." Ed. John Moss. *Future Indicative: Literary Theory and Canadian Literature.* Ottawa: U of Ottawa P, 1987. 71–84.

Ortiz, Simon, ed. *Speaking for the Generations: Native Writers on Writing.* Tucson: U of Arizona P, 1998.

Pivato, Joseph. "A History of Italian-Canadian Writing." Accessed 2 Jan. 2008. <http://www.athabascau.ca/cll/research/hisitcan.htm>.

Razack, Sherene. *Dark Threats and White Knights: The Somalia Affair, Peacekeeping, and the New Imperialism.* Toronto: U of Toronto P, 2004.

Rees, William, and Mathias Wackernagel. *Our Ecological Footprint: Reducing Human Impact on the Earth.* Gabriola Island, BC: New Society Pub., 1995.

Riegel, Christian, ed. *Twenty-First-Century Canadian Writers.* Detroit: Thomson Gale, 2007.

Robinson, Harry. *Write It on Your Heart: The Epic World of an Okanagan Storyteller.* Ed. Wendy Wickwire. Vancouver: Talonbooks/Theytus, 1989.

Said, Edward. *Culture and Imperialism.* New York: Vintage, 1994.

Sankar, Celia. "Neil Bissoondath: Hungering for an Imperfect Homeland." *Sunday Guardian* 25 Feb. 2001: 7.

Smyth, Heather. "Sexual Citizenship and Caribbean-Canadian Fiction: Brand's *In Another Place, Not Here* and Shani Mootoo's *Cereus Blooms at Night.*" *ARIEL* 30.2 (1999): 141–60.

Steffler, John. "A Piece of Hard Light: Excerpts from Michael Crummey's *Hard Light.*" *Labour/Le Travail* 50 (2002). Accessed 30 May 2008. <http://www.historycooperative.org/journals/llt/50/steffler.html>.

Steeves, David. "Maniacal Murderer or Death Dealing Car: The Case of Daniel Perry Sampson, 1933–1935." Unpublished manuscript, n.d.

Sugars, Cynthia. "Original Sin, or, The Last of the First Ancestors: Michael Crummey's *River Thieves.*" *ESC: English Studies in Canada* 31.4 (2005): 147–75.

—. "Strategic Abjection: Windigo Psychosis and the 'Post-Indian' Subject in Eden Robinson's 'Dogs in Winter.'" *Canadian Literature* 181 (Summer 2004): 78–91.

—, ed. *Unhomely States: Theorizing English-Canadian Postcolonialism.* Peterborough, ON: Broadview, 2004.

Taylor, Timothy. *Stanley Park.* Toronto: Knopf, 2001.

Walcott, Rinaldo, ed. *Rude: Contemporary Black Canadian Cultural Criticism.* Toronto: Insomniac, 2000.

"Whose Voice Is It, Anyway?" *Books in Canada* Jan./Feb. 1991: 11-17.

index

Author and artist names appear in **bold**; entries for figures are followed by the letter "*f.*"

Grateful acknowledgement is given to the following copyright holders for permission to reproduce material in this text.

Section V

Page 1: A.J.M. Smith, "Wanted—Canadian Critics," *Canadian Forum*, vol. 8 (1927–28), n.p. Reprinted in Malcolm Ross, ed., *Our Sense of Canadian Identity* (Toronto: Ryerson Press), 220. Permission to reprint granted by William Toye, Literary Executor for the Estate of A.J.M. Smith. **Pages 53–66:** From *Selected Poems: E.J. Pratt*, Edited by Sandra Djwa, W.J. Keith, and Zailig Pollock. University of Toronto Press © 2000. Reprinted with the permission of the publisher. **Page 67:** Lawren S. Harris, "Revelation of Art in Canada," *The Canadian Theosophist* (July 15, 1926). By permission of the Family of Lawren S. Harris. **Page 78:** Laura Goodman Salverson, "Those Child Transgressions" from *Confessions of an Immigrant's Daughter*. Copyright © 1939. Reprinted by permission of the Estate of Laura Goodman Salverson. **Pages 85–91:** From *F.R. Scott: Selected Poems*. Copyright © 1966. Permission to reprint granted by William Toye, Literary Executor for the Estate of F.R. Scott. **Pages 91:** F.R. Scott Notebook of Minutes from *Preview* meeting (Montreal, March 13, 1944). National Library Archives, F.R. Scott founds, MG 30 D211, Vol. 87. Permission to reprint granted by William Toye, Literary Executor for the Estate of F.R. Scott. **Pages 96, 98:** From A.J. Smith, *Collected Poems*. Copyright © 1962. Permission to reprint granted by William Toye, Literary Executor for the Estate of A.J.M. Smith. **Pages 96, 97:** A.J.M. Smith, "The Lonely Land." Copyright © 1926, 1936. Permission to reprint granted by William Toye, Literary Executor for the Estate of A.J.M. Smith. [The 1936 version is from *New Provinces: Poems of Several Authors* (University of Toronto Press), p. 50. The 1926 version is from *McGill Fortnight Review*, vol. 1, no. 4, p. 30.] **Page 99:** A.J.M. Smith, "A Rejected Preface" from *New Provinces: Poems of Several Authors* (University of Toronto Press). Permission to reprint granted by William Toye, Literary Executor for the Estate of F.R. Scott. **Page 103:** Morely Callaghan, "Loppy Phelan's Double Shoot" from *The Complete Stories—Volume Two* (pp. 97–112), published 2003. Reprinted with permission of Exile Editions and the Estate of Morley Callaghan. **Pages 114–119, 121, 124:** Earle Birney, *One Muddy Hand: Selected Poems* (Harbour Publishing, 2006). Used with the permission of the Estate of Earle

Birney. **Page 120:** Earle Birney, *Collected Poems* (McClelland & Stewart, 1975). Used with the permission of the Estate of Earle Birney. **Page 126:** Hugh MacLennan, "Boy Meets Girl in Winnipeg and Who Cares?" From *Scotchman's Return and Other Essays by Hugh MacLennan*. Copyright © 1960 Hugh MacLennan. Reprinted with permission of McGill-Queen's University Press. **Page 135:** "The Painted Door" from *The Lamp at Noon and Other Stories* by Sinclair Ross © 1968. Published by McClelland & Stewart. Used with permission of the publisher. **Pages 152–158:** From *Complete Poems: A.M. Klein, Part I: Original Poems 1926–34* (University of Toronto Press, 1990). Reprinted with permission of the publisher. **Page 159:** "A Modest Proposal" from *A.M. Klein Beyond Sambation: Selected Essays and Editorials 1928–1955*, ed. M.W. Steinberg and Usher Caplan. (University of Toronto Press, 1982). Plus editorial footnote on page 495. Reprinted with permission of the publisher. **Pages 164–168:** From Dorothy Livesay, *Selected Poems of Dorothy Livesay (1926–1956)*. Copyright © 1957 by Dorothy Livesay. Reprinted with permission of Jay Stewart for the Estate of Dorothy Livesay. **Pages 169–172:** From *Dorothy Livesay, Collected Poems: The Two Seasons*. Copyright © 1972 by Dorothy Livesay. Reprinted with permission of Jay Stewart for the Estate of Dorothy Livesay. **Pages 174–178:** From *A Wild and Peculiar Joy* by Irving Layton © 1982, 2004. Published by McClelland & Stewart. Used with permission of the publisher. **Page 178:** From *The Collected Poems of Irving Layton* © 1971. Published by McClelland & Stewart. Used with permission of the publisher. **Page 182:** From *This Is My Own* edited by Muriel Kitagawa and Roy Miki, © 1985 Muriel Kitagawa and Wes Fujiwara. Talon Books Ltd., Vancouver, BC. Reprinted by permission of the publisher. **Pages 188, 189, 190:** Copyright © The Estate of Douglas LePan, c/o Don LePan. **Pages 193–198:** Reprinted from *The Hidden Room* (in two volumes) by P.K. Page by permission of the Porcupine's Quill. Copyright © P.K. Page, 1997. **Pages 201–202:** Reprinted from *Always Now* (in three volumes) by Margaret Avison by permission of the Porcupine's Quill. Copyright © Margaret Avison, 2003. **Page 205:** *Report of a Royal Commission on National Development in the Arts, Letters & Science 1949–1951*.

Section VII